A HISTORY OF CHICAGO
1848–1871

By BESSIE LOUISE PIERCE
THE UNIVERSITY OF CHICAGO

✵

A HISTORY

OF

CHICAGO

VOLUME II
FROM TOWN TO CITY
1848–1871

New York · ALFRED A KNOPF · London

MCMXL

TO MY SISTER
ANNE

" A little while ago . . . the wilderness stood here, and the child of the forest thought of it as a prepared abiding place for himself and his people forever. The red man has gone; and these structures, and vehicles, and busy crowds have come into their places magically, like the new picture in a dissolving view."

Rev. E. H. Chapin, *Humanity in the City* (1854)

ACKNOWLEDGMENT

For assistance in all stages of the preparation of this book I am under great obligation to Dorothy Culp, Alan Bliss, and Herbert Wiltsee, and for help in checking data to Kirsten Richards, the University of Chicago Research Staff; and for aid in research to Joe L. Norris, Richard O. Cummings, Georgia Watson Craven, and Tracy E. Strevey, sometime members of the Research Staff.

B. L. P.

PREFACE

THIS IS THE SECOND of several volumes to be devoted to the history of Chicago. It covers approximately the years from 1848, the coming of the first railroad, to 1871, the destruction of the city by fire. During these years Chicago passed from a town economy to the economy of a metropolis and began to exercise a many-sided leadership over the far-flung Middle Valley of America.

I have been unable to sketch the story of these crowded years in as much detail as they deserve. The most that the historian can hope to do is to gather his facts, sift, consider, and reassemble them in the light of relationships he may have discovered. He must also decide whether he will make his selections with an eye focused upon the group or whether his narrative will pivot about outstanding members of the community. I have chosen to do the former in the hope that at some future time I may write about some of the leaders of these fast-moving years.

The national crisis of a civil war from 1861 to 1865 interrupted in Chicago, as elsewhere in America, the normal flow of life. But it accelerated rather than altered a development which the coming of the railroads had ordained. Because this seems so I have treated the war as a very important but not the chief factor in the evolution of the city. The war, in a very real sense, impinged upon the thoughts and acts of Chicagoans, but their city would have eventually emerged as the " great emporium " of the Mississippi Valley had there been no struggle between the North and the South.

Many sources which might have been used in weaving the colorful pattern of these years were destroyed by the fire of 1871, but an effort has been made to survey all that are available. The printed bibliography does not include a complete list of all materials at hand, but some are cited in the footnotes. Those who wish a better understanding of state and city relationships will find helpful Arthur C. Cole's *The Era of the Civil War, 1848–1871* in the *Centennial History of Illinois.*

In the preparation of this volume I have had the advice of many friends. I have again called upon Professor Arthur M. Schlesinger, Harvard University, who read a large part of the manuscript. I have had the counsel of Professor Charles E. Merriam, the University of Chicago, through whose offices this study was begun. Professor Merle Curti, Columbia University, and my colleagues Professor Louis Wirth and Professor Chester Wright made helpful suggestions on the entire manuscript. Portions of the book were read by Professor Paul W. Gates, Cornell University, Professor Roy Nichols, the University of Pennsylvania, Professor William T. Hutchinson and Professor Leonard D. White, the University of Chicago. I have benefited by the points of view and broad information of my colleagues in the other social sciences as well as in history. Whenever I have called upon them Dean Edith Abbott, Professor Avery Craven, Professor Edward A. Duddy, Professor Earl S. Johnson, Professor Simeon E. Leland, and Professor Harry A. Millis have responded generously.

I am under special obligation to the staffs of Newberry Library and the libraries of the Chicago Historical Society and the University of Chicago as well as those in other cities. I am indebted to Mr. Joseph T. Ryerson for access to his rare collection of Chicagoana. Many other Chicagoans have also been helpful in various ways in this writing of the history of their city. I want to thank, in particular, my friend Mr. Lloyd Lewis for suggestions on two chapters of the manuscript, Mr. I. M. Labovitz for criticisms on sections dealing with the subject of taxation, and Mr. M. S. Parkhurst for sources on the stockyards.

An indebtedness to my research assistants and students in my seminar extends to all who for the last several years have been associated in a study of urban history. Besides those mentioned elsewhere I wish to thank Miss Ella P. Levett, Miss Rae Rips, Mr. Samuel R.

Mohler, and Mrs. Mary Mohler. Dr. Richard Burks assisted in trans-
lations from German sources, and Mr. Gustav Elwood Johnson performed a similar service in Swedish sources. The Social Science Research Committee, the University of Chicago, has made generous
grants for research, and the manuscript has been prepared by Miss
Dorothy Mapes under the direction of Miss Diane Greeter.

B. L. P.

VOLUME II

CONTENTS

VOLUME II

MAPS AND ILLUSTRATIONS

A HISTORY OF CHICAGO
1848–1871

CHAPTER I

THE STRUCTURE OF SOCIETY

WHEN CHICAGO was incorporated as a town in 1833, it was a hamlet of but 350 souls; by mid-century it was a city of nearly thirty thousand. Amazing as this growth was, the increase which took place in the next twenty years was equally so; for by 1870 the population had reached the imposing total of almost three hundred thousand. At the same time the little village of 1833, with its area of less than one square mile, had pushed its boundaries out to include over nine square miles in 1850 and more than thirty-five square miles at the time of the great fire in 1871. And beyond the actual limits of the city many people were crowding into suburbs, some of which were, in the last quarter of the century, to become part of Chicago, sharing her economic life and copying or helping to produce the social and cultural patterns of the great midwestern center.

The years from 1833 to 1848 had been, in every sense, elemental. They had plainly borne the earmarks of frontier experience. They had been years in which men had created new things and had been forced in the light of the new needs to adapt the legacies of their past to a new environment. With unwavering faith in the future of Chicago, these pioneering spirits looked to a day when their town would be the great emporium of the growing central valley.

At times, man-induced obstacles, such as the panic of 1837, halted temporarily the march forward and seemed to conspire with physical barriers to retard progress. Even in 1848 the dominance exercised by Chicago over the near-by region was assured only in the dreams of her boosters. True, her geographic position, in the center of a rich and expanding agricultural section and at the junction of the Illinois and Michigan Canal and Lake Michigan, guaranteed a continuous importance in the water-borne commerce of the Middle West. But this strategic position in relation to the two great water routes was significant for the future chiefly because it made certain that the railroads from the East and those tapping the West would make Chicago the point where the rails of the nation stopped and began in the east to west passage.

As the railway network lengthened, Chicago reached out into a widening hinterland from which products of the farm were drawn to be exchanged for the manufactures of the East, and these same products became the basis of a phenomenal commercial development. Because the rail and water routes to the east offered more advantages than did the outlets to the south, Chicago increasingly directed her trade eastward. Before the great fire had reduced her to ruins in 1871, she had excelled her most persistent rival, St. Louis, in the volume of the wholesale trade; she had outdistanced Cincinnati in the packing of meats; and she had surpassed, in the bulk of business, Milwaukee and other western towns which had hoped for commercial leadership.

This urban expansion, to which Chicago proudly pointed, was colored by the great national crisis of a civil war from 1861 to 1865. The city, throughout these years and those which immediately preceded and followed them, fashioned its thoughts and actions in terms of a national pattern. Local political issues in themselves appeared drab and uninteresting unless they drew in or were linked with aspects of national happenings. Just as elsewhere money and men were poured into a struggle many believed a moral crusade. And during these same years business leaders quickened their step and advanced toward economic success perhaps more rapidly than they might have had there been no war.

The period 1848 to 1871 was robust and ambitious. Chicago advanced from a town economy to the economy of the city. With the passing from the home market and the emergence of a metropolitan economy came greater sophistication in all avenues of life. An urban civilization with its busy and restless crowds, its complex ways of living, its brightness and its darkness appeared, as if by magic, in the short span of little more than a score of years upon a people still rural in point of view and untutored in the solution of urban problems.

This startling urban development was attended by the characteristics of the growth of established communities.[1] In 1837 nearly one half of the white population had been males twenty-one or more years of age, but by 1850 this group had shrunk to about one third, and the percentage of children had grown to nearly one half, although that of women was almost the same as in 1837.[2] As the years marched on, the difference between the number of men and that of women gradually decreased,[3] the number of children increased, and society gave signs of replenishment not only by a continued immigration of families rather than of single persons but by the establishment of family life within the city.[4]

This expansion in numbers was due in part to natural causes, but a more important cause was the continuing stream of newcomers

---

[1] Bessie Louise Pierce, *A History of Chicago* (New York, 1937), I, 44; United States, *Statistical View of the United States . . . Being a Compendium of the Seventh Census* (J. D. B. DeBow, comp. Washington, 1854), p. 347. The population in 1850 was 29,963 and, by 1860, had risen to 109,260. By 1870 it was 298,977. Even the older large cities of the East experienced a rapid increase in population — New York, Boston, and Philadelphia nearly doubling their numbers during these two decades. In the cities of the Northwest, the gain was even greater. *Ibid.*, pp. 342, 347, 350, 360, 369, 372, 375; United States, *Eighth Census, 1860*, "Population," pp. 121, 246, 378, 381, 539, 608, 609, 610, 613; United States, *Ninth Census, 1870*, I, "Population," 127, 176, 229, 231, 292, 380. Except when indicated otherwise population statistics for 1850, 1860, and 1870 are found in the three census volumes listed above.

[2] Pierce, *A History of Chicago*, I, 172–74.

[3]

TABLE SHOWING SEX OF INHABITANTS

Year	Sex	Number	Per Cent of Aggregate Total
1850	Male	16,300	54.40
	Female	13,663	45.60
1860	Male	55,474	50.77
	Female	53,786	49.23
1870	Male	152,828	51.12
	Female	146,149	48.88

These figures include both white and Negro populations.

[4] At the beginning of 1854 the population of the city was 60,652 with 9,435 families. In 1870, the population was 298,977 with 59,497 families. In these sixteen years the population nearly quintupled, but the number of families increased more than sixfold. *The Daily Democratic Press*, December 31, 1853; *Weekly Chicago Democrat*, January 7, 1854. See Appendix, pp. 481–82.

which had begun pouring into the city in the years before 1848. The movement was accelerated by improved transportation facilities, notably the extension of the rail network. No longer need the migrant from the East await patiently the coming of the summer when ice had fled the lakes and rivers and roads were passable. "Who can wonder," remarked the *Daily Democratic Press,* "that in the enjoyment of facilities like these, the young and enterprising men of the older States are seeking by thousands for homes in our almost boundless and fruitful West?"[5] By 1849, the Michigan Central Railroad, by using on part of the route steamboats crowded from "stem to stern," was carrying large numbers of immigrants, chiefly English, Irish, and German, from Buffalo to Chicago at very low rates, and in the early part of May alone, twelve hundred persons were reported en route to points on Lake Michigan.[6]

By spring, 1855, the transfer of population from the old to the new states was heralded as one which would far exceed in numbers all former precedents. Within twenty-four hours in the summer of 1857, thirty-four hundred emigrants were reported as arriving over the Michigan Central alone. With her eastern and western connections, Chicago naturally became the principal receiving and distributing point for all this immigration, and the hearts of real estate promoters and other enterprising citizens warmed to the advantages of vacant lots and houses for rent and for sale. On to neighboring Iowa, Nebraska, Minnesota, and Wisconsin, as far south as Texas and even to the West Coast swept peoples of all classes and conditions, stirred by an impulse to partake of a life dreamed of as free and untroubled, where homesteads could be had from the government or at second-hand from companies and speculators.[7]

Mormons, a despised people, bound for Utah, to whom an unwilling city for a short time opened its gates;[8] entire families to people

[5] *The Daily Democratic Press,* December 12, 1855.

[6] *Daily Democrat,* May 8, 11, 15, 28, July 30, 1849. There were three classes of tickets, the holder of which was entitled to passage to any point on Lake Michigan. Foreign immigrants were charged three dollars, American steerage passengers, five dollars. First-class cabin fare was seven, eight, and nine dollars.

[7] *The Daily Democratic Press,* March 8, April 9, December 12, 1855, January 11, 1856.

[8] For the attitude of Chicago toward Brigham Young's government of Utah, see *ibid.,* August 25, October 26, 1857; *Oquawka Spectator,* July 18, 1856; *The Press and Tribune,* May 20, 1859. From July 17 to August 20, 1868, foreign converts to Mormonism to the number of 2,950 from Scotland, Wales, England, Germany, and the Scandinavian countries passed through Chicago. *Chicago Tribune,* August 20, 1868.

GREAT CENTRAL DEPOT GROUNDS, 1868

The view is north and east from the vicinity of Adams and Michigan. In the right center is the grain warehouse of Sturges and Buckingham which survived the fire of 1871.

VIEW ALONG LAKE STREET BETWEEN CLARK
AND LASALLE, 1857

the prairies of Illinois or perhaps to pause for some time within the city in quest of a better livelihood than known before;[9] groups of orphaned children, under the protection of missionary societies and charitable undertakings, seeking new homes where sometimes they could add to the labor supply as apprentices to foster parents;[10] domestic female servants sent on their way by a Women's Protective Immigration Society [11] — all these and others came under the lure of well-phrased advertisements which sketched in bright outline the promised land. Bankers and dealers in foreign exchange joined with real estate promoters in distributing pamphlets describing the abundance and fertility of land near by, not to mention the opportunities provided by the city itself. Through the Roche Brothers and Company of New York and similar firms, persons brought from Liverpool to New York on the Black Ball or Old Line of Liverpool packets and sometimes on first-class American ships were provided by their agents with "the cheapest and most expeditious mode of conveyance" to Chicago or farther west.[12] A "European Passage Department," by which immigrants not only from Liverpool, but from Havre, Bremen, and Hamburg were brought to America, was operated by Henry and Elias Greenebaum in connection with their banking business in Chicago. Hoffman and Gelpcke, bankers and ex-

---

[9] Within a few months in 1849, for example, fifteen families from the neighborhood of Wilmington, Delaware, came to Chicago. *Chicago Commercial Advertiser,* October 24, 1849.

[10] *The Daily Democratic Press,* September 28, 1854. The Rev. Van Meter of the Five Points Mission, New York, was among those who placed children in Illinois homes. (*Chicago Daily Democratic Press,* November 14, 1857; Arthur Charles Cole, *The Era of the Civil War, 1848–1870* [Clarence W. Alvord, ed., *The Centennial History of Illinois,* III. Springfield, 1919], p. 15.) The Children's Aid Society of New York under the direction of Charles Loring Brace performed a similar service. See *The Children's Aid Society of New York; Its History, Plan and Result* . . . (New York, 1893), pp. 32–34, 39–40.

[11] Arthur Charles Cole, "Illinois Women of the Middle Period," Illinois State Historical Society, *Transactions, 1920,* p. 85.

[12] *The Daily Democratic Press,* May 2, 1854; *Daily Democrat,* April 15, 1848. The city council was asked to buy 5,000 copies in German and 5,000 in English for distribution in the United States and Europe of the pamphlet entitled "Railroads, History and Commerce of Chicago." When the council did not act favorably the pamphlet was translated into German as *Geschichte, Eisenbahnen und Handel von Chicago.* It was printed by the *Illinois Staats-Zeitung.* (See *The Daily Democratic Press,* October 3, 1854.) Among the promoters were R. K. Swift, banker and dealer in foreign exchange, and Rees and Kerfoot, real estate agents. (See also *The Free West,* July 12, 1855.) Charles McDonnell in the 'forties was the Roche representative in Chicago. In 1850 he became the agent of P. W. Byrnes and Company. (*Chicago Daily Democrat,* October 14, 1850.) John C. Dodge was the Chicago representative of Harden and Company. *Ibid.,* January 1, 1849.

change brokers, circularized prospective German settlers,[13] and many an individual, successful in the new land, proved the most convincing of all through letters back home.

Colonization projects under the aegis of railroad companies, such as the Illinois Central, tempted the restless to leave established homes for new adventures connected with the great metropolis of the West. Well-phrased descriptions by foreign capitalists interested in lands near railroad routes convinced many farmers and artisans of the British Isles and the continent that the American Garden of Eden lay in the state of Illinois,[14] while colonization schemes designed to capitalize on the importance of Chicago as a distribution center for immigrants were promoted by agencies such as the Egg Harbor City Society, the Eudora Colonization Society, and the German Colonization Company of Colfax, Fremont County, Colorado.[15]

[13] In New York, the Greenebaums made arrangements with the general emigrant agent of the New York and Erie Railroad to forward immigrants to points west. (John Gager, comp., *Gager's Chicago City Directory for the Year Ending June 1st, 1857* . . . [Chicago, 1856], "Prominent Business Houses," p. 4 [hereafter referred to as Gager, *Directory, 1857*]. See also *The Workingman's Advocate*, April 24, May 22, 1869.) On May 16, 1862, the *Chicago Tribune* listed nineteen persons who left Liverpool on the packet *John Bright* and whose passage was paid at the Chicago office of Greenebaum Brothers. Georg von Bosse, *Das deutsche Element in den Vereinigten Staaten unter besonderer Berücksichtigung seines politischen, ethischen, sozialen und erzieherischen Einflusses* (Stuttgart, 1908), p. 186; *Die Fackel. Literaturblatt zur Förderung geistiger Freiheit* (1856), pp. 268–73.

[14] *The Workingman's Advocate*, March 12, 1870. For the story of the colonization of the Illinois Central lands see Paul Wallace Gates, *The Illinois Central Railroad and its Colonization Work* (Harvard Economic Studies, XLII. Cambridge, 1934). See the letters of Sir James Caird, *Chicago Daily Press and Tribune*, March 2, 31, April 1, 2, 4, 8, 9, 1859; also his *Prairie Farming in America* . . . (London, 1859). After 1857 financial misfortune led British bond and stockholders of the Illinois Central to form "protective committees" and send representatives to America to study the books and lands of the road. Caird was sent in 1858 and waxed enthusiastic over Illinois lands. Gates, *The Illinois Central Railroad*, pp. 80, 214–18, 232.

[15] *Illinois Staats-Zeitung*, March 16, April 2, 1861. A German land agency advertised Sigel, a new town about 190 miles south of Chicago during the 'sixties. (*Ibid.*, January 12, 1864.) In the spring of 1862, it was reported that many wealthy German landowners were about to emigrate to Illinois, Wisconsin, and Minnesota. Twenty thousand acres in these three states had already been bought for them, it was asserted, and the party was expected to arrive about the middle of July. Most of the land purchased was in Illinois. (*Chicago Tribune*, May 9, 1862.) In 1870, the German Colonization Company of Colfax, Fremont County, Colorado, said to be a Chicago organization, petitioned Congress for forty thousand acres upon which to colonize some Germans. It was urged that it cost too much for immigrants to move into the territory unaided, but if they joined the organization at $250 each, the society could move them and put them in possession. *Ibid.*, February 5, 1870; James F. Willard and Colin B. Goodykoontz, eds., *Experiments in Colorado Colonization 1869–1872* . . . (University of Colorado, *Historical Collections*, III, Colony Series II. Boulder, 1926), pp. 57–58, 60–66.

Herded into already overcrowded steamers with others who could speak no English and with whom the only means of conversation was through a pocket edition of an English dictionary, eager men, women, and children sought out the much-talked-of Chicago, traveling in the late 'forties and early 'fifties by way of the Hudson River, the Erie Canal, and the Great Lakes. When the railroad came, the ten days sometimes consumed in this journey were cut in half, later to be reduced without, however, much improvement in comfort, for emigrant ships and trains still seemed "little better than hog pens." [16] Sharpers, under the pretense of being "licensed forwarders," fleeced the unsuspecting by the sale of bogus railroad tickets as they entered New York harbor; imposters in Chicago operated in like manner upon those who were bound farther west; and illegal agents in Chicago extorted charges from immigrants as they docked. [17] Yet on they came, wretched, ill, and exploited, and the march into the new city and its surrounding country seemed unending. Thus it happened that Chicago became a more cosmopolitan city than New York, for the native-born population of the latter in 1850 was nearly 54 per cent of the total, while in Chicago it was but 46 per cent. [18] By 1860, Americans and their adopted brothers appeared in approximately equal numbers, and by 1870 the former slightly exceeded the latter. [19]

The section of the country which contributed the largest number of native born to the growing population of Chicago was the Old Northwest, the states of Illinois, Indiana, Ohio, Michigan, and Wisconsin. Those born in this region made up nearly a fourth of the total population and nearly half of the native born of the city in 1850, more than one fourth of the former and over half of the latter in 1860, and a third of the former and almost two thirds of the latter in 1870. Within this territory, Illinois was naturally the largest con-

---

[16] *The Workingman's Advocate,* June 11, 1870; Eric Johnson and C. F. Peterson, *Svenskarne i Illinois* (Chicago, 1880), p. 235; Ernst W. Olson and others, eds., *History of the Swedes of Illinois* (2 v. Chicago, 1908), I, 306–7; Eric Norelius, *Early Life of Eric Norelius* . . . (Emeroy Johnson, trans. Augustana Historical Society, *Publications,* no. 4. Rock Island, Illinois, 1934), pp. 106–10, 212–13.

[17] *The Daily Democratic Press,* March 2, 1854; *Daily Democrat,* May 11, 17, 1849; unsigned circular, enclosed in letter of B. A. Froiseth to Stephen A. Douglas, January 12, 1859, *Papers of Stephen A. Douglas, 1845–1861* (*Ms.* The University of Chicago).

[18] DeBow, *Statistical View of the United States,* p. 399.

[19] See Appendix, pp. 481–82.

tributor, followed by Ohio, although the latter and other north-western states furnished a very small proportion of their sons and daughters to swell the number of Chicago dwellers.[20]

From the Middle Atlantic and New England states came the next largest group, and it is probable that a good proportion of those born in the Northwest were descended from families originally from this area, cherishing and bequeathing their distinctive ways of living and patterns of thought. Together, in 1850, men and women of this region made up approximately 22 per cent of the total population and 47 per cent of the native born, or almost as many as those whose birthplace was the Northwest. Although Easterners resident in Chicago increased from 6,544 in 1850 to 44,162 in 1870, the proportion of eastern born to total native born gradually grew smaller, dropping in the decade 1860 to 1870 over 8 per cent. During the same period an almost equivalent increase of Northwesterners took place. By far the largest number of Easterners came from New York, followed by those from Pennsylvania in 1850 and by Massachusetts in 1860 and 1870. United by memories of their former abode, they kept alive local allegiances by the organization of societies; New Yorkers, for instance, joining hands in the Excelsior Society, while New Englanders perpetuated their friendships in the New England Society, whose celebration of the anniversary of the landing of the Pilgrims proved a gala occasion in the social life of Chicago.[21]

Few people came from the region across the Mississippi, of course. In 1850, there were only nineteen who had dared to reverse the general movement of the day, and they came from near-by Iowa. The number in 1860 reached only 138, and by 1870 slight migrations raised the number to what at that time was the least from any section, or 1,589. Those who arrived in Chicago from the South or from the so-called border states composed a very small part of the population, although their numbers grew in the years 1850 to 1870 from about 3.6 per cent to over 4.7 per cent of the native born. At first Virginians led, but in 1860 and in 1870 settlers from Kentucky stood first numerically. By 1870, those who came from Missouri and Maryland

[20] For detailed statement about population discussed in this chapter, see Appendix, pp. 481–82.

[21] Excelsior Society to Lyman Trumbull, January 29, 1859, *The Papers of Lyman Trumbull, 1855–1877,* XV (*Ms.* Library of Congress); *Daily Democrat,* January 9, 11, 1849; Gager, *Directory, 1857,* Appendix, pp. xxii–xxiii.

had shown a considerable gain. Most of these Southerners were whites.[22]

Only 323 Negroes, about 1 per cent of the total population, were in Chicago in 1850. Although this number increased in the next ten years to 955, Negroes made up a still smaller proportion of the total population — being less than 1 per cent. In 1870, however, their 3,691 represented an increase of over 286 per cent in ten years in their own numbers, but they still formed a group of slightly more than 1 per cent of the total population.[23] Almost two thirds of the native-born blacks living in Chicago in 1870 came from the South, and of these not quite a third were from Kentucky, with the next largest number, or a little over one fifth, from Virginia. The Old Northwest sent 955, or almost 27 per cent of the total native-born black population, and, as in the case of the white inhabitants, Illinois, with 606, furnished the most of any state in this region. To these were added 312 from the Middle Atlantic and New England states and the 22 Negroes who came from Iowa and Minnesota.[24]

The Negro population though small was fairly well concentrated, for 82 per cent, in 1850, lived in the South Division, particularly in the First and Second wards.[25] Ten years later about 72 per cent congregated in the First, Second, and Third wards, and, according to the federal census of 1870, almost 80 per cent lived in the area bounded by Sixteenth Street, the lake front, and the main and south branches

[22] DeBow, *Statistical View of the United States,* p. 399; United States, *Eighth Census, 1860,* " Population," p. 613; United States, *Ninth Census, 1870,* I, " Population," 380–85.

[23] In 1850, Negroes made up 1.08 per cent of total population; in 1860, .87 per cent; and in 1870, 1.23 per cent. Although there was an increase of 1,042.72 per cent in the colored population from 1850 to 1870, the proportion to the total population remained practically the same.

[24] In 1870, the Middle Atlantic states furnished 7.50 per cent and the New England states 1.26 per cent of the total native Negro population.

[25] United States, *Seventh Census, 1850,* p. 705. The following table shows the number of Negroes in the South Division:

Wards	Male	Female	Total
First	48	26	74
Second	32	41	73
Third	32	26	58
Fourth	27	33	60
Total	139	126	265

The boundaries of these wards were as follows: First (lake shore, Twenty-second, State, Chicago River); Second (State, Twenty-second, Clark, Chicago River); Third (Clark, Twenty-second, Wells, Chicago River); Fourth (Wells, Twenty-second, South Branch of the Chicago River). For a map showing the boundaries, see Pierce, *A History of Chicago,* I, 326, also this volume p. 307.

of the Chicago River.[26] Upon their black brethren Chicagoans, like many other Northerners, showered kindliness and intolerance. Politically Republican during the Civil War and generally hostile to slavery expansion earlier, they wished to protect Negroes in their civil rights, but not to the point of elevating them to the plane of equality.[27] Opposing the further extension of the "Black Code" of Illinois in 1848, disapproving of the law of 1853 which prevented the immigration of free Negroes into the state,[28] these protectors of fugitive slaves raised no objection to the exclusion of Negro testimony against a white person in the courts of law; they seemed to see no inconsistencies in providing a separate section in the theaters for Negroes,[29] and in segregating the races in the common schools.[30] Even in the late 'sixties labor-union organizers hesitated to receive colored workmen into their fraternity, and white laborers openly opposed Negro competition in the labor market. At the same time common carriers took into consideration what must have been the public will of the day and excluded Negroes from the accommodations provided others, just as the owners of property found it undesirable to rent to them.[31]

Indians made up an even smaller portion of the population than

---

[26] This area formed the First, Second, and Third wards at this time.

[27] See, for example, the speech of Douglas on the Compromise of 1850 as reported in James W. Sheahan, *The Life of Stephen A. Douglas* (New York, 1860), pp. 156–57. Typical of the discussions regarding Negro equality is the editorial in *Chicago Evening Post*, September 9, 1868.

[28] See p. 383; also Pierce, *A History of Chicago*, I, 393.

[29] For example, in 1854, charges in the police court against a white woman for adultery were dismissed because the witnesses were Negroes. *The Daily Democratic Press*, February 2, 1854; *Daily Democrat*, November 18, 1848.

[30] In the midst of a war to free the slaves, a mulatto girl with an average grade of ninety-seven was not permitted to receive her diploma with others at the regular commencement exercises. (*Chicago Evening Journal*, July 11, 1863.) In 1861, there was a controversy about admitting a Negro girl to the Normal Department of the High School. She was finally admitted. (*Chicago Tribune*, July 28, 1861.) In 1863, a separate school for colored children was opened in accordance with an act of the state legislature. The revised charter of 1865 repealed this law, however, and the separate school was abolished in April of that year. [Shepherd Johnston], "Historical Sketches of the Public School System of the City of Chicago," *Twenty-fifth Annual Report of the Board of Education for the Year Ending July 31, 1879* (Chicago, 1880), p. 38; Act of February 13, 1863, *Private Laws of Illinois, 1863*, p. 129 (*Private Laws of Illinois* hereafter cited as *Private Laws*); Act of February 15, 1865, *Private Laws, 1865*, I, 287.

[31] Charles H. Wesley, *Negro Labor in the United States* (New York, 1927), p. 99; *The Irish Republic*, May 18, 1867; *Chicago Tribune*, January 4, 1868, July 27, 1870. See also *ibid.*, July 15, 17, 1862, which described an episode known as the "omnibus riot case" in which W. E. Walker, colored, was put off a "bus" driven by an Irishman, Richard Kelly.

the Negroes. As early as 1851, a number of Pottawattomies, encamped a short distance south of the city, was so unusual a sight that school children were taken to pay them a visit. By the mid-'fifties these "wild tenants of the forest," the victims of the white man's civilization, seemed to a visiting circus manager worth advertising in a community which had known them well little more than a score of years before.[32] Within the city itself six Indians lived in 1860, and by 1870 there were only five.

Early settlement and urban development had been, on the whole, the work of native Americans. But by the late 'thirties heavy foreign migrations had taken place, so that by mid-century over half of the city was made up of foreign immigrants. As in the 'forties, the largest foreign group in the city in 1850 was the Irish, numbering over six thousand, more than 20 per cent of the total population and nearly 39 per cent of all foreigners. Their numbers continued to mount during the next two decades, although the ratio in proportion to total population and to other foreign born decreased. Driven to seek release from political oppression, large numbers came, particularly from Waterford, Cork, and Limerick. By the late 'forties in one week £9,000 in separate sums of £1 each were paid to one house in Liverpool "as head money for so many separate families emigrating to America." Still others, blessed with more of this world's goods, including some Dublin shopkeepers and some industrious farmers from Waterford, joined in the search for a better life across the seas.[33]

In Chicago, many of the Irish went to make up the unskilled labor so important to the growing community. Often crowded in insanitary shanties which provided little shelter from the cruelties of the weather, they tended to congregate on the North Side and in Bridgeport, the slaughterhouse district located along the line of the canal, where offensive odors befouled the air, apparently to the unconcern of what one writer called the "unwashed Dimmycrats."[34]

Whether of the lowly or of the more prosperous, the Irish were intensely loyal to their native land, for which independence was craved

[32] *Chicago Daily Journal*, March 29, 1851; *The Daily Democratic Press*, June 29, 1855.

[33] *Daily Democrat*, January 15, 16, 1849.

[34] *Chicago Daily Journal*, August 20, 1850; *Chicago Evening Journal*, October 3, 1863. See also E. L. Peckham, "My Journey Out West," *The Journal of American History*, XVII (3rd quarter, no. 3, 1923), 228.

even to the point of large offerings of money and the proffer of personal service.[35] Assistance for this purpose was frequently sought in mass meetings of Irish nationals, who, making merry on St. Patrick's Day or holding high festival on other occasions such as the visit of Jeremiah O'Donovan Rossa, the Irish rebel, demonstrated for Irish independence. By the early 'sixties the Fenian Brotherhood, whose chief aim was Irish independence, could boast a membership of at least three hundred, anxious to " trample in the dust the blood-stained banner of England." In November, 1863, the national convention of the organization was held in Chicago, where Irishmen made up almost one fifth of those living in the city. But the sessions were secret and the deliberations, therefore, not known.[36]

A National Fair, opening in March, 1864, addressed by Lieutenant Governor Francis A. Hoffman and John Wentworth, was the largest of several gatherings to get money to promote plans for Irish independence. Receipts of $54,000 in one week gave a touch of realism to the professions of these romantically nationalistic people. Exhibits from every state in the Union and even from Ireland betokened graphically the unity of purpose, the hope that

> The patient dint and powder shock
> Will blast an empire like a rock.[37]

Continued activity on the part of these green- and black-garbed Irishmen provoked the charge that they were attempting to set up a republic within a republic. Large sums of money poured into the

[35] Among prominent Irish citizens of the community were John E. McGirr, physician and outstanding in educational work; William J. Onahan, produce commission merchant and leading Catholic layman; Dr. William B. Egan, physician and real estate dealer; James H. Collins, attorney; and James A. Mulligan, attorney and colonel of the famous Irish Brigade in the Civil War.

[36] *The Daily Democratic Press,* September 13, 1855; *Daily Democrat,* March 14, 19, 1849, March 18, 21, 1850; *Chicago Tribune,* March 8, 1865, March 19, 1866, April 17, 1871; *Chicago Evening Journal,* March 18, 1863. A purpose of the Fenians was to get arms and munitions and to hold military drill. The exact date of the organization in Chicago is not known. Their hall was located in 1863 at the northwest corner of Wells and Randolph streets, where meetings were held twice each week. The Fenians were of like mind with the Irish Republican Brotherhood founded in Dublin in 1858. (T. M. Halpin, comp., *Halpin & Bailey's Chicago City Directory for 1863-64* [Chicago, 1863], " City and County Register," p. xxi [hereafter cited as *Halpin & Bailey's Directory, 1863-64*].) At this time there were forty " circles " in Illinois. *The Chicago Times,* November 4, 1863, February 8, 1864; *The Irish Republic,* May 4, 1867.

[37] *Chicago Tribune,* March 29, December 24, 1864; *Chicago Evening Journal,* January 18, March 28, 29, 1864; *The Chicago Times,* January 21, 26, March 17, April 2, 5, 13, 1864.

central office of New York, and by 1866 Chicago was reported to have the finest regiment in the Fenian army, which, with others from the state, moved toward Buffalo under General Thomas W. Sweeny to strike at Canada. But the movement was doomed to failure, for President Johnson forbade Americans to engage in such an enterprise, and the United States Circuit Court declared the invasion a violation of the Neutrality Act of 1818, still in force.[38]

Despite these curious activities of the Fenians, little opposition arose, aside from the frank denunciation by Bishop James Duggan of the group as a secret society fostering revolution through the use of arms, of which the Church disapproved. The *Tribune*, too, raised a somewhat querulous voice in 1864 when it protested the proposal of the Chicago Circle for America to declare war on England. And when four years later the Brotherhood urged high tariffs instead of the reduction proposed by the *Tribune*, the editor prescribed "less crochetty" principles for the members.[39]

Avowedly opposed to political party alignment, the Fenians, however, were generally found in the Democratic ranks, although their loyalty was tenuous whenever Irish sensitivities were touched. An article in the *Chicago Times* in 1865, which criticized their poor brethren in what they held "contemptible" terms, led to some slight defection from Democratic columns, a defection willingly encouraged by Republicans. This encouragement led to a split in the Irish vote in the election of 1866, and by 1868 a Republican club endeavored to deliver Irish votes in the national election. The following year a national Republican convention made up of discontented sons of the Emerald Isle met in Chicago and vented spleen against England in resolutions of vitriolic tone. By 1870, however, the Fenians in Chicago as elsewhere seemed to have lost something of the vigor of mid-'sixties, although the years immediately prior had seen

[38] *Chicago Evening Journal*, August 14, 1865; *The Chicago Times*, November 4, 1863; *Chicago Republican*, May 12, 1866; *Chicago Tribune*, February 12, November 3, 1866. Not only Irish, but Americans, Poles, and Germans contributed to the fund for an invasion of Canada. The Chicago Brotherhood raised $10,000 for military preparation. (*Chicago Republican*, March 5, 13, 1866.) Canadian volunteers from Chicago were rushed to the assistance of Canadians. *Chicago Evening Journal*, June 4, 5, 6, 14, 22, 1866; *Chicago Tribune*, June 22, 1866.

[39] *The Chicago Times*, February 3, 8, 1864. Bishop Duggan declared that a secret inner circle controlled the organization activities. He forbade members to take the sacrament. *Chicago Evening Journal*, February 3, 1864; *Chicago Tribune*, December 25, 1864, January 13, 26, 1866, July 7, 9, 1869.

an enthusiastic welcome accorded John O'Neill, national president, who was still driving for enlistments, and Chicago Fenians still donated to the cause of the homeland.[40]

Besides the Irish, the British Isles contributed English, Welsh, and Scotch. Altogether these four groups made up almost 29 per cent of the total population and about 55 per cent of the foreign born in 1850. By 1870 they composed 18 per cent of the total and nearly 38 per cent of the foreign-born population, while in actual numbers they had increased over six-fold. Next to the Irish, emigrants from England were the largest group. In 1850 they numbered 1,883, and by 1860 they had increased to 4,354 and to 10,027 in 1870. They, too, kept alive memories of the homeland by dining on Queen Victoria's Birthday and by associations with their fellows in St. George's Society of Illinois, founded in the spring of 1847 and designed for both benevolent and social purposes. The quick amalgamation of the English into American ways was demonstrated in no more effective manner than by the attendance of the Society at the services at the Church of the Atonement on the occasion of the National Fast declared for September 26, 1861, by President Lincoln after the Union military reverses of that year. But this ready assimilation had not dimmed an inbred love for the ruling house of England, and when the Prince of Wales paid Chicago a brief visit in 1860 he was received with customary warmth and pomp.[41]

Next came the Scots, who numbered 610 in 1850. In 1860, this group had increased to 1,641 and by 1870 to 4,197.[42] To serve their

---

[40] *The Chicago Times,* August 10, 1865; *Chicago Tribune,* August 11, 1865, August 16, 17, 1866. John Pope Hodnett, editor of the *Irish Republic* in Chicago, with John F. Scanlan and Alderman Arthur Dixon was active in the attempt to win over Irish votes. Some of the meetings of the Republican Club were attended by loyal Irish Democrats who wielded clubs and threw stones upon the deserters. *Ibid.,* February 20, April 22, July 27, August 28, 1868, July 7, 9, 1869; *The Chicago Times,* August 2, 3, 10, 12, 1867, May 25, 31, 1870. See p. 287.

[41] *The Daily Democratic Press,* May 26, 1856; *Daily Democrat,* April 12, 1849, September 21, 1860; *Chicago Tribune,* September 24, 27, 1861, June 25, 1868, May 25, 1871; *The Press and Tribune,* September 22, 24, 1860; *Oquawka Spectator,* August 16, September 6, 27, 1860.

[42] Among the prominent Scotchmen who were citizens of Chicago were George Armour, grain merchant; George Smith, banker; James S. Kirk, soap manufacturer; Allan Pinkerton, detective; George MacPherson, pharmacist; John Crighton, grain merchant; John Clark, manufacturer; James Ballantyne, first commercial editor in Chicago, connected with the *Daily Democratic Press, Tribune,* and *Republican;* James Chisholm, journalist with the *Times, Tribune,* and *Inter Ocean;* Robert Fergus, publisher; James Barnet, printer. A. T. Andreas, *History of Chicago from the Earliest Period to the Present Time* (3 v. Chicago,

brothers in distress they founded the Illinois St. Andrew's Society in January, 1846, and its yearly festival became a gala occasion where the "sweetest and purest" Scotch music regaled these sturdy Caledonians and kept them mindful of Burns, Scott, Ramsay, Wallace, and Bruce. The Caledonian Club served as another link in the chain of loyalty to homeland, and by 1869 its library of several hundred volumes provided reading materials in a day when there was no public library.[43]

Least in numbers from the British Isles were the Welsh, so few indeed that the census of 1850 counted them with the English. In 1860, there were only 222 in Chicago and ten years later only 565, in both instances forming less than a half of 1 per cent of either the total or foreign-born population. But numbers seemed unimportant when it came to St. David's Day, which as early as 1837 was celebrated in Chicago. A St. David's Society was organized in 1852, and at the second anniversary dinner it was reported that only one Welshman "had been found in circumstances requiring assistance during the past year." This the editor of the *Democratic Press* regarded "as a high compliment to the industry and prudence" of the Welsh citizens.[44]

The single nationality which added most to the population of Chicago after 1850 was the German. In 1850, the 5,094 Germans in the city comprised 17 per cent of the total population. Their numbers grew rapidly, and in the census of 1860 German born represented more than 20 per cent of the total population. In the next ten years the German-born group more than doubled, but their percentage of the total population decreased slightly to a little less than 20 per cent. On the other hand, they made up over 41 per cent of the foreign

1884–86), II, 492, 497–98; Thomas C. MacMillan, "The Scots and their Descendants in Illinois," Illinois State Historical Society, *Transactions, 1919*, pp. 55, 56, 57, 73, 76, 81, 83, 84.

[43] Pierce, *A History of Chicago*, I, 184; *Weekly Chicago Democrat*, December 9, 1854; *Daily Democrat*, January 8, 1848, January 20, 1860; *The Daily Democratic Press*, November 29, 1855, November 27, 1856; *Chicago Tribune*, November 29, 1860, December 1, 1863, December 1, 1870, August 16, 1871. At the annual meeting of the St. Andrew's Society in November, 1868, it was reported that $359.15 had been spent during the year in relieving fifty-three cases of needy Scotchmen. (*Ibid.*, November 13, 1868.) The celebration of the birthdays of Scott and Burns served to call the Scotch together.

[44] Pierce, *A History of Chicago*, I, 184; *The Daily Democratic Press*, March 3, 1854, March 1, 1855. By 1860, there was also the Cambrian Benevolent Society which was to look out for the welfare of the indigent Welsh. *Chicago Daily Democrat*, March 2, 1860.

born, exclusive of those born in the United States of German parentage. Unlike the Irish, they were, on the whole, Protestant in religion, although immigrants from the German-speaking sections, Baden, Bavaria, Austria, and Bohemia, were, for the most part, Catholic.[45]

A consciousness of common origin led them to prefer German-made goods, German hostelries, German churches and theaters, German trade unions, and even patent medicines wearing a German label. It was, therefore, the better part of wisdom for native business organizations to employ German clerks, to carry German goods, and to advertise their wares in the German language.[46] In some way this subservience to group consciousness laid open the way for Germans to proclaim that they were " the most energetic, most enlightened and cultivated citizens of the union," and the " counterpoise against the corrupting influence of American materialism and its excrescence." [47] Nor was it unnatural that these newcomers, stirred by the events of 1870 in the Fatherland, expressed individually and collectively a sympathy for Bismarck and took from their purses some of their earnings to aid those engaged in the Franco-Prussian War.[48] In these activities Americans sometimes played a part, both directly and indirectly lending support to the German cause. Indeed, political and business acumen, as well as affection for their German brothers, frequently seem to have motivated protestations on the part of some Americans. When peace came, the city went wild. A reported thirty thousand demonstrated in a colorful procession ten miles long under the eyes of two hundred thousand spectators.[49]

[45] By 1860, 26 per cent of the Germans in Chicago came from Prussia, with Bavaria furnishing nearly 12 per cent; in 1870 the former composed 42 per cent of the German population, and Bohemians ranked second with almost 11 per cent. (DeBow, *Statistical View of the United States*, p. 399; United States, *Eighth Census, 1860*, " Population," p. 613; United States, *Ninth Census, 1870*, I, " Population," 386, 387.) In 1860, there were 22,230 German born; in 1870, there were 59,299, including 6,277 Bohemians.

[46] *Illinois Staats-Zeitung*, January 15, February 20, April 5, 11, August 25, October 30, 1861, October 10, 1864; *Deutsch-Amerikanische Geschichtsblätter*, VII (1907), 44–45. Among the German hotels may be listed the New York Haus, the Franklin Haus, Schall's Haus, and North Western Haus. *Illinois Staats-Zeitung*, May 16, 28, June 10, November 1, 1861, October 11, 1864.

[47] *Ibid.*, December 3, 1861.

[48] On July 17, 1870, a large meeting took place, at which Caspar Butz, Edmund Jüssen, and Hermann Raster spoke. Resolutions of sympathy were adopted and $3,000 collected. *Chicago Tribune*, July 18, 1870.

[49] On August 19, 1870, a meeting in Farwell Hall was addressed by Governor Edward S. Salomon of Wisconsin, Hermann von Holst, the historian, Edmund Jüssen, Norman B. Judd, and J. Y. Scammon. Benefit fairs were held, and picnics and similar demonstrations of

Despite such manifestations, the walls of national solidarity were not so impregnable that eventually they did not crumble, in part at least, under the siege of daily contact with things American. Americanisms such as *smarte* (smart) became a part of their daily expressions, restaurants served *excellente* lunches, *Grocereien* supplanted the *Materialwaren, und so fort* succeeded *und so weiter.* Within four months in 1861 one fourth of the marriage ceremonies performed by German justices of the peace were intermarriages with Americans.[50] The call for volunteers in the Civil War reduced them irretrievably to the American amalgam and consigned them to the nationalism of a Republican North.

Next in numbers was the Scandinavian group — the Swedes, Norwegians, and Danes — although, in 1860, they were only 2,279. This was about 2 per cent of the total population and a little more than 4 per cent of the foreign born. Throughout the years from 1850 to 1870, the most came from Norway, followed by those from Sweden, with the Danes trailing.[51] These hardy and frugal Northmen had come to Chicago in appreciable numbers by the 'forties,[52] and before 1850 Norwegians alone were estimated at six hundred. "We get no better population," declared the editor of the *Daily Democratic Press,* "and we most cordially welcome them to the land of 'liberty, equality, and fraternity.'"[53] By mid-'fifties the stream seemed in full flood, fourteen immigrant ships filled with seekers of more "numerous chances" than were provided at home crossing the Atlantic at one time in the early summer of 1856. Economic security was the goal of some, political allurements of others. Here, indeed, work was no disgrace; class interests and conventional prejudices placed few obstacles in the way of him who would work. And those who dis-

---

cultural unity took place. (See, for example, *ibid.,* August 3, 20, 30, September 1, 1870.) The monster parade to celebrate peace was held on May 29, 1871. It proceeded to the Court House Square, where the marchers were received and reviewed. The assembled masses repaired to Wright's Grove, where they were welcomed by Franz Arnold and John B. Rice (mayor, 1865–69). *Ibid.,* May 27, 30, 1871; August Lueders, *Sechzig Jahre in Chicago* (Chicago, 1929), pp. 24–26.

50 *Illinois Staats-Zeitung,* July 19, 20, August 2, 5, September 2, December 6, 1861.

51 The census of 1850 does not list Scandinavians in Chicago.

52 Within ten weeks in the summer, 1861, five thousand Scandinavians arrived in Chicago, having traveled over the Grand Trunk Railroad from Quebec on their way westward. Most of them went farther west via the Galena and Chicago Union. *Chicago Tribune,* July 18, 1861.

53 *Chicago Daily Democrat,* July 30, 1849; *The Daily Democratic Press,* June 21, 1856.

agreed with the preachments, particularly of the Swedish Lutheran Church, could find release from the tyranny of convention. That these benefits came to those who dwelt in America was not doubted by these intrepid wayfarers, for they had been told so in numerous letters from trusted kinfolk and friends who had dared to adventure.[54]

During 1854 the Chicago Scandinavian Union was organized at the behest of prominent citizens who wished to care for their brethren who were emigrating to America and to encourage " a more intimate intercourse and knowledge of each other." [55] Despite the design of the founders and the bond of unity which might have existed, the Norwegians, Swedes, and Danes tended to become more particularized as time went on.[56] What might have been common endeavor was carried on by separate organizations such as the Svea Society, which, besides its social and humanitarian objects, was founded to prevent fraudulent practices on the Swedish immigrant. It maintained a house on Illinois Street which eventually became inadequate, a new home being provided in 1868.[57] But common hardships failed to unite the conservative church faction with the liberal element represented in the Svea Society, and the national unity of some other groups seemed lacking. This division went so far as to prove a handicap in raising money by the Svea Society for the destitute in the

[54] Bessie Louise Pierce, ed., *As Others See Chicago* (Chicago, 1933), p. 178. One group of 309 arrived in June, 1856, carrying drafts on R. K. Swift and Company amounting to $12,000. This group reported that 1,300 from the same part of Norway were en route. *Ibid*. See also John S. Lindberg, *The Background of Swedish Emigration to the United States* . . . (Minneapolis, 1930), pp. 1–3; George M. Stephenson, " The Background of the Beginnings of Swedish Immigration, 1850–1875," *The American Historical Review*, XXXI (July, 1926), 710; George M. Stephenson, " The Stormy Years of the Swedish Colony in Chicago before the Great Fire," Illinois State Historical Society, *Transactions, 1929*, pp. 167–70, 172.

[55] *The Daily Democratic Press*, February 10, December 23, 1854.

[56] In 1869, for example, a mass meeting of all Scandinavians was called not only to consider the question of immigration but to find means by which to cement the three groups into a harmonious whole. *The Workingman's Advocate*, May 1, 1869.

[57] T. M. Halpin, *Halpin's Eighth Annual Edition Chicago City Directory, 1865–6*, " City and County Record," p. xxv (hereafter cited as Halpin, *Directory*). The Svea Society (Sällskapet Svea) was organized in 1857 by a non-Lutheran group. In two weeks in 1868, it was reported, 1,800 persons were cared for. Funds for a new home were increased by the usual " fair." In 1870, rivalry between Swedish factions, an allegedly incompetent management, and opposition from emigration agents caused the abandonment of this home as well as the one maintained by the Scandinavian Aid Society. *Chicago Tribune*, July 12, October 21, 1868; Stephenson, " The Stormy Years of the Swedish Colony in Chicago before the Great Fire," *loc. cit.*, pp. 173, 177.

homeland in 1867, at a time when the influx of Swedes into Chicago was at its peak.[58]

Despite divisive influences and although the use of English even in church services became more and more common,[59] the Swedes retained a national consciousness which sought to perpetuate both language and culture. Retention of their folkways and mores was not difficult, on the whole, for most Swedes lived together on the swampy prairie of the North Side in their homes of logs and rough boards. Gradually they spread from the "Swedish Town" to the South Side, and from their midst came outstanding and useful citizens.[60]

In fewer numbers were the French, making less than 1 per cent of the total population in the years up to 1870. Of those who reached Chicago many passed to homes on the prairies, and a colony on its way to Bulbonia's Grove in Will County, where already was a considerable number of "the sons of La Belle France," paused in Chicago momentarily in 1848. In 1850, there were but 234 French in Chicago. By 1860 the number had increased to 883, enough, it was felt, to justify the establishment of a vice-consulate in the city. By 1870 there were only 1,418 Frenchmen, constituting less than .5 per cent of the total population.[61] Events in the homeland aroused their

---

[58] *Ibid.*, p. 177; Olson, *op. cit.*, I, 888–89, 890. The Svea Society had a library in which could be found the leading Stockholm newspaper, *Aftonbladet*, which cost the society fifty-six dollars annually.

[59] *Hemlandet*, the Swedish newspaper, under the editorship of T. N. Hasselquist, a young Lutheran clergyman, was particularly desirous that his countrymen should not be considered as foreigners. Fritiof Ander, "Some Factors in the Americanization of the Swedish Immigrant, 1850–1890," Illinois State Historical Society, *Journal*, XXVI (April–July, 1933), 139–47.

[60] The original location of the Swedish colony was in the section bounded by Division Street and Grand Avenue on the north and south, and by Wells Street and the North Branch of the Chicago River on the east and west. After 1850, Swedes located between Indiana Avenue and Erie Street along the North Branch of the River. In 1853 and 1854 Swedes purchased lots from W. B. Ogden and W. L. Newberry, and scattered over the North Side. By this time some moved to the South Side. (Johnson and Peterson, *op. cit.*, p. 241; Olson, *op. cit.*, I, 310–11. See also Vivien Marie Palmer, *The Primary Settlement as a Unit of Urban Growth and Organization* [unpublished Ph.D. Thesis, The University of Chicago, 1932], pp. 114–16, 141–42.) Two outstanding members of the Swedish group were Captain Polycarpus von Schneidau, who was the first Swedish consul in Chicago, and the Rev. Gustaf Unonius. These two men did much to alleviate the sufferings of newcomers. *Chicago Daily Democrat*, July 14, 16, 1852.

[61] *Daily Democrat*, June 20, 1848. C. A. Ravin D'Elpeux was the first consul to be appointed. (*Ibid.*, March 13, September 21, 1860.) Most of the French resided on the South Side. The center of the colony was the French Catholic Church of St. Louis, which stood at Polk and Sherman streets. *L'Écho des Deux Mondes* . . . , VII (October, 1909), 13.

sympathy, just as happenings elsewhere stirred the emotions of others of foreign birth. The establishment of the Third Republic led to a rousing mass meeting at Farwell Hall, at which Americans joined in extolling the spread of republican institutions; and the celebration of the birthdays of French heroes became the occasion for fanning the flame of national pride.[62] La Société Française de Secours Mutuels, organized in 1859, served to keep alive native lore and to assist the needy. Other societies with like purpose were organized, and they, too, resorted to charity balls and lectures as ways to gain funds to carry on their work.[63]

Belgians, Italians, Spaniards, Poles, and Russians were here in relatively small numbers. Indeed, no one of them made up as much as 1 per cent of the population from 1850 to 1870.[64] After the Revolution of 1848, Hungarians came, Anthony Poleski, a lieutenant of Hussars, reaching Chicago in 1850 in search of employment. In the same year, refugees under Laisdlaus Ujhazy [sic] paused long enough on their way west to be offered the hospitality of the city. In the autumn of 1851, 128 bound for New Buda, Iowa, remained for a time to earn money to proceed on their journey. By 1870 Chicago had only 159 Hungarians as residents, but their racial cohesion was such that in 1858 they organized to foster memory of country and language, as well as to care for their indigent sick and to promote accord among the Magyars. In 1865, a Slavic Union was the expression of a sense of unity among Slavs in the city, just as two years prior the Slovanska Lipa Benevolent Society represented their feel-

---

[62] The celebration of the Third Republic was addressed by W. F. Coolbaugh, banker; Leonard Swett, lawyer; Wirt Dexter, lumber merchant; Edward G. Asay, lawyer; J. F. Finerty representing the Irish Literary Society; and Gen. Hasbrouck Davis, lawyer and editor. (*Chicago Tribune,* September 23, 1870.) At a celebration of the birthday of Napoleon I in 1865 it was the feeling of the speakers that the United States dare not " touch a hair of the imperial head of Maximilian," for fifty thousand Frenchmen could dispose of the entire American military force. This boast, said the *Tribune* (August 18, 1865), was but " a piece of impertinence," and it counselled greater discretion in speech.

[63] *L'Écho des Deux Mondes,* VII (October, 1909), 13; Halpin, *Directory, 1865–66,* " City and County Record," p. xxiv; *Chicago Tribune,* February 18, 1861, November 20, 1868, May 28, 1870. The Société Française de Bienfaisance was organized in February, 1861. Its officers were F. G. Berteau, president; J. Leduc and G. DeLoynes, vice-presidents; A. Spink, treasurer; A. Fredin, secretary.

[64] In spite of their small numbers the Italians paid homage to Victor Emmanuel, Garibaldi, and Cavour and joined with Americans in celebrating Columbus Day. *Ibid.,* June 9, 1868, October 3, 12, 1870.

ing of oneness in their avowal of responsibility to care for poverty-stricken nationals.[65]

In the building of the Chicago of this time Jews, although few in numbers, played a praiseworthy part.[66] By the late 'fifties their number seemed sufficient to have warranted consideration in the search for votes by political parties, and Abraham Kohn was nominated in 1859 for clerk of the Common Council, later serving during 1860–61 under Mayor Wentworth in that capacity. By 1853, too, the Jewish Synagogue, Kehilath Anshe Mayriv, established in 1847, had outgrown its second synagogue and moved into a two-room building, where, in the basement, a day school was held. That a Jewish public school, provided for in 1859, gave instruction in the Hebrew and English languages indicated the attempt of this group not only to perpetuate its own tongue but to master that of the new homeland.[67] At an early time, too, Jews became prominent in the economic life of the city, where, for instance, the success of the Greenebaum banking house bore witness to a business acumen which aided in the material expansion of the city. Little anti-Semitic feeling seems to have existed in Chicago. In 1867, an order of New York insurance companies that all applications from Jews for insurance on stocks of merchandise had to be referred to the general agent aroused both Jews and gentiles to the point of boycotting the agents of companies engaged in such action.[68]

[65] *Chicago Daily Democrat*, February 14, April 24, 25, October 10, 14, 1850; *Chicago Daily Press and Tribune*, August 17, 1858; *Chicago Tribune*, January 21, 23, 1865; Halpin, *Directory, 1865–66*, " City and County Record," p. xxv. About eighty of these Hungarians bound for Iowa obtained employment on the Illinois Central Railroad. Their work was so satisfactory that the contractor proposed to keep them to work on the Rock Island Railroad. *Chicago Daily Democrat*, April 17, 1852.

[66] *Ibid.*, June 14, 1851; *Oquawka Spectator*, October 17, 1854. There are no enumerations at this time which list Jews.

[67] *Chicago Weekly Democrat*, June 11, 1859; Herman Eliassof, " German-American Jews," *Deutsch-Amerikanische Geschichtsblätter*, XIV (1914), 366. The first synagogue in 1851 was at Adams and Wells streets. (Harold Korey, " The Story of Jewish Education in Chicago Prior to 1923," *Jewish Education*, VI [January–March, 1934], 37, 38.) The spelling varies. In the act of incorporation, for instance, it appears as Kehilath Anshe Mayrib. Act of February 12, 1855, *Private Laws, 1855*, pp. 584–85.

[68] The insurance companies concerned were the Hanover, Germania, Niagara, Republic, and Manhattan, according to the *Chicago Tribune*, April 12, 1867. At a meeting, April 11, 1867, presided over by Levi Rosenfeld, the action was condemned by Henry Greenebaum, Jewish banker, Francis Hoffman, J. Y. Scammon, gentile bankers, and·J. C. Dore, gentile commission merchant and insurance agent.

But if the citizenry in general did not indulge in racial discrimination, the Jews themselves were not free from discord. In the late 'fifties reformers within Kehilath Anshe Mayriv caused dissension there. German Jews, who seemed in the majority, sometimes would not allow the Hebrew Relief Society to care for Jews of other than German nativity.[69] The Independent Order of B'nai B'rith, a benevolent association organized in Chicago in 1857, at one time permitted only German Jews as members. Separate congregations arose to permit Polish Jews and Jews from Bohemia to worship God, since they found no welcome from the members of Kehilath Anshe Mayriv.[70]

Within this mosaic of many climes and countries, one lone Turk could be found in 1860, and in 1870 he had been joined by two others. Malta, Greece, and the Duchy of Luxemburg added their contributions. Negroes, Canadians, and others from British America, Mexicans and other Latin Americans, went into the pattern now being drawn.[71] By 1855 so great was the incoming that a consideration of how to distribute labor seemed the better part of wisdom. The "honest and industrious," it was urged, should be cared for, but those who had been paupers in their own lands should be sent back. To provide for the deserving, directed immigration and settlement were advised through the offices of the port of reception. During the 'fifties a Labor Exchange was in existence in New York, but it languished during the Civil War and was not revived until 1868.[72]

In the meantime the problem had reached such a state that the Chicago Lyceum debated the advisability of the federal government's encouraging more foreigners to come to America. Steps to further

[69] Korey, loc. cit., p. 38. An illustration of German antagonism toward other Jews can be found in Chicago Tribune, December 29, 1866.

[70] In 1867, there were three hundred members in the two Chicago lodges, Ramah and Hillel of B'nai B'rith, both under the jurisdiction of the Grand Lodge No. 2 at Cincinnati. Hillel Lodge in 1867 protested some of the rules of the Grand Lodge, including the prohibition of intermarriage between Jews and gentiles. The following year Chicago was placed in Grand Lodge No. 6, her own district. Jews of other groups were later admitted to membership. (Philip P. Bregstone, Chicago and Its Jews . . . [Chicago, 1933], p. 19; The Jewish Encyclopedia, III, 275–76; Chicago Tribune, October 15, 1866, November 11, 1867; Letter to the author from Mr. Otto G. Felton, August 17, 1937.) In the early years of this period, a Polish congregation organized the Congregation Kehilath B'nai Sholom, and in 1870 the Bohemian Jews organized B'nai Abraham. Korey, loc. cit., pp. 39–40.

[71] United States, Eighth Census, 1860, "Population," p. 613; United States, Ninth Census, 1870, I, "Population," 386–91. See also Appendix, p. 482.

[72] The Daily Democratic Press, January 23, 1855; Friedrich Kapp, Immigration, and the Commissioners of Emigration of the State of New York (New York, 1870), pp. 115–16.

assimilation were urged by others, and rapid induction into citizenship was promoted. On the whole, foreigners in the vicinity of Cook County responded eagerly, in one year in the early 'fifties taking out 799 naturalization papers.[73] A federal bill declaratory of the rights of naturalized citizens abroad, proposed in 1868, was objected to by the *Tribune* on the ground that it took protection from citizens abroad when charged with crime and that it withdrew protection from naturalized citizens who had escaped military service in the homeland. The final form of the bill proposed by the House Committee on Foreign Affairs, however, met the sanction of its chief adversary in that it declared expatriation an inherent right and that naturalized citizens were free from claims of their former sovereigns, that they had in truth the rights of the native born.[74]

The need of a labor supply, particularly in this expanding Middle West, served to convince the larger portion of the people that immigration should be assisted, if need be, by the federal government. This point of view was freely preached in the columns of the *Tribune,* which not only would bring young men and young women, but would finance such an undertaking by bonds from those benefited, with interest payments pledged from earnings made here.[75]

In 1864, E. B. Washburne introduced a bill in Congress to promote immigration to the United States and to provide for a branch of the foreign emigration service at Chicago.[76] Four years later the German Emigrant Aid Society addressed the Common Council on the importance of Chicago as a distributing point of the Northwest and on the lack of facilities for incoming foreigners. The need of an emigrant depot with bathing rooms and temporary sleeping quarters for at least a thousand, under the supervision of the Board of Health,

---

[73] *The Daily Democratic Press,* August 31, 1854, January 23, March 5, 1855.

[74] *Congressional Globe,* 40 Cong., 2 sess., pt. 2, p. 1797, pt. 5, p. 4454; *Chicago Tribune,* February 15, 21, 1868. The bill was passed and enrolled July 25, 1868. Immigration from Prussia was said to be stimulated by a treaty with the North German Confederation in 1868. *Ibid.,* July 9, 1868; United States, *Statutes at Large,* XV, 615–17.

[75] See message of President Lincoln, December 8, 1863, in support of this view. James D. Richardson, comp., *A Compilation of the Messages and Papers of the Presidents* (10 v. Washington, 1908), VI, 182; *Chicago Tribune,* December 12, 1863. The attitude of Chicago toward the problem of immigration was like that in many other places. See Edith Abbott, *Historical Aspects of the Immigration Problem; Select Documents* (Chicago, 1926).

[76] B. A. Ulrich to E. B. Washburne, April 21, 1864, *The Papers of Elihu B. Washburne, 1829–1882,* XXXVII (*Ms.* Library of Congress); *Cong. Globe,* 38 Cong., 1 sess., pt. 2, pp. 1764, 1793, pt. 4, pp. 3495, 3547.

recommended by the Aid Society, indicates the magnitude of the problem presented by these newcomers.[77] The Society itself for fourteen years had provided for its own sick, had served as an employment agency, had tried to protect immigrants from imposters, and had forwarded many to their destinations. These recommendations for an emigrant depot sprang from a wealth of experience, and it was the belief of the Society and of others that part of the cost of upkeep should be borne by the railroads entering the city.[78]

Aside from a common faith in the opportunities and happiness to be found in the New World held by all these newcomers, the bonds of unity were often slender. Labor antagonism toward the Negro led to numerous riots by the Irish and others; Hungarian laborers found honest labor had its dangers when the Irish wanted their jobs; in turn, the Irish sometimes found that they were excluded from applicants considered for workmen;[79] and Scandinavians, despite a common heritage, were not always one in sympathies. German Catholics were not consistently of like mind with their Protestant brothers, and Protestants, in general, intolerantly weighed the Catholics in the scale of public opinion and found them wanting. Nativist sympathizers organized into Know-Nothing groups, and the needy immigrant was sometimes contemptuously described as lacking the independence and self-respect characteristic of native born, not to mention an advanced state of "physical degeneration" which foreigners had reached.[80]

[77] *Chicago Tribune*, June 16, 1868. The Society addressed the Committee on Finance. Chicago, *Council Proceedings, 1868–69*, pp. 74, 451.

[78] *The Daily Democratic Press*, May 9, June 19, 1854, November 5, 1857; *Chicago Daily Press and Tribune*, July 3, 1858; *Chicago Tribune*, February 5, 1866, March 7, 1867, January 14, June 16, 1868. The Society employed an agent to devote all his time to the care of German immigrants, the first such agent being Henry Kompe. For a survey of the history of the German Society see *Abendpost*, February 9, 1930.

[79] In 1862, for example, occurred the anti-Negro "Omnibus Riot." (*Chicago Tribune*, July 15, 17, 18, 19, 1862, August 5, 1863.) In 1864, a mob of five hundred Irishmen assaulted a dozen Negro laborers working in a lumber dock. (*Ibid.*, July 15, 1864. See also *ibid.*, August 11, 1862, November 13, 1866.) In 1851, some Hungarian laborers working on the Michigan Southern Railroad were set upon by a group of Irish. *Watchman of the Prairies*, November 25, 1851. See also advertisement in *Chicago Tribune*, February 26, 1866, in which appeared the statement "No Irish need apply." Also editorial in the *Chicago Evening Post*, September 9, 1868, which indicates antagonism toward the Irish.

[80] *Prairie Farmer*, n.s. IV (July 14, 1859), 25. See also as typical of anti-foreignism the attitude expressed toward the Germans in E. C. Hubbard to "My dear Sister," April 12, 1862, E. C. Hubbard to Adolphus S. Hubbard, May 9, 1862, *Gurdon S. Hubbard Papers* (*Mss.* Chicago Historical Society). See pp. 211–12, 218.

But all, despite differences in habits of thought, like the American of the day, endorsed movements for democracy throughout the world. Particularly was this true of the Germans who had come after the Revolution of 1848 and who, in the early 'fifties, saw an opportunity to demonstrate their faith by endorsing the activities of Gottfried Kinkel and his Revolutionary Committee. To them Kinkel personified the principles of democracy, for had he not attempted, while a member of the Prussian diet in the days of Frederick William IV, to aid in arming his fellows in order to liberalize the government by force if necessary? The Revolutionary Committee with headquarters in London knew full well that Kinkel's chances for raising money to destroy monarchy in Europe were good in America.[81]

After visiting New York and other cities Kinkel arrived in Chicago, December 4, 1851, where he was met by the mayor and other leading citizens. The next night with torch lights blazing he addressed a " whirl of humanity," gathered under the balcony of the Tremont House, whose cheers approvingly punctuated his remarks. The following day he again spoke at a mass meeting presided over by Mayor Gurnee, who had so warmly welcomed this apostle of democracy a short time earlier.[82] Before adjourning, those assembled recorded their undying adherence to the principle that government exists by the consent of the governed and only for their welfare; and that when governments become subversive of these ends, it is the right as well as the duty of the people to alter or abolish them. Indeed, so emboldened were they in this land of the free that they de-

[81] Carl Schurz, The Reminiscences of Carl Schurz, 1829–1869 (3 v. New York, 1907–8), I, 117, 129–30, 159; Joseph Schafer, Carl Schurz, Militant Liberal (Wisconsin State Historical Society, Publications, Wisconsin Biography Series, I. Evansville, Wisconsin, 1930), pp. 26–30. Kinkel participated in an abortive attack on the Siegburg arsenal. (Schurz, op. cit., I, 179, 191.) He was captured by government troops, court-martialed, and sentenced to life imprisonment but escaped with the help of Schurz in November, 1850, and the two fled to England. (Engels to Jenny Marx, July 25, 1849, in V. Adoratsky, ed., Karl Marx and Friedrich Engels Correspondence, 1846–1895 [London, 1934], pp. 24–25; Claude Moore Fuess, Carl Schurz: Reformer, 1829–1906 [New York, 1932], pp. 30–35; Oswald Garrison Villard, " Carl Schurz," Dictionary of American Biography, XVI, 466–70.) Revolutionary exiles in London joined Schurz and Kinkel in their plans for revolution. Friederick Althaus, " Beiträge zur Geschichte der Deutschen Kolonie in England," Unsere Zeit, n.s. IX (1873), pt. 2, 227; Schurz, op. cit., I, 393.

[82] Among those who had marched to hear Kinkel were Masons, Odd Fellows, Sons of Temperance, the Fire Department, members of the German Song Union, and numerous prominent citizens. Chicago Daily Journal, December 5, 6, 8, 1851.

clared that "resistance to tyranny is obedience to God." To apply
these abstractions to the situation at hand seemed the part of honesty
and kindness. Further resolutions, therefore, announced the concern
of Americans over hostility manifested in Europe toward the spread
of democracy; and demands were voiced that the political and moral
power of the government of the United States should be "systemati-
cally exerted in behalf of the people struggling for the common rights
of humanity in all lands." [83]

Americans, both native and naturalized, had spoken. Like patriots
in other parts of the country they saw no inconsistency in their zeal
to indoctrinate the world with the philosophy of their form of government and an equal zeal to prohibit in their midst preachments
which espoused a form of government thought less democratic. If
they recognized any intolerance, they gave no sign. Moved even to
the point of financial offerings, these crusaders for government by
all the people pinned their hopes in leaders of revolt like Kinkel and
Lajos Kossuth, whose words seemed to them prophetic of the day
when democracy would enfold the world, a day to which both native
and adopted sons looked with longing eyes. [84]

Despite scars upon the social body which an increasing urbanism
seemed to inflict, Chicagoans appeared as happy as most Americans.
On the whole, both aliens and natives who had come to the city were
content to remain, not adventuring beyond its environs in the quest

[83] *Ibid.*, December 8, 1851. Resolutions endorsing the "German National Loan," the
appointment of committees to collect pledges, and similar matters gave further evidence of
the good faith and anxiety of Chicago Germans for Germans across the Atlantic. Kinkel's
scheme of raising money failed. In November, 1852, the treasurer of the German National
Loan reported $7,717.35 in his treasury. He had spent $2,705.37 and called upon the
various committees to come forward and claim the amounts due them minus expenses already incurred. The amounts collected and forwarded to London by the various committees
were: London, $13.25; Germany, $45; New Orleans, $800; Baltimore, $805.35; Cincinnati,
$1,821.41; Pittsburgh, $300; Cleveland, $800; Alleghany County, Pennsylvania, $100;
Buffalo, $400; St. Louis, $1,035.27; Chicago, $184.50; Detroit, $175; Belleville, $720.68;
Milwaukee, $275.91; Dayton, $201.31; private contributions, $15.41. *Chicago Daily Demo-
crat*, November 23, 1852; C. F. Huch, "Revolutionsvereine und Anleihen," *Mitteilungen
des deutschen Pionier-Vereins von Philadelphia*, no. 18 (1910), pp. 15–17.

[84] An official invitation from the city council to Kossuth to visit Chicago failed to
bring the Hungarian patriot thither, to the great disappointment of these aggressive exponents of liberty. Resolution of the Common Council, January 21, 1852, and Letter from
Kossuth to the city of Chicago, February 21, 1852, in *Common Council Documents, no.
1657*, Council Year 1851 (*Ms.* Chicago City Hall). See also *Western Citizen*, January 6,
1852, and *Watchman of the Prairies*, November 25, 1851, for attitude toward Kossuth. For
comment of a German on American interest in democratic movements abroad see *The Press
and Tribune*, July 11, 1859.

of the things which sustained life. But there were those who saw the star of empire rising elsewhere. Stories of gold, late in 1848, in which as much as $800 a day could be had by treasure hunters whose only capital need be a sheath knife, a wooden trough, a sieve, a tin pan or an Indian basket, crowbar, pick, and shovel, drew men from Chicago as well as from other parts of the country. Indeed, so many were the departures to " the Golden West " that the editor of the *Democrat* feared that Chicago stood " a fair chance of depopulation." [85] Plans to organize a company were formulated as early as January, 1849, and a committee appointed to collect information on the best route to be taken. Throughout the spring of that year the rush continued without abatement.[86]

Some went overland in covered wagons; others by way of the Welland Canal and the St. Lawrence and thence around Cape Horn; still others crossed eastward to New York to take a boat to Chagres on the Isthmus of Panama.[87] By February, 1850, the number preparing to start westward appeared to be " double or treble " that of 1849 and included some of the most promising young men of the city and a number of businessmen who had been attacked " so severely with the fever " that they had lost " all apparent regard for home and family in their eager desire to grasp at the gold of the modern El Dorado." [88] That some did not realize their dreams is the solemn tale in the frequent death notices in the press. Others found the abundance of gold had dwindled or had been grossly overestimated and returned to Chicago sad and disillusioned. But there were others, said to have reaped a fortune, who came back with their pockets " full of the rocks " or with " a good-sized pile." [89]

[85] *Daily Democrat,* December 4, 18, 22, 29, 30, 1848, January 1, 3, 4, 10, 16, February 6, 1849. See especially *ibid.,* December 15, 1849. Among the first to leave the city were Major James B. Campbell and Captain James Averell, who went as agents for a company started in the city, and W. W. Barlow and H. Pike, who served their own interest. *Weekly Chicago Democrat,* January 2, 1849.

[86] *Daily Democrat,* January 18, 1849; *Chicago Daily Journal,* March 29, 1849.

[87] *Daily Democrat,* March 10, December 25, 1849; *Chicago Commercial Advertiser,* October 3, 1849. In the group going by way of New York and Panama were Charles M. Gray, John P. Foss, Asa F. Bradley, Dr. W. B. Herrick, J. Coburn, E. J. Chapin, H. M. Stow.

[88] *Chicago Daily Democrat,* February 25, 1850. In April, 1850, Starr Foot, Henry Norton, and Alfred P. Wurts, all well-known Chicagoans, left for California by way of the Isthmus of Panama. Professional men, including doctors, were among those who left Chicago for California. *Ibid.,* March 20, 1849, April 10, 1850.

[89] *Ibid.,* February 19, 25, December 14, 17, 24, 1850, January 8, February 4, March 22, May 20, June 19, 1851, July 16, 1852.

But the rush had made money for some of the enterprising who remained at home, even if it had not profited all who left. The call for pistols raised the price of these weapons from ten to fifteen and twenty dollars; wagonmakers worked overtime to produce vehicles optimistically christened "Sacramento" and "San Francisco" or realistically named "Gold Hunter." Sailcloth for wagon covers, blankets, carpetbags, and trunks skyrocketed in price. R. K. Swift and his brother Elijah found it advantageous to increase their banking business by opening the California Loan and Exchange Office to facilitate business transactions between Chicago and California.[90]

The lure of the golden metal of California was shortly put to rout by the lure of rich agricultural lands lying in the new territories of Kansas and Nebraska. Relatively high prices of some farm lands in Illinois had, as early as 1853, started an invasion of more virgin soil.[91] Soon individual enterprise was accompanied by collective endeavors, some of which were abortive and were said to be fraudulent.[92] But seekers of economic betterment, filled with the spirit of venture, paid little heed to a poor beginning. On May 30, 1854, the Kansas-Nebraska Bill was passed, and in the early autumn a trustee of the New England Emigrant Aid Society and Henry Dwight of the Kansas Emigrant Society visited Chicago to explain how emigrants could be forwarded to Kansas through the auspices of the Society. "There is but one feeling we believe among the people," declared the editor of the *Democratic Press*, "and that is, that in spite of machinations of corrupt politicians, this territory consecrated by our fathers to freedom *shall be free.*"[93]

90 *Ibid.*, February 5, 6, March 10, 26, 1849; *Chicago Daily Journal*, March 29, 1849; *Weekly Chicago Democrat*, November 13, 1849. Wagons fitted out for the gold fields excited much curiosity. (See [Abby Farwell Ferry], *Reminiscences of John V. Farwell by his Elder Daughter* [2 v. Chicago, 1928], I, 102.) They were generally large enough to afford shelter at night and stow away large quantities of provisions and luggage. (*Daily Democrat*, March 10, 1849; *Prairie Farmer*, IX [July, 1849], 212.) Elijah Swift was the representative of the California Loan and Exchange Office in California. For early activities see Pierce, *A History of Chicago*, I, 158–59.

91 *Weekly Chicago Democrat*, November 26, 1853; Cole, *The Era of the Civil War*, p. 10.

92 In February, 1854, a Captain Gibbs arrived in Chicago to raise a company to settle Nebraska. Supported by a gullible press, Gibbs obtained from thirty-five young men amounts of money varying from $50 to $100 each. Plans were laid to leave Chicago March 17, despite rumors that the Indian titles were not extinguished. On the eve of departure Gibbs disappeared with the funds. *The Daily Democratic Press*, February 28, March 10, 11, 15, 17, 1854.

93 *Ibid.*, September 14, 15, 1854. A meeting of interested citizens was held September 14, to organize a society in Chicago. For political aspects, see pp. 205–10.

By the spring of 1855 a group of Scotchmen with an eye to economic gains planned to found a town in Kansas with the aid of all men who loved freedom, liberty, and social happiness. In spite of this earnest effort the first Illinois company left Quincy in March, 1855, sponsored by the Nebraska Colonization Society. But the day which would ignite the spark of forceful penetration by the North was near at hand. On May 26, 1856, Lawrence was sacked, and Chicago was aflame. A mass meeting took note, among other things, of the persecution of the Kansans, and donations began with a $500 gift. The shout that accompanied its announcement opened the purse strings of others. At the stroke of midnight $12,000 had been given; motions for adjournment proved ineffectual in the surge of emotion which swept all before it. By one o'clock $15,000 had been contributed, as "prolonged cheers" for "the liberty of free speech, freedom of the press, and the perpetuity of the Union" rent the quiet of the night.[94] Chicago had spoken.

Within the month the executive committee of the Kansas Settlers' Society of Illinois opened offices in the city "to answer all inquiries in relation to the state of Kansas and the aid proffered by the Settlers' Society, to such able-bodied, industrious and sober men" as desired "to seek a home in that country." A company of about sixty-six willing to undertake the hazards of actual settlement left the city June 17 for Alton, whence they were to proceed to Fort Leavenworth.[95]

In excellent spirits they boarded the *Star of the West* and proceeded up the Missouri River. They had gone but a short way when at Lexington the boat was boarded by armed men who threatened death to all who would not surrender their arms. Upon giving over their guns, the passengers were allowed to continue the journey as far as Kansas City, where they were met by David R. Atchison and

---

[94] *The Free West*, April 5, 1855. The meeting, following the incidents at Lawrence, was called to ratify nominations for state officers made at Bloomington (see p. 215), and, according to Peter Page of Chicago, it was one of the longest held up to that time in the city. (Peter Page to Lyman Trumbull, June 3, 1856, *Trumbull Papers*, IV.) It was estimated that three thousand people were present. General J. H. Lane and others from Kansas spoke. *The Daily Democratic Press*, June 2, 1856.

[95] *Ibid.*, June 13, 18, July 1, 1856; *Weekly Chicago Democrat*, June 14, 1856. The Kansas Settlers' Society of Illinois was organized May 29, 1856. A. H. Andrews was elected president and S. P. Hand, secretary, of the group bound for Kansas. Ralph V. Harlow, "The Rise and Fall of the Kansas Aid Movement," *The American Historical Review*, XLI (October, 1935), 13.

Benjamin F. Stringfellow, who accompanied the emigrants to Leavenworth. Here, relieved of their provisions, tents, farming utensils, and other freight except trunks and carpetbags, they were sent on to Weston, later returning to Leavenworth, where they were placed under the guard of armed men and returned to a point within five miles north of Alton and landed during the night.[96] Would Illinois "quietly pocket the insult and let the outrage go unredressed," or would she "with becoming spirit demand reparation for the wrong, and in the event of refusal, demonstrate her ability to defend her people against insult and outrage, from whatsoever quarter" it might come?[97] These were the questions on the lips of Chicagoans in these soul-disturbing days.

On July 5, 1856, at the call of the executive committee of the Kansas Settlers' Society "a large concourse of citizens" gathered at Dearborn Park and heard Peter Page, Isaac N. Arnold, J. C. Vaughan, and others demand that both federal and state authorities protect those going into Kansas.[98] A little later, at Buffalo a convention of the organized societies assembled and recommended the appointment of a committee to be made up of a representative from each state and five from Chicago, where regular meetings were to be held. It was proposed that county committees raise funds to keep free settlers in Kansas, to induce free-state absentees to return to Kansas, to provide, if necessary, passage and clothing for them, and to induce free-state emigrants to go into the territory as rapidly as possible.[99] But bickering within and obstacles without the committee deterred it from accomplishing its program. By summer of 1857 the move-

[96] *The Daily Democratic Press,* June 18, 30, July 1, 2, 1856; affidavit of Charles H. Ward, sworn to before Louis D. Hoard, clerk of the Cook County Circuit Court, August 1, 1856, *Trumbull Papers,* VII. The rumor that these men were bent on making trouble in Kansas was denied, the defenders declaring them men of good reputation, farmers, printers, and mechanics. Peter Page, George W. Dole, H. B. Hurd, N. B. Judd, and C. H. Ray to Lyman Trumbull, July 31, 1856, *ibid.*

[97] *The Daily Democratic Press,* July 2, 7, 9, 1856.

[98] *Ibid.,* July 9, 1856.

[99] Harlow, *loc. cit.,* pp. 14–16; W. F. M. Arny to Lyman Trumbull [n.d.], *Trumbull Papers,* VI. H. B. Hurd of Chicago was on the committee which prepared this plan. Abraham Lincoln was first named as the representative of Illinois, but he was finally replaced by W. F. M. Arny of Bloomington, who became "General Transportation Agent." H. B. Hurd was made secretary of the committee, and Horace White of Chicago was named assistant secretary. Other Chicago committee members were Isaac N. Arnold and J. Young Scammon. *The Daily Democratic Press,* July 8, 1856.

ment seemed near collapse, with some of the members counselling violence to accomplish their ends.[100]

To those who wished other lands to conquer the movement to Pike's Peak furnished opportunities by the spring of 1859. Chicago merchants rallied to the new demands and set about to supply hard bread and crackers, " Pike's Peak Stoves," traveling equipment, rifles, revolvers, and bowie knives. But it was nearly a decade before a noticeable exodus for Colorado took place. By 1870, under the leadership of the Chicago Colorado Company, pamphlets eloquently pleaded the cause of colonization in this new region, and in February, 1871, a site was chosen and land bought in the Boulder Creek country near the Big and Little Thompson creeks, twenty miles from Denver.[101]

Emissaries from the West, too, wooed Chicagoans as settlers of Washington and Dakota territories. A real estate company known as the National Land and Migration Company of America was organized " to stimulate migration to the undeveloped regions of the Great West," [102] and opportunities in the South especially after the war beckoned a few.[103] Emigration of Negroes who, before the close of 1865, found it desirable to seek homes outside the United States

---

[100] Harlow, *loc. cit.*, pp. 17, 24–25. For the activities of the Chicago committee see its statement in *Weekly Chicago Democrat*, February 28, 1857. The committee furnished advice on routes, how to get land, and what provisions to take to Kansas, as well as describing markets and resources.

[101] *Oquawka Spectator*, March 24, 1859; *The Press and Tribune*, April 16, 1859; *Chicago Tribune*, December 13, 1870, February 23, 1871. It was said that William Bross was interested in the movement to Colorado. The Rev. Robert Collyer of Unity Church promoted it also with the idea of establishing a temperance colony. For German settlement in Colorado, see p. 8.

[102] *Chicago Tribune*, September 2, 1871. Governor Edward S. Salomon of Washington Territory and former governor of Wisconsin visited Chicago in 1870 and set on foot a colonization scheme. A colony of 120 persons was organized, and it was planned that 200 more would follow. (*Ibid.*, July 28, 1870.) In 1870, John P. Hodnett urged people to go to Dakota. This movement was sponsored by the Irish Colonization Society with the intention of getting Irishmen to go West. Charles King was president of the society. (*Ibid.*, August 5, 1870.) The officers of the National Land and Migration Company of America included George S. Bowen, president; Ambrose W. Clark, treasurer; Channing Sweet, secretary; and C. N. Pratt, general manager. *Ibid.*, September 2, 1871.

[103] In 1850, a few Chicagoans moved to Texas. (*Chicago Daily Democrat*, November 26, 1850.) In 1850, only 2,855 persons living in Texas were from Illinois. (United States, *Seventh Census, 1850*, p. xxxvi.) By 1860, the number was 7,050. (United States, *Eighth Census, 1860*, " Population," pp. 328–29.) In January, 1870, Col. George of Mississippi spoke at Farwell Hall and urged settlement in his state. *Chicago Tribune*, January 21, 1870.

also took place. About three hundred free colored persons were said to have left Chicago in April, 1861, for Canada, and shortly thereafter forty-seven departed for Haiti.[104]

On the whole, however, the movement from Chicago of those who had cast their lot here seemed relatively small. By 1870 it was the fifth city in the United States — a place where "broken English" and foreign languages were heard almost as frequently as the English of the original Easterners who had made up the first substance of its social body. Much that was true of Chicago was true of other cities of the time where the stage of development was similar. But Chicago, more than many other cities, was not a unit in its ethnic composition. Its human energy, originally drawn from eastern America, was, during these years, abundantly reinforced by those who came from northern Europe and who made common cause with others to reach the goal of urban greatness.

The coming of urbanism to Chicago was the result of several factors, but it was accelerated by the faith of all these Chicagoans in the future of their city, a faith so assertive and boastful that it became contagious. To Chicagoans, pride in city seemed natural. In their own eyes they were not inordinate braggarts when they confidently declared: "Chicago does not go to the world. The world comes to Chicago. . . . Should Chicago pay people to come hither when it is for their advantage to come? Does Rome pay the expenses of the everlasting crowds of pilgrims that are journeying to its shrines? If Rome does not pay, why should Chicago pay?"[105]

[104] Wesley, *op. cit.*, p. 98; *Chicago Tribune,* June 18, 1861. This was almost one third of the 955 Negroes resident in Chicago in 1860. In 1859, an invitation from the president of Haiti to emigrate to that island was considered by the Negroes of Chicago. *The Press and Tribune,* April 25, 1859.

[105] *The Chicago Times,* March 25, 1868.

CHAPTER II

HIGHWAYS OF TRADE AND TRAVEL

ON NOVEMBER 20, 1848, a number of prominent Chicagoans boarded a crudely built baggage car fitted with seats and for the first time rode out of the city on a train drawn by a steam locomotive. Less than a month before, the first Chicago railroad, the Galena and Chicago Union, had sent out a tender and two cars in an experimental trip of five miles, and those who dwelt on the sprawling, thinly-wooded prairie had heard the whistle of a locomotive. Now, on a crisp November day "the iron horse," fittingly christened the "Pioneer," puffed confidently westward for eight miles. Sighting a farmer heading cityward behind a pair of slow-moving oxen, two of the passengers purchased his load of wheat and hides, making these commodities the first rail freight delivered to Chicago.[1] This exciting excursion passed off without mishap, but it was a journey pregnant with meaning as to what this new form of transportation would mean to the thriving little city, for it symbolized the emergence of Chicago as the metropolis which would soon dominate and direct the commercial growth of an ever-widening hinterland.

Besides the Galena's ten miles of track, Chicago in late 1848 had only the Illinois and Michigan Canal and the dirt roads over which

[1] *Daily Democrat,* October 24, 26, November 22, 1848; *Chicago Daily Journal,* October 26, November 21, 1848. The earlier run was made on October 25. Charles Walker, forwarding and commission merchant, bought the wheat. Jerome Beecher, boot, shoe, and leather dealer, purchased the hides. The first ten miles of track were not completed until December, 1848. Galena and Chicago Union Railroad Company, *Second Annual Report, April, 1849* (Chicago, 1849), p. 10.

the city could receive the products of field and woodland which she craved to exchange for her imports from the East. Roads were unimproved and frequently impassable — deep ruts in winter and beds of sticky muck in the spring. When these were blocked with ice or mud, the farmers of the back country had to hold their grain, although vessel owners in the harbor near by clamored insistently for cargoes to carry back east.

Plank roads seemed one solution. The Barry Point Road was opened in September, 1848, and its immediate financial success led to the construction of others. From 1848 to 1854 six more were built from Chicago, three in a southerly and three in a northerly direction. The Southwestern was finished to a point near Naperville in 1851. The Northwestern, the Western, and the Northern roads were built toward the west and the north in 1849, and the Southern and the Blue Island were projected southward in 1851 and 1854.[2]

But the day of the plank road was over almost as soon as it had begun. Although good roads were believed locally to be of greater commercial importance than railroads, and the planks were held to be "perfection," their shortcomings were quickly revealed. Weather warped and twisted the lumber; rain washed out sections; and farmers, sometimes disgusted with the state of the highway, bore away the planking for their own use. In 1860, when traveling south, one had little choice whether to pass over the Southern Road with every other plank missing or to drive in the deep, shifting sand by the side. During the short time of their use, however, the roads performed

---

[2] The Southwestern Plank Road had extensions running to Naperville, Oswego, St. Charles, Warrenville, and near-by places, making a total of sixty miles of such road to the southwest of Chicago. The Southern ran by way of the line of State Street to Kyle's Tavern ten miles out. The Blue Island Road ran from Blue Island due north on the line of Western Avenue to Blue Island Avenue and followed the latter into the heart of the city. Its total length was about thirteen miles. The Northwestern was completed by July, 1850, to Dutchman's Point. At Oak Ridge, eight miles northwest of Chicago, the Northwestern Road connected with the Western which ran to the east side of DuPage County there connecting with the Elgin and Genoa Plank Road. The Northern ran parallel with the lake shore to Hood's Tavern on the Green Bay Road, a distance of five miles. *Daily Democrat*, January 22, October 2, 1848, January 10, 1851; *The Daily Democratic Press*, March 16, 1854; Pierce, *A History of Chicago*, I, 113; Act of February 10, 1849, *Private Laws, 1849*, pp. 70–71; *Weekly Chicago Democrat*, February 2, 1850; *Prairie Farmer*, X (July, 1850), 229; The Daily Democratic Press, *The Railroads, History and Commerce of Chicago*, [1853] (Chicago, 1854), pp. 52–53 (hereafter cited as The Daily Democratic Press, *Annual Review, 1853*); Milo M. Quaife, *Chicago's Highways Old and New* . . . (Chicago, 1923), pp. 123–37.

service, for in a measure they extended the commercial area and stabilized trade conditions during thaws and rainy periods.[3]

But the commercial ascendancy of Chicago was not based on such slight extensions of mercantile endeavor as were afforded by these facilities. Rather it rested on the greater avenues of transport — the canal and the railroads — which reached the grain fields rimming the city and extending as far south as Kansas and Missouri, as far west as Iowa and Nebraska, and as far north as Minnesota and Wisconsin.

Tapping the fertile area to the southwest of the city and drawing bounteous offerings of corn and other cereals into the local warehouses, the Illinois and Michigan Canal with the Illinois River provided a continuous waterway between Chicago and the Mississippi. It made available an extensive market for goods forwarded from Chicago, for farmers who entered the newly opened region turned to the city for supplies; and it strengthened commercial relations with St. Louis whose trade in maize until 1849 was far greater than that of Chicago.[4] The effect of the canal upon the corn trade of Chicago was immediate, and until the late 'sixties the canal remained, with the exception of 1854, the city's greatest single corn feeder. Shortly afterwards, however, it was outdistanced by the Illinois Central and the Chicago, Burlington and Quincy railroads.[5] Although it greatly swelled the volume of wheat receipts in 1849, it was eclipsed as a

---

[3] *Chicago Daily Democrat,* June 8, 1849; Quaife, *op. cit.,* pp. 134–37; Judson Fiske Lee, *Transportation as a Factor in the Development of Northern Illinois Previous to 1860* (Chicago, 1917), pp. 29–30.

[4] For receipts and shipments by the canal and other means of carriage for selected years (1852, 1859, 1864–65, and 1871) see Appendix, pp. 492–98. For a statement of chief articles carried and tolls collected at Chicago, Lockport, Ottawa, and La Salle see also " Twenty-first Annual Report of the Board of Trustees of the Illinois and Michigan Canal, 1865," *Reports Made to the General Assembly of Illinois . . . , 1867* (2 v. Springfield, 1867), I, 291–442 (hereafter cited as Illinois, *Reports, 1867*); Freeman Hunt, ed., *The Merchants' Magazine and Commercial Review,* XXVI (March, 1852), 325 (hereafter cited as *Hunt's Merchants' Magazine*); Chicago Board of Trade, *Fifteenth Annual Report of the Trade and Commerce of Chicago for the year ending December 31, 1872,* p. 35 (hereafter cited as Chicago Board of Trade, *Fifteenth Annual Report, 1872*).

[5] The Daily Democratic Press, *Fourth Annual Review, 1855,* p. 11. By 1852 *DeBow's Review* noted the decline of St. Louis as a grain market. That year Chicago received over four times as much corn as St. Louis. (James D. B. DeBow, ed., *DeBow's Review, and Industrial Resources, Statistics, etc.,* XIV [April, 1853], 394 [hereafter cited as *DeBow's Review*].) In 1868, the receipts of corn by canal were 6,106,016 bushels, by Illinois Central, 6,027,490, and by Chicago, Burlington and Quincy, 4,774,227 bushels. Chicago Board of Trade, *Eleventh Annual Statement, 1868–69,* p. 39. For receipts in 1871 see Appendix, p. 497.

wheat carrier after 1851 by the Galena and Chicago Union Railroad.[6] Other grains and dairy products in smaller quantities came up the canal, but there were few direct importations except sugar and molasses from the deep South.[7]

Southward the canal carried great quantities of lumber, chiefly to communities situated along its route and the Illinois River.[8] Until 1863–64 it was the greatest single carrier of lumber from Chicago. Then its prestige waned as a result of the competition of the railroads leading to the southwest.[9] Through the canal went merchandise, such as groceries, hardware, and wearing apparel in comparatively small quantities,[10] in part for the needs of the communities along its way and the Illinois River, in part for distribution from St. Louis, whose wholesale trade gained by reason of greater expedition and cheapness in shipment. In addition, St. Louis obtained an enlarged market in Illinois and the lake ports for southern products, such as coffee, sugar from Louisiana, and hemp, pork, and bacon.[11] Thus both cities profited from the construction of the canal, and, as the *Daily Democrat* remarked in 1849, "the asperity which at first appeared ready to kindle into a flame of strife" was "dissipated in a commercial friendship," a relationship which was, however, of unfortunately slender proportions.[12]

Soon after the canal opened, a line of packets for passenger travel made daily trips, thereby providing what was considered an improvement over land travel. From Chicago to La Salle, a distance of ninety-nine miles, one could spend twenty or more hours, dragging

[6] In 1849, the canal brought 560,200 bushels of wheat to the city, the Galena only 171,365. *Chicago Daily Democrat*, December 30, 1851; B. F. Johnson to W. H. Osborn, August 8, 1855, *Johnson Papers* (Ms. Illinois Central Railroad Company). For later figures see Appendix, pp. 492–98.

[7] During the Civil War the bulk of the sugar came through eastern routes. Following the war this was also true. Unless otherwise stated, the annual reviews of business and annual statements of the Board of Trade constitute sources used for receipts and shipments.

[8] Some lumber went to St. Louis to be distributed from that point. *Daily Democrat*, January 27, 1849, December 30, 1857; Illinois, *Reports, 1867*, I, 302.

[9] In 1863–64 the canal was eclipsed as a lumber carrier by the Illinois Central and in 1864–65 by the Burlington and the Illinois Central. See Appendix, p. 496.

[10] See Appendix, pp. 492–98.

[11] *Daily Democrat*, January 27, February 23, August 23, 1849; *Weekly Chicago Democrat*, August 1, 1848. Putnam points out that during 1845–53 the grocery business of St. Louis advanced from $1,134,367 to $5,018,677, and the hardware business from $251,259 to $904,316. James William Putnam, *The Illinois and Michigan Canal. A Study in Economic History* (Chicago, 1918), pp. 103–4.

[12] *Daily Democrat*, January 27, 1849.

along at the rate of five miles an hour. But even so, this was a more comfortable procedure than by stagecoach. Crowded vessels in increasing numbers attested to the popularity of this water travel until the railroad usurped the transport of men just as it did the carriage of freight.[13]

While the canal was a significant factor in the development of Chicago, it did not become the artery for intersectional trade which its promoters had prophesied. With the exception of strictly southern commodities, such as sugar, molasses, and cotton, most of the canal receipts in Chicago during the 'fifties were the agricultural products of the northern part of Illinois.[14] In part this was due to natural deficiencies of the route, for in the winter ice choked its waters, and at other times the Illinois River was too shallow for boats drawing even less than five feet of water — a condition which proved a greater cause of anxiety to the canal commissioners than did the competition of railroads.[15]

Because of these natural handicaps the improvement of the Illinois River was pressed by the Board of Trade in 1850, and in the following year delegates were sent to a convention in Peoria which considered the matter. Five years later the Board co-operated with the St. Louis Chamber of Commerce in an effort to obtain betterment, and in 1857 the Illinois River Improvement Company, which included among its incorporators William B. Ogden, was formed to provide a navigable channel.[16] These efforts failed to engage the attention of Congress, but with the outbreak of the Civil War and the closure of the lower Mississippi, national defense was urged as a new reason for appropriations for the improvement. A deep waterway from the Great Lakes to the Mississippi, it was argued, would permit the passage of war vessels and so aid the North in the contest with the South, and in the event of war with England would serve

[13] Quaife, op. cit., p. 85; Harlan H. Barrows, Geography of the Middle Illinois Valley (Illinois State Geological Survey, Bulletin, no. 15. Urbana, 1910), pp. 96, 102–3; Daily Democrat, April 26, September 3, December 31, 1849, May 5, 1852.

[14] A. L. Kohlmeier, The Old Northwest as the Keystone of the Arch of American Federal Union (Bloomington, Indiana, 1938), pp. 122, 152, 194.

[15] Charles Walker and others to Captain Swift, October 3, 1849, William H. Swift Papers, 1843–1865 (Ms. Chicago Historical Society); Barrows, op. cit., pp. 102–3.

[16] E[lias] Colbert, Chicago: Historical and Statistical Sketch of the Garden City . . . (Chicago, 1868), p. 49; Act of February 14, 1857, Laws of Illinois, 1857, pp. 212–18 (hereafter cited as Laws); Chicago Tribune, January 1, March 29, December 6, 1861; Putnam, op. cit., pp. 51, 131.

both sections. A bill for this purpose introduced in Congress in February, 1862, was defeated a year later, however, and although in June, 1863, the National Ship-Canal Convention, meeting in Chicago, stressed the military and commercial importance of the work and the desirability of ownership and control of the route by the national government, Congress again failed to act.[17] Like the national, the state legislature procrastinated in taking steps. Finally in February, 1867, it gave its approval to the improvement of the Illinois River channel, and in 1872 the first lock for this purpose was opened.[18]

Roughly paralleling the canal and the Illinois River to Peru was the Chicago and Rock Island Railroad, whose rails led from there across the state to Rock Island on the Mississippi. Begun April 10, 1852, and completed on February 22, 1854, these "iron bands of commercial intercourse," in the words of an enthusiast of the day, henceforth could turn the stream of commerce eastward to Chicago, thence to the cities of the seaboard.[19] Although some of the citizens of Chicago regarded this road as the most important thoroughfare to join the city with the western portions of the state, they really had little to do with the inauguration of the undertaking, which was conceived by venturesome promoters of Rock Island and Davenport.[20] On May

[17] The delegates to the Ship-Canal Convention were from Illinois, Indiana, Wisconsin, Michigan, Iowa, Missouri, Kansas, Ohio, New York, New Jersey, Maryland, the District of Columbia, Connecticut, Rhode Island, Massachusetts, Vermont, and Maine. (*Chicago Tribune*, June 3, 1863; Putnam, *op. cit.*, pp. 133–35; *Cong. Globe*, 37 Cong., 2 sess., pp. 902, 3023–27, 3033, 3056; *ibid.*, 3 sess., pp. 812, 830–31.) The national government, for example, was petitioned, in 1868, to issue 6 per cent bonds to improve and complete the canal. *Chicago Tribune*, February 11, 1868. For the attitude of advocates of the canal improvement, see J. H. Dunham to Hon. James R. Doolittle, February 8, 1865, William Bross to Doolittle, February 6, 1865 (*Mss.* Chicago Historical Society).

[18] *Chicago Tribune*, June 29, 1867; Putnam, *op. cit.*, pp. 135–36; Act of February 28, 1867, *Public Laws of Illinois, 1867*, pp. 81–88 (hereafter cited as *Public Laws*); Illinois, *Reports, 1869*, I, 409–24. For lowering of summit level of the canal as a sanitary measure for Chicago see p. 331.

[19] *The Daily Democratic Press*, February 17, 1853; The Daily Democratic Press, *Fourth Annual Review, 1855*, p. 70.

[20] *Chicago Daily Democrat*, July 10, 1851; Chicago and Rock Island Railroad, *Reports of the President, Chief Engineer and Consulting Engineer of the Rock Island Railroad Company presented to the Board of Directors at their Meeting in Chicago, December 22, 1851* (New York, 1852), pp. 3, 6, 10. In 1847, the state legislature approved the Rock Island and La Salle Railroad to run between La Salle and Rock Island. (Frank J. Nevins, "Seventy Years of Service," *Rock Island Magazine*, XVII [October, 1922], 6; Act of February 27, 1847, *Private Laws, 1847*, pp. 139–42.) The project languished for three years but in 1851 the legislature authorized an extension of the road to Chicago by way of Joliet. At the same time, to meet opposition from the Illinois and Michigan Canal interests the legislature provided for compensation for losses in freight traffic which they might suffer. The canal

26, 1851, the Common Council consented to the laying of tracks within the city.[21] The depot was located at first at Twelfth Street between Clark and Buffalo, but in 1853, in company with the Michigan Southern, the Rock Island began to build a $60,000 station between Clark and Sherman streets on Van Buren. In 1866, an enlargement, dignified as a Union Depot, constructed at a cost of $225,000 with five car tracks, the "largest baggage room" in the country, a large dining room, and ladies' and men's waiting rooms, not to mention twenty-six skylights, stirred the pride of all civic-minded citizens. At the formal opening of the road in June, 1854, one thousand invited guests, including ex-President Millard Fillmore, Charles Dana, Thurlow Weed, and George Bancroft, toured the city and were shown "what western enterprise" could accomplish "in less than twenty years." Then, drawn by engines decked with flags, flowers, and evergreens, trains carried the notables to the terminus of the line whence they went up the river by steamboat to St. Paul.[22]

To enterprising Chicagoans were thus unlocked vast new stores of corn and other grains. Shortly after, in 1856, they beheld broadened spheres of endeavor as the Rock Island Bridge Company, in spite of the spirited opposition of water carriers and of St. Louis businessmen, united by means of a bridge across the Mississippi the Rock Island with the Mississippi and Missouri Railroad.[23] In 1866, con-

trustees, however, failed to make a formal grant of the right of way by the stipulated first Monday in June, 1851, since they were advised that the right of eminent domain could not be exercised in the case of land granted for public use. The railroad company successfully instituted condemnation proceedings for a right to construct their road through canal lands without the payment of tolls to the canal. Putnam, *op. cit.*, pp. 109–11; Act of February 7, 1851, *Private Laws, 1851,* pp. 48–51; Isaac N. Arnold to William H. Swift, December 23, 1850, E. A. Prescott to Swift, January 30, 1851, *Swift Papers.*

[21] The ordinance was like, in principle, those passed for other roads in the 'fifties, with the exception of that for the Illinois Central. It prescribed the speed of locomotives (in this case five miles per hour), permitted the procurement "otherwise" of land and the construction of depots. Legislation designed to care for railroads in the future, it was prescribed, could apply to this system. *The Charter and Ordinances of the City of Chicago (to Sept. 15, 1856, inclusive)* . . . (George W. and John A. Thompson, comps., Chicago, 1856), pp. 344–45.

[22] William Bross, *History of Chicago* . . . (Chicago, 1876), p. 46; The Daily Democratic Press, *Annual Review, 1852,* p. 11; *Chicago Tribune,* August 13, December 18, 1866. The depot was near the LaSalle Street Station site in 1940. *The Daily Democratic Press,* June 1–14, 1854.

[23] The Daily Democratic Press, *Fourth Annual Review, 1855,* p. 70; Franc P. Wilkie, *Davenport Past and Present* . . . (Davenport, 1858), pp. 117–18. Court action was a means of hindering construction. Litigation was first directed to prevent construction across the

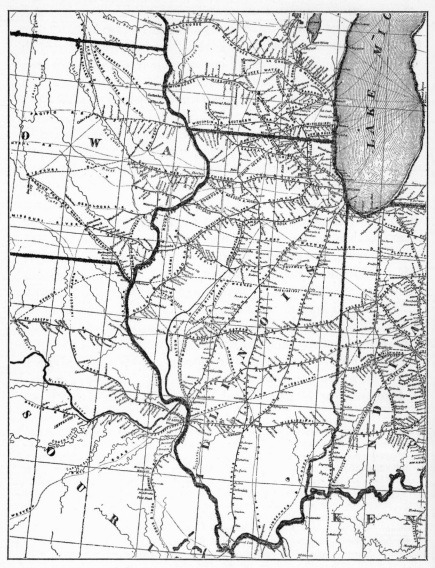

RAILROAD MAP OF THE UPPER MISSISSIPPI
VALLEY, 1859

(From J. Sage & Sons, *New & Reliable Rail Road Map, Travelers Edition. Western.*
New York, 1859.)

solidation made these railroads one under the name of the Chicago, Rock Island and Pacific; by 1869 Council Bluffs was reached whence the Omaha connection with the Union Pacific led to California. It was indeed only a short twenty-four years after the little group of Davenport planners had obtained the charter as a speculation and sold it to the group of eastern capitalists controlling the Michigan Central that the Rock Island and Pacific Railroad had linked San Francisco to Chicago even as Chicago was linked to New York.[24]

Over the Rock Island in 1854 came more than half a million bushels of corn, contributing to the rise from the total receipts of less than three million bushels the year before to more than seven million bushels. In succeeding years almost constantly increasing offerings of both corn and wheat rolled into Chicago, and out of the city in return went carloads of merchandise, especially dry goods, iron, and lumber. Where the railroad touched the Illinois River, some sugar and groceries from New Orleans were picked up in the 'fifties, but this trade did not attain an importance which challenged the Rock Island traffic in grains.[25]

The Illinois Central was the third great route to tap the region to the southwest of Chicago. Advocates of a north to south railway eventually became convinced, when the efforts of a group of speculators bore no fruit, that governmental aid was essential to a successful prosecution of the plan. With Stephen A. Douglas in the United

---

government property at Rock Island and a bridge across the river. The opinion of the judge who reviewed the case was that entry of the company on the island was authorized by act of Congress granting the railroad the right of way through public lands. (United States v. Railroad Bridge Co., Circuit Court N. D. Illinois, July term, 1855. Case no. 16, 114. The Federal Cases Circuit and District Courts of United States [St. Paul, 1896], Book 27, pp. 686–94.) One month after the construction had been completed a packet, The Effie Afton, crashed into the bridge and was completely destroyed by fire resulting from the impact. The owner brought suit against the bridge company. Among the counsel for the defendant were Norman B. Judd and Abraham Lincoln. The case dragged on five years. At the same time St. Louis interests continued their attack, but the bridge remained despite opposition. The laws of progress proved inexorable. Albert J. Beveridge, Abraham Lincoln 1809–1858 (4 v. Boston, 1928), II, 301–8; The Daily Democratic Press, February 14, 1853, July 3, August 4, 1855, April 25, September 9–15, 1857; Chicago Daily Press and Tribune, March 2, 1859; Chicago Tribune, December 13–17, 1860.

[24] Henry V. Poor, Manual of the Railroads of the United States . . . for 1871–72 (New York, 1871), p. 223 (hereafter cited as Poor's Manual). By 1867 the route reached Kellogg, Iowa, 314 miles from Chicago. Poor's Manual, 1868–69, p. 212; W. H. Swift to Thomas Ward, February 16, 1851, Baring Papers (by courtesy of Professor Paul W. Gates).

[25] The Daily Democratic Press, Fourth Annual Review, 1855, pp. 10–11; The Daily Democratic Press, March 15, 1853.

States Senate the project took on new vigor by the 'fifties, about fifteen years after the first undertaking had been proposed. Motivated, so his political opponents charged, by the desire for profits in the sale of his own real estate which lay along the route, Douglas nonetheless saw in the road both national and state benefits.[26] Pointing out that a connection southward from the Great Lakes to Cairo by way of Chicago would serve as a trunk line between the Atlantic seaboard and the Mississippi River, he urged Congress to grant lands to the state of Illinois for the construction of such a railroad, but his bill and a similar measure of his colleague, Sidney A. Breese, were defeated by the opposition of strict constructionists and landless states. Nothing daunted, Douglas and his Illinois confreres pushed through another bill which became law on September 20, 1850, for the opposition of the South had been dissipated somewhat by land grants to Alabama and Mississippi and by the desire of the South to strengthen economic bonds with the Northwest. Thus was the " Chicago and Mobile railroad " measure made possible.[27]

Under the aggressive promotive skill of Robert Rantoul of Massachusetts and other eastern capitalists, the project moved forward with vigor and expedition. To the state, the company promised to pay 5 to 7 per cent of its gross revenues.[28] With other citizens of Illinois Chicagoans rejoiced, for they saw mounting returns on their real estate investments and an expanding sphere of enterprise and trade to the south. On December 23, 1851, ground for the new road was broken in Chicago and Cairo, and during the next five years con-

[26] Howard Gray Brownson, *The History of the Illinois Central Railroad to 1870* (University of Illinois, *Studies in the Social Sciences*, IV. Urbana, 1915), pp. 17 ff.; Gates, *The Illinois Central Railroad,* pp. 23–34. Douglas disposed of sixteen acres of his Chicago property to the Illinois Central for its right-of-way for the sum of $21,310. Thirteen were under water. *Ibid.,* p. 64.

[27] Breese as well as Douglas had a personal interest in lands which would be served by the railroad. Breese's bill included provisions to grant to the builders of the road pre-emption rights to a portion of the public lands through which the railroad would pass rather than a direct land grant to the state. Cole, *The Era of the Civil War,* pp. 36–38; United States, *Statutes at Large,* IX, pp. 466–67; *Chicago Daily Democrat,* September 30, 1850.

[28] From March 24, 1855, to April 30, 1880, the state received $7,938,868.51. (Thomas Donaldson, *The Public Domain* . . . [47 Cong., 2 sess., H. Misc. Doc. 45, pt. 4. Washington, 1884], p. 264; Act of February 10, 1851, *Private Laws, 1851,* pp. 61, 71, 72–73.) By this act of the legislature the Illinois Central was incorporated " as a body politic and corporate." For details of the struggle between competing groups of capitalists to obtain a charter from the state for the road, see Paul Wallace Gates, " The Struggle for the Charter of the Illinois Central Railroad," Illinois State Historical Society, *Transactions, 1933,* pp. 55–66.

struction went on apace.[29] By autumn of 1856 direct traffic was established between these points.[30] Douglas had dreamed of an unbroken line of rail linking Lake Michigan with the Gulf, but this dream did not become a reality until the 'seventies.[31]

During the 'fifties the trade of Chicago with the South over the Illinois Central remained secondary in importance to the corn and wheat receipts from regions closer to the city. To be sure, high hopes were held for this southern outlet, and these hopes were not without some substantiation, for the first large consignment of sugar arrived in November, 1857, and two years later the president of the road reported the movement of an " unusually large quantity " of this and other southern products to the North together with " a heavier return traffic than ever before." [32] And, when in 1860 Illinois was " literally overflowing " with a " remarkable harvest " for which there was " an active demand, especially for the Southern markets," because of a serious drought in the South, the president of the road concluded that a large and profitable through traffic was permanently established.[33]

In spite of this optimism, the trade of Chicago with the South was, in 1860, more a hope for the future than a reality of the present. Wishful thinking on the part of those whose roots lay deep in the South rather than in the East was reflected by the editor of the *Times,* who hoped that politicians would not " by their loud mouthed in-

[29] *Gem of the Prairie,* June 28, 1851; The Daily Democratic Press, *Annual Review, 1852,* p. 11; Brownson, *op. cit.,* pp. 47–48. Work on ten divisions proceeded simultaneously.

[30] William K. Ackerman, *Historical Sketch of the Illinois-Central Railroad* . . . (Chicago, 1890), p. 88; The Daily Democratic Press, *Fourth Annual Review, 1855,* p. 73; *The Daily Democratic Press,* October 3, 1856.

[31] The New Orleans-Jackson and Great-Northern Railway stretched 206 miles northward from New Orleans. From the terminus of this line the Mississippi-Central Railroad went to Jackson, Tennessee. From there north there was a gap. To connect with the Gulf it was necessary for the Illinois Central to ship over the Mobile and Ohio Railroad which led south from Columbus, Kentucky. A distance of twenty miles between Cairo and Columbus was covered by ferry. (Ackerman, *op. cit.,* pp. 112, 116.) On December 24, 1873, direct rail connection between Chicago and New Orleans was established. Thomas D. Clark, *A Pioneer Southern Railroad, from New Orleans to Cairo* (Chapel Hill, 1936), p. 125.

[32] Illinois Central Railroad Company, *Reports and Accounts, 1859,* p. 5. See Appendix, pp. 493–94.

[33] It was estimated sixty million bushels of corn would be needed. (*Hunt's Merchants' Magazine,* XLIII [October, 1860], 412.) The Illinois Central arranged for a regular line of steamers from Cairo to New Orleans to expedite the corn shipments. *Prairie Farmer,* n.s. VI (December 27, 1860), 406; Illinois Central Railroad Company, *Reports and Accounts, 1860,* p. 1; Chicago Board of Trade, *Third Annual Statement, 1860,* p. 74.

tolerance prevent the establishment of a large commercial business between Chicago and Memphis."[34] But the tide of Republicanism was running strong, and war was soon to check the plans of those looking southward for a profitable and varied market.

Still, during the early months of 1861, the amount of commerce between Chicago and the lower Mississippi Valley showed a satisfying increase. Shipping cotton to the East by way of Chicago grew in popularity, and local factories imported this commodity for their own use, to the great delight of the commercially-minded editor of the *Tribune*. But by April encouragement of trade with the South had given way to condemnation of traffic with "traitors," for, on April 12, southern batteries opened fire on Fort Sumter. Farmers of the Northwest were urged to withhold their grain and produce from southern purchasing agents whose money, it was asserted, was of very doubtful value anyway.[35] But regardless of an order of the Treasury Department in May which prohibited the shipment of arms, munitions, and other supplies to the states in insurrection, goods continued to be exchanged. The economic urge had, for the moment anyway, a firmer hold than patriotism. The Confederates by their free trade policy encouraged the importation of supplies, while the federal government, anxious to keep the good will of Kentucky, allowed large quantities of goods to pass into that state whence they were forwarded to southern destinations. Yet the immediate effect of the opening of hostilities was a considerable decrease in the amount of commerce carried on with the South.[36] Wartime prosperity was to come from another source.

Under the terms of the land grant the government was entitled to use the Illinois Central as an open highway in time of war. By an arrangement with the railroad the government was charged one third less than the regular rate for freight carried, and during the next four years the Illinois Central formed an important life line for the Union armies in Kentucky and Tennessee. Thousands of men were sent south to Cairo, and large supplies of grain, meat, ammunition,

---

[34] *The Chicago Times*, January 28, 1860.

[35] *The Cincinnati Daily Enquirer*, January 19, March 3, 1861; *The New York Times*, January 25, February 4, 1861; *Chicago Tribune*, January 1, April 19, 25, 1861.

[36] *Hunt's Merchants' Magazine*, XLIV (June, 1861), 786; E. Merton Coulter, "Effects of Secession upon the Commerce of the Mississippi Valley," *The Mississippi Valley Historical Review*, III (December, 1916), 282–83; Illinois Central Railroad Company, *Reports and Accounts, 1861*, p. 1.

and other materials were forwarded in the same direction, such shipments being given precedence over regular traffic. So heavy was this carriage that the loss of any former trade with the South was offset, and enough revenue was gained in these years for the Illinois Central to pay its first dividends.[37]

As the war in the West progressed and more territory fell into Union hands, trade with the lower Mississippi revived. Self-denial for the sake of a patriotic principle seemed praiseworthy enough in the first fervor of the war spirit, but why, held the practical-minded Chicagoans, should they lose a profitable business when other cities such as Cincinnati and Louisville were gaining by the war.[38]

By 1862 Memphis cotton factories and sugar merchants again advertised in Chicago newspapers, an evidence of "a renewal of civilization" in the opinion of the *Tribune*. Corn, pork, and beef were reported to command almost fabulous prices, and exports to the South revived. In June, 1862, a shipment of hats re-opened the trade with New Orleans, and in July, 1862, a consignment of flour was sent to that city. With the cessation of hostilities came new demands from the South for products of the Northwest.[39] Though trade at first was retarded because of the impoverished condition of the defeated section, by 1870 it was reported that sufficient cargo space could not be obtained on the Mississippi to forward accumulated rail freight

[37] W. H. Osborn to Simon Cameron, April 26, 1861, in United States War Department, *The War of the Rebellion: A Compilation of the Official Records* . . . (Washington, 1880–1901), ser. 3, I, 121–22, 752 (hereafter cited as *Official Records of the Rebellion*); Brownson, *op. cit.,* pp. 66–67, 98; *Hunt's Merchants' Magazine,* XLVI (May, 1862), 464; Emerson David Fite, *Social and Industrial Conditions in the North during the Civil War* (New York, 1910), p. 44. In 1863, 4 per cent dividends were paid; in 1865, two cash dividends of 5 per cent and a stock dividend of $10 a share. Net profits in 1860 had been $850,630, and in 1864 they were $2,463,194. *Hunt's Merchants' Magazine,* LV (July, 1866), 48–49; Illinois Central Railroad Company, *Reports and Accounts, 1865,* p. 10.

[38] *Chicago Tribune,* March 14, 1862. In 1862, the largest amount of cotton thus far brought was received. Three and one-half million pounds of cotton were received by the Illinois Central in 1861. Chicago Board of Trade, *Fourth Annual Statement, 1861,* p. 74, *Fifth Annual Statement, 1862,* p. 74.

[39] No receipts of cotton were reported in 1863. In the late 'sixties, Chicago cotton receipts on the Illinois Central declined irregularly. (Chicago Board of Trade, *Eighth Annual Statement, 1865–66,* p. 98, *Ninth Annual Statement, 1866–67,* p. 108, *Tenth Annual Statement, 1867–68,* p. 118, *Eleventh Annual Statement, 1868–69,* p. 118, *Fourteenth Annual Report, 1871,* p. 90; *Chicago Tribune,* July 2, March 14, June 16, July 2, 1862.) Flour shipments from Chicago declined markedly during the war years, for in 1862 the number of barrels shipped on the Illinois Central was little more than half of what it had been in 1859. After the war this trade again expanded. Chicago Board of Trade, *Fifth Annual Statement, 1862,* p. 74; see also Appendix, pp. 495–98.

at river ports, and that several hundred loaded freight cars filled the side tracks at different stations north awaiting opportunity to be moved into Cairo. Cash was now paid on delivery at southern destinations; the traders of that region were considered to be the " best customers "; and trade with them was indeed most welcome.[40]

The trade of Chicago with the South, however, remained subordinate in actual value to the less spectacular commercial intercourse centering around the agricultural products of the North. The liberal land policy of the Illinois Central built up the farming region through which the road passed and thus provided a wide market for Chicago merchandise and a large supply area for grains and provisions.[41] Over the southern branch of the road came great quantities of corn, largely from the northern third of Illinois. In addition to this service as a corn route, the road became, as a result of its westward extension, an important supply line for wheat.[42] To the Chicago market also were brought the fruits of southern Illinois, Jonesboro and Makanda apples and peaches, as well as tomatoes, blackberries, and melons. By 1866, special cars attached to passenger trains to carry these delicacies were no longer considered an innovation. The following year four hundred thousand boxes of fruit found their way from " Egypt " to the Chicago market, as well as 6,775 bushels of vegetables.[43]

The entrance of the Illinois Central into Chicago had been the signal for a bitter local controversy. Residents of the North and West divisions, seeking relief from the tax burden incident to maintaining the lake shore, allied themselves with the railroad to silence the protests of wealthy landowners along Michigan Avenue, who feared depreciation of their property and sought to defend the scenic beauty of the shore.[44] The council and legislature yielded to the pressure of

[40] Illinois Central Railroad Company, *Reports and Accounts, 1865*, p. 1; *ibid., 1866*, p. 1; *ibid., 1868*, p. 1; *Chicago Tribune*, March 18, 1870. Hay, meats, and agricultural implements, besides flour, were the chief articles desired by the South.

[41] *United States Economist*, V (June 17, 1854), p. 164. See for full discussion Gates, *The Illinois Central Railroad*, pp. 140–42 and *passim*.

[42] See Appendix, pp. 493, 495, 497.

[43] B. J. Johnson to W. H. Osborn, July 10, 11, 1855, *Johnson Papers*. The fruit came through by passenger train at $1.50 per hundred pounds. On July 25, 1857, one farmer alone shipped to Chicago fifty bushels of tomatoes. Paul Wallace Gates, " The Promotion of Agriculture by the Illinois Central Railroad, 1855–1870," *Agricultural History*, V (April, 1931), 57–78.

[44] Brownson, *op. cit.*, pp. 51–54.

the railroad, and in 1851 and 1852 the Illinois Central was given liberal rights along the lake front as far north as the south pier of the inner harbor.[45] Further legislation in 1869 confirmed the original grant of land lying four hundred feet east of the west line of Michigan Avenue, and at the same time the legislature handed over the property adjoining the Avenue between Monroe and Randolph streets for use as a depot by the Illinois Central, the Michigan Central, and the Chicago, Burlington and Quincy roads, with the understanding that the three roads pay the city $800,000. Violent opposition arose to the grant of property adjoining the Avenue, and at a later session of the legislature the measure was repealed. But the Illinois Central was unwilling to give up this valuable depot property and for many years contested the rescinding of the act.[46]

To the southwest also went the Chicago, Alton and St. Louis, which with other lines gave Chicago its first rail connection with the Mississippi River.[47] Like the Illinois and Michigan Canal, it formed a direct link between Chicago and St. Louis. The former city, however, gained more than did the latter. While more wheat was brought to Chicago at first, corn, by 1871, exceeded wheat receipts, and in the carriage of corn the Alton was exceeded only by the Illinois Central and the Burlington. In the transport of coal to Chicago the Alton was, by 1871, excelled only by the lake. Like other roads lead-

[45] *Ibid.*, p. 54; Andreas, *History of Chicago*, I, 255. The Illinois Central wanted in return for lake shore protection not only a right of way but also a prohibition of the opening of any public street east of the railroad's west line. (R. Schuyler to Mason Brayman, November 3, 1851, *Mason Brayman Papers* [Ms. Chicago Historical Society]; *Chicago Daily Democrat*, December 31, 1851.) The ordinance did not contain this provision, however. *Ordinances of the City of Chicago; passed since the Publication of the Revised Ordinances of 1851, and now in Force* (Arno Voss, comp., Chicago, 1853), pp. 51–55; Act of June 22, 1852, *Laws, 1852*, pp. 130–31. See pp. 200–1.

[46] Chicago, *Charter and Ordinances, 1856*, p. 539; Act of April 16, 1869, *Public Laws, 1869*, pp. 245–48; Andreas, *History of Chicago*, III, 190–92; Ackerman, *op. cit.*, pp. 96–105; Illinois, *Reports, 1869*, II, 1053–67. The state was upheld in Illinois *v.* Illinois Central Railroad, 246 Ill. 188 (October 28, 1910).

[47] The Chicago, Alton and St. Louis had its beginnings in a Springfield to Alton Railroad, authorized in 1847. By September, 1852, it operated trains between these points. (Act of February 27, 1847, *Private Laws, 1847*, p. 144; *Chicago Daily Democrat*, September 2, 1852.) The Alton was extended toward Chicago reaching Normal (near Bloomington) on October 18, 1853. Rail connection thus was made with the Illinois Central to La Salle and with the Rock Island from La Salle to Chicago. On July 31, 1854, through service for 260 miles between Alton and Chicago was possible, trains entering the latter place over the tracks of the Joliet and Northern Indiana and Illinois Central. Cole, *The Era of the Civil War*, p. 42; *The Daily Democratic Press*, July 31, 1854; The Daily Democratic Press, *Fourth Annual Review, 1855*, p. 71; *United States Economist*, IV (November 12, 1853), 56.

ing to the southwest it carried in return considerable quantities of merchandise, lumber, and iron.[48]

Another southwestern artery, the Chicago, Burlington and Quincy, joined Chicago with the Mississippi and brought to the city vast stores of grain as well as large shipments of hogs.[49] This railroad had its beginnings in the plans of an Aurora group assisted by Stephen F. Gale of Chicago, who obtained a charter in February, 1849, for the construction of the Aurora Branch Railroad.[50] Short lines joined Chicago with Burlington and Quincy, and in February, 1856, through passengers from Quincy arrived in Chicago. In the next decade a connection was made at Burlington between the Chicago, Burlington and Quincy and the Burlington and Missouri Railroad which led to Council Bluffs and thence by the Omaha connection to the Pacific; while a bridge at Quincy connected with the Hannibal and St. Joseph Railroad which ran to Kansas City.[51] The Burlington was one of the most important freight lines with its terminal in Chicago, for by 1871 it led in volume of oats, wool, hides, cattle, live hogs, and lard received in the city over its tracks. It was second only to the Alton in the carrying of lumber and to the North Western and Illinois Central in the shipment of merchandise and sundries, and was crowding the Illinois Central for leadership as a corn supply route.[52]

To the west and northwest of Chicago a great carpet of wheat spread across the states of Wisconsin and Minnesota and extended southward into northern Illinois and Iowa. Although these fields continued in the 'sixties as they had in the 'fifties to provide the city with the greater part of her wheat supply, after 1862 Chicago was eclipsed by Milwaukee, "Queen of the Lake," as a wheat market.

[48] The Daily Democratic Press, Fourth Annual Review, 1855, p. 11, Fifth Annual Review, 1856, p. 22; see Appendix, pp. 493–98.

[49] See Appendix, pp. 493, 495, 497.

[50] Daily Democrat, February 28, 1849. The Michigan Central was interested in the construction of this road and the other roads which made up the Chicago, Burlington and Quincy system. (Gates, The Illinois Central Railroad, p. 87.) In the early years the Burlington used tracks belonging to the Galena, from the junction, thirty miles west, into the city. (The Daily Democratic Press, Fifth Annual Review, 1856, p. 56.) By an ordinance of December 15, 1862, permission to lay its own tracks into Chicago was granted. (Laws and Ordinances Governing the City of Chicago . . . [Murray F. Tuley, comp. Chicago, 1873], pp. 263–64.) Ordinances of November 2, 28, 1864, January 30, 1866, further defined privileges and restrictions. Ibid., pp. 264–66.

[51] The Daily Democratic Press, Fourth Annual Review, 1855, p. 69; The Daily Democratic Press, July 11, 1856; Poor's Manual, 1870–71, p. 39.

[52] See Appendix, pp. 497–98.

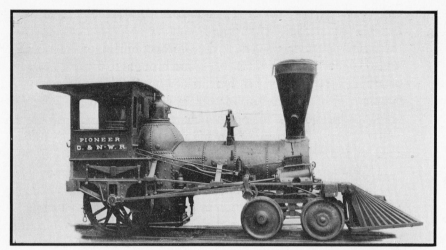

Courtesy of the Chicago and North Western Railway.

"THE PIONEER," FIRST RAILROAD ENGINE IN CHICAGO
It was used on the Galena and Chicago Union Railroad, October, 1848.

Courtesy of the Illinois Central Railroad.

ENGINE NO. 31 ON THE ILLINOIS CENTRAL RAILROAD
First built in 1856. The photograph was taken on the Chicago lake front, 1862. It shows the engine rebuilt to burn coal.

Over the rails leading from this section came more wheat than from all other sources.[53] On the eastern edge of this wheat area lay the lumber forests of Wisconsin and Upper Michigan, and farther to the north were the mineral deposits of the Superior region, which were later to provide raw material for one of the leading industries of Chicago.

The beginning of what later became the Chicago and North Western Railroad system, the great wheat feeder of Chicago, was the Galena and Chicago Union Railroad. This road entered Chicago by permission of a generous city council which imposed few restrictions. True, the council insisted upon the right to regulate the running of locomotives within the city limits and wanted the tracks to be so constructed that carriages could pass conveniently, but there were no time limits of rights granted and no bonds required to indemnify the city for damages arising from entrance.[54] In 1848 the Galena stretched to a point ten miles from the city; by September, 1853, it was extended westward to Freeport, where it permanently halted.[55] Although the Galena and Chicago Union did not reach the Mississippi along the route originally planned, work was started in 1853 on a branch which ultimately became the main line of the North Western Railroad to the Missouri River. Two years later a road known colloquially as the Dixon or Galena Air Line laid open a new route to Fulton, a point on the Mississippi opposite Clinton, Iowa,[56] whence eventually the North Western system reached Council Bluffs.

The Chicago and North Western Railway Company, which was to absorb the Galena in 1864, was an amalgamation of a number of

[53] Bayrd Still, " The Growth of Milwaukee as Recorded by Contemporaries," *The Wisconsin Magazine of History*, XXI (March, 1938), 275; The Daily Democratic Press, *Fourth Annual Review, 1855*, p. 10; Chicago Board of Trade, *Third Annual Statement, 1860*, p. 16, *Fourteenth Annual Report, 1871*, p. 51. In 1852 the Galena and Chicago Union was the only line which tapped the area; in 1860 the lines were the Galena and Chicago Union, the Chicago and North Western, the Chicago and Milwaukee, and the Iowa Division of the Illinois Central; and, in 1871, the Chicago and North Western and the Iowa Division of the Illinois Central.

[54] Chicago, *Charter and Ordinances, 1856*, pp. 341–43.

[55] For the building of branches from this road, see William Larrabee to C. S. Hempstead, March 7, 1855, *Hempstead Papers* (Ms. Chicago Historical Society); Galena and Chicago Union Railroad Company, *Seventh Annual Report, 1854*, p. 6; [Chicago and North Western Railway Company], *Yesterday and Today; a History of the Chicago and North Western Railway System* (3d ed. rev., Chicago, 1910), pp. 21–25, 75.

[56] Act of February 15, 1851, *Private Laws, 1851*, p. 254; The Daily Democratic Press, *Fourth Annual Review, 1855*, p. 68.

small lines. The Rock River Valley Union, started to provide a city market for the fertile Rock River Valley of Wisconsin, was consolidated in 1855 with the Illinois and Wisconsin Railroad under the leadership of William B. Ogden. The hope that the trade of Minnesota might be diverted from Milwaukee to Chicago led to the establishment of the Chicago, St. Paul and Fond du Lac Railroad, but that road fell victim to the panic and was taken over in 1859 by the Ogden interests, newly organized as the Chicago and North Western Railway Company. When in 1864 the North Western added the Galena to its network, hoping thereby eventually to effect a connection with the Pacific, Ogden controlled a rail empire of 836 miles. To this the North Western in 1866 added a line to Milwaukee by the perpetual lease of the Chicago and Milwaukee. But Ogden was not destined to control this coveted prize long, for in 1868 Wall Street, in the person of Henry Keep, who was already an important figure in the Rock Island, took control. There followed under the leadership of the Vanderbilts a period of co-operation between the two western roads, typified by the election in 1870 of John F. Tracy, president of the Rock Island, to the same position on the North Western.[57]

These lines controlled by the North Western formed a great L-shaped system with Chicago at the intersection of the long and short bars. From Chicago the short bar reached northward to Marquette, and from Chicago westward the long bar stretched to Fulton on the Mississippi River. With the Chicago, Iowa and Nebraska, the lease

---

[57] For the details of these consolidations see Act of August 19, 1848, *Laws of Wisconsin, 1848*, pp. 161–65; Acts of February 4, 9, 1850, *Acts and Resolves . . . of Wisconsin, 1850*, p. 175; Acts of March 11, 13, 1851, *Acts and Resolves . . . of Wisconsin, 1851*, pp. 203–4; Act of March 10, 1855, *Private and Local Acts of Wisconsin, 1855*, pp. 179–81; Act of March 6, 1857, *Private and Local Laws of Wisconsin, 1857*, pp. 798–99; Acts of February 12, 17, 1851, *Private Laws of Illinois, 1851*, pp. 108–9, 266; Act of March 5, 1853, *Private Laws of Illinois, 1853*, p. 9; Illinois and Wisconsin Railroad Company, *Record Book*, pp. 3–5, 13, 14, 16, 20, 24, 35–38; Madison and Beloit Railroad Company, *Record Book*, pp. 1, 121–22, 131; Chicago, St. Paul and Fond du Lac Railroad Company, *Record Book*, " A," pp. 6–16, *Record Book*, " B," p. 145; Chicago and North Western Railway Company, *Record Book*, no. 2, pp. 46, 74, 629–30, *Record Book*, no. 3, pp. 57–63, 307–20 (*Mss.* in the office of the vice-president and secretary of the Chicago and North Western Railway Company); Galena and Chicago Union Railroad Company, *Record Book*, " B," pp. 570–85; Wisconsin Railroad Commissioners, *First Annual Report* (Madison, 1874), Appendix, p. 151; Chicago and North Western Railway Company, *Sixth Annual Report, 1865*, pp. 13–15, 26–27, 34–35; Chicago and North Western Railway Company, *Documents Relating to the Formation of the Chicago and North Western Railway Company* (New York, 1860), pp. 9, 17, 26–28; *Yesterday and Today*, pp. 55–56, 57, 60–61, 65–66; Isaac N. Arnold, *William B. Ogden; and Early Days in Chicago . . .* (Fergus Historical Series, no. 17. Chicago, 1882), pp. 20–21.

of which was acquired in 1862 by the Galena, it encompassed the entire northwest quadrant of the trade area of Chicago, and through it, like a funnel, the products of the Northwest, particularly wheat, cattle, and meat, poured into the city by the lake.[58]

The significance of the great North Western system in the commercial development of Chicago was foreshadowed in the service of its component part, the Galena and Chicago Union Railroad. In 1849, the Chicago wheat receipts from this road were 171,365 bushels, and each year succeeding 1854 millions of bushels were brought to the city. Consignments of corn were also large during the first few years after the opening of the road, but at no time following 1855 did they equal in magnitude those of wheat.[59] The direct result of the successful service of the Galena as a freight carrier took the form of extremely liberal dividends to its stockholders, a fact which did not escape the notice of eastern capitalists, particularly after 1857 when most railroads were suffering from the depression.[60]

While the North Western was the great supply line for the wheat of the area to the west and northwest of the city, the Iowa Division of the Illinois Central, extending westward from the abrupt turn of the main line at Freeport, also sent considerable contributions to the Chicago mart over the tracks of the Galena Railroad. When other railroads were constructed parallel to the Galena, the Illinois Central was provided with new inlets to Chicago, but in 1889 it built its own line from Freeport to the city and kept the profits of its western business.[61]

Although western business in general suffered from the depression of 1857, grain receipts of the Iowa Division at the river port, Dunleith, to which products from the upper Mississippi were brought and thence forwarded to Chicago, increased ninefold in the years between

[58] By 1871 the North Western was the unquestioned leader among the western roads as a wheat carrier, had wrested supremacy in the meat trade from the Burlington which still excelled it in the eastward carrying of live hogs, and was second to the Burlington, the Alton, and the Illinois Central in the transport of cattle. See Appendix, pp. 497–98.

[59] See Appendix, pp. 492–93.

[60] Dividends declared by the Galena were as high as 22 per cent in 1856. In 1861, however, they fell to 5 per cent. Galena and Chicago Union Railroad Company, *Ninth Annual Report, 1856*, p. 20, *Sixteenth Annual Report, 1862*, p. 5.

[61] Brownson, *op. cit.*, pp. 95–97; *Memorandum of an Understanding Relative to Proposed Relations Between the Illinois Central Railroad and the Galena and Chicago Union Railroad, March 6, 1855* (Ms. Illinois Central Railroad Company); Illinois Central Railroad Company, *Reports and Accounts, 1858*, p. 9; *ibid., 1897*, pp. 22, 80.

1855 and 1860.[62] In the meantime the Dubuque and Pacific Railroad had been extended westward from Dubuque opposite Dunleith. In 1867 as the Dubuque and Sioux City Road it was leased for twenty years by the Illinois Central, under whose direction the two lines were connected by the Dunleith to Dubuque bridge in 1869.

Four railroads leading from Chicago now bridged the Mississippi.[63] In 1869, also, the Union Pacific closed the gap in the route between California and Omaha, which lay but a few miles from the termini of the Chicago and Rock Island and the Chicago and North Western.[64] The dream of Chicagoans for more than a score of years had come true. Now could their city become the central link of a continuous chain from East to West, "the New York of the West," the culmination of a burning desire for economic empire.[65] When the last spike was driven in May of 1869, Chicago businessmen celebrated to the ringing of bells and the shrieking of whistles as they rode through the streets in a parade of more than eight hundred vehicles. For did they not believe that "the commerce of the Indies and the East, which, for a thousand years, has found its way over its accustomed circuitous paths to Europe and the West," would break away, and "by a direct route across the Pacific, the mountains and the plains, pour itself into the lap of Chicago, to be distributed to the Atlantic cities, and thence to the European markets?"[66]

[62] Total receipts from the Iowa branch at Chicago in 1855 were approximately 531,920 bushels; in 1860, approximately 1,186,430 bushels. *Ibid., 1855; ibid., 1860,* pp. 11–12.

[63] The Daily Democratic Press, *Fourth Annual Review, 1855,* p. 68; *Poor's Manual, 1869–70,* p. 435; *ibid., 1870–71,* p. 257. The Chicago and Rock Island, the Chicago, Burlington and Quincy (at both Burlington and Quincy), the Chicago and North Western, and the Illinois Central bridged the Mississippi.

[64] The Missouri River was not bridged at Omaha in 1870. To make through shipments without breaking bulk, goods were sent via the Sioux City and Pacific which crossed the river at Blair, Nebraska. From Chicago, the Iowa Division of the Illinois Central connected with the Sioux City and Pacific. *Chicago Tribune,* April 14, 1870.

[65] *Prairie Farmer,* XI (January, 1851), 20. Chicagoans made declarations in favor of a grand trunk line with branches at St. Louis and Chicago at the National Railroad Convention at St. Louis in 1849 (*Chicago Daily Journal,* October 12, 1849). William B. Ogden was active enough in plans for a Pacific Railroad to be chosen president of the Pacific Railroad Convention at Philadelphia in 1850 (*New York Evening Post,* May 3, 1850). In 1853, John Wentworth introduced a resolution into Congress for such a railroad (*Cong. Globe,* 33 Cong., 1 sess., pt. 1, p. 38). During the 'fifties the project was tied in with politics in which Douglas played a stellar rôle. George Fort Milton, *The Eve of Conflict* . . . (Boston, 1934), pp. 99, 104; Frank H. Hodder, "The Railroad Background of the Kansas-Nebraska Act," *The Mississippi Valley Historical Review,* XII (June, 1925), 3–22.

[66] Despite expressions of hope, Chicago commercial interests clamored for another transcontinental route which would insure low rates by competition, and they enthusiastically sup-

The completion of the Union Pacific Railway brought Chicago within about 106 hours of travel from San Francisco and marked for a time the last major extension of the transportation system leading west. Fresh fruit from California could now be found on the Chicagoan's table, and merchants talked of sending such things as drugs in return. The domestic trade of the city expanded, and the vision of Chicago as an entrepôt for the trade of the Orient was also fulfilled. In June, 1870, the *Tribune* enthusiastically noted the arrival of "tons of raw silk" en route to Liverpool from China, and in the following year reported that thousands of chests of tea had been sent directly from Yokohama and Hongkong by way of San Francisco.[67] The opening of transportation routes westward brought to Chicago, to be sure, the exotic products of the distant lands of the Orient, but these products were far excelled in quantity and in total value by the more commonplace livestock, grains, meat, lumber, and merchandise from the areas which lay near at hand.

At the same time rapid increases in shipments took place to the East. But the extension of the railroads eastward was brought about only after a major conflict between the Michigan Central and the Michigan Southern had been resolved in 1852, thereby ending the virtual monopoly which lake carriers had exercised. Officials of both railroads, with an eye on profits which they might gain were one line to monopolize Chicago rail traffic, fought each other in the legislatures and courts of Indiana and Illinois, and in the Common Council of Chicago.[68]

Even before it sought charter rights in Illinois, the Michigan Central had made an agreement with the Galena and Chicago Union, which granted the eastern line the Galena's somewhat doubtful right to build a track from Chicago to the Indiana border.[69] In 1851

ported the Congressional appropriation and land grant to the Kansas Pacific Railway in 1870 in the belief that it would open up trade with New Mexico. Union Pacific Railway Company (Eastern Division), *Action of the Board of Trade of Chicago* . . . (Chicago, 1868), pp. 7–9, 16, 18–19; *Chicago Tribune,* January 26, 1868, May 10, 11, 1869.

[67] The Chicago Tribune, *Chicago Tribune's Annual Review, 1869,* p. 71 (hereafter cited as Chicago Tribune, *Annual Review*); *Chicago Tribune,* October 13, 1869, June 2, 1870, October 5, 1871.

[68] Brownson, *op. cit.,* p. 49.

[69] The clause in the Galena charter which seemed to give a right to build a track from Chicago to the Indiana line was as follows: sec. 6 ". . . and it shall be lawful also for the said corporation to unite with any other rail road company already incorporated, or which may be incorporated, upon any part of the route of the said rail road upon such terms as may

these allied roads suggested that the Michigan Southern use this proposed line jointly with the Central, the Galena to act as arbitrator in case of a dispute.[70]

As the Southern refused the compromise offer, the scene of battle shifted to the halls of the Illinois legislature, convened in January, 1851. Each road had its advocates among western leaders, some of whom held financial stakes. Philip Maxwell and Thomas Dyer of Chicago worked in the lower house to further the requests of the Michigan Central, the latter interested in railroad development through holdings in the Galena. In the columns of the *Daily Democrat* John Wentworth openly made powerful appeals in behalf of the Central. State Senator Norman B. Judd, later a director of the Rock Island Railroad which was dominated by men with investments in the Southern, vigorously attacked the claims of his opponents.

The Southern group was supported also by Alfred Dutch of the *Commercial Advertiser* just as earnestly as Dutch was accustomed to support causes which he sponsored. Chicago land interests, controlling the probable site of the Michigan Southern depot, lent their influence to the side of the Southern, while the *Tribune,* in spite of favoring the Central, joined the *Journal* in asking that both roads be permitted to enter Chicago on equal terms. Businessmen of the city vainly tried to settle what seemed an insolvable problem by obtaining charters independent of either interest, but so keen was the rivalry among the various groups that neither road could gain an advantage.[71]

Consequently the two lines were forced to seek private agreements with roads already enjoying charter privileges in Illinois. These agreements of the Michigan Central with the Illinois Central and the Michigan Southern with the Rock Island were made easy by the financial interests in the western roads of the capitalists controlling

---

be agreed upon by the directors of said companies, and also to construct such other and lateral routes, as may be necessary to connect them with any other route or routes, which may be deemed expedient." Act of January 16, 1836, *Laws, 1836,* p. 26.

[70] *Chicago Daily Democrat,* January 4, February 1, 1851; Gates, *The Illinois Central Railroad,* pp. 87, 90.

[71] *Chicago Daily Journal,* January 9, 18, 24, 25, 1851; *Chicago Daily Democrat,* January 4, 21, 29, 31, February 3, 1851. Wentworth's interest in the Michigan Central was probably affected by the fact that he was involved in the activities of the Illinois Central. Gates, *The Illinois Central Railroad,* p. 63.

the eastern lines. John Murray Forbes, John Thayer, George Griswold, and James F. Joy among the Michigan Central group were also active investors in the Illinois Central; and in the Michigan Southern group, George Bliss, Edwin C. Litchfield, John Stryker, and John B. Jervis were directors of the Rock Island.[72]

The proposal of the Michigan Central to meet the Illinois Central at the state line aroused instant opposition in Chicago lest this arrangement divert traffic from the city. The Common Council appropriated $10,000 to fight the scheme, and Mayor Gurnee and Stephen A. Douglas, whose aid in the protection of Chicago had been enlisted, went to New York and successfully urged that the plan be abandoned.[73]

Meanwhile the Michigan Southern, while it pushed forward toward its goal, attempted also to frustrate its rival. In June, 1851, it had refused to accept the proposal to allow the Michigan Central to build an Illinois line which the Southern could lease, and was reported as going so far as to try to prevent the floating of Illinois Central loans in Europe. In August, 1851, the Michigan Southern obtained an injunction to keep the Michigan Central from completing its lines across Indiana. The injunction, however, was dissolved by the supreme court of the state.[74]

The tactics of the Michigan Southern were successful in giving it the advantage in the race to enter Chicago, and on February 20, 1852, its first train came into the city over the Rock Island tracks. Three months later, on May 22, its first through passenger train ran into Chicago, the day after the Michigan Central had sent its first train into the city. In June, 1852, the special session of the Illinois legis-

[72] *Ibid.*, pp. 44, 49, 91; *Chicago Daily Democrat*, February 22, April 14, 22, 26, May 12, 14, 27, June 25, 1851; "Contracts between the Michigan Central and Illinois Central Railroad," *Brayman Papers*; *American Railroad Journal*, XXIV (October 18, 1851), 664; Chicago and Rock Island Railroad Company, *Reports of the President, Chief Engineer and Consulting Engineer . . . 1851* (New York, 1852), p. 5; Gates, "The Struggle for the Charter of the Illinois Central Railroad," *loc. cit.*, pp. 55–56; *Statements and Replies in Reference to the Compensation for the Use of the Road of the Illinois Central R. R. Company . . .* (Boston, 1860), pp. 86–91, 93–94.

[73] Mason Brayman to William H. Osborn, April 14, 1860, *Brayman Papers*; Gates, *The Illinois Central Railroad*, p. 92.

[74] *Chicago Daily Democrat*, June 23, 25, October 13, 1851. One man accused of attempting to block the Illinois Central loans in Europe was Charles Butler, a brother-in-law of William B. Ogden, who had long been interested in Chicago development. *Ibid.*, October 13, 1851; Pierce, *A History of Chicago*, I, 146; *American Railroad Journal*, XXIV (September 13, 1851), 582; *Weekly Chicago Democrat*, February 4, 1854.

lature authorized the Union Railroad Company, a Michigan Central corporation, and the Chicago and Northern Indiana Railroad Company, a Michigan Southern organization, to build their own tracks in Illinois if they wished.[75] The struggle now centered on getting the through business, and a heated competition developed which was finally resolved in 1857 when they made a pooling agreement by which the Southern agreed to divide equally with the Michigan Central all its through freight business over 42 per cent, whereas the latter divided with the Southern only its business over 58 per cent.[76]

The Pittsburgh, Fort Wayne and Chicago, the third great line to the East, was formed in 1856 by a merger of the Fort Wayne and Chicago, the Ohio and Indiana, and the Ohio and Pennsylvania Railroad and ran its first through train to Pittsburgh from Chicago on Christmas Day, 1858. Linked with the Pennsylvania at Pittsburgh, it provided the shortest route between Chicago and New York. From its station on the West Side at the corner of Canal and Madison streets a traveler could also go by the most direct route to Baltimore or Washington.[77]

The entrance of the Pittsburgh and Fort Wayne in 1858 broke the monopoly of rail shipments to the East which the Michigan Central and Michigan Southern lines had enjoyed. But in ten years it too suffered at the hands of a competitor when the Pennsylvania Railroad acquired control of the Pittsburgh, Cincinnati and St. Louis Railroad, a parallel route to Chicago which entered the city in 1868. The strangle hold which the Pennsylvania Railroad had not only on its eastern terminus but also on the competing route to Chicago probably influenced the Pittsburgh and Fort Wayne to relinquish its

[75] *Chicago Daily Democrat,* February 20, May 22, 27, 1852; Gates, *The Illinois Central Railroad,* p. 92; Brownson, *op. cit.,* p. 53; Acts of June 16, 22, 1852, *Laws, 1852,* p. 14.

[76] Through passenger business was divided equally. Michigan Central Railroad Company, *Annual Report, 1858,* p. 9; Michigan Southern and Northern Indiana Railroad Company, *Annual Report, 1857–58,* p. 13.

[77] The Daily Democratic Press, *Fifth Annual Review, 1856,* p. 60; H. W. Schotter, *The Growth and Development of the Pennsylvania Railroad Company* . . . (Philadelphia, 1927), p. 38; *Chicago Daily Press and Tribune,* January 11, 1859; Richard Edwards, *Fifteenth Annual Directory of Chicago* . . . *1872* (Chicago, 1872), p. 753 (hereafter cited as Edwards, *Directory*). The station of the Pittsburgh, Fort Wayne and Chicago was also used by the Chicago, Alton and St. Louis. (*Chicago Tribune,* November 29, 1860.) The ordinance providing for the terminal was passed August 15, 1858. Chicago, *Council Proceedings, 1858– 1861,* p. 33. See also City of Chicago, *The Municipal Code of Chicago* . . . (Chicago, 1881), pp. 649–50, 652–53.

independent existence, and in July, 1869, its directors signed a 999 year lease to the Pennsylvania.[78]

Welding the Pittsburgh, Cincinnati and St. Louis Railroad out of the Steubenville and Indiana, Holliday's Cove, and Pan-Handle railroads, together with the leased lines, the Little Miami and Columbus and Xenia railroads and the Columbus, Chicago and Indiana Central, was one of the last major developments during these years in the transportation system leading from Chicago to the East.[79]

East of Chicago stretched the trunk lines which connected the young midwestern city with the great cities of the East. To a small extent these roads shared with the lake the east-bound grain traffic, particularly in the less bulky cereals. The transport of cattle and meat products to the seaboard came increasingly to be the province of the railroad, especially after the introduction of the refrigerator car in the late 'sixties facilitated the traffic in cut meats. Merchandise and sundries led all other types of commodities in the west-bound freight, the three leading roads carrying approximately similar amounts. From the East also came iron and nails, to be used in the growing manufactories of Chicago and in the construction of new homes on the prairies to the west. The transportation of coal also helped to effect a balance between east and west traffic, this commodity being carried primarily on the Pittsburgh, Cincinnati and St. Louis.[80]

The railroads quickly gained the passenger traffic between Chicago and the East. The Michigan Central was particularly active in this respect, running boats in 1849 from Chicago to its western terminus, New Buffalo, and then carrying passengers over the rails to Detroit whence they again embarked on a Michigan Central boat for Buffalo, a trip which took them thirty to forty-five hours.[81] Through travel by rail to Toledo became possible in May, 1853, by way of the Michigan Southern, in the same year the lines east of Buffalo were consoli-

---

[78] Michigan Central Railroad Company, *Annual Report, 1858*, pp. 19, 22; Pittsburgh, Fort Wayne and Chicago Railway Company, *Seventh Annual Report, 1868*, p. 17; John S. Wright, *Chicago: Past, Present, Future* (Chicago, 1868), p. 362; *Poor's Manual, 1871–72*, pp. 332, 352.

[79] *Ibid.*, p. 332.

[80] See Appendix, pp. 493–98.

[81] *Daily Democrat*, April 10, 1849, February 16, 1852; *Weekly Chicago Democrat*, March 26, 1853; Michigan Central Railroad Company, *Annual Report, 1854*, p. 4, *Annual Report, 1858*, p. 21.

dated in the New York Central, and in 1858 both freight and passengers could go on the Pittsburgh and Fort Wayne to Cleveland, Buffalo, Cincinnati, and Pittsburgh without changes. By 1870 through connections with the Pennsylvania system enabled Michigan Southern ticket holders to go to New York without change of cars.[82] The preponderance of passenger travel was westward. Thus in 1857 the Michigan Central and the Michigan Southern alone brought to the city about ninety-five thousand more passengers than they took east. This was also true of the travel on the western lines. In the same year four roads, the Galena and Chicago Union, the Chicago, St. Paul and Fond du Lac, the Chicago, Burlington and Quincy, and the Chicago and Rock Island carried west 76,387 more passengers than they brought back to the city. Chicago had become a focal point in migration to the West. As early as 1854, its ten railroads were said to be pouring crowds of over thirteen thousand a week into the city.[83] Chicago prospered and rejoiced that her streets were crowded and her hotels were filled.

Frequent excursions to Niagara Falls, to political conventions, and to other national and local events, as well as those for pleasure, stimulated patronage, fares sometimes being little more than one cent a mile.[84] Despite accidents, often the result of carelessness, people developed a travel-mindedness which broke chains of provincial self-interest and opened to them broadened horizons of culture through contacts with distant regions. Yet, notwithstanding the advantages of the railroad over other methods of transport, traveling was not

[82] *Chicago Daily Democrat*, May 27, 1852; *Chicago Daily Press and Tribune*, November 30, 1858; *The Workingman's Advocate*, January 8, 1870. See advertisements in *Chicago Daily Democrat*, 1852, and after; *Chicago Press and Tribune*, November 8, 1858.

[83] Chicago Daily Democratic Press, *Sixth Annual Review, 1857*, p. 46. The total of the westward through and way traffic on the Michigan Central and Michigan Southern in 1857 was 565,996, the total of the eastward through and way traffic was 470,941. In 1870, the ratio was about the same. (*Poor's Manual, 1871–72*, pp. 202, 539.) On four western railroads the total of the western through and way travel was 752,061, that of the eastern 675,224. (Chicago Daily Democratic Press, *Sixth Annual Review, 1857*, p. 46; *The Daily Democratic Press*, October 3, 1854.) Travelers from the South came especially in the summer, bound for Canada and Niagara Falls. *Ibid.*, July 10, 1854; *Weekly Chicago Democrat*, July 15, 1854; *The Press and Tribune*, August 2, 1860.

[84] For example, in 1860, the Pittsburgh, Fort Wayne and Chicago Railroad had excursion rates to the Democratic Convention at Baltimore for twenty-four dollars. (*Chicago Daily Democrat*, June 12, 1860.) In 1870, the *Workingman's Advocate* (July 16, 1870) reported the fare to New York as eighteen dollars over the Michigan Central. Twenty dollars was the usual one-way fare to New York in the 'sixties, but at the time of the Democratic National Convention in 1868 round-trip tickets were sold at that price. *Chicago Tribune*, July 4, 1868.

attended by speed and comfort. Dust in the " dry times " nearly suffo-
cated " the unhappy wight " who, in the words of a contemporary,
was " hurried through the world at the rate of forty miles an hour,"
and in the cold months, heat from a single wood-burning stove extended but a short distance in a car.[85] The first hardship, however,
sometimes was relieved by an early form of air conditioning, Dr.
George F. Foote's ventilator system. This, when the car was in motion and the windows were closed, permitted air to circulate from
chambers at the sides of the car and up through grates in the floor.[86]

Winter travelers in the late 'sixties were comforted by Baker's
patent car warmer by which salted hot water circulated through
pipes under the car seats. This device seems to have been an improvement, even over the Pittsburgh and Fort Wayne system by which
heat from a stove was piped along the floors of sleeping cars.[87] The
Pittsburgh and Fort Wayne also sent out separate smoking cars on
its runs as early as 1860, thereby eliciting from the press a word of
gratitude on behalf of the " lovers of the weed."

The most important advance toward travel comfort was the introduction of the sleeping car. In 1856, cars which could be converted
into sleeping quarters on one side with " a row of seats with revolv-
ing back, similar to barber's chairs," on the other led to the prophecy
that " railroading" would soon become as easy and comfortable as
riding upon the most luxurious steamers. In 1858, the Galena line
put on a sleeper between Chicago and Freeport and Dubuque. In
the same year, cars were built for the Chicago and Alton, whose
plush seats could be converted into sleeping sections at night if a
traveler wished to pay fifty cents.[88] By 1861 the Michigan Southern
cars not only provided similar accommodations, but had a " raised
ventilator roof " which was an improvement over the flat roof of a
short time before. Within a few years more, richly curtained sections

[85] *The Daily Democratic Press*, May 26, 1854. See also *The Press and Tribune*, May 11,
1860. The rate of travel was usually thirty miles or less.

[86] *The Daily Democratic Press*, May 26, 1854. Before circulation the air was " washed "
in a shower of water which came from a storage tank kept under pressure by a pump run
with power from the car axle. This system was said to have been successful on the Michigan
Southern.

[87] *Chicago Tribune*, June 10, 1868. The Michigan Southern in 1868 installed this system
of heating. *Ibid.*, January 29, 1862.

[88] *The Daily Democratic Press*, June 23, 1856; *Chicago Tribune*, November 12, 1860;
Yesterday and Today, pp. 45, 46. George M. Pullman, Norman J. Field, and Benjamin Field
of Albion, New York, had the contract.

containing " spring mattresses " were available for those who wished to go from Chicago to New York. Dining cars likewise added to comfort and speed since it was no longer necessary to stop at " eating stations " to accommodate passengers.[89]

Experiments with cast iron cars for freight and with steel rails likewise heralded a new and better day in transportation. Ways of shipping freight were also improved. Almost as soon as the eastern lines had opened, cattle cars passed over the rails.[90] Quick and efficient carriage and savings on insurance captured traffic for the rail companies despite higher charges than those demanded by lake carriers.[91] By the late 'sixties the installation of a third rail permitted narrow gauge cars to go directly from Chicago to the seaboard without breaking bulk, and the introduction of refrigerator cars facilitated the transportation of fresh meats. By the 'sixties, also, gas-lighted coaches with trucks and wide tread wheels made the run from Chicago to New York without change of cars and the breaking of gauge.[92]

Facilities for the transportation of money and light packages were developed by 1850 by the American Express Company to New York, Milwaukee, St. Louis, Cincinnati, and Buffalo. Five years later this service was extended to Detroit, Sault Ste. Marie, and Ontonagon by co-operation with the Lake Superior Express Company, and by 1860 messengers went daily over nine railroads connecting with other roads and expresses leading to " all parts of the United States, Canada and Europe." Soon express facilities had been provided Iowa and Minnesota; and Wells, Fargo and Company had brought California

[89] *Chicago Tribune,* April 2, 1861, May 15, 1862, February 28, 1866; Illinois Railroad and Warehouse Commission, "First Report," Illinois, *Reports, 1871,* II, 436–37. On March 30, 1868, the *Tribune* carried the story of a trip on the C. B. and Q. taken by George M. Pullman and thirty guests, who rode in the new dining car "Delmonico," constructed at a cost of $20,000 for Pullman and able to accommodate twenty-four persons at black walnut tables placed near the windows. *Chicago Tribune,* March 30, 1868.

[90] *Chicago Daily Democrat,* October 31, 1860; *Chicago Tribune,* February 9, 1861, March 19, 1868; Michigan Central Railroad Company, *Annual Report, 1867,* p. 24.

[91] Chicago Board of Trade, *Fourteenth Annual Report, 1871,* pp. 84–85; George G. Tunell, "The Diversion of the Flour and Grain Traffic from the Great Lakes to the Railroads," *The Journal of Political Economy,* V (June, 1897), 348; Michigan Central Railroad, *Opening of Road to New Buffalo* . . . (Bulletin, Chicago Historical Society); *Chicago Daily Democrat,* September 8, 1849.

[92] *Chicago Tribune,* February 17, 1864; Michigan Central Railroad Company, *Annual Report, 1867,* p. 22. It was not until the 'nineties that there was a well-developed tendency to standardize the gauge to four feet, eight and one-half inches, the standard today. J. L. Ringwalt, *Development of Transportation Systems in the United States* (Philadelphia, 1888), p. 136.

and Oregon within reach.[93] Express service was also furnished by the
United States Express Company, whose Chicago office opened in 1854
and whose route at first followed the Chicago, Rock Island and
Pacific and the South Shore from the Mississippi to New York. Small
companies, such as Kellogg's Western Express, offered carriage of
parcels along the Galena, just as Abbott and Company did along the
Illinois Central and the Chicago, Rock Island and Pacific.[94] Local
expresses to serve the immediate neighborhood developed, particularly after 1859.[95]

Speed, safety, and care in express shipments meant increasing business. Gradually money-order, commission, collecting, and letter-of-
credit services were added. As early as 1855 one exchange broker
was reported as having shipped from Chicago by express nearly three
and one-half million dollars.[96]

By the 'fifties forces were at work to eliminate the difficulties encountered when freight was transported over separate railways.[97]
Chicago shippers of perishable goods had every reason to agitate for
fast and uninterrupted transit to the seaboard. Express companies
responded by extending their services to bulky products. The "fast
freights" which they provided led to the establishment of fast freight
organizations which owned their own cars and furnished through
bills for goods sent over various connecting lines. These fast freight
companies by the mid-'fifties were advertising the transportation of
goods at the rate of $1.75 per hundred pounds to New York in eight
days.[98] So well did they perform their duties that on some lines they

[93] *Chicago Daily Democrat*, April 10, June 15, 1850; Andreas, *History of Chicago*, I, 263;
Western Railroad Gazette, February 4, 1860, April 18, June 20, 1863. In 1861, the American
Express Company's Chicago office received currency shipments of $700,000, largely in gold
coin. *Chicago Tribune*, June 24, 1861; *The Daily Democratic Press*, March 14, 1855.

[94] Andreas, *History of Chicago*, II, 127; *Weekly Chicago Democrat*, March 1, 1850; *The
Daily Democratic Press*, January 2, June 27, 1854, August 13, October 30, December 11, 29,
1855. By 1861, the United States Express had made connections with Wells, Fargo and
Company and with the Pony Express. *Halpin & Bailey's Directory, 1861–62*, p. 180.

[95] Forrest Crissey, *The Romance of Moving Money* . . . (Chicago, 1929), pp. 13–15.

[96] *The Daily Democratic Press*, March 27, 1855. This was F. G. Adams, exchange broker.

[97] Railways had different gauges. Freight transported over two or more railroads had
to have a separate bill of lading for each. Forwarding companies arranged with railways
over which goods were shipped for special cars for their use and performed the services necessary for the carriage of goods between producer and consignee. Logan G. McPherson, *Railroad
Freight Rates in Relation to the Industry and Commerce of the United States* (New York,
1909), pp. 161, 163.

[98] The first company to offer "fast freight" services was Kasson's Dispatch, purchased
soon after its organization in 1850 by the American Express Company to operate as the Mer-

shortly came to have a virtual monopoly of first- and second-class trade to New York and Boston.[99]

These years of railroad beginnings were hard. The retarding effects of competition of railroad with railroad and of railroad with water carrier sometimes threatened the prosperity which otherwise might have prevailed. The vexatious problem of rates seemed ever-present, and provisions for the comfort and safety of passenger travel and for the effective handling of specialized types of freight demanded constant attention. Taking advantage of the increased dependence of shippers resulting from the closure of the Mississippi during the early years of war the railroads generally raised their rates, charging all that the traffic would bear and maintaining these rates at a high level after the emergency of the war had passed.[100] Protests were not long delayed. In January, 1866, the real estate brokers of the city passed resolutions directed against high railroad rates, pointing out that unless concessions were made " serious mischief to all classes of business " would result, and that the prosperity of Chicago as the leading market of the Northwest would be threatened. Already, it was asserted, " shippers, merchants and business men generally in the towns and cities West and Southwest " were looking toward other cities and other avenues of trade. In the same year, a group of 123 business firms addressed to all railroads centering in Chicago a memorial about the comparative freight rates charged for transportation of produce and merchandise.[101]

chant's Dispatch. (New York [State], *Proceedings of the Special Committee on Railroads,* . . . [5 v. Albany, 1879–80], III, 2960; *The Daily Democratic Press,* April 17, 1855.) The Merchant's Dispatch in 1857 was followed by the Great Western Dispatch in connection with the United States Express Company. (New York [State], *Proceedings of the Special Committee on Railroads,* . . . , III, 2961.) The Great Western shipped by way of the Erie and Lake Shore and Michigan Southern. *Western Railroad Gazette,* January 23, 1864.

[99] Pittsburgh, Fort Wayne and Chicago Railway Company, *Fifth Annual Report, 1866,* pp. 135–37. Lesser express companies offered similar services. Spalding's Express operated over the New York and Erie, Michigan Southern, and C. R. I. and P. to points west of Chicago. (*The Daily Democratic Press,* September 10, 1855.) The Valentine Express Company also carried freight from New York to Chicago. *The Press and Tribune,* September 26, 1859.

[100] *Chicago Tribune,* September 17, 23, 1861. In 1866, the *Prairie Farmer* pointed out that from Pittsburgh to Chicago, a distance of over 500 miles, a lot of freight cost $4.64, but from Sterling, Illinois, to Chicago, a distance of 110 miles, it cost $6.41. (*Prairie Farmer,* n.s. XVII [January 13, 1866], p. 24.) Persons could ship more economically from Chicago to New Orleans than from Chicago to Kankakee. Lumber could be shipped from Chicago to St. Louis and from St. Louis more cheaply than directly to Springfield from Chicago. *Debates and Proceedings of the Constitutional Convention of the State of Illinois, convened* . . . *December 13, 1869* (2 v. Springfield, 1870), II, 1646.

[101] *Chicago Tribune,* January 9, 11, 1866.

Nor were high rates the only distressing feature in the situation. To Chicago businessmen and farmers of the surrounding country equally disconcerting was the fluctuation of charges. The cost of carriage between New York and Chicago varied in 1869 and 1870 from $5.00 to $37 per ton, while the Erie for a short time charged as little as two dollars. The abnormally low rates were not sufficient to cover the cost of transportation, and the roads made up the loss by charging exorbitant prices between non-competitive points. The Union and Central Pacific railroads, unhampered by rail competition to San Francisco, in some cases charged more for freight carriage between that city and Chicago than between San Francisco and New York, so that the historian of the Board of Trade wrote that " Chicago may well complain of discriminations on this line." [102]

As the 'sixties grew old, the farmer, who saw his product the pawn of the carriers, demanded that the government take action in his behalf. In the halls of the state legislature his voice was heard, ineffectually at first it is true, but strongly enough in 1869 that an enactment, although without teeth, was passed to pacify the elements of discontent. [103] Three years before, businessmen of Chicago, alarmed at the tone of public opinion, had asked the railroads to explain the reasons for excessive rates and the causes of complaint on the part of shippers. It was, indeed, a matter of considerable concern to have farmers upon whose produce and trade their economic well-being rested speak of them as the allies of capitalists and promoters of

[102] Passenger rates were also a source of irritation and objection. Illinois Railroad and Warehouse Commission, " First Report," Illinois, *Reports, 1871,* II, 22; Joseph Hinckley Gordon, *Illinois Railway Legislation and Commission Control since 1870* (University of Illinois, *The University Studies,* I, no. 6, March, 1904. Urbana, 1904), p. 228; Charles H. Taylor, ed., *History of the Board of Trade of the City of Chicago* (3 v. Chicago, 1917), I, 393; *Chicago Tribune,* February 4, 1868, April 27, 1870.

[103] In 1861, a bill to punish discriminations by railroads passed the lower house. (Illinois, *Journal of the House of Representatives of the . . . General Assembly of the State of Illinois, 1861,* p. 937 [hereafter cited as Illinois, *House Journal*].) The bill was introduced but never acted upon in the Senate. (Illinois, *Journal of the Senate of the . . . General Assembly of the State of Illinois, 1861,* p. 583 [hereafter cited as Illinois, *Senate Journal*].) In 1863, a bill for the appointment of railroad commissioners, passed by the Senate, was tabled in the House. (*Ibid., 1863,* pp. 89, 193–94, 210; Illinois, *House Journal, 1863,* pp. 117, 502–3, 681.) In 1865, the House passed a bill for the appointment of a railroad commission and also one limiting passenger fares to three cents a mile. In the Senate the bills died in committee. (*Ibid., 1865,* pp. 133, 164, 467, 520, 701, 778, 833, 982; Illinois, *Senate Journal, 1865,* pp. 548, 675, 683, 711.) Bills were presented in 1867 but none passed both houses. *Ibid., 1867,* pp. 173, 200, 446, 1231; John Moses, *Illinois, Historical and Statistical* . . . (2 v. 2d ed. rev. Chicago, 1895), II, 769; Solon J. Buck, *The Granger Movement (Harvard Historical Studies,* XIX. Cambridge, 1913), pp. 125, 126; Gordon, *op. cit.,* p. 225.

monopoly. And when merchants found that these high prices actually drove the products of Iowa and Minnesota down the Mississippi to St. Louis rather than to Chicago, it seemed time to put a stop to such practices.[104]

But the problem was complicated, and the way to its solution seemed full of pitfalls. In 1866, an investigation by the Board of Trade and the Mercantile Association showed that not only the railroads but also the steamboats on the upper Mississippi had effected combinations with each other. Thus it appeared that the farmers of the upper Mississippi had either to send their crops to Chicago and pay the high rates or else to let them rot, unless some way out of the difficulty were found. This way, it seemed, might lie in the constitutional convention called for December, 1869. Meetings of the Chicago group of the Patrons of Husbandry, as well as others interested, were but counterparts of similar assemblages held elsewhere in the state, which aroused sentiment to the point that the Constitution of 1870 provided for the regulation of what rebellious agriculturalists liked to call "wealthy, rich and purseproud" corporations.[105]

From the standpoint of the commercial interests of Chicago, a remedy for the distress of producers was the construction of a water route connecting the Illinois and Michigan Canal with the Mississippi River at Rock Island, which should, by offering competition, force the railroads to lower rates. For the survey of the route the Board of Trade appropriated $500 in 1866, but the outlet was not completed at this time.[106] The canal, however, had a salutary effect

[104] *Prairie Farmer*, n.s. XVII (January 20, 1866), 33; *ibid.*, n.s. XV (January 7, 1865), 3; *Chicago Tribune*, April 5, 1864; *Chicago* [Tri-Weekly] *Tribune*, December 15, 1865.

[105] Joint Committee of the Board of Trade and Mercantile Association, *Produce and Transportation: The Railway and Warehouse Monopolies* . . . (Chicago, 1866), p. 9. The Chicago Patrons of Husbandry was organized in April, 1868, by O. H. Kelley. (*Prairie Farmer*, n.s. XXI [May 2, 1868], 288. See the call of Henry C. Wheeler to farmers to unite in *ibid.*, n.s. XXV [April 30, 1870], 130. See also Jonathan Periam, *The Groundswell. A History of the Origin, Aims, and Progress of the Farmers' Movement* . . . [Cincinnati, 1874], pp. 225–28.) The Constitution in Article XI makes provisions, among other things, for the General Assembly to legislate regarding maximum rates of charges for passengers and freight, and to pass laws to correct abuses and unjust discrimination. (*Debates and Proceedings of the Constitutional Convention, 1869–70*, II, 1646, 1877–78.) The legislature following this passed such measures. See pp. 84–87.

[106] *Chicago Tribune*, January 9, 11, November 8, 1866; Joint Committee of the Board of Trade and Mercantile Association, *Produce and Transportation, passim;* Colbert, *op. cit.*, p. 56. The Senate Committee on Transportation Routes to the Seaboard recommended construction of this waterway, the Rock Island and Hennepin Canal, in 1874, but it was not completed until 1907. Putnam, *op. cit.*, p. 142; United States Senate, *Report of the Select*

on railroad rates during the season of navigation. In 1870, for example, corn could be shipped by canal from Henry in Marshall County, a distance of 130 miles to Chicago, for five cents a bushel, and wheat could be sent for six cents. Over the Rock Island the rate was about seven cents for corn and ten cents for wheat. After the close of navigation the railroad charged almost ten cents for corn and over twelve cents for wheat. On the railroads which did not have to compete with the canal, the price for corn was regularly from eleven to fourteen and one-half cents and from fifteen to eighteen cents for wheat for the same distance.[107]

The demand of Chicagoans for an improved water route was not surprising in a day when it was customary to think of water carriage as affording relief from hardships inflicted by the railroads. Then, too, transport by river and lake had been, for a long time, the way to market. Even during the 'fifties and 'sixties the lakes retained ascendancy in the forwarding of bulky commodities when speed was no object.

North of the city stretched the great natural water route, Lake Michigan, which lapped the shores of the giant forest lands of Wisconsin and Michigan. Commercial contacts with this section developed slowly until 1848 when the Illinois and Michigan Canal provided an outlet by which the products of the lumber mills, which lined the shores of Green Bay, might be distributed to the settlers of the prairies. The number of ships engaged in this trade almost immediately multiplied, and by 1855 the lumber fleet was proudly pointed to as "immense." Two years later ships so engaged alone were valued at one and one-half million dollars and carried over 444,000,000 feet of lumber to the city. The lake retained its ascendancy in the lumber traffic until the opening of competing timber lands diverted it to other routes.[108]

Trade between the Lake Superior region and Chicago over this route unfolded more slowly. Some provisions were carried to Lake

---

Committee on Transportation-Routes to the Seaboard . . . , 43 Cong., 1 sess., S. Rept. 307, II, pt. 1 (2 v. Washington, 1874), 229–33.

[107] Barrows, *op. cit.*, p. 108.

[108] The Daily Democratic Press, *Fourth Annual Review, 1855*, p. 16, *Sixth Annual Review, 1857*, p. 22. From facts in his own books a manufacturer estimated that for every million feet of lumber cut the lumber promoter expended $2,490 in supplies from the Chicago market for his workmen. *Weekly Chicago Democrat*, February 18, 1854. See also Appendix, pp. 492–98.

Superior in the early 'fifties, but the rapids in St. Mary's River proved a hindrance to the commercial development of the shores of the lake. Believing that the area of Chicago commercial enterprise would be expanded by the construction of a ship canal, the local press urged a Congressional appropriation for this improvement. When the Sault Ste. Marie Canal was opened in 1855 the belief was freely expressed that the copper and iron of the region would now flow to Chicago and aid in developing metal manufactures — a belief unwarranted until the late 'sixties.[109]

The lake trade of Chicago with the East, despite the competition of the railroads, increased greatly during these years. In the brief period of four years after 1851, the fleet making regular trips to and from Chicago more than doubled, and by 1870 Chicago stood third among the customs districts of the lakes. Only at Buffalo and Oswego were more vessels owned.[110] An expanding tonnage of arrivals at the port also took place, mounting almost three times from 1854 to 1871, and in only a score of years duties collected at the Customs House vaulted from a mere $5,615 to $724,565.[111] By 1857 seven lines of propellers ran east to Buffalo and beyond. The bane of combinations was less felt after eastern rail lines entered into competition with lake carriers, although the sums realized by them for transportation services were decidedly neat and far more than were received by the farmer who produced the grain.[112]

For this important commerce, maintenance of an open and deep harbor at Chicago was essential. Meetings of the Board of Trade to

[109] *The Daily Democratic Press*, March 20, 1854; *Chicago Daily Democrat*, March 22, 1852; *Cong. Globe*, 32 Cong., 1 sess., pt. 3, p. xi; The Daily Democratic Press, *Fourth Annual Review, 1855*, p. 5. See pp. 114–16.

[110] *Chicago Daily Democrat*, January 17, 1852. Before 1852 estimates rather than exact counts are generally cited in sources. In 1851, Chicagoans owned thirty-five of the eighty-four steam and sail craft engaged in making regular trips from Chicago. In 1856, there were 188 steam and sail vessels with a tonnage of over 56,670. (The Daily Democratic Press, *Fourth Annual Review, 1855*, p. 18.) In 1870, there were eighty-one steam vessels and 563 sail and unrigged vessels with a tonnage of 94,216.99. Chicago Board of Trade, *Fourteenth Annual Report, 1871*, p. 116.

[111] In 1854, the tonnage was 1,092,644; in 1863 it was 2,172,611; and in 1871 it was 3,096,101. The Daily Democratic Press, *Fifth Annual Review, 1856*, p. 28; Chicago Board of Trade, *Tenth Annual Statement, 1867–68*, p. 135, *Fourteenth Annual Report, 1871*, p. 109; Andreas, *History of Chicago*, I, 578–79.

[112] *Chicago Tribune*, October 21, 1861. This issue pointed out that vessel owners realized about nineteen cents per bushel for carriage from Chicago to Buffalo to the ten cents or less received by the farmer. A shortage of vessels was a frequent cause of complaint. *Ibid.*, August 27, 1861. For early steamboat combinations, see Pierce, *A History of Chicago*, I, 76–77, 84–88.

consider harbor improvement, the dispatch of delegates to care for local harbor interests at Washington, newspaper editorials and appeals, and appropriations for dredging were concrete evidences of a firm belief in the desirability of an unobstructed harbor. The appropriations of $1,000 made now and then by the city fathers and Board of Trade seemed but a pittance to clear away sandbars which all too often choked the entrance. Finally, in 1859 Congress under pressure appropriated $87,000 to repair the works and piers and to preserve the lighthouse erected by the federal government.[113]

Though the harbor was of immediate importance to Chicago commercial interests, the improvement of navigation facilities all along the lake route was also of vital concern. In 1853, the Board of Trade sent representatives to Detroit for a convention of delegates from all the lake cities to consider means to lessen the hazards of the St. Clair flats. Attention was next directed to the idea of a canal from Georgian Bay on Lake Huron through Lake Simcoe to Lake Ontario, a plan endorsed by the Board of Trade in the belief that it would aid also in direct trade with Europe and Asia, thus making Chicago merchants, in the language of a contemporary, real merchant "princes."[114] This project would have provided a direct route to the East by way of the St. Lawrence or Oswego Canal, thus cutting out Lake Erie, the Welland Canal, and a portion of the Erie Canal. Although such a plan was again suggested at the Ship-Canal Convention of 1863, it was not carried into effect.[115]

From an early day the Erie Canal had provided an important route for Chicago shippers, who often were troubled by its rate policies.

[113] *Daily Democrat*, March 10, 14, 17, 1849, April 29, 1850, March 21, 25, 1851; Colbert, *op. cit.*, p. 50; *Cong. Globe*, 35 Cong., 2 sess., "Index," p. 343; *Daily Democrat*, March 19, September 7, 1849; *The Daily Democratic Press*, March 9, 11, 1854, December 11, 1856. For lake disasters see *ibid.* Chicago was not so fortunate in her natural harbor as was Milwaukee. The boosters of the latter city were sure that this advantage, together with the fact that Milwaukee was closer to the eastern lake route, would insure her emergence as the economic capital of the Middle West. A. C. Wheeler, *A Chronicle of Milwaukee* . . . (Milwaukee, 1861), pp. 208–9, 274–75.

[114] Colbert, *op. cit.*, p. 50; *The Daily Democratic Press*, February 10, 1853, June 12, 1855. William Bross was the prime mover and was a member of the Board of Trade committee to raise funds and to co-operate with Canadian promoters. He attended a meeting held at Toronto which resulted in a survey of the route by Kivas Tully and Col. Roswell B. Mason of Chicago, as consulting engineer. The survey indicated the practicability of the route but pointed out its great cost. The panic of 1857 put a temporary damper on plans. *Ibid.*, September 18, 1855; Bross, *History of Chicago*, p. 70; *Chicago Tribune*, January 20, 1866; Mrs. Bross to "My dear Cousin," March 22, 1871 (*Ms.* Chicago Historical Society).

[115] Wright, *Chicago*, pp. 343–44; Colbert, *op. cit.*, p. 50.

Although its northern competitor, the Welland, was too shallow to permit the passage of large vessels, the latter carried the direct foreign trade of Chicago as well as a considerable domestic commerce.[116] To choke off the competition of the Welland, the Erie Canal interests introduced a bill in the New York legislature which would have established discriminatory rates against shippers who used the Welland rather than the Erie for shipments to the sea. Against this the Chicago Board of Trade offered strong protests. Among proposals to avoid such handicaps was the construction of a deep water canal around the American side of Niagara Falls even as the Welland cut around the Canadian side.[117]

In the early 'fifties the lakes and the Erie Canal furnished the principal route whereby the products of Chicago travelled to the seaboard. But by the close of the decade the lake had lost its lead in the shipment of provisions to the eastern rail routes. The provision trade was the first to go, followed closely by the flour trade. This relative decline in the carrying trade of the lakes does not indicate that the rail routes offered more advantageous freight rates to Chicago shippers, but rather that they furnished quicker and safer carriage for perishable products.[118] But there were times when the rivalry between rail and water carriers resulted in the reduction of rates. In 1851 the New York Central gained an advantage over the Erie Canal when it was released by the New York legislature from paying railway tolls to the canal. Although this was a blow to the canal interests, it worked to the advantage of the shipper who was charged lower rates by the railroad and consequently by the canal.[119] In return for their cargoes of grain and other agricultural products, lake transports brought to Chicago coal, iron, salt, and merchandise. They had provided practically the sole means whereby Chicago received

---

[116] *Chicago Tribune,* January 20, 1866, October 6, 1870; Chicago Board of Trade, *Thirteenth Annual Report, 1870,* p. 14. Grain shipments were carried by way of the Oswego and Erie canals to New York. Completion of the Northern (Ogdensburg) Railroad in the early 'fifties made possible shipments via the Welland, Lake Ontario, and St. Lawrence to Ogdensburg, whence they were sent by railroad to Lake Champlain, thence to New York or Boston. *Chicago Daily Democrat,* March 30, 31, April 17, 1852.

[117] Construction was advocated by the Board of Trade in 1853 and frequently thereafter, but it was never carried out. Colbert, *op. cit.,* p. 51; Wright, *Chicago,* p. 344; Taylor, *op. cit.,* I, 328; *Chicago Tribune,* January 9, December 13, 1866, March 27, 1868, October 1, 1870.

[118] Tunell, *loc. cit.,* p. 348. See Appendix, pp. 492, 494, 496, 498.

[119] Noble E. Whitford, *History of the Canal System of the State of New York* . . . (2 v. Albany, 1906), I, 194–95, 205, 207.

eastern goods in 1850, but by the mid-'sixties eastern merchandise was brought to Chicago largely by rail.

The lake was also an important avenue of foreign trade, particularly during the life of the 1854 treaty of reciprocity with Canada. Among other things, the treaty provided for the free exchange of the natural products of Canada and the United States, that is, products of the farm, the mine, the sea, and the forest, and gave American ships free access to the St. Lawrence River and the Canadian canals.[120] To residents of northern Illinois it seemed a dream come true, for within two years twenty-two times as many vessels from Canada reached Chicago as had come in 1854, and exports and imports showed an equally amazing upturn. Immediately branches of Canadian grain and lumber firms could be found in Chicago, and so enthusiastic did Chicagoans become over the glamorous present that it was proposed to make permanent such trade relations by annexing Canada to the United States.

The high water-mark of entrances and clearances in the port of Chicago came during 1862 and 1863 when 626 vessels entered and 696 cleared, most of which were engaged in trade with Canada.[121] Timber and lumber made up the bulk of imports. Fish, firewood, fruit, animals, unwrought stone and marble, nursery products, some grains and dairy products, tea, sugar, rice, and wines were also among the incoming cargoes. Although imports from Canada represented a good share of all the imports of Chicago, their value was considerably less than the exports of the city.[122] Thus the balance of trade

[120] Chalfant Robinson, *History of the Reciprocity Treaty of 1854 with Canada,* 62 Cong., 1 sess., S. Doc. XXVII, no. 17 (Washington, 1911), p. 10. The Board of Trade led the movement for free navigation of the Canadian waters. Douglas and Shields, senators from Illinois, promoted bills to this end in the United States Senate. Colbert, *op. cit.,* p. 49; *Cong. Globe,* 31 Cong., 2 sess., p. 203; *Chicago Daily Democrat,* March 31, July 10, 1851; United States House of Representatives, *Extracts from Congressional Debates on the Reciprocity Treaty of 1854 with Canada,* 61 Cong., 3 sess., H. Doc. CXXIV, no. 1350 (Washington, 1911), pp. 5, 7, 9, 10, 49; *The Daily Democratic Press,* March 16, 17, 1855.

[121] In 1854, there were five arrivals of Canadian vessels in Chicago. In 1856, 110 reached there. In 1854, exports in Canadian vessels were valued at $82,145 and in 1856 they amounted to $975,297. Canadian imports in 1854 were valued at $24,855 and in 1856 duty-free goods alone reached $2,060,546. Chicago Daily Democratic Press, *Sixth Annual Review, 1857,* p. 26; *The Daily Democratic Press,* October 18, 1855; *Report of the Secretary of the Treasury on the Commerce and Navigation of the United States for the Fiscal Year ending June 30, 1863* (Washington, 1865), pp. 287, 291 (hereafter cited as *Report on Commerce and Navigation*).

[122] For example, in the fiscal year 1868–69 imports from Canada amounted to $410,259, almost the total amount of foreign imports ($423,889). Exports from Chicago to Canada that year were $3,742,256. The next year out of a total of $735,894 worth of foreign imports Canada sent $717,862 and received from Chicago $2,611,678. *Ibid., 1869,* pp. 6, 36.

throughout was hers. This served undoubtedly to whet desires for a renewal of the treaty when the time of expiration drew near. Despite a strongly worded memorial to Congress and the efforts of many of the Illinois delegation, the resolution to terminate the treaty was passed in 1866. The opposition to continuance certainly was influenced by antagonism toward Canada because of expressions of sympathy with the Confederacy, but an even greater cause was the realization throughout the country that the balance of trade was in favor of Canada.[123]

Nor was the foreign trade of Chicago confined to Canada. By 1855 European representatives had established contacts with Chicago business houses in order to promote relations which would be mutually profitable.[124] At the same time plans to carry purchases directly to Chicago from Great Britain by means of sailing vessels and propellers received the endorsement of commercial interests, and in 1856 the schooner *Dean Richmond* sailed with a cargo of wheat to Liverpool with the blessings of the Board of Trade. Direct contact with Norway came in 1862 when the brig *Sleipner* dropped anchor in the Chicago harbor, with 110 passengers and 200 barrels of herring. When the *Sleipner* returned, her cargo was the grain from the fields of the great Northwest. In the spring of 1866 shipments to Liverpool were made with regularity, and by 1871 through bills of lading showed flour, grain, lard, provisions, and miscellaneous items finding a market across the Atlantic.[125]

Congressional action permitting Chicago as a port of entry to receive bonded goods marked the passing of the day of dependence on eastern cities, and on September 30, 1871, two cars reached Chicago over the Michigan Central with imported dry goods for Field, Leiter

[123] Chicago Board of Trade, *Third Annual Statement, 1860,* p. vii; Chicago Tribune, *Annual Review, 1860,* p. 5; Colbert, *op. cit.,* pp. 52–53. See arguments for and against renewal in *Extracts from Congressional Debates on the Reciprocity Treaty of 1854 with Canada,* pp. 49–145, *passim,* 184; *Chicago Tribune,* December 21, 1864; Emory R. Johnson and others, *History of Domestic and Foreign Commerce of the United States* (2 v. Washington, 1915), II, 340–41.

[124] The editor of the *Democratic Press* noted that an agent of the Dutch East India Company was also in Chicago hoping to open a direct trade through the St. Lawrence. *The Daily Democratic Press,* January 2, 12, 1855.

[125] Rates on freight direct from Europe to Chicago were seventy-five cents per hundred pounds, which was twenty-five cents less than the usual rate from New York to Chicago. (*Ibid.,* January 20, 27, May 12, 1855.) It took the *Dean Richmond* twenty-three days to reach Liverpool. *Ibid.,* July 19, October 3, 1856; *Chicago Tribune,* August 4, 1862; Chicago Board of Trade, *Eighth Annual Statement, 1865–66,* p. 95, *Fourteenth Annual Report, 1871,* p. 54.

and Company. Small wonder was it that a day of celebration was declared by Customs House officials, members of the firm, and others, and the seal for inspection broken to the tune of clinking glasses of champagne.[126]

Developments in communication supplemented those of transportation. The telegraph reached Chicago from Milwaukee on January 15, 1848, and a few days later a tariff had been worked out. In the same month a connection with Michigan City was opened, which, in the words of the *Journal,* brought Milwaukee and Michigan City so near that Chicagoans began "to feel a little crowded."[127] On April 6 the first through messages from the East arrived by wire and thus began the transformation of the commercial life in the pattern of the marts of the East.[128] Competing lines soon put Chicago in communication with other cities, and in 1849 the Illinois and Mississippi Telegraph Company was organized, shortly falling into the control of John D. Caton. Projection into outlying regions tied the agricultural communities even more closely to the growing city. Competition between various short lines gradually subsided as the several systems passed into the hands of the rapidly growing Western Union Telegraph Company.[129]

In 1861, the Pacific Telegraphic Company completed its lines to San Francisco. A date line for October 19 in the *Tribune* indicated communication as far west as Utah; and on the twenty-fifth the paper noticed the formal opening of the line to San Francisco. Shortly

[126] United States, *Statutes at Large,* XVI, 270–71; *Chicago Tribune,* October 1, 1870, October 3, 1871. In 1871, the Treasury Department ruled that duty-free foreign goods could be carried in bonded cars with goods on which duty would be collected in Chicago. (*Ibid.,* October 5, 1871.) The firm of Wright and Taylor, tea importers, received in October, 1870, what was described by the *Chicago Tribune* as the "first arrival of bonded goods direct to a resident firm." *Ibid.,* October 4, 1870.

[127] Ten words cost twenty-five cents, each extra word two cents, and two cents was charged for delivery from Chicago to Milwaukee. *Chicago Daily Journal,* January 17, 20, 29, 1848.

[128] Ezra Cornell and the Swift brothers got subscriptions for the telegraphic enterprises. F. O. Smith with their aid financed the Erie and Michigan Telegraph Company which built a line from Buffalo to Detroit and thence to Chicago and Milwaukee. The Milwaukee line was completed January 15, 1848. Alvin F. Harlow, *Old Wires and New Waves, The History of the Telegraph, Telephone, and Wireless* (New York, 1936), pp. 138–39.

[129] In 1852 Caton got control of the Illinois and Mississippi Telegraph Company. *The Daily Democratic Press,* March 25, 1854; James D. Reid, *The Telegraph in America, Its Founders, Promoters and Noted Men* (New York, 1879), pp. 152, 233, 235–40; John Gager, comp., *Case & Co.'s Chicago City Directory for the Year Ending June First, 1857* (Chicago, 1857), p. 84 (hereafter cited as *Case & Co.'s Directory*); Andreas, *History of Chicago,* II, 125.

thereafter Chicago was made the eastern terminus of the new transcontinental line and, in the words of the editor of the *Tribune,* thus became " the focus from which all news reports will be received from and sent to California and the Pacific Coast. News agents and reporters from every principal city in the Union will be located in this city." [130]

In 1864, the United States Telegraph Company made available to Chicago the facilities of its sixteen thousand miles of wire, but in two years the Western Union had purchased them, thus monopolizing business. Further acquisitions by this organization led to apprehension as to the future, and the *Tribune* agitated for government ownership of the network of telegraphic communication. Resolutions by the Board of Trade denouncing mismanagement and monopoly on the part of the Western Union, however, were followed by expressions of satisfaction when the Atlantic and Pacific Telegraph was completed to the seaboard in 1868.[131] The opening of the Atlantic Cable on August 26, 1866, gave Chicago quick access through the seaways, and happenings of the great grain markets of Europe caused vibrations along the shores of Lake Michigan.

A slower but cheaper avenue of information than the telegraph was the postal service. In 1848, the city, when the weather was good, was two and one-half days by post from New York, but with the coming of the railroad, time of mail carriage decreased as the speed of the trains increased. Chicago became the distribution point of mail particularly to the great central valley and the Far West, but even in 1854 a good share remained within the city.[132] In 1864, a city carrier system for distribution and collection was inaugurated, eliminating the necessity for calls at the post office or deliveries by special messengers.[133] By mid-'sixties, instead of a daily service, Detroit, Toledo, Milwaukee, St. Louis, Davenport, and Clinton, Iowa, had twelve mails a week to Chicago, and eastern cities were similarly connected.

---

[130] *Chicago Tribune,* October 19, 26, 31, 1861.

[131] *Ibid.,* May 10, 1865, June 9, 1867, November 11, 1868; Andreas, *History of Chicago,* II, 125; Reid, *op. cit.,* p. 521; Taylor, *op. cit.,* I, 365. In 1868, a monthly paper was started to advocate new telegraph lines and reduced rates. *Chicago Tribune,* April 1, 1868.

[132] *Chicago Daily Journal,* March 23, 24, 25, April 24, 1848; The Daily Democratic Press, *Annual Review, 1854,* p. 36.

[133] Halpin, *Directory, 1865–66,* " City and County Record," p. x; Edwards, *Directory, 1866,* p. 785; *Chicago Tribune,* April 8, 1865; *Chicago* [Tri-Weekly] *Tribune,* August 23, 1865.

By 1868 Council Bluffs, Iowa, had also been tied to Chicago.[134]

A little more than a score of years had thus seen Chicago emerge from a dependence on two water routes, the lake and the canal. Throughout the state more miles of railroad were constructed than could be found in any other commonwealth of the Union,[135] and railway systems of some ten thousand miles bound her to all the important commercial centers of the country. Indeed, by the late 'sixties no farm in Illinois was more than fifty miles from a railroad station and the average distance was seven. So far flung was the Chicago rail network that no less than sixteen points on the Mississippi had railroad communications with the city. Every fifteen minutes a passenger train whistled arrival or departure.[136] From 820 locomotives and 14,681 cars in 1864 the eight major carriers in 1870 had 1,473 locomotives and 32,130 cars, while gross earnings from passenger fares and freight receipts had skyrocketed from $39,521,101 to $64,758,434.[137]

All this had come about though Chicago as a city had made no railroad investments, and Chicagoans as a whole had not unduly loosed their purse strings to finance railway construction. There had even been some who opposed this form of carriage because of a fear of the new or because of a desire to protect their investments in water carriers. But it appeared unnecessary for Chicago to pour her resources into what others seemed anxious to finance. It was men of fortune and daring from the East such as William H. Osborn and Erastus Corning who staked their money on the future of western lines running into Chicago, and by holdings in more than one rail-

[134] United States, " Report of the Postmaster General," *Message of the President of the United States* . . . 38 Cong., 2 sess., H. Ex. Doc. 1 (6 v. Washington, 1864), V, 813–14; United States, " Report of the Postmaster General," *Message of the President of the United States* . . . 40 Cong., 3 sess., H. Ex. Doc. 1 (4 v. Washington, 1868), IV, 55.

[135] Illinois Railroad and Warehouse Commission, " First Report," Illinois, *Reports, 1871*, II, 435.

[136] Arithmetically the rail system extending from Chicago increased a thousandfold in this period. In 1848, ten miles of rail extended from the city, in 1852 about forty miles, in 1855 tributary lines amounted to about three thousand miles (The Daily Democratic Press, *Fourth Annual Review, 1855*, p. 77); in 1857 about four thousand miles (Chicago Daily Democratic Press, *Sixth Annual Review, 1857*, p. 46); in 1867 about seven thousand miles (Colbert, *op. cit.*, p. 71); in 1871 over ten thousand (Andreas, *History of Chicago*, II, 157). James Parton, " Chicago," *The Atlantic Monthly*, XIX (March, 1867), 330.

[137] These figures are for the Michigan Central, the Burlington, the Rock Island, the Illinois Central, the Pittsburgh, Fort Wayne and Chicago, the Michigan Southern, the North Western, and the Chicago and Alton. *Poor's Manual, 1868–69; Poor's Manual, 1871–72, passim.*

road were able to exert an immeasurable influence on the economic development of the Middle Valley. Their confidence generated similar confidence in men across the Atlantic. When the Civil War came, these capitalists feared the outcome of a Southern victory and worked with well directed zeal to insure the success of the Union.[138] To the larger holdings of investors from the East were added the purchases of railroad stock by people living along the route, who hoped that their own little center would be a great metropolis. But it was Chicago, with her superb geographical position at the foot of Lake Michigan, which reaped the harvest of the rails.

This vast network of iron was the greatest single factor in the phenomenal commercial development of Chicago during these years. By 1854 the Mississippi was reached; by 1859 the railroad system of the country extended to the Missouri; and ten years later the Pacific Coast was united to the growing metropolis of the West. Months were added to each year of the commercial life of Chicago as the railway poured bountiful stores of domestic products into her lap. Now the depressions of closed navigation were routed, isolation, the handmaid of winter and ice, vanquished, and the money markets no longer choked by the frigid fingers of "Old Man Winter." The rails which brought Chicago the harvests of an increasing area brought her also the commercial hegemony which her hopeful promoters had frequently foretold.[139]

[138] Those named below were among the railroad leaders. William H. Osborn was president of the Illinois Central during the Civil War years and was also a director of the Chicago, St. Louis and New Orleans Railroad. Henry Farnam was a construction engineer who aided in the construction of the Michigan Southern, the Rock Island, and the Mississippi and Missouri Railroad and who served as president of the Rock Island. Erastus Corning, long president of the New York Central, was interested also in the Michigan Central and the Burlington. The New York speculator, Robert Schuyler, added an interest in the Illinois Central to his holdings in eastern lines such as the New York and New Haven and the Harlem roads. H. H. Hunnewell was a director in the Illinois Central and Michigan Central roads. James F. Joy of Detroit had substantial interests in the organization of the Michigan Central, Illinois Central, and Burlington roads. See pp. 56–57. See also Appendix pp. 483–91.

[139] Farm as well as city dweller felt the effects of these changes. In the homely words of the farmers:

Our horses now freed from the road-dragging toil,
We will keep on the fallows, and till well the soil,
And when we have leisure the city to greet,
With our ladies we'll then in the cars take a seat.
Now free from the dread of the mud and the slough,
Feeling sure that the rail-car will carry us through;
Then welcome the steam horse with sinews so strong,
Ourselves and our produce can now move along.

Prairie Farmer, X (March, 1850), 101.

CHAPTER III

THE COMING OF A
METROPOLITAN ECONOMY

THE EXTENSION of the transportation network made Chicago the commercial center of the great Middle Valley. Dealers and commission men who sent eastward abundant stores of produce gathered from neighboring plains and fields amassed large fortunes and became the potentates of a far-flung back country. Speculators won and lost on the exchanges. Wholesalers who sent finished commodities out to the farms became prosperous. By 1851, the volume of grain coursing through Chicago had so swollen that the city came to be the greatest primary corn market of the country; three years later it was the greatest primary wheat center; in 1856, it attained preeminence as the foremost lumber mart of the United States; and during the Civil War it emerged as the greatest packing point. By 1871, the city had surpassed St. Louis in the wholesale trade and had become the chief commercial emporium to which the farmers of the West turned to satisfy their needs.

The mainspring of this commercial greatness lay in the grain trade. While on the one hand this yielded indirect benefits such as the stimulus to the lumber and the forwarding trades, on the other it made possible direct profits to speculators and the interests engaged in warehousing, processing grain, and financing its movements.

The center of grain speculation was the Board of Trade, the "Altar of Ceres" in the words of a contemporary.[1] Organized in 1848, it carried on a feeble struggle for eight years. Then, in 1856, its mem-

[1] *Chicago Tribune,* August 11, 1865.

bers set up grades and standards, lending thereby greater surety to the quality of grains. Speculators deserted the streets, where formerly they had inspected the farmers' offerings, for the Board of Trade rooms. They now made their trade with warehouse receipts specifying the amounts and grades of the grain which changed hands. In the same year the Board rented more commodious quarters and promoted plans for a building of its own. Two years later the services of its trading rooms were offered to Lee and Armstrong to sell stocks; market information was regularly received by telegraph from New York; and the organization was dignified enough to publish its own reports.[2] No idealistic aims gave direction to this evolutionary process. The association was of, by, and for the money-makers. Held together by the lure of speculation despite political differences and bitter factional struggles for economic advantage, the members — grain dealers, warehousemen, lumber dealers, and businessmen who were attracted by the hope of profiting through speculation — dominated the commercial life of the city.

In the middle 'fifties the high pitch of grain speculation came during the Crimean War, when Chicago traders gambled, bought, and sold as the telegraph flashed news of the wavering fortunes of sultan and tsar. During the panic of 1857 speculation fell off, but when Napoleon III declared war on Austria in 1859 another flurry agitated buyers and sellers. With peace, speculation subsided; traders led a less hectic life until the conflict between the North and the South, 1861–1865, plunged them into an orgy of hazardous undertakings.[3]

For the duration of the Civil War Chicago speculators — the assortment of bulls, bears, and lambs which had appeared before 1860 — struggled together, engaging in "spot trading," trading in "privileges," and many different types of future trading, including buyers' and sellers' options.[4] During hours of business traders crowded the

[2] The Board of Trade reorganized in 1850 under a general law for the establishment of boards of trade. Chicago Board of Trade, *First Annual Statement, 1858,* p. 5; *Chicago Daily Journal,* April 21, 1848; Colbert, *Chicago,* p. 51.

[3] A general résumé which shows the fluctuation of Chicago wheat prices, and, to a limited extent, its causes, can be found in James Boyle, *Chicago Wheat Prices for Eighty-One Years* . . . (n.p., 1922).

[4] Henry C. Emery, *Speculation on the Stock and Produce Exchanges of the United States* (Columbia University, *Studies in History, Economics and Public Law,* VII, no. 2. New York, 1896), pp. 39–50.

Board rooms, and, after the gong struck, transactions sometimes were continued on the sidewalk, in the saloon of the Tremont House, and in the rooms of the Sherman House. In 1865, the Stock Exchange facilities were adopted for this purpose, and in the same year the Masonic Temple was utilized for nighttime transactions.[5]

The membership of the Board increased during the war from 665 to 1,462. It cost only five dollars to become a member, and one could trade with an empty pocket, for margins were not required.[6] Some who entered the organization at this time became outstanding figures in the commercial life of the city, others turned away broken and disheartened. In a long, narrow room, " unbroken by pillar or column," on the second floor of a South Water Street building, the traders clustered. There was no pit; there were no signals. When quotations were called, a babel burst from the group as members made verbal contracts with each other. Pushing and jostling, as excitement relaxed they sometimes threw samples of wheat, corn, and flour into the air to cascade over the heads of jubilant members.[7] This wild fever, some hoped, would abate when the war closed. In 1865 and subsequent years, regulations were drawn up to limit speculation to responsible parties and to place the methods on a more reputable foundation. Membership qualifications were raised by the requirement of higher dues, margins were established, and some of the more questionable practices were discountenanced.[8]

Rules and regulations marked a forward step in curbing speculation, but they were not enough to cope with the schemes which professional speculators had developed during the war period. Cornering the market, for example, became common. In 1868, at least seven corners in grain were put through. After one had squeezed a number of prominent members, including E. V. Robbins, the president of the Board, the organization resolved that corners were " essentially improper and fraudulent," and that those who engaged in them were

[5] Taylor, *History of the Board of Trade*, I, 311–12, 325.

[6] In 1861, the Board excluded non-residents of Chicago from membership. Outsiders desired to become members to avoid payment of brokers' commissions. Colbert, *op. cit.,* p. 54; Chicago Board of Trade, *Third Annual Statement, 1860*, p. 104, *Eighth Annual Statement, 1865–66*, p. 9.

[7] *The Press and Tribune*, July 20, 1859; Taylor, *op. cit.*, I, 333, 414.

[8] Chicago Board of Trade, *Seventh Annual Statement, 1865*, p. vii; United States Federal Trade Commission, *Report . . . on the Grain Trade* (5 v. Washington, 1920), II, 72; Taylor, *op. cit.*, I, 325, 331–32, 368–69.

liable to be expelled. But, despite attempts by the Board to do away with them, corners and various other forms of price manipulation continued unchecked not only on a local but, perhaps, on an international scale, for following the completion of the Atlantic Cable, Chicago operators were accused of working hand in glove with the brokers of Liverpool in raising and depressing prices.[9] The effects of these combinations on the commercial life of the city were so important that, when a combination raised the price of wheat in August, 1871, the press asserted that the day of the peak was almost comparable to the panic of Black Friday.[10]

As price manipulations increased in number and consequence, an aroused public feeling made known its opposition to such conduct. Particularly outspoken were the farmers, upon whom Chicago depended so much, who held grain speculators " leeches upon commerce and the community " that sucked " the life blood of the farmers and dealers in grain without contributing anything towards the general wealth or productions of the country." Most bitterly accused were warehousemen, who not only speculated but also laid heavy tariffs on all grains entering the city.[11] At times the public mind looked upon their operations as buccaneering and piracy on a grand scale. As the power and fortunes of the warehousemen came to light, farmer and businessman found it difficult to separate the scrupulous from unscrupulous. Monopoly in the handling of grain, exorbitant storage rates, deception as to quality, and the playing with marked cards even among themselves were frequent enough to place owners of the drab-gray structures near the canal and railways among the suspected, despite the fact that all may not have belonged there.

Until 1854 the warehouses of the city were small, and the warehousemen useful but not powerful figures.[12] In that year, however,

9 *Ibid.*, I, 333, 342, 343, 357, 370–73, 384.

10 *Chicago Tribune*, August 3, 1871. On August 2, short sellers were called on to deposit fully $2,000,000 of margins with the treasurer of the Board.

11 *Debates and Proceedings of the Constitutional Convention, 1869–70*, II, 1623; *Chicago Tribune*, December 26, 1865; *Prairie Farmer*, n.s. XIV (July 2, 1864), 8.

12 R. C. Bristol's elevator, the first in the city equipped with steam power, was opened in September, 1848. (*Weekly Chicago Democrat*, September 19, 1848.) It had a capacity of ninety thousand bushels, but, like the other elevators of the city until 1855, it was primarily a convenience for the transfer of grain. The following shows the growth of grain warehousing in Chicago: total warehouse capacity of Chicago area: 1848, 600,000 bu.; 1854, 750,000 bu.; 1855, 1,550,000 bu.; 1856, 3,500,000 bu.; 1857, 4,095,000 bu.; 1858, 4,095,000

the improved supply system, bumper crops, and heavy demands from Europe resulted in more than twice as much grain pouring into the city as before. During the navigation season, warehouses and mills were filled to overflowing, and though vessels and railway cars were utilized for storage space, the streets were littered with bursting bags and uncovered piles of grain. The press cried for "room," and enterprise supplied the need. In 1855 two mammoth structures — the warehouses of Gibbs, Griffin and Company and Munger and Armour, with a capacity of five hundred thousand and three hundred thousand bushels respectively — rose on the Chicago landscape. By the close of 1856 Sturges, Buckingham and Company, T. W. Alexander and Company, and the Galena elevators added to warehouses already completed a two million bushel capacity.[13]

Following the close of the Civil War, charges of undue profiteering were heard more frequently than before. In the 'fifties there had been considerable competition among the warehousemen. But during and immediately after the war consolidation took place. In 1860 there were thirteen firms; in 1868 there were nine, five of which exercised a major control.[14] Their grip on the business seemed to rest on agreements with the railways, near which they were located, to deliver to their bins all grain carried, regardless of consignments. So tight was this monopoly that they raised rates for grain storage almost at will. Resentment against their exorbitant charges came from both the grain merchants of the city and the farmers of the country round about; during the 'sixties complaints became increas-

---

bu.; 1861, 5,915,000 bu.; 1862, 6,815,000 bu.; 1863, 10,010,000 bu.; 1865, 10,055,000 bu.; 1868, 10,680,000 bu.; 1871, 11,375,000 bu. Taylor, *op. cit.*, I, 199, 201, 203, 218; Andreas, *History of Chicago*, I, 581, II, 376; Chicago Board of Trade, *First Annual Statement, 1858*, p. 7, *Tenth Annual Statement, 1867–68*, p. 33.

[13] Gibbs, Griffin and Company, and Munger and Armour were near the Galena; Sturges, Buckingham and Company near the Illinois Central; and T. W. Alexander and Company near the Rock Island. *The Daily Democratic Press*, April 5, September 2, 23, 1854; Taylor, *op. cit.*, I, 201–2, 218, 222; Gager, *Case & Co.'s Directory, 1857*, "Advertisements," p. 5, "Business Directory," p. 83. For a discussion of the grain elevators see Guy A. Lee, "The Historical Significance of the Chicago Grain Elevator System," *Agricultural History*, XI (January, 1937), 16–32.

[14] In 1868 the five firms exercising major control were Munn and Scott receiving grain from the Chicago and Alton, the Chicago and North Western, and the canal; Armour, Dole and Company from the Chicago, Burlington and Quincy; Flint, Thompson and Company from the Rock Island; Munger, Wheeler and Company from the Galena division of the North Western; J. and E. Buckingham and Company from the Illinois Central and the canal. Chicago Board of Trade, *Eleventh Annual Statement, 1868–69*, p. 25, *Third Annual Statement, 1860*, p. 9.

ingly common, and early the *Tribune* was led to declare that there seemed "no limit to the bounds of cupidity." [15]

In an attempt to stop the destruction of competition, the legislature in 1865 ordered railroads, in so far as possible, to deliver grain to the consignee. Two years later railroads were required to transfer grain at intersection points and run cars of connecting roads over their tracks at reasonable rates, and warehousemen were instructed to accept grain consigned to them, and prohibited from discriminating in charges against grain received by different railroads.[16] From 1865 the charters granted warehouse corporations were drawn so as to lessen the opportunities for making exclusive contracts with the railroads. Despite these regulatory measures, discriminations continued until after the passage of the Warehouse Act of 1871.[17]

Besides fattening on high storage rates, elevator owners were alleged habitually to defraud customers and to increase their own incomes by an elaborate technique of mixing. When the volume of trade had been small, grain had been usually purchased directly from farmers, and each consignment had been given separate treatment, binning, and sale. But as volume increased it became necessary to grade the many lots and store similar grades in the same bin. Inasmuch as the standards of the various warehouses did not correspond, confusion resulted. Consequently, in 1856 the Board of Trade set up standards for wheat.[18] But maintenance of standards was a more difficult matter than their formulation, for warehousemen could not be depended on to enforce the Board's regulations. Therefore, the Board prescribed an inspection system. Inasmuch as inspectors checked grain only at the railroads and canal and not in the warehouses, unscrupulous warehousemen continued mixing high and

---

[15] *Chicago Tribune*, October 22, 1861, October 3, 1863; *Prairie Farmer*, n.s. XIII (April 2, May 7, 1864), 225, 321, XVI (November 18, 1865), 365; Taylor, *op. cit.*, I, 460; *Debates and Proceedings of the Constitutional Convention, 1869–70*, II, 1622–23.

[16] Act of February 14, 1865, *Public Laws, 1865*, p. 75; Act of February 16, 1867, *Public Laws, 1867*, pp. 177–82; Benjamin F. Goldstein, *Marketing: A Farmers' Problem* (New York, 1928), p. 22.

[17] Acts of February 15, 16, 1865, *Private Laws, 1865*, II, 674, 685. For instance, in 1868 the Chicago and Alton discriminated against the National Elevator in favor of the Union, with which it was identified, and two years later the North Western refused to deliver grain to the Iowa Elevator on the ground that by so doing it would violate its agreement to deliver all grain to the Wheeler Elevator. Taylor, *op. cit.*, I, 364, 400–2. See p. 87.

[18] Colbert, *op. cit.*, p. 51; Andreas, *History of Chicago*, II, 376–77; Taylor, *op. cit.*, I, 146–47.

low grades, shipping the composite product to fill orders for high quality grain in the eastern markets. The result was a loss of confidence in the character of the Chicago product, which injured all concerned.[19]

In grain speculation the warehousemen had advantages possessed by no other group. Grain contracts in the 'forties were settled by the actual delivery of grain. After grades had been established, however, buyers no longer required actual delivery and were satisfied with the endorsement of a warehouse receipt for a specified amount and grade of grain stored in one of the Chicago warehouses. These receipts, which were issued by the warehousemen, supposedly were as good at the current market rates as gold, and they circulated freely from hand to hand.

To aid their speculations, however, warehousemen sometimes issued fraudulent receipts. At other times they spread reports that the grain in their elevators was heating (spoiling). No one was certain as to the accuracy of these reports, but nervous holders threw their receipts on the market, and, as prices fell, the elevator interests bought up their own receipts at desirable figures.[20]

Obviously, outsiders labored under serious disadvantages. To better conditions, the grain interests, in the years following the war, tried to extend the Board of Trade inspection system to the interiors of the warehouses, to compel warehousemen to post information regarding the kinds and condition of grain in their elevators, and to establish under the supervision of the Board a bureau which would register and cancel all warehouse receipts. The warehousemen, their commission agents, and allied speculators vigorously fought these attempts at regulation.

---

[19] Andreas, *History of Chicago,* II, 376–77; *Chicago Daily Democratic Press,* June 23, 1857; Taylor, *op. cit.,* I, 227–28; *Chicago Tribune,* November 7, 1870. An example of the results of mixing is found in 1858, when the quality of Chicago wheat in eastern markets was so dubious that it sold from five to eight cents below a similar grade from Milwaukee. Taylor, *op. cit.,* I, 241–43.

[20] *Ibid.,* I, 328, 333, 342, 382. In 1869, according to the *Chicago Tribune,* July 28, 1870, corn advanced forty cents a bushel, and the outstanding receipts were worth several millions of dollars. Immediately " hot corn " was announced, and the elevators refused to permit their stock to be examined or to state the amount of receipts outstanding. It was generally believed that the issue of bogus receipts was very large and the profits of the fraud were enormous. In 1851, an attempt at regulation had been made by the legislature. It declared that warehousemen might issue receipts only for grain in store, and it prohibited the transfer of lots without consent of owner. Act of January 28, 1851, *Public Laws, 1851,* p. 9.

In 1865, the Board of Trade gained some control over the situation when the warehousemen consented to permit inspectors within their establishments, but complaints of false reports of heating after this date show how futile was this extension of the system. The inspectors apparently were suborned by the elevator men, and, in 1870, the Board abandoned these efforts.[21] Some owners began in 1867 to publicize weekly the quantity and kind of grain in their establishments, but the statute requiring such publicity was generally disregarded, and such figures as were recorded were not dependable. Three years later they agreed to comply with the law and post accurate statistics, but once again they balked the aims of the grain interests by giving the aggregate quantity in several elevators without specifying the kinds, thus defeating any attempt to check their figures. An attempt to ascertain the number of warehouse receipts outstanding in Chicago was made in 1870, when the grain interests proposed that the warehousemen register all their receipts at an agency to be established by the Board.[22] The warehousemen, however, refused to cooperate, asserting that to do so would be equivalent to acknowledging that they were rascals. This explanation, " the answer which a rascal would naturally make when driven into a corner," they published in the *Tribune*.[23]

The obduracy of the warehousemen in withstanding attempts at control paved the way to a downfall. The business interests of Chicago had failed to regulate their actions by Board of Trade rules.[24] They had also been unable to get airtight legislation through the Assembly at Springfield. There was another group, however, from whom they might expect sympathy — the farmers, who, too, had grievances. An alliance with them, it was held, might bring about the passage by the Constitutional Convention meeting in December, 1869, of a measure with teeth in it.

---

[21] Taylor, *op. cit.,* I, 341, 369, 403, 405–10; Chicago Board of Trade, *Ninth Annual Statement, 1866–67*, p. 10.

[22] Act of February 16, 1867, *Public Laws, 1867*, p. 178; Taylor, *op. cit.,* I, 397–402.

[23] *Chicago Tribune*, January 30, 1870.

[24] That the elevator proprietors, who numbered only about twelve among the members of the Board of Trade, were able to defy regulation by the organization appears remarkable. An explanation is suggested by the *Chicago Tribune*. In 1870, the editor of the financial page remarked that the warehousemen wished the inspection system left in the hands of the Board, " being well enough satisfied that they can always hire a sufficient number of the scalpers to enable them to carry a vote on any measure they may wish, from the appointment of an important officer down to the meanest regulation adopted." *Ibid.,* November 18, 1870.

The making of such an alliance, however, was attended by difficulties. The businessmen of Chicago, particularly the grain interests, were identified by many farmers with speculation, and speculation in agricultural commodities was the bane of the farmer's existence. Apparently to allay rural suspicions, the grain interests and businessmen devised a roundabout method of bringing pressure on the delegates. A measure giving the Board of Trade sweeping powers to institute an inspection system, to open the books of warehousemen, and at any time to examine under oath the warehousemen or their employees as to both their records and the quantity and condition of their grain was submitted to the Committee on Miscellaneous Corporations; and William Cary, delegate from Jo Daviess County, was persuaded to act as sponsor. J. M. Richards, president of the Board, presented a petition from the businessmen of Chicago for action against the abuses of the warehousemen and the railroads, but, except for this single expression, the grain interests did not bother to send petitions from Chicago. Instead, they let their customers throughout the state set forth their views in the barrage of protests directed to delegates at the convention.[25]

In spite of these maneuvers, however, not all were convinced of the validity and honesty of the proposals made. Some agreed with Thomas Turner of Stephenson that the measure was " the most dangerous element " in the convention — the article of the grain gamblers. To him it was a device to give the grain interests of Chicago knowledge of the amount of grain in the warehouses and thus aid them in their speculations. Others felt the matter one for the consideration of the General Assembly, on the ground that warehouse control required police regulation and should not be thought of as a fundamental or elemental law to be taken up by a constitutional convention.[26] In speaking for the article, delegate Joseph Medill, editor of the *Chicago Tribune,* eloquently pleaded the cause of the farmer and urged the curbing of " the grand ring," the combination

[25] *Ibid.,* May 7, 1870; *Debates and Proceedings of the Constitutional Convention, 1869–70,* II, 1622–25, 1695–96. After charges that members of the Board prepared the bill had been made on the floor of the convention a member of the Committee on Miscellaneous Corporations, James McCoy of Whiteside, conceded, " It is true, to a certain extent, that this report came from the city of Chicago; that it came from there in form and in substance, and had its manliness and all its garments laid on there; and I am willing to concede further that I am willing to receive anything good, that may come out of evil." *Ibid.,* p. 1631.

[26] *Ibid.,* pp. 1623–25, 1635.

of warehousemen and railways that was squeezing "the sweat and blood out of the producers of Illinois." "There is no provision in the fundamental law standing between the unrestricted avarice of monopoly and the common rights of the people," said he, "but the great, laborious, patient ox, the farmer, is bitten and bled, harassed and tortured, by these rapacious, blood sucking insects. It is the bounden duty of this Convention to step between these voracious monopolies and the producers, and give them protection, in some degree, at least." The moral effect of this article, he concluded, would be " great, good and happy." [27] Medill's colleague from Cook, Samuel S. Hayes, joined in the argument for the proposed measure and attempted to show that the interests of farmers were identical with those of the grain interests to whom the farmers looked for their market [28] — a relationship which the urban traders emphasized whenever possible.

The weight of objection was not sufficient to prevent the inclusion in the constitution of an article for the regulation of warehouses. Control was lodged in the state instead of in the Board of Trade. All warehouses that stored grain for compensation were designated as public warehouses. Their managers were prohibited from mixing grain without the consent of the owner, who was given the right to inspect the grain when he so chose, and they were enjoined against the issuance of fraudulent warehouse receipts. They were also required to post weekly reports of the kind, grade, and quantity of grain in store. This provision was applied only to Chicago, for the delegates believed that compelling warehousemen throughout the state to do so would result only in advantage to Chicago speculators. Combinations between warehousemen and railroads were guarded against by requiring the latter to permit all warehouses to connect with their tracks and to deliver all shipments to the consignee if so connected. To abate the abuse of short weights, the railway companies were required to weigh and give receipt for grain at the point of shipment.

[27] *Ibid.*, p. 1629. Medill's paper, the *Chicago Tribune*, was plain-spoken in explaining its support of the Warehouse Article. An editorial pointed out that it "was a question, as Bastiat says, ' between robbery, half-robbery and quarter-robbery.' When this venerable abuse became a matter of public controversy, a short time since, we adopted the opinions of those members of the Board of Trade in whom we had been accustomed to place most confidence. They were going in for quarter-robbery, and so we went in for quarter-robbery." *Chicago Tribune*, May 7, 1870.

[28] *Debates and Proceedings of the Constitutional Convention, 1869–70*, II, 1630.

And finally, the General Assembly was empowered to pass laws to make these provisions effective and to protect the producers, shippers, and receivers of grain and produce.[29]

Although there was a minority who continued in the belief that the article was a "humbug," and who doubted the advisability of incorporating the regulation of warehouses in the Constitution, the revised article, designated Article XIII, was passed by the delegates and approved by the people in July, 1870. In April of the following year, the legislature in three acts gave effect to the article. They provided that the warehousemen should be supervised by a board of three railroad and warehouse commissioners to be appointed by the governor, prescribed maximum rates for storage, required all public warehousemen to obtain a state license and a bond on which they might be sued for violation of state regulations, forbade discrimination among warehousemen and railroads in the handling of grain, and provided that in order to guard against short shipments the latter must weigh and receipt for grain at the point of delivery.[30]

The three members of the Warehouse Commission were appointed in July, and in the same month the chief grain inspector of the state opened his Chicago office. The commissioners adopted, with but slight changes, the system of inspection and registration of warehouse receipts which the Board had attempted to put into effect. The warehousemen, however, refused to observe the maximum storage rate requirement and also neglected to take out licenses.[31] To force compliance with the law the commission instructed the state's attorney in September to bring action against Ira Y. Munn and George L. Scott, leading warehousemen of Chicago. Because of the fire in October, 1871, a decision was not rendered until the next year when the defendants were found guilty of a violation of the warehouse act. An appeal was then taken, but not until 1876 was the famous Munn *v.* Illinois decision finally handed down by the United States Supreme Court.[32]

The glamour and excitement of speculation and the publicity given

[29] *Ibid.*, pp. 1697, 1878. The article applied to warehouses in any city or town of not less than one hundred thousand inhabitants.

[30] *Ibid.*, p. 1628; Acts of April 13, 25, 1871, *Public Laws, 1871–72*, pp. 618–19, 636–39, 762–73.

[31] Illinois Railroad and Warehouse Commission, "First Annual Report," Illinois, *Reports, 1871*, II, 15–17, 70.

[32] 94 U. S. 113 (1876); Goldstein, *op. cit.*, pp. 48–56.

to warehousing obscure the fact that a portion of the grain which streamed to the city was being converted into flour, distilled beverages, and malt liquors. The manufacture of flour had been the most important feature in the industrial development of the 'forties. Though the output grew gradually until 1868, Chicago during these years was led by St. Louis in milling, perhaps because Chicagoans found it more profitable to sell the crude grains in the East than to expend time and money in processing. The flour interests in 1867 founded the "Millers' Association of the City of Chicago," an organization which established grades for flour and agitated against the exactions of the warehouse interests. But the milling industry began to decline after 1868, and by 1870 Milwaukee forged ahead of Chicago to join St. Louis as a leading flour-milling center of the West.[33]

More important than the trade in home-manufactured flour was the flour-forwarding trade. The receipts of flour from country mills exceeded the quantity manufactured in the city in 1854, and by the middle of the 'sixties even St. Louis was sending a portion of her flour through the Chicago market. Some of this flour may have been used to increase the home supply, but most of it was forwarded by rail, principally to the East and Canada. Little flour was shipped to the South except in 1860 and at the close of the war, when a dearth of foodstuffs existed in that section.[34]

Little grain appears to have been converted into distilled beverages during the 'forties. By 1854, however, eight distillers and rectifiers were utilizing a portion of the corn, barley, and rye supply.[35] Be-

[33] *Chicago Daily Democrat*, March 11, 1851; *Chicago Tribune*, January 8, 1867; Taylor, *op. cit.*, I, 382; *The Chicago Times*, November 7, 1870; Chicago Board of Trade, *Fourteenth Annual Report, 1871*, pp. 9–10. St. Louis, 1852, 383,184 barrels; 1861, 694,110 barrels; 1871, 1,507,915 barrels; Chicago, 1852, 70,979 barrels; 1861, 291,852 barrels; 1871, 327,-739 barrels. (St. Louis Merchants' Exchange, *Report, 1889*, p. 118; Chicago Board of Trade, *Fourteenth Annual Report, 1871*, p. 36.) Milwaukee, 1870, 530,049 barrels; Chicago, 1870, 443,967 barrels. Milwaukee Chamber of Commerce, *Report, 1870*, p. 20; Chicago Board of Trade, *Fourteenth Annual Report, 1871*, p. 36.

[34] Chicago Tribune, *Annual Review, 1864*, p. 9; Chicago Board of Trade, *Eighth Annual Statement, 1865–66*, p. 32. In 1870, total manufactured in city, 443,967 barrels, home consumption and unaccounted for, 404,036 barrels; 1871, total manufactured in city, 327,739 barrels, home consumption, destroyed by fire, and unaccounted for, 492,477 barrels; 1872, total manufactured in city, 186,968 barrels, home consumption and unaccounted for, 364,772 barrels. Chicago Board of Trade, *Thirteenth Annual Report, 1870*, p. 53, *Fourteenth Annual Report, 1871*, pp. 36, 51, *Fifteenth Annual Report, 1872*, p. 49.

[35] Hall & Co., *Chicago City Directory and Business Advertiser for 1854–55* . . . (Chicago, 1854), Appendix, p. 11 (hereafter cited as Hall & Co., *Directory, 1854–55*). In 1860, there were seven distilleries. (United States, *Eighth Census, 1860*, " Manufactures," p. 86.) In

tween 1860 and 1870, the value of liquors annually produced increased nearly 500 per cent, rising from $477,480 to $2,751,221. In quantity, the manufacture mounted from 1,653,000 gallons in 1856 to 7,082,364 by 1870. Though a good share of these liquors was consumed in the city, some of the home manufactures were shipped to other markets, and agents sold the Chicago products in the principal cities of the Middle West.[36] There was also a considerable trade in forwarding the products of the country distilleries. Thus, 62,126 barrels were received, principally from the western and southwestern hinterland in 1860, and some 65,223 barrels were forwarded, chiefly to the East. From 1862 to 1864 high wines were objects of great speculative activity among the businessmen of Chicago, who gambled on whether the government would levy an excise tax on the whiskey then on hand or only on that to be distilled after the act. The speculators shared in the profits, which ranked high in the gains on commercial transactions up to that time.[37]

The brewing industry of the city developed rapidly as the German population of the city increased. The eight brewers of 1854 found their market invaded by fifteen more by 1870. During the 'sixties, the value of the annual output increased more than 300 per cent, amounting to $2,523,945 in 1870. In spite of this considerable gain, Chicago ranked below St. Louis and Cincinnati as a brewing center. The wartime excise on distilled liquors caused a change in consumption habits, the poorer classes turning from high-priced whiskey to comparatively low-priced beer as a palatable drink. Eager to retain the patronage which resulted from this price derangement, the beer manufacturers united in the Brewers' Association of Chicago. This group, in 1867, entertained the convention of the National Beer Brewers' Association, which had for one of its purposes resistance to " the encroachments upon the social and political freedom of individuals by the Total Abstinence party."[38]

1860, there were 3,744,000 gallons. Chicago Board of Trade, *Fourteenth Annual Report, 1871*, p. 79.

[36] *Ibid.;* Chicago Daily Democratic Press, *Sixth Annual Review, 1857*, p. 18; United States, *Ninth Census, 1870*, III, " Wealth and Industry," 649; I[saac] D. Guyer, *History of Chicago . . .* (Chicago, 1862), p. 41.

[37] Chicago Board of Trade, *Third Annual Statement, 1860*, p. 49; *Chicago Tribune*, July 24, 1862; Taylor, *op. cit.*, I, 321; Elmer A. Riley, *The Development of Chicago and Vicinity as a Manufacturing Center Prior to 1880* (Chicago, 1911), pp. 120–21; Fite, *Social and Industrial Conditions*, p. 81.

[38] Hall & Co., *Directory, 1854–55*, Appendix, p. 7; United States, *Ninth Census, 1870*,

Trade in live animals came to be a significant factor in the economic development of Chicago during these years. Although that in cattle and swine was the most important, a brisk exchange in horses took place. At the same time some sheep were sold.[39] By 1851, Chicago was noted as a horse market, and, as the years passed, larger and larger numbers of horses were required for use in the city or were forwarded to points east, west, and south. During the Civil War, this trade boomed when army contractors entered the market, and Chicagoans heeded the injunction, " Brush up the nags and trot them out." The bringing of "broken down" and "spavined and wheezy old hacks" all the way from Pennsylvania to sell at high prices with those from the Midwest led the *Tribune* to declare that evidences of collusion between horse contractors and inspectors were too glaring to admit of doubt.[40] But a few weeks before, it had happily seen the city and section the recipient of "the handsome sum of two hundred thousand dollars" from army contracts to supply horses not only to Illinois troops but to the regiments of other states. From June 30, 1861, to September 30, 1862, the government purchased almost four thousand horses in Chicago, and in the six months ending December 31, 1864, over five thousand horses were bought in the city for war purposes.[41] After the war, Chicago continued to be a forwarding point, and, in 1871, about ten thousand horses and mules were received and shipped by rail from the city. Besides, a lively trade was carried on within the city itself, for by the late 'sixties fine

III, " Wealth and Industry," 649, 689, 714; Fite, *Social and Industrial Conditions*, p. 82; *Chicago Tribune*, June 6, 7, 1867.

[39] The sheep trade grew from 2,085 sheep received and 174 shipped in 1853 to 315,053 received and 135,084 forwarded in 1871. The Daily Democratic Press, *Annual Review, 1853*, pp. 70–71; Chicago Board of Trade, *Fourteenth Annual Report, 1871*, p. 67.

[40] *Chicago Daily Democrat*, June 21, 1851; The Daily Democratic Press, *Annual Review, 1854*, p. 18; *Chicago Tribune*, August 23, October 18, 1861.

[41] *Official Records of the Rebellion*, ser. 3, II, 810; " Government Contracts," *Reports of Committees of the House of Representatives*, 37 Cong., 2 sess., H. Rept. no. 2 (Washington, 1862), pp. lvi, 1118–25; United States, *Report of the Quartermaster General, 1865*, p. 49. One contract in August, 1861, called for a price of $110 for each horse at a time when the Union Defense Committee stated horses could be purchased for $95. (*Chicago Tribune*, August 23, 1861; *Official Records of the Rebellion*, ser. 1, VIII, 388.) The latter part of August, 1861, fifty-nine carloads of horses and cattle were shipped east via the Michigan Southern on one day. (*Chicago Tribune*, August 27, 1861. See also *Washburne Papers*, XXII, advertisement from Chicago.) The *Prairie Farmer* reported in 1865 that during the past year over fifteen thousand horses had been bought in Chicago for army use at a cost of $2,400,000. (*Prairie Farmer*, n.s. XV [May 20, 1865], 400.) Rail shipments of horses from Chicago in 1864 amounted to 6,372. Chicago Board of Trade, *Seventh Annual Statement, 1864*, pp. 95, 103, 105.

horses were possessed not only by wealthy citizens but by clerks and even butcher boys.[42]

As rail lines were extended to the East and as the center of livestock production moved westward, the traffic in cattle and swine expanded appreciably. In 1856, the number of cattle shipped from the city topped the number packed; by 1871 it was nineteen times as many.[43] In the case of hogs, however, the proportion of packed to shipped during these years remained more nearly constant.[44]

Business dealings in livestock proved very profitable. Beginning a colorful career by making heavy hog shipments to New York during a decline in the local market in 1860, Samuel W. Allerton emerged as a leader in the early 'sixties. Nelson Morris and Hugh Maher were at the same time becoming rich, benefiting by contracts with the federal government during the war. Still others, engaged in supplying the government, mounted the ladder of wealth, their progress at times sullied by selling what the press characterized as "the offscourings of Sodom and Gomorrah" instead of "good looking steers."[45]

The growth of the Chicago livestock trade was naturally accompanied by changes in the method of buying and selling. At first, stockmen and drovers sold directly to the packer, but as the volume of business expanded the middleman played an important rôle. In

[42] Receipts of horses and mules in 1871 were 10,109; shipments were 10,221. These figures do not include the numbers driven to and from the city. *Chicago Tribune,* February 24, 1868; Chicago Board of Trade, *Fourteenth Annual Report, 1871,* pp. 86–105.

[43] In 1856, 22,502 cattle were shipped, and 14,977 packed. (Chicago Daily Democratic Press, *Sixth Annual Review, 1857,* pp. 16–17.) In 1871, 401,927 cattle were shipped, and 21,254 were packed. Chicago Board of Trade, *Fourteenth Annual Report, 1871,* p. 44.

[44] Thus, in the packing season of 1856–57, 74,000 hogs were packed; in 1862–63, 970,-264; and in 1870–71, 919,197. In the year 1857 a total of 123,568 live and dressed hogs were shipped; in 1863, 862,190; and in 1871, 1,331,759. *Ibid.*

[45] Rudolph A. Clemen, *The American Livestock and Meat Industry* (New York, 1923), pp. 87–88, 156–58; Taylor, *op. cit.,* I, 253; *Chicago* [Tri-Weekly] *Tribune,* January 31, 1862; [Inter Ocean], *A History of Chicago* . . . (Chicago, 1900), p. 194; *Chicago Tribune,* May 31, July 17, 1861, October 24, 1866. Said the *Tribune,* " Among the drovers — mercenary as they are said to be — there was no small amount of indignation expressed that any man could be found heartless enough to offer such a mass of skin and bone to our soldiers for beef. . . . If the Government accepts such stock the inspectors ought to be sentenced to eat them and nothing else." The prices paid ranged from $2.25 to $2.75 per hundred pounds, while the quality of beef furnished under a former contract by Samuel Allerton was sold at $3.75. This, to the editor, offered some justification for the kind purchased, since delivery at Harrisburg had to be made at $3.90 per hundred pounds, with freight costing about $1.00 per hundred pounds, to say nothing of shrinkage and the expense of feed and care en route. *Ibid.,* July 16, 17, 1861. See, however, for the shipment of good cattle, *ibid.,* July 30, 1861. For further contracts see *Official Records of the Rebellion,* ser. 2, VI, 928–29.

the early 'fifties, a commission firm appeared, and by 1865 eight commission houses were carrying on business. The next year, some of the leading commission men and cattle purchasers formed a Chicago Livestock Board of Trade which conducted transactions secretly, so that farmers, kept in ignorance of the market value of their cattle and hogs, accepted whatever prices were offered by the drovers acting as agents of the commission houses. Price movements were hidden also from the press, which labeled the association the " Dark Lantern Board " and maintained that it was morally "the basest kind of fraud " to withhold information on prices from those engaged in agriculture. Farmers were advised not to sell to the combination. Acting upon this advice, they diverted to other markets the cattle which might have come to Chicago. Confronted with appreciably reduced receipts, the association gave up its plan and, at the close of 1866, agreed to furnish reporters with all desired information concerning sales.[46]

As cattle crowded into the city, facilities for their care were necessarily enlarged. In the early days, when cattle were brought " on the hoof " along the several roads leading into the city, owners of taverns, which catered to the drovers and stockmen, provided enclosed pastures and pens as an accommodation until arrangements for sale were made.[47] In 1837, Myrick's Tavern, located in the neighborhood of present-day Cottage Grove Avenue and Twenty-ninth Street, had a yard for the brawny, rollicking drovers to keep stock brought to Chicago. By the 'fifties, other tavern keepers furnished similar accommodations. Sidney L. Darrow fenced off a pasture of fifty acres near his hotel along the Southern Plank Road (later State Street), and Matthew Laflin, located on the Southwestern Plank Road (now Ogden Avenue) at West Madison Street, offered his Bull's Head Tavern drover-guests "bunks to feed and tie up the cattle." " The most extensive cattle yards in the West " were advertised in 1854 at the junction of Western Avenue and Archer Road in the village of Brighton, whence cattle could be driven into the city " without danger of fright from locomotives." [48]

[46] *Chicago Daily Drover's Journal*, June 28, 1939; Clemen, *op. cit.*, p. 88; Halpin, *Directory, 1865–66*, p. 798; *Chicago Tribune*, October 24, 25, November 6, December 27, 1866; *Prairie Farmer*, n.s. XVIII (November-December, 1866), 289, 321, 337, 353, 384.

[47] *Chicago Daily Drover's Journal*, June 28, 1939.

[48] *Chicago Daily Democrat*, January 1, April 17, July 8, 10, 17, September 18, 1851, May

THE CHAMBER OF COMMERCE BUILDING

Southeast corner of LaSalle and Washington, completed in 1865. The wires strung along the street are fire alarm telegraph wires.

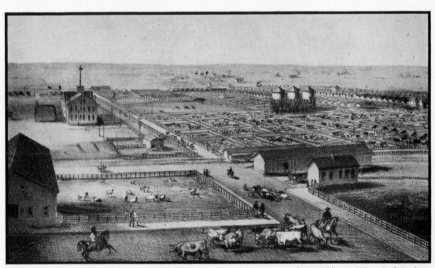

CHICAGO UNION STOCK YARD IN THE LATE 'SIXTIES

Although tavern yards were used even after the coming of the railroads, the advantages offered by the new means of transportation could not long be ignored. In 1856, the construction along Sixteenth Street of a track joining the eastern and western lines so expedited the shipping of livestock through the city that the advantages of stock yards adjacent to railroads became obvious. Before the mid-'sixties yards were served by the Michigan Central, the Illinois Central, the Michigan Southern, the Rock Island, the Pittsburgh and Fort Wayne, the Alton, the Chicago and North Western, and the Burlington.[49]

With business accelerated during the war, no one concerned with traffic in hogs and cattle felt that the several terminals scattered over the city proved the best and most economical arrangement. Owners and dealers saw injury to the hooves of their stock in driving the animals from yard to yard over the rough, ungraded streets; the railroads incurred considerable expense in switching cars from one yard to another; and the packers found it difficult to obtain their supply of livestock as needed. When the Pork Packers' Association suggested in 1864 the desirability of a means to facilitate more efficient handling of livestock, it found a ready response on the part of the railroad officials. Negotiations for the consolidation of the several yards into a Union Stock Yard followed immediately.[50] The company was capitalized at $1,000,000, of which all but $75,000 was subscribed by the railways. Thus was organized " The Union Stock Yard and Transit Company of Chicago." On Christmas Day, 1865, the yards were opened for business.[51]

15, 25, November 3, 25, 1852; *The Daily Democratic Press,* October 5, 17, 1853, October 28, 1854; The Daily Democratic Press, *Annual Review, 1853,* p. 53.

[49] *Chicago Daily Drover's Journal,* June 28, 1939; Jack Wing, *The Great Union Stock Yards of Chicago* (Chicago, 1865), pp. 9–10; Joseph G. Knapp, " A Review of Chicago Stock Yards History," *The University Journal of Business,* II (June, 1924), pp. 333–34.

[50] Among the packers, Col. R. M. Hough and John Hancock appear to have been especially active in initiating the negotiations, while John W. Brooks of the Michigan Central was the spokesman for the railroads. *Chicago Evening Journal,* June 29, 1864; *Chicago Tribune,* June 29, July 31, 1864.

[51] *Ibid.,* July 31, 1864; Knapp, *loc. cit.,* p. 335; [Anon.], " The Union Stock Yards of Chicago," Illinois State Agricultural Society, *Transactions,* VI (1865–66), 314–24. The amount of $75,000 not taken by the railroads was cared for by the packers, who provided $50,000, and by the public, $25,000. The $1,000,000 was, however, insufficient for the purpose. A total of $1,650,000 was expended in construction. (*Prairie Farmer,* n.s. XIX [January 5, 1867], 9.) The sum of $400,000 was borrowed on note and mortgage. The remainder was provided by earnings and stock dividends. (David W. Wood, ed., *Chicago and its Distinguished*

Located on the west side of Halsted Street at Thirty-ninth, and covering some 345 acres, the Union Stock Yard was the most modern in the United States. More than one hundred thousand head of livestock could be accommodated; an ample supply of pure water was assured by the drilling of two artesian wells; a hotel was provided for drovers, and a bank for the convenience of those doing business at the market.[52] Such facilities guaranteed a practical monopoly of the stock-yarding business, and the several isolated yards soon ceased operations.

The spread of the railway network also changed the history of meat packing. Before the building of the railroads it was more profitable for the stock raiser to sell his cattle to a drover, who took it overland to the East, or to have his hogs packed at some near-by center, such as Beardstown or Alton, whence they were floated down the river to New Orleans. Indeed, until the season of 1851–52 Beardstown led Chicago in the packing of pork. The entrance of the railroads from the west, north, and south changed the situation completely.[53]

Within a few years direct trunk lines to the East had been completed, marketing facilities of the Board of Trade had been improved, and the credit structure of the Chicago banks had been so developed that funds released in autumn, when grain contracts were settled, could be readily transferred to the packers. These factors had so contributed to the growth of the packing industry that Chicago in 1861 snatched from Cincinnati the pork-packing crown of the United States.[54]

Citizens . . . [Chicago, 1881], p. 357.) The incorporators included nineteen packers and railroad officers. The first directors were Martin L. Sykes, John B. McCullough, James F. Joy, John F. Tracy, Timothy B. Blackstone, John L. Hancock, Roselle M. Hough, Charles M. Culbertson, and Virginius A. Turpin. Act of February 13, 1865, *Private Laws, 1865*, II, 679–83.

[52] *Chicago Tribune*, December 27, 1865, January 1, 1866. By 1868 the capacity was 175,350. There were thirty-five miles of underdrains, streets and alleys ten miles in length, one thousand covered pens for hogs and sheep, and two thousand open pens for cattle. There were a fire department and a gas plant, a hospital for the sick and injured livestock. " The Union Stock Yards of Chicago," *loc. cit.*, pp. 314–21; [Anon.], " Review of the Chicago Live Stock Trade, during the Year 1868," *Griffith's Live Stock Reporter*, quoted in Illinois State Agricultural Society, *Transactions*, VII (1867–68), 402–10.

[53] Clemen, *op. cit.*, p. 107. In 1850, Illinois stood sixth among the states in the production of swine; in 1860, second; and in 1870, it led the Union. In 1850, Illinois ranked seventh in cattle on farms; by 1860 she had gained second place, a lead kept ten years later. United States, *A Compendium of the Ninth Census (June 1, 1870)* . . . (Francis A. Walker, comp. Washington, 1872), pp. 708–10. For figures, see Appendix, pp. 492–98.

[54] In 1860–61, Cincinnati packed 433,799 hogs, and Chicago packed 271,805. In 1861,

During the decades of the 'fifties and 'sixties, meat packing was perhaps the most important industry of Chicago, the value of the output mounting steadily. This growth was accompanied by a great increase in capitalization and in expenditure for raw materials. In contrast with the cost of materials, wages were a comparatively small item: in 1860, the 146 hands engaged received $27,885, and in 1870, 2,129 workers got $425,560.[55] Large profits were the order of the day in packing as in many other endeavors, and in 1860 packers as a whole realized almost 100 per cent on their investments. By 1870 about 50 per cent in profits rewarded their efforts.[56]

It is not strange that firms and individuals from other cities were thus lured into the Chicago industry. The packers of an early day, such as Sylvester Marsh, Wadsworth and Dyer, and Gurdon S. Hubbard, who had operated primarily on commission for eastern wholesalers and exporters during the 'fifties, were obscured by new firms, among which were Cragin and Company, commission merchants of New York, and Jones and Culbertson, later Culbertson and Blair, who began packing in 1858. The outbreak of the Civil War led firms from other places to establish themselves in the city, and the great activity in packing from 1862 to 1865 caused still others to enter the industry. The number of packers increased from about thirty in 1860 to about fifty-eight in 1864, a number which remained more or less fixed until after 1871.[57]

At the close of the war, the meat-packing industry of Chicago was distributed among a large number of comparatively small firms led

the former packed 474,167 and the latter 514,118. *Hunt's Merchants' Magazine*, LIII (September, 1865), 193, LIV (May, 1866), 382; Taylor, *op. cit.*, I, 361.

[55] In 1860, in Cook County, the capital laid out in the industry amounted to only $155,-000. By 1870, $6,361,000 was invested in the plants. United States, *Eighth Census, 1860*, " Manufactures," p. 87, *Ninth Census, 1870*, III, " Wealth and Industry," 649.

[56] Records of the firm of Armour and Company lend credence to these startling figures. This firm made between 1869 and 1873 respectively, 75, 24.5, 7.5, 28.8, and 77.1 per cent profit on the net worth of the company. United States Federal Trade Commission, *Report . . . on the Meat Packing Industry* (6 v. Washington, 1920), V, 21.

[57] *Daily Democrat*, September 26, 1848. Cragin and Company established a packing house in 1854. Jones and Culbertson had been packers in Muscatine, Iowa, in 1856. Lyman Blair was associated with them in 1863–64. [Chicago Daily Press and Tribune], *Seventh Annual Review of the Trade and Commerce and of the Public and Private Improvements of the City of Chicago . . .* (Chicago, 1859), p. 20 (hereafter cited as Chicago Daily Press and Tribune, *Annual Review*); John Moses and Joseph Kirkland, *History of Chicago, Illinois* (2 v. Chicago, 1895), I, 390; Chicago Board of Trade, *Fifth Annual Statement, 1862*, p. vii, *Third Annual Statement, 1860*, pp. 37–38, *Sixth Annual Statement, 1863–64*, pp. 46, 53, *Fourteenth Annual Report, 1871*, pp. 146–47; Andreas, *History of Chicago*, II, 335, III, 756.

by Culbertson, Blair and Company and Cragin and Company. But consolidation was soon to take place, just as it was destined to in other fields of human endeavor. The leadership in this movement was in the deft hands of Benjamin P. Hutchinson, one-time shoe manufacturer of Lynn, Massachusetts, who had come west, as had others after the panic of 1857, to begin life anew. A five-dollar membership on the Board of Trade opened the door to a successful career in the grain trade, followed soon by his entrance into the lucrative field of pork packing. In 1863 huge profits in speculative dealings in high wines and whiskey, before the passage of the federal revenue tax, marked him as one of the most discerning and daring of the businessmen of Chicago. Banking yielded other rich returns, and, with a considerable fortune, " Old Hutch " or " the Prince of Scalpers," as he was familiarly known, entered the meat-packing business. In 1868 he consolidated several small companies into the Chicago Packing and Provision Company. At once this company attained the lead among Chicago packers, a position which it held until the season of 1878–79.[58]

Armour and Company, which sprang from a branch of Plankinton and Armour, packers of Milwaukee, in 1878–79 took the leadership from the Chicago Packing and Provision Company. The Chicago branch was organized in 1867 and was at first conducted by Joseph F. Armour, a brother of the founder of the family fortune, Philip D., who did not leave Milwaukee to make his home in Chicago until later. In 1865, Herman O. Armour, who had been a commission merchant in Chicago since 1862, turned over its management to his younger brother Joseph and went to New York to take over a new firm, that of Armour, Plankinton and Company. In 1869, the house of Armour had a branch in Kansas City, Missouri, under the direction of Simeon B. Armour; and when Philip D. Armour moved his headquarters to Chicago, in 1875, his organization covered the two lesser supply points, Milwaukee and Kansas City, and the great marketing point, New York.[59]

---

[58] Hutchinson came to Chicago in 1859 from Milwaukee where he had gone from Massachusetts. *Ibid.*, II, 331; Chicago Board of Trade, *Ninth Annual Statement, 1866–67*, p. 53, *Eleventh Annual Statement, 1868–69*, p. 50, *Fourteenth Annual Report, 1871*, p. 146, *Twenty-second Annual Report, 1879*, pp. 54–55; Inter Ocean, *op. cit.*, p. 201.

[59] Clemen, *op. cit.*, pp. 151–53; Harper Leech and John Charles Carroll, *Armour and His Times* (New York, 1938), pp. 36–37.

More preserved beef than preserved pork was produced by the local packers in 1848. Indeed, Chicago at that time was credited with leading the cities of the United States in salt-beef production. The growing demand for this article came mainly from England, where the salt beef of Wadsworth and Dyer excited much favourable comment at the London World's Fair in 1851. During the Civil War a strong domestic demand appeared, and in the 1864–65 season a slaughter of 92,459 cattle marked the high point in beef packing, a considerable gain over the 21,806 for 1851 and the 34,623 for 1860. In the season of 1865–66 the number packed dropped to 27,172, and by 1870 the business was reported to have dwindled into comparative insignificance in Chicago. The decline resulted partly from the fact that it was more profitable to ship than to pack cattle, and partly because the industry was centering at Kansas City, which lay near the new great cattle supply, and whither a number of Chicago beef packers transferred their business. The canning of beef which had started under the guidance of Arthur A. and Charles P. Libby and Archibald McNeill in 1868, however, continued to grow, the firm becoming later the internationally known Libby, McNeill and Libby.[60]

Pork packing was less important than beef packing in the early 'fifties, for it was easier to drive cattle long distances on the hoof to the Chicago market than to bring the swine. After railroads opened up a new way of carriage, however, great numbers of swine came into the city, the season's hog pack in 1854–55 being three times as great as that of cattle.[61] Pork packing continued its lead. So important did it become that when the meat packers of the city organized in 1862, they named their association the " Pork Packers' Association," laying no stress whatever on beef.[62]

[60] *Prairie Farmer*, IX (December, 1849), 382; *Chicago Daily Democrat*, May 20, 1851; Chicago Board of Trade, *Seventh Annual Statement, 1864–65*, p. 43, *Ninth Annual Statement, 1866–67*, p. 59, *Eleventh Annual Statement, 1868*, p. 56, *Thirteenth Annual Report, 1870*, p. 13; Riley, *op. cit.*, p. 131; Andreas, *History of Chicago*, III, 757. In the first year of operation sales amounted to about $60,000 in the Libby firm.

[61] In 1851–52, the number of cattle packed had grown to 21,806, the number of hogs to 22,036; in 1854–55, 73,694 hogs and only 23,691 cattle were packed. Chicago Board of Trade, *Fourteenth Annual Report, 1871*, p. 44.

[62] The Pork Packers' Association was formed by the pork and beef packers of the city about 1862 for the " mutual protection and the advancement of the packing interests." In March, 1865, the association drew up regulations for cutting and packing Chicago meats and provided for a voluntary system of inspection to improve the market for Chicago meats. The inspection was of samples, not of all packages. *Chicago Tribune*, March 20, 1865, January 1, 1866; Chicago Board of Trade, *Eighth Annual Statement, 1865–66*, pp. 16–21.

The city was aided in gaining and retaining its position as the greatest pork-packing center of the country by new methods adopted by Chicago packers. To meet the demands of the English market after 1862 English methods of pork curing were adopted on a large scale. Instead of packing the pork in a barrel of brine, the pieces sometimes were laid in dry salt in a light, cheap wooden box. For the year ending June 30, 1860, 218 barrels worth $3,382 were exported, and three years later 25,895 barrels worth $293,468. Chicago pork packers also started summer pork packing in 1858 in refrigerated rooms, having stored ice during the winter for this purpose. Their product commanded top prices in the New York market, and, in 1860, the fifteen days required to cure meats in icehouses seemed remarkable in the light of an outside temperature sometimes as high as one hundred degrees.[63]

Important as was this business in cured and other preserved meats, it, of course, did not satisfy the demand for fresh products. In the 'fifties the desirability of shipping dressed fresh meats rather than live hogs and cattle became increasingly apparent, but before the development of the refrigerator car this was hazardous business because of the danger of spoilage. This risk was relatively small when the meat could be kept cool, but before the coming of the railroad the closed navigation season so nearly coincided with the period when fresh meats could be shipped without spoiling, that it was impossible for Chicago fresh-meat interests effectively to invade the markets of the East. After the building of rail lines, however, dressed hogs were forwarded over them during the freezing temperatures of winter.[64] This traffic increased after the fast freight lines applied the quick through-shipment system, which they had devised for grain, to dressed meats. By the 'seventies their volume of business in this field was large.[65]

The day of greater safety in carrying perishable commodities throughout the year was hastened in 1865 when William W. Chandler, the superintendent of the Star Union Fast Freight line, fitted

---

[63] *Reports on Commerce and Navigation, 1859–60*, p. 337; *ibid., 1862–63*, p. 30; Chicago Daily Press and Tribune, *Seventh Annual Review, 1858*, p. 23; Chicago Board of Trade, *Third Annual Statement, 1860*, p. 36.

[64] For figures on this trade, see Appendix, pp. 492, 494, 496, 498.

[65] D. C. Brooks, " Chicago and Its Railways," *Lakeside Monthly*, VIII (October, 1872), 275; Taylor, *op. cit.*, I, 369–70.

up some thirty boxcars with insulated walls and ice bins, which were experimentally used for the shipment of dairy products, meats, and vegetables. In 1869, a refrigerated carload of dressed beef reached New England in good condition, and the secretary of the Board of Trade reported that so successful was the method that the dressed-meat traffic " promises to increase and grow in favor." [66] Thus was the stage set for the entrance of Gustavus Swift, whose large-scale application of this method in the 'seventies and 'eighties revolution-ized the livestock and meat industry of Chicago.

Quantity production of meats was accompanied by the rise of spec-ulation. During the early 'fifties the packers usually operated on orders from eastern houses or consigned their products to the East on commission, but by the middle of the decade contracts for future delivery were becoming common. In the spring of 1856 it was ob-served that settlements of contracts made in the preceding fall had left speculators in an " extremely unfortunate position." [67] Three years later they so manipulated prices that legitimate traders for a time withdrew from the market. And during the wartime excite-ment, many entered the speculative market for provisions. Upon the belief that " Grant and the Union are going to win before long," Armours sold short, profiting an estimated $500,000 to $1,500,000 only a few years before a branch of Plankinton and Armour was set up in Chicago.[68]

Following the war, the Board of Trade continued to be the scene of great speculative activity. In the spring of 1868 three to five mil-lion pounds of pork sometimes changed hands daily. A corner in April sent prices skyrocketing, and fortunes were won and lost. While these operations were in themselves hazardous, they were rendered even more so by the fact that the products traded in were not of uniform quality; the buyer who contracted for a number of barrels of mess pork sometimes received barrels containing unequal quantities of an unevenly cured product which would bring, on re-sale, a return which varied accordingly. This condition could be remedied only by setting up grades for provisions.

[66] Andreas, *History of Chicago*, III, 337; Riley, *op. cit.*, p. 130; Taylor, *op. cit.*, I, 369–70, 396.

[67] The Daily Democratic Press, *Fifth Annual Review, 1856*, pp. 25–26.

[68] Leech and Carroll, *op. cit.*, pp. 31–33; Andreas, *History of Chicago*, II, 331; Taylor, *op. cit.*, I, 255–56, 317; *Chicago Tribune*, November 16, 1863; Clemen, *op. cit.*, p. 152.

Grades had been established for grain in 1856, but no effective system was devised for enforcing grades in provisions until 1870. In that year, meat packers and provision dealers, in the hope of improving the position of Chicago meats in world markets, adopted rules for grading and inspection and submitted them to the Board of Trade for adoption. Acceptance by all was not to be expected, for speculators were more interested in making money than in improving quality, and the whole problem was complicated by the lack of a standard weight, for pork changed weight according to the length of time it was packed in salt. Opponents lost their fight in November, 1870, for they were outvoted on the Board, and that body thereupon set up exacting standards for Chicago provisions.[69]

One of the reasons for the subsequent supremacy of Chicago as a meat center was the development of industries making use in large quantities of the by-products of slaughtering and packing. The use of these by-products enabled the great Chicago firms to put their meats on the market at lower prices than local butchers in the East could offer. For soap, cooking, and illuminating purposes, lard and tallow not only served Chicagoans, but were shipped to the hinterland and sometimes to New York, Boston, and Montreal.[70] Concentration of the manufacture of those particular by-products within the packing industry became apparent before the close of the 'fifties, although earlier manufacture had been carried on by independent houses. About 1854, R. M. and O. S. Hough and Company, a packing concern, installed tanks and boilers in their packing house. Others followed this example, and three years later Charles Cleaver, who had had a practical monopoly of the rendering business, abandoned the field largely to the packers themselves.

With the exception of oils and tallow, however, by-product manu-

---

[69] Taylor, *op. cit.,* I, 372; *Chicago Tribune,* July 7, 8, 1870. The following example shows the attitude of some speculators. Early in 1870, a speculator sold and delivered two hundred barrels of pork to another speculator. A few weeks later in the course of his speculations he repurchased two hundred barrels from the latter, but, when offered the identical lot which he had sold, he refused to accept it on the grounds that it was light weight. *Ibid.,* July 13, 14, November 30, 1870; Chicago Board of Trade, *Thirteenth Annual Report, 1870,* pp. 20–23.

[70] Clemen, *op. cit.,* pp. 57, 131; Wright, *Chicago,* p. 214; Charles Cleaver, *Early-Chicago Reminiscences* (Fergus Historical Series, no. 19. Chicago, 1882), p. 50; *The Daily Democratic Press,* December 13, 1852. The value of the manufacture of animal oils in 1870 amounted to $1,473,700; of grease and tallow to $1,412,000; and of candles and soap to $1,050,150. United States, *Ninth Census, 1870,* III, " Wealth and Industry," 649.

facture appears to have remained independent of the packers during the years 1848 to 1871. Although in 1850 some of the offal went into the river, most of the miscellaneous material except blood was carted off for hog food. By 1851 the press exulted that individuals had appeared in the city negotiating for the blood to use in the manufacture of Prussian blue. A brush manufactory existed in 1850, and a curled hair manufactory by 1867. Bones were utilized for bone black and bone dust and in the manufacture of whips. Portions of the beeves served various purposes: beef gall was sold in 1848 at thirty-seven and a half cents a gallon, a beef extract plant was found by 1867, and glycerine and gelatine came upon the market. By 1867 the manufacture of offal into fertilizer was a large-scale industry, and by 1871 there were three glue factories in the city.[71]

As the supply of hides from slaughtered animals increased, the hide and leather trades developed. In 1855, three establishments were engaged in tanning, and by 1870 the number had multiplied nine times. This leather, cured with hemlock brought from Michigan, was sometimes manufactured into finished products in Chicago establishments, although some of it was shipped along with green hides to the East and Europe. The trade became increasingly important as the years advanced. Leather merchants also dealt in wool, a trade which increased from a half million pounds in 1848 to over twenty-four million in 1871.[72]

Leather working was an industry of great importance, and leather manufacturers turned out harness and saddles, a business stimulated in 1861 by wartime demands for cavalry equipment. Condict, Woolley and Company operated twenty-four hours a day for a while in order to furnish saddles to the army, and Turner and Sidway made a contract calling for $150,000 worth of material by summer of the first year of the war. In September, 1861, the latter was said to be shipping daily no less than 102 cavalry equipments, proudly proclaimed to be about equal to any three other manufactories in the

[71] Illinois State Agricultural Society, *Transactions*, VII (1867–68), 162; Cleaver, *op. cit.*, pp. 50–51; Clemen, *op. cit.*, pp. 127, 133; *Chicago Daily Democrat*, December 13, 1850, June 2, 1851; Wright, *Chicago*, pp. 203–4.

[72] Tanning establishments had a capital investment of $150,000 and an output in 1855 worth $290,000. (The Daily Democratic Press, *Fourth Annual Review, 1855*, p. 39.) Twenty-seven firms representing $991,400 of capital turned out hides valued at $3,333,121 by 1870. United States, *Ninth Census, 1870*, III, "Wealth and Industry," 649. For figures on shipments and receipts of hides see Appendix, pp. 492–98.

United States. In so doing their employment list grew to four hundred, about fifty employees being women. In 1863, it was reported that they had furnished the government nearly a million dollars' worth of leather equipment.[73]

On the supplying of the army with leather goods, for which Chicago gained huge contracts, the shadow of charges of irregular practices fell just as in other cities and just as it did on the furnishing of nearly all other types of material by contractors, particularly during the early years of the war.[74] Some Chicagoans were reported as having profited to an unconscionable degree, not only by selling goods of inferior quality but by the payment demanded. Profits pocketed not only by the firm furnishing supplies but at times by the agents promoting the transaction sometimes left the taint of irregularity, although not all Chicagoans were guilty.[75]

The boot and shoe industry likewise felt the force of the demands of the federal troops and received its full share of criticism as to the poor quality of product delivered. One lot purchased for the Irish Brigade lasted but two weeks, and other soldiers had similar experiences.[76] The impetus given to the manufacture of footwear during the war was such that by 1870 the output was valued at $1,666,723, and Chicago proudly pointed to the removal from the East of factories which recognized the advantage of being near the place where the hides were tanned. Miscellaneous items such as hose, belting, and carriage trimmings were also manufactured.[77]

Subsidiary to meat packing were also the cooperage industry and the salt trade. Growth in cooperage was a concomitant of increased activity in meat packing, and in 1870 thirty-one establishments turned out wooden containers valued at $295,000. Large quantities of salt were at first imported from Europe by the packers. In the

---

[73] *Chicago Tribune*, July 25, August 16, 17, 23, 27, September 3, 6, 16, 18, 26, 1861, March 12, 1863.

[74] For example, it was alleged in 1861 that the sum of $10 each was added to the price of cavalry equipment furnished the government by Condict, Woolley and Company through an agent. *Ibid.*, November 6, 1861.

[75] United States, "Government Contracts," *op. cit.*, pp. LI, LII, LVI, 62, 65–66, 1118, 1137.

[76] *Chicago Tribune*, June 24, 1861.

[77] United States, *Ninth Census, 1870*, III, "Wealth and Industry," 649. In 1862, a Lynn, Massachusetts, firm gladdened Chicagoans by moving to their city and giving work to three hundred employees. *Chicago Tribune*, May 14, 1862; *Chicago Daily Democrat*, December 3, 1851.

'fifties, however, Syracuse salt came into growing favor, and the Michigan salt springs were looked to as a source of supply. The surplus was shipped to the towns north and west of Chicago, and during the war the east-to-west commerce in this article was furthered when supplies from Kanahwa and other places were cut off by the blockade of the southern ports. In 1871, the fact that over seven hundred and three thousand barrels were received in Chicago and about four hundred and fifty thousand were shipped indicated that salt had become an item of considerable importance in the wholesale trade of the city.[78]

In return for agricultural products, Chicagoans sent back to the farmers building materials, a wide variety of consumers' goods, and agricultural machinery. The dwellers on the near-by prairies had great need for lumber, and as the network of rails was extended, they turned chiefly to Chicago. Lumber then poured into the city from the north in such quantity that receipts in 1856 exceeded the amount passing through Albany, which until then had been the greatest primary lumber market in the United States. Supplies also came from Canada and the valley of the Susquehanna in Pennsylvania.[79] Lining the banks of the Chicago River from the Fort Wayne depot at Madison and Canal streets to the vicinity of Bridgeport, the lumber yards, with stacks as high as thirty feet, constituted, with the possible exception of the grain elevators, the most impressive outward sign of the commercial greatness of Chicago. In 1865, the receipts were over 606,645,000 feet, exclusive of shingles and laths, posts, railroad ties, and telegraph poles. The capital invested was reported as " immense," and it rendered rich rewards to its beneficiaries. Sometimes enterprising yard owners, such as Turlington W. Harvey, Jesse Spalding, and Freeland B. Gardner, extended their sphere of operations to planing and saw mills lying along the banks of the Wisconsin rivers which touched the shores of the timber lands. Prosperity spread investments in other yards which fed the center of operations at Chicago. Success led to the control of carriers to market which

[78] United States, *Ninth Census, 1870*, III, "Wealth and Industry," 649; *Chicago Daily Democrat*, March 4, 1850; Chicago Board of Trade, *Third Annual Statement, 1860*, p. 47, *Fourth Annual Statement, 1861*, p. 46, *Fourteenth Annual Report, 1871*, pp. 38–39.

[79] *Chicago Daily Democrat*, January 26, December 30, 1850, December 30, 1851; "Documents relating to the Organization of the Illinois Central Rail Road," *Brayman Papers*; *Hunt's Merchants' Magazine*, LIV (February, 1866), 102–3, 105; Taylor, *op. cit.*, I, 215.

anchored at docks owned by the lumber dealers, who also frequently held wide stretches of land in Michigan and Wisconsin from which the timber was cut.[80]

Inasmuch as lumber was primarily an article sent to the agriculturists in exchange for the products of the soil, the statistics of lumber shipments show a remarkably close correspondence to the increases in the grain and meat trade. Thus, except for five lean years following 1857, the number of feet of lumber shipped from Chicago almost constantly increased.[81] As in other fields of endeavor, charges of questionable contracts with the government during the war cast a shadow over some transactions. Demand, however, stimulated sales during these years to such an extent that in the fiscal year ending July 1, 1868, Chicago shipments reached the impressive total of 1,401,-635,124 feet, a figure which did not include supplies of laths and shingles.[82]

After the depression of 1857, the lumbermen believed that they could improve the condition of their business by setting up a special organization, and in 1859 they withdrew from the Board of Trade to form the Lumber Manufacturers' Association. They rented rooms and opened an exchange for the use of resident and non-resident manufacturers, dealers, vessel captains, and others interested in the

[80] *Hunt's Merchants' Magazine*, LIV (February, 1866), 104; *Chicago Daily Democrat*, August 30, 1849. Harvey came to Chicago in 1854 at the age of nineteen with very little capital. At the height of his career he had lumber mills in Wisconsin and Michigan, owned boats for lake transportation, and held thousands of acres of timber land. In 1867 his taxable income was reported as $33,681. Spalding came to Chicago in 1857 because he desired more opportunities than the Susquehanna River lumber trade offered him. He bought a sawmill at the mouth of the Menominee River in Wisconsin. By 1871 his business was extensive. He was also interested in railways and water transports. Gardner came to Chicago in 1852 from Wisconsin where he had lumber yards and timber lands. Soon he built two boats to carry lumber to Chicago. His business grew rapidly. His taxable income in 1867 was reported as $64,831. Eli Bates, E. L. Jillett, Nathan Mears, and George R. Roberts also laid the basis for fortunes in lumbering. In 1867 their taxable incomes were all reported to be over $30,000. Martin Ryerson laid the basis of a fortune in timber lands around Muskegon, Michigan. Josiah Seymour Currey, *Chicago: Its History and Its Builders, a Century of Marvelous Growth* (5 v. Chicago, 1912), IV, 295; *Biographical Sketches of the Leading Men of Chicago* . . . (Chicago, 1868), pp. 495–98; Andreas, *History of Chicago*, II, 691–92, III, 369, 373; *Dictionary of American Biography*, XVI, 272; *Chicago Tribune*, May 2, 1867; *The Chicago Times*, May 2, 1867.

[81] The *Daily Democratic Press, Fifth Annual Review, 1856*, p. 27; Chicago Board of Trade, *Third Annual Statement, 1860*, p. 62, *Eleventh Annual Statement, 1868–69*, p. 63, *Fourteenth Annual Report, 1871*, p. 80.

[82] The amount of laths was 217,433,288 and of shingles was 927,969,775. *Report of the Commissioner of the General Land Office, 1868*, p. 15; *Chicago Tribune*, December 12, 31, 1861, January 13, 1864; "Government Contracts," *op. cit.*, pp. 1090, 1124, 1134–35.

trade. The exchange functioned poorly and, though the organization dragged on for seven years, closed its doors in 1867, when the members returned to the Board of Trade.[83]

Much of the lumber received in Chicago was used in the city. One enterprising manufacturer, Lyman Bridges, turned out prefabricated houses, stores, and school buildings which could be put together by any "ordinary mechanic." By 1866 buildings made by this firm were scattered through Indiana, Illinois, Iowa, and Nebraska. The local need of lumber for building purposes was considerable, and finishing of furniture, trimming, and similar products emancipated Chicago from an earlier dependence on the East. Furniture manufactories, too, had multiplied between 1860 and 1870 more than three times, with their products increasing in value from less than a quarter of a million to one and one-half millions of dollars. Production of sash, doors, and blinds, though of less importance, nearly trebled.[84]

Wagon and vessel building and repairing sometimes made men wealthy, or at least "well-to-do"; and during the war many steam tugs belonging to Chicagoans passed into the hands of the government.[85] Brick manufacture by 1852 had attained importance enough to give business to five firms, one of which, Penny's, occupied about fifteen acres of land on the west side of the South Branch of the river. Sandstone brick, made at Cleaverville, found ready sale for building purposes at a later day. By 1870, the number of concerns engaged in this business had quadrupled; in that year twenty turned out a product valued at more than half a million dollars. Limestone for trimming city buildings was quarried at Athens, twenty-five miles to the southwest, and carried northward by canal. The Merchants and Mechanics Bank used it for facing in the early 'fifties, and others,

---

[83] Chicago Tribune, *Annual Review, 1860,* p. 25; *The Press and Tribune,* April 12, 1859; *Chicago Tribune,* January 19, April 2, 1867.

[84] *Ibid.,* November 10, 1866. Six planing mills which existed in 1860 had grown to thirty-four ten years later, and the value of their products had increased from $417,828 to $6,755,580. United States, *Eighth Census, 1860,* "Manufactures," p. 86; United States, *Ninth Census, 1870,* III, "Wealth and Industry," 649.

[85] A leading wagon builder, Peter Schuttler, furnished the Mormons with wagons to cross the plains. (*Gurdon S. Hubbard Papers,* XII.) In 1870, only St. Louis and Philadelphia ranked ahead of Chicago in wagon production. Production and repair of vessels reached a value of more than $200,000 in 1870. United States, *Ninth Census, 1870,* III, "Wealth and Industry," 649, 728; *Official Records of the Rebellion,* ser. 1, XXIV, pt. 3, 172–73; *Chicago Tribune,* September 13, 28, 1861.

impressed by the result, followed suit. Lime in large quantities was also brought by canal from Athens and used for a variety of purposes in addition to building.[86]

Until 1848, the Chicago trade in consumer's goods was chiefly retail. Merchants ordered supplies from eastern wholesale houses and sold them to their fellow citizens. An exception, of course, was the perishable food supply, which was drawn from the immediate vicinity and retailed. These continued to be sold in the city markets, whose offerings expanded as the wants and wealth of the community grew.[87] Gradually, as transportation improved, many city retailers developed a wholesale business. Country merchants who had purchased most of their goods directly from New York began to turn to Chicago dealers for supplies.[88] By 1853, improved carrying facilities were held to have increased the business of some local wholesale firms by at least 40 per cent. Five years later, the *Press and Tribune* boasted that the city was " mistress of commerce," adding that buyers from Wisconsin towns flew thither as to the center of the universe. The income of one local house, it was asserted, was as great as that of the best eastern firms, and a dozen wholesale houses were said, in 1859, to have business which in the aggregate was " counted by millions." When the 'sixties closed, the position of Chicago as a wholesale supply center seemed well established. As an editor pointed out, thousands of merchants in the budding country towns which the railroad tapped could now step into a car at night, be in Chicago the next morning, and reach home again within a day.[89]

Contacts of wholesalers grew more frequent, of course, as the rail lines extended. But they were immeasurably strengthened by the dispatch to outlying districts of traveling salesmen, who slowly began to usurp what had been the prerogatives of representatives from the

[86] *Daily Democrat,* January 1, May 10, 1849, July 12, 1851; *The Daily Democratic Press,* October 31, 1855; United States, *Ninth Census, 1870,* III, " Wealth and Industry," 649; Chicago Daily Democratic Press, *Sixth Annual Review, 1857,* pp. 19–20.

[87] See pp. 48, 460–61. A general discussion of the early trade in consumer's goods is given in Pierce, *A History of Chicago,* I, 124–37.

[88] Direct appeals of New York wholesalers to country merchants appear in advertisements. *Daily Democrat,* March 17, 1848, September 4, 1849, December 30, 1851; *The Daily Democratic Press,* September 28, 1852.

[89] The Daily Democratic Press, *Annual Review, 1853,* pp. 42–43; *Chicago Daily Press and Tribune,* August 25, 1858; Chicago Board of Trade, *Second Annual Statement, 1859,* p. 75; Wright, *Chicago,* p. 152.

East. Until the 'seventies, however, Field, Leiter and Company carried on their contacts by means of circulars.[90] By 1864, the number of traveling men had grown to such a point that the Mercantile Association, composed of small businessmen, debated the good or evil arising from the employment of such salesmen. Some of the members emphasized the fact that the practice had been condemned in the past when the "runners" of eastern houses had taken from Chicago merchants some of the trade they craved. Others cited advantages in the form of increased business. The opinions of those who favored this method of selling goods prevailed, and the grocers, to whom the subject was referred, decided to drop the matter.

In 1866, the traveling salesmen banded together in an association known as the Commercial Travellers Association of Chicago, the chief object of which was to obtain better rates and accommodations from the railroad companies.[91] This organization was supplanted in 1869 by the Merchants and Commercial Travellers Association, which had a broad platform — the benefiting and protecting of merchants, commercial travelers, and manufacturers of Chicago and the Northwest. This group occupied a suite of rooms on Dearborn Street, subscribed to three hundred daily and two hundred weekly papers, magazines, and price reports, and was prepared to supply reliable commercial information to its members. The traveling salesman had come to stay, a storied figure, a symbol of the dominance of Chicago over the wholesale trade of the Mississippi Valley.[92]

Most important of the jobbing lines was dry goods. Twelve houses in 1859 catered to the wholesale trade alone, and within five years after that Chicago stood next to New York as the most important dry goods market in the country, with an estimated trade of $35,000,-000. The cloth and sundries so distributed by Chicago merchants were imported from the East. Small quantities of cotton were

[90] Marshall Field, *Papers* (Typescript. Marshall Field and Company. Hereafter cited as *Field Papers*); *Chicago Tribune*, July 14, 1871.

[91] Chicago Board of Trade, *Second Annual Statement, 1859*, p. 75. The Mercantile Association was established in 1861. (Colbert, *op. cit.*, p. 57; *Chicago Tribune*, February 2, March 8, 1864, January 3, 1866.) The executive committee of the Commercial Travellers Association was made up of a representative of dealers in liquor, boots and shoes, confections, groceries, fancy dry goods, hardware, and clothing. See *Daily Chicago Post*, January 3, 1866.

[92] The association also aimed to get lower traveling and hotel rates and to do away with unclean politics. *Chicago Tribune*, May 25, 1869; Fred C. Kelly, *Seventy-Five Years of Hibbard Hardware* . . . (Chicago, 1930), p. 32.

brought from the South during the late 'fifties, but cotton milling, though considered, was not carried on.[93]

Greatest among the dry goods firms of Chicago by the 'sixties was that of Potter Palmer, Marshall Field, and Levi Leiter, now known as Marshall Field and Company. Palmer came to Chicago in 1852 from Albany County, New York, and with a capital of $5,000 opened a retail dry goods store on Lake Street, in a frame structure where tobacco chewers loafed with their feet on top of the stove. Advanced methods of merchandising were introduced, by which customers could have goods sent to their homes on approval; satisfaction was guaranteed, or their money refunded. Palmer made trips abroad to bring back the dry goods and carpets of European markets, thereby gaining glittering encomiums from the press. By 1857, he had added a wholesale branch to his store. At the outbreak of the Civil War he purchased huge bills of goods and, operating in New York as well as in Chicago, profited by the rise in prices, often never moving the goods at all. After selling his store to Field, Leiter and Company in 1865, he devoted his energies to real estate speculation and hotel management. But it was as Palmer the merchant that he won his early fame. Never before his time had advertising been used so widely, or window and counter displays so effectively. Other merchants were literally forced to adopt his methods of doing business.[94]

The men to whom Palmer sold his business, Marshall Field, known as " Silent Marsh," and Levi Leiter, had also come to Chicago during the 'fifties. They both had entered the dry goods business and had become partners in the firm of Farwell, Field and Company when they bought out Palmer. Pursuing the general plans established by Palmer, the new firm prospered. It showed a profit at the end of 1865, despite the fact that a $300,000 loss had been suffered because of

[93] Colbert, op. cit., p. 74; Chicago Tribune, Annual Review, 1864, pp. 21–22. In 1869, a report of the Cotton Manufacturers' Association indicated that Illinois was the smallest producing state in cotton milling in the country. Hunt's Merchants' Magazine, LXI (November, 1869), 378–79; Chicago Daily Democrat, March 11, 1851; The Daily Democratic Press, October 8, 1856; Chicago Tribune, January 1, 1861; Smith & DuMoulin, Chicago City Directory, for the Year Ending May 1, 1860 (Chicago, 1859), pp. 77–78 (hereafter cited as Smith & DuMoulin, Directory, 1859–60).

[94] [Andrew MacLeish], The Life of Andrew MacLeish, 1838–1928 (Chicago, 1929), pp. 28–29; The Press and Tribune, June 8, 1859; Chicago and Marshall Field's (Chicago, 1937), p. 50; Chicago Tribune, October 13, 1868; Chicago Daily News, June 17, 1931. During the war Potter Palmer sold to the government principally flannels and blankets. The amounts sold from Chicago were apparently not large. See " Report of the Board of Army Auditors," Illinois, Reports, 1865, II, 595–808.

falling prices at the close of the war. In 1868, Chicago boasted that Field's stood third in the United States, with sales of over ten millions, only Claflin's and Stewart's in New York exceeding the local firm. During that year, Field's moved into "Palmer's Marble Palace" on State Street. This emporium, six stories high, with marble columns, beautiful lighting, and spacious floors, set a new standard for the buying public of Chicago. Everything from hoop skirts and ready-made clothing to notions and perfumes was sold by specially trained clerks, while entire floors were devoted to various classes of goods.[95] Thus, not only was Field's a leader in the dry goods business, but it pioneered as a department store — a development in business organization which was to be of importance in the late years of the nineteenth century.

The rapid growth of this firm is shown by mounting sales even during the postwar period, the gross receipts increasing from $9,447,000 in 1867 to more than $12,000,000 in 1868. Among its competitors were the outstanding wholesale and retail houses of Carson, Pirie and Company, J. V. Farwell and Company, Hunt, Barbour and Hale, and Bowen, Whitman and Winslow. Each of these houses, with the exception of the first, which averaged $700,000 for the two years, had sales in 1866 and 1867 amounting to more than $1,000,000, and Farwell's, next to Field's in prominence, did a business valued at about $7,000,000.[96]

Of importance, too, was the trade in ready-made clothing. Henry A. Huntington, pioneer of the wholesale clothing trade, opened a store on Water Street in 1852. Other firms followed his lead, and by 1859 the ready-made clothing business was considered one of the most extensive in both the wholesale and retail traffic of the city, doing a

---

[95] Marshall Field arrived in Chicago at the age of twenty-two and received $400 for his first year's work as a clerk. In three years he was a partner, and in five years he was the head of a great firm. Field's brother Milton became a partner in the new enterprise for two years, but he then withdrew, Henry Field, H. J. Willing, and L. G. Woodhouse entering the firm, which became known as Field, Leiter and Company. *Chicago Tribune,* October 13, 1868; *Field Papers;* Ferry, *op. cit.,* II, 122.

[96] Ed. S. Austin, comp., *John C. W. Bailey's Chicago City Directory for 1867–68* (Chicago, 1867), pp. 7–8 (hereafter cited as Austin, *Bailey's Directory, 1867–68*); *Chicago Tribune,* January 23, 1868. Of Field's the capital stock from 1869–72 was $1,200,000. (*Field Papers;* Wright, *Chicago,* p. 148.) In 1867, the dry goods houses which reported similar sales were John V. Farwell and Company, $7,109,714; Bowen, Whitman and Winslow, $2,422,505; Hunt, Barbour and Hale, $1,667,946.

business valued at two and one-half millions annually. Wartime demands for uniforms and the changes brought by the introduction of the sewing machine jumped sales of clothing in 1863 to $12,000,000.[97] Many doing business at this time depended on eastern manufacturers for their supplies, but some established their own factories. By 1870, eighty-five firms with a capitalization of nearly $2,000,000 turned out men's and women's clothing valued at $6,469,590.[98]

The opening of the 'fifties saw the establishment of the first exclusively wholesale boot and shoe houses, and by 1864 sixteen firms were engaged in the manufacture and wholesaling of boots and shoes. Two hundred dealers supplied the retail trade of the city, and the amount of goods sold by the jobbing firms was estimated at $3,000,000 annually. Wartime demands stimulated the business, and in 1864 sales amounted to $14,000,000, the greater part accruing from articles of local manufacture.[99]

Hats and caps were also important in the wholesale trade, sales by 1864 approximating $5,000,000. In addition to the retail dealers, nine firms were engaged in merchandising headwear. Often associated with the hat and cap trade was the fur business, which declined as the frontier was pushed farther west. H. B. Smith and Company, however, shipped eastward in the mid-'fifties nearly seventy-five thousand skins of fox, muskrat, raccoon, and other wild animals, as well as thirty-five thousand pounds of deer skins. But the real magnitude of the trade was unknown because of "the secrecy and mystery" with which it was conducted. In the 'sixties a shipment of three thousand buffalo robes from the Rocky Mountain country was said to have been the first brought directly from there. Besides importations from the country roundabout, Chicago merchants sometimes received furs from Europe and the East to be fashioned into finished articles. In 1862, F. W. Lasak and Son of New York, who

97 *The Press and Tribune*, January 2, 1860. There were six wholesale clothing merchants handling the bulk of the business. Among the more prominent were Foreman Brothers, H. W. Hunt and Company, Barrett, King and Company, and Huntington, Wadsworth and Parks. (The Press and Tribune, *Eighth Annual Review, 1859*, p. 32.) Some of the hustling clothiers who gained contracts to furnish large numbers of uniforms were, in 1861, accused of the use of shoddy in outfitting soldiers. *Chicago Tribune*, July 25, 1861; Chicago Tribune, *Sixteenth Annual Review, 1864*, p. 22.

98 United States, *Ninth Census, 1870*, III, " Wealth and Industry," 649.

99 The Press and Tribune, *Eighth Annual Review, 1859*, p. 32; Smith & DuMoulin, *Directory, 1859–60*, p. 33; Chicago Tribune, *Annual Review, 1864*, p. 22.

made extensive purchases in Europe at the Hudson's Bay Company's sales, opened a branch in Chicago under the name of T. B. Morris and Company.[100]

The wholesale grocery trade developed rapidly during the 'sixties, for processed foods of other than local origin were important wants of rural dwellers. By 1860 thirty-four firms, with annual sales averaging from ten to twelve millions of dollars, were underselling St. Louis and drawing trade from all the Northwest. The establishment of the Grocer's Exchange in 1864, located in the Smith and Nixon Building on Washington Street, aided materially in the promotion of business. In these headquarters, telegraphic dispatches of the New York grocery and gold markets were posted daily, and job lots of groceries were sold to out-of-town buyers. This institution supplied a real need and expedited transactions to the satisfaction of both buyer and seller.[101] Some sugar was forwarded, and in 1858 the Chicago Refining Company was established in the city. Salt, sold chiefly to the meat packers, coffee, and tea swelled the number of items not found near at hand which were made available in the Chicago market.[102]

A starch factory utilizing wheat and an establishment for the production of pearlash saleratus appeared. At an early day drugs were supplied to the hinterland by H. Bowman and Company and others; later, Chicago distributors were sending these necessities to California, and, during the war, medical stores for the army were forwarded in large amounts from Chicago. By 1864 those engaged in this trade had formed the Druggists' Trade Association in order to establish fair practices and prevent legislation unfavorable to their interests.

A similar trade was the patent medicine business. Numerous advertisements for these nostrums crowded the pages of the city papers, and the Chicagoan, Walter B. Sloan, who manufactured cures for both man and beast, proudly proclaimed that his medicines were sold in nearly every town in the western states. Tobacco, brought from the South and processed in Chicago by the more than one hundred establishments at the close of the 'fifties, made glad the hearts of

100 *Ibid.; Weekly Chicago Democrat*, June 21, 1856; *Chicago Daily Democrat*, April 5, 1860; Guyer, *op. cit.*, pp. 80–81. The skins were said to bring a profit of 100 per cent at times. Raccoon skins in particular were sent to Europe. *Chicago Tribune*, October 2, 1861, August 7, 1862.

101 *The Press and Tribune*, January 2, 1860; Edwards, *Directory, 1866*, p. 762.

102 *The Press and Tribune*, March 22, December 15, 1859; Wright, *Chicago*, p. 204; *Chicago Tribune, Annual Review, 1869*, p. 69. See pp. 45, 102–3.

smokers, snuffers, and chewers, not only in the city but also in the out-lying territory.[103]

The diversity of products made and distributed by Chicago ex-panded as the years passed. Stoves, hardware, and nails, especially horseshoe nails, went to near-by regions, to which Chicago agents also sold Sheffield cutlery and other imports. A hot-air cooking stove with a double oven, "the Queen of the Prairies," was manufactured in Chicago as early as 1848. By the close of the Civil War there were thirty-nine stove founders, manufacturers, and dealers in the city, dispensing their products from Minnesota to Kansas, and selling their wares in Indiana, Michigan, and Wisconsin, as well as in Il-linois.[104]

In addition to stoves, Chicago foundries manufactured pipe, store fronts, "fire-proof" safes, posts, and bells. Among the brass founders was Richard Teller Crane, who, at twenty-three years of age, poured castings for brass couplings and copper points for lightning rods in a small frame building of his own in a corner of his uncle's lumber yard. Sole employer and employee of the R. T. Crane Brass and Bell Foundry, he probably did not dream, even in his most imaginative yearnings, that some day his name would represent a $100,000,000 corporation.[105]

City foundries turned out lead pipes and fittings, their supplies being drawn from the lead mines at Galena. Much miscellaneous hardware, including lightning rods, refrigerators, and coffee roasters manufactured in the East, was also distributed from Chicago. So

---

[103] *Chicago Daily Journal,* July 1, 3, October 3, 1848, July 6, 1849; *Chicago Daily Press and Tribune,* July 10, 1858; *Chicago Weekly Democrat,* October 15, 1859; *Chicago Tribune,* September 11, 28, 1861, February 2, 1864; *Chicago Daily Democrat,* August 9, 1849, Oc-tober 16, 1851; Chicago Tribune, *Annual Review, 1869,* p. 71. See pp. 440, 451–52.

[104] Guyer, *op. cit.,* p. 52. Hibbard and Spencer, wholesalers, had sales of $200,000 in nails in 1866. (Kelly, *op. cit.,* p. 27; *Daily Democrat,* March 31, 1848; Halpin, *Directory, 1865,* pp. 860–61; Charles H. Atkinson, *Diaries, 1867–68* [*Ms.* Chicago Historical Society].) In 1871, there were fourteen stove manufacturers and wholesale dealers, while sixty-five firms were listed as retail. Richard Edwards, comp., *Chicago (Merchants') Census Report; and Statistical Review* . . . (Chicago, 1871), p. 1240 (hereafter cited as Edwards, *Merchants' Census Report, 1871*).

[105] *Chicago Daily Democrat,* May 16, 1849, October 31, December 24, 1850, April 17, 1851; B. W. Raymond, *Letter Book, 1853–56,* April 19, 1853 (*Ms.* Chicago Historical Society); [Anon.], *History of Crane Company* (Typescript, Crane Company, Chicago); Currey, *Chicago,* II, 259. In 1867, the United States Clock and Brass Company could roll out one ton of brass a day. The *Tribune,* which reported this, pointed out that copper, zinc, and brass could be prepared in Chicago much more cheaply than in the eastern foundries. *Chicago Tribune,* February 20, 1867.

important had the vending of hardware, such as Russian Iron for stovepipes, copper for the bottom of washboilers, well buckets, guns, cutlery, and felloe oilers, become that after the middle 'sixties Hibbard and Spencer advertised and sold its ware in Iowa through a traveling salesman.[106]

The manufacture of agricultural implements was destined to be one of the greatest enterprises of Chicago. Its market extended to the tip of the western agricultural settlement as well as to the older parts of the country. During the 'sixties the value of the products of the four Garden City firms increased nearly 300 per cent. Civil War enlistment, which resulted in a diminution of man power on the farms and made imperative increased use of machinery, contributed greatly to this progress.[107]

Most prominent of the manufacturers of agricultural implements in Chicago was the reaper magnate, Cyrus Hall McCormick, whose business after the dissolution of a partnership with O. M. Dorman, in 1850, became a family concern. McCormick's inventive genius was accompanied by a business ability which increasingly manifested itself during the 'fifties and 'sixties. The number of his machines sold grew from 700 in 1848 to 4,561 by 1858, and ten years later more than twice as many reapers were distributed through the country. The Civil War years found McCormick reapers scattered from coast to coast. Shortly through prizes for demonstrations at the London, Paris, and Hamburg expositions international recognition came to McCormick, who was made a Chevalier of the Legion of Honor in 1868. Although the actual sales in Europe were small at this time, the foundations were laid for the McCormick reaper's conquest of the world market for harvesting machines.[108]

Reapers were also manufactured by the enthusiastic booster, John

[106] The Daily Democratic Press, *Fourth Annual Review, 1855*, p. 17; *Chicago Daily Democrat*, May 16, 1849, January 21, May 19, September 19, 1851; *Chicago Daily Journal*, June 16, 1859; Kelly, *op. cit.*, p. 32. For the amount of lead received, 1853–54, see *Hunt's Merchants' Magazine*, XXXII (June, 1855), 692.

[107] The value of agricultural implements manufactured in 1860 in Chicago amounted to $529,000; in 1870 to $2,081,000. (United States, *Eighth Census, 1860*, "Manufactures," p. 86.) In 1870, Canton, Ohio, however, produced agricultural machinery valued at more than that made in Chicago. United States, *Ninth Census, 1870*, III, "Wealth and Industry," 719; Frederick Merk, *Economic History of Wisconsin During the Civil War Decade* (State Historical Society of Wisconsin, *Studies*, I. Madison, 1916), pp. 145–46.

[108] William T. Hutchinson, *Cyrus Hall McCormick* (2 v. New York, 1930–35), I, 268, 369, 388–89, II, 360–61, 405–22, 435, 440–47.

S. Wright. His firm, established in 1853, turned out the Atkins' Self-Raking Reaper and Mower. Plow making, too, was important, among the promoters being Henry Witbeck, who sold the Premium Steel Clipper Plow and Cultivator. Seed drills, corn shellers, and threshers, bearing the imprint of Chicago, were likewise sent to agriculturists.[109]

The manufacture of railway iron and iron for structural purposes logically followed the establishment of Chicago as a key point in railroad extension. In 1857, Captain Eber B. Ward, who came from Detroit, saw a potential profit in manufacturing rails at this central point and established the Chicago Rolling Mill for the purpose of rerolling iron bars. In 1864, the capacity of the plant, about one hundred tons of iron rails daily, was doubled, and a puddling department was added. Renamed the Chicago Rolling Mills Company, the enlarged enterprise had a capital of $500,000. In the following year it produced the first steel rails manufactured in Chicago, bringing steel blooms for the purpose from Wyandotte, Michigan.[110]

Iron work for bridges, turntables, and other railroad equipment was brought out by the Union Car and Bridge Works, whose plant was built in 1852. In the second year of its existence this company carried on operations for some twenty-four lines of railroads in Illinois, Missouri, and Wisconsin. In Illinois alone, 11,897 linear feet of bridges were completed, and 7,000 feet were partly finished in 1854.[111] This plant furnished the iron for the first railroad bridge across the Mississippi at Rock Island, which was completed in 1856. In 1853, the American Car Company, which led a short existence from 1852 to 1855, when it was absorbed by the Union Car and Bridge Works, turned out seven hundred cars. Locomotives, too, were constructed in Chicago, the first of these, "the Enterprise," being completed by the Chicago Locomotive Company after the building of the Galena

---

[109] The Daily Democratic Press, *Fourth Annual Review, 1855,* p. 27; *Daily Democrat,* January 16, May 16, 1849, January 9, June 16, 28, July 17, 1851.

[110] *The Daily Democratic Press,* September 23, December 24, 1856, September 21, 1857; *The Press and Tribune,* January 6, 1860; *Chicago Tribune,* March 7, 1863; Moses and Kirkland, *op. cit.,* II, 410; Andreas, *History of Chicago,* II, 674; Riley, *op. cit.,* p. 103. A leader in the iron business was Joseph T. Ryerson, a Philadelphian who arrived in Chicago in 1842. By mid-'fifties he had entered the iron business and purchased a dock lot at 218-24 South Water Street where boats unloaded at his warehouse and factory. Joseph T. Ryerson, *Recollections* (Ms. Joseph T. Ryerson Private Collection, Chicago, 1880), p. 1.

[111] In 1853, 250 freight, 30 passenger, and 10 baggage and mail cars were built. *The Daily Democratic Press,* February 16, 1855.

and Chicago Union Railroad. By the late 'sixties the press reported purchases of locomotives by railroads centering in Chicago and noted that the " Henry Keep " and " Rufus Hatch" were among the " very beautiful " ones produced.[112]

In 1867, the Pullman Palace Car Company was organized with a capital of $1,000,000. By 1870 its capital assets were no less than $8,-000,000. This enterprise of George M. Pullman had cars running over fifteen thousand miles of road, and the plant employed three thousand men. The surplus earnings of Chicago capitalists poured in to promote the Pullman Company, whose future at the very beginning appeared bright enough to attract the services of men of railroad experience like H. R. Pierson.[113]

No pig iron was manufactured in Chicago before the Civil War, the rolling mills and other iron works importing their main supplies from Ohio and Pennsylvania and small amounts from Missouri and Scotland. To the north, however, lay the great iron ore deposits of Upper Michigan, which became readily accessible in the last half of the 'fifties. The opening of Escanaba meant that Chicago could tap one of the greatest ore distributing points on the lakes more easily than could Cleveland, an iron-manufacturing point which within a decade was to be eclipsed by Chicago. Moreover, Chicago was advantageously situated so far as freight rates from the Upper Peninsula were concerned, for the ore might serve as ballast cargo for vessels on their return from carrying agricultural produce east.[114]

Fuel for Chicago blast furnaces could also be brought cheaply from the East, for Pennsylvania and Ohio coal were ballast for carriers westward. This coal trade had developed before the war, for the Chicago Gas Works, dating from 1851, required large quantities for fuel. As late as 1871, however, more than half of the coal received came through the lakes. Coal was also carried to the city by the Illinois Central, the Chicago and Alton, and other roads leading from the

[112] The Daily Democratic Press, *Annual Review, 1853*, p. 54, *Annual Review, 1854*, p. 54, *Fourth Annual Review, 1855*, p. 28, *Fifth Annual Review, 1856*, p. 34; *The Daily Democratic Press*, February 16, 1855; *Chicago Tribune*, April 18, 1869.

[113] *Ibid.*, March 19, June 14, 1870; *Field Papers.*

[114] *Memorial to the Government of the United States from the Citizens of Chicago, Illinois, Setting Forth the Advantages of that City as a Site for a National Armory and Foundry* (Chicago, November, 1861), pp. 12 ff.; *Chicago Tribune*, January 3, 1869; Riley, *op. cit.*, pp. 104–5. On February 4, 1864, the *Tribune* proposed to publish a series of articles showing why iron manufactures should be profitable in Chicago. See especially issues of February 5 and March 8, 1864.

southern Illinois coal fields. This coal, however, could contribute little to the development of the iron industry, for it was unfit to use in the blast furnaces of the day.[115]

Recognizing the advantage of a ready market for pig iron, as well as of convenient supplies and satisfactory freight rates for raw materials, a group of capitalists headed by Arthur B. Meeker organized the Chicago Iron Company, whose blast furnaces, with a capacity of thirty-five to forty tons of pig iron daily, were completed in December, 1868. Two years later the Chicago Rolling Mills, which were to grow into the great Illinois Steel Corporation, set up two furnaces at a cost of $250,000. In 1871, Chicago, with four blast furnaces, seemed to a contemporary writer on the verge of a great expansion in the realm of manufacturing.[116] In this industry, as elsewhere, resourcefulness and unified effort were working hand in hand to achieve desired ends. Demands for supplies during the war were, like other supplies furnished, responsible for lifting Chicago high on the ladder of economic achievement.[117]

The leadership which Chicago had in 1871 was, of course, hers, but many of the forces which carried the city to pre-eminence were operative elsewhere in America. The years from 1848 to 1871 were years of economic change and expansion. Other cities situated as was Chicago along water and rail routes joined in the rapid march. At times rival claimants to superiority surpassed the ever ambitious Illinois city. In 1860 Cleveland, for example, was forwarding more livestock than Chicago, and Toledo, Detroit, and Cleveland were sending eastward more flour.[118] In the course of the next ten years, as the center of the wheat-producing area moved west, St. Louis and Milwaukee

---

[115] *Chicago Daily Democrat*, June 7, 1849; Chicago Board of Trade, *Second Annual Statement, 1859*, p. 72, *Fourteenth Annual Report, 1871*, pp. 90–108; *Chicago Weekly Democrat*, May 23, 1857; Ernest Ludlow Bogart and Charles Manfred Thompson, *The Industrial State, 1870–1893* (Clarence W. Alvord, ed., *The Centennial History of Illinois*, IV. Chicago, 1920), p. 421.

[116] *Chicago Tribune*, February 20, 1868, January 3, 1869; Andreas, *History of Chicago*, II, 674; Chicago Board of Trade, *Fifteenth Annual Report, 1872*, p. 9.

[117] From the making of lead bullets, powder pills for "the treatment of rebellion," magazines, and cannon, to the furnishing of subsistence and other supplies, Chicago had profited greatly, leading the *Tribune* to rejoice that there was no danger that grass would grow in the streets. (*Chicago Tribune*, April 29, May 1, 4, 14, 24, June 6, 1861, January 8, 1862.) In 1863, the ammunition fabricated at Chicago cost $8.00 per hundred, while at Springfield it cost $1.125 per hundred. "Reports of the Quartermaster General of the State of Illinois," Illinois, *Reports, 1863*, III, 15–16.

[118] Kohlmeier, *op. cit.*, p. 193.

challenged Chicago as a leading flour-producing center of the West.[119]

The westward direction of agricultural expansion was of great significance in the history of all these cities. It was partially responsible for Chicago's seizing the pork-packing crown from Cincinnati during the Civil War, and in turn for the fact that Chicago was outdistanced in 1870 by Kansas City as a beef-packing center. All Middle America felt the effect of the increased tillage of the soil, and all its cities grasped eagerly the opportunity to be the exchange center of the products of the field for the merchandise and manufactured goods of the East and Europe.

But in spite of the success of her rivals, Chicago was in 1871 the mistress of western commerce. Her advantageous position as the terminal point on lake, canal, and railroad was unique, and her location in the center of a rich farming region was enviable. These were, indeed, important causes of her success. But her success was partly due to the spirit of her citizens, who acknowledged no barrier to progress. And why should they admit any drawbacks, they argued, for did not " the difference between Chicago and St. Louis business men " lie in the fact that the latter wore " their pantaloons out sitting and waiting for trade to come to them," while the former wore " their shoes out running after it "? Indeed, fantastic as it may have seemed, the fulfillment of Mayor Rice's prophecy was not far distant when long lines of spacious storehouses would be filled with the products and manufactures of China, Japan, and the islands of the sea, along with the manufactures of the region near at hand.[120]

[119] United States Treasury Department, *Report on the Internal Commerce of the United States, 1878* (Washington, 1879), Appendix, p. 170; Mildred Eversole, *The Commercial Development of Chicago 1865-75* (unpublished M.A. Thesis, The University of Illinois, 1926), pp. 69-85.

[120] *Chicago Tribune,* August 5, 1868, April 28, 1870.

CHAPTER IV

BANKING, INVESTMENTS, AND FINANCE

A SOUND and abundant currency and a credit machinery adequate for her expanding commerce and industry were great needs of Chicago as the 'forties ended. There were no state banks of issue in the city or in Illinois. Little specie was available, and businessmen were forced to depend on a motley array of currency, which included the fluctuating paper money of other states, city scrip, Cook County warrants, canal scrip, Michigan scrip, railroad scrip, and Indiana land scrip, as well as such miscellaneous business paper as warehouse receipts, and " I.O.U.'s." Counterfeits, at times, were " thick as musquitoes [sic] in dog days," and the general instability of a debased currency racked nerves and hampered progress. Merchants who sent goods east suffered especially. They often needed more than their shipments to cancel indebtedness to eastern creditors, and they could purchase exchange only at a heavy premium.[1]

The provision in the Constitution of 1848 that a state banking law might be framed and submitted for popular approval afforded an opportunity to remedy the situation.[2] Chicago businessmen at once began working for the needed legislation. In December, 1848, the

---

[1] *Chicago Daily Democrat*, December 12, 1849. Monetary quotations given daily in the local press show wide variations in discount and premium. See, for example, *ibid.*, September 30, 1848, April 27, July 16, September 14, November 17, 1849, January 4, 1850, December 11, 1851; *Chicago Daily Journal*, January 22, 1848, December 2, 1850, January 6, 1851.

[2] Emil Joseph Verlie, ed., *Illinois Constitutions* (Illinois State Historical Library, *Collections*, XIII. Constitutional Series, I. Springfield, 1919), p. 84.

Board of Trade framed a general bank bill which provided for the chartering of state banks to be banks of issue, their notes secured by federal or state bonds deposited with the state treasurer and by reserve funds in the banks themselves. Another group of merchants met in January, 1849, and endorsed the proposed creation of state banks, although they disagreed as to the deposit of bonds with the state treasurer. Walter L. Newberry, interested in many business undertakings, reflected the opinion of others when he held that the public should have " generous confidence " in the " honesty and capacity " of bank managers.[3] Downstate Democrats, in alliance with "Long John " Wentworth, suspicious of all banks and looking upon banks of issue as " monsters," were, however, so influential that the legislature failed to enact a law in 1849.[4]

Chicago businessmen were not to be deterred, however, and persisted in protesting the evils of insufficient and unregulated currency and prohibitive rates of interest. Memorials to state legislators to enact a law which would protect the citizen from the flood of paper money from all parts of the United States and Canada continued. In the legislative session of 1851, bank and antibank cohorts clashed again. On January 14, Thomas Dyer of Chicago presented in the General Assembly a new bill, which, with minor alterations, became law in spite of the veto of Governor French.[5]

This law of February 15, 1851, modeled on the New York State free banking system, provided for the deposit with the state auditor of national or state bonds for which circulating notes were to be received. It contained no specific provision for a specie reserve. Banks, set up on a minimum of $50,000 of capital stock, could conduct a general banking business, using notes received from the auditor equivalent to the market value but not above the par value of the deposited federal or state bonds. Illinois securities were to be accepted at 20 per cent less than the average market price during the previous

[3] *Chicago Daily Journal,* December 23, 30, 1848, January 4, 8, 1849. See also *Chicago Commercial Advertiser,* May 16, June 13, October 24, 1849, March 27, April 30, May 29, 1850.

[4] Antibank arguments are given in the *Daily Democrat,* January 10, 11, 17, March 27, November 17, 1848, January 27, February 5, 7, April 12, May 8, December 6, 1849. Wentworth, in spite of his attitude toward banks in general, was not opposed to the creation of banks of deposit and discount and for savings. *Ibid.,* January 27, September 21, 1849.

[5] *Chicago Commercial Advertiser,* March 27, April 30, 1850; *Chicago Daily Journal,* July 29, 1850; William Hudson Harper and Charles H. Ravell, *Fifty Years of Banking in Chicago* . . . (n.p., [1907]), p. 83; Illinois, *House Journal, 1851,* p. 62. For the text of the veto message, see *ibid.,* pp. 474–77.

six months in New York. The auditor was forbidden to issue bills on bonds upon which less than 6 per cent was regularly paid, unless there were deposited at least two dollars in bonds for every dollar in bills issued. Bank notes were payable in legal tender at the "place of business," between the business hours of ten and three o'clock, failing which the holder of the notes presented could start proceedings to close the issuing bank.

The "free" banks established under this law were allowed to exercise general banking powers, but were limited in the amount of real estate they might hold and were allowed to charge not more than 7 per cent interest on loans. Stockholders were individually liable to the amount of their respective shares of capital stock. Quarterly bank reports were required. Supervision of the system was assigned to three bank commissioners, the state treasurer, and the auditor.[6]

In accordance with the constitution, the measure was presented to the people for approval. Chicago voted 2,122 to 79 for ratification. The disappointed (Springfield) *Illinois State Register* called for the names of the seventy-nine who looked to the interest of the state rather than "to the aggrandizement of the brokers' clique of the 'garden city.'" The *Times* of St. Louis declared that the Democrats of Chicago had been cheated into supporting Whigs and Abolitionists. In Chicago, the *Democrat* gave the state majority as seven thousand. "The law is safe," said the editor sarcastically. "Now bring on your 'two dollars a day and roast beef,' gentlemen!" Yet when the Democratic press of the state tried to revive the bank issue, Wentworth advised against it. "These issues have all passed away," he said, "and it appears to us that he does not act very wisely who attempts to recall them." In Chicago, even the antibank Democrats found it a wise policy to accept the mandate of the community and avoid the charge that they were hostile toward the business of the growing West.[7]

The first Chicago bank of issue organized under the new law was the Marine Bank, incorporated by the backers of the Chicago Marine

---

[6] A digest of Dyer's bill is given in the *Chicago Daily Journal*, January 27, 1851. For the text of the law, see Illinois, *General Laws of the State of Illinois . . . 1851* (Springfield, 1851), pp. 163–75 (hereafter cited as *General Laws*).

[7] *Chicago Daily Journal*, November 5, 20, December 5, 1851; *Chicago Daily Democrat*, November 5, 21, 25, December 3, 1851. The state majority for the bill, as computed from figures in the newspaper, was 6,257, the number voting for the bill totaling 37,578. *Ibid.*, December 11, 1851.

and Fire Insurance Company in January, 1852. The charter of the latter company had been revived in 1849, and in 1850 it had resumed business with J. Y. Scammon as president.[8] Its directors established the Marine Bank to profit by a circulating medium. In April, 1852, it received from the state auditor $49,875 in circulating notes, the first such notes sent to Chicago. By autumn, added deposits of bonds had increased this bank's circulating note issue to over $99,000. The chief activity of the Marine Bank, like that of most of the Illinois " free " banks, was the issuance of bank notes. These notes were loaned by the banks to agents who reloaned to borrowers at the market rate of 10 per cent interest, a device adopted to evade the law which forbade " free banks " from receiving more than 7 per cent on their note issues.

Virtually all of the free banks authorized for Chicago before 1860 were organized by private bankers who wished to profit by the control of a circulating medium. They did not, as a rule, carry on commercial banking.[9] By 1854 twenty-nine banks had been organized under the Illinois law of 1851. Ten of these were in Chicago.[10] Their legal notes were redeemable in specie. But the issue of unauthorized currency, subject to discount on redemption, had not ceased. Canny

---

[8] *Ibid.*, February 19, December 6, 1849, January 23, 1850; Andreas, *History of Chicago,* I, 536–37. For the early development of the Chicago Marine and Fire Insurance Company, see Pierce, *History of Chicago,* I, 157, 159–60. An Act of February 12, 1849 (*Private Laws, 1849,* p. 47), extended the act of January 13, 1836, which incorporated the Chicago Marine and Fire Insurance Company, until 1870.

[9] Illinois, *Reports, 1853,* pp. 52–53; United States, *House Executive Documents,* 33 Cong., 1 sess., XII, Doc. 102, p. 162; Rollin G. Thomas, *The Development of State Banks in Chicago* (unpublished Ph.D. Thesis, The University of Chicago, 1930), pp. 34–35; F. Cyril James, *The Growth of Chicago Banks* (2 v. New York, 1938), I, 232–33; Don Marcus Dailey, *The Development of Banking in Chicago before 1890* (unpublished Ph.D. Thesis, Northwestern University, 1934), pp. 116–17; George William Dowrie, *The Development of Banking in Illinois, 1817–1863* (University of Illinois, *Studies in the Social Sciences,* II, no. 4. Urbana, 1913), pp. 138, 143, 160. The Chicago Marine and Fire Insurance Company was the agent for the Marine Bank.

[10] Cole, *The Era of the Civil War,* p. 97. Among the free banks were the City Bank sponsored by D. Ogden Bradley and Charles B. Curtiss, the Bank of America organized by George Smith, the Commercial Bank which the Southwestern Plank Road Company used to legalize its note issue, I. H. Burch's Chicago Bank, the Merchants and Mechanics Bank of Bronson and Company, the Union Bank of Messrs. Forrest, H. A. Tucker and Company's Exchange Bank, and Chase Brothers' Farmers' Bank. Another free bank established in the city was the Phoenix Bank of N. C. Roe and Company. (*The Bankers' Magazine,* VII [November, 1852], 345; United States, *House Exec. Docs.,* 33 Cong., 1 sess., XII, Doc. 102, pp. 165–66; Illinois, *Reports, 1853,* p. 54; Thomas, *op. cit.,* pp. 34–36.) By 1854, the Commercial Bank had gone out of business, but had been replaced by the Bank of Commerce of Davisson and McCalla. James, *op. cit.,* I, 218–20.

George Smith's Wisconsin Marine and Fire Insurance Company put out a great deal of this money. As Smith redeemed his notes at 1 per cent discount while the "free" bankers had to redeem theirs at par, the latter suffered loss of specie and determined to drive Smith out of business. A "tiger fight" against him, captained by Scammon of the Marine Bank, was carried into the city election in the early months of 1852 and led to a contest for municipal deposits. Scammon, who was backing Gurnee, Democrat, for mayor, persuaded Governor Leonard J. Farwell of Wisconsin to bring *quo warranto* proceedings against Smith's insurance company, but nothing came of this action.[11]

In May, 1852, the chartered bankers, reluctant to start a drive for specie payment on Smith's institution for fear of reprisals, tried to bring the redemption value of all notes up to one hundred cents, by means of an exchange of notes each Saturday. This plan was unsuccessful, for Smith would consent only to an arrangement whereby he and Scammon promised that they would each exercise "forbearance toward [the] other," that they would not attempt to hamper the note circulation or create a run on each other's bank. An armed truce followed. The circulation of Smith's insurance company increased to $1,470,000 by December.[12] Some of the banks were beginning to accept Smith's methods. On December 23, Scammon and his allies forced the finding of true bills of indictment against George Smith and other bankers guilty of irregular practices. The accused retaliated by instituting a run for specie payment on their accusers. None of the persons indicted was convicted, and the proceedings were apparently dropped.[13]

Seth Paine, ardent Fourierite, spiritualist, and abolitionist of the

[11] *Chicago Daily Democrat*, February 2, 3, 14, 16, 17, March 3, 1852; Andreas, *History of Chicago*, I, 539; Dowrie, *op. cit.*, p. 140.

[12] Wentworth called on the Board of Trade to take matters in hand and induce the banks to pay specie. Besides other fears on the part of Chicago bankers was the rumor that Smith would use the Bank of America in Washington, D. C., which he had recently acquired, to issue additional notes not payable in specie. Smith denied this rumor. *Chicago Daily Democrat*, April 24, May 4, 6, 24, 1852; Andreas, *History of Chicago*, II, 617; Dailey, *op. cit.*, p. 66a.

[13] *Chicago Daily Democrat*, December 25, 1852; *The Daily Democratic Press*, December 25, 1852. Those indicted were Henry T. Adams and Charles L. Chase of the Farmers' Bank, Levi D. Boone and Stephen Bronson of the Merchants and Mechanics Bank, Thomas McCalla of the Bank of Commerce, W. T. Muir and Seth Paine of the Bank of Chicago, John R. Valentine of the Bank of America, and George Smith and E. W. Willard of the Wisconsin Marine Insurance Company. (*Weekly Chicago Democrat*, January 1, 1853.) It was observed that the indictment did not include certain irregular bankers who were allied with the Scammon group. *Chicago Daily Democrat*, December 25, 1852; Dowrie, *op. cit.*, pp. 140–41.

first degree, added more worries to the load of Chicago bankers when, in October, 1852, he established the Bank of Chicago. Ira B. Eddy soon became its president, and the bank began to issue notes, unique as specimens of art even if quite illegal. According to Paine's pronunciamento, his bank would make no loans for payment of debts, for aiding "in murder of anything which has life," for "speculating in that which is necessary to life," for making or dispensing intoxicating liquors or tobacco, or for the use of gamblers and usurers. No money would be loaned on real estate, for the officers believed that such property could not be bought and sold since "possession with use, is the only title."[14] This basis for banking was unusual enough in itself, but aside from its oddities it was vastly different from the general interest and practice of Chicago during the 'fifties.

The Bank of Chicago charged 6 per cent on its loans, which was considerably less than the usual rate. It aggressively championed the cause of the "mechanic and the common people" who were "crushed by the aristocracy of the money power." Its affairs were so completely intertwined with the religious activities of the Spiritualists, who met in "Harmony Hall" on the floor above the bank, that Chicagoans called it the "Spiritual Bank" and held serious doubts about the sanity of its management. All these circumstances contributed to the animosity with which the more orthodox Chicago bankers regarded this strange institution. In early January, 1853, they threw out its notes. The local railroads took their cue and did likewise.[15] Paine fought bitterly and used the columns of his weekly, the *Christian Banker,* for venomous attacks on his enemies.[16] But the spiritualistic

[14] *Chicago Daily Democrat,* October 18, December 18, 1852; Andreas, *History of Chicago,* I, 540–44.

[15] *The Daily Democratic Press,* December 14, 25, 1852, January 6, 10, 1853; *Chicago Daily Democrat,* December 25, 1852; Andreas, *History of Chicago,* I, 541.

[16] One such personal attack appeared during the final run on the Spiritual Bank: "If a cigar-smoker or a rum-sucker, or hog-eater comes in (for there are such men in Chicago yet), who not only have so little respect for themselves, but actually intrude such offensive influence before us . . . we refuse to do business with them, but send them right over to [R. K.] Swift, who smokes to drown conscience, which has been violated so long by huge shaves [excessive discounts on notes] of his fellow-men, that the hair has all come off over that organ. . . . There all smokers can find sympathy." *Christian Banker,* January 29, 1853, quoted in Andreas, *History of Chicago,* I, 541–42. Eight issues of the *Christian Banker* appeared, according to Franklin William Scott, *Newspapers and Periodicals of Illinois, 1814–1879* (Illinois State Historical Library, *Collections,* VI. Bibliographical Series, I. rev. ed. Springfield, 1910), p. 65.

advice of Alexander Hamilton and George Washington apparently failed Paine and Eddy in the crisis. A run on their bank occurred. During this run, Mrs. Herrick, a medium, sat behind the counter and indicated which depositors should be allowed to redeem notes. When the bank officers were brought to trial, the mediums relied on their spiritual counselors to defend their case. There was a hectic court scene, Eddy was found insane, and Paine was jailed for assault and battery. The doors of the bank were closed by court order in February.[17]

Revision of the banking laws came before the state legislature in 1853. There was strong sentiment in favor of the repeal of the law of 1851, although most Chicago business groups, including the Board of Trade, vigorously opposed such action on the ground that it would cause a derangement of state finances, embarrass business, and disturb property values. The legislature, however, modified certain provisions of the law of 1851, in order to restrict the many issues of unauthorized currency, both domestic and foreign. The act forbade, under heavy penalty, the issuing in Illinois of any medium designed to pass as money other than the bills authorized by the general banking law of 1851. It provided also that the only foreign bank notes which could circulate in the state were those of regular specie-paying banks in the various states and territories and in the provinces of Canada, and that only notes in denominations of five dollars or more were to be received from these. The act was successful in stopping illegal issues, although some small foreign bills continued to circulate. George Smith, finding that he could no longer use the Wisconsin Marine and Fire Insurance Company to issue evidence of debt, sold out his interest.[18]

Under the banking act of 1853 bankers, dealers in merchandise, and others were forbidden to receive or pay out Illinois currency which did not comply with the act of 1851, but they could use notes

[17] The notes submitted by men who were smoking tobacco were categorically refused, and one man was accorded similar treatment on the ground that he was dishonest because he was wearing a gold ring. Despite its many vagaries, this bank occasioned none of its creditors any loss. *The Daily Democratic Press*, February 5–14, 1853; Andreas, *History of Chicago*, I, 543–44.

[18] Act of February 10, 1853, *General Laws, 1853*, p. 30; Dowrie, *op. cit.*, pp. 141–42; *The Daily Democratic Press*, February 9, July 18, August 3, September 12, 1853; "Report of the Bank Commissioners," Illinois, *Reports, 1859*, I, 197; *The Bankers' Magazine*, IX (August, December, 1854), 102–13, 462–66; James, *op. cit.*, I, 231. This act stipulated also that no bank could be incorporated until the paid-in capital amounted to at least $50,000.

issued by specie-paying banks in any other state. Illinois currency must still be redeemed at par, but the notes of other states might be taken up at a discount. Obviously, if a banker were to issue legally in another state notes which he could redeem in Chicago at a discount, he would have the advantage of the free banks.

Late in March, 1853, rumors began to circulate that George Smith and Company had purchased a bank in Georgia and were planning to issue bills there. These rumors were substantiated in April when Smith sent S. C. Higginson to Georgia to take charge of his Atlanta bank.[19] Almost at once the bills of the Atlanta Bank of Georgia appeared in Chicago, and bills from other Georgia banks followed. By mid-1855, Georgia currency made up a large part of the notes in circulation in the city.[20]

So popular were Smith's notes and so widely were they distributed through his Chicago firm and its branches in Galena, St. Louis, and Detroit, that his business enemies joined forces for a concerted attack. A group of brokers and bankers in the lead district of Illinois and southwestern Wisconsin started the fight. Among them were N. Corwith and Company and Elihu B. Washburne of Galena. They soon drew the support of Governor Matteson, Scammon, R. K. Swift, the *Tribune,* and the *Times.* Their first move was to bring about a sustained run on Smith's Atlanta and Griffin banks, beginning in the late summer of 1855. They organized also a press campaign which was successful in so depressing the value of Georgia bank notes in rural districts that the anti-Smith group was able to obtain them at substantial discounts and profit by redemption. Chicago merchants and railroad men divided into opposing camps. Some deprecated the run; others called loudly upon the banks of the Northwest to join them in throwing out Georgia notes. Scammon, Swift, and Officer

[19] George Smith and Company announced that they were personally liable for the bills of the Atlanta Bank which they would receive at Chicago on the same terms as notes of Ohio and Indiana banks, i.e., at 1 per cent discount. In 1855, Smith advertised that he had purchased the majority control of another Georgia bank, the Interior Bank of Griffin, Georgia. *The Daily Democratic Press,* March 28, April 5, 25, 1853, March 14, August 29, 1855.

[20] Other Georgia expansionists included I. H. Burch and Company through the LaGrange Bank, the Merchants and Mechanics Bank through the Cherokee Insurance and Banking Company of Dalton, Georgia (later purchased by N. B. Curtiss and Company of Peoria), H. A. Tucker and Company through the Merchants' Bank of Macon, and David Preston and Company through the Planters and Mechanics' Bank of Dalton, Georgia. (*Ibid.,* April 26, 1853, April 10, October 7, 27, 1854, June 16, 1855, October 22, 1856, November 9, 1857; *The Weekly Democratic Press,* April 26, 1856.) At the beginning of 1855, the circulation of Georgia banks amounted to $2,750,000. Dailey, *op. cit.,* p. 83.

and Brother, of Chicago, and Corwith and several other Galena, Davenport, and Dubuque bankers responded to this call with haste. The run, lasting for four months, forced the redemption of an estimated $500,000 of notes a month and caused a strain on gold reserves in New York. The number of Georgia bank notes decreased greatly. In their stead, notes from Ohio, Indiana, Pennsylvania, Maryland, and other eastern states flowed into the city. The "Georgia War" marked the end of Smith's large-scale note issues.[21]

The free banks were put to a severe test by a minor panic in 1854 which affected the whole nation. Thousands of dollars worth of their notes were presented for redemption. Five of the ten banks in Chicago were forced to close their doors, although the Merchants and Mechanics was later able to reopen with J. H. Woodworth as president. But Chicagoans, fortified by the belief that the city would keep growing until railroads stopped running and inhabitants stopped coming, did not worry greatly about the present condition. Merchants, sharing the optimism, advertised their acceptance of all Illinois bank notes at par, but a scramble for gold soon led them to repent.[22]

In 1857, the legislature attempted to strengthen the free banking system by raising the limit on the interest rate from 7 to 10 per cent. It tried to appease those who had held that bankers should be permitted, in the words of the press, to " receive the same interest which private individuals " were allowed for money loaned, that is " *ten per cent.*" The law prescribed that banks must transact all business at the place specified in their certificates of registration, and that the place must have a population of at least two hundred. This, it was hoped, would do away with the practice of organizing banks where they were not likely to be visited for note redemption. Further pro-

[21] *Ibid.*, pp. 73, 86, 87; *The Daily Democratic Press,* June 16, August 29, September 4, 5, 8, 24, October 1, 9, 16, December 10, 27, 31, 1855, January 5, 7, 21, March 3, 6, 1856; *Weekly Chicago Democrat,* September 8, October 6, 1855; *The Weekly Democratic Press,* December 22, 1855; *Chicago Daily Democrat,* October 1, 9, 1855; *The Bankers' Magazine,* X (January, 1856), 572. Washburne, himself, in late September, 1855, visited Atlanta with notes for redemption and was kept waiting while the bank redeemed the bills one at a time. (*The Daily Democratic Press,* October 1, 1855.) Discount and deposit banking were becoming more important than note issue, and this may also have determined Smith's withdrawal from the field. Thomas, *op. cit.,* p. 44.

[22] *The Free West,* November 23, 1854; James, *op. cit.,* I, 236–37; *The Bankers' Magazine,* IX (April, 1855), 822; *The Daily Democratic Press,* November 17, 18, 20, 27, December 5, 1854, June 16, 1855. The banks which were liquidated at this time were the City Bank, Union Bank, Phoenix Bank, and Farmers' Bank. *Ibid.,* November 16, December 12, 1854.

visions were designed to eliminate the practice of "wearing out" those who presented notes for redemption by forbidding the banks to pay out legal tender on only one bill at a time instead of in a lump sum.[23]

Strengthening the banking system was well justified, for in a short time Chicagoans heard rumblings of the financial storm breaking in the East. But threatening rumors were dismissed with the usual spirit of optimism. No year in history, said journalistic observers, had opened with such brilliant promise for business. Suppose there were unnecessary extravagance, as eastern critics asserted. Had that not always been true? Warnings that Chicago would soon have to pay for her speculations were discounted as nothing more than wails of jealousy from Easterners who resented the heavy migration to the West. To Chicagoans, an estimated half dozen failures in as many months meant only that adventurous and unstable businesses were collapsing. Chicago was not "an experiment, but a success," declared her citizens. Her destiny was "still onward." By summer, however, exchange had become so scarce and loans so difficult to obtain that hard times had to be admitted. By September the panic hit in deadly earnest. The failure of several eastern banks had sad repercussions in Chicago. Runs on Chicago banks started, and private banks began to close their doors. It was slight comfort then to blame the disaster on the duplicity of eastern speculators and "the machinations of Wall street." By October, exchange sold for 10 per cent premium, and gold had reached a premium of 10 and 15 per cent.[24]

The defects of the currency afloat in Illinois daily became more evident. "Wildcat" and "stump tail" issues, unredeemable now in specie, slumped to complete worthlessness. Bank notes of other states were accepted only at large discounts. Even the issues of some eastern banks were discredited. Southern currency was in still "worse repute." Fear surrounded the firesides of rich and poor. Merchants struggled to eliminate Georgia "red-dog currency" and to bar shinplasters. Wholesalers tried to discontinue the acceptance of Nebraska

---

[23] *Ibid.*, November 16, 1854; Act of February 14, 1857, *Laws, 1857*, pp. 23–25. This act also ended the discrimination against Illinois state stocks as the basis for the circulating notes. It made them acceptable on the same conditions as federal and other state stocks.

[24] *Chicago Daily Journal,* April 17, June 10, 1857; *The Daily Democratic Press,* March 21, May 18, 30, September 5, 11, 14, 29, 30, October 1, 5, 12, 19, 1857. Among the private banks which failed were E. I. Tinkham and Company, and R. K. Swift, Brother, and Johnston.

wildcat currency which had become an important part of the circulating medium of the Northwest. When St. Louis merchants discredited Illinois currency and forced it home for redemption, Chicago citizens were faced with grim reality. Higgenbotham and White, important dry goods wholesalers, and Frost and Bradley, lumber dealers, failed early that autumn. Shortly thereafter E. R. Kellogg and Company, dealers in hats, suspended operations with liabilities amounting to $115,000. During 1857 and 1858, 204 business houses were reported to have gone under, leaving debts amounting to over $10,000,000. But although the panic was second only to "the perilous times of 1836–7," the Marine Bank and the Chicago Bank came through unshaken, and so did some of the private institutions. Some note issues were retired, and Chicago bankers accepted the notes of Illinois banks at par. Although the state bonds on which the currency was based declined in value, the decline was covered by additional securities. By mid-December, 1858, the bank commissioners reported that the banking system had weathered the blighting two years just passed and recommended that the legislature allow it to stand, albeit with some modifications.[25]

Only one of the local free banks, the Marine, remained in 1860. Notes of the closed Chicago banks still circulated, but the currency in the city consisted chiefly of the notes of Illinois banks outside the city and issues from other states. The currency of the Illinois banks was backed in considerable part by securities of southern states on deposit with the auditor.[26] As threats of secession multiplied, these securities fell in value, and the note issues became unreliable. To check this fault, leading bankers and businessmen suggested that the banking law be amended to permit issues based on Illinois or United States stocks only. These issues, they suggested, should be redeemable at

[25] *Chicago Daily Democratic Press,* September 19, October 5, 6, 7, 9, 10, 14, November 3, 1857; *Chicago Tribune,* July 28, December 24, 1857; *Chicago Weekly Democratic Press,* November 14, 1857; Cole, *The Era of the Civil War,* pp. 99–100; "Report of the Bank Commissioners," Illinois, *Reports, 1859,* I, 193, 196–97; Dowrie, *op. cit.,* p. 153. The *Bankers' Magazine* reported for the rest of the state of Illinois a total of 504 failures during the biennium, with liabilities of $7,744,200, and for the United States 9,157 failures with liabilities of $387,499,600. *The Bankers' Magazine,* XIII (February, 1859), 641.

[26] On January 1, 1861, there were outstanding notes of the Bank of America, $1,162; Bank of Commerce, $137,170; Chicago Bank, $4,903; Exchange Bank, $493; Marine Bank, $50,000. While the total circulation of Illinois banks at this time amounted to some $12,310,-694, notes of Chicago banks accounted for only $193,728. Chicago Board of Trade, *Third Annual Statement, 1860,* pp. 63–65. See also *Chicago Tribune,* April 4, 1861.

Springfield or Chicago. The Chicago bankers also requested the Illinois banks to curtail circulation of notes.[27]

The legislature responded to these demands and passed the banking law of 1861, which prescribed that notes must be redeemed at Chicago or Springfield, that the only state stocks which could be received as security for note issues were to be Illinois stocks, receivable at par, on and after February 14, 1861, and that, after January, 1862, banks of issue could not discount notes presented for redemption more than .5 per cent. The new law could not take effect immediately. Pending its application, Chicagoans nervously passed bills from hand to hand. So disordered was the condition of banks throughout the country that, after consulting a bank list, a man was liable at any moment to find that the various issues in his wallet were worth less than half their face value. To add to other monetary troubles, counterfeits circulated freely. Even the bank-note detectors which were issued for guidance were not much of a protection. Currency lists, published by merchants, railroads, lumbermen, the Board of Trade, and others seldom were in agreement.[28]

Bankers were so uncertain about the value of state currency that by spring they were discriminating against bills of some Illinois and Wisconsin banks. In mid-May they were charged with hoarding bills based on the bonds of the northern states and circulating debased currency secured by southern state issues, thus advancing the price of exchange. No man, wrote the editor of the *Democrat,* was " safe in sleeping over night with a dollar of Illinois currency in his pocket," while bankers were fertilizing their resources "by grinding to the dust the widows and orphans of Chicago," and by paying laborers in " miserable wild cat." Even the schoolteachers faced the possibility of having their wages paid with depreciated currency worth about 65 per cent of the money due them. The banking system was on the verge of a collapse.[29]

---

[27] *Ibid.,* November 10, 21, December 8, 1860, January 14, 16, 1861; *The Bankers' Magazine,* XV (January, 1861), 584–85.

[28] Act of February 14, 1861, *Public Laws, 1861,* pp. 39, 41. Until January, 1862, state banks could redeem their notes at .75 per cent discount. William O. Scroggs, *A Century of Banking Progress* (New York, 1924), pp. 160–61; *Chicago Weekly Tribune,* May 23, 1861; *Chicago Bank Note List,* July 15, October 15, 1862, June 1, November 16, 1863.

[29] *Chicago Weekly Tribune,* May 2, 16, 1861; *The Bankers' Magazine,* XV (May, 1861), 916; *Chicago Weekly Democrat,* May 18, 1861; *Chicago Tribune,* July 6, 9, 13, 1861; Dailey, *op. cit.,* pp. 146–47. By November, 1866, the total bank-note circulation of the Illinois free

Establishment of a specie basis seemed the only solution, even though it would mean hardship for a community whose " pecuniary necessities have overridden their pecuniary sense." When, in the summer of 1861, Congress authorized the issue of $50,000,000 of demand notes, the *Tribune* welcomed them as the salvation of the money system of the country and declared that they would be opposed only by the " debt factories " called banks.[30]

The suspension of specie payments by New York banks in December, 1861, and by the federal government in January, 1862, and the issue of greenbacks, under the act of February 25, 1862, brought about a rise in the premium of gold in terms of notes. Notes of state banks increased in circulation when the treasury notes were made legal tender, and state bank notes could be redeemed in a medium other than specie. Such notes and the new greenbacks were absorbed by the West in considerable amounts.[31] To meet the great need for fractional currency, tradesmen's tokens, postage stamps, city railway tickets, and " postal currency " in the form of small greenbacks were introduced. Even the " promises to pay " or " shinplasters " issued by retailers and tradesmen passed from hand to hand.[32] Until the close of the war, the prices of products tended to vary with the quotations of gold in terms of greenbacks, and the value of the greenbacks rose and fell as the fortunes of the federal government waxed or waned. Wide fluctuations increased the ever present speculative zeal, and inflationists and contractionists carried on a running battle.[33]

In January, 1865, a group of businessmen, including members of the Board of Trade, established the first Chicago Stock Exchange to bring together the buyers and sellers of gold, government bonds, and

---

banks had declined to $35,046, of which only $8,361 were issued by Chicago banks. Illinois, *Reports, 1867*, I, 114–15.

[30] *Chicago Weekly Tribune*, May 23, 30, October 17, 1861; *Chicago Weekly Democrat*, May 25, 1861; *Chicago Tribune*, September 14, 1861.

[31] Don C. Barrett, *The Greenbacks and Resumption of Specie Payments, 1862–1879* (Harvard Economic Studies, XXXVI. Cambridge, 1931), pp. 14, 18, 24; Wesley Clair Mitchell, *A History of the Greenbacks, with Special Reference to the Economic Consequences of their Issue: 1862–65* (Chicago, 1903), pp. 40–41, 145–48, 182–83, Appendix A, p. 425. From the time the banks suspended specie payments until the introduction of the currency provided for in the National Banking Act, state bank notes were the chief circulating medium in Chicago. Thomas, *op. cit.*, p. 61.

[32] *Chicago Tribune*, December 4, 1860, July 14, 16, 18, 1862, January 1, 9, 25, 1863, January 10, 1868; *Prairie Farmer*, n.s. X (July 26, 1862), 57.

[33] Taylor, *History of the Board of Trade*, I, 347–48; Mitchell, *op. cit.*, Appendix A, pp. 425, 428.

various securities.[34] In buying and selling gold for profit, Chicago
followed the example of New York, where dealing in gold began
as early as January, 1862, and where a formal gold exchange was established in October, 1864. The prices of gold were telegraphed to Chicago and served to govern operators in this city.[35] The Chicago transactions in the spring of 1865 were large, but when, with the close of
the war, the premium on gold steadied, interest in the exchange declined. By the spring of 1866 it was practically defunct. The premium on gold remained steady until 1869. Then in April, May, and
June of that year there were wide fluctuations, as Gould and Fisk
and their associates began the operations which led to " Black Friday "
in September. Once again Chicago businessmen and speculators
were impelled to buy gold to protect themselves or to make a profit.
On April 27, the incorporators of the second stock exchange met and,
in October, the exchange opened for business. Its transactions were
extremely small, and it failed to reopen after the fire of 1871.[36]

The solution of the currency problem in Chicago finally came with
the establishment of the National Banking System in 1863. Secretary
of the Treasury Chase had paved the way toward such a system by
his suggestion, in December, 1861, that certain organizations be given
permission to circulate bills furnished by the federal government.
For more than a year this project languished, but in February, 1863,
the National Currency Act was passed by Congress and signed by the
President. Under the provisions of this act, rightly hailed by the
Tribune as the dawn of the " era of true banking," the First National
Bank of Chicago was organized, and approved, June 22, 1863, by
Comptroller of the Currency Hugh McCulloch. This institution, the
second national bank in the country to begin business under the new
act, opened its doors on July 1, 1863. One year later, Chicago had
seven national banks with an aggregate capital of nearly $2,000,000.

[34] John C. Hilton, president, Calvin T. Wheeler, first vice-president, Solon McElroy,
secretary, and William H. Goodnow, treasurer, were officers of the exchange as well as members of the Board of Trade. Halpin, *Directory, 1865–66*, Appendix, p. xii; Wallace Rice, *The
Chicago Stock Exchange, A History* (Chicago, 1928), p. 9.

[35] Mitchell, *op. cit.*, pp. 183–85; Taylor, *op. cit.*, I, 313–14.

[36] On May 13, 1865, rooms of the exchange were opened at 57 Dearborn Street. Four
seats under the railing were auctioned off for $100, $105, $135, and $115. Other seats were
sold as high as $425 and as low as $30. (*Chicago Tribune*, May 15, 1865, January 1, 1866;
Rice, *The Chicago Stock Exchange*, pp. 9–11; *Chicago Republican*, October 19, 1869.) The
incorporators of the second stock exchange elected D. H. Denton, president, Christian Wahl,
vice-president, J. J. Richards, secretary, and James E. Tyler, treasurer. Taylor, *op. cit.*, I, 383.

By 1871 there were seventeen. In less than six years their loans and discounts and individual deposits had increased over threefold, and their invested capital had nearly doubled. During the same period bankers' balances quadrupled, and the total resources of these national banks increased 141 per cent.[37]

The establishment of a Chicago clearing house naturally followed the stabilizing of banking. Previously, porters had daily carried back and forth the checks drawn and the money to settle balances between the banks. The Chicago Clearing House, similar in many respects to the New York Clearing House, and headed for the most part by officials of the national banks, began business on April 6, 1865. The clearances for the first three days amounted to some $3,039,400, and by 1870, annual clearances of more than $810,676,000 and balances of over $80,910,400 represented the usefulness of this aid to financial steadiness.[38]

The establishment of a sound currency removed the problem of excessive rates of exchange. It had been at times extremely difficult for Chicago merchants to liquidate their eastern indebtedness because of the balance of trade against Chicago.[39] When financial blocks had occurred in seaboard cities and dealers there had ceased produce purchases, exchange had been extremely scarce and very expensive in Chicago. In 1856, for example, exchange on New York sold in Chicago at .75 to 1.5 per cent premium, but when the panic struck in 1857 it rose to 10 per cent. During 1859 it ranged from par to 3 per cent. Political disorder in the following year sent it again to 10 per cent. In New York the Illinois banks were regarded as so insecure

[37] Henry C. Morris, *The History of the First National Bank of Chicago* . . . (Chicago, 1902), pp. 40–44, 52–54. On January 1, 1866, the *Chicago Tribune* rejoiced that the national tax on state notes had effected a sound currency. From 1861 until passage, the *Tribune* had advocated a national law taxing the state bank notes out of existence. *Chicago Tribune*, January 18, 1862; *Chicago Weekly Tribune*, October 17, 1861, January 1, 1863. See also J. Medill to Lyman Trumbull, January 28, 1863, *Trumbull Papers*, LIII; J. Medill to E. B. Washburne, May 24, 1862, April 12, 1864, *Washburne Papers*, XXV, XLV; James, *op. cit.*, I, 341–42; *The Bankers' Magazine*, XIX (October, 1864), 314; Thomas, *op. cit.*, pp. 63–64; Edwards, *Directory, 1871*, pp. 980–81.

[38] The first president of the Chicago Clearing House Association was W. F. Coolbaugh, president of the Union National Bank. *Chicago Tribune*, January 1, 1866, January 4, 1868; Edwards, *Merchants' Census Report, 1871*, p. 1231; *The Bankers' Magazine*, XIII (January, 1859), 586.

[39] In 1860, for example, Chicago's imports were valued at about $97,000,000 and its exports at $72,700,000. Chicago Board of Trade, *Third Annual Statement, 1860*, p. 93. See also p. 136.

that their notes at times were accepted only at ruinous rates of discount. This further aggravated the exchange condition. When neither currency nor produce could be sent to the East, the only other medium of exchange was the scarce specie, which also sold at a premium. With the establishment of a uniform currency in both East and West, notes were exchanged at par, and the rate of exchange became a negligible factor.[40]

In addition to the banks of issue organized under the Free Banking Act of 1851 and the national banks which came into existence in 1863 and after, one other class of legally authorized banks carried on business in the city. These were the specially chartered state banks. Some were primarily commercial banks, others were chiefly savings banks, and some combined features of both types of banking. The Merchants' Savings, Loan, and Trust Company, chartered in 1857, was principally a commercial bank. It had large loans and discounts and large deposits subject to check, but a relatively small total of savings deposits. The Illinois Savings Institution, also chartered in 1857, and sponsored by such men as John H. Kinzie, William B. Ogden, and Gurdon S. Hubbard, was of the savings type. At one time it had an estimated $4,000,000 in deposits. It has been said that the chief significance of these specially chartered banks was that they helped to undermine " the dominance of the private bankers " during the 'fifties and 'sixties and " bridged the gap between the collapse of Illinois' first general banking system " (that of 1851 and after) and her second banking system inaugurated in the 'eighties. By 1871, Chicago had sixteen special charter banks. They were, however, far less important than the national banks.[41]

While banks of issue were attempting to supply the currency needs of the city, private banks were doing much of the commercial bank-

---

[40] *Chicago Tribune*, January 1, 1861. The *Tribune's Annual Review, 1864,* p. 1, stated: " In former years, in the best times, Exchange on New York has ruled from 1 to 5 per cent, liable to be carried by the lightest panic to 18 or 20 per cent. This burden and this peril have been lifted from our trade. Exchange on New York throughout the year has averaged at par." At the close of this period the difference for exchange was due chiefly to the express charges for shipment of money, a margin which was not always in favor of the East. Colbert, *Chicago*, p. 81.

[41] The Illinois Savings Institution was later known as the State Savings Institution. (Dailey, *op. cit.*, pp. 159–61, 163–66, 168–69, 174, 190, 261–64; James, *op. cit.*, I, 256–57, 377; Thomas, *op. cit.*, pp. 49, 68, 70, 75–79.) Something of the relative strength of the state and national banks can be gathered from the fact that the capital, surplus, and profits of the former in 1871 were about $3,729,000; of the latter, $10,745,500. *Ibid.*, pp. 70, 72–73.

ing. The directory of 1849–50 lists ten such firms in the city. At the outbreak of the Civil War there were thirty-one, but by the close of the struggle the number had shrunk to twenty-one. These ephemeral private banks were a little like old-fashioned country stores in that they handled a miscellaneous array of business. They sold exchange, received deposits, discounted notes, cared for investments, conducted a pawnshop business, handled real estate, solicited immigrants in Europe, and engaged in the produce trade. Each tended, however, to have its own specialty. They were subject to no legal regulation and were organized and liquidated with little " formality." Important among them were the firms of George Smith, R. K. Swift, Hoffman and Gelpcke, and Greenebaum Brothers.[42]

The field of finance and commercial banking in Chicago was dominated by these private banks until the national banks, with their greater capital, largely took it over. The specially chartered state banks, particularly at the close of the 'sixties, also engaged in the financing of Chicago's produce, provision, lumber, and wholesale trades.

Bankers found financing the produce trade comparatively simple as long as the producers brought their own grain to market and received currency in return. But as the transportation system was extended and country dealers from remote points began consigning large quantities of grain to Chicago dealers, it was not always practical to return currency to these middlemen. The use of checks drawn against the proceeds of loans made by the Chicago banks had become an accepted practice by the early 'fifties. E. H. Hadduck, a commission merchant, to pay for purchases of wheat during the first three weeks of November, 1855, drew checks on the Marine Bank which amounted to over $1,200,000. One of his checks was for $92,000. Country banks, as correspondents of the Chicago banks, held produce drafts on Chicago houses and used these bills to obtain currency from the city banks.[43]

The produce was financed while in storage in the city by loans secured by the goods in store. The forerunners of such loans were

[42] *The Bankers' Magazine*, XV (June, 1861), 956–57, XIX (March, 1865), 710–11; Harry L. Severson, *History of Investment Banking in Chicago* (Ph.D. Thesis in progress, The University of Chicago), pp. 84–85. See pp. 7, 122, 124–26, 146.

[43] *The Daily Democratic Press*, September 12, 1853, July 23, November 19, December 19, 1855; Dailey, *op. cit.*, pp. 177–78; *The Press and Tribune*, August 25, 1859.

"the advances on property left on sale" by the commission houses, which at times were similar to banks in their operations. Gradually a regular system of loans on warehouse receipts developed. Up to the mid-'sixties warehouse receipts served as collateral for bank loans as well as readily negotiable paper among commission merchants. But they could easily be forged, and when the Supreme Court decided that mere deposit or transfer of warehouse receipts without actual transfer of grain or other property was a transaction conveying no responsibility, their value as collateral was impaired.[44]

The banks probably furnished funds also for various speculative activities. When, in 1865, a "close" money market made it difficult for legitimate dealers to operate, the *Tribune* charged that bank directors and heavy stockholders were "the leading operators in gambling transactions," as speculation in grain was sometimes called.[45]

Although a considerable part of the eastward produce shipments was financed by the seaboard banks, local institutions also carried a share of this financing. Bills of exchange were commonly used by Chicago bankers for this purpose. They were referred to in the newspapers as "bills on New York," "short produce bills on New York," and, after 1856, simply as "produce paper." Bankers liked them because of their self-liquidating characteristics and period of short maturing, and often took them "to the exclusion of promissory notes."[46] This was particularly true in the grain trade, which was carried on from April to November when lake navigation was open. The Chicago dealer shipped his grain, had his bill discounted, and used the currency or credit so obtained to purchase more grain.[47]

In the meat trade, because packing was done in a season when navigation was closed and meat products could not go forward at once,

---

[44] *The Bankers' Magazine*, XX (June, 1866), 986, XXI (January, 1867), 556. See also Dailey, *op. cit.*, pp. 208–9; *The Daily Democratic Press*, September 17, 1856.

[45] *Chicago Tribune*, September 19, 1864, September 15, 18, 19, 1865, March 31, 1871.

[46] *Weekly Chicago Democrat*, October 26, 1847; *Chicago Tribune*, October 10, 1869; Dailey, *op. cit.*, pp. 196, 217–19. See *The Daily Democratic Press*, August 20, September 10, 1856, August 22, 1857, for credit facilities offered the lumber trade. The lumber dealers received much help from local capital.

[47] It is interesting to note that in August, 1857, Chicago bankers were accommodating dealers with local discounts to a fair extent only if they were regular customers. But these same bankers were accepting all the produce paper on Buffalo, Oswego, and New York that was offered. (*The Weekly Democratic Press*, August 8, 1857.) In September, 1860, some banks paid out currency on more than $100,000 worth of produce paper a day "besides paying the checks of their customers." *The Press and Tribune*, September 12, 1860.

a long-term form of credit, the promissory note, was used.[48] So large were the demands of the packers during the packing season that though currency released from the grain trade was then available and the banks acted " with all the liberality in their power," it was sometimes difficult to meet their needs. After the completion of the eastern rail lines, provisions could be shipped eastward without regard to the navigation season. Then bills of exchange, which could be quickly redeemed, were sold against meat products. As these winter shipments eased the credit facilities of the Chicago banks, Chicago packers gradually found it possible to adjust shipments to demands. To avoid payment of exchange they agitated for a local financing of their operations by means of the promissory note. Although local banks were reluctant to tie up their funds in this manner the packers gained their point in the autumn of 1860, when produce shipments dropped sharply and the banks had large quantities of currency. In December, large discounts payable in Chicago were given reliable houses which then did not have to make payments in New York.[49]

The currency which Chicago bankers furnished to the produce merchants of the city was paid out by them to the producers and flowed back to the city to finance the mercantile trade. Further aid to this trade was given through the correspondents of Chicago banks. Trade carried on primarily with the East received part of its support locally. Much of it, however, was financed in the eastern cities. When holders of notes given by Chicago merchants got short of funds, they sometimes had the notes sold at high rates in the Chicago market, a practice which led to eastward currency shipments and contributed to currency shortages in Chicago.[50]

A widening of the Chicago money market occurred as the extension of the produce, provision, lumber, and wholesale trades drew Chicago bankers into closer relationship with the country banks. As the trade area expanded through railroad development, Chicagoans

---

48 The promissory note was referred to in the financial columns as " business paper," " local paper," " general commercial paper," and commonly, in the late 'fifties and subsequent years, as " commercial paper." See *The Chicago Times*, July 16, September 9, 1859; Dailey, *op. cit.*, p. 199.

49 *The Chicago Times*, November 28, 1858; *Chicago Daily Democratic Press*, November 23, 1857; *The Press and Tribune*, March 30, 1859; Dailey, *op. cit.*, pp. 220–25; *Chicago Tribune*, December 24, 28, 1860.

50 *The Daily Democratic Press*, January 7, 1856, June 15, November 9, 1857; Dailey, *op. cit.*, p. 197; *Chicago Daily Democrat*, August 20, 1853; *Chicago Tribune*, March 11, 1871.

began to dream of making their city a great financial center. In 1854, it was proposed that the western bankers should come to an understanding which would protect their common interests and decide upon a financial center for their operations. Chicago boosters pointed to economies in time, travel, transfer of funds, and adjustment of balances between the different banking houses, which would be possible if their city were selected. If Chicago were chosen, they declared, the Wall Street stock and bond market would be transferred to the West; "Hither would come the 'bulls and bears' with their capital and shrewdness"; hither, too, would come "European orders for investment."[51]

Despite this wishful pronouncement, the development of Chicago as a banking center came about slowly. Gradually, however, the banks of Illinois, Iowa, and Wisconsin began to solicit Chicagoans for the business of making collections in country towns. Because Chicago was a great export point, funds were sent from Indiana, Missouri, Wisconsin, and other places to purchase the exchange on New York which the Chicago banks were able to accumulate. Rediscounting notes for country correspondents and the redemption of uncurrent note issues for other banks became a service. By the spring of 1861, it was reported that many of the deposits in Chicago banks belonged to country banks, although it is improbable that the aggregate of bankers' deposits in the city was more than $1,000,000.[52]

An impetus was given interbank relations when the Illinois Banking Act of 1861 designated the banks of Chicago, as well as of Springfield, as agents for the redemption of state bank notes; and a great step forward was taken when the National Banking acts of 1863 and 1864 named Chicago as a reserve or redemption city. Under the requirements of the 1864 revision of the National Banking Act, banks outside the redemption cities were permitted to count deposits in reserve city banks as three fifths of their required 15 per cent reserves, a privilege of which they took advantage increasingly during the succeeding decade.[53]

By the middle of 1871, some 245 national banks had been estab-

[51] *The Daily Democratic Press,* September 6, 1854.

[52] *Ibid.,* October 1, 1855; *The Weekly Democratic Press,* October 18, 1856; *The Press and Tribune,* August 22, 1860; *Daily Chicago Journal,* November 4, 1854; *Chicago Tribune,* April 13, 1861; Dailey, *op. cit.,* p. 358.

[53] Margaret G. Myers, *The New York Money Market: Origins and Development* (New York, 1931), pp. 223, 226, 227, 235–36.

lished in the Chicago trade area. Most of these probably had their Chicago correspondents. Chicagoans proudly pointed to the report of the Comptroller of the Currency for 1871, which showed Chicago bank balances due national banks as $5,272,168, and to state banks, as $4,429,832; while St. Louis banks had $1,139,572 of the former and $852,165 of the latter, and Milwaukee had $421,956 of the former and $199,269 of the latter.[54] By 1868, currency was being shipped from the city to Milwaukee and to northern Iowa, Wisconsin, and Minnesota. It needed no more than this to prove to Chicagoans that their city was the " money center of the West." [55]

Such investment banking as was carried on in Chicago during the 'fifties was handled in the main by the private bankers, but later state and national banks also engaged in this business. Much of this activity had to do with real estate, for mortgages and other building investments appeared to be the chief form of long-time loans which appealed to Chicagoans of that day.

As canal and railroad opened avenues of settlement and trade, real estate as an investment became increasingly attractive, not only within the confines of the city but in the outlying region as well. By 1853, territory had been added by the legislature to the three natural divisions of Chicago formed by the Chicago River and its two branches. In 1853, 1863, and 1869, acts of the legislature extended the corporate limits of the city still farther in all directions. The South Side, the center of early investments, outgrew its old limits. The West Side, considered " country " but a few years earlier, became the scene of great activity, especially after the opening of the Illinois and Michigan Canal in 1848. At the same time, the North Side experienced a commercial development stimulated by the coming of the Galena and Chicago Union Railroad. People moved here and there, new centers of fashion and of business grew up, and amid the bustle and change fortunes were made.

The main business district, lying in the South Division in the 'forties, had its wholesale center on South Water Street and its retail

[54] These figures are of October 2, 1871, and include the trade of Chicago with the states of Illinois, Wisconsin, Minnesota, Iowa, Missouri, Kansas, and Nebraska. United States Comptroller of the Currency, *Report . . . to the Second Session of the Forty-Second Congress of the United States, December 4, 1871* (Washington, 1871), pp. 628–29, 630, 632–33, 634–36.

[55] *Chicago Republican*, September 27, 1866, October 16, 1867; *Chicago Weekly Journal*, May 13, August 26, 1868.

center on Lake Street until after the Civil War. By the mid-'fifties, Lake Street was without a vacant lot from the river on the west to the Illinois Central depot on the east, and retailers were extending south-ward along the north-south streets from State Street west. Business blocks replaced the "rookeries" that had lined LaSalle, Dearborn, and near-by streets; and iron fronts, which permitted the enlarge-ment of display windows, took the place of heavy stone store fronts with their forbidding square brick columns. In the postwar years Lake Street lost its leadership as a business avenue. When, in 1865, the Board of Trade moved from LaSalle and South Water to LaSalle and Washington, it created a new financial center. About this time retailers of men's clothing made a similar southward move to Clark and Madison, which in 1869 was considered one of the leading retail business corners of Chicago.

But the shift of retail trade to State Street in the later 'sixties proved to be the most lasting in importance. Potter Palmer, with a fortune of several millions derived from the sale of his retail business and from cotton speculation during the Civil War, purchased large front-ages along State, widened the street by moving back the buildings which faced it, and built a hotel at State and Quincy and a large store at State and Washington. Then he persuaded Field, Leiter and Com-pany to move into this new store. Other retailers followed their lead to this section, and wholesalers rushed into the Lake Street area thus vacated.[56]

During the postwar years, too, business began to encroach on Wa-bash and Michigan avenues, which, up to that time, had been a neigh-borhood of fashionable and well-to-do homes. As early as 1866, com-merce, "progressing eastward," had reached Michigan Avenue; four wholesale houses were put up a short distance south of Lake Street. A year and a half later, retail and wholesale establishments appeared as far south on Wabash as Jackson Street, and on Michigan they sprang up between Madison and Washington streets.[57]

As business areas expanded, the homes of both rich and poor were

[56] Homer Hoyt, *One Hundred Years of Land Values in Chicago* (Chicago, 1933), pp. 89–90; The Daily Democratic Press, *Fourth Annual Review, 1855*, pp. 55–57; *Chicago Daily Democrat*, April 23, 1850; *The Daily Democratic Press*, June 6, 1855, January 1, 1856; Taylor, *op. cit.*, I, 329–30.

[57] E[lias] Colbert and Everett Chamberlin, *Chicago and the Great Conflagration* (Cin-cinnati, 1871), pp. 174–75; *Chicago Tribune*, August 9, 1866, January 5, 1868. In 1871, real and personal property north of Harrison Street, in the business section of the South Division,

pushed into what had once been thought "the country." The fashionable avenues of the 'fifties, Michigan and Wabash, lengthened; and Prairie and Calumet came to be the locale of the wealthy. On Michigan Avenue was the much-talked-of Terrace Row, limestone-front dwellings designed in 1856 by W. W. Boyington for eleven families, at costs ranging from eighteen to thirty thousand dollars. On Prairie Avenue, between Twentieth and Twenty-first, Louis Wahl's stately sandstone mansion with its mansard roof and costly frescoing, commenced in 1871, stood among other edifices of the rich.[58] In spite of this South Side development, other men of wealth and prominence, including William B. Ogden, E. B. McCagg, Julian Rumsey, and Walter L. Newberry, lived on the North Side, called by some "the seat of the real aristocracy of the city." In the western section of the city among less pretentious dwellings was the $200,000 house of Peter Schuttler, whose wagon business had returned rich dividends. During these years expensively built homes appeared on Washington, Ashland, Park, and Warren streets.[59]

Throughout the city those who had bought land in 1848 or 1850 saw their investments multiply three to ten times in less than ten years. A boom which began in 1853 in three years raised the prices on property at the corner of Clark and Lake streets from $400 a front foot to $1,250. Land near State and Twelfth streets which had sold for $200 an acre in 1845 brought $20,000 in 1856. Much of this appreciation was, however, wiped out during the panic of 1857, which destroyed the equities of many investors, especially of those who had bought "on time." Land sales moved slowly until 1862, when the stimulus of wartime profits led to renewed buying.

During 1862, large sales of land in Chicago and in the near-by country were heralded as proof that a new era of prosperity was dawning. Building took on new life. In 1864, improved business

---

was considered worth about one third of all property in the city. This area covered about three fourths of a square mile.

[58] Homes in Terrace Row were owned, among others, by P. L. Yoe, J. Y. Scammon, H. T. Dickey, P. F. W. Peck, B. F. Sherman, and Tuthill King. Bross, *History of Chicago*, p. 117; Samanda King Farlin, *Account, Terrace Row Papers* (Ms. Chicago Historical Society); Ferry, *Reminiscences of John V. Farwell*, II, 249; W. Thorn & Co., *Chicago in 1860; a Glance at its Business Houses* (Chicago, 1860), p. 202; Hoyt, *op. cit.*, pp. 93–94; Everett Chamberlin, *Chicago and its Suburbs* (Chicago, 1873), pp. 240–43, 258; [Anon.], *Chicago, A Strangers' and Tourists' Guide* . . . (Chicago, 1866), pp. 92–94.

[59] *Ibid.*, pp. 90–92; Pierce, *As Others See Chicago*, p. 157; Hoyt, *op. cit.*, pp. 94–95; Chamberlin, *op. cit.*, pp. 253–57; W. Thorn & Co., *op. cit.*, p. 203.

property in the downtown district rose 20 per cent, and rents went skyward. Some seven thousand buildings had been constructed or remodeled in 1863, and the next year expenditures on eight thousand reached $4,700,000. The boom seemed almost "like a dream." In spite of higher costs of labor and materials, the next three years witnessed greatly increased activity.[60] Labor unrest and high costs of material tended in 1867 to retard the expansion so well started, but the next year brought a revival of building. The erection, in 1868, of large business blocks, such as those put up by Cyrus H. McCormick at Michigan Avenue and Lake Street, the Merchants' Insurance Company at Washington and LaSalle streets, and Potter Palmer's block on State Street, indicated that general conditions had really improved. Workingmen's cottages, especially in the Bridgeport and Holstein districts and in the section between Twenty-second and Thirty-second streets, relieved a shortage of dwellings for laborers and served to reduce rents about one third.

Orgies of speculative buying and selling continued throughout 1868 and 1869. Owners of lots south of Twenty-second Street got from $100 to $150 a foot, or five times the 1866 price. In February, 1868, the "Douglas Tract," two miles south of Hyde Park along the lake, was auctioned off at prices as high as $2,000 an acre for land which had cost about $200 an acre in 1857. By the middle of March, weekly transfers of property of $757,098 were hailed as probably the largest in the history of the city, but even this figure was dwarfed in May when real estate exchanges for a single week reached $1,-133,526.[61]

As transportation facilities improved, owners of property in the suburbs profited by a rapid rise in prices. In Hyde Park, land at the corner of Fifty-first Street and Hyde Park Avenue, which had cost $8.00 a front foot in 1865, skyrocketed to $50 in 1870 and to $100 three years later. Paul Cornell, who had laid out Hyde Park in 1856, also pushed his interests farther south. In 1865, he bought land in the neighborhood of Grand Crossing for $25 an acre, and eight years later

[60] Hoyt, op. cit., pp. 67, 69, 74–76, 80, 82, 86, 340; Colbert, op. cit., p. 21; Chamberlin, op. cit., pp. 201–2; John S. Wright, Investments in Chicago (Chicago, 1858), p. 1; Chicago Daily Press and Tribune, September 2, 1858; Chicago Tribune, May 10, 1862, October 8, 9, 1863, January 1, 1864, November 22, 1865, November 10, 1866.

[61] Ibid., January 4, 1861, January 6, 1862, January 31, February 19, 29, March 17, 20, April 22, May 12, August 18, 1868, May 20–24, 1869; Hoyt, op. cit., p. 73. Bridgeport was near Ashland and Archer avenues; Holstein was at Western and Fullerton.

he sold it for $3,000 an acre. About the same time Cleaverville experienced a similar rise, land which had cost Charles Cleaver $625 an acre in 1866–67 bringing him $1,600 an acre in less than five years.[62]

The capital invested in real estate rendered good returns not only when sold, but also when rented. In 1848, rentals in the business section were said to bring from 6 to 9 per cent on the original investment, with taxes paid by the lessee. Good brick stores in the business district and constructed for $3,000 rented for $800 to $850 a year. After deducting a tax allowance, this amount was equivalent to a return of about 10 per cent on both the building and the land. By 1856, rents had appreciated so much that the initial costs of building were reported frequently paid in two or three years, and as much as 18 per cent was earned at times on the total expended. Houses seemed an equally lucrative investment, their rental in one year sometimes almost matching the original cost of the building.[63]

The panic of 1857 occasioned reductions, but for five or six years beginning in 1862, rents appreciated rapidly. Houses became scarce as early as 1863, and, by the end of the war, small three to five room apartments were let for $10 to $15 a month. Rents were said, early in 1866, to be twice as much as they had been in 1862. Dwellers in cottages near the city limits paid between $250 and $500 a year, families in moderate circumstances leased houses for $400 and $600, the wealthy spent $1,200 to $2,000 a year when renting their homes. In 1867, small cottages, far from the center of town, rented for about $300 a year, and the "average for respectable residences" was $700 to $800. During the 'sixties possessors of business blocks enjoyed similar rewards, sometimes enough to pay off costs of original construction in less than three years.[64]

In 1870, despite a fall in the prices of many necessities, real estate held relatively firm. The confidence of Chicagoans in the expansive

[62] *Ibid.*, p. 108; Chamberlin, *op. cit.*, pp. 220, 308. Cleaverville was in the neighborhood of Thirty-ninth Street and the lake.

[63] Wright, *Chicago: Past, Present, Future*, p. 8; Chamberlin, *op. cit.*, p. 51; *Weekly Chicago Democrat*, April 7, 1855; *The Press and Tribune*, April 6, 1860; Hoyt, *op. cit.*, p. 340; The Daily Democratic Press, *Fourth Annual Review, 1855*, pp. 55, 56, 60, *Fifth Annual Review, 1856*, p. 8.

[64] Chamberlin, *op. cit.*, pp. 225–26; *Oquawka Spectator*, May 7, 1863; *Chicago Tribune*, January 16, 1865, February 22, November 10, December 31, 1866, April 23, 1867, May 24, October 18, 1868; *The Workingman's Advocate*, June 12, 1869. The high rentals led in the spring of 1868 to widespread construction of homes by tenants. By the fall of that year landlords had cut rents at least 30 per cent.

possibilities of their city was always hard to dim, but at that time a general belief that Chicago would " ultimately be benefited more by the completion of the Pacific Railroad than any other city on the continent except San Francisco " helped to keep land values high. Chicagoans considered real estate investments the royal road to fortune. Potter Palmer and other financial giants increased their millions in this way, and every second man and one woman in four were reported in 1871 to be owners of realty.[65]

Many early fortunes had such a foundation. John S. Wright, John H. Kinzie, William B. Ogden, William E. Jones, Edward H. Hadduck, and Asahel Pierce had important holdings in the original town, and Gurdon S. Hubbard, Allen Robbins, S. S. Smith, Charles B. Farwell, John Frink, and John Murphy were large owners in the school section.[66] John Wentworth had over 120 acres of valuable city property in addition to thousands of acres along the Illinois and Michigan Canal.[67] Walter L. Newberry had large holdings including his forty acre addition to Chicago which was bounded by Franklin, LaSalle, and Illinois streets, and Chicago Avenue. This he purchased for about $1,000 in 1833; twenty years later it was worth half a million. Jason Gurley, another prominent Chicagoan whose fortune was acquired through real estate speculation, purchased a thirty acre tract lying south of Twelfth Street and east of State Street for $110,000 in June, 1855. Two years later he had sold part of it for $254,000 and held the remainder which was valued at $150,000. William B. Egan, Hugh T. Dickey, Buckner S. Morris, Hugh Maher, and Cyrus Hall McCormick, leaders in the civic and economic life of Chicago, owned large properties in and near Chicago. Of all, the McCormicks were said to be the heaviest holders, the reaper king, in 1867, having real property valued at $1,350,000.[68]

[65] *Chicago Tribune*, January 9, 1870, July 9, August 6, 27, September 24, 1871; Hoyt, *op. cit.*, pp. 100–1; Colbert, *op. cit.*, p. 21. For examples of increases in real estate values, see Chamberlin, *op. cit.*, pp. 214–23, 298–310.

[66] Cook County Tax List, 1849, *Autograph Letter Book*, XVII, 253–57 (Ms. Chicago Historical Society). The original town comprised the south half of section 9, township 39 and range 14, or the area bounded in 1939 by Kinzie, State, Madison, and Desplaines streets. Pierce, *A History of Chicago*, I, 33; Rufus Blanchard, *Guide Map of Chicago, 1867* (Chicago, 1867). See also map, p. 307.

[67] Gates, *The Illinois Central Railroad*, p. 112. Wentworth's holdings included a large part of section 7, township 38, range 13 east. See also E. S. Prescott to David Leavitt, September 26, 1853, Prescott to W. H. Swift, March 30, 1854, *Swift Papers*.

[68] Ed. Mendel, lith., *Map of Chicago and its Southern & Western Suburbs* [1853] (in possession of author); Rufus Blanchard, *Map of Chicago, 1857* (Chicago, 1857); Hutchinson,

Stephen A. Douglas, too, saw the opportunities in such investments. Before 1850 he owned 160 acres in the neighborhood of Thirty-first Street and Cottage Grove Avenue, a tract of land described as partly wooded and partly prairie, the timbered area covering eighty acres on the shore of the lake. Later he acquired 2,964 acres near Lake Calumet for $2.50 an acre, and in 1855 he bought from the Illinois Central Railroad, at $10 an acre, 4,610 acres which lay in the neighborhood of his other holdings.[69]

So widespread and general was the interest in real estate investment that many organizations sprang up to guide and direct the flow of capital from pockets of rich and poor alike. Real estate promoters, by well-timed and convincing advertisement, loosened the purse strings of prospective purchasers eager for the almost fabulous returns promised. Among their functions land agencies sometimes included the procuring and trading of soldiers' land warrants, the drawing of abstracts, and even the lending of money. As early as 1854, forty-three such agents were listed in the city directory, and this number did not include those who dealt in land as a branch of other business. Homestead associations, appealing particularly to the low-income groups, by 1870 were advertising suburban lots for sale on monthly payments. Associations such as the Riverside Improvement Company undertook to enhance the marketability of their holdings by landscaping, road improvement, and the laying out of parks. So profitable was the selling of land in and near Chicago that realty promoters from other places joined those resident in the city.[70]

A Board of Real Estate and Stock Brokers, organized " to promote just and equitable principles " in trade, admitted only " legitimate dealers in Land " and betokened a maturity in the conduct of this business not expected in the speculative atmosphere of commercially-minded Chicago in the early 'fifties. But unethical realtors still swin-

---

Cyrus Hall McCormick, II, 121–25, 133, 494–98; *Chicago Magazine: The West as It Is*, I (June 15, 1857), 312.

[69] *Weekly Chicago Democrat*, July 26, 1851; Milton, *The Eve of Conflict*, pp. 7, 33; Gates, *The Illinois Central Railroad*, p. 112. Douglas's property at Cottage Grove was sold on a mortgage foreclosure in November, 1863, the sixty acres sold bringing $83,160, or an average price of $1,386 per acre. *Chicago Tribune*, November 25, 1863.

[70] See, for instance, an investment circular of John S. Wright, October 14, 1852, *Autograph Letter Book*, XVII, 291–94 (Ms. Chicago Historical Society); S. S. Fuller and others, comps., *Riverside, Then & Now* . . . (Riverside, 1936), pp. 75–80; Hoyt, *op. cit.*, pp. 91–92; Chamberlin, *op. cit.*, pp. 370, 415–16; *The Workingman's Advocate*, October 1, 8, 1870; *Chicago Daily Democrat*, August 20, 1849. See also advertisements in the newspapers.

dled small investors, particularly laborers. Albert Colvin, the owner of a large tract of land three miles northwest of Washington Heights, discovered, in 1869, that a firm known as Halleck and Company had subdivided and " sold " his land to mechanics and laborers without his knowledge and decamped with several thousand dollars. The Common Council was under the frequent pressure of " rings " for improvements to benefit sections in which they were particularly interested.[71]

The Chicago Building Association, one of the early organizations to combine the functions of a real estate board and a loan association, made its first loan in April, 1849. This loan was for $200 at 45 per cent premium. The principal on such loans was never called, for the shareholder reimbursed the association of which he was a member by payment of interest and dues. By the 'sixties similar organizations such as the Chicago Cottage Building and Loan Association, the Chicago Mutual Homestead Association, and the Chicago Loan and Building Association, enabled those of " small means " to acquire their own homes. The Merchants, Farmers and Mechanics Savings Bank, in the belief that a home might be " placed within the reach of most industrious and frugal persons in Chicago," offered prizes for designs of workingmen's " tenement " cottages and used part of its funds to finance the building of such houses.[72]

Some of the money invested in Chicago real estate was borrowed by local promoters directly from eastern capitalists on long-time loans. John S. Wright, trumpeter of the progress of Chicago, was a master of the art of coaxing investors. He issued pamphlets which set forth glowing accounts of his operations and of the profits in store for those who would finance them. One of his circulars, issued in February, 1849, explained how a piece of property would appreciate in fifteen years. The result was " so enormous " as " almost to stagger " his own belief. In 1861, in order to diversify the risks involved in realty deal-

---

[71] Gager, Directory, 1857, Appendix, p. xvi; Chicago Tribune, July 8, 1869; Colbert and Chamberlin, op. cit., p. 446; Hoyt, op. cit., pp. 91, 92. See also Daily Democrat, February 20, 1849; Oquawka Spectator, December 19, 1854.

[72] Merchants, Farmers and Mechanics Savings Bank, The Labor Question . . . Labor, Trades Unions, Co-operative Societies, and Model Houses and Cottages . . . (Chicago, 1867), pp. 128–30; Daily Democrat, February 10, March 19, April 11, 1849, April 18, 1851; Chicago Daily Journal, January 9, 1852; Halpin, Halpin & Bailey's Directory, 1863–64, " City and County Register," p. xxi; The Chicago Times, July 19, 1868, July 4, 1869; Chicago Tribune, July 19, 23, 1868; The Workingman's Advocate, July 17, 1869.

ing, Wright obtained a charter for "The Land Improvement Company," with a capital stock of $200,000 which might be increased to $2,000,000 divided into shares of $100 each.[73]

Another method of attracting capital into Chicago real estate was by issuing mortgage coupon bonds. Probably the first of these bonds were introduced to the Chicago market in 1855 by the private banker Richard K. Swift. During the last half of the 'fifties they were handled by several private bankers, including Greenebaum Brothers, G. C. Whitney and Son, and Hoffman and Gelpcke.[74] Private bankers and realtors in general found it a profitable enterprise to act as agents for eastern and southern capitalists who wished to take advantage of the high rates offered on western mortgages. Travelers who paused momentarily in Chicago were caught by the contagion and either for themselves or for their friends spent their savings in real or hoped-for profits.[75]

Providing funds for railroad development was not an important banking activity in the Chicago of 1850 to 1870. It is true that the promotion of the Galena and Chicago Union Railroad had early engaged the interest of local investors, and an average return of 16 per cent on its capital stock from 1850 to 1855 proved an incentive to further investment in the expansion of that road.[76] In the early

[73] Act of February 22, 1861, *Private Laws, 1861*, pp. 451–52; Wright, *Chicago*, pp. 9–10, 13–14. For an autobiographical account of Wright, see *ibid.*, pp. 289–96.

[74] *The Weekly Democratic Press*, April 14, 1855; *Chicago Daily Democratic Press*, September 17, 1857; Henry E. Greenebaum, *Henry E. Greenebaum Papers* (*Mss.* Chicago Historical Society).

[75] *The Weekly Democratic Press*, April 25, 1857, May 1, 1858; *Chicago Daily Democrat*, September 16, 1857; *Weekly Chicago Democrat*, January 1, May 21, 1853; *The Daily Democratic Press*, February 21, 1853, March 16, September 29, November 17, 1854, March 31, April 7, August 7, 11, 1855; *The Press and Tribune*, June 23, 1859; *Chicago Tribune*, April 6, 1861; Chamberlin, *op. cit.*, pp. 200–1; Colbert, *op. cit.*, p. 21.

[76] Gates, *The Illinois Central Railroad*, p. 86. See Pierce, *A History of Chicago*, I, 116–18, for the early financing of the railroad. By spring, 1848, citizens of Chicago and Cook County had taken over 35 per cent of the stock, their holdings amounting to 1,244 shares out of the total of 3,547 subscribed. Thirty-one residents of Chicago and Cook County owned ten or more shares each, those having fifty shares being William H. Brown, Thomas Dyer, I. V. Germain, Augustus Garrett, Walter L. Newberry, William B. Ogden, Allen Robbins, George Smith and Company, J. Young Scammon, and E. S. Wadsworth. Others, including James Collins, E. H. Hadduck, Norman B. Judd, B. W. Raymond, R. K. Swift, and Charles Walker, had ten or more shares. (List of subscribers to the capital stock of the Galena and Chicago Union Rail Road Company in William B. Ogden, *Report of W. B. Ogden, President of the Galena and Chicago Union Rail Road Company . . . April 5, 1848* [*Ms.* Chicago Historical Society], pp. 97–121.) In the 'fifties Richard K. Swift, the private banker, was active in obtaining from eastern and foreign correspondents funds for the Galena Railroad. *The Daily Democratic Press*, August 22, 1854.

'fifties the stock of the short-lived Savanna Branch Railroad was also taken in the city, and the Dixon Air Line (Galena Air Line) to Fulton, Illinois, was controlled by the promoters of the Galena and Chicago Union.[77] But other railroads gained little financial support from Chicago citizens. Perhaps $150,000 of capital stock of the Illinois Central was held in Chicago, and of the $100,000 loan of the Rock Island in 1851 the *Democrat* reported that $30,000 was subscribed in the city.[78]

Investors in way stations on routes to Chicago and capitalists from the East and from Europe supplied most of the capital for railroad building. Frequently the story of their investments was a sad tale. The Chicago and Mississippi Railroad Company, chartered to extend the Alton and Sangamon (later Chicago, Alton and St. Louis Railroad) to Joliet and thus connect with Chicago, authorized several millions of mortgage bonds which Henry Dwight of New York sold in the East. Apparently funds were misappropriated, and when the bottom fell out of the company in 1856, extensive lots of these "promises to pay" were left in the hands of farmers, tradesmen, college professors, clergymen, widows, and school teachers in and about New Haven, where the desire for the bonds had been as "infectious as the itch." John B. Turner, J. Young Scammon, Walter L. Newberry, and other leading Chicagoans promoted railroads to some extent. Wentworth and Douglas put some of their money in such enterprises and were at times accused of directing legislation toward the betterment of their holdings.[79]

By the end of the 'sixties Marshall Field was reported to have become interested in the Chicago, Milwaukee and St. Paul Railroad

[77] *Ibid.*, January 17, 1853, December 19, 1854; The Daily Democratic Press, *Fifth Annual Review, 1856*, pp. 53, 54.

[78] *Weekly Chicago Democrat*, April 5, 1851; *Chicago Daily Democrat*, July 14, 1851. The indexes and ledgers of stockholders up to and including 1870 recorded the following holdings of Illinois Central stock by residents of Chicago: John M. Douglas, 56 shares, acquired in 1864–65; Solomon A. Smith, 100 shares, acquired in 1866; E. H. Sheldon, 1 share, acquired in 1867; Byron Laflin Smith, 10 shares, acquired in 1868; George Armour, 100 shares, acquired in 1869; J. F. Tracy, 2,100 shares, acquired in 1870; F. H. Kales, 100 shares, acquired in 1870. (Letter to the author from George M. Crowson, assistant to the President, Illinois Central Railroad, Chicago, August 29, 1938.) In 1862, only one Chicagoan was a member of the Board of Directors. See Appendix, p. 485.

[79] The records of railroads entering Chicago do not, on the whole, record the stockholders, but a list of directors who were Chicagoans will be found for selected railroads and selected years in the Appendix, pp. 483–91. See also p. 76; *Weekly Chicago Press and Tribune*, January 20, 1859; Gates, *The Illinois Central Railroad*, pp. 63, 269.

as a part of his program to strengthen the sales and shipping of his wholesale business.[80] But the only Chicagoan whose operations were in any way comparable in scope to those of eastern magnates like Jay Gould and Jim Fisk was William B. Ogden, interested not only in the Galena and Chicago Union, but also in the North Western and the Union Pacific roads. His right to the title "railway king" was admitted even by those who opposed him.[81]

An overweening eagerness to get rich motivated most Chicagoans to embark upon enterprises from which a quick return could be expected. When the Civil War came, however, they patriotically forgot their dislike for long-time investments and subscribed to government loans. In April, 1861, Chicago bankers agreed to lend $500,000 to the state before the legislature assembled. Local bonds for war purposes and federal loans received support. After the war, with the patriotic incentive removed, bankers of the city found that federal bonds at times did not move as well as other securities.[82]

Acquaintance with federal bonds, however, made purchasers more receptive to municipal issues. Such securities were frequently available, since the city required many improvements. These, with bonds from other new communities in the Middle West, were handled by several Chicago private bankers. But the greater part of the municipal financing of Chicago was done through eastern firms and with eastern money.[83]

Investments in manufacturing lagged far behind those in real estate and enterprises such as the produce trade. Slowness in industrial

[80] *Field Papers; Chicago Tribune,* December 19, 1872.

[81] In 1866, James Parton, author of numerous biographies, brought out a sensational pamphlet entitled "Manual for the Instruction of 'Rings,' Railroad and Political; with a History of the Grand Chicago and Northwestern 'Ring' and the secret of its success in placing an over-issue of twenty millions, with a margin of three millions, in three years." Parton sought to describe the activities of what he considered the North Western Railroad "ring," headed by Ogden as "Grand Concocter," Samuel J. Tilden as "Grand Legalizer," and Perry H. Smith as "Special Legislative Promoter," among which activities were watering the railroad's stock, forcing the purchase by the railroad at exorbitant figures of properties held by members of the ring, raising transportation rates on farmers and towns, obtaining special legislation, and making a profit of some $3,000,000 for the ring. The *Republican* felt that the effect of this pamphlet would be to increase the respect of Wall Street for Ogden, for "Wall street is looking not after moralists, but after 'grand concocters.'" *Chicago Republican,* October 25, 26, 27, 1866. Parton's pamphlet was reprinted in *ibid.,* October 26, 1866.

[82] *Chicago Tribune,* April 19, May 1, 2, 3, 10, 1861, *passim.* See p. 255.

[83] *Chicago Tribune,* October 8, December 12, 1862, September 16, 1863, September 30, 1864; *The Daily Democratic Press,* April 7, May 21, 28, August 20, 1856.

investment was undoubtedly due to the large immediate returns provided by many speculative undertakings. In 1860, capital invested in manufacturing in Cook County was only $5,571,025. But during the Civil War large sums poured into the city from an expanded agricultural trade, part of which was directed into industry. By 1870, the capital laid out in manufactures in Cook County had increased to $39,372,276.[84] How much of this came from Chicagoans is problematical, but the experience of Chicago with her two stock exchanges seems to indicate that the amount of local capital thus invested was relatively small. The members of both the first and second exchanges apparently paid little attention to local manufacture. Their chief concern was hedging or deriving quick profit from fluctuations in the price of gold.

But even so, Chicago was maturing in financial skills and knowledge. As a metropolitan economy developed the city expanded its financial influence to outlying regions. Financial items in the newspapers served a useful educational purpose. As early as 1853 the *Daily Democratic Press*, under the editorship of John L. Scripps and William Bross, placed special emphasis on its commerical department. Other newspapers followed. Annual reviews of trade and commerce appeared and stressed this phase of municipal development. During the 'sixties, interest in securities grew, and their sale attained importance. But real estate remained the most popular form of investment. In spite of rapidly mounting wealth within the city itself, capital from the East continued for years to assist Chicago in its commercial and industrial undertakings.

[84] United States, *Eighth Census, 1860*, "Manufactures," pp. 86–87, *Ninth Census, 1870*, III, "Wealth and Industry," 509; *The Daily Democratic Press*, August 9, 1853; *Chicago Daily Journal*, May 18, 1857; *Chicago* [Tri-Weekly] *Tribune*, May 12, 1862.

CHAPTER V

THE RISE OF LABOR
CONSCIOUSNESS

THE COMING of large numbers of people in the 'fifties spared Chicago the retarding effects of labor famines. A remarkable commercial and industrial expansion gave to this army of workers ample means of employment. "No one need here beg the poor privilege, or vainly assert the right to toil," declared the editor of the *Democrat*. Indeed, at times it seemed as if the tillers of the fields near by and laborers for the increasing number of other occupations came all too slowly. "Let the starving thousands of our eastern cities, whom poverty is driving to crime and the alms-house, swarm and scatter over the busy, teeming west," proclaimed Wentworth. "Here their labor will be appreciated and receive its just reward, and they will find themselves the citizens of a land abounding in gold more plentiful than California and Australia, and flowing with milk and honey."[1]

Such widely heralded opportunities eventually led to a well-supplied labor market. By 1870, Chicago had about the same average employment as had cities farther east, betokening a maturity in labor needs common to older communities. Of the total population of 298,-977 in 1870, nearly 38 per cent, or 112,960, sold their services. Of these slightly over one third were Americans.[2] Among the foreigners

---

[1] *Weekly Chicago Democrat,* October 1, 1853; see also *The Daily Democratic Press,* August 12, 1854, February 12, 1855.

[2] In 1870, New York had about 37 per cent employed, Boston 41 per cent, Brooklyn 35 per cent, Cincinnati 36 per cent, and Philadelphia and Cleveland about 32 per cent. In Chicago, workers were about 35 per cent native and 64 per cent foreign born. About 26 per cent

who worked there were more from the British Isles than elsewhere. Of these the Irish led. Then came Germans, Scandinavians, British Americans, French, Italians, and other immigrants who had come in smaller numbers.[3]

More people were engaged in manufacturing and mechanical industries than in other pursuits.[4] Of these, over 34 per cent performed unskilled work, followed in order by such skilled workmen as carpenters, tailors, painters, brickmasons, milliners, and bootmakers. In a city expanding physically to keep pace with an amazing economic growth, it is not strange that among skilled artisans and laborers those in the building trades led in numbers, with wearing-apparel makers, machinists and iron workers, and wood workers and finishers following. Indeed, these four occupational groups accounted for over 80 per cent of all skilled workmen in manufacturing and the mechanical industries in Chicago.[5]

Fewer Americans than foreigners in proportion to their total number gained their living in manufacturing and mechanical industries, which took care of 61 per cent of the Germans and 54 per cent of the Irish. More than one half of the Irish, less than one third of the Germans, and more than one fourth of the Americans so employed were unskilled laborers.[6] From the Germans, more than from any others,

of the native born and about 50 per cent of the foreign born hired their services. This was probably due to the composition of the total population. United States, *Ninth Census, 1870*, I, "Population," 110, 167, 211, 212, 229, 231, 254, 778, 779, 782, 783, 784, 793, 794. The *Ninth Census* provides information for labor figures in 1870 unless otherwise noted.

[3] See Appendix, p. 499.

[4] The 17,717 unskilled laborers in Chicago in 1870 were listed, according to the census of that year, in the category "Professional and Personal Services." The same was true of public servants. With this confusing situation in mind, a regrouping of the various occupations on the basis of classifications used in the census of 1930 has been worked out in order to make the figures more nearly applicable to present-day conditions. Thus reclassified, slightly over one half of the total itemized workers in 1870 were in manufacturing and mechanical industries. This number included laborers and those in the manufacturing and mechanical industries except clerks, miners, fishermen, and lumbermen, who, in the 1930 census, appear in other categories. The itemized occupations for 1870, it should be noted, add up to a total of only 101,152 persons according to the regrouping, instead of 112,960 as given in the *Ninth Census* (1870). This latter figure includes 11,808 persons of unknown occupation. See Appendix, p. 499. For the computations on the following pages, the itemized totals as shown on p. 499 have been used.

[5] Including brickmasons and brickmakers, carpenters, painters, plasterers, and plumbers, the building trades employed about 24 per cent of those in manufacturing and mechanical industries. Boot- and hatmakers, milliners, and tailors accounted for about 16 per cent; blacksmiths, carmakers, ironworkers, machinists, and tinners, 10 per cent; cabinetmakers, coopers, saw-mill operators, and wheelwrights, about 4 per cent.

[6] Of the Americans, 36 per cent were employed in manufacturing and mechanical indus-

came the skilled workers, and within these handicrafts, so largely manned by Germans, the movement for unionization gained great headway.[7]

Trade provided for the next largest number, or over 21 per cent of all the workers in the city.[8] Americans made up 53 per cent of all so employed, while their nearest competitors, the Germans, had less than 20 per cent. Not only did Americans give service more largely than other groups in trade, but about 34 per cent of their employed turned to that type of work,[9] in which they appeared chiefly as clerks, salesmen, and accountants in stores, and as traders and dealers. In banking and insurance, too, the native born predominated. Transportation, the handmaid of trade, absorbed about 9 per cent of all employed. Although native Americans contributed about one third of these, approximately half of whom were railroad officials and employees, the Irish were close competitors, with many engaged as carmen, draymen, and teamsters. Scandinavians had more mariners than any other group.[10]

Domestic and personal service claimed the time of about 14 per cent of those employed in 1870.[11] Approximately 87 per cent in this type of work were domestic servants, of whom a little less than one third were native Americans. Among immigrant workers a greater proportion of Irish and Scandinavians than of others took part in this kind of work.[12]

Less than 3 per cent of all workers in 1870 earned a living through professional services. Here Americans predominated, for over 71 per cent were native born. In contrast to the 1,905 Americans so en-

tries. Of the Irish in these industries, about 58 per cent were unskilled laborers; of Germans, about 30 per cent; of Americans, about 28 per cent. See Appendix, p. 499, for numbers in various employment groups.

[7] By 1870 skilled workingmen who were active in promoting unions and were largely native Americans rather than Germans included printers, metal workers, painters, and machinists (but not blacksmiths).

[8] This classification included hotel and restaurant keepers and employees, persons engaged in insurance, banking, and brokerage, store clerks, salesmen, and accountants, hucksters, peddlers and commercial travelers, and traders and dealers.

[9] The Germans had about 18 per cent of their group employed in trade, the Irish had about 11 per cent, and the English and Welsh about 20 per cent.

[10] Included in transportation were officials and employees of express companies, railroad companies, street-railroad and telegraph companies, carmen, draymen, and teamsters, sailors, steamboatmen, and watermen, and livery-stable keepers and hostlers.

[11] Included in this classification were domestic servants, launderers and laundresses, barbers, boardinghouse keepers, and billiard and bowling alley keepers.

[12] For details, see Appendix, p. 499. The exact number of domestic servants was 12,279.

gaged stood 279 Germans, their nearest competitors in number. In spite of the relatively few engaged in the professions, a notable increase occurred in the years from 1848 to 1870. During these years, for example, the number of physicians and surgeons increased from 49 to 649. In 1849, 69 attorneys dispensed the lore of Blackstone, but by 1870 their number had reached 629, "a sentry for every loop-hole of the law," to quote the *Democrat*.[13] Booksellers, daguerreotype artists, and photographers added to the small group of specially trained residents, and the presence of architects of ability and training, including W. W. Boyington, Otto H. Matz, John M. Van Osdel, and Edward Burling, seemed to promise the rescue of Chicago from the unsightly and drab appearance of its early years.[14]

Even fewer than those in the professions were persons in the public service, where Americans again furnished a majority or nearly 52 per cent, followed by the Irish with 19 per cent and the Germans with 15 per cent.[15] Still smaller was the group entering agriculture and mining, for in 1870 less than 1 per cent of all Chicago workers followed these pursuits. Of these, Germans and Americans made up the greatest numbers. Not many were found in clerical services. In this line of work Americans constituted over 68 per cent of the total.[16]

In these occupational groups, except in domestic and personal service, men were most numerous. By the early 'fifties, however, women found avenues of earning a living reaching beyond the restricting confines of marriage, teaching, and domestic service. "Female" clerks "after the manner of New York, Boston, Philadelphia," and other cities, and women in both skilled and unskilled industry took their places in pursuits that had been solely the prerogative of men.

[13] *Chicago Daily Democrat*, December 19, 1850. See also Pierce, *As Others See Chicago*, pp. 162–63. Included among the professions were teachers, clergymen, lawyers, physicians and surgeons, and journalists. See Appendix, p. 499.

[14] For statistics on these occupations see O. P. Hatheway and J. H. Taylor, *Chicago City Directory and Annual Advertiser, for 1849–50* (Chicago, 1849), *passim* (hereafter cited as Hatheway and Taylor, *Directory, 1849–50*); Hall & Co., *Directory, 1854–55*, "Business Directory," pp. 4, 7, 10, 24; Smith & DuMoulin, *Directory, 1859–60*, pp. 433, 437, 446, 483; Edwards, *Merchants' Census Report, 1871*, pp. 1239, 1240.

[15] See Appendix, p. 499. Included in this form of employment were officials and employees of the civil government and soldiers, all of whom formed less than 1.5 per cent of the total working population.

[16] Included in agriculture and mining were all types of farmers and gardeners, as well as fishermen, miners, and lumbermen. Only clerks in manufacturing establishments were listed separately in 1870. Clerks in stores were listed with accountants and others engaged in trade. Therefore, the exact number of clerks in trade cannot be determined. See Appendix, p. 499.

That women were engaged in cigar making and the preparation of confections and in milling, baking, and bookbinding pointed hopefully to expanding industrial horizons. But, in general, such occupational opportunities came only when men were not available for the same hire, and the age-old tendency of women to abandon positions for marriage proved conclusively to some employers the inadvisability of their employment.[17]

Pay for women was low in all these fields of work. In 1860, seamstresses averaged $3.00 or $4.00 a week, but by 1865 they were getting as high as $8.00. Even this gain was not enough in the light of costs of living, and a " protective association," sponsored by ministers and mission workers, sought to get sewing for girls directly and thus prevent the jobbers and middlemen from holding all the profits.[18]

Engagements outside the home were, of course, generally in domestic service, and almost 92 per cent (or 11,288) in that work in 1870 were women.[19] Here again wages were never very high, sometimes not more than $1.25 a week for doing the family washing and ironing, cooking, and general housework, as well as milking the cow if one were kept.[20] Women, too, could earn something as laundresses, for commercial laundries had not then appeared to any great extent.[21] But many women seemed to feel that domestic services and work of like nature offered not only poor pay but an unalluring place in the social scale. It often seemed the last work which women wanted to perform, and the cry for willing servants plaintively reflected the dilemma of many mistresses.[22]

[17] *Chicago Daily Democrat,* October 21, 1852; *The Daily Democratic Press,* October 20, 1852; *Chicago Tribune,* January 1, 1867. The total number of females of all ages in manufacturing in 1870 was officially listed as 3,763. The detailed list totals only 3,444. There were 1,490 milliners, dress and mantua makers, and 1,686 tailoresses and seamstresses. A few were found as steel workers, textile and paper mill operatives, and similar workers. *The Chicago Magazine of Fashion, Music, and Home Reading,* I (April, 1870), 14–15.

[18] *The Workingman's Advocate,* August 11, 1866; *Chicago Tribune,* September 4, October 23, 1865; Chicago Tribune, *Annual Review, 1865,* p. 11.

[19] See note 12, p. 152. Working women of all ages, in 1870, numbered 18,300. They formed about 16 per cent of the entire working population of 112,960.

[20] This rate of pay in 1852 had reached only $1.50 to $1.75 in 1858. In 1858 hotels paid $1.50. Presumably domestic servants also received board and, often, room. (*Chicago Daily Democrat,* July 10, 1852; *Chicago Weekly Democrat,* May 1, 1858.) In 1865, kitchen girls in the hotels received $3.00 a week, but the following year they got fifty cents to one dollar more. *Chicago Tribune,* December 14, 1866, January 1, 1867.

[21] In 1865, in spite of a population of two hundred thousand, there were only nine laundries listed in the city directory. Halpin, *Directory, 1865–66,* pp. 45, 793.

[22] *Chicago Tribune,* February 24, 1866.

Children from ten to fifteen years of age, although among the wage earners of the day, made up in 1870 less than 3 per cent of the gainfully employed, a proportion below the average of the country.[23] By 1870, over half of these children were found in manufacturing and mechanical industries, many of them boys from ten to fifteen, who labored chiefly as common laborers and in cotton and woolen mills and cigar factories.[24] Girls in manufacturing generally served as seamstresses, but when girls needed to earn a living they usually became domestic servants.[25] The fields of trade and transportation gave employment to others, but again boys were in the majority. Agriculture took care of less than 1 per cent.[26]

Regardless of age, national origin, and sex, skilled and unskilled felt the leveling effects of enforced idleness and the exhilaration of boom days. In spite of the inexorable operation of the law of supply and demand, wages lagged behind rising costs of housing and other necessities.[27] Accountants in commercial establishments who were able to get about $1,800 a year in the mid-fifties found under the influence of the depression of 1857 that this figure sometimes shrank to about $1,200. It was not before the end of the war that the general level of pay rose to $2,000 or more. Most bookkeepers received far less; John V. Farwell's salary of $250 in 1849 was not unusually low for that time. By 1860 bookkeepers were reported to be getting $600 to $800 a year, and by 1865 they were paid $1,000 to $1,200.[28]

By 1856, skilled carpenters and masons were receiving from $1.50 to $2.00 a day, and day laborers, $1.25 to $1.50. Because of the panic

[23] The average of the nation was 5.91 per cent. Only in fourteen of the thirty largest cities did children form a smaller percentage of the employed than in Chicago. The average for these thirty cities was 2.7 per cent of the total employed, while that of Chicago was 2.5 per cent.

[24] According to the 1930 census classifications, a total of 2,251 girls and boys were at work in the various itemized occupations in 1870, of whom about 55 per cent were employed in the manufacturing and mechanical industries. Of the total of 1,553 boys employed at this time, a little over 64 per cent were in these industries.

[25] About 61 per cent of the itemized total of girls employed (698) in 1870 were domestic servants, and 22 per cent were seamstresses.

[26] In 1870, trade and transportation took care of 23 per cent of the working children. Most of them were boys who were employed chiefly as clerks, salesmen, or accountants.

[27] See Appendix, p. 500, for table showing wages of selected workers in the 'fifties and 'sixties. Rents in Chicago in the mid-'fifties were said to be more than 50 per cent higher than elsewhere. *Weekly Chicago Democrat*, February 10, 1855; *The Daily Democratic Press*, June 19, 1854.

[28] Kelly, *Seventy-Five Years of Hibbard Hardware*, p. 36; *The Chicago Times*, November 25, 1865; Ferry, *Reminiscences of John V. Farwell*, I, 48, 61.

the next year, the labor market was glutted, just as it was throughout the country. Somber forecasts that the slackening of production in such a crisis would affect adversely the 1,000,000 factory workmen in the nation and that in Chicago alone 20,000 workers and their families faced starvation were heard everywhere during that autumn and winter. Such a situation seemed little short of calamitous at a time when the country was said to have a surplus of 40,000,000 bushels of wheat, corn enough to feed 100,000,000 people, and twice as much beef, pork, and other articles of food as it needed for its own consumption. With the coming of the panic, merchants abandoned the happy anticipation of profits, transmuting stocks on hand as quickly as possible into cash, while lowered prices seemed to the man out of work relatively dearer than those of the year before.[29]

With workers being laid off daily as the winter of 1857 approached, aids to recovery were grasped at by all the afflicted. In November, German workers assembled at West Market Hall and discussed unity of action as a means of meeting threatening conditions. Those out of work were advised by the press to seek the virgin fields to the west. The city reduced the pay for labor on its streets from seventy-five cents to fifty cents a day, in order to give work to more men.[30] But these noble attempts to decrease unemployment were doomed to failure and served little to solve the problem, which continued most vexatious through the spring of 1858. Some hope, however, during depression years, came from the farms, where planting and harvest hands at good wages were in demand, although not enough were needed to take up all the slack.[31]

By 1860, wages on the whole had not been lifted out of the slough of 1857, and they remained lower than in the palmy year of 1856.

[29] *Chicago Tribune*, October 8, 1863; *Chicago Daily Democratic Press*, October 10, 19, 21, November 14, 1857; Cole, *The Era of the Civil War, 1848–1870*, p. 203. Lowered prices were reflected in such necessities as eggs, which cost on the average eleven cents a dozen in June, 1856, but dropped to an average of seven to eight cents two years later, while butter fell from an average price of twelve and a half cents to ten cents a pound over the same period. *Chicago Daily Democrat*, June 16, 1856, June 16, 1858.

[30] *Chicago Daily Democratic Press*, November 12, 1857; *The Weekly Democratic Press*, February 21, 1857; *Chicago Daily Democrat*, June 12, 14, 1858. The city gave work to a man only two days each week in order to spread employment.

[31] In the spring of 1858 when those Chicago laborers who could find employment received seventy-five cents a day, farmers were reported to be offering eight-month contracts at $10 and $12 a month, plus board and room. (*Chicago Weekly Democrat*, May 1, 1858.) During the harvest season of 1860, farm hands in Wisconsin were in such demand as to warrant a daily wage of $1.00 to $3.00 a day. *Chicago Daily Democrat*, July 19, 1860.

Those who were unemployed were still urged to seek the rural areas, which by 1861 were said to be "oppressed by an ungathered corn crop." Nor were these conditions bettered by the unsettlement which came out of the presidential contest of 1860, with its attendant disruption of trade caused by secession and the subsequent outbreak of war. The only fortunate aspect of an otherwise wretched scene was the cheapness of provisions, which were said to cost about one fourth of what they did in prosperous times.[32]

As time went on, war necessities, however, stimulated employment, while the cost of living skyrocketed an estimated 30 to 60 per cent by November, 1862, the result of currency inflation and other war factors.[33] Wages rose appreciably in terms of greenbacks. Machinists, for example, who had received $1.75 in gold a day in 1860, got $2.35 in greenbacks by 1863, and the wages of house painters advanced from about $1.25 to $2.00 in the same period. Day laborers in the meantime doubled their pay. By 1863 the heavy drain of war demands on farm labor left women to carry on much of the work and, where funds were available, induced the purchase of additional machinery. Factories running full time, commerce and trade moving at top speed, and building booming gave the city a prosperity it had never before known.[34]

At once living costs rose, working a tremendous hardship on the thirty thousand heads of families in Chicago. Between 1860 and 1863 while wage increases were reported as ranging from 15 to 100 per cent, clothing costs went up at least 100 per cent; fuel costs, from 85 to 122 per cent; rent, 66 per cent; and the prices of certain foodstuffs, 133 per cent. By March, 1863, mechanics were holding meetings to voice their demands for wage increases of from 10 to 30 per cent.[35] Even so, propaganda as to the advantages of the West over the East continued, and the unemployed in the eastern states were urged to turn their faces toward Chicago.[36]

[32] *Chicago Tribune*, January 9, 1861.
[33] *The Chicago Times*, November 26, 1862. By November, $13.18 in paper was worth but $10 in gold. For the effect of Civil War inflation, see p. 130.
[34] See Appendix, p. 500, for table on wages. See also *Chicago Tribune*, August 16, October 8, 1863.
[35] *Ibid.*, March 15, 1863, January 14, 1864; Cole, *The Era of the Civil War*, p. 368; Francelia Colby, *Our Family* (Typescript. Chicago Historical Society), p. 110. See also pp. 142, 463–64.
[36] The Rev. E. B. Tuttle of St. Ansgarius Church was dispatched to Baltimore and other

High prices continued. By September, 1864, it was estimated that a list of commonly used goods which cost $12.99 in 1860 or 1861 had reached $33.81. Rents, too, mounted until by May 1, 1864, they seemed to one observer to " approach the infinite." [37] But the following year saw some improvement in the pay of working men and women, and the returns on their labor were said to range from 50 to 75 per cent above those for corresponding work in 1860. Some wages had advanced as high as 100 per cent, although, of course, there were great variations in the rates of increase among different groups of workers. Indeed, in general, wages in Chicago were reported as higher than those in other parts of the country.[38]

In late 1865, troops began to return home. Demobilization meant dislocation and readjustment. The winter of 1865–66 was hard; business houses retrenched; country boys looking for white-collar jobs were warned not to come to the city. Adventurers from Canada and other seekers of fortune, unless skilled mechanics, found their search unrewarded. During this winter and the next, Chicago had many hungry, many cold, and many scantily clothed. A rainy autumn made it difficult to carry on outdoor work, so that carpenters, bricklayers, and outside painters, as well as common laborers, teamsters, and others were unable to save for what proved to be a time when the unemployed walked the streets. Credit from butchers and grocers occasionally saved the former wage earners from seeking public charity, and " odd jobs," such as cleaning sidewalks and sawing wood, sometimes kept formerly skilled and semiskilled, as well as common laborers, from the humiliation of begging.[39]

To those in such straits it must have been a bit tempting when,

---

eastern points to encourage migration during the summer of 1863. *Chicago Tribune,* August 16, 1863.

[37] *Ibid.,* May 1, July 20, September 21, 1864. The following joke was frequently told: Said O'Flaherty on his knees when informed that his landlord had raised the rent, " A thousand thanks to your honor for that same, for sure and I can niver raise it mesilf." See also pp. 142–44.

[38] *The Chicago Times,* November 25, 1865. See Esther E. Espenshade, *The Economic Development and History of Chicago, 1860–65* (unpublished M.A. Thesis, The University of Chicago, 1931), pp. 134 ff. Blacksmiths, boat builders, shoe repairers, bricklayers and plasterers, and boiler makers had wage increases amounting to about 100 per cent, while railroad employees, coppersmiths, dyers, and others received increases of about 50 per cent. Women employees received increases, but these were less uniform than among male employees. Bricklayers received $2.00 a day in Massachusetts, $4.00 in Ohio, and $4.50 in Chicago.

[39] *Chicago Tribune,* October 18, December 11, 1865, January 30, 1866, January 1, 17, 1867.

early in 1866, an employment agency advertised for three thousand men to go south to work for $50 a month besides board. At the same time good wages and transportation were offered for two hundred able-bodied Negroes who would labor as field hands on plantations near Vicksburg; and in the spring calls for men to become railroad laborers and farm hands again opened up a labor market for those willing to leave the city.[40]

The years from 1867 to 1870 were still more unhappy, for skilled and unskilled alike at times found it difficult to gain employment. Even plenty of work could not long stand the depressing effect of the importation of workers to which Chicago employers sometimes resorted in order to reduce labor costs. This, coupled with other conditions, made it inevitable that by the winter of 1869–70 it could be said that one half of the mechanics and other workingmen were idle and that want and unemployment transcended any similar experiences for ten years.[41]

These moments of uncertainty and distress stimulated again the search for remedies for wrongs, real and imaginary. At an early day employment agencies set about to find work for the industrious. " Intelligence offices," sometimes none too scrupulous, furnished to employers individuals or groups of workers.[42] Religious and charitable organizations lent a hand. Robert Collyer, minister-at-large of the Unitarian Church, was particularly interested in placing not only boys from six to thirteen years of age, but also adult carpenters, farmers, painters, and tradesmen.[43] The Chicago Christian Union, an

---

[40] *Ibid.*, January 1, 29, March 24, 1866. The offer to the Negroes was made by the American Emigrant Company.

[41] *The Workingman's Advocate*, July 2, 31, 1869, January 8, June 18, 1870.

[42] As early as 1844, James W. Norris, lawyer and compiler of the first city directory, operated a " General Intelligence and Agency Office." (J. W. Norris, *General Directory and Business Advertiser of the City of Chicago, for the Year 1844* [Chicago, 1844], p. 65 [hereafter cited as Norris, *Directory, 1844*]. See, for other examples, advertisements of " Intelligence Offices," in *Chicago Tribune*, February 18, 1867; *Chicago Daily Democrat*, July 14, 1851.) The swindling of applicants apparently was common. For instance, in 1866, sixty Chicago masons and carpenters paid $2.00 each to one agency and were sent to Memphis at their own expense. When they reached Memphis they found no work, and no refund was made to them. Housewives were victimized sometimes by agencies which charged a fee of from fifty to seventy-five cents for a servant, when the latter would remain but a few hours, thereby necessitating another appeal to the agency. *Chicago Tribune*, January 22, 1866.

[43] *Prairie Farmer*, n.s. V (January, 1860), 88. See *Chicago Tribune*, June 28, 1861, for a sample notice: " Ministry at large. — I want to find work for two stout Swedish [*sic*] men just landed from the old country; they can speak no English, but are well up in all kinds of farm work, and will be capital harvest men. Parties wanting them had better come

organization of liberal churches interested in social work, the Chicago Ladies' Christian Union, and the Young Men's Christian Association also helped in obtaining jobs. The Young Men's Christian Association was especially active in the placement of discharged soldiers, war widows, and foreigners.[44]

Such endeavors were, on the whole, not directed by workers themselves. As early as the 'fifties, however, they turned their attention toward united action for "self-protection and for charitable purposes generally."[45] Printers took the lead, organizing, in October, 1850, one of the first unions in Chicago, and working actively for better pay. In 1851, when the wage of a few journeymen reached twenty-five cents per thousand ems over a prevailing sixteen cents, employers hoped for peace.[46] But the next year found organizers still busy. In June, 1852, fifty-eight determined unionists obtained a charter from the National Typographical Union as Local No. 16, and by 1860 they had added eighty-four other members. More than one third of all printers in Cook County were now enrolled in the union, a notable number considering the youth of the city and the newness of the national organization.[47] The problem of increased wages, how-

---

for them directly, to 177 Randolph street, second floor, as they will hardly do to go alone. Apply to Robert Collyer, Minister at large."

[44] *Ibid.*, December 4, 1864, September 25, 1865, August 20, 1866, March 29, 1867, August 1, 1868. "EMPLOYMENT FOR BOYS. — Persons requiring the help of boys from twelve to eighteen years of age can be furnished at the rooms of the Christian Union, No. 2 Washington street, as large numbers are applying there daily for situations and work of every kind." (*Ibid.*, June 27, 1868.) The Chicago Ladies' Christian Union was organized in 1870 at the suggestion of a number of charitable organizations for the purpose of finding employment for women and girls. Within a short time it had placed 2,352 persons, chiefly as domestic servants. (*Ibid.*, November 3, 1870.) The Young Men's Christian Association through its Employment Department found jobs for 3,411 in 1867–68, for 5,081 in 1869–70, for 3,490 in 1870–71. *The Advance,* March 19, April 30, 1868, April 15, 1869, June 23, 1870, May 25, 1871. See pp. 377–78.

[45] *Chicago Daily Democrat,* July 8, 1851.

[46] The organization took shape October 26, 1850, with Carver Butterfield as president and Benjamin Franklin Worrell as vice-president. (Andreas, *History of Chicago,* I, 415; Hall & Co., *Directory, 1854–55,* Appendix, p. 12; International Typographical Union, *Official Souvenir of the International Typographical Union, Forty-First Session at Chicago, June 12–17, 1893* [Chicago, n.d.], p. 37.) This organization was apparently short-lived, for in the next summer another was suggested because of the prevalence of the pay of sixteen cents per thousand ems. Twenty cents as a standard was proposed by the employers at this time. Apparently this was not satisfactory to the workmen. Later, employers nipped in the bud a workers' movement by raising the pay to twenty-five cents for all journeymen. Wentworth declared himself in favor of the new wages in his establishment, in the hope that other employers would follow. *Chicago Daily Democrat,* July 8, 30, 1851.

[47] The preamble of the constitution gave as among the purposes of the organization the establishment and maintenance of an equitable scale of wages, the protection of just employ-

ever, remained unsolved. Employers were not receptive to the demands made upon them and even resorted to the hire of women compositors.[48] In 1854, the scale of pay reached thirty cents per thousand ems, or about $1.67 a day, a rate still operating in 1861.[49]

As early as 1858 the strength of this Chicago group was manifested when it became host to the annual convention of the National Typographical Union, six years after the national group effectively organized and Chicago printers affiliated with it. That its interests were not bounded by a consideration merely of wages for its members is seen in the appointment of a committee to memorialize Congress for the establishment of a national printing bureau, an international copyright law, and the restriction of so-called unworthy foreign publications.[50] Despite the faith in the union which its members showed when they toasted it as " the citadel " of strength and " the source " of the printers' prosperity, it failed to accomplish what was desired after the panic in 1857. But the Civil War helped to bring about increased pay when 20 per cent of the union's men enlisted in the Northern army.[51]

Chicagoans found further dissatisfaction when they compared the

---

ers from cheap-labor-huckstering rivals, the protection of toilers, the encouragement of conciliation and arbitration in the settlement of labor disputes, the improvement of working hours and conditions. It was estimated in 1860 that four thousand printers were members of the national union. International Typographical Union, *op. cit.*, p. 40; Gager, *Directory, 1857*, Appendix, p. xxiii; *Chicago Daily Democrat*, October 25, 1860; United States, *Eighth Census, 1860*, " Manufactures," p. 87.

[48] In 1853, employers attempted to induce Miss Harriet Case to organize a corps of women compositors to displace dissatisfied men. She refused to do so unless women were paid the rates demanded by men. The union thereupon presented her with a " beautiful ring." (*Weekly Chicago Democrat*, May 14, 1853.) The *Free West*, in its advance notice for volume two, appealed to women subscribers on the ground that type was set by " females." *The Free West*, November 23, 1854.

[49] *The Daily Democratic Press*, March 16, 1854; *Hunt's Merchants' Magazine*, XXXII (June, 1855), 693. See wage table, Appendix, p. 500.

[50] J. M. Campbell to S. A. Douglas, April 11, 1858, *Douglas Papers;* George A. Tracy, *History of the Typographical Union* . . . (Indianapolis, 1913), pp. 136–38, 143–44, 173–74. At this convention Sam Slawson, of Chicago, was appointed to write a brief history of the union.

[51] *Ibid.*, p. 169; International Typographical Union, *op. cit.*, p. 40. In the newspaper offices in 1862 rates for piece work were raised to thirty cents per thousand ems, with an extra ten cents an hour after ten o'clock at night, and thirty cents an hour after midnight. The daily wage in 1863 was about $2.33. In 1864, the rate rose to fifty cents per thousand ems, but without extra compensation. In St. Louis and Cairo, it was said that sixty-five cents per thousand ems, in Memphis seventy-five cents, and in New York sixty cents, prevailed in 1864 as wages, while Chicago printers received only fifty cents. *The Workingman's Advocate*, September 17, 1864; *Chicago Tribune*, January 14, 1864.

higher returns for labor in other cities with their own. It seemed, indeed, a never-ending struggle to maintain "the dignity of Labor against the grasping exactions of the Capitalists of the country," to educate employers in regard to the wages that laboring men should receive, and to emancipate laborers themselves from the "plausible statement" that if wages were raised other costs rose too.[52] Apathy on the part of workmen themselves and suspicion on the part of employers formed a combination nearly impossible for unionists, still few in number, to break.

The failure of the *Times* in 1864 to recognize the printers' union and the *Tribune's* tacit endorsement of the *Times'* attitude weighed heavily upon the minds of the members of the organization and eventually drove them into open revolt.[53] In an attempt, it was charged, to break up the union, the *Times* employed women typesetters and nonunion men compositors to replace the union men who struck in September, 1864. This threat to the principle of unionization was met by a mass assemblage of "at least one thousand five hundred hard-fisted Workingmen," who discussed the situation particularly as it "applied to the female sex," and warned "Capitalists" that the day had gone when they could use "the prejudices of Laboring men to fatten and enrich themselves." In this case capitalists were again "the aggressors," declared these aroused laborers, and such "sweat and blood-suckers" would soon find out what they might expect from "the honest working men of Chicago."[54] In this mass meeting of the General Trades Assembly, said to be the first since the organization of this central body of trade union representatives, discontented laborers cited other instances of the alleged aggressions of capital. The treatment accorded by the *Times* they added to their catalogue of other wrongs laid at the door of employers, such as the Illinois Central Railroad, which, they said, had grown so rich from the government's donation of land that it had forgotten the original purpose of the grant. They heatedly charged that the Illinois Central

[52] *The Workingman's Advocate,* September 17, 1864.

[53] International Typographical Union, *op. cit.,* p. 40. Said the *Workingman's Advocate* of the *Tribune:* "Oh! you hypocritical, unprincipled and lying sheet, how dare you blister your lips with the lying declaration that you are the friend of the Labor cause?" *The Workingman's Advocate,* September 17, 1864.

[54] *Ibid.; Chicago Tribune,* September 8, 10, 11, 1864. George K. Hazlett, president of the General Trades Assembly and a member of the Typographical Union, so spoke. The meeting was September 10.

imported machinists from Belgium who worked for much less than was demanded by native workers.[55] The irate unionists heard, too, of the difficulties which had faced molders, bakers, and the Brotherhood of the Footboard.[56] A list was read of the " depraved sneaks " among the printers who had broken their pledge not to work with men outside the union. To break faith with the union was bad enough, but it seemed even more despicable to fall victim to the blandishments of Wilbur F. Storey, publisher of the Copperhead *Times,* a man whom the strikers held a " traitor to his country, to his God, and to the Workingmen " of Chicago.[57]

With Storey, the workers arraigned all members of the Northwestern Publishers' Association who had sought to break up units of the Typographical Union in the Northwest. To this end publishers were said to have educated women in the art of typesetting solely to make them useful as strikebreakers, and not from any desire to improve " the condition of persons of the female persuasion." The printing trade was wholly unsuited to women, their brother printers insisted. Not even the strongest women could endure the effects of working from fifteen to nineteen hours a day in overcrowded shops where the air was rendered impure by the breath of other workers and exhausted by the thirty or forty gas burners used in the small, unventilated rooms. And when these union men considered the medievalism of the five-dollar-a-week wage paid by the *Times* to its women employees, their indignation mounted still more. No longer, they declared, should society condone the payment of a bare subsistence wage. Why should workmen be denied the right to educate their children, to buy Bancroft and Hildreth, and to take the periodicals of the day " to keep posted upon current events," and to lay up " something against times of adversity "? Indeed, it seemed opportune

[55] *The Workingman's Advocate,* September 17, 1864. The General Trades Assembly was organized in April, 1864. (See p. 168.) According to Gates, the Illinois Central did not profit unduly from the lands, but because many speculators and farmers had bought more than they could pay for, the company, after making generous extensions of time, urged the farmers to cancel their contracts and take smaller amounts. Currency inflation made new prices seem higher. Gates, *The Illinois Central Railroad,* pp. 269–73, 279.

[56] *The Workingman's Advocate,* September 17, 1864; John R. Commons and others, *History of Labour in the United States* (4 v. New York, 1918–35), II, 62.

[57] *The Workingman's Advocate,* September 17, 1864. The account in the *Times* is, on the whole, moderate in tone. (See *The Chicago Times,* September 12, 13, 1864.) In 1861, Wilbur F. Storey purchased the *Times.* His experience in newspaper work included the New York *Journal of Commerce,* the La Porte, Indiana, *Herald,* and papers in Mishawaka, Indiana, and Jackson, Michigan. In 1853, he became part owner of the *Detroit Free Press.*

to remind the rich that their wealth was not "rendered more secure in consequence of being surrounded by hungry, desperate people."[58] Resolutions embodying sentiments such as these were unanimously adopted at the mass meeting, but an attempted boycott of the *Times* failed to achieve the end desired.[59] In the spring of 1867 the *Times* printers again struck.[60]

Such activities did not, however, represent the sole interest of the Chicago Typographical Union. Its national influence was such that several Chicago printers served as officers of the national body,[61] and, in 1866, forty-one local unions sent delegates to a national convention in the city.[62] Benevolences and annual festivals also engaged their attention. The celebration of Franklin's birthday was a gala occasion when speeches, often touching upon national events, punctuated the lighter moments of dancing and feasting.[63]

Although the printers' union seems to have been the most vociferous, other organizations presented a united front for similar reasons

[58] Upon the attitude of Storey and the Northwestern Publishers' Association Albert Griffin, a member of the Typographical Union, spoke. Men were said to work fifteen to nineteen hours for three or four days a week. *The Workingman's Advocate*, September 17, 1864.

[59] For the text of these resolutions see Appendix, pp. 501-3. The mass meeting of September 10 was followed by another on the seventeenth, at which agitation against the *Times* and *Tribune* was carried on. (*Chicago Tribune*, September 18, 1864.) The Typographical Union, however, frowned upon recourse to political party organization as a means of gaining their ends. They urged, instead, that people attend "the preliminary caucuses of the party" to which they belonged and see that none except the friends of labor received nomination. *The Workingman's Advocate*, September 17, 1864.

[60] *Chicago Tribune*, April 6, 1867; *The Chicago Times*, April 6, 7, 1867. In 1864, the Trades Assembly of Detroit tendered its sympathy to the Chicago printers and condemned Storey and the Northwestern Publishers' Association. *The Workingman's Advocate*, September 17, 1864.

[61] See *Chicago Tribune*, May 2, 1863, for statement as to Chicago delegates present at the Cleveland convention in 1863. At the Nashville convention in 1860, John M. Farquhar of Chicago was elected national president and served until 1863, when he resigned. Other Chicago men who served as officers were: James P. Woodbury, corresponding secretary (1853); B. C. Sanford, first vice-president (1856); M. C. Misener, first vice-president (1857); George W. McDonald, second vice-president (1868); Fred K. Tracy, corresponding secretary (1871). Tracy, *op. cit.*, p. 152, *passim; The Chicago Times*, June 6, 1871.

[62] Ninety-one locals had been given charters up to 1866. At this meeting the *Printers' Circular*, published at Philadelphia, was made the official organ. Tracy, *op. cit.*, pp. 215, 219, 220.

[63] *The Daily Democratic Press*, January 17, 1853, January 9, 1855, December 16, 1856, January 19, 1857; *Oquawka Spectator*, January 16, 1855. In 1861, at the Franklin day celebration the following toasts were given: "The Federal Government: May its authority never be abrogated, nor the estates of the realm be a rood less "; " *Union of States, and the Union of Printers.* — Let the people *stick* to the one, and the craft *stand* up to the other, and liberal institutions and well organized labor will *rule* the world." This latter was from fellow unionists in Washington, D. C. *Chicago Tribune*, January 18, 1861.

and with varying degrees of success and permanence. As early as 1852 shipwrights and caulkers opposed employers who would pay less than $2.00 a day,[64] but no very lasting organization seems to have been found until 1860. Then a group of these workers associated themselves for mutual benefit, including sick care and annuities to the aged and infirm, and the maintenance of a wage standard.[65] A mutual protective society for mechanics showed an early craft consciousness on the part of these skilled workmen, and the Chicago Seamen's Mutual Benevolent Society was the beginning of greater solidarity among lake sailors.[66]

In 1856, a convention of master mechanics of the railroads organized to hold monthly meetings where they could discuss "the performance of engines and machinery under [their] direction." [67] By 1863, locomotive engineers had strengthened their ties of common interest by forming the Brotherhood of the Footboard, which a year after its founding became the Brotherhood of Locomotive Engineers.[68] Association for better operation of their engines led to exchanges of other ideas. Strikes on the railroads became more common. One, when the Galena and Chicago Union Railroad failed to keep a wage agreement with its engineers in 1864, occasioned considerable concern because it interfered with the transport of military supplies.[69] At the same time the union called a general strike of all locomotive engineers on lines entering Chicago. But the railroads imported strikebreakers from the East, and the anxiety of those de-

---

[64] *Chicago Daily Democrat,* March 25, 1852. Other strikes took place within the next few years, such as one by ship carpenters in March, 1857, when wages of $2.50 a day were asked, an increase of fifty cents. The employers gave the protestants $2.25. *The Daily Democratic Press,* March 14, 1857.

[65] *Chicago Tribune,* January 17, 1862. Employers were inclined to pay only part of the weekly wage in cash and to retain the balance until it was convenient to settle with their workmen. This grievance the association tried to rectify.

[66] In 1852, journeymen mechanics met to organize. The Mechanics Union Association became their society. (*Chicago Daily Journal,* May 1, 21, 1852.) The Chicago Seamen's Mutual Benevolent Society was founded first for purely benevolent purposes. It was incorporated in 1861. (Act of February 22, 1861, *Private Laws, 1861,* p. 46.) Strikes of seamen were not uncommon. (See *Chicago Tribune,* November 20, 1863, April 13, 1864.) Stronger unionization of sailors was sought in 1869. *The Workingman's Advocate,* April 24, 1869; *Chicago Evening Post,* April 12, 1869.

[67] *The Daily Democratic Press,* April 5, 1856.

[68] Commons, *History of Labour,* II, 62; Frank T. Carlton, *The History and Problems of Organized Labor* (Boston, 1911), p. 58.

[69] *Chicago Tribune,* March 15, 16, 1864.

siring to use the railroads was quickly dispelled. Again the employ-ers came out victors.[70]

Iron molders, machinists and blacksmiths, those engaged in the building trades, and others likewise allied themselves with those of similar vocational experience and sometimes affiliated with their national organizations.[71] Ethnic kinship often helped direct this associative movement.[72] Chicago German workingmen, steeped in the philosophy of the "Forty-eighters," found common cause in the programs of the *Wagner-Verein* (coachmakers), the *Schreiner-Verein* (carpenters), and the *Schneider-Verein* (tailors). By 1855, German members sought articles of incorporation for the Cabinet Makers Society of Chicago and for the Association of Tailors of Chi-cago, each gaining thereby the right to sue and be sued, and to ac-quire, hold, and convey property not in excess of $5,000.[73] The Chi-cago *Arbeiter-Verein,* organized in 1857, could boast, by 1865, a

[70] The lines out of Chicago on which strikes were called were the Galena, the Rock Island, the Michigan Southern, the Illinois Central, and the Chicago and Alton. (*Ibid.,* March 16, 17, 1864.) The Brotherhood later moved more cautiously.

[71] The Iron Molders Union grew out of the conditions brought about by the panic in 1857. (Commons, *History of Labour,* II, 5–6.) The Chicago union was not important in the national union. No Chicago delegates were present at the organization of the National Iron Molders at Philadelphia in 1859. As early as 1855, brass molders, finishers, grinders, and foundry employees organized, but the union was short-lived. (Frank T. Stockton, *The Inter-national Molders Union of North America* [Johns Hopkins University, *Studies in Historical and Political Science,* XXXIX, no. 3. Baltimore, 1921], pp. 15–16, 19.) The first annual ball of the Chicago union was in February, 1861. (*Illinois Staats-Zeitung,* February 16, 21, 1861.) With fifteen foundries and 250 skilled workmen in Chicago, the organization had developed in 1860 until it was able to dedicate its " Library Hall and Reading Room " in Joy's marble building on Lake Street. (*The Press and Tribune,* October 8, 1860. For further information on the union see *Illinois Staats-Zeitung,* February 21, 1861; *The Workingman's Advocate,* April 30, 1870.) The machinists and blacksmiths organized a national union in 1859, and shortly thereafter Chicago had its local unions. By 1869 there were three locals of the national group in Chicago. (*Ibid.,* October 30, 1869.) In 1863, an increase in pay of 20 per cent was asked. (*Chicago Tribune,* March 10, 1863.) On June 8, 1859, the Masons' and Bricklayers' Association was formed. (*The Press and Tribune,* June 9, 1859.) This was evidently short-lived, for in 1864 another union was established. (Royal E. Montgomery, *Industrial Relations in the Chicago Building Trades* [Chicago, 1927], pp. 14, 15.) In 1868, another attempt at unionization was made. (*Chicago Tribune,* June 2, 1868.) In 1863, a Journeymen House and Sign Painters Association was organized, which asked a wage of $1.75 a day as a minimum. (*Ibid.,* March 12, 1863.) As early as 1851 there had been a joint request for increased wages by journeymen painters. (*Chicago Daily Democrat,* Oc-tober 20, 1851.) By 1864 plasterers had organized. Montgomery, *op. cit.,* p. 15; *The Work-ingman's Advocate,* April 2, 1870.

[72] The Irish attitude toward unionization can be found in *The Irish Republic,* June 1, 1867.

[73] Gager, *Case & Co.'s Directory, 1857,* Appendix, p. xxvii; Acts of February 12, 15, 1855, *Private Laws, 1855,* pp. 612, 726–27.

membership of 1,000, which proudly possessed in its library 3,000 volumes.[74]

To the union's hall on Sundays, men, women, and children came to enjoy the social festivities of their club. Here they could drink their beer and sing their songs in peaceful obscurity, unreproved by puritanical Americans. Lectures and an evening school, held twice a week, accelerated the desired adjustment to the ways of a new homeland. Such activities of the union were undoubtedly the most common, but as time went on the ventilation of opinions on political and economic questions became increasingly important. Through Edward Schläger and other Chicago disciples of a radical labor philosophy, German workmen, in particular, were made conscious of the constantly widening gulf between the capitalist and the laboring man.[75]

Conventions of the national organizations in Chicago brought to the city labor leaders chiefly from the urban centers of the East, and made for a greater solidarity along the labor front.[76] But even so, these associations, aside from their benefit and social offerings, were not very effective. Unionization was yet in its infancy. Many workmen were not convinced of the advantages of organization, and even those who were a part of it were, at times, lukewarm in its support. Individual employers and organized employer groups fought the movement with all the weapons at their command. Nevertheless, when, in 1864, some iron molders successfully carried through a city-wide strike for higher pay, and when, in 1868, the national organization promised aid to bricklayers striking for $5.00 a day in place of the prevailing $4.00 or $4.50, employers began to perceive in the unions a strength not known before.[77] The ends desired by work-

[74] Halpin, *Directory, 1865–66*, Appendix, p. xxi; Act of February 15, 1865, *Private Laws, 1865*, I, 63.

[75] *Illinois Staats-Zeitung*, February 12, August 8, 1861; *Chicago Tribune*, August 22, 1864; *The Workingman's Advocate*, July 31, 1869.

[76] Among others, the sixth annual national convention of the cigar makers was held in Chicago in 1869. (*Ibid.*, September 18, 1869.) In January, 1870, the National Bricklayers' Union was entertained by Chicago. (*The Chicago Times*, January 12, 1870.) The convention of the National Labor Union, or the National Labor Congress, in 1867 was held in Chicago. Commons, *History of Labour*, II, 115; *Chicago Tribune*, August 22, 1867; *The Chicago Times*, August 20–24, 1867.

[77] *Chicago Morning Post*, April 19, 30, 1864; *The Chicago Times*, June 11, 1868; *Chicago Tribune*, June 2, 3, 4, 8, 11, 12, 1868; *The Workingman's Advocate*, April 24, 1869. As was the case in many other groups, benefit provisions enticed more workmen into the association of bricklayers. (*Ibid.*, March 12, 1870.) The Bricklayers and Masons Benevolent

ingmen were not always gained by peaceful means. Violence and intimidation sometimes became tools in preventing production; employers who persisted in hiring those unacceptable to a union were, at times, blacklisted.[78] But the drive for the closed shop seems to have had, at best, only temporary and fleeting success.[79]

In 1864, the General Trades Assembly was organized to coordinate the activities of more than a score of unions in the city, following the example of Rochester, Boston, New York, St. Louis, and other places. A plan of organization, drawn up by a delegate from each union, placed the direction of the Assembly in the hands of representatives from the subordinate unions, each of which paid to the Assembly a tax of twenty-five cents a member. By 1865, the General Trades Assembly proudly announced that it represented eighty-five hundred workingmen, and shortly thereafter it reported that twenty-four unions made up its constituency.[80]

High costs of living and excessive war profits impelled the Assembly to announce, in the summer of 1864, a program which demanded an equalization of the influence of labor and capital in the government of the country; an equalization of the tax load, which

Association of the City of Chicago was incorporated February, 1865. Act of February 16, 1865, *Private Laws, 1865,* I, 65–66.

[78] See, for example, the activities of strikers in quarries along the Illinois and Michigan Canal in 1854, when nonstrikers were driven out. The sheriff with a " sufficient retinue, thoroughly armed and provided with cords, hand cuffs, and other implements," was called to the scene of the disturbance. The quarries affected were those of Singer and Talcott, David G. Skelley, and the Illinois Stone and Lime Company. The men were getting ten shillings (about $1.25) a day and asked for twelve ($1.50). *The Daily Democratic Press,* June 2, 5, 6, 1854.

[79] In 1863, the carpenters and joiners, who were in the process of unionizing at the time, drew up a list of employers who persisted in hiring incompetent workers and presented the list to various architects with the request that such persons not be employed to do any work upon plans and specifications let from their offices. (*Chicago Tribune,* March 7, 13, 1863.) The closed shop entered the list of issues at stake in strikes by the carpenters in 1864, and by the shoemakers in 1869. (See p. 173.) In 1867, men employed at Magill and Company's Mechanics' Dry Dock walked out because a man not a member of the shipwrights' and caulkers' union had been employed. *Chicago Tribune,* March 19, 20, 1867.

[80] *Ibid.,* April 27, 1864; John C. W. Bailey, *Chicago City Directory, 1864–65* (Chicago, 1864), " City and County Register," pp. xl-xlv (hereafter cited as Bailey, *Directory, 1864–65*); Commons, *History of Labour,* II, 21–22. In Chicago, on April 26, 1864, representatives from the various trade unions met. George K. Hazlett, president of the General Trades Assembly, and Elisha W. McComas, lawyer and one-time editor of the *Herald* and the *Times,* addressed the meetings. (*Chicago Tribune,* April 25, 27, 1864.) Permanent organization was effected on May 10. (Bailey, *Directory, 1864–65,* " City and County Register," p. xlv; *Chicago Tribune,* April 27, 1864.) The *Workingman's Advocate* was the official organ. Chicago Tribune, *Annual Review, 1865,* p. 12.

seemed to labor to fall unjustly on the poor; a gold basis for wages; and shorter hours of work. Under the influence of Virginia-born Elisha W. McComas and those who held that war profits were of little benefit to the workingman, the Assembly insisted that a greater number of officials, including President Lincoln and Governor Yates, shoulder muskets just as the laborer was obliged to do; and they wanted the war terminated at once. To bring about these ends the Trades Assembly resolved to encourage the formation of a labor party.[81]

Throughout 1864, the Trades Assembly proved a provocative and irritating source of opposition to the proponents of war, as it frequently allied itself with those critical of Republican leadership. In the campaign it electioneered against William Bross as lieutenant governor because of his antiunionism, it supported Cyrus H. McCormick against John Wentworth in the contest for Congressman because McCormick promised more to labor, and it attacked the stand of Republican candidates for the state legislature on the labor question.[82]

The radical labor organ, the *Workingman's Advocate*, had demanded in early autumn that candidates for the legislature give unequivocal answers to the following questions:

Will you use your utmost endeavor to have the present system of farming out the convict labor of the State Penitentiary *totally and forever abolished?* Will you endeavor to procure the repeal of the " La Salle Black Laws "? Will you endeavor to use all your powers to procure a rightful portion of the Public Lands for the purpose of founding institutions of education, by the U.S. [*sic*] Congress, so that our children may be benefitted by it? Will you labor earnestly that all

81 *Chicago Tribune,* August 22, 1864. In the meeting of the Chicago General Trades Assembly both German and English were spoken. Among the grievances nursed by labor was the failure of the state legislature to pass a mechanics' lien law satisfactory to workingmen. In 1861, the German Social Laborers' Society of the Tenth Ward joined with the Union of Clubs of South Chicago in a request to the state legislature that such a law be passed. (*Ibid.,* January 29, 1861.) In 1867, the National Labor Union at Chicago adopted a resolution of similar import, directed to the various state legislatures. (John R. Commons and others, eds., *A Documentary History of American Industrial Society* [11 v. Cleveland, 1910], IX, 192–93; *The Chicago Times,* August 23, 1867.) In Illinois, the legislature passed a general lien law satisfactory to labor in 1869. *The Workingman's Advocate,* May 29, 1869; Illinois, *The Revised Statutes of the State of Illinois, A. D. 1874* (Springfield, 1874), p. 668 (hereafter cited as *Revised Statutes, 1874*).

82 *Chicago Tribune,* August 22, September 3, November 2, 1864; *The Workingman's Advocate,* September 17, November 5, 1864. See pp. 281–83.

working men may, before all others, become preferred creditors in case of failure of assignment of corporate bodies or individuals? Will you agree to introduce and advocate the passage of a bill to *shorten the hours of labor?*

Democratic candidates answered in the affirmative, with the reservation that they were unwilling to advocate shorter work hours since less worktime might reduce wages and thus lower standards of living. Republican candidates, on the other hand, gave less satisfactory assurance of sympathy with labor. The workers, therefore, served notice on the *Tribune,* allegedly hostile to unions, that they no longer would be made " dupes of " by " false statements and past hypocritical catch-words." [83] In the campaign, the Trades Assembly played a conspicuous if unsuccessful part. After the results of the election were known, it turned its attention to other ways of achieving its desires. Throughout 1866 and 1867 the strength of the Trades Assembly seemed unimpaired, but by 1870 it had " died a natural death," just as it did in cities of the East. Later it was re-formed as the Trade and Labor Council which still later became the Trade and Labor Assembly.[84]

Like the movement in general, Chicago unionization until mid-'sixties was not in the direction of national federation. In 1864, however, delegates were sent to Louisville to meet with those from seven other cities to consider means of national co-operation.[85] The constitution, framed by a committee composed of a delegate from each state represented, decried the attempt of the " secret organization " of capitalists which was trying to crush the workers' " manhood."

[83] *The Workingman's Advocate,* September 17, October 22, November 5, 1864. The La Salle Black Law passed February 13, 1863, as a result of a series of coal mine strikes. It made possible the imposition of a fine of $100 upon anyone guilty, by threat, intimidation, or otherwise, of preventing any other person from working at any terms he saw fit. It also made illegal a combination of two or more persons to deprive an owner of property from its lawful use or management, or to keep anyone from working. The penalty was $500 or six months in jail. Earl R. Beckner, *A History of Labor Legislation in Illinois* (Chicago, 1929), p. 8.

[84] *Chicago Tribune,* January 1, 1867; Austin, *Bailey's Directory, 1867–68,* " City and County Register," pp. xxxviii–xxxix; *The Workingman's Advocate,* February 6, October 8, 1870. In 1877, the Trades Assembly became the Trade and Labor Council, and in 1880 the Trade and Labor Assembly. Trade and Labor Assembly of Chicago, Illinois, *Constitution, By-Laws and Rules of Order . . . adopted May, 1880* (Chicago, 1886).

[85] Commons, *History of Labour,* II, 35–36, 38–39. See *ibid.,* pp. 33, 34, for earlier attempts to effect a national union movement. The cities represented were Evansville, St. Louis, Buffalo, Boston, Detroit, Louisville, Cincinnati, and Chicago. John Blake, a printer and a member of the staff of the *Workingman's Advocate,* was the delegate from Chicago. Commons, *Documentary History,* IX, 120.

The workers' statement pointed out that employers had taken for granted that they had "the right to own and control labour." But even after this rather hostile pronouncement the delegates recommended conferences, in so far as possible, to adjust disputes over wages between capital and labor. Under the name of the International Industrial Assembly of North America, the men in attendance at the convention proposed that local assemblies help sewing women to organize; that legislation be enacted prohibiting convict labor and the system of wage payment by store orders; that agitation for an eight-hour day be continued; and that consumers' co-operative stores be established by trades assemblies. An especially heartening note for the Chicago delegates was sounded when the convention in strong language condemned the *Chicago Times* for its attitude toward the Typographical Union, a few days after a similar sentiment had been voiced by the Trades Assembly of Detroit.[86]

In spite of the interest manifested at the meeting, the Louisville convention did not promote effectively the nationalization of trade unions, for at the time labor was often able to obtain wage increases through its local organizations. The trades assembly, furthermore, in Chicago as elsewhere, seemed to many an adequate means of settling difficulties between the different trade unions. But conditions were less favorable after the war, and Chicago delegates gladly joined in a movement for a national convention at Baltimore in August, 1866. Here Andrew C. Cameron, representing the Chicago Trades Assembly and the Illinois Grand Eight Hour League, as chairman of the Committee on Trades' Unions, Organization and Strikes, endorsed trade organization of skilled workmen, general workingmen's associations for the unskilled, and the formation of an international organization. The convention supported arbitration rather than strikes in disputes between employer and employee and recommended that the machinery of settlement be in charge of a committee on arbitration set up by each trades assembly.

Agitation and organization for an eight-hour day were suggested as "the two great levers" to bring to the workingman "more time for moral, intellectual and social culture" to which it was felt he was entitled. Edward Schläger and Cameron urged the inaugura-

[86] Commons, *History of Labour*, II, 36–37; *The Workingman's Advocate*, November 5, 1864; Commons, *Documentary History*, IX, 123.

tion of a new political party so forcefully that the fighting Cameron was instructed to embody the sentiment in a report. As finally presented, the report declared that " the time has come when the workingmen of the United States should cut themselves aloof from party ties and predilections, and organise themselves into a National Labor Party " pledged to the passage by Congress and state legislatures of laws making eight hours a legal day's work. The Baltimore Congress also sympathetically discussed the place of women in industry, it recorded its conviction that the public domain should be disposed of to settlers only, and it approved co-operative stores and workshops.[87]

The next year the National Labor Congress met in Chicago and again considered these matters. Embattled delegates appeared more interested than ever before in the problems common to laborers, farmers, and small businessmen. At the moment, the Labor Congress, newly christened the National Labor Union, wanted monetary reform more than anything else. Under the leadership of Cameron, chairman of the Committee on Political Organization, the convention espoused greenbackism and recommended that the industrial classes organize a political party which should name candidates, both national and local, to combat the national banking system or " money monopoly," which was to them " the parent of all monopolies — the very root and essence of slavery — railroad, warehouse and all other monopolies." [88] This endorsement of greenbackism mirrored the reactions of workingmen to the economic factors then believed to be

[87] *Ibid.,* IX, 126–32, 134–35, 137–38; Commons, *History of Labour,* II, 86–87, 96–102. Among workers' newspapers which were endorsed at this time were the *Workingman's Advocate* and *German Reform,* of Chicago.

[88] Sixty-four organizations were represented by seventy-one delegates. Among the committees which reported were those upon the questions of eight hours and public employment, Negro labor, public lands and agriculture, apprentices, mechanics' liens, and local unions. Resolutions were adopted calling on the federal Congress for the " speedy restoration of the agricultural industry of the Southern States," as " of vital importance to the industrial classes of the north "; one declaring that " a direct exchange of produce and imports ought to be established between the workingmen of the east and producers of the west, and that the labor associations in the west ought to take the place of the middle men, who now increase unduly the price in the necessaries of life, and that measures be established by said associations to effect the desirable exchange, and furnish workingmen with produce and imports, such as coffee, etc., at a cost price as near as possible." The Labor Congress authorized the president to employ lecturers when finances would permit. It also favored the taxation of government bonds and, at the instigation of the Tailors' International Union, protested against the extension of the patent for the Howe sewing machine. Commons, *Documentary History,* IX, 40, 45, 173–94; *The Chicago Times,* August 20–24, 26, 1867; Commons, *History of Labour,* II, 87, 101, 115, 119, 121–22.

depressing labor in America. In their search for a means to cure their ills, workers had now turned to a political rather than a purely economic weapon. Political unity among laboring men based on financial reform was the American expedient which for a few years held the promise of a good life for those who toiled.

In the late 'sixties trade unionism made appreciable gains, penetrating into fields of labor hitherto untouched and reinvigorating faltering organizations of an earlier day.[89] No group felt more keenly than did the shoemakers the ruinous results of the substitution of machines for men. In the face of this crisis the Chicago Shoemakers Union, piloted by aggressive and gregarious German workers, turned, in 1868, to the Order of the Knights of St. Crispin and made their lodge the third in the West.[90] Other craftsmen took a similar stand under like conditions.

Common laborers, whose pay was least and whose strikes for better working conditions and pay had generally turned out unfavorably, established, in February, 1865, the Laborers' Benevolent Association.[91] White-collar workers, such as clerks in mercantile establishments, banded together sporadically, seeking a half holiday a week or an earlier closing hour.[92] How, they asked, could clerks with a fourteen-hour workday possess even as much information as mechanics whose apprenticeship usually required only eleven hours of work? The Chicago Mercantile Early Closing Association, in 1855, and the Dry Goods Clerks' Early Closing Association, in 1861, followed by others, strove for a shorter day, sometimes appealing to the " fair ones " not to trade with merchants who denied their clerks

[89] For example, unionization was attempted under the Car Drivers' Protective Union and by the laundrymen in 1869. (*The Workingman's Advocate,* July 17, December 2, 1869.) A union of musicians attempted to regulate the activities of orchestra players and to dictate to employers. *Chicago Tribune,* June 9, 14, 1868.

[90] Don D. Lescohier, *The Knights of St. Crispin* . . . (University of Wisconsin, *Economics and Political Science Series,* VII, no. 1. Madison, 1910), p. 6; *The Workingman's Advocate,* December 11, 1869. See also *Chicago Tribune,* March 30, 1869.

[91] Act of February 13, 1865, *Private Laws, 1865,* I, 82; A. T. Andreas, *History of Cook County, Illinois* . . . (Chicago, 1884), p. 391; Halpin, *Directory, 1865–66,* Appendix, p. xxiii. The Laborers' Association was reorganized in 1870, at which time there were over five hundred members. *The Workingman's Advocate,* May 21, 1870.

[92] For example, in 1848, by petition clerks asked for an eight o'clock closing hour. (*Daily Democrat,* April 20, 1848.) In 1855, leading grocers under the force of public opinion announced an eight o'clock closing hour during the winter. At the same time some shoe dealers and clothiers followed this practice except on Saturday evenings. (*The Daily Democratic Press,* October 2, December 18, 1855.) Throughout the 'sixties agitation continued. *Chicago Tribune,* May 21, 1861, July 17, 23, September 24, 1864; *Illinois Staats-Zeitung,* May 22, 1861.

"the perfume of the flowers" and "the fresh lake breeze." Sometimes their plea was for Sunday free from toil. The barbers, in 1855, turned at last to the Common Council, begging that body to close by ordinance all shops on that day, a request which the city fathers felt impelled to deny.[93]

As in other places where the urban-industrial impact was becoming manifest, Chicago, by the mid-'sixties, looked to an eight-hour day for the wage earner. The laboring classes, pleading that their intellectual and social well-being would be advanced by a shorter workday, found their efforts opposed just as had been other attempts to improve their condition. The employing groups raised the bogy of ten hours' pay for eight hours' work and the consequent increase in the cost of living; and rising prices, they made clear, would touch wage earners as well as employers.[94]

In spite of these objections, the movement in Illinois did not lag behind that in the East, possibly because the tireless Cameron maintained a running fire, never losing sight of his legislative goal. His leadership in the national congresses after the war reflected in somewhat broader outline his activities in Chicago and in turn kept alive the movement in the Midwest. By 1865, under his chairmanship, a city-wide meeting of dissatisfied workmen preceded Chicago ward organizations, soon called the Eight-Hour Leagues. In March, 1866, these leagues had become organized well enough to test their strength in the municipal election of that spring by demanding from some of the regular party candidates an expression of their attitude toward the movement. The power of the leagues was clearly apparent when the votes were counted, for nearly one third of the aldermen chosen, according to the *Workingman's Advocate,* were committed to the Cameron forces.[95] Success in the city election also encouraged the

---

[93] This attempt by the barbers is undoubtedly among the earliest attempts made to get such support from the council. (*The Daily Democratic Press,* June 12, July 25, December 8, 12, 1855; *Chicago Tribune,* May 21, 1861.) In 1864, the Association of Salesmen on South Clark Street was successful in getting employers to close at eight o'clock between October 1 and January 1, and at seven o'clock between January 1 and March 1. *Ibid.,* September 24, 1864.

[94] *Ibid.,* September 18, October 9, 1865.

[95] *Ibid.,* September 15, 1865, March 25, 1866. Aldermen held to be favorable to the movement were elected from the Second, Fourth, Seventh, Twelfth, and Fourteenth wards. Credit for the return to office of Stephen Barrett in the Third Ward was taken. The municipal election was April 17, 1866. (*The Workingman's Advocate,* April 21, 1866; *Chicago Tribune,* April 18, 1866.) There were sixteen wards at this time. See also p. 288.

leagues to seek pledges from Congressional candidates to support the movement in Congress.[96]

Before they had gained the much-heralded seats in the Common Council, Cameron and his followers petitioned the council for an eight-hour ordinance to apply to all employees of the city and to be effective after April 1. They based their appeal on the precedent of regulation by law of labor on the roads, which could be demanded of all males between twenty-one and fifty. Bowing to what appeared the will of a majority, the council instructed the judiciary committee to prepare such an ordinance to apply, as workmen requested, to all laborers and mechanics hired by the city. This hopeful action Mayor John B. Rice stopped short through parliamentary tactics, declaring that a previous petition had been received and appropriately referred, and that this, therefore, was out of order. A subservient council sustained Rice's ruling. In April, Alderman Charles G. Wicker of the Third Ward, where many laborers lived, tried again to bring about the passage of such an ordinance. But his resolution was defeated when the mayor broke a tie vote by siding with the negative.[97] The perseverance of the workingmen, however, was rewarded a few months later when the council could no longer resist pressure and passed the ordinance desired.[98]

Success also attended the league's efforts in the state, for early in 1867 the legislature acceded to workers' demands, enacting a law affecting all mechanical trades and arts and "other cases of labor and service by the day, except in farm employments," where there was no agreement to the contrary. The act, however, in no way affected service by the year, month, or week; nor did it prevent persons from doing overtime work or making their own contracts. Cameron's aggressive leadership had borne fruit. Illinois, his state, was the first to pass such legislation.[99]

[96] Norman B. Judd, who was elected, gave such a promise. *Chicago Tribune*, October 9, 1866.

[97] Chicago, *Council Proceedings, 1866*, pp. 252, 253, 273. See, for further eight-hour agitation in the council, *Chicago Tribune*, January 1, 1867; Chicago, *Council Proceedings, 1866*, pp. 103, 209, 230. Failure to get such legislation in the county is discussed in *The Workingman's Advocate*, January 1, 1867. See also Cook County Board of Supervisors, *Reports, 1866–71* (n.p., n.d.), p. 3. For the attitude of the Irish see *The Irish Republic*, June 1, 8, 1867.

[98] *The Workingman's Advocate*, January 1, 1867; *Chicago Evening Journal*, April 10, 1867; *Chicago Tribune*, January 1, 1867; Chicago, *Council Proceedings, 1866*, p. 230.

[99] Act of March 5, 1867, *Public Laws, 1867*, p. 101; *Revised Statutes, 1874*, p. 478. For Illinois legislation regulating labor on the roads and used as precedent for eight-hour laws,

Chicago employers, on the whole, heartily disapproved of the new statute. Within a short time over seventy of them decided to adopt the practice of paying workmen by the hour instead of by the day. On the ground that shorter hours meant a lower standard of living, they decried any attempt to lighten the day's work. Eventually, they declared, under such a plan both " workmen and the capitalists must suffer a diminution of wealth in the same proportion." [100]

The open hostility of employers and their declarations of intended nullification of the law spurred labor to a greater unity of spirit than might otherwise have developed. Meetings of workmen were held. On March 30 they gathered to endorse the new law and heard the redoubtable Cameron and other labor leaders counsel vigilance. The assembled workingmen and their wives listened also to the governor of the state, Richard J. Oglesby, who held that eight hours a day were enough for a man to work. With a sense of satisfaction they heard Robert G. Ingersoll, recently appointed attorney general of the state, declare that he thought that a workday should be still less. [101] Threats by the General Trades Assembly of strikes, if the law were not put into operation, left both employers and employees fearful. Conditions prevailing especially in the building trades, reaper and boiler manufactories, foundries, shipyards, and railroad shops boded ill for employers of workmen trained to perform tasks in these lines, if the law were not obeyed. The prevalence of strikes in Pittsburgh, New York, and other eastern cities bred a " numbness " in business entrepreneurs, as class arrayed itself against class. [102]

With prices falling, some employers were led to make concessions. The City Railway Company of the South and West divisions proposed for its employees an eight-hour day with proportionately reduced pay; the Illinois Stone Company, Singer and Talcott, and Edwin Walker offered to raise the wages of quarrymen from $1.75 to $2.25 for a ten-hour day; and the McCormick reaper factory

see Illinois, *A Compilation of the Statutes of the State of Illinois of a General Nature in Force January 1, 1857* (N. H. Purple, comp. 2d ed. 2 v. Chicago, 1857), II, 1046. Missouri followed Illinois in eight-hour legislation on March 13, and New York passed such a law May 9. Commons, *Documentary History*, IX, 330; *Laws of the State of Missouri . . . 1867* (Jefferson City, 1867), p. 132; *Laws of the State of New York . . . 1867* (2 v. Albany, 1867), II, 2138.

[100] *Chicago Tribune*, March 10, 17, 22, April 18, 24, 1867. Among the employers who passed resolutions against the eight-hour law were manufacturers and the master builders.

[101] *Ibid.*, March 31, 1867; *The Chicago Times*, March 31, 1867.

[102] *Chicago Tribune*, April 18, 21, 25, 26, 1867.

reached an amicable arrangement with its men.[103] But the Rock Island and North Western railroads announced that if Chicago could not provide enough men willing to work ten hours, their shops would be moved to Iowa.[104] Because of the issue, Ford and Fuller discharged about one fourth of their employees from their machine shop; the Northwestern Manufacturing Company dismissed one third of its workmen; employers of painters notified their journeymen that eight hours' work meant eight hours' pay; and some manufacturers of heavy goods gave notice that after May 1 those averse to working ten hours need not return.[105]

On May 1 thousands of men from Chicago and from the towns of Illinois tramped for hours over the streets of the city in a " grand civic procession " to celebrate the inauguration of the new law. Forty-four unions proudly bore banners inscribed with sentiments appropriate to the day, or piloted colorful floats and models suggestive of the crafts which had worked so earnestly for the law. At the lake shore they paused long enough to hear Mayor Rice implore them to consider "with reason, calmness, and conciliation" the situation which faced the city, and to be receptive to compromise in case employers felt unable to reduce the hours of work.[106] They heard their own spokesmen warn, in both English and German, of the alleged desire of capital to control the fruits of labor, the wealth of the whole nation. Then they defiantly resolved to maintain at all hazards the principle that eight hours constituted a legal day's work, and they boldly denounced "the high-handed action" of employers who had discharged or proposed to discharge workmen for declining to work more.[107] Thus with denunciations of the employing group ringing in their ears, thousands of tired marchers went their separate ways,

[103] *Ibid.*, April 19, 1867; *The Chicago Times*, May 1, 1867. Several quarries were located about twenty-five miles from Chicago along the canal. In the case of the McCormick reaper factory, employees agreed to work for the time being ten hours for the same wages they were receiving, calling two of these hours " extra " time.

[104] *Ibid.*, April 30, 1867. It was said a total of three thousand men were employed by these railroads. The Illinois Central and the Chicago and Alton took a somewhat similar stand on the ten-hour day.

[105] *Ibid.; Chicago Tribune*, April 28, 1867. It was said that about one half of those affected acceded to these demands. The examples cited are typical of the situation which had developed.

[106] Governor Oglesby, who had felt eight hours sufficient for a day's work when he addressed Chicago laborers on March 30, now urged workmen not to insist too strongly on their rights and thereby cause business to suffer. *Ibid.*, May 2, 1867.

[107] *Ibid.*

unconscious that they may have been responsible for the designation, at a later time, of May 1 as the day for the annual world-wide demonstration of labor solidarity.[108]

Dawn of the next day found much of the business of the city palsied by strikes in carshops, freight depots, planing mills, and lumber yards. To men, many of whom had but a short time before emerged from a war where violent death had been a constant expectation, the use of force to gain ends desired seemed a logical course of action. Sometimes those who had stayed by their jobs were obliged to abandon work; some nonconformist shop owners, rather than brave the bludgeons of these determined men, submitted to the closing of doors. In the lumber yards and other establishments of Bridgeport, along the South Branch of the river, control passed almost completely for a time into the hands of an infuriated mob whose visits to the saloons had so filled it with "fight" that all laborers were forced to cease work at the point of "fence-pickets, pieces of lath, and short sticks." [109]

Despite efforts of the police to keep order, despite the general impression that laborers could be brought in from outside if none could be found near at hand, despite agreements reached especially by lumber dealers to employ only men who would work ten hours a day, despite threats to quell the strike by force, riots and the destruction of property kept the populace in a state of panic — a panic fanned to fever pitch not only by actual happenings but by terrifying rumors.[110]

[108] When the eight-hour movement was revived in mid-'eighties, workers chose May 1 as the day to inaugurate their campaign. When the American Federation of Labor sought to further the movement, with a campaign to begin May 1, 1890, it made known its attitude to the Second International in Paris in 1889. The International endorsed the American Federation of Labor plan and went on record in favor of an international manifestation. By this action it started the international May Day. See Lewis L. Lorwin, *Labor and Internationalism* (New York, 1929), p. 71; Commons, *History of Labour*, II, 376 ff.

[109] *Chicago Tribune*, May 3, 1867; *The Chicago Times*, May 3, 1867. The freight depots of the Rock Island, North Western, and Michigan Central railroads, many of the lumber yards and several planing mills, and the Illinois Central Railroad carshops and roundhouse were among the places closed by the strikers. At the lumber yard of Ferry and Son, the men were told that if they worked more than eight hours they would be whipped on the way home. At the sash and door factory of Richards and Hunt, the employers told their workmen that because of the trouble they would work only eight hours that day, but that they would resume the ten-hour basis the next. One man at the Kretsinger and Farr lumber yard who continued to work was badly beaten. Two men at the Newaygo Lumber Company were also injured. *Chicago Tribune*, May 3, 1867.

[110] *Ibid.*, May 3, 4, 5, 1867; *The Chicago Times*, May 3, 4, 5, 1867. The *Tribune* as-

By May 8, the main strength of labor's opposition was broken. Men must eat. Many accepted a wage reduction in proportion to a reduction in hours; many remained unemployed, their places now held by strikebreakers. Machine shops reopened on a ten-hour plan; some of the railroads took much of their repair work to Indiana, Iowa, downstate Illinois, and Wisconsin. It was estimated that during the first two weeks of the strike $125,000 in wages had been lost by those striking. Labor seemed defeated on all fronts. Although agitation for an eight-hour workday continued for the next few years, the backbone of opposition to the employers' scheme of pay was paralyzed at least for the time being.[111] Not until 1886 was the eight-hour movement to take the attention of the city, this time in connection with the tragic episode of the Haymarket riot.

Acceptance by the mass of workers of such an outcome militant labor leaders saw as a form of moral inertia. In Cameron's eyes, retreats were "craven." To the outside observer, however, these retreats seemed at times inevitable under the prevailing economic philosophy, for on all counts organized employers seemed to command the balance of power. In the 'fifties, employers' associations as such, of course, had experienced far less trouble with employee groups than in the 'sixties. In both decades those who controlled wages, on the whole, seemed to act collectively to their greatest advantage in times of crisis.[112] There were instances of unity, however, in times of industrial peace. In 1853, the master horseshoers com-

---

sured its readers that the Dearborn Light Artillery as well as an increased police force was in readiness to protect property. Both the *Times* and *Tribune* reported the availability of outside men for work. Employers at a meeting at the Tremont House asserted their right to contract for ten or more hours and declared that it was impossible to increase wages. They voted acceptance of the eight-hour day as legal, however. Among the acts of violence and destruction for which strikers were said to be responsible, though without proof, was the burning of the Armour and Dole grain elevator. The burning brought a second proclamation by the mayor urging strikers to desist. Among the rumors which proved especially terrifying, but which had no basis in fact, was one to the effect that the Dearborn Light Artillery had opened fire on several hundred men gathered near Twelfth and Canal streets and had killed scores of people.

[111] *Chicago Tribune*, May 5, 7, 8, 9, 11, 1867; *The Chicago Times*, May 8, 15, 1867; *The Workingman's Advocate*, April 9, 1870. By May 5 the strikes began to subside. Freight companies, for example, replaced all strikers. At the same time railroad shop employees out on strike received from shopmen at Amboy and Centralia heartening news that they were also still on strike.

[112] *Ibid.*; Commons, *History of Labour*, II, 26. For opposition of employers of stone cutters who were on strike, see *The Daily Democratic Press*, March 16, May 30, 1854, July 18, 1855; of bricklayers, see *The Chicago Times*, June 11, 1868.

bined to set a price on their work and to provide for the inspection of their books, and in 1856, vessel owners met with the standing committee of the Board of Trade and agreed upon a rate of wages to be paid seamen.[113] In the 'sixties the Northwestern Publishers' Association, the Canal Boat Owners' Association, and the Chicago Iron Founders' Association operated successfully in their own interests, holding, in the words of the Iron Founders' Association, that it was "not only the *right* but the *duty* of employers to check and suppress" by "any lawful means" movements of employees to enter the sphere of employers in determining pay for labor.[114]

At a time when trade unionism met almost universal opposition from the employers of labor, forms of co-operation between employers and employees sometimes received open endorsement.[115] By the late 'sixties, some business promoters were reported to be acting with workmen with a view to "arriving at some method of co-operation" which would give to each man employed "an interest in the establishment" with which he was connected, thereby insuring better products and also retarding the expansion of the trades union. The movement had "assumed an active shape" at the Eagle Works, the foundry of P. W. Gates, an early manufacturer in Chicago. Although a portion of the stock for some time had been held by employees, Gates planned in 1867 to give each workman a semiannual dividend of 5 per cent upon the wages he earned.[116] The Northwestern Manufacturing Company, through its president, Richard T. Crane, offered employees a share in the fortunes in its metal foundry after its incorporation by the legislature in 1865.[117] This form of copartnership between employers and employees met approval

---

[113] *The Daily Democratic Press*, February 17, 1853, May 24, 1856. The master horse-shoers, in 1853, also agreed that they would make no contracts to shoe horses at a reduced rate. The prices agreed upon were thirty-seven and one-half cents for setting new shoes, twenty-five cents for setting secondhand shoes, and eighteen cents for resetting shoes.

[114] Italics in the quotation are in the original. Organizations such as a Master Tailors Association in 1864 served both social and commercial purposes. (Carlton, *op. cit.*, p. 89; *Chicago Tribune*, April 25, 1864; Andreas, *History of Chicago*, II, 348. See also Halpin, *Directory, 1865-66*, Appendix, p. xxi.) After the strike of engineers in 1864 on the Galena and Chicago Union Railroad the Board of Directors resolved, among other things, that combinations of labor endangered property and should be discouraged. Galena and Chicago Union Railroad Company, *Record Book B*, pp. 559-61.

[115] *The Chicago Times*, April 22, 1867, April 3, 1869; *Chicago Tribune*, April 11, 1867.

[116] *Ibid.*, May 11, 1867; Pierce, *A History of Chicago*, I, 142. The Eagle Works was originally the foundry of Scoville and Gates.

[117] Merchants, Farmers and Mechanics Savings Bank, *The Labor Question*, pp. 42-43.

from the press, which considered such a method of co-operation fair to both parties concerned and a sure way to kill a movement toward unionization.[118] A painters' association, on the basis of this arrangement, had by 1867 demonstrated the practicability of this means of settling the ever-pressing problem of satisfying employees with the returns they received for their labor.[119]

But there were few manufactories or other forms of business where the laborers shared with employers in the profits. Co-operative undertakings generally rested upon mutual interests among workers trying to provide the necessaries of life. Sometimes stock ownership made possible enterprises which otherwise might not have been carried on, as the building of a hall by the *Aktien-Gesellschaft* chiefly for the purpose of German entertainments on the West Side.[120] By 1865, co-operatives to bring within the workingman's means those things he most needed found some willing sponsors, who followed the lead of Philadelphians who had set up in April, 1864, their "Union Coöperative Number 1" upon the principles of the Rochdale Pioneers of England.[121] In November, 1865, "a joint stock store to furnish stockholders provisions at cost" was opened according to the British plan, under the superintendency of C. Riley, at 213 East Washington Street.[122]

A Citizens Protective Fuel Company was organized in the late 'sixties to provide coal to its members at fifty cents a ton above cost price, but the venture was ill-starred and was pointed to by opponents of such endeavors as further proof that departures from orthodox selling methods were unwise. In this case arguments seemed entirely on the side of exponents of common practice, for the superintendent and treasurer of the fuel company were accused of embezzling the funds. But hope sprang eternal in the hearts of these innovators, and shortly the fuel company was reorganized as the Citizens Protective Fuel Association, with a capital stock of $200,000 to be distributed into eight thousand shares, for the purpose of purchasing

[118] *The Chicago Times*, April 28, 1867.
[119] *Ibid.*, April 29, 1867.
[120] *Illinois Staats-Zeitung*, February 23, 1864. See also *The Chicago Times*, February 22, 25, March 3, 1864.
[121] Edward W. Bemis, "Coöperation in the Middle States," *History of Coöperation in the United States* (Johns Hopkins University, *Studies in History and Political Science*, VI, pt. 3. Baltimore, 1888), p. 141.
[122] *Chicago Tribune*, October 11, November 20, 1865.

and selling coal, coke, and wood, and of engaging in mining operations if it were deemed necessary. In 1869, another fuel association
was organized for similar purposes.[123] About the same time that efforts were directed toward providing fuel at reasonable prices, a co-
operative laundry, for the use of fifty families, attempted to eliminate
"the dread of every well-regulated household," washing and ironing.
Still other enterprises represented the growth of the co-operative
movement. Even the field of life insurance was invaded, the Provi-
dent Life Insurance Company of Chicago paying a member's family
$5,000 in the event of his death.[124]

Most of these co-operative endeavors were for the purposes of distribution. But just as in other places where co-operation was tried,
production co-operatives were developed in Chicago in the late
'sixties. One of the most conspicuous undertakings grew out of a
strike carried on in 1869 by journeymen tailors for increased wages.
Rather than accede to the demands of the union, Ely and Brothers,
employers, declared their willingness to sell out — "a proposition,"
in the words of the *Workingman's Advocate,* "favorably entertained by the union," which was anxious "to test the principles of
co-operative industry." In about a month the tailors opened their
shop and advertised that they were prepared "to execute orders in
the highest style of the art at 20 per cent. below the prices" charged
by fashionable establishments.[125] This co-operative experiment had
been preceded by a co-operative shop of carpenters and joiners, and
boilermakers, machinists, molders, and other trades had made like
attempts, some of which lasted but a short time.[126]

The Germans, in the workingmen's associations, were especially
willing to undertake such experiments in the hope of more nearly
equalizing the cost of living and the returns of labor. At times they
linked co-operation with the eight-hour question, as they sought
a way to abolish "the system of hired labor" from which they
thought they got too little. Through co-operatives, declared the German Workingmen's Association in 1867, the blessings and benefits of

[123] *The Chicago Times,* July 2, 8, 15, 1868, September 2, 3, 5, 1869. See also regarding
fuel associations *The Workingman's Advocate,* October 22, 1870.

[124] *Chicago Tribune,* November 17, 1867; *The Workingman's Advocate,* October 10,
1868.

[125] *Ibid.,* November 6, 13, 27, 1869; *The Chicago Times,* October 29, November 13,
14, 1869.

[126] Merchants, Farmers and Mechanics Savings Bank, *op. cit.,* pp. 42–43.

capitalism might be had. But the *Tribune* realistically pointed out
to them that it seemed improbable that in America the system of
" wage-hiring" would ever die out.[127]

The Chicago undertakings were, on the whole, joint stock enterprises rather than counterparts of the Rochdale plan. As attempts
in production developed, the problem of capital and credit plagued
even the most ingenious promoters. In spite of the difficulties experienced, Cameron, through the columns of his *Workingman's Advocate,* continued to urge his readers to hold co-operation as an ob-
jective of every labor organization and to make good such intentions
by a weekly contribution to the cause.[128] But like many efforts of
the laboring class, the co-operative program proved to be more idealistic than real, and the 'seventies found trade unionism generally
seeking remedies for labor ills by other means.

When other endeavors to ameliorate their condition failed, laborers could always let their thoughts turn hopefully to the vast public
domain, with the assurance that they would receive support from
men of wealth as well as from those whose possessions were few.
All Chicago rejoiced or sorrowed as prospects of passage of homestead bills by the national legislature rose or fell.[129] Labor congresses
joined political rallies in resolutions pointing out that the freeholder
was " the natural support of a free government." [130] With more than
a billion acres of public lands not yet distributed, workingmen of
the day beheld an untouched largess to which they claimed " a natural right." [131] When they could wrest from the capitalist this " his
last stronghold, the monopoly of the soil," then and only then, they

[127] *Chicago Tribune,* April 11, 1867.

[128] *The Workingman's Advocate,* July 3, 1869.

[129] Among the proponents were Dr. Charles A. Helmuth, editor of the *Illinois Staats-
Zeitung;* James H. Collins, lawyer; Charles V. Dyer, physician; J. K. C. Forrest, of the
Chicago Democrat; William B. Ogden, entrepreneur and president of the Free Soil League
of Chicago; Fernando Jones, real estate operator and secretary of the aforementioned league;
Nathan H. Bolles, realtor; W. B. Snowhook, dry goods merchant; John L. Scripps, publisher;
William Sampson, realtor and one of the vice-presidents of the Industrial Congress of 1850;
and the Rev. William Barlow, pastor of Trinity Episcopal Church. *Daily Democrat,* April
29, May 19, 30, September 8, 1848, May 9, 1850; *Chicago Commercial Advertiser,* September
6, 1848; Joe L. Norris, " The Land Reform Movement [in Chicago]," Illinois State Historical Society, *Papers in Illinois History and Transactions for the Year 1937,* pp. 73–82.

[130] *Daily Democrat,* January 22, 1848.

[131] In 1850, the total unsold and unappropriated land in the United States was set at
1,444,636,265.09 acres; in 1860, 1,055,911,288 acres. United States, " Letter from the Secretary of the Interior," *Land Office Report,* 31 Cong., 2 sess., p. 38; United States, *Report of the
Secretary of the Interior,* 36 Cong., 2 sess., Sen. Exec. Doc., I, no. 1, 65.

declared, would come an equitable division of the fruits of industry, and labor be rewarded in proportion to the services rendered.[132] Promoters of this form of relief for the needy were successful in 1862. The new legislation which provided 160 acres for any head of a family who would settle and improve the land brought general satisfaction. The Free Homestead Club, a successor of the Free Labor Club of Chicago, could now join hands with others who had, throughout the years, valiantly endorsed the theory that free homesteads would stabilize the labor market and give to the laborer an opportunity to have that much-prized possession of Americans, his house and the land upon which it rested.[133]

This widespread acceptance echoed, in a very real sense, the demands of the industrial congresses of the 'forties and 'fifties, supported by associationists, abolitionists, and ten-hour advocates. When the 1850 Industrial Congress convened in Chicago, the dominating theme of their discussion was land reform that would abolish land monopoly — a monopoly which laborers and mechanics held the cause of " over toil, and the loss of opportunities for study and self-improvement and consequent ignorance and degradation; the poverty of the masses; the unjust accumulation of wealth and power by a privileged few; and the corruption of the morals of the rich by luxury, pride and sensuality." [134]

Unions, co-operative enterprises, land reform, and like measures represented indeed the lines of defense and offense by which increasing numbers of laborers sought to maintain what they considered their rights. Woven into the laborer's pattern of discontent were low wages and long hours of work, the prospect of competition from coolie labor, and apprehension as to the effects of the coming of the Negro. In the late 'sixties the wave of opposition to convict labor fed the turbulent stream enough so that the National Labor Con-

[132] *Daily Democrat*, March 29, 1848. This is from an editorial written by John Wentworth. Wentworth's endorsement of homestead legislation when he went into the Republican party was attacked by Democrats as a device to win German and other votes from the Democratic party. The latter claimed to be the original sponsor of such a program. Ellis Smalley to Stephen A. Douglas, January 20, 1858, *Douglas Papers*.

[133] For act of 1862 relating to homesteads, see United States, *Statutes at Large*, XII, 392–93.

[134] *Chicago Daily Democrat*, June 17, 1850. At the Industrial Congress held in Chicago in 1850, women were given the privilege of participating in the sessions, and woman suffrage was endorsed. Commons, *Documentary History*, VIII, 23; *Chicago Daily Democrat*, June 8, 1850.

gress at Chicago in 1867 resolved that the legality of convict labor not performed on public works should be challenged in the courts. Resolutions in like vein continued through the next few years, even though the Illinois Manufacturing Company surrendered its contract for convict labor because of its unprofitableness.[135]

Especially plagued were the coopers and stonecutters. Under the instigation of the former, the General Trades Assembly in March, 1868, asked Chicago workingmen to eat no bread made from flour manufactured by any miller who bought his barrels from the state prisons. Again the bonds of labor failed to encompass their fellow-men, who, willy-nilly, reduced the pay of other wage earners. Indeed, argued the editor of the workingman's paper, criminals were enriched by the system and " consequently benefited by their crime." Penitentiaries, under the prevailing labor philosophy, were erected, it was true, to protect society and to reform criminals, but the protection of society and the reformation of wrongdoers did not, to their minds, include plans to make busy minds and busy hands.[136] This sentiment was spread far. Under its banners were enrolled enough members of the Constitutional Convention of 1869–70 to force through an article which prohibited the leasing of convicts. Labor, however, did not succeed in amassing votes in its favor, and the article was rejected by popular referendum.[137]

The years 1848 to 1871 were in every sense transitional in the history of the laboring class in Chicago, just as these years were transi-

---

[135] *The Workingman's Advocate*, January 2, March 27, June 12, August 21, 1869, January 1, April 9, 30, 1870; *The Chicago Times*, August 22, 1867; Illinois, *Senate Journal*, *1867*, pp. 24–32. This fear on the part of Chicago labor regarding coolie labor was scarcely justified but reflected an apprehension spreading throughout urban centers. (See Wesley, *Negro Labor in the United States*, pp. 159–60, for the attitude taken by National Labor congresses toward the Negro.) By 1862, Negroes were reported as being brought to Chicago to work. (*Oquawka Spectator*, October 16, 1862.) In the 'fifties the threat of importing cheap Irish labor was used by employers when employees asked wages large "enough to support a family on." (William P. Caton to John D. Caton, March 6, 1854, *John D. Caton Papers* [Ms. Library of Congress].) Competition from cheap Irish labor was dreaded just as later that of Negro labor was feared. The attitude of labor toward the Negro, therefore, was not entirely racial. See pp. 12, 266, 267.

[136] *The Workingman's Advocate*, February 20, 1869; *Chicago Tribune*, March 11, 12, 1868. The coopers were pledged to support no political candidate who would not advocate and vote for a bill to abolish the mechanical departments of the state prison. *Ibid.*, July 24, 1868.

[137] *The Workingman's Advocate*, January 1, 1870. It was not until 1886 that an amendment relating to convict labor was added to the constitution. Verlie, *Illinois Constitutions*, p. 167.

tional in other parts of the country. At the close of the period, business was enthroned and the machine age entrenched firmly in America. While vainly trying to stem the course of events which no one fully comprehended, a few restive Chicago workingmen turned at first to the socialist philosophy of the Marxian Germans, who, after 1848, had settled in the city. To a greater degree than American workmen they saw the new age as one of conflict between the forces of labor and capital. Strikes and mass meetings revealed an unrest dangerous to the continuation of happy relations between paymaster and wage earner. In spite of their short residence and small number, these Germans expounded the tenets of scientific socialism through the columns of *Der Proletarier,* edited by Henry Rösch in 1853. Their forces were strengthened by the coming, about 1859, of Josef Weydemeyer, who was both friend and apostle of Karl Marx and a power in the radical labor movement in America. In Chicago, Weydemeyer found the soil of discontent well fertilized by the panic of 1857, and the way open to canalize the dissatisfaction of troubled workmen, who already had organized their *Arbeiter-Verein.*

In 1858, representatives of German workers in Chicago appeared at the first congress of the *Allgemeiner Arbeiterexekutivausschuss* which had been organized in New York the year before. Along with delegates from St. Louis, Chicago workers joined New York workingmen in reaffirming the platform drawn up at the time of organization. They held that the right of revolution was guaranteed them by the Declaration of Independence. They announced their belief that scientific, technical, commercial, and industrial progress had reached a stage which necessitated a change in the American form of government. They demanded the right to organize, and they protested against the treatment of labor by capital — treatment they described as slow murder. They attacked political party platforms and the programs of private charities as offering no remedies for the ills of poverty. And since labor had been maltreated by the politicians, they insisted that it must "build its own house," and elect candidates who would swear to uphold the cause of labor and humanity. A countrywide labor organization was urgently recommended, an organization in control of newspapers printed not only in German but in English.

In 1859, Chicago representatives again mingled in New York with men of like belief from Cleveland, Philadelphia, Boston, Louisville, Charleston, New York, and Williamsburg. Soon afterward the *Arbeiterbund* moved its executive offices to Chicago from New York, and the *Stimme des Volkes,* under the guardianship of Weydemeyer, began to spread the gospel of socialist labor. But the small group of German radicals under Weydemeyer's leadership failed to carry their program beyond this point.

In their 1859 meeting in Chicago, the *Turnvereine* officially withdrew their support of the socialist position. Six years later they had dropped the name *Socialistischer Turnverein* and had substituted *Nordamerikanischer Turnerbund,* which more exactly described their purpose. Along with the greater number of American workmen, many Germans were quietly accepting the bourgeois philosophy of the day. In 1860, the question of slavery and a civil war blotted out other issues, however pressing and important they had previously appeared. Even Weydemeyer let his thoughts stray from his revolution to reconstruct society for the white laborer of the North to a war to set free the Negro of the South.[138]

As in the 'fifties so in the 'sixties foreign elements furnished the most recruits to a radical labor philosophy. Before the end of the 'sixties Chicago ranked next to New York in the activity of its socialist groups. Although native-born workers joined their foreign brothers in demanding that labor receive rewards commensurate with its contribution to society, the voices of native sons were softer and their spirit weaker than those of alien stock. Life for the latter had perhaps been harder.

The small but vocal group of Marxian followers of the 'fifties was superseded in the 'sixties by disciples of Lassalle whose teachings were expounded ably by Edward Schläger, who, during these years, was connected with German newspapers and had assisted in putting out a German supplement of the *Workingman's Advocate* in 1864.[139] Andrew C. Cameron, as editor-in-chief of the *Advocate,* joined hands

---

[138] Hermann Schlüter, *Die Anfänge der deutschen Arbeiterbewegung in Amerika* (Stuttgart, 1907), pp. 83–214; *Illinois Staats-Zeitung,* December 5, 1861; Commons, *History of Labour,* II, 227.

[139] Schläger was at one time connected with the *Illinois Staats-Zeitung,* the *Union,* and the *Telegraph. The Workingman's Advocate,* September 17, 1864; Scott, *Newspapers and Periodicals of Illinois, 1814–1879,* pp. 61, 69, 99.

with Schläger in spreading through a nationwide circulation of his newspaper the gospel of political action in the Lassallean sense. They believed in the force of the ballot as one way to effect the cures desired (in 1874 they were to launch a labor party); and they preferred arbitration to the strike in the settlement of labor disputes. To the Lassallean ideology Cameron and his followers in the late 'sixties added the American greenbackism and the issue of an eight-hour day. It was not in their plan that individualism be subservient to the interest of the state, nor did they believe that the salvation of labor rested in the destruction of property. In the words of Cameron, " Between communism and property the foundation of a new world order has to be laid, [and] it is only by the combination of State and individuals that the great problem of the future can be solved." [140]

In their attempts to cement loyalties to the cause of labor, leaders militantly built their structure of co-operation upon portrayals of invidious tactics on the part of employers, dubbed the autocrats of the city.[141] The so-called " better class " was accused of acquiring wealth by extortion, oppression, and the rise in real estate rather than by industry; and it was denounced as the tireless enemy of the producing classes. Charges of an unholy alliance between organized religion and the employer group, leading to the championship by the church of the rights of property; of acquittals in courts of law said to have been bought by gold while poor men were forced to pay the penalty for their misdemeanors; of city officials chosen by " the sovereigns," marked the day of growing class antagonisms.[142] Try as they would, employers sometimes found their powers of persuasion far less effective than the burning words of labor leaders — words which rang true to the laborer when he looked into the weekly pay envelope. The gulf between him and the capitalist seemed all the more real when he found himself excluded from boarding houses where an aristocracy stipulated that no mechanic

[140] See Cameron's editorial, " The Law of Social Reform," *The Workingman's Advocate*, October 30, 1869. Cameron quoted Proudhon in part.

[141] *Daily Democrat,* March 20, 1849.

[142] *Oquawka Spectator,* October 31, 1854, January 16, March 20, 1855, April 17, July 10, 1857, March 24, 1859, May 8, 1862, May 26, September 24, 1863; *The Chicago Times,* September 9, 1864; Lyman E. DeWolf, *The Social Evil* . . . (Chicago, 1870), pp. 3, 7; *Watchman of the Prairies,* November 21, 1848, November 5, 1850; *Northwestern Christian Advocate,* March 30, 1853; *The Advance,* May 26, 1870.

could be admitted even to the second table, and when he discovered that his name was not included in the list of those socially the equal of the "First Families." [143]

With the workman of the East the laborer of the West made common cause, drawn nearer to him, as the years advanced, by increased trade and improved communication. When the question of slavery reached harassing proportions, the workman of Chicago, like the workman of other northern cities, denied "the right of the slave holder to plant slavery at pleasure in any free territory," territory he held to be the common property of freemen, where he and his fellows might go if slavery were excluded. Capitalists of the North and slaveowners of the South seemed to the protesting laborer to be cast in the same mold, an opinion strengthened during the war when exemptions from service appeared to be only for those who could buy them.[144]

Despite what appeared to be growing class distinctions in the two decades succeeding 1850, manhood suffrage served to neutralize to some degree their destructive effects. Conditions peculiar to a new and rapidly growing city, furthermore, hindered a too rigid stratification. Whether rich or poor, most men in Chicago worked. There were the leveling influence of a universal pride in the growing and thriving community and enough instances of philanthropy to prove that wealth had not made all possessors unmindful of those less favored. Examples of the rise to high fortune from low estate, too, gave to many poor workmen a faith that eventually they would be beneficiaries of the rapidly expanding wealth of the city.

---

[143] *Chicago Tribune,* September 18, 1865, May 5, 1867, June 11, 1868, May 18, 1871; *The Chicago Times,* April 22, 1867; *The Daily Democratic Press,* February 3, 1855; *Oquawka Spectator,* November 9, 1853, September 11, 1857. By the late 'sixties a directory of those eligible for "first-class society" was available. Colbert and Chamberlin, *Chicago and the Great Conflagration,* pp. 179–80. See also for discussion of cliques in Chicago: editorial, "Western Conservatism," *Chicago Record,* I (May 1, 1857), 12; editorial, "Tyranny," *The Irish Republic,* May 11, 1867.

[144] *Daily Democrat,* February 14, April 14, 1848; *Chicago Daily Press and Tribune,* January 29, 1859. In stating his opinion of those Chicago capitalists who had shown great reluctance in aiding the federal government during the first Civil War year, Quartermaster William A. Webb said: "All the rich men in this city, all the men who have capital, have not contributed a cent to the war. They are a damned set of sneaks." (United States, "Government Contracts," *op. cit.,* II, 66.) Of course, this "name-calling" was not altogether justified. See pp. 90, 91, 249–50, 272.

CHAPTER VI

THE MOLD OF POLITICS
1848–1860

WHILE ECONOMIC LIFE expanded and grew strong, new political alliances were also taking form. Until 1848 the Democrats could well claim Chicago as their own, for after 1837 most local contests had adopted the pattern established by the nation, and both the humble and the mighty sought refuge within the fold of Jacksonian Democracy. Land reform, banking, the tariff, and internal improvements had been and were to continue vital issues to be determined without regard to political party label, as the circumstances of the time demanded.[1] Before the late 'forties, however, decisions came more and more to be resolved in the light of attitudes toward the extension of slavery. This question was to divide both Democrats and Whigs and sever irrevocably ties of loyalty to these old parties. No longer was the bony finger of " King Andrew's " ghost to point the way to docile followers. New coalitions based on similarities of economic pattern were to be formed. The long struggle of Northeast and South for the economic allegiance of the Northwest was soon to be decided in favor of the Northeast.

Within Chicago, a much vaunted belief in democracy had been quickened by frontier conditions in which each man appeared the equal of his neighbor. Any "feeling of superiority," based on the fact that one had " either grown up without engaging in useful labor,

---

[1] See Pierce, *A History of Chicago*, I, chap. xi, for a discussion of these issues prior to 1848.

or, through some fortuitious [*sic*] circumstance " had been able " to dispense with it," evoked in many Chicagoans what the press described as nothing but contempt. This " feeling of superiority," although held not entirely southern, was believed to be more prevalent in that region than in the North, " a direct consequence of the presence of slavery." [2] Adding to abstractions on free and forced labor signs of what he considered a greater prosperity in his section than in the South, the horny-fisted Chicagoan thus sat in judgment on his neighbor's institutions. Like many of his fellows throughout the North he was none too willing to accept a continuation of " a Southern influence " in political life. He was now ready to serve notice on the slaveholder of the nation, " Hitherto mayest thou come, but no further, and here shall the blighting influences be stayed." [3] Herein were the seeds of a new party, seeds embedded in the soil of what was conceived to be the essence of democracy, the equality of all men black or white.

By this watchword could the animus of Chicago be stirred against a section whose votes in the national legislature had checked economic benefits held vital to the development of the West. When the slavery question came to overshadow schemes for the extension of carriers of men and goods, warning voices protested the election of a Douglas man or one backed by the South. It was easy enough to clothe the issue of improvements and that of slave labor in the same mantle. And it was equally easy to elevate the political to the plane of a great moral crusade.[4] Here was an issue which could not be shunned, which was to shape the destinies of hamlets, of states, and even of the nation itself. In determining schemes of settlement leaders from Chicago and Illinois were to play a large part, and were so to mold sentiment that western ideas and desires eventually severed sectional and political ties and brought about four years of bloody

[2] *The Daily Democratic Press*, August 7, 1854.

[3] " He has read the history of his country in vain who does not know that for most of the time since the adoption of the constitution the controling [*sic*] influence has been a *Southern* influence . . . the Northern people, with the exception of a few fanatics, are content that they should enjoy their ' peculiar institution,' so long as it is not sought by breaking solemn compacts to enlarge and extend it. They shall have all their rights to the fullest extent of the compact; but duty to themselves and to the Union require [*sic*] that the people of the free States should say to slavery ' hitherto mayest thou come, but no further, and here shall the blighting influences be stayed.' " *Ibid.*, October 14, 1854.

[4] See, for example, *Weekly Chicago Democrat*, May 10, 1856; *Chicago Daily Press and Tribune*, July 5, 1858.

conflict.[5] In this mood Chicagoans voted for Martin Van Buren, Free Soil candidate for the presidency in 1848, preferring him to Zachary Taylor or Lewis Cass.

The opening of Congress in December, 1849, found Chicago playing the rôle of both agitator and peacemaker through two of her citizens — gargantuan John Wentworth, fighting free soiler and Democratic member of the House of Representatives, and his physical antithesis, Senator Stephen Arnold Douglas. In the autumn of 1843, when these two men had entered the halls of Congress, they were one in political spirit and aims, but in the years that followed they were to drift hopelessly apart.[6]

As questions of territorial status arose which would affect the vast stretches of land acquired in the administration of President Polk, Douglas boldly advocated popular decision within the territory itself; and Wentworth clung persistently to his Wilmot Provisoism.[7] To Oregon, Douglas at first sought to apply the Missouri Compromise but finally agreed to territorial bills which, Wentworth insisted, gave tacit approval to the principles of the Wilmot Proviso.[8] In March, 1849, as the Thirtieth Congress drew to a close, Wentworth helped defeat a proposal for the admission of California which did not contain provisions to exclude slavery, and in the early days of Taylor's administration, although saying little, he continued his maneuvers to exclude slave labor in the recently acquired lands.[9]

President Taylor's message to the new Congress, recommending the admission of California and New Mexico regardless of constitutional provisions about slavery, raised a storm of protest and warnings of disunion from slavery extremists in Chicago as elsewhere. On January 29, 1850, Henry Clay presented to the Senate a series of resolutions designed to restore peace to a troubled nation. To Chi-

---

[5] For a discussion of the situation in Illinois, during these years, see Cole, *The Era of the Civil War*, chaps. iii, v-viii.

[6] Douglas at that time was from Quincy. In 1847 he moved to Chicago.

[7] Douglas was chairman of the Senate Committee on Territories from the first session of the Thirtieth Congress to the second session of the Thirty-fifth Congress, when he was removed because of his disagreement with Buchanan.

[8] "Instead of the Wilmot Proviso Douglass [*sic*] put in what southern men try to stigmatize as the 'Cass Proviso.' . . . The twelfth section of the Oregon bill, as reported by Judge Douglass [*sic*], endorses the action of the people and continues the Wilmot Proviso in force there." *Daily Democrat*, June 21, 1848. See also United States, *Senate Journal*, 30 Cong., 1 sess., pp. 562–64.

[9] Wentworth believed that the general government had power over slavery in the territories and the District of Columbia. *Weekly Chicago Democrat*, January 9, April 3, 1849.

cagoans, his suggestion that California be admitted as a free state appeared the reassertion of the principles of the Wilmot Proviso, but to organize the new territories of New Mexico and Utah with no restrictions as to slavery seemed the greatest unwisdom.[10] And when the sentiments of the most authoritative spokesman of Cotton-Capitalism, Calhoun, were learned, even the Whig organ, the *Chicago Journal,* prophesied that the effect of his speech would be to " consolidate into union all of whatever faith."

> The open stand taken [declared the editor] will by no means intimidate the North. If efforts of concession, compromise and conciliation, are spurned by the South, and its chosen champion boldly avows their object to be disunion, even from within its own borders will come up a voice as of many waters, in solemn protest, . . . This age shall behold, and history shall write it; how two old men, sons of the same land, baptized in the same font, pledged to the same sacred cause, did stand up, the one ignobly to immolate the Union which had been nursed and fostered through long and perilous years — . . . — the other pleading in tones of thrilling eloquence, with a voice sounding like " a prophet's word," by the memory of the past, by the blessings of the present, by the hopes of the future, that the Union may be preserved in all its integrity and beauty, the richest legacy to coming time. CLAY AND CALHOUN! Let the mantle of charity and the chain of silence be thrown over this last act of the one; for the other, he already hears " the thanks of millions yet to be! " [11]

As the debate progressed, sentiment for compromise grew. To Wentworth and others of the Chicago Democracy the question, " Does God want men and women raised up to be sold and separated like cattle, and kept in ignorance of the Scriptures and everything else? " was one to which only one answer would be made, for they would in no way subscribe to the dogmatic formula, "the will of God," as the means of settlement.[12]

Douglas supported the compromise although he believed any all-inclusive measure such as Clay had proposed was foredoomed to failure. On March 25, the younger statesman presented his bills for the territorial governments, framed with the aid of his Illinois colleague in the House, John A. McClernand, and in conference with

10 *Ibid.,* February 23, March 9, 1850.
11 *Chicago Daily Journal,* March 6, 1850.
12 *Weekly Chicago Democrat,* April 6, 1850.

representatives of the South.[13] On April 18, 1850, the compromise resolutions were transmitted to a Senate committee of thirteen, with Clay as chairman. On May 8, three bills were reported. In the meantime, fear as to the outcome had caused an aroused Chicago to denounce Douglas as the betrayer of his section, willing to hand over territory "to the blight of slavery." Under the chairmanship of Mayor James H. Woodworth, a partyless, antislavery group adopted resolutions which condemned any compromise leading toward the extension of slavery. On May 15, a call for a meeting for the Congressional District to take action in the interests of freedom was signed, among others, by the editor of the abolition paper, the *Western Citizen,* and the three editors of the *Tribune.* But Wentworth's name was not there. He still maintained that "the confinement of slavery to its present limits was not only the quickest and surest way to stop the progress of fanaticism and abolitionism, but it was the only possible way in which it could be done." The editors of the *Chicago Tribune* soon withdrew from the free soil group, following similar action by individuals as yet unwilling to break with the past.[14]

Clay's proposals, somewhat modified, passed Congress in September. This outcome Wentworth had prophesied in August. Even in the eyes of a not unfriendly critic, "Southern bigots" and "Northern fanatics" had been still further estranged rather than brought together.[15] Could the Union be preserved under the pressure of opposing views? Did the South really want a dissolution? John Wentworth, outwardly acquiescing in the Compromise, declared that threats of disunion were "all gas." Yet for the first time in eight years he failed to be the Democratic candidate for Congress. He let the mantle fall upon Dr. Richard S. Moloney of Joliet, whose campaign was based on opposition to slavery extension in the territories,

[13] *Chicago Daily Journal,* February 11, 1850. According to Alexander Stephens, he and Robert Toombs were called into conference with John A. McClernand and William A. Richardson of southern Illinois and others. McClernand was chairman of the House Committee on Territories while Douglas was chairman of that committee of the Senate. Alexander H. Stephens, *A Constitutional View of the Late War between the States* (2 v. Philadelphia, 1868–70), II, 202–4.

[14] *Weekly Chicago Democrat,* February 23, 1850; *Chicago Daily Journal,* May 15, 1850; *Cong. Globe,* 31 Cong., 1 sess., p. 1444. The *Journal* held that Wentworth was given to misstatements in the *Democrat* regarding the Compromise, and that he ignored the fact that it was for " the high and holy object of preserving the Union." *Chicago Daily Journal,* January 31, 1850; *Chicago Tribune,* May 29, 1850, quoted in *Western Citizen,* June 4, 1850.

[15] *Chicago Daily Journal,* August 1, October 2, 1850.

abolition of slavery in the District of Columbia, and the repeal of the Fugitive Slave Law.[16]

Into this highly charged atmosphere, a month after the passage of the Compromise, came Uriah Hinch seeking a slave escaped from Missouri. His presence set on fire smouldering hostilities toward that part of the compromise which was held most hateful by Chicagoans. Since the authorities would give no official protection from a threatened coat of tar and feathers, Hinch did not tarry long within the city gates.[17]

On October 21, the Chicago Common Council met to transact business. It informed all senators and representatives from the free states who had had any part in the passage of the Fugitive Slave Law that they were considered " fit only to be ranked with the traitors, Benedict Arnold, and Judas Iscariot who betrayed his Lord and master for thirty pieces of silver." Since the law represented nothing less than a suspension of the time-honored rights of habeas corpus and trial by jury, why, they argued, should the city police or other officers interfere with fugitives? Why should not citizens exercise ordinary humanity in abstaining from " the capture and delivering up of the fugitives from unrighteous oppression, of whatever nation, name or color?" Having adopted resolutions, the council adjourned to attend a meeting the following evening at the City Hall where citizens of all classes were expected to endorse their action and organize resistance. Thomas Richmond was chosen to preside. But the meeting failed to accomplish all that its vitriolic sponsors had hoped. Douglas, just home from Washington, asked to be heard publicly on the subject the next night.[18]

The immense crowd which assembled the next evening taxed the City Hall to its utmost capacity. Before them appeared " the Little

[16] In 1848, Wentworth wrote that he would not be a candidate in 1850 because of the opposition of his wife and father-in-law, who, he said, were " deadly hostile " to his candidacy. (John Wentworth to Edmund S. Kimberly, June 26, 1848. Edmund Stoughton Kimberly, *Papers, 1811–63* [*Ms.* Chicago Historical Society].) Moloney was endorsed by William B. Ogden whose support had been sought for Churchill Coffing, the choice of the *Journal*. Ogden had been a candidate himself but withdrew when Moloney espoused free soil principles. Moloney won in Chicago and in Cook County. *Weekly Chicago Democrat*, April 6, October 12, November 16, 1850.

[17] Charles W. Mann, *The Chicago Common Council and the Fugitive Slave Law of 1850* (Chicago, n.d.), p. 69; *Western Citizen*, October 22, 1850.

[18] The council also rebuked all senators and representatives from the free states " who basely sneaked away from their seats, and thereby evaded the question." Douglas was absent on the final roll call. *Chicago Daily Journal*, October 22, 23, 1850.

Giant," discredited and hated. Squarely facing the accusation of cowardice because of his absence on the final roll call on the compromise, he declared his vote would have been affirmative. For three and a half hours he endeavored to point out that the law did not abolish the right of trial by jury and that it did not suspend the writ of habeas corpus; that it was in fact "a protection to the slave." In scathing terms he criticized the council resolutions.

An act of the American Congress nullified by the Common Council of the city of Chicago! Whence did the Council derive their authority? I have been able to find no such provision in the city charter, nor am I aware that the Legislature of Illinois is vested with any rightful power to confer such authority. I have yet to learn that a subordinate municipal corporation is licensed to raise the standard of rebellion, and throw off the authority of the federal government at pleasure! This is a great improvement upon South Carolinian nullification. It dispenses with the trouble, delay, and expense of convening Legislatures and assembling conventions of the people, for the purpose of resolving themselves back into their original elements, preparatory to the contemplated revolution. It has the high merit of marching directly to its object, and by a simple resolution, written and adopted on the same night, relieving the people from their oaths and allegiance, and of putting the nation and its laws at defiance! It has heretofore been supposed, by men of antiquated notions, who have not kept up with the progress of the age, that the Supreme Court of the United States was invested with the power of determining the validity of an act of Congress. . . . But the spirit of the age is progressive. It is not long since that I heard an eminent lawyer propose an important reform in the admirable judicial system of our state . . . that our judicial system should be so improved as to allow an appeal, on all constitutional questions, from the Supreme Court of this state to two justices of the peace! When that shall have been effected, but one other reform will be necessary to render our national system perfect, and that is, to change the federal Constitution, so as to authorize an appeal, upon all questions touching the validity of acts of Congress, from the Supreme Court of the United States to the Common Council of the city of Chicago! [19]

Douglas's ironical oratory did not entirely silence Chicago citizenry. Several unconvinced members of the audience challenged

[19] *Ibid.*, October 24, 1850; Sheahan, *The Life of Stephen A. Douglas*, pp. 168–86. See also Mann, *op. cit.*, pp. 70–80.

him to explain parts of the law upon which he had not touched. The spell of his personality, however, carried most of his listeners into camp. A series of resolutions which he presented were passed without dissent. These pledged support to the Fugitive Slave Law and asserted that it was the sacred duty of all to maintain and preserve every provision of the Federal Constitution. Then contrite Chicagoans in ringing tones repudiated the action of their council and "adjourned with nine cheers — three for Douglas, three for the Constitution, and three for the Union." Bowing to the popular will, the council on the twenty-fifth voted twelve to one "to reconsider the vote on the passage of the resolutions in regard to the fugitive slave law, passed at their last meeting," although a motion to expunge the resolutions from the record was tabled.[20]

Within two days, so fickle is man and so passing his fancy, it was possible for strong antislavery exponents to call an assembly which gave sympathetic ear to James H. Collins, long-time abolitionist, and Edwin C. Larned, and passed a series of resolutions which, although more moderate in tone than those previously offered, expressed condemnation of the obnoxious law. When a defense of Douglas was attempted from the floor "noise and confusion" forced the speaker to give way for a motion to adjourn.[21] The magic of Douglas's presence of a few nights before had fled.

Neither oratory nor the desire for peace restrained those intent on ignoring the law. Throughout the 'fifties the Underground Railroad did "a large business," and many fugitives made their way to freedom through the aid of Chicago citizens. The press called the law a benefit to professional slave-catchers and suggested that advice not to agitate for fear of endangering the Union was merely an application of "the gag." Before December, 1850, the council again held that in saving "fugitives from oppression," Chicagoans could in no sense be charged with treason against the government.[22]

[20] Sheahan, op. cit., p. 160. The resolutions which repudiated the council action were presented by Buckner S. Morris, Whig mayor in 1838 and later candidate for governor on the Know-Nothing ticket in 1856. Morris supported the Bell-Everett ticket in 1860. He was a Kentuckian by birth. He actively opposed war with the South. The council motion to reconsider was presented by Alderman John C. Dodge and the motion to expunge the resolutions from the record was made by Alderman R. J. Hamilton. Chicago Daily Journal, October 24, 25, 1850.

[21] The resolutions were presented by Isaac N. Arnold. The speaker who attempted to defend Douglas was S. S. Hayes. Ibid., October 26, 1850.

[22] The Free West, October 14, 1854; [Samuel May], The Fugitive Slave Law and its

When, in 1851, one Moses Johnson was nabbed "in broad daylight" and thrown into "a carriage like a stick of wood," to be taken into "the little U. S. Court room instead of the capacious City Hall," indignation knew no bounds. The agent for the alleged owner "narrowly escaped chastisement from the crowd in the street as he passed from the Court Room," fully aware that it was "best to make himself scarce as quickly as possible." As the Commissioner discharged the defendant, he was snatched from the hands of officers by a shouting crowd and hurried to safety.[23]

Other fugitives came to the city and, more frequently than not, were sent on their way to freedom. Some reached Chicago through the help of Allan Pinkerton, then a cooper in the little town of Dundee. In 1854, 482 were reported to have been run safely through the city within seven months. By 1855 Pinkerton was in Chicago aiding Philo Carpenter, Dr. Charles V. Dyer, and other abolitionists, having established himself here as a night watch.[24]

To the Illinois statutes regarding Negroes much the same type of obedience was given as was paid to the national law. In 1850, petitions were circulated for the repeal of enactments which permitted the admission to the state of only those Negroes able to produce certificates of freedom and to post bonds or security of $1,000. In 1853, however, a new bill, even more offensive to antislavery forces, passed the legislature making the state conspicuous, said its opponents, "for one of the meanest laws ever enacted."[25]

For the time being, however, the Compromise of 1850 checked in a measure the animus of Chicago toward the South. In the minds

---

Victims (rev. ed. New York, 1861), pp. 41, 121–23; *Western Citizen,* December 3, 1850, January 7, 1851. The December, 1850, action of the council was by a vote of ten to three.

[23] The Negro was defended by George Manierre who showed him to be five feet five and one-quarter inches tall and very black whereas the fugitive was described as five feet eight inches and copper colored. Three companies of militia had been called out before the trial. *Chicago Daily Democrat,* June 4, 5, 7, 1851.

[24] Verna Cooley, "Illinois and the Underground Railroad to Canada," Illinois State Historical Society, *Transactions, 1917,* pp. 78–79; *The Free West,* September 21, 1854; *Western Citizen,* July 20, 1852; *Chicago Weekly Democrat,* July 30, 1859, November 17, 1860, April 13, 1861; Richard Rowan, *The Pinkertons . . .* (Boston, 1931), p. 23; Luther Laflin Miles, *In Memory of Allan Pinkerton* (Pamphlet, n.d., Chicago Historical Society). The number of real fugitives was undoubtedly exaggerated. In 1850, there were 3,200,364 slaves in the country, of which there were 1,011 fugitives. This amounted to one out of 3,165. (United States, *Preliminary Report on the Eighth Census, 1860* [Washington, 1862], p. 137.) In 1860, there were 3,950,511 slaves and 803 fugitives, or one out of 4,919.

[25] *The Free West,* February 9, 1854; Act of February 12, 1853, *Laws, 1853,* pp. 57–60.

of some a dissolution of the Union would prevent the conquest of markets of which Chicagoans dreamed; the preservation of the Union, on the other hand, would inevitably accelerate the much desired commercial achievements. With eyes thus focused on the national capital, voters found most local happenings uninteresting and even trifling. Through the year 1854 those wearing the label "Democrat" were, on the whole, successful in municipal elections, but sometimes so issueless was the campaign that all candidates were of this one party, running without formal party nomination. This was true in 1849 and the two elections directly following. In that year little interest attended nominations, aside from meetings of workingmen, convinced that their part in producing the wealth of the community had been greater than that of any other class, and that they ought, therefore, to pass on the fitness of those presenting themselves for office. After a dull campaign, James H. Woodworth, Independent Democratic mayor in 1848, was re-elected, and in 1850 he was succeeded by James Curtiss, Democrat, who in 1848 had run against him. Walter S. Gurnee, of the same party, was chosen in 1851.[26]

In 1852, the local campaign was, however, rescued from the monotony of the four preceding mayoralty elections, for moralists, with the fervor common to their kind, urged repeal by the legislature of the licensing clause in the city charter. Rally after rally called for support for only those candidates pledged to refuse to anyone the privilege to sell liquor. So aroused did the public appear that other candidates took the pledge and, according to the *Democrat,* quite the worst habitués were induced to stay away from even "the smell of ardent spirits."[27] Burdened with propaganda of what "drink" might do to a man's physical and moral powers, voters went to the polls. They had to decide also about a grant to a proposed water company and one of lake-shore lands to the Illinois Central Railroad for an entry into the city; they must consider the effect of these decisions on the city treasury.

Into the campaign were injected personal animosities, honest differences of opinion as to the desirability of municipally financed pub-

[26]. Pierce, *A History of Chicago,* I, 398, 421; *Daily Democrat,* February 21, 26, March 1, 3, 5, 6, 8, 1849, March 1, 1850, March 6, 1851; *Weekly Chicago Democrat,* March 16, 1850. For figures on all elections, see Appendix, pp. 506-9.

[27] *Weekly Chicago Democrat,* February 28, 1852; *Chicago Daily Democrat,* February 5, 1852. For a further discussion of the Temperance question, see pp. 435-40.

lic utilities, and tormenting repercussions of the Michigan Central-Michigan Southern struggle for entrance into the city.[28] Wentworth led the forces opposed to the Chicago City Hydraulic Company, authorized by the legislature in 1851 and now asking permission to construct a plant which would compete with the private water company, the Chicago Hydraulic Company. His trenchant pen described what he considered the folly of a municipal plant in the light of an increased city debt; and his antagonism toward Ebenezer Peck, attorney of the board of three water commissioners who had recommended the new plant, was cloaked under the charge that the board had been named in an undemocratic manner.[29]

Equally important was the answer voters were asked to give regarding the entrance of the Illinois Central Railroad into the city. For months preceding the day of balloting the electorate had been subjected to arguments for and against granting the company a right of way along the lake shore. The exchange of reasons for and against this grant must have proved disturbing indeed to those not fully conversant with the details of the bitter struggle between politicians and capitalists interested in the Michigan Central and those concerned in the Michigan Southern — a struggle that had gone on for at least two years, and in which the Illinois Central became involved because some of its promoters were allied with the Michigan Central interests.[30]

In the columns of the *Democrat* Wentworth ventilated his opinion and that of other interested persons that liberal terms to the railroad would create jobs for the jobless, and that the taxpayers' money would be saved if the railroad bore the expense caused by lake erosion. Indeed, so eloquently did Wentworth plead the cause of the company that the Common Council, on December 29, 1851, passed an ordinance acceptable to the Central promoters. It gave the Central a right of way of three hundred feet along the shore of Lake Michigan from Twelfth Street to the river in exchange for the rail-

---

[28] See pp. 55–58.

[29] *Chicago Daily Journal*, February 25, March 3, 1852; *Chicago Daily Democrat*, March 2, 1852. The differences between Peck and Wentworth included a contest for leadership in the Democratic party. Peck represented the antiabolition wing and " Long John " headed the free soil group. They were reported to have indulged in fisticuffs in one disagreement. Peck's friendship with Norman Judd also marked him as *persona non grata* to Wentworth. *Chicago Tribune*, May 26, 1881. See pp. 240–41.

[30] See pp. 48–49, 55–58.

road's promise to assume the expense of protecting the shore from the encroachments of the lake between the river and Hyde Park. The ordinance was promptly vetoed by Mayor Gurnee in a message which the *Democrat* had earlier reported would be drafted by the attorney of the opposing railroad, the Michigan Southern.[31] The mayor's motives were also suspected because he lived on Michigan Avenue among wealthy Chicagoans who feared that the proximity of a railroad would bring down the price of their property. But the forces favorable to the Illinois Central and residents of the North and West divisions, glad of relief in tax levies, succeeded in getting the council to override the mayoral veto, only to have that body reconsider their action and adopt, on January 5, a franchise less favorable to the railroad. The second ordinance the Illinois Central refused to accept.[32]

Such was the state of affairs when the municipal election occurred in March. Wentworth, who later openly declared himself an owner of one fortieth of the Illinois Central stock, opposed Gurnee and endorsed James Curtiss for chief executive of the city.[33] Although Gurnee was the successful candidate, the choice of aldermen was satisfactory to the *Democrat* and the railroad forces. The construction of the new water plant was approved overwhelmingly, but the Temperance cause suffered defeat, the nominee, Amos G. Throop, running third.[34]

From 1848 to 1850 voters in county contests assumed an attitude similar to that taken in municipal campaigns. By autumn, 1849, it seemed certain that those Democrats who had voted the Free Soil ticket in 1848 had not strayed permanently from the fold. Canvasses were conducted and concluded without much reference to party, and, on the whole, the Democrats outdistanced the Whigs in all contests for office.[35] During the early years of the 'fifties, political strategists,

[31] *Chicago Daily Democrat,* January 1, 1852.

[32] *Ibid.,* October 13, 17, December 3, 30, 1851, March 1, 2, 1852; *Chicago Daily Journal,* March 1, 1852; Brownson, *op. cit.,* pp. 50–54; Gates, *The Illinois Central Railroad,* pp. 63, 90–92; J. S. Wright to R. Schuyler, September 29, October 4, 1851, *Brayman Papers;* J. W. Wentworth to W. K. Ackerman, William K. Ackerman, *Collection, 1839–83* (*Ms.* Chicago Historical Society). The matter of the entrance of the Illinois Central into Chicago was settled June 14, 1852, when the ordinance of December 29 was re-enacted.

[33] *Chicago Daily Democrat,* March 1, 1852.

[34] *Ibid.,* March 3, 4, 1852; *Chicago Daily Journal,* March 3, 1852.

[35] *Weekly Chicago Democrat,* March 27, November 13, 1849, February 16, 1850; *Daily Democrat,* January 16, 1849.

when considering issues beyond purely local concern, preferred to toy with the old issues of land reform, banks, internal improvements, and the tariff rather than permit the intemperate in speech to cultivate seeds of disunion.

This strategy was apparent in the county election held November 4, 1851, when the proposed state banking law was the only item of importance upon which voters were called to act. An overwhelming vote in Chicago for the measure implied an abandonment of a hostility of earlier days, for the pressure of commercial needs seems to have outweighed an abstract political theory.[36]

Again in 1853 and 1854 the city and county elections were fought without regular party nominations or conventions. Indeed, the small number of candidates for office indicated either an indifference to the political concerns of the community or, perhaps, as the *Democratic Press* put it, was "an indication of the prosperity of our citizens." So little was the prize of office sought that it was not even necessary for contenders to indulge in the time-honored custom of "treating" to convince the public of fitness for office.[37] In the county, in 1853, with one exception, Democrats were chosen, and in the city all offices went Democratic. Charles M. Gray, a newcomer in politics but well-known to Chicagoans as an associate of Cyrus H. McCormick in the reaper business, was named mayor.[38] In 1854 the Temperance forces suffered another defeat. Their candidate, Amos G. Throop, who had run in 1852, was beaten by Isaac L. Milliken, Democrat,[39] for temperance, as a political issue, had little appeal in a community where about one half the people were of foreign extraction.

[36] *Chicago Daily Democrat*, November 5, 1851. In Chicago, the vote on the bank law was 2,122 for to 79 against. Democrats of southern Illinois were antibank men. Cole, *The Era of the Civil War*, p. 103. For a discussion of the banking act, see pp. 119–20.

[37] A request, in 1853, to Josiah L. James, who had been a member of the council, to run for mayor was signed by about three hundred followers and publicized through the press, a common practice of the time. *The Daily Democratic Press*, February 1, 22, 23, 1853; *Weekly Chicago Democrat*, April 9, 23, November 12, 26, 1853.

[38] *The Daily Democratic Press*, March 4, 1853; *Weekly Chicago Democrat*, November 12, 1853. In April, 1853, the Whig candidate, Buckner Morris, won the special judicial election. *The Daily Democratic Press*, April 25, 1853.

[39] *Ibid.*, February 7, March 9, 1854; *Weekly Chicago Democrat*, March 18, 1854. On June 8, 1855, the choice of two state judges and a prohibitory liquor law for the state were before the people. John D. Caton had a large majority for supreme court judge, and George Manierre was elected circuit judge without opposition. *Ibid.*, June 9, 23, 30, 1855. For a discussion of the liquor question see pp. 435–40.

While municipal problems, on the whole, seemed solvable without the blessing of specific political parties, detachment as to issues beyond local concern appeared, by November, 1852, no longer possible. Both the Democrats and the Whigs, however, realized the danger of permitting discussion about the extension of slavery. Availability for nomination, therefore, was based not on policies expressed but on silence. Indeed, it was said that, throughout the state, a man to receive consideration for office on the Democratic ticket must be able to carry Democrats of " all the shades of opinion." [40] And when the Whigs met in May in county convention, they felt impelled to announce with a renewed vigor their undying attachment to the Union, as they endorsed the policies of the national Whig administration.[41]

In this mood both major parties prepared to nominate a president. With the exception of Wentworth, most prominent Democrats of Illinois favored Douglas. As the candidate of " Young America," he was garbed in the raiment of liberalism and acclaimed the opponent of reaction, the foe of European monarchies, the promoter of railroads, and the champion of prosperity. But Illinois Democrats, allied with what liberal forces could be summoned outside the state, were unable to obtain for him the nomination of the Baltimore convention. Franklin Pierce was named, and Douglas, acquiescing in the decision of his party, pledged to the new nominee the undivided loyalty of the Democrats of Illinois. To Douglas, as to most other Democrats of Chicago, unified action seemed all-essential, and Wentworth warned that even the Democratic victories of 1851 in the city and the county should not " exhilarate " the party " too much," for lack of unity would surely put " whiggery in the ascendant " the next four years.[42]

The Whigs, on the whole, accepted General Winfield Scott, nominated for the presidency at Baltimore.[43] But they were troubled by fears of the length to which the feud might go which had existed

[40] *Chicago Daily Democrat*, January 23, 1852.

[41] *Ibid.*, May 17, 1852.

[42] Merle E. Curti, " Young America," *The American Historical Review*, XXXII (October, 1926), 34–55; Merle E. Curti, " George N. Sanders — American Patriot of the Fifties," *South Atlantic Quarterly*, XXVII (January, 1928), 79–87; *Chicago Daily Democrat*, November 5, 1851; *Chicago Daily Journal*, April 29, May 6, 1851; *Weekly Chicago Democrat*, June 12, 1852. Wentworth had wanted to nominate Thomas H. Benton of Missouri for president because of his antislavery leanings. But in the southern part of the state there was little enthusiasm for Benton, and Wentworth, the pragmatist of 1852, bowed in acquiescence. *Chicago Daily Democrat*, March 31, 1852.

[43] *Chicago Daily Journal*, June 22, 1852.

between Alfred Dutch, editor of the *Commercial Advertiser,* and Richard Wilson of the *Journal,* Chicago postmaster under President Taylor. Dutch had favored George W. Dole who was the Fillmore appointee for the postmastership; Wilson had wished to hold what had been his under Taylor. Dutch had clung to Fillmore and Webster, but Wilson had refused to desert a Scott delegate to the national convention. Outmaneuvered by the Wilson forces, the fiery editor of the *Commercial Advertiser* then entered the race for Congress as an independent against Cyrus Aldrich, only to withdraw in a little while, probably because defeat was imminent.[44]

The Democrats, too, were uneasy when they considered their candidates for Congress. In April, Ebenezer Peck had attempted to introduce into the state Democratic convention a series of resolutions asserting that no one hostile to the Compromise of 1850, including the Fugitive Slave Law, should be entitled to sit in the convention. This was aimed at Wentworth, who was directly named in another resolution as one whose presence should be prohibited on the convention floor. Peck's resolutions were tabled and failed to accomplish the end desired. Wentworth, feared and hated by his foes, but able to get votes, was returned to Congress, his antislaveryism bringing him victory.[45]

Strife was further intensified by the persisting cry for internal improvements. In 1851, the failure of Congress to grant $15,000 for the improvement of the harbor at Chicago aroused antagonism toward Southerners and others voting against the bill.[46] By this time, Douglas had hopefully proposed that Congress permit local authorities to levy tonnage duties on imports and exports in order to collect funds needed for local improvements. But only those apprehensive of the stand which Pierce might take seemed favorable.[47]

---

[44] *Weekly Chicago Democrat,* October 2, 1852; *Chicago Daily Democrat,* September 22, October 9, 13, 18, 22, 1852. Dutch's name does not appear in the final returns. Richard L. Wilson and Charles L. Wilson were editors of the *Journal.* During the former's postmastership, the latter was editor.

[45] Peck was not a delegate. He, however, induced a delegate to introduce his resolutions. *Ibid.,* April 28, 1852. The results of the election are found in *ibid.,* November 9, 1852.

[46] The grant to Chicago was part of a bill carrying appropriations for river and harbor improvements in various parts of the country. *Cong. Globe,* 31 Cong., 2 sess., p. 529; *Western Citizen,* March 18, 1851.

[47] *Chicago Daily Democrat,* September 2, October 2, 8, 1852; *Chicago Daily Journal,* June 23, August 24, 27, 1852. Alderman Thomas B. Dwyer presented a resolution to the legislature to petition Congress to allow Chicago to collect a tonnage duty on vessels entering

Thus, with both old parties shaken by internal dissension, the election of Franklin Pierce took place. True to its past, Chicago went Democratic, voting against a party declared to hold as its " pet doctrine" that it was the duty of the government to "take care of the rich and the rich will take care of the poor." Young men's associations formed to renew life in both parties added vigor to the campaign.[48] Songs and ditties gave it a sprightliness reminiscent of the election of 1840.[49] The Democratic party had worked hard to draw into its ranks all of alien parentage and birth and had sought to convert others by charging that the Whig national administration had stolen $20,000,000 a year from the federal treasury through contracts to its favorites. The defeat of the Whigs was generally interpreted as the death knell of the party, and in the next few weeks Whigs of southern Illinois sparred with those of the northern sections, who seemed to turn in increasing numbers to free soil principles.[50]

The growing tension between those who once had held like party views was further increased by a rivalry between sections as to a proposed transcontinental railroad. The Compromise of 1850 had healed sectional wounds only superficially. On January 4, 1854, Douglas, as chairman of the Senate Committee on Territories, roused even more serious controversy when he presented a bill for the creation of the " Territory of Nebraska," accompanied by a report specifying that the issue of slavery be determined by the principles embodied in the

Chicago, but the resolution was defeated, eleven to two. Thomas B. Dwyer to S. A. Douglas, February 10, 1853, *Douglas Papers*. For Pierce's stand on internal improvements and other western demands, see Roy Franklin Nichols, *Franklin Pierce* (Philadelphia, 1931).

[48] *Chicago Daily Democrat*, October 15, 1852. The Young Men's Democratic Union Club was formed August 10, 1852, and was open to men under thirty-five. (*Ibid.*, August 12, 1852.) The Chicago Scott Club was organized August 9, 1852. It had no age limitations. *Chicago Daily Journal*, August 7, 16, 1852.

[49] For example:
> "Our cause is just, so win we must,
> And this we mean to do;
> The Whigs we *Polked* in '44
>   We'll *Pierce* in '52."
>   — *Chicago Daily Democrat*, September 29, 1852.

The *Democrat* (September 18, 1852) printed a chorus which it described as "a return of the horid [*sic*] excruciating Whig poetry of 1840."
> "D--n the Locos,
> Kill 'em — slay 'em!
> Give 'em h-ll!
> With Scott and Graham."

[50] *Ibid.*, July 20, 22, September 16, 21, October 2, November 1, 5, 1852; *Weekly Chicago Democrat*, August 6, 1853; Cole, *The Era of the Civil War*, p. 112.

Compromise of 1850. Before the bill reached its final form, two territories, Kansas and Nebraska, were authorized and the repeal of the Missouri Compromise was specified.[51]

The truce between North and South was ended. "The free people of Illinois thus have the mortification of seeing one of their Senators acting as the tool of southern slave-drivers," wrote the irate editor of the abolitionist *Free West*. Using political capital common to Douglas's foes, he declared that there was in the whole United States no man more fit "to present such an infamous proposition" than Douglas, "a North Carolina slaveholder," spokesman for a state which had "prostituted itself" for "the purpose of these lordly dealers in human flesh." [52]

In late February, the state legislature under the party lash passed resolutions endorsing the Nebraska Bill. Norman B. Judd in the Senate joined the Whigs in the opposition, but Homer Wilmarth, representing Chicago in the Assembly, voted for the resolutions. To the *Free West*, the vote showed that Douglas had got "the rolling hitch" on the Democrats, but that paper believed they had secretly sworn "it should be his death." [53] Although not entirely without the support of Chicagoans, Douglas's bill encountered more and more the opposition of general public, pulpit, and press. Petitions asking representatives to oppose the annulment of the Missouri Compromise were circulated freely, and protest meetings of native and foreign born alike recorded objection to "the repeal or modification of an act which time and the public faith" had "made sacred." On February 8, a large meeting sponsored in part by "old-line" Democrats at South Market Hall declared against any bill which would tend to destroy harmony between North and South and "create sectional distrusts." What right had a representative in Congress, demanded S. S. Hayes, to repudiate "a solemn contract" without the advice of "the people of this sovereign state" who were by no means Russian serfs, and who had sent him to Congress to vote for measures they wanted? [54]

[51] Milton, *The Eve of Conflict*, pp. 99–143; *Cong. Globe*, 33 Cong., 1 sess., p. 115.

[52] *The Free West*, January 19, February 2, 9, 1854.

[53] Illinois, *House Journal, 1854*, p. 168; Illinois, *Senate Journal, 1854*, p. 79; *The Free West*, March 2, 1854. The other Cook County representative in the Assembly, William B. Egan, also a Democrat, was absent when the vote was taken. Illinois, *House Journal, 1854*, p. 168.

[54] *The Daily Democratic Press*, February 7, 9, 13, 1854. Among those who spoke against

Under the leadership of George Schneider, editor of the *Illinois Staats-Zeitung,* the Germans of the city massed in almost unbroken ranks against repeal of the Missouri Compromise. When the state legislature visited Chicago in February, a committee presented Lieutenant Governor Gustave Koerner with a petition signed by several hundred of his fellow Germans expressing their views. Confident of the strength of their votes, in a mid-March meeting they denounced Democratic leaders who " by their sycophancy to the South called forth this outrage," and publicized their intention of getting rid of that " ambitious and dangerous demagogue," Stephen A. Douglas, who was a " blemish upon the honor of the State of Illinois." The thought that a proposed amendment to the already malodorous bill would curtail the political privileges of even the foreign-born residents in the territories, who had taken the oath of citizenship, further enraged them. They burned Douglas in effigy. But this act was not condoned by either the native-born or many foreign opponents of the bill, and the stand of Schneider in deprecating the act reassured those who feared a reign of violence and disorder.[55]

Democratic party organs like Wentworth's *Democrat* and Bross's *The Daily Democratic Press* joined the opposition in an emphatic rejection of Douglas's course. Wentworth was slow to condemn the bill openly, and until late spring he hoped that " all that portion " which related " directly or indirectly to slavery or the repeal of the Missouri Compromise " would be stricken from the final form. He believed, however, that, although the North was, on the whole, opposed to the Nebraska Bill and that most Democrats in the free states regretted its introduction, there would be an acquiescence to the will of the majority if it passed, and he apprehended " nothing " that would disturb " the amicable relations of the different sections of the Union." [56]

---

the bill were Hugh T. Dickey, Mark Skinner, Peter Page, Robert S. Blackwell. A meeting on February 11 was addressed by Isaac Cook, C. S. Cameron, Elisha W. Tracy, and others in favor of Douglas's bill.

[55] *Ibid.,* February 20, March 17, 1854; Milton, *op. cit.,* p. 132. As early as January 29, the Germans held a protest meeting. (F. I. Herriott, " The Germans of Chicago and Stephen A. Douglas in 1854," *Deutsch-Amerikanische Geschichtsblätter,* XII [1912], 381–404; see also Otto C. Schneider, " Abraham Lincoln und das Deutschthum," *ibid.,* VII [1907], 65–75.) Douglas was burned in effigy Thursday evening, March 16. *The Daily Democratic Press,* March 20, 1854. For protest of the clergy, see p. 384.

[56] *The Free West,* March 30, 1854; *Weekly Chicago Democrat,* May 27, 1854.

On May 30, Pierce signed the bill. " One thing is now made clear, what comparatively few have hitherto apprehended," prophetically declared the editor of the *Free West,* "either Slavery or Liberty must fall." On June 5, proponents of the bill paraded the streets of Chicago, but the line was thin and wavering compared with that which, on July 4, formed to celebrate national independence and resolved itself into a demonstration against the new legislation. Hibernian Society members marched with German Turners and swung into line with the Scandinavian Union. Cassius M. Clay, Kentucky abolitionist, whose impassioned oratory was heard throughout the summer months in hamlet and countryside in central and northern Illinois, spoke to the crowds.[57]

During the summer excitement ran high, and on the streets of Chicago the dread word "disunion" was whispered. Rumor had it that northern antagonists of the Kansas-Nebraska Act looked to "a confederacy of the Northern States" and the annexation of Canada, an arrangement which the commercially-minded were not loath to consider. Against this spirit Democracy issued warnings, at the same time endeavoring to stem the tide against the formation of a new party.[58]

Traveling westward in August, after Congress adjourned, "the Little Giant" was able, as he later declared, to go from Boston to Chicago by the light of his own burning effigies. His arrival at the Tremont House on the evening of August 23, however, was received quietly despite the unpopularity of his activities in Congress. With characteristic courage Douglas announced that he would speak on the evening of September the first. At one o'clock that afternoon, flags in the harbor were lowered to half-mast, and from six to seven o'clock church bells tolled, heavily indicative of the mood of the citizenry of Chicago as it gathered to the number of eight or ten thousand in the Public Square on that hot September night. An unwelcome silence greeted Douglas as he began to speak. He had uttered but few words when a storm of hisses and groans, mingled with shouts and cheers, drowned his voice. He stood his ground, declaring that

57 *The Free West,* June 1, 8, July 6, 20, August 3, 1854. For Wentworth's statement see *Weekly Chicago Democrat,* June 3, 1854.
58 *The Daily Democratic Press,* May 5, June 7, 1854.

he would remain until heard. Whereupon the raucous voices of his adversaries rose in the song:

> We won't go home until morning,
> Till morning, till morning,
> We won't go home until morning,
> Till daylight doth appear.

Against the tumult, Douglas shouted his attack on the press and some of the citizens of Chicago. Until nearly midnight he boldly and insistently defended his position before an unruly crowd alleged to be armed and bent on violence.[59] Out of patience at last, he hurled his final words at his hecklers: "Abolitionists of Chicago! It is now Sunday morning. I'll go to church and you may go to Hell."[60] Abolitionists were blamed for this demonstration, but they were by no means Douglas's only adversaries. Throughout northern Illinois "the Little Giant's" visits that autumn were received with similar reactions, and even to the south of Chicago anti-Nebraskaites roundly took their former leader to task for the revival of the question of slavery extension.

On October 3, 1854, at the state fair in Springfield Douglas began a series of talks. The next day he was answered by Abraham Lincoln, an anti-Nebraska Whig. With Lincoln were allied one-time political cohorts of Douglas, including Lyman Trumbull, who was to become a Chicagoan in 1863, and Edmund D. Taylor, Chicago lawyer. Later that month Lincoln spoke in Chicago to "a large auditory at

[59] See Milton, *The Eve of Conflict*, pp. 175–76; *The Daily Democratic Press*, August 25, September 2, 4, 1854; *The Free West*, September 7, 1854; Sheahan, *op. cit.*, pp. 272–73. Sheahan declares that the press of the city had inflamed the Know-Nothings to such a degree that "every revolver and pistol in the stores of the city had been sold, and that there were orders for a large number yet unfilled." It was likewise reported that Douglas intended to enforce silence by a bodyguard of five hundred Irishmen.

[60] Allen Johnson, *Stephen A. Douglas* (New York, 1908), p. 259; *The New York Times*, September 6, 1854. [Henry M. Flint], *Life of Stephen A. Douglas . . .* (New York, 1860), p. 74, has it "while you can go to the devil in your own way." See Milton, *The Eve of Conflict*, p. 176. There seems to be division of opinion as to the length of time Douglas tried to speak, some writers giving it as about two hours, others indicating that he tried to address the disorderly crowd for nearly four. The size of the crowd as reported reflects the feeling of the writer also. Chicago newspapers of the time, according to political color, describe Douglas as irritable and insulting, or as good-tempered under insults. See also *New York Semi-Weekly Tribune*, September 8, 1854, which says that Douglas measurably lost his self-control; hence much of the disturbance which followed. The *Tribune* also reported that the meeting was not packed with anti-Nebraska men, as his followers alleged, but that feeling was so high in Chicago that it was impossible to obtain a calm statement.

the North Market Hall," engaging their attention with his "witty argumentative" and "happy hits upon poor Bill Nebraska." If the Kansas-Nebraska measure were Union-saving, he declared he would support it.[61]

In the course of the autumn, political activity increased through the county conventions. The Democrats met on October 3 in Chicago and endorsed "the great landmarks of the party as laid down by the Baltimore convention of 1852 and supported uniformly . . . since the days of Jefferson." A resolution of opposition to "any new tests" gave notice of Democracy's fear of divided ranks.[62] Wentworth pleaded earnestly for a continuation of the caucus system and party regularity, in the face of being called by William Bross an "unscrupulous demagogue and political Ishmaelite." Outside the fold, however, antislavery forces commended "Long John's" stand on the issue of slavery and lent support to plans of his making.[63] On October 5, the Congressional Democratic Convention met at Aurora, reaffirmed the Baltimore platform of 1852, and nominated Edward L. Mayo of De Kalb County for Congress after Wentworth had declared he did not wish to run since it might injure Judge Douglas. Nebraskaites broke from this group and nominated John B. Turner of Chicago, president of the Galena and Chicago Union Railroad.[64]

These meetings had been preceded by the People's Convention at Aurora, September 20, 1854, in which was striking proof of the disintegration of parties under the impact of slavery. The name "Republican" was taken by the delegates, a designation having appeal to those who opposed the Kansas-Nebraska Act, and intended to attract both Whigs and Democrats. But the fusion did not materialize because an agreement on terms could not be reached. James H. Woodworth, a free soiler since 1848, former mayor of Chicago for two terms and a member of the General Assembly, was nominated for Congress by the so-called Republicans. At the same time the Whigs chose Robert S. Blackwell. Woodworth won over his rivals

---

[61] Cole, *The Era of the Civil War*, pp. 132–33. Lincoln spoke at Chicago, October 27, 1854. *The Daily Democratic Press*, October 28, 1854.

[62] Thirty delegates were chosen for the Second Congressional District Convention. *Weekly Chicago Democrat*, October 7, 1854.

[63] *The Free West*, September 7, 1854; *The Daily Democratic Press*, September 5, 22, 1854. Bross, the editor of the *Democratic Press*, repeatedly charged Wentworth with selfish motives and with methods "the most corrupt and detestable."

[64] *Ibid.*, October 6, 7, 1854; *Weekly Chicago Democrat*, October 7, 14, 1854.

in a quiet contest which editor Bross characterized as conducted with qualities unusual in elections — intelligence and dignity.[65]

In their campaigning the Democrats had tried to avoid the issue of slavery, but they could not prevent the popular vote from reflecting current opinion of the Kansas-Nebraska Bill. Anti-Nebraska men won all offices for which votes were cast in Chicago, and the state legislature showed similar complexion. The choice of a United States senator fell upon Lyman Trumbull, whose defeat of General James Shields the *Times* held to be " the severest blow " the Democrats had yet received.[66]

The municipal election of 1855 mirrored, in general, the uncertainty attending old-time political attachments. Enough voters turned to the Know-Nothings to bring about a flurry of success in the annual bout for municipal offices, garnering all the important places and carrying Dr. Levi D. Boone, one-time city physician, into the mayoralty.[67] Although candidates did not openly announce themselves many days before the time of balloting, the *Democrat,* in late February that year, printed a list of office seekers alleged to be of the Know-Nothing party. The strength of the Native Americans in Chicago was apparent when later in 1855 the city was selected as the home of the *Native Citizen,* official organ of the party. Despite the plan to issue a daily paper under the management of W. W. Danenhower, a weekly with Washington Wright, late editor of the *Capital City Enterprise,* as editor, was undertaken. After about six months it was obliged to suspend publication.[68]

In the state, also, the spread of Know-Nothingism reflected the lack of harmony prevalent in Democratic and Whig circles. The state council meeting in May, 1855, dissolved into two discordant groups: the Jonathans and the Sams. The former were supposed to

[65] *Ibid.,* September 30, November 18, 1854; *The Free West,* September 21, 1854; *The Daily Democratic Press,* September 22, November 8, 15, 1854; R. L. Wilson to E. B. Washburne, September 19, 1854, *Washburne Papers,* II. " Fusion " and " Coöperation " were used interchangeably. Dr. John Evans, the independent Democratic candidate, withdrew September 21, because his stand coincided with that of James H. Woodworth. *The Daily Democratic Press,* September 22, 1854.

[66] *Ibid.,* January 13, February 9, 1855; *Weekly Chicago Democrat,* November 11, 1854; J. W. Sheahan to S. A. Douglas, February 8, 1855, *Douglas Papers.*

[67] The chief officers selected in addition to the mayor were attorney, John A. Thompson; collector, Jacob Russell; treasurer, William F. DeWolf. *Weekly Chicago Democrat,* March 10, 1855.

[68] *The Daily Democratic Press,* March 1, August 6, September 8, October 9, 1855; *Weekly Chicago Democrat,* February 24, 1855. See p. 420.

hate slavery worse than they hated foreigners, and to be willing to admit any alien who would disavow "temporal allegiance to the Pope." In Chicago the Jonathans outnumbered the Sams, who, backed up by Douglas, found their most ardent recruits among anti-foreign and anti-Catholic residents of southern Illinois. The gourmand-like Jonathan threatened, however, to swallow up Sam completely, since the latter was supported by "the old Hunker Whigs, old Hunker Democrats and old fogies generally"; and the bright success which had been confidently predicted for the American party faded when state returns came in.[69]

Throughout the summer of 1855 solicitude regarding the peopling of the new territories grew, and in like degree the popularity of "the Little Giant" waned. Many antislavery men of all political labels were looking forward to the day when they would have a party similar to the Republican of Wisconsin and Michigan, under whose banner all of like faith could find refuge. But party loyalty held in bondage Wentworth and many others sharing his views, and slackened the speed of any attempted organization. For the moment local organizations were the chief means of carrying on any program. In January, 1856, the *Morgan Journal* of Jacksonville led in a movement to unite editors of antislavery leanings. Twenty-five men concurred in the proposal, but the *Chicago Democrat* and the *Democratic Press* failed to join. A heavy snow storm blocked railroads so effectively that only twelve reached their destination for the meeting on February 22, but Chicago was represented by Dr. Charles H. Ray of the *Tribune* and George Schneider of the *Staats-Zeitung,* who, with several other members of the resolutions committee and with the assistance of Abraham Lincoln, drew up resolutions objecting to the repeal of the Missouri Compromise and the further extension of slavery, while disavowing any desire to interfere in any state's internal affairs.[70]

The municipal election of 1856 in a very real sense turned on national issues. It was marked by the efforts of Douglas to obtain a

[69] *Weekly Chicago Democrat,* May 5, 1855.

[70] Before adjournment, it was decided to hold a state convention at Bloomington on May 29. Among the members chosen for the state central committee was William B. Ogden of Chicago, whose absence from the state later necessitated the appointment of Dr. John Evans. Paul Selby, "The Editorial Convention of 1856," Illinois State Historical Society, *Journal,* V (October, 1912), 346.

vote which would appear a ratification of the Kansas-Nebraska Act by this important group of his constituency. The Douglas candidate for mayor was Thomas Dyer, described by his enemies as holding "in his right hand . . . the Nebraska Bill," and "in his left hand . . . the message of President Pierce, showing why he could sign bills to improve Savannah harbor in Georgia, and the Cape Fear river in North Carolina, and why he could not sign bills to improve the Chicago harbor and the St. Clair Flats." [71] Dyer was opposed by Francis C. Sherman as standard bearer of the Democracy against slavery extension, the discussion of which was entangled with the old and vexatious question of internal improvements. [72]

Throughout the state the election was watched as a barometer of sentiment for or against "the Little Giant," who with other Northerners charged with Southern sympathies came to be called derisively a "Boo Hoo." [73] Laborers were appealed to on the ground that the attack of the *Times,* supporter of Dyer, on the credit of the city would discourage investors in public works by which employment was provided. And freemen "one and all" were besought to vote for Sherman if they wished "commerce expanded, . . . prosperity promoted," and "credit and honor preserved." [74] And what plea could touch a Chicagoan's heart more than this?

Extensionists, on the other hand, found grist for their mill in charges that the anti-Nebraska group was hostile to aliens and favored the prohibition of liquor, while they themselves showed their real feeling toward the Maine Law when they chose Cook's Saloon as their headquarters. [75] Violence, intimidation, rowdyism, and bribery marked the campaign. Respected citizens indulged in fisticuffs, openly engaging in street fighting and in property destruc-

[71] Dyer was a merchant and a vessel owner. *Weekly Chicago Democrat,* February 2, 9, 16, 1856; *The Daily Democratic Press,* February 19, 1856.

[72] Francis C. Sherman was urged to run by about 250 citizens including George Schneider, R. L. Wilson, J. L. Scripps, John Wentworth, Mark Skinner, J. C. Vaughan, and William B. Ogden. The signers of the petition declared they would not refuse to make slavery extension the only issue in the municipal campaign, if such a policy were forced upon them by anti-Nebraska men. (*Ibid.,* February 12, 1856.) Sherman, who had been Democratic mayor in 1841, was a man of considerable wealth. Dyer was one of the earliest warehousemen in Chicago and first president of the Board of Trade.

[73] Southern extensionists were called "Sams," Northern antislavery men "Sambos," and Northern men with Southern "principles" were dubbed "Boo Hoos." *Weekly Chicago Democrat,* June 30, 1855.

[74] *The Daily Democratic Press,* February 29, 1856.

[75] *Weekly Chicago Democrat,* March 1, 8, 1856.

tion, thus providing for Douglas's enemies evidence of "the identity of Douglas, Kansas outrages and border ruffianism generally."[76]

Although a vigilance committee had been appointed for each ward by the anti-Nebraska party "to ensure the getting out the full anti-Nebraska vote," the electorate chose Dyer. The old-line Democracy had stemmed the tide of revolt. Almost 9,000 votes were cast, said to be nearly 1,500 more than could be legally polled. According to the fighting editor of the *Democrat,* Douglas had probably spent $50,000, and "all the saloons in the city which were for sale for political purposes were kept free." When a comparison of the vote in this election was made with that in the municipal election of 1855, the defeated felt sure that fraud had been the order of the day. A special committee of the Common Council appointed to investigate election irregularities reported the colonization of voters from four near-by counties, the sending of teams to Bridgeport and other points outside the city to bring in illegal voters, the payment of fees for naturalization papers in return for votes, bribes to aldermen for votes on election judges. To prevent a repetition of such practices, not unique in this election, the committee recommended a registry law.[77]

But under the sting of defeat, the unity of antislavery forces was achieved. Names came to mean "nothing," and principles "everything." Soon antislavery extension clubs were receiving the endorsement of "Maine Law men and Anti-Maine Law men, Americans and foreigners, Old Line Democrats, Old Line Whigs, Old Line Abolitionists and Republicans." In May, a call was issued by a county committee for all persons "opposed to the extension of slave territory, now free," to choose delegates for a county convention to be held in South Market Hall, Chicago, May 23, to select seventeen delegates to the anti-Nebraska state convention to be held at Bloomington, May 29.[78]

[76] *The Daily Democratic Press,* February 28, 29, March 3, 1856. One of the most publicized encounters took place on Clark Street between United States District Attorney Thomas Hoyne and Charles L. Wilson, editor of the *Chicago Daily Journal,* in which Mr. Wilson was reported to have " pummeled Mr. Pierce's official pretty effectually," Hoyne being knocked through the " show window of the State Bank, and safely deposited among the other 'small coin,' to the great consternation of the man of mammon." *Ibid.,* February 29, 1856.

[77] *Weekly Chicago Democrat,* March 8, 15, 1856; *The Daily Democratic Press,* March 4, 6, 14, 1856.

[78] *Weekly Chicago Democrat,* February 16, April 26, May 17, 1856; *The Daily Democratic Press,* May 7, 1856.

Wentworth was the leading spirit of the Chicago convention, and Francis C. Sherman its president. Resolutions avowing hostility to expanding slave territory were passed; Francis A. Hoffman, one-time Whig and a Chicago banker, was endorsed as candidate for the lieutenant governorship; and Trumbull and Woodworth were commended for the "punctuality and correctness" of their votes in Congress.[79] Six days later the Bloomington convention charged the administration at Washington with using "all its energies" to secure the spread of slavery and with attempting to curb freedom of speech and to subvert liberty, and demanded the immediate admission of Kansas and the recognition of the equality of all men regardless of religion or place of birth. William H. Bissell of St. Clair County was nominated for governor and Francis A. Hoffman for lieutenant governor, and delegates were named for the Republican convention to be held in Philadelphia in June. Chicago expressed its delight over the achievements of the Bloomington convention in "a large and enthusiastic rally presided over by Norman B. Judd" on the evening of May 31, at which the nominations were enthusiastically ratified.[80]

While antislavery sentiment had thus been coming to a focus, the Democrats held their state convention at Springfield on May 1. Its resolutions glorified squatter sovereignty and denied the right of Congress to legislate upon the matter of slavery in any way.[81] A month later James Buchanan was named at the national Democratic convention at Cincinnati as candidate for president on a squatter sovereignty platform. Again the hope of Douglas was blasted. A Chicago rally on June 10 endorsed the nomination, but with "very thin" enthusiasm, according to the *Democratic Press*.[82] The reception accorded the news of Buchanan's nomination seemed the more ominous in Chicago when later in the month word came of the naming of John C. Frémont by the Republicans. Salutes by guns from morning until night, fireworks thrown in Dearborn Park, and "bonfires kept burning until midnight" accompanied the cheers and applause which greeted endorsements voiced in the speeches of

[79] *Ibid.*, May 24, 1856; *Weekly Chicago Democrat*, May 31, 1856.
[80] *Ibid.*, June 7, 1856; *The Daily Democratic Press*, May 31, June 2, 1856.
[81] *Ibid.*, May 1, 7, 1856; C. H. Ray to E. B. Washburne, May 4, 1856, *Washburne Papers*, II. Colonel William A. Richardson was nominated for governor.
[82] *The Daily Democratic Press*, June 11, 1856.

William Bross, John Wentworth, Francis A. Hoffman, and General James H. Lane of Kansas.[83] As the conviction grew "that Frémont and Freedom" were synonymous, clubs for young men, as well as for the old and tried, were organized. On July 19, Abraham Lincoln spoke to "a large meeting" in Dearborn Park. For a long time the audience listened to his calm, clear, and forceful "references to indisputable facts in our political history" which supported the anti-Nebraska platform.[84] So convincing was he that the editor of the *Democrat* felt that this orator of the so-called Black Republicans ought to be kept "on the stump" until the campaign closed.[85]

The canvass was spirited, sometimes vituperative. The Democrats were accused of repudiating the principles of Washington, Jefferson, Madison, and Jackson, and of being purely sectional in point of view. In fair and foul weather Republican meetings were well attended, and each gathering seemed to show increased strength for "the cause of Frémont and Freedom." Poets, song writers, and vocalists of national and local fame made their contributions. One could have "The Banner of the Free" for twenty-five cents, not to mention the popular "Give 'em Jessie Polka." Street corner, assembly hall, and parlor resounded with the song:

> Yankee Doodle keep it up;
> It is as plain as figures,
> Buchanan is the candidate
> To raise the price of niggers.

Campaign circulars to "get out the vote" importuned Illinoisans to "Push on the column in Illinois! Organize — bring up every man to the polls, and by the blessing of Almighty God, Freedom and Frémont will obtain a signal triumph one week from Tuesday next." [86]

Dr. William B. Egan, spokesman of the sons of the Emerald Isle who wanted "free land or no land," and who therefore now looked more favorably on the Republicans than upon the Democrats, George Schneider of the *Staats-Zeitung,* Zebina Eastman of Aboli-

[83] *Ibid.,* June 19, 20, 1856; *Weekly Chicago Democrat,* May 31, 1856.

[84] *The Daily Democratic Press,* July 12, 21, 22, 1856.

[85] *Weekly Chicago Democrat,* July 26, 1856.

[86] *The Daily Democratic Press,* July 28, August 9, October 2, 1856; *Tri-Weekly Democratic Press,* August 4, 9, 1856; *Weekly Chicago Democrat,* September 13, 1856; Circular from Truman Smith, New York, October 23, 1856, *Washburne Papers,* II.

tion fame, John Wentworth, erstwhile Democrat, and Jonathan Young Scammon, Wentworth's Whig opponent in 1848, represented the old-time and diverse political creeds and dogmas now being woven into the new fabric of antislaveryism. The variegated design may have pleased all, but none more than it did Wentworth, who had wanted an organization dedicated to "anti-slavery extension," which would "receive all anti-slavery extensionists on an equality" and not be merely the party of Horace Greeley with all his "isms." [87]

While these activities were going on under Republican auspices, Douglas and his followers canvassed Illinois from Yankee Chicago to remotest Egypt, urging the election of Buchanan "upon the ground that the Democratic party and its candidates were pledged in the most solemn manner to secure to the people of the Territories the right of having slavery or not, as they of their own free action might determine." [88] In September, when he returned from Washington, Douglas brought several of "the most rampant fire-eaters of the South" to aid, so his enemies said, in "subduing" the people of Illinois. Their presence irritated many in Chicago. "Now suppose we were to test the 'nationality' of the proslavery Democracy," indignantly wrote the editor of the Daily Democratic Press, "by sending Mr. Dayton to stump South Carolina for his ticket, and Mr. Trumbull and Joseph Knox, Esq., to Georgia and Alabama. Would they come back with whole skins and sound limbs? Nobody will imagine for a moment that they would. No; there is no reciprocity. It is all fierce sectionalism on one side, and free, courteous toleration on the other. Until there is something like equality between the North and South in this regard, let Douglas and other exponents of African Democracy have the decency to hold their peace about 'nationality' and 'sectionalism.'" [89]

Not to be outdone by the fanfare of the Republicans, the "Buchaniers" held mass meetings, some designed to catch the foreign vote, others addressed to native Americans. In August, the Customs House was adorned with a "Buchanier flag, with more black than any other color on it," causing the opposition press to inquire, "Has

[87] Weekly Chicago Democrat, April 5, June 7, July 19, 1856; The Daily Democratic Press, June 28, 30, 1856.

[88] Sheahan, op. cit., p. 312.

[89] The Daily Democratic Press, September 15, 1856. William L. Dayton was candidate for vice-president with Frémont in 1856. Joseph Knox was a Republican from Rock Island.

the Collector destroyed the Flag of Our Union? Is the banner of
Slavery Extension to be flaunted above our National offices and
edifices? . . . Are the Stars and Stripes torn from the Capitol at
Washington, and the black flag unfurled in its place?"[90]

Meanwhile both Know-Nothings and Whigs raised their battle
cries and tried to draw recruits from the ranks of other parties.
Fillmore and Donelson clubs, vying with those supporting other
candidates, pledged Chicagoans to oppose "all sectional parties"
and to enroll under the standard, "The Constitution and the
Union."[91]

Political connivance and chicanery were on all sides. Followers
of Buchanan often were charged with inciting religious animosities
by reports that Frémont was a Catholic. Fillmore Know-Nothings
were said to have tried to entice Bissell, later candidate for governor
on the Republican ticket, into their state council in order to fix on
him "the stain of 'Americanism,'" and thus ruin him with the
Germans. "Doughface" Democrats raised the cry that Republicans
had formed an unholy alliance with abolitionism. With a large
foreign element in Chicago, candidates of nativist sympathies stood
small chance of success. Fearing that the stigma of Native Americanism, with its twin sister the Maine Law, would bring ruin to the
Republicans, antislavery promoters who wished to remove such a
"scare-crow" suggested that they be called "free or white Democrats."[92]

Old fears and old allegiances were routed as the conflict grew
more furious. The traditional alliance of the Germans with the
Democracy was undermined when the Kansas-Nebraska Bill seemed
to open a way for slave labor to threaten the position of the German
proletarian. Under the guidance of George Schneider, Frémont
clubs among the Germans made capital of this antislavery sentiment until "no German in the city" was "willing to advocate

[90] *Ibid.*, August 18, 27, 30, 1856. "The Buchanier flag" was not shown on the following day. *Ibid.*, August 19, 1856.

[91] In the minds of some, Know-Nothingism was identified with the South. Among 180
signers of the Fillmore and Donelson club call were Levi D. Boone, Buckner S. Morris, B. L.
Honoré, H. H. Honoré, W. W. Danenhower, J. B. Blair, James L. Allen, and S. D. Childs,
Jr. *Weekly Chicago Democrat*, May 17, July 26, 1856; *The Daily Democratic Press*, July 31,
1856.

[92] *Weekly Chicago Democrat*, August 2, 16, 1856; C. H. Ray to E. B. Washburne, May
4, 1856, *Washburne Papers*, II.

publicly the doctrines of slavery extension."[93] Indeed, the defection of German Democrats had so enraged the Nebraskaites that in March they had attempted to wreck the office of the *Staats-Zeitung* after having burned in effigy its editor, the indomitable Captain Schneider.[94] Failing this and convinced that the pen should be mightier than the sword, the Douglas forces started a rival paper, the *Demokrat,* in the hope that the word Democrat would still have the appeal of the days of 1848.[95] Scandinavians, Swiss, and other foreign groups, influenced by the prevalent propaganda that slave owners were the instinctive enemies of foreigners, identified them-selves with the Republicans. But the Irish, with few exceptions, obedient to the party whip, cast their fortunes with the Democracy.[96]

By early June, "bleeding" Kansas captured the fancies of all and became the dominant issue in the presidential campaign. Lecturers who denounced "outrages" in Kansas and who came out in favor of freedom in the territories were enthusiastically received. Resolu-tions of resentment at the treatment in Kansas of former residents of Chicago who had emigrated to the scene of battle, and the selec-tion of delegates to a "Kansas Convention" in Buffalo for late July were direct and simple manifestations that the heat of midsummer was matched by that of the incensed citizenry.[97]

The issue of slavery seemed enough, but the need of internal im-provements still vexed nervous Chicagoans. Of what avail was it, they inquired, to have Congress pass harbor and river improvement bills only to have them vetoed by the President? Votes in Congress against this requisite of happiness for Chicago, moreover, they noticed generally came from "the Buchanan party," which was "the only party, therefore, opposed to the interests of the West," — a party "arrayed under the leadership of the abstractionists of the South," which was "seeking to make Mr. Buchanan President."[98] Closely

---

[93] *The Daily Democratic Press,* July 23, 30, August 9, 1856; Herriott, *loc. cit.,* p. 381. See also C. H. Ray to Lyman Trumbull, March 21, 1856, *Trumbull Papers,* II.

[94] The attempt to wreck the office was prevented by the German Turners. *Weekly Chicago Democrat,* March 15, 1856.

[95] *The Daily Democratic Press,* July 12, 1856.

[96] *Ibid.,* August 5, 22, 25, 1856; *Weekly Chicago Democrat,* May 12, June 14, 1856.

[97] *The Daily Democratic Press,* June 2, July 7, 1856; *Weekly Chicago Democrat,* July 12, 1856. Among the delegates were Grant Goodrich, William B. Ogden, J. Young Scammon, William Bross, John H. Kinzie, Isaac N. Arnold, William B. Egan, Charles L. Wilson, and Peter Page.

[98] *Ibid.,* August 16, 1856; see also *ibid.,* May 10, June 21, 1856.

allied to river and harbor improvements was the persisting desire of the West for railroads. Both the antislavery group and Douglas favored a transcontinental line. In spite of this apparent agreement between opposing forces, debate about its route and methods of financing caused postponement until another day.[99]

In the autumn of 1856 conventions to nominate county, state, and Congressional officers chose candidates whose political views reflected the national. A Republican county convention met in Chicago in September to appoint delegates to the Congressional convention to be held at Dixon on the eighteenth. This assembly praised James H. Woodworth's course in Congress and recommended to the district convention that he be renominated, but their recommendation was overruled and the district convention named John F. Farnsworth. Resolutions were passed endorsing the principles embodied in the platform of the anti-Nebraska party, announcing opposition to slavery extension, favoring the admission of Kansas at once as a free state, and declaring its faith in the right of Congress to legislate regarding slavery in the territories. The delegates opposed all laws to restrict or diminish the rights of foreign-born residents to become citizens, and approved internal improvements at federal expense and government aid in the construction of a " National Railroad to the Pacific." [100]

On October 15, the Republicans in county convention drew up what they believed "a most capital ticket" of officers, including Norman B. Judd for state senator, A. F. C. Mueller, Isaac N. Arnold, J. H. Dunham, and George W. Morris for representatives. The Fillmorites earlier in the month had nominated T. J. S. Flint for state senator, and Archibald Clybourn, B. F. James, J. E. Crane, and Eliphalet Wood for the lower house, although they had previously felt it inexpedient to run a ticket.[101]

Election day came November 4. The last week of October had been filled with rancor and bickering about the appointment of election judges. So tense was the feeling between factions that the

[99] Ibid., August 23, 1856. See the Republican party platform of 1856, which approved a railroad by " the most central and practicable route " through aid by the federal government. Thomas V. Cooper and Hector T. Fenton, American Politics (Chicago, 1884), Book II, p. 40; Sheahan, op. cit., p. 371. See p. 54.

[100] The Daily Democratic Press, September 16, 20, 1856. The county convention met September 15.

[101] Ibid., September 29, October 6, 16, 1856.

only safety lay in the choice of a nonpartisan board of inspectors. On election day all the saloons and drinking houses were ordered closed. Frémont vigilance committees for some time had been meeting daily, anticipating need for watchfulness on November 4. By mid-October it had been reported that "the Ruffian Democracy" had commenced colonizing the wards of the city with imported voters. This rumor led to the appointment of a "Central City Committee," who offered a reward of twenty-five dollars for the detection and conviction of every nonresident attempting to vote, or for the detection and conviction of anyone who falsely swore in a vote. On the third of November "squads of illegal voters" were said to have arrived and to have been met at the depot by the Buchaniers and accompanied to the boarding houses provided for them. The opposing groups tried to spot their faces and to learn their names so that arrests could be made and "free lodgings" provided for them "a longer time than La Rue, Dyer, and Douglas" had guaranteed. The sheriff took the precaution of appointing five hundred deputies, part openly wearing a sheriff's badge and "the balance in citizen's dress" as "a reserve posse." Despite undercurrents of excitement and alarm, the election was comparatively quiet, except in the Seventh Ward, where Irish protagonists of Douglas and his party were reported to have tried forcibly to prevent the opposition from casting their votes.[102]

Chicago went for Frémont, while Buchanan carried the state; the county voted in favor of Frémont and all antislavery candidates; and the Second Congressional District sent the Republican Farnsworth to victory. State officers were likewise Republican. Egypt joined with northern Illinois to place in the executive mansion William H. Bissell, a Catholic, instead of Col. William A. Richardson, who had been Douglas's choice. The national Democratic victory was thus dulled by state and local returns.[103]

The defeat of the national ticket in Illinois did not dim Republican faith in ultimate success. Within a week, the Young Men's Frémont

[102] Ibid., October 21, 24, 29, November 3, 1856; Chicago Daily Journal, October 23, 25, 30, 31, November 1, 5, 1856. The Seventh Ward had a high proportion of foreign born as residents. Many Irish lived there.

[103] The Daily Democratic Press, November 10, 20, 1856; Chicago Daily Journal, November 8, 1856. The story of charges made against Bissell in the campaign in connection with the Illinois Central Railroad grants can be found in Weekly Chicago Democrat, March 22, August 9, 1856.

Club had met to consider whether the organization should continue. The German Republican Club had already set an example of uninterrupted activity by deciding to present a series of lectures on the all-absorbing theme of slavery extension. The Frémont Club followed their lead and proceeded to lease " for permanent occupancy " the quarters they had occupied, to adopt a constitution, and to create an executive committee. They endorsed their defeated candidate for the presidency in 1860, and recorded that their confidence in the ultimate success of Republicanism was undiminished. But they offered assurances that they did not wish to interfere with slavery in the states where it existed, although they were opposed to extension in territory then free.[104]

In early December, Republican delegates from all parts of Illinois "joined with one voice and heart " in a great banquet to inaugurate "the principles of right and justice" in their state government. At the head of the table sat Jonathan Young Scammon, one-time Whig, who had come to Chicago in 1835. Near by was Abraham Lincoln, whose gaunt figure towered above the well-laden board as he rose, " amidst most deafening cheers," to answer the toast, " The Union — The North will maintain it — The South will not depart therefrom." Then came toasts to the various Republican candidates, the Free Press, the Northwest, Kansas, "Our adopted Citizens," " There's a good time coming," Illinois and Chicago, and the party itself. To states rights was offered " States Rights — Maintained by unity of purpose and action, differences of locality will not weaken. Executive encroachments or imbecility will not destroy them." [105]

The Democrats had celebrated their national victory a month before with bands of music, torches, banners, and flags. Opposite the Tremont House they kindled a bonfire and listened to a short speech by Douglas, who assured them that " Chicago would yet redeem herself — she would do so at the next election, and after that she would be right at every election." [106]

Both Republicans and Democrats held conventions on February 28, 1857. The Republicans named Wentworth for mayor. Re-

[104] *Chicago Daily Journal,* November 11, 1856; *The Daily Democratic Press,* November 12, 13, 1856.
[105] *Ibid.,* December 11, 1856.
[106] *Ibid.,* November 13, 1856.

sults of the Democratic convention were not published until March 2, when the party announced that Benjamin F. Carver, cashier of the Marine Bank and of the Chicago Marine and Fire Insurance Company, would carry its ensign for the mayoralty. On February 28 the " Hon. Abram Lincoln of Springfield " addressed all friends of city reform who were demanding " more efficiency in the Police Department — more care and economy in the disposition of finances — more *honest* men in the Common Council — in short . . . more regard paid to the duties of the offices to which the incumbents " were elected, and " less personal and party manoeuvring [*sic*] for the ' spoils.' " Lincoln's well-disposed listeners, sensitive to the local debacle into which they thought the Democrats had plunged the city administration, were likewise suspicious of the motives back of " the Little Giant's " interest in Chicago politics, for they believed he was making " one more desperate effort " to obtain success for " his partisan friends " in order that it might seem " an endorsement of his own political course." [107]

The election on March 3 was stormy. Violence and disorder ruled, especially in the Seventh and Tenth wards, where only Democrats seemed safe. And it was particularly dangerous to be Germans, for " they were singled out and set upon as a class " because they had " so largely contributed " to the defeat of the Democrats in the autumn. Little protection was provided by the city police, moreover, and many a voter found it unwise to exercise his rights as a freeman unless he subscribed to the tenets of the Democracy. When the count was made, however, Wentworth put to rout his Democratic opponent by a vote of 5,933 to 4,842, and the other city offices went to the Republicans. Chicago again rejoiced that she had shown central and southern Illinois her real attitude toward Douglas and slavery, although " Long John " as mayor was " a bitter pill " for some of the party " to swallow." [108]

Two days after the inauguration of Buchanan, the Dred Scott Decision increased concern over national affairs. In the minds of many, the " sectional bias " of the decision ill became a federal judiciary which " ought ever to be untrammelled and uninfluenced

[107] *Chicago Daily Journal*, February 25, 28, March 2, 3, 1857; D. Harner to S. A. Douglas, March 1, 1857, *Douglas Papers*.

[108] *Chicago Daily Journal*, March 4, 5, 1857; W. H. Brown to Lyman Trumbull, February 28, 1857, *Trumbull Papers*, VIII. See also *Chicago Daily Journal*, February 25, 1857.

by any other considerations than those of impartial justice and righteous judgment." [109]

Chicagoans were somewhat prepared for the momentous judgment. As early as December the *Journal* had prophesied that the court, being " pro-slavery " in the majority, would decide that Congress had no power to prohibit slavery in a territory, " that the Missouri prohibition was unconstitutional," and that Scott was " lawfully held as a slave." In early January, the *Daily Democratic Press* went even further and foretold that seven of the nine judges would be in favor of a decision " declaring the unconstitutionality of the Missouri Compromise, and by implication affirming the right of slaveholders to hold their slaves in all the free territory of the Union." By June, " the infamous decision " was talked of by antislavery men as likely to be incorporated in the Democratic national platform. " Is Freedom national, as the Republicans contend," they asked, " or Slavery, as ' Democracy ' asserts ? "

These expressions of disapproval of the court Douglas, on the other hand, considered as " poisonous shafts of partisan malice," and vehemently urged all " friends of order and constitutional government . . . to organize themselves . . . under the glorious banner of the Union " in the event of resistance to the court's order. [110]

In this atmosphere, surcharged with the hate which only political partisanship can generate, Chicago approached the county election of 1857. Rallies and other demonstrations, especially on the part of Republicans, protested what they chose to call Douglas's breaches of national faith and national honor, and declared in unequivocal terms against " the nominees of pro-slavery democracy," who could carry the election only by default or by fraud. A well-organized vote gave Republicans the victory both in Chicago and in Cook County. [111]

Both parties began to prepare for the municipal contest in January, 1858, and each soon prescribed its slate of officers, the Republicans naming John C. Haines and the Democrats Dr. Daniel Brainard. During the winter, even in the council meetings attacks on Wentworth, representative of the old-time Democracy and now of the

---

[109] *Ibid.,* March 9, 1857.

[110] *Ibid.,* December 20, 1856, March 9, June 13, 1857; *The Daily Democratic Press,* January 9, 1857; Mark Skinner to Lyman Trumbull, March 8, 1858, *Trumbull Papers,* XII; Sheahan, *op. cit.,* pp. 283–84.

[111] *Chicago Daily Democratic Press,* November 2, 3, 5, 1857.

antislavery faction, superseded the business of city government, and endangered, in the opinion of some, the new Republican party. But the comptroller's report, published just before the election, showed achievements in economy during Wentworth's mayoralty and served to clinch the votes of the wavering. Events at the national capital had, during the weeks of municipal campaigning, tended further to intensify loyalties to the new alignments. In spite of a large campaign fund of the Democrats, to which it was alleged hundreds of dollars had been contributed by houses of prostitution, saloons, and those desiring concessions from the government, victory went to Haines, a former flour miller and several times a member of the Common Council.[112]

Outside of Chicago, as well as within the city, the Republican victory created a profound impression. "The Court faction," or administration forces, looked upon it as a defeat of the Douglas Democrats, but Mark Skinner declared it more "the result of deep hostility to the Lecompton Swindle" than "anything else." Certainly it represented collective opinion against the Lecompton Constitution, endorsed by the local Democracy at a meeting in the North Division, February 23, 1858.[113]

Controversy over the Kansas constitution had begun in December, 1857. Like other northerners of antislavery bent, Chicagoans, on the whole, considered the Lecompton Constitution a grant to slavery dangerous to the free settlers of Kansas. They also felt that the method of presenting it to popular vote was fraudulent. In this opinion Douglas concurred. On December 9, he stated his position in the Senate and thus broke with Buchanan. In so doing, "the Little Giant" imperiled his influence in garnering the spoils of office for his supporters. Indeed, the Democracy of Chicago had not been pleased at all times with the Buchanan selections, which in the future were to prove even less acceptable to Douglas and his friends.[114]

The stand on Lecomptonism taken by Douglas was the signal to aspirants for leadership in the party to endeavor to undo him.

[112] *Ibid.,* January 7, 8, 26–29, February 2, 3, 8, 13, 15, 22, 25, March 7, 10, 1858; *Chicago Weekly Democrat,* March 13, 1858.

[113] Mark Skinner to Lyman Trumbull, March 8, 1858, W. H. Stickney to Trumbull, March 6, 1858, N. B. Judd to Trumbull, March 7, 1858, *Trumbull Papers,* XII; *Chicago Daily Democratic Press,* February 25, 1858.

[114] *Chicago Daily Journal,* March 19, 20, 1857; Charles P. Button to S. A. Douglas, March 20, 1857, *Douglas Papers.*

Whether because of expediency or because of honest agreement with promoters of Lecomptonism, Iram Nye, Dr. Daniel Brainard, Thomas Hoyne, and Isaac Cook deserted the Democracy of Douglas and became leaders in the administration's faction. To each of them a reward from Washington came in the form of an office. Cook's appointment as postmaster, replacing William Price, raised a storm of protest in Chicago, not only because of his alleged association in the past with "stews, low gambling," and other disreputable surroundings, but also because he was accused of having been "a defaulter" during his earlier term in the same office. The administrative ax fell on other "Lecompton Rebels" and soon "the names of the beheaded" were "too numerous to mention." In their places appeared new leaders, Owen McCarthy and Philip Conley, able to draw to themselves most of the Irish of the town. Further strength was gained by the anti-Douglas faction when, in March, the *National Union,* later succeeded by the *Chicago Herald,* assumed the responsibilities of the party's journal.[115]

Douglas's attitude toward the Lecompton Constitution laid him open to attack from both sides. Republicans mistrusted his motives; Democrats often misunderstood them. His acceptance of the Dred Scott Decision, his enemies declared, was a substitution for his much discussed theory of popular sovereignty; and his stand on the Lecompton Constitution seemed to some inexplicable and to others inconsistent with his political philosophy. He was forced, many thought, either to rebel openly against the administration or "to acquiesce and be hamstrung by it." He chose the former course, angling for Republican support by confiding in men of that political faith in Chicago that "he intended to get Kansas in as a free state." These overtures caused much confusion, though they led to increased strength among the new party's members in the East.[116]

[115] *Chicago Daily Democratic Press,* February 22, March 20, 1858; *Chicago Daily Democrat,* March 5, 8, 13, 1858; Sheahan, *op. cit.,* pp. 386–87; Mark Skinner to Lyman Trumbull, March 8, 1858, C. H. Ray to Trumbull, March 9, 1858, *Trumbull Papers,* XII, XIII; James W. Sheahan to S. A. Douglas, February 10, 1858, *Douglas Papers;* Milton, *The Eve of Conflict,* p. 303. Among the appointments made by Buchanan in 1858 were Owen McCarthy to succeed Paul H. Dennis as special mail agent and Alderman Philip Conley to succeed General Jacob Fry as collector of the port of Chicago. *Chicago Daily Democratic Press,* March 20, 1858.

[116] *Chicago Daily Press and Tribune,* August 11, 1858; N. B. Judd to Lyman Trumbull, December 1, 1857, *Trumbull Papers,* IX. ". . . he really made some of their eyes stick out at his zeal — or in other words it was an attempt to disorganize us by drawing off some

The split in the Democratic ranks which in December, 1857, the *Press and Tribune* had declared could never be brought about had come. The still youthful Republican party saw its strategic opportunity. To consolidate anti-Lecompton forces, bargains were suggested and some were consummated. Through Horace Greeley, editor of the *New York Tribune,* who had welcomed " Black Douglas " into Republicanism, Elihu B. Washburne, Congressman from Galena, was sent to Springfield to suggest that Douglas's path be cleared by dropping Lincoln, who was to contest the senatorship with " the Little Giant." [117]

On April 17, 1858, the Cook County Democrats held their convention preparatory to the state meeting at Springfield on the twenty-first. They gave sanction to the Cincinnati platform, advised the submission of the Lecompton Constitution to the people of Kansas, and condemned the administration's attitude on that constitution. Two days later an anti-Douglas convention, dominated by Isaac Cook, now controller of patronage, also named delegates to Springfield. There two antagonistic groups, one a so-called " Douglas " convention and the other made up of Buchanan's followers, adopted similar resolutions adhering to the Cincinnati platform, for the Douglas faction feared openly to denounce Buchanan and his use of the patronage.[118]

The nomination of Douglas for the senatorship solved a problem for the Republicans. All through the spring it was feared that Douglas's " declaration of intentions " might obligate the party to receive him, and therefore mean a defeat of Lincoln for the Senate. If that did not happen, they still feared that Douglas would cast his

---

of the old democracy. . . . You have already been informed by some of your correspondents of his plans of sending back the Constitution with the enabling bill so that all the people of Kansas may vote. I want you to introduce such a bill before he does. . . . Lincoln was here yesterday and he thinks in any event Douglass [*sic*] will loose [*sic*] ground here — and notwithstanding his boldness I think the party will be too strong for him." See also C. H. Ray [*Chicago Tribune*] to Trumbull, December 18, 1857, E. L. Baker [*Illinois State Journal*] to Trumbull, May 1, 1858, *ibid.,* X, XIV; *Chicago Daily Democratic Press*, December 9, 1857; *Chicago Daily Press and Tribune*, July 2, 1858; *Cong. Globe*, 35 Cong., 1 sess., pt. I, pp. 14–18.

[117] Cole, *The Era of the Civil War*, p. 161; *Chicago Daily Democratic Press*, December 21, 25, 1857.

[118] *Ibid.,* April 19, 22, 1858; Cole, *The Era of the Civil War*, p. 162. The Cincinnati platform declared that " the people of all the territories, . . . acting through the legally and fairly expressed will of the majority of the actual residents," possessed the right " to form a constitution, with or without domestic slavery, and be admitted into the Union upon terms of perfect equality with the other states." Cooper and Fenton, *op. cit.,* Book II, p. 38.

eye upon Lyman Trumbull's place, and thus create discouragement among many of the earnest workers who would think that all their hard work would result only in keeping a warm place for him whom they all hated. How to dispose of Douglas was, therefore, a problem of great concern. Perhaps, it was suggested, he would be willing to withdraw if promised "a place in the cabinet of the next Republican President," a promise which apparently those who "hated" him thought might "stimulate him to extra exertions" in their behalf. On the night of the convention prominent Republicans drew up a program for future action and declared that it would be their moral duty to nominate Abraham Lincoln as senator when they assembled at Springfield, June 16.[119]

To that Republican convention Chicago sent about 7 per cent of the fifteen hundred in attendance. The platform condemned, as was expected, the policies of the Buchanan administration and the Dred Scott Decision, and glorified free labor as the only sound basis of a republican government. Planks in support of river and harbor improvements, a Pacific railroad by a central route, and homestead legislation were included. The keynote was struck for a campaign of propaganda designed to dignify labor and ennoble toil, a campaign in which adroit use was to be made of the belief that the South, because of "hatred of Free Labor" and "jealousy of Western growth" was the home of "inflexible opposition" to the West. The convention did not, however, set forth an aggressive program to check slavery extension.[120]

On the day on which Lincoln delivered his memorable speech of acceptance, the Senate of the United States adjourned and Douglas left Washington for New York, where he remained a few days while preparations went forward for an "imposing" demonstration in Chicago, alleged to be financed by "the Little Giant" himself. In New York he was in "consultation with his friends," prominent among whom, according to a dispatch to the *Daily Press and Tribune,* were "many of the leading spirits of Old Tammany, the

[119] C. H. Ray to Lyman Trumbull, March 9, 1858, *Trumbull Papers,* XIII; Cole, *The Era of the Civil War,* p. 163.

[120] Among the delegates from Chicago were Joseph Medill, William Bross, Horace White, John Wentworth, Charles L. Wilson, John L. Scripps, George Schneider, Caspar Butz, Hermann Kreismann, Thomas Hale, and Ebenezer Peck. *Chicago Daily Journal,* June 9, 1858. See also *ibid.,* June 18, 1858; *Chicago Daily Press and Tribune,* July 3, 5, 1858; *Chicago Weekly Democrat,* June 26, 1858.

very high church faction of modern Democracy." Republicans, therefore, "who, at the outset of his rebellion, were ready to welcome him into their ranks, and even to make him their leader," began to "doubt his sincerity . . . and look for his speedy restoration to the fold of the faithful," since he "so ostentatiously clung to the skirts of Democracy."[121] And when Republicans discovered that Douglas took occasion to speak sneeringly of them in public and contemptuously in private, they were inclined to accept the opinion of one of his harsher critics and call him a "Mongrel Democrat," "the greatest charlatan and humbug in the country."[122]

On July 9 Douglas reached Chicago. How different his reception from that accorded the Nebraska champion less than four years before! From the Tremont House to the Central Depot in early evening gathered a crowd estimated at thirty thousand, the air of "an intensely hot day" fanning their cheeks.[123] Democrats from Egypt and others from central Illinois joined with northern Democracy to celebrate the return of "the champion of Popular Sovereignty." Through banner-lined streets and flag-bedecked buildings and with cannon booming, Judge Douglas, "in an open barouche drawn by six horses" and followed by "the Committee of Arrangements in other carriages," was escorted by Irish military organizations, the Montgomery Guards and Emmett Guards, up Lake Street to Wabash Avenue, thence to Washington Street, down Dearborn to the Tremont House.[124]

As the milling throng shouted their welcome, "the Little Giant" started a defense of his opposition to the Lecompton Constitution. He held that it violated the right of self-government, a right he had chosen to call "popular sovereignty." He disclaimed the desirability of "uniformity" in local laws as he answered Lincoln's "house divided" statement, and took issue with his opponent's attack on the Supreme Court. When he declared that he yielded obedience to and

---

[121] From New York correspondent, July 2, 1858, to *Chicago Daily Press and Tribune,* July 7, 1858.

[122] *Chicago Daily Democrat,* October 11, 1858.

[123] The *Times,* a Douglas organ, estimated the crowd at thirty thousand (*The Chicago Times,* July 10, 1858, quoted in Sheahan, *op. cit.,* p. 400), but the *Tribune* said there were only twelve thousand present. The *Press and Tribune* declared the estimate of thirty thousand fantastic in the light of Chicago's adult male population. *Chicago Daily Press and Tribune,* July 10, 12, 1858.

[124] Sheahan, *op. cit.,* pp. 398, 400. The Douglas reception was reported as costing $1,252. *Chicago Daily Press and Tribune,* July 10, 1858.

acquiesced in the final determination of the highest tribunal of the nation upon the Federal Constitution, loud salvos rose from the throats of men, many of whom less than a year before had loosed torrents of abuse upon the venerable judges of that tribunal. Douglas could not, he said, like Lincoln, condemn the court because it did not affirm that the Negro was the equal of the white man, for the government of the United States "was made by white men for the benefit of white men, to be administered by white men in such a manner as they should determine." The audience roared its thunderous assent; the band struck up "Yankee Doodle"; rockets and pieces of fireworks blazed forth. The scene, in the words of a contemporary, "was glorious beyond description." [125]

Quick to sense the warmth of his reception, Douglas then attacked the "unholy, unnatural alliance" which Republican leaders and "unscrupulous federal office-holders" had made against him. "I shall deal with these allied forces just as the Russians dealt with the allies at Sebastopol," said he. "The Russians, when they fired a broadside at the common enemy, did not stop to inquire, whether it hit a Frenchman, an Englishman, or a Turk, nor will I stop." Again there were "cheers and cries of 'Bravo.'" [126] Chicago, a depot of the Underground Railroad, the refuge of fugitive slaves, had, at least for the moment, endorsed the tenets of Douglasism.

The die had been cast; the issues between Lincoln and Douglas were clear. The next night Lincoln spoke at the same place, dealing especially with popular sovereignty and the Dred Scott case before a crowd estimated at nine thousand, whose "enthusiasm," to a partisan editor, seemed "about four times as great" as that at the Douglas meeting.[127] Of an alliance between Republicans and administration forces, Lincoln knew nothing; nor did he believe one existed. The defeat of the Lecompton Constitution he maintained was not to be credited solely to Douglas. At this point, the applause which greeted him was mingled with heckling; his listeners were not entirely converted.

He repeated his prophecy that "a house divided against itself can-

---

[125] *Ibid.;* Sheahan, *op. cit.,* pp. 406–15.

[126] *Ibid.,* pp. 414–15. Lincoln was a listener to Douglas's speech. The *Chicago Daily Democrat,* July 9, 1858, declared that he was in Chicago to try a case in court, and other papers said that his presence was purely accidental.

[127] *Chicago Daily Press and Tribune,* July 12, 1858.

not stand," and declared that he had no desire to set "the sections at war with one another." Turning to the foreign born, he assured them that their European forebears were in very truth spiritually "blood of the blood, and flesh of the flesh of the men" who wrote the Declaration of Independence and pronounced the equality of man. This principle, he held, should be as nearly reached as possible. "If we cannot give freedom to every creature, let us do nothing that will impose slavery upon any other creature," he concluded. And "let us discard all this quibbling about this man and the other man, this race and that race and the other race being inferior, . . . and unite as one people throughout this land, until we shall once more stand up declaring that all men are created equal." Here was the touchstone of American political faith — the equality of man. As Lincoln finished his address, "cheers like blasts of a thousand bugles" came from the throats of his listeners.

A partisan press declared that Lincoln had "demolished Douglas" and "knocked him higher than a kite," but the leaders of the party were not overconfident. The repeated charge that they believed in "a war of sections," "negro equality," and "amalgamation" plagued them beyond measure.[128] "If there be one rock more dangerous than another in the pathway of the Republican party it is this [Negro equality]," declared Charles L. Wilson, editor of the *Journal*. "For myself," said he, "I am opposed to Slavery not only because it is a wrong to the downtrodden and oppressed but that it blights and mildews the white man whose lot is toil, and whose capital is labor. . . . I am resolutely opposed to the 'equallizing [*sic*] of the races' and it no more necessarily follows that we should fellowship with Negroes because our policy strikes off their shackles, than it would to take felons to our embraces, because we might remonstrate against cruelty to them in our penitentiaries."[129]

Throughout the summer and early autumn, Douglas and Lincoln carried forward their campaign, Lincoln trailing "the Little Giant" who seemed to have the advantage. In addition to the speeches of early July in Chicago the contenders spoke from the same platform in seven towns during the famous debate series. Senator Lyman Trumbull also took the stump for his party. In early August he laid

[128] *Ibid.*, July 12, 13, 16, 23, 1858; Norman B. Judd to Lyman Trumbull, July 16, 1858, Charles L. Wilson to Trumbull, May 12, 1858, *Trumbull Papers*, XIV.
[129] *Ibid.*

before the citizens of Chicago his views on the political questions of the day, all of which, he believed, centered in the understanding of the institution of slavery, to which "all the great powers" of government were then subordinated. The Republicans, he declared, did not wish to interfere with slavery where it was, but to prevent its expansion, and to leave it "exactly where the men who framed the Constitution left it." [130]

The Buchanan forces, or Danites, were also active. They presented candidates for the legislature and put Judge Sidney Breese into the running for the senatorship. On July 23, a "Grand Rally of the 'Nationals'" was held at Metropolitan Hall, presided over by Col. R. J. Hamilton and addressed by Col. R. B. Carpenter, Henry S. Fitch, and John S. Dougherty of Jonesboro. Here Douglas was arraigned as a deserter from the ranks of Democracy and charged with "taking up house with Seward, after making himself at home with Hale, fresh with the kiss of Giddings on his cheek." He had, the "Nationals" indignantly asserted, come to Chicago "and through his magnificent gift of perversion and assurance" accused the Danites of "having formed an unholy alliance with the Republicans," an accusation fortified by Wentworth's efforts to broaden the chasm in the Democratic ranks.[131]

In August, John Slidell of Louisiana visited Chicago, where he was "assiduously courted and generously feasted by the friends of Mr. Buchanan" but "looked upon with scowls and frowns" by the Douglasites. Out of his visit grew a report that slaves said to be owned by Douglas were mistreated; that they were hired out "in lots," were "ill-fed," "over-worked," and in every way so badly treated that they were spoken of in the neighborhood where they were held "as a disgrace to all slaveholders." Douglas's opponents used the story as effective political capital even though at the end of the campaign it was denied by its originators.[132]

Following Slidell came Alexander H. Stephens, friend of Bu-

[130] *Chicago Daily Press and Tribune,* August 9, 1858.

[131] *Ibid.,* July 24, 1858; J. W. J. Cone to S. A. Douglas, February 18, 1858, J. W. Sheahan to Douglas, May 30, 1858, *Douglas Papers.* Dougherty was candidate for state treasurer.

[132] *Chicago Daily Press and Tribune,* August 11, December 24, 1858. John Slidell was reported to have told the story of the slaves to Dr. Daniel Brainard, a professor of Rush Medical College and a federal office-holder. Both denied their parts as chronicled in the *Chicago Daily Press and Tribune.* See Sheahan, *op. cit.,* pp. 441–42 and the *Chicago Daily Press and Tribune,* December 24, 1858.

chanan, "playing the part of peace-maker between the raging, roaring, swearing Democratic factions in Illinois." Stephens wanted, according to the press, to point out that, regardless of personal differences between the senator and the chief executive, Douglas was not only competent, but was "ardently devoted to the South and her institution." But the peacemaker seemed to accomplish little among "the Lazzaroni and Buzzard crew," as the Douglas organs chose to call their administration foes.[133]

By September, Carl Schurz joined his nationals in Chicago in the fight to elect Lincoln, and, with others, addressed a meeting at Mechanics' Institute Hall, where he engaged in an analysis of popular sovereignty, which, he contended, was "the first successful attempt" to raise slavery "from an obnoxious fact to a national principle." In ringing tones he explained his defense of Republicanism on the ground of his love of the Union and his fear that the South was abandoning herself to despotism. Like Koerner, Hoffman, Schneider, and others holding the political philosophy of the 'Forty-eighters, Schurz felt he must, therefore, discard the party of the South and accept Republicanism, for the struggle had come to mean a struggle indeed between a hated aristocracy and a beloved democracy.[134]

As the campaign drew to a close, Chicago was visited in the cause of freedom by Francis Blair, Senator James R. Doolittle, Cassius M. Clay, and ex-Governor William F. Johnston, representing Missouri, Wisconsin, Kentucky, and Pennsylvania.[135] Opposing them and appealing to old-line Whigs and others to put down the agitators of the slavery question and to save the Union from their onslaughts, slave-state Democrats poured into Illinois to the number of forty-one, according to the *Chicago Democrat*.[136]

Speakers and newspapers on both sides indulged in misrepresentation and innuendo. Rancor mounted. Crop failures throughout the state added discontent to the distortion of outlook persisting from the panic of 1857; and the rumor that Douglas had reaped a fortune during his service in Congress did not serve to reassure or convert the financially distressed. Mrs. Douglas's Catholicism

[133] *Ibid.*, August 11, 1858.
[134] *Ibid.*, September 29, 30, 1858; Schurz, *op. cit.*, II, 188–90.
[135] *Chicago Daily Press and Tribune*, October 7, 14, 28, 1858.
[136] *Ibid.*, October 11, 1858; *Chicago Daily Democrat*, November 1, 1858.

stirred the hostility of bigoted Protestants, and gossip that he drank excessively also weighed heavily against "the Little Giant." [137]

Chicago went Republican on election day, November the second, except in the choice of Congressman. The city gave Thomas Dyer a slight plurality, which was wiped out by the Cook County vote. The Democrats, however, through an outworn apportionment law, retained a majority in the legislature, which assured the re-election of Douglas to the Senate. To the victor in the senatorial struggle the fruits were indeed sweet. Douglas could now look with optimism to 1860 for a still greater race. "It is the triumph of the Constitution over faction," he declared. "It is the triumph of the glorious principles of this Union over fanaticism and sectionalism; it is the triumph of the principle of self government over congressional interference and executive dictation." [138]

His Republican townsmen he assured that he had "no peace to make with Buchanan and his gang," because he had made "no war"; that if a bill were introduced to reopen the slave trade he would oppose it at once; that he would be "the first to denounce any legislation" designed for the protection of slavery in the territories; that Buchanan and his ilk had "reduced niggers to the status of mules"; and that, so far as he was concerned, "they must be content with the legislation which would protect mules — not persons owing service or labor"; that he would "stand by the decision of the Court" that slavery might go into a territory; and that he would not give up his notion that settlers might refuse to legislate for it after it was there; that he would not oppose a revenue tariff affording "all necessary incidental protection"; and that he did not expect to be "a candidate for the Presidency in 1860." [139]

In spite of his avowed disinclination, many, including Illinois Republicans, realized that Douglas stood a good chance for the 1860 nomination, although a whispering campaign among the Douglas Democrats as to irregularities in the post office and attempted re-

---

[137] Beveridge, *Lincoln*, IV, 277–78; *Chicago Daily Journal*, December 2, 1856. See p. 380.

[138] *Chicago Daily Press and Tribune*, November 5, 6, 18, 1858. The apportionment law was based upon the census of 1850 and framed by a Democratic legislature. It favored southern and middle Illinois.

[139] C. H. Ray to E. B. Washburne, November 22, 1858, *Washburne Papers*, IV. Ray concluded: "Beyond that everlasting cackle about 'my great principle,' I found little to object to in his talk. I send you these items that you may know how he talks to his enemies. You can judge as well as I of the man's reliability."

prisals by Buchanan appointees checked the Democratic cohesiveness so much desired.[140] Traveling in the East after the election, Horace White, a correspondent for the Press and Tribune, found so much sentiment for Douglas among the masses of the people that he concluded that "hardly anything short of an interposition of Providence" would prevent Douglas's nomination at Charleston and his election by a larger majority than Buchanan received in 1856.

To prevent such a catastrophe, White declared, he had evolved a scheme to induce the Kansas legislature, about to assemble, "to put the doctrine of 'unfriendly legislation' in force to the extent of abolishing slavery in the Territory and nullifying the Fugitive Slave Law at the same time both of the measures to be argued from texts in Douglas's Freeport speech, and his still later one at Memphis — we should hit the Charleston target nearly in the center of the bull's eye." This scheme to block Douglas was submitted to Norman B. Judd, who had managed Lincoln's campaign, and, according to White, "considerably impressed" Judd. "Even though we should fail of securing the passage of the measure in either territory," White added, "we could make a 'devil' of a blow with it — fill the newspapers North and South; and perhaps this broad suggestion of what possible fiends are lurking in the Freeport dogma, will do Mr. Douglas' business at Charleston without any positive enactment." [141]

The discomfiture of Chicago Republicans was increased when they considered that Seward and Greeley had, by their friendliness toward Douglas, "contributed so much" to their party's defeat. If the East expected the Lincoln protagonists "to return good for evil," it was mistaken. "If the vote of Illinois can nominate another than Seward [in 1860] — I hope it will be so cast," declared Ebenezer Peck. "The coals of fire I would administer will be designed to raise a severe blister." [142]

---

[140] See, for example, John P. Heiss to S. A. Douglas, July 13, 1858, and C. P. Button to Douglas, December 26, 1858, Douglas Papers. Although written in 1858 these letters are typical of some complaints.

[141] White thought this might be done in both Nebraska and Kansas. He hastened to add: "Of course if we make any use of these suggestions we shall have to keep all knowledge of it to ourselves." Horace White to Lyman Trumbull, December 8, 1858, Trumbull Papers, XV.

[142] E. Peck to Lyman Trumbull, November 22, 1858, ibid. Peck was a member of the Illinois legislature at that time.

Little excitement marked the municipal election of 1859, for again purely local concerns seemed unimportant in the light of more colorful national events. In spite of charges of bad faith and extravagances in the management of city affairs made against him, Mayor John C. Haines, supported by the *Tribune,* was re-elected for another year. Part of the re-election propaganda of the *Tribune* was designed to woo the so-called dependents of the city and to catch the eye of the laborer, promising the one relief from distressing conditions and the other steady employment.[143] Judicial elections were also carried on. Fear of the Republicans of the influence of the Democrats in the judicial organ of government was clearly expressed. It was with considerable relief that the Republicans heard the election returns as favorable to their candidates.[144]

As the year 1859 grew older, the threatening shadows of a maturing hostility toward the South lengthened and deepened. In October occurred the raid of John Brown on Harpers Ferry, an act condemned by conservative Northerner and Southerner alike. "No man in his senses can say that it is not the most crazy development which the slave history of this country affords," declared the *Press and Tribune.* "We desire to see all parties engaged in that bloody *emeute* brought to punishment. . . . No matter who has been drawn into the treason, let it apply to all, and favor none. If hanging is the penalty — hang; if imprisonment — imprison; but give us no accusations of innocent men."

Still, the Chicago press could not resist pointing out "the ridiculousness of the precautions to prevent the escape or rescue of the three wounded and dying rioters," men led by a man of "addled brains." The "fearful array of cannon" and "crowds of threatening and excited men" provided too good an opportunity to overlook. The *Press and Tribune* inquired why, "if the attachment of the slaves to their masters" were "as sincere as the journals of the South" represented, "the niggers" were not told the truth, "that Brown's purpose was their freedom — the thing which, masters assure us, their slaves hate above all things else?"[145]

---

[143] *Chicago Weekly Democrat,* March 5, 1859; *Chicago Daily Press and Tribune,* February 26, March 1, 8, 17, 1859; *Christian Times and Illinois Baptist,* March 9, 1859.

[144] *The Press and Tribune,* March 25, April 6, 1859. Van H. Higgins and Grant Goodrich, Republicans, were successful.

[145] *Ibid.,* October 20, 21, 24, 27, 1859.

As the days passed and horror over the madness of the episode itself gradually faded, men began to see its political consequences and implications. Douglas laid the blame squarely upon the Republicans.[146] The Republicans countered by accusing the Democratic party of attempting to implant in the minds of Southerners the widespread belief that the people of the North were ready, at a moment's warning, to take up arms in behalf of slaves if an insurrection occurred. Such rumors, they held, were ill-founded and dangerous to the perpetuation of the Union. Indeed, in the opinion of the Republicans the whole unfortunate affair was the offspring of Democratic folly in its treatment of the slavery issue. In the eyes of a partisan Republican press, the only objection of the Democrats was "to Old Brown . . . running niggers *North* instead of *South*." "It was simply the *direction* in which he was traveling the colored persons," declared the *Tribune,* "that the Democracy take exceptions to. Had he been running darkies out of Canada into Virginia, instead of *vice versa,* the chivalry would be elevating him to Congress rather than on a gallows."[147]

As Friday, December 2, approached, Wentworth, through the columns of his antislavery paper, called the people of his city and of the Union to assemble in meetings "to let the world know how unanimous public sentiment" was in the free states against "the outrages of the slave power." He prophesied that there were thousands who would be too much excited to attend to any business while one of their fellow citizens was being executed "for violating laws in favor of human slavery," while "slavery propagandists" were "hourly trampling the laws of their country under foot."[148] While Chicagoans "waited and yet shrunk to hear the tidings from Charleston, Virginia," on that cold December day, public meetings indicated the tenseness of the moment. As prayers were offered for the souls of the hangmen, the telegraph flashed the news across the country that Ossawatomie and Harpers Ferry had been avenged; martyrdom had come to John Brown.[149]

---

146 *Cong. Globe,* 36 Cong., 1 sess., pp. 553–54.

147 *The Press and Tribune,* October 31, November 5, 1859. Italics are in the original.

148 *Chicago Weekly Democrat,* November 12, 1859. *The Press and Tribune,* December 2, 1859, while extolling Brown's martyrdom, declared that he should be made to answer for the legal consequences of his act.

149 *Ibid.,* December 3, 1859.

During the autumn and winter of 1859 and 1860, the fateful events just past increased tension between the North and the South. Southern threats of secession resounded through the halls of Congress. "But," said the *Press and Tribune,* "who's afraid? . . . Dissolution of the Union is not dreamed as among human possibilities. . . . We have no inclination to give heed to that wildest of all apprehensions, which some of our Democratic friends indulge, that the triumph of the Republicans in 1860 will be the signal for the dissolution of the Union. . . . Of all *bosh,* that is the most ridiculous." The implication that the Republican party was sectional had already been disproved, thought the editor, whereas the entire "significance of the Democratic party as a political organization" consisted in its "adherence to Southern interests." On the other hand, Republicans were "anxious for" legislation to promote the commercial and industrial interests of the whole people. And was it not the Republicans who recognized "the insufficiency" of the tariff, who hoped for the passage of a Pacific Railroad bill and for the improvement of western rivers and harbors? [150]

Playing to the fancies of commercial and industrial interests in all walks of life the Republicans cried out for a revision of the tariff "in favor of American industry" which would put "manufactures on a healthy, permanent basis." Free trade, a Democratic policy of the past, had, in their opinion, become outmoded and should be discarded if national prosperity were to continue. Further attempts should be made also to secure "reciprocity of trade with Cuba," which, the *Press and Tribune* believed, could be done if the United States would withdraw her proposal to purchase the island and insure Spain against "the designs of American filibusters." The granting of homesteads would further redound to the benefit of the white laboring man, although such grants seemed improbable in the light of past experience. [151]

Both Republicans and Democrats viewed the local elections of early 1860 as having special significance in the light of the coming

---

[150] *Ibid.,* September 9, November 9, December 8, 1859; italics in the original. See also *Chicago Daily Journal,* February 6, 1860.

[151] *Chicago Daily Press and Tribune,* January 29, July 26, August 15, October 12, 1859. Said the editor on August 15: "If this will not bring it, then a retaliatory tariff upon the productions of Cuba would be the next method available to us. As more than two-thirds of her exports now find a market in our ports, such a tariff would not be long in producing the desired result."

presidential campaign. In February, 1860, at a Republican nominating convention, bitter antagonism arose between those who wanted as mayoralty candidate Isaac N. Arnold and those who supported John Wentworth.[152] The contest became desperate. Overtures to both Arnold and Wentworth that they withdraw were without avail. The Wentworth machine ran smoothly and "Long John . . . swept the board," creating uneasiness as to the political future of Judd, aspirant for the governorship, and inflicting a political body blow upon Arnold. To many of the stalwarts it looked "very dark" indeed — like a Democratic victory of the Douglas brand. If this happened, some thought the fault would be Wentworth's, for he had "forced himself upon the party" and was reported as favoring Simon Cameron for the presidency.[153]

The Democrats had swung into line a few days earlier, nominating for the mayoralty Walter S. Gurnee, endorsed by the Isaac Cook machine but also acclaimed as a Douglasite. Just as Republicans desired to carry the city because of the effect of the outcome on the coming presidential convention, so did the Democrats. Party regularity led administration and Douglas forces to join hands in the support of "Count" Gurnee, whose previous administration in the city was painted in the blackest colors by his opponents. They accused him of mishandling $100,000 in municipal funds so that he gained the interest on the deposit. They charged also that Gurnee's bank, using municipal funds, had bought city certificates of indebtedness, many of them at fifty cents on the dollar, from laborers who had worked for the city. The profit on this adversely publicized transaction was reported to be "some $25,000."[154]

In contrast, the Republicans declared that their guardianship of the city was above reproach. "Before the inauguration of a Republican city government," they asserted, "our streets were vocal with brawls, and our elections but another name for riots, bloodshed and murder. Then, the O'Malleys and Prendergasts and Fords pursued, unchecked and unrebuked, their official plunderings, the debt under

<hr/>

152 *Chicago Daily Journal*, February 10, 18, 1860. The *Journal* declared in a later issue that Arnold did not want the nomination but was being saved as the next representative in Congress.

153 H. Kreismann to E. B. Washburne, February 6, 9, 19, March 1, 1860, *Washburne Papers*, VII.

154 *Chicago Daily Journal*, February 14, March 2, 3, 1860; J. W. Sheahan to S. A. Douglas, February 15, 1860, J. B. Taylor to Douglas, February 17, 1860, *Douglas Papers*.

which we are now groaning was contracted, and the name of Chicago was a by-word and reproach throughout the nation." Although Mayor Haines had not liquidated the city debt, he had avoided the raising of taxes, which certainly, said the propagandists, should "appeal to the property owners." And since the Republican constituency included most of the businessmen of the town, it need not be chronicled that the appeal was effective.[155]

Republicans as well as Democrats found it necessary to bury internal dissensions in that election. The report that Republicans in the national capital would be glad to have Wentworth defeated led to a denial and to an earnest exhortation that all Chicagoans of this credo support their standard bearers.[156] The party was more important than the man! "Unusually heavy voting" brought victory to the Republicans, a forecast, it was exultantly declared, of the national election only a few months away. Throughout election day rumors had been rife that Bridgeport was again donating some of her citizens to the cause of Democracy, but fears of unusual violence at the polls were dissipated as the hours passed.[157]

Administration Democrats ascribed their defeat to the discord stirred in the ranks of the Douglasites, who persisted in the nomination of Gurnee rather than McCormick or Marcus D. Gilman. But the Republicans assured them that the result was "the natural fruit of the 'irrepressible conflict' coupled with the attempt to carry the election by *hireling votes*."[158] In both parties internal dissension seemed bound to bring "a plague on both their houses," and the far-seeing counseled peace and harmony.

After the mayoralty race, eyes turned toward state offices. Here was more trouble for the Republicans. Southern and central Illinois demanded that the nominee for governor be chosen from their midst and, in spite of Wentworth's opposition, Chicagoans wished to name Judd. By early April the lines were tightly drawn between

---

[155] *Chicago Daily Journal*, February 24, 1860; George Lester to Lyman Trumbull, February 24, 1860, *Trumbull Papers*, XVIII.

[156] Wm. H. Bradley to E. B. Washburne, March 14, 1860, *Washburne Papers*, VIII; F. Linder to S. A. Douglas, February 26, 1860, *Douglas Papers*; *Chicago Daily Journal*, March 1, 3, 5, 1860.

[157] *Ibid.*, March 1, 5, 6, 7, 1860; *The Press and Tribune*, March 7, 1860; *Chicago Weekly Democrat*, March 10, 1860; D. L. Phillips to Lyman Trumbull, March 6, 1860, *Trumbull Papers*, XVIII. See Appendix, p. 506.

[158] Italics are in the original. *Chicago Daily Journal*, March 8, 1860; Hutchinson, *Cyrus Hall McCormick*, II, 44.

the newly chosen mayor and his opponent. Wentworth was charged with training his guns upon a place in the Republican cabinet of 1860, notably the postmaster-generalship because of the patronage connected with it, as well as hoping to stop Judd's gubernatorial aspirations. On May 9, when the state convention met at Decatur, the forty-seven Chicago delegates had been instructed for Judd, but they had been told not to split the party over his nomination. He went to defeat before Richard Yates.[159] The platform included the time-worn plank of more economy in state administration, support of a pending homestead law, and a declaration against discriminations between natives and aliens. The assembled delegates before adjournment joined harmoniously in endorsing Lincoln for the presidency.[160]

While the state political game was being played with an eye to the stakes of the national election, events moved toward the nominating conventions at Chicago and Charleston. In the Democratic ranks the Douglas-Buchanan split was still wide, and Douglas found his position particularly difficult. What had seemed to some a Janus-like attitude on slavery had cost him friends both in the North and in the South. To court the slaveholding interests he arrayed himself with others coveting Mexico, Central America, and Cuba, declaring himself "in favor of expansion as fast as consistent with our interest." "It is our destiny to have Cuba," he said in New Orleans in December, 1858.[161] In general, Illinois Democrats accepted his position on Cuba, but the *Chicago Democrat* thought that island would be an expensive possession. Since the government had failed to enact a reciprocity agreement with Cuba, the *Press and Tribune* pointed out, something ought to be done, for America, it declared,

---

[159] *Chicago Daily Journal,* March 29, May 1, 1860; Horace White to Lyman Trumbull, March 10, 1860, *Trumbull Papers,* XVIII; *Chicago Daily Democrat,* November 7, 1859. Said Judd: " There is not a prominent man in the state but that he [Wentworth] hates, including our friend Lincoln, and there is only one mode of dealing with him and that is open opposition." (N. B. Judd to Lyman Trumbull, April 2, 1860, *Trumbull Papers,* XIX.) Judd's defeat, according to Kreismann, was brought about " by the deep personal feeling of the Swett men, which had been created by Wentworth and his blowers." (H. Kreismann to E. B. Washburne, May 13, 1860, *Washburne Papers,* IX.) Leonard Swett, from Bloomington, was a candidate. He was a former Whig. Yates was from Jacksonville. Francis A. Hoffman of Chicago was nominated for lieutenant governor. *Chicago Daily Journal,* May 4, 10, 1860. See Cole, *The Era of the Civil War,* pp. 190–91, for a discussion of state politics in this election.

[160] *The Press and Tribune,* May 11, 1860.

[161] Sheahan, *op. cit.,* pp. 122–23; Milton, *The Eve of Conflict,* p. 362; J. P. Campbell to S. A. Douglas, April 12, 1860, P. A. Hoyne to Douglas, April 12, 1860, *Douglas Papers.*

was forced to pay $15,000,000 annually to settle American trade balances.[162]

To increasing Southern demands for Congressional intervention in the territories, however, Douglas could not accede, and Southern opposition to his candidacy grew. If he were to win at Charleston, he realized that he must summon all available support at the North, particularly in his own state, where, in spite of his rejection of Southern demands, many, including the *Press and Tribune,* still held him a staunch ally of the slave interests in "counseling the felonious seizure of Cuba." [163] To consolidate his position, Douglas published in *Harper's Magazine* an article on the "Dividing Line between Federal and Local Authority" which became the text of editorials in Chicago papers as well as elsewhere.[164] The *Press and Tribune* believed that "the pith and marrow of the essay . . . is the promulgation by Mr. Douglas of another change in his sentiments"; and Lincoln, in his campaigning, was not slow to point out Douglas's silent recognition of his opponent's thrusts in the Freeport speech.[165]

The Democratic Convention at Charleston was hopelessly divided. From Douglas's own state two sets of delegates attended, one selected by the Democratic State Convention on January 2, and the other by the administration forces on January 8. Not until the convention had been broken up and reassembled at Baltimore in June was the nomination of Douglas for the presidency accomplished by a group from which members of eight Southern states had seceded. Immediately the seceders, in a rump convention of their own, nominated John C. Breckinridge as their candidate. The hopes of the party for success in 1860 had been sacrificed to an internal feud. Votes were further scattered by the naming of John Bell on a Constitutional-Union ticket.

In mid-May, Chicago received the "very flower of the leaders of the Young Republican party" in what its enemies chose to call "a sectional convention," although it included delegates from Kentucky, Maryland, Virginia, Missouri, and Texas.[166] By the thir-

---

[162] *Chicago Weekly Democrat,* September 4, 1858; *The Press and Tribune,* August 15, 1859.

[163] *Ibid.,* February 2, 1859.

[164] Stephen A. Douglas, "The Dividing Line between Federal and Local Authority," *Harper's New Monthly Magazine,* XIX (September, 1859), 519–37.

[165] *The Press and Tribune,* August 27, September 7, October 6, 1859.

[166] Henry Villard, *Memoirs* (2 v. Boston, 1904), I, 136–67. It had been decided in De-

"RECEPTION OF JUDGE DOUGLAS AT CHICAGO,
OCTOBER 4TH, 1860"

A cartoon from The Rail Splitter, *October 27, 1860, a Lincoln campaign paper
printed in Chicago.*

"CAIUS MARIUS ELONGATUS"

"Long John" Wentworth caricatured in the Chicago Tribune, *June 26, 1862.
Signpost points to Wentworth's farm at Summit. Wentworth's slogan, "Liberty and Economy," flies at half-mast.*

teenth the town was "full of people," for whose comfort hotel facilities proved so inadequate that private homes throughout the city opened their doors, and billiard tables sometimes provided the only available place for sleep. Chicago was in gala attire, her buoyant spirits expressed in the gaily decked buildings and festooned streets. On the twelfth had occurred the dedication of the "Great Wigwam" on Lake Street, especially constructed to care for the delegates and said to be capacious enough to house ten thousand; indeed, in the eyes of local Republicans, a truly "magnificent hall." Newspapers applied for nine hundred tickets for their reporters alone, an indication of the public interest the convention had aroused.[167]

Illinois sought to promote the candidacy of her favorite son with street parades, in which bands led the marchers shouldering rails. Seward supporters heavily laden with streamers and banners with slogans for their hero and accompanied by brass bands proclaimed the merits of the man who had seen throughout the 'fifties the coming of an "irrepressible conflict." "No end of champagne and cigars" was consumed. Money flowed freely for the winning of converts. Raucous-throated serenaders shouted each other down, while the more temperate took refuge on the lake in boats provided by the Chicago Board of Trade.[168]

Back of these gay and boisterous manifestations, however, lay grim determination to nominate some popular hero, some favorite son. Horace Greeley endorsed Edward Bates of Missouri, but the Germans would have none of him. The Simon Cameron forces were early on the ground, angling for support to add to the instructed Pennsylvania delegation. Many leading exponents of Re-

cember, 1859, to hold the convention in Chicago. According to Koerner, the influence of Norman B. Judd was effective enough to convince leaders in the party that Chicago was "neutral ground" and that Lincoln's candidacy was not threatening to other better known men. Gustave Koerner, *Memoirs of Gustave Koerner, 1809-1896* . . . (2 v. Cedar Rapids, Iowa, 1909), II, 80, 85.

167 H. Kreismann to E. B. Washburne, May 13, 15, 17, 1860, *Washburne Papers*, IX. Among the delegates-at-large from Illinois was N. B. Judd. George Schneider represented the Second District. The *Press and Tribune* boasted that its building was illuminated at night from "turret to foundation . . . by a thousand lights," and over the main door was suspended an "immense transparency" with the inscription, "For President, Honest Old Abe. For Vice-President, Hannibal Hamlin." *The Press and Tribune,* May 11, 17, 19, 1860.

168 The Pennsylvanians, as well as Illinoisans, carried old rails on the night of the eighteenth. Schurz, *op. cit.,* II, 176-77; Murat Halstead, *Caucuses of 1860* . . . (Columbus, 1860), pp. 121, 132, 141, 144; *The Press and Tribune,* May 17, 18, 19, 1860.

publicanism, including prominent Germans, held Seward the most suitable nominee, and by the fifteenth it looked as if the choice would fall upon him or Lincoln. On that morning Wentworth announced that he was for Seward. It was privately reported that Thurlow Weed had made "a bargain with him." [169]

The Illinois delegation pushed the nomination of Lincoln on the grounds of availability, and even before the convention opened Medill reported that half the Indiana delegation had been won over to him. Though Lincoln, who was absent, opposed dickering for votes, political bargains were made with Ohio, Pennsylvania, and Indiana. The *Press and Tribune* carried a series of editorials advocating him as the one man upon whom all delegations could unite, and these were placed in the hands of delegates from the doubtful states in an effort to build up a strong body of opinion for the Illinois candidate before the voting began. [170]

Political strategy on the part of Judd, Joseph Medill, Isaac N. Arnold, and other leading Republicans had much to do with Lincoln's nomination. Judd and Medill had charge of seating the delegations, and in the final arrangements they isolated New York in such a way that the doubtful states and those necessary to the nomination of Lincoln were placed some distance away from the enthusiastic supporters of Seward. Lincoln protagonists found it easy to get tickets, but endorsers of other candidates sometimes had difficulty in gaining entrance to the great hall. [171]

On the third ballot, Lincoln took the lead and was nominated as the Republican candidate for President. The announcement was greeted "with the most enthusiastic and thunderous applause. The entire crowd rose to their feet, applauding rapturously . . . cheering again and again," "stout men wept like children," reported the *Press and Tribune.* Through the skylight word was passed to the messenger on top of the Wigwam, who announced it to the mass of

[169] H. Kreismann to E. B. Washburne, May 13, 15, 1860, *Washburne Papers,* IX; G. Koerner to Lyman Trumbull, March 15, 16, 1860, *Trumbull Papers,* XVIII.

[170] Tracy Elmer Strevey, *Joseph Medill and the Chicago Tribune during the Civil War Period* (unpublished Ph.D. Thesis, The University of Chicago, 1930), p. 79; George Washington Julian, *Political Recollections, 1840–1872* (Chicago, 1884), p. 183; *The Press and Tribune,* May 14, 15, 16, 1860.

[171] H. I. Cleveland, "Booming the First Republican President, A Talk with Abraham Lincoln's Friend, the Late Joseph Medill," *Saturday Evening Post,* CLXXII (August 5, 1899), 85–86; Koerner, *op. cit.,* II, 85.

humanity jamming the streets. Cannon boomed. Men took up the cry for "old Abe," and, as it echoed and re-echoed throughout the city, the news was flashed by telegraph to a waiting country.[172] "Honest Abe," whose modesty led him to voice what his opponents thought, "Just think of such a sucker as me as President," was to make the race against Douglas, Breckinridge, and Bell.[173]

[172] *The Press and Tribune,* May 19, 1860; Koerner, *op. cit.,* II, 91–92; Schurz, *op. cit.,* II, 186; Halstead, *op. cit.,* p. 154; T. J. Wright to S. A. Douglas, May 18, 1860, *Douglas Papers.*

[173] H. Villard, *op. cit.,* I, 96.

CHAPTER VII

WAR AND ITS AFTERMATH
1860–1871

THE NOMINATION of Lincoln was received with conflicting emotions. Eastern Republicans and men of the lake region could not but wonder why events had turned as they had in Chicago on that May day of 1860. But those of foresight and wisdom realized that it was better that no "radical" like Seward, or even Chase, should be their standard bearer against the best-known political figure of the day. Far better was it that a man without national distinction had been chosen, one who could attract the timid who, for economic reasons or because of lack of interest in the slavery crusade, would have none of abolitionism. Out of the West had come great things, just as Douglas had prophesied of his beloved section.

The Republican platform adopted at Chicago was more conservative than that upon which "the great Pathfinder" had stood only four years before. It did not allude to slavery and polygamy as the "twin relics of barbarism," but it did assert that neither Congress, a territorial legislature, nor any individuals had the right to establish slavery in any United States territory, and it roundly condemned the opening of the slave trade. Among its resolutions was an avowal of a desire to preserve the Union. A protective tariff, a free homestead policy, river and harbor improvements, and governmental aid for a railroad to the Pacific were planks that were broad enough to capture the special interests of Chicago businessman, laborer, and expansionist alike; and the foreign born of Chicago looked with favor upon the pronouncement that their rights should not be restricted.

Within two weeks organized Republican activities were in full swing. Wide Awake Clubs, made up of young men pledged by their constitution to advance the tenets of Republicanism, tramped the streets in military order to the strains of martial music. And when Seward came to Chicago one October night, an estimated five to ten thousand lit the streets with their torches or small tin lamps perched on the pine sticks which they carried, as they paraded before the seventy-five to one hundred thousand visitors. Uniformed in short, cape-like cloaks of black enameled waterproof cloth, and specially designed " glazed cap, bound around with a white, red and blue ribbon " they aided the campaign speaker throughout the summer and autumn of 1860 in educating the masses in the political philosophy of the day. With ward clubs, national alliances, and workingmen's associations, Wide Awakes and others distributed literature on political issues especially prepared by the Republican organ, the *Tribune*. Party identification was made easy by white satin badges bearing candidates' portraits.[1] Claims and counterclaims not only by the political orator but by the ordinary voter filled the thoughts of young and old. When there seemed no other way of voicing his political sentiment the Republican could always join his fellows in singing " Poor Little Doug " or huzza in the " Wide Awake Song."[2]

[1] *The Press and Tribune*, April 4, May 12, 29, June 8, 1860; Colby, *Our Family*, p. 46; Julian, *Political Recollections, 1840–1872*, pp. 178–79; Schurz, *Reminiscences*, II, 194; *Chicago Daily Democrat*, July 23, August 7, October 3, 1860; *The Rail Splitter*, October 6, 1860; *Chicago Daily Journal*, January 7, 1860, *passim;* Strevey, *Joseph Medill and the Chicago Tribune during the Civil War Period*, pp. 85–86.

[2] " Poor Little Doug " was sung to " Old Uncle Ned," a well-known song. Its first verse and chorus ran as follows:

> Dere was a little man and his name was Stevey Doug,
> To de White House he longed for to go;
> But he hadn't any votes fru de whole of de Souf,
> In de place where de votes ought to grow.
>
> So it ain't no use for to blow —
> Dat little game of brag won't go;
> He can't get de vote 'case de tail ob de coat
> Is hung just a little too low.

The " Wide Awake Song " was as follows:

> Oh, hear you not the wild huzzas,
> That come from every State?

Neither Douglas nor Breckinridge nor the Constitutional Union candidate, John Bell, put forth much effort in Chicago, for more likely votes could be wooed in central and southern Illinois. To help to bring victory to the Democrats, Chicago's Irish laborers contributed their services as colonists in other parts of the state and with many others of the Catholic faith gave their support to " the Little Giant." [3]

On the sixth of November, Chicago went early to the polls and gave Lincoln ten thousand votes and Douglas only two thousand less. By ten o'clock that evening, the telegraph had brought an excited city enough reports to assure the followers of Lincoln that the Midwest had gone Republican; and by midnight, the overjoyed throngs gathered about the telegraph office heard that the electoral vote of New York would be " Old Abe's." [4]

The anxiety of the last few weeks as to the new President was now at an end. Along with Lincoln went candidates for the state offices, and Lyman Trumbull was sent to the United States Senate, in spite of Wentworth's alleged desire for this place.[5] But Republican success seemed less glamorous in the light of threatened secession by the South, and by mid-November the *Tribune* reluctantly and at times satirically predicted the withdrawal of at least five cotton states unless concessions were made by the North.[6] Secession became the all-engrossing subject of discussion. If secession must

---

For honest Uncle Abraham,
The People's candidate?
He is our choice, our nominee,
A self-made man, and true;
We'll show the Democrats this fall
What honest Abe can do.

George W. Bungay, ed., *The Bobolink Minstrel: or Republican Songster, for 1860* (New York, 1860), pp. 41, 70–71.

[3] Amos C. Babcock to Lyman Trumbull, August 27, 1860, *Trumbull Papers*, XXIII; William J. Onahan, " A Civil War Diary," *Mid-America*, n.s. III (July, 1931), 66; *The Press and Tribune*, July 19, 21, 1860.

[4] Bell polled only 107 votes in Chicago; Breckinridge, only 87; Lincoln received 10,697; Douglas, 8,094. *Chicago Tribune*, November 13, 1860; Koerner, *Memoirs of Gustave Koerner, 1809–1896*, II, 102–3.

[5] *Ibid.*, p. 103; W. H. Stickney to Lyman Trumbull, September 13, 1860, *Trumbull Papers*, XXIII; *The Press and Tribune*, October 13, 1860; Cole, *The Era of the Civil War*, chap. viii.

[6] *Chicago Tribune*, November 7, 8, 1860; J. Medill to Lyman Trumbull, November 17, 1860, *Trumbull Papers*, XXVII. See, for example, *Chicago Tribune*, November 15, 1860, in which activities on the part of Southerners are satirized by recording a mythical secession of the Tenth Ward of Chicago, the only one which voted the whole Democratic ticket.

come, Medill counseled the readers of the *Tribune* to accept "a bloodless separation."[7] There were those who opposed holding a state within the Union against its will, but the leaders of Republicanism wanted neither compromise nor concession. Under either plan what would happen to the rich party rewards which the election had promised?[8]

On December 20, radicals and moderates were faced with the end of conjectures as to what South Carolina might do. Secession was a fact. To Horace White of the *Tribune* this was cheering news, for he saw "the prospect of a good hearty fight on or about the 4th of March — a square knock-down and drag-out." White believed even John B. Turner, a delegate to the Charleston Convention of 1860, was "raging for an opportunity to equip a volunteer company" to "take the field in person." As the days passed, an increasing number of men joined White in blessing "the revolution" which was upon them. The Union must be preserved at all costs. By late December, many citizens of Chicago and the state looked to a policy of coercion, which many of them realized meant war and only war.[9]

Not all were willing, however, to abandon the time-honored method of conciliation, and attempts to adjust differences of opinion within the next few weeks resulted in what Schurz described as an "epidemic" of compromise.[10] Followers of Douglas went with him in supporting the Crittenden proposals, introduced into the Senate two days before the fateful move of South Carolina on December 20.[11] Businessmen, who their critics declared were more interested in preserving profits gained by trade with the South than in preserving the Union, urged some form of compromise such as an amendment to the Constitution which would separate free from

---

[7] Th. Richmond to Lyman Trumbull, December 14, 1860, *Trumbull Papers*, XXVII; W. A. Baldwin to E. B. Washburne, December 13, 1860, *Washburne Papers*, XI; *Chicago Tribune*, December 1, 1860.

[8] Th. Richmond to Lyman Trumbull, December 14, 1860, *Trumbull Papers*, XXVII.

[9] Horace White to Lyman Trumbull, December 30, 1860, *ibid.*, XXVIII; John A. Clarke to E. B. Washburne, January 9, 1861, *Washburne Papers*, XII; *Chicago Tribune*, December 19, 29, 31, 1860.

[10] Schurz, *op. cit.*, II, 211.

[11] Douglas was a member of the Committee of Thirteen of the Senate. Trumbull opposed the measures. *Chicago Daily Journal*, December 19, 21, 1860; *The Chicago Times*, July 30, 1861; Grant Goodrich to Lyman Trumbull, January 21, 31, 1861, *Trumbull Papers*, XXX.

slave territory at 36° 30'.[12] Pork packers and wholesale grocers, meeting to consider the critical situation of the day, heard Roselle M. Hough, a packer, roundly denounce the *Tribune* for its uncompromising attitude toward the South. William B. Ogden was said to be " an awful Union-saver "; Cyrus H. McCormick joined with fellow Democrats in resolutions for compromise on January 14 when they gathered to elect delegates to a state convention;[13] and there were also those who talked again of the grandiose scheme of a northwestern republic, at one time discussed to frighten New England, but now revived as a confederacy to be aloof from entangling alliances.[14]

But as banks withdrew loans, as securities fell, and as money became tight, other men of commercial bent welcomed coercion in the belief that it would drive people from the border into the interior " as far as possible from the scene of strife and bloodshed." Such a migration would inevitably bring about " an enormous rise in their Lake City lots and Northwestern lands "; their dream of Chicago as " the great interior city of the Continent " would come true.[15] With the South no longer in the Union and with hope of reunion gone, the Northwest would become the ruling power of the republic. Indeed, the *Chicago Record* pointed out, when this shifting of influence from the South to the Northwest came about, then would Congress " vacate the palatial halls of the Potomac for a new Washington on one of those noble lakes," and " as sure as ' the United States ' ever comes to comprise the free North alone, Chicago will be the Capital of the New Republic."[16]

Differing opinions were expressed through rallies; union prayer

[12] J. J. Richards to Lyman Trumbull, January 23, 1861, *ibid.; Chicago Tribune,* January 1, February 14, April 19, 25, 1861. See pp. 45–46.

[13] Hutchinson, *Cyrus Hall McCormick,* II, 49, 83–84; N. B. Judd to Lyman Trumbull, January 8, 1861, *Trumbull Papers,* XXVIII; *Chicago Tribune,* January 15, February 14, 1861. Ogden, although a Republican in 1860, was a moderate. During the war he doubted the wisdom of Lincoln's use of his war powers, and the Emancipation Proclamation alienated him from the party. Arnold, *William B. Ogden,* p. 31. See for resolutions passed by Democrats later that month *Chicago Weekly Tribune,* January 24, 1861, and C. H. McCormick to S. A. Douglas, December 28, 1860, *Douglas Papers,* for McCormick's opinion about the Crittenden plan.

[14] Kohlmeier, *The Old Northwest,* pp. 223–33; S. S. Hayes to S. A. Douglas, December 18, 1860, *Douglas Papers.*

[15] See *Cincinnati Daily Enquirer,* January 31, 1861, editorial entitled, " The Kind of Men who control Lincoln — Heartless Speculators in Lake Shore Lots and Wild Lands."

[16] *Chicago Record,* March 1, 1861.

meetings by the churches and by organizations like the Young Men's Christian Association, resolutions by national alliances and others having kindred interests betokened how completely men's thoughts were absorbed in the question of peace or war.[17] Although the discussion became less restrained as the winter days passed, moderate Republicans still hoped that there would be enough " patriotism and wisdom " to save the nation.[18] Some joined Democrats in an endorsement of the stand of William Kellogg of Peoria, who, as Illinois representative on the House Committee of Thirty-three, bravely struggled to stem the tide of coercion.[19] But before March the counsels of the *Tribune* and those who shared its opinion had proved so effective that it seemed as if " 99/100 of all Republicans . . . and a large portion of the Democrats " were " for giving Southerners what they want and plenty of it." [20]

In the chariot of hate with the Southerners rode President Buchanan, for had he not flung "the gauntlet in the face of the North," spit " upon the land that bore him," and taken " his party in the Free States by the throat " and leaped "with it into the ditch "? [21] His dilatoriness in re-enforcing Major Robert Anderson in the federal forts in Charleston Harbor and his passivity in the face of other hostile acts on the part of the South appeared to Chicagoans reasons for impeachment.[22] When Major Anderson occupied Fort Sumter, Mayor Wentworth heralded the event with a proclamation setting aside January 8 as a day when Chicago stores should close their doors, when flags should be flown and cannon be fired in honor of the Union, Andrew Jackson, and Major Anderson. It seemed also a propitious time to the mayor to urge young men to join some military organization to be ready for the emergency he felt certain would arise.[23]

---

[17] See pp. 258, 386–87.

[18] John A. Clarke to E. B. Washburne, February 19, 1861, *Washburne Papers*, XIV.

[19] *Cong. Globe*, 36 Cong., 2 sess., p. 690; *Chicago Tribune*, February 4, 6, 11, 14, 18, 1861.

[20] Wm. T. Barron to Lyman Trumbull, February 2, 1861, *Trumbull Papers*, XXXII; *Chicago Tribune*, February 14, 1861.

[21] The Chicago Tribune, *The W. G. N.* . . . . (Chicago, 1922), p. 31.

[22] *Chicago Weekly Tribune*, January 3, 1861, " Progress of the Treason." For a general discussion of national events, see J. G. Randall, *The Civil War and Reconstruction* (Boston, 1937).

[23] *Chicago Weekly Democrat*, January 12, 1861. Wentworth's proclamation was issued January 5.

In this atmosphere of passion and prejudice Abraham Lincoln became President of the United States. As he placed his hand upon the Bible that fourth of March in 1861, "his rugged face, appearing above all those surrounding him, calm and sad" and so "unlike any other in that distinguished assemblage," many must have wondered, as did Carl Schurz, how these men, some of whom soon were to be Lincoln's advisers and associates in the great task of government, would work together.[24] Near by was his able political opponent for over a decade, Stephen A. Douglas of Chicago. There, too, was Roger B. Taney, chief justice of the Supreme Court, which the *Tribune* described as "the last entrenchment behind which Despotism is sheltered," and which it hoped would be reformed by the Republicans through the "appointment of better men in their places."[25] And there was James Buchanan, white-cravated as was his wont. Lincoln's forthright argument against the constitutional right of secession left no doubt in the minds of his listeners as to his intention to execute the federal laws in all the states.

In selecting his cabinet, Lincoln tried to satisfy the various elements in his party by naming four of his one-time rivals for the presidential nomination. But he passed by Norman B. Judd. Later an appointment as minister to Prussia seemed scant acknowledgment of Judd's effective work at the Chicago convention. The disappointment of his followers was sharpened as they thought of the influence which Wentworth might have in the distribution of the patronage; and Judd's own unhappiness was heightened by a realization of what he felt was ingratitude and the effect of Lincoln's reported dislike of him.[26]

Others of the inner circle of Lincoln's Chicago promoters felt that they, too, had a vested interest in the distribution of the spoils, and from them poured unnumbered requests to the President that he recompense Hermann Kreismann for the delivery of German votes by giving him the consulate at Frankfort, and that he make Captain George Schneider of the *Staats-Zeitung* collector of the port. They

[24] Schurz, *op. cit.*, II, 219.

[25] *Chicago Tribune*, March 4, 1861. See also *The Press and Tribune*, September 11, 1860, which speaks of "eight capricious slave drivers and doughfaces who cannot maintain one set of opinions for five years in succession."

[26] N. B. Judd to Lyman Trumbull, January 3, 1861, *Trumbull Papers*, XXVIII; Horace White, *The Life of Lyman Trumbull* (Boston, 1913), pp. 146–51; Koerner, *op. cit.*, II, 114–15; *Chicago Tribune*, March 7, 1861.

also asked that men of the "original Liberty Party," such as Zebina Eastman, be treated with proper consideration and implied that the Republican party would be more certain of perpetuation if the Irish received as many favors as the Germans. But the rewards so ardently desired failed to materialize, in most cases, and when there was any recognition of the services rendered by Chicago men to Lincoln, it generally came in the form of a minor appointment.[27]

One of the juiciest plums to be awarded in Chicago was the post-mastership, for which Ebenezer Peck, Charles L. Wilson of the *Journal,* and John L. Scripps, among others, yearned. The *Tribune* demanded the appointment of Scripps as a reward for the aid it had given Lincoln and the Republican cause. "We want the office," declared Ray, "not wholly for the money there is in it, but as a means of extending and insuring our business and extending the influence of the *Tribune."* To this Medill added the frank, if un-necessary, explanation that, if Scripps received the appointment, the country postmasters of the Northwest would work to extend the paper's circulation, which would not only fill the *Tribune's* coffers but would "benefit the party" and promote the legitimate influence of the paper. Medill felt it desirable to mention also that, in the last senatorial canvass in the state legislature, Lyman Trumbull, to whom were directed some of these telling requests for Scripps's appoint-ment, had been the beneficiary of one half of a two thousand dollar fund distributed by the *Tribune.* Scripps was given the coveted prize, and the disappointed Peck was led to prophesy dire misfortune to the Republicans in the spring election.[28]

[27] N. B. Judd to Lyman Trumbull, December 21, 1860, Alonzo Huntington to Trumbull, March 12, 1861, *Trumbull Papers,* XXXIV; Otto C. Schneider, "Abraham Lincoln und das Deutschthum," *loc. cit.,* pp. 65–75; Zebina Eastman to E. B. Washburne, July 14, 1861, J. L. Scripps to Washburne, July 15, 1861, *Washburne Papers,* XVIII; *Chicago Weekly Democrat,* March 16, 1861. Julius White was named collector of customs for the port at Chicago, in which post he served from March to October, 1861, when he was mustered into service. He was followed by Luther Haven who served until March 9, 1866. George Schneider was sent in September, 1861, to Helsingör, Denmark, as consul; Zebina Eastman was given a consul-ship at Bristol, England. (*The Chicago Times,* September 25, 1861; United States, *Sen. Exec. Doc.,* 37 Cong., 2 sess., IV, Doc. 12, p. 4.) Hermann Kreismann was commissioned Secretary of Legation at Berlin on March 8, 1861. On December 18, 1865, he was commis-sioned consul at Berlin, assuming charge February 1, 1866. Files, National Archives, Wash-ington.

[28] C. H. Ray to Lyman Trumbull, February 25, 1861, J. Medill to Trumbull, March 4, 1861, William Bross to Trumbull, February 13, 1861, E. Peck to Trumbull, March 21, 1861, *Trumbull Papers,* XXXVI, XXXVII, XXXIV, XXXIX; *Chicago Weekly Democrat,* March 16, April 6, 1861.

Peck's prophecy, however, failed to come true, for the municipal election on April 16 resulted in a victory for nearly all Republican candidates. So disorganized had the Democratic machine become in the face of an impending war that no official ticket was put in the field. Instead, on April 9, a group of Chicago citizens, regardless of the brand of their Democracy or of party in general, had drawn up a slate, the "People's Union Ticket." Thomas B. Bryan, lawyer and real estate promoter, was induced to be a candidate for the mayoralty. His running mates included Charles M. Gray, regular Douglas Democratic mayor in 1853, and Philip Conley, a "Buchanier" of the late 'fifties, for the Board of Public Works, besides others representing like differences of opinion in Democratic ranks. This ticket was ratified by outstanding citizens such as Cyrus H. McCormick, Roselle M. Hough, and Melville W. Fuller on April 12, the day before the Republican city convention nominated Julian S. Rumsey as mayor.[29]

No local issues were discussed aside from the usual pledge of economy in the use of city funds, for on April 12 the South began the bombardment of Fort Sumter. On the thirteenth Major Anderson surrendered. The day of compromise was past. To vote Republican seemed a patriotic duty. Only three aldermen and Frederick Letz, Democratic candidate from the West Division for the Board of Public Works, edged out their rivals. Letz's success came solely through massed German votes protesting no representation on the police board and hoping that his election would give a German majority on the Board of Public Works, thereby insuring jobs for Germans.[30]

Lincoln called for troops on April 15. A hysterical Chicago could find in its heart "no toleration towards traitors."[31] Pulpit and press joined in declaring that loyalty in thought and word was every man's duty. "Lenity and forbearance have only nursed the viper into life," cried the editor of the *Tribune*. "Let expressed rebuke and contempt rest on every man weak enough to be anywhere else in this crisis than on the side of the country against treason — of Lincoln and Scott against Davis and Twiggs, of God against Baal.

[29] *Chicago Daily Journal*, April 10, 13, 1861; *Chicago Tribune*, April 15, 16, 1861. The Republicans ratified their ticket April 15.
[30] *Ibid.*, April 16, 18, 1861.
[31] *Ibid.*, April 15, 1861; *Chicago Daily Journal*, April 20, 1861.

We say to the Tories and lickspittles in this community, a patient and reluctant, but at last an outraged and maddened people will no longer endure your hissing. You must keep your venom sealed, or *go down!* The gates of Janus are open, the storm is on us. Let the cry be, *THE SWORD OF THE LORD AND OF GIDEON!* " [32]

On the evening of the fall of Fort Sumter thousands of men of all political creeds gathered at the Wigwam to consider the distress of the nation. Here Judge George Manierre administered to them an oath of fealty to the constitutions of the nation and the state, in what William Onahan described as "a solemn spectacle." [33] Appeals for men, money, and arms, voiced at gatherings in Bryan Hall, Metropolitan Hall, in churches, and on street corners, resounded amidst the footsteps of men marching to drum and fife. Representative bankers tendered to Governor Yates the sum of about $500,000 for war purposes in advance of the assembling of the legislature. By the evening of the twentieth, $36,000 was given, "not loaned," for "fitting out the city volunteers." The volunteer fund grew daily, and committees from the Board of Trade, the bench and bar, railroads, citizens, and military organizations offered their services and resources to the cause of the hour. Southern sympathizers were warned that it was the part of wisdom that "treason must be dumb," and businessmen were urged to cease any trade with the South. Newspapers reflected the fervor so prevalent in editorial columns and in advertisements designed to awaken any laggards in enlistment.[34] On April 26, thousands of dollars were poured into the war coffers of the city, as a great mass meeting heard Wentworth describe the scenes of excitement he saw as he approached the city the night of Fort Sumter's fall.[35] Men clamored to enlist, and by late May it was urged that Illinois be permitted to enlarge her quota.[36]

Even before Lincoln called for troops, Chicago military organizations, long a part of the social and recreational life of the city, experienced a revival of interest in things martial. The Irish Mont-

---

[32] The words of an editorial in the *Chicago Tribune*, April 15, 1861. Italics are in the original. For a discussion of the part of the churches see pp. 386-88.

[33] Mary A. Livermore, *The Story of My Life* (Hartford, 1898), pp. 466-67; Onahan, *loc. cit.*, p. 69.

[34] *Chicago Tribune*, April 16, 19, 20, 1861; *Chicago Daily Journal*, April 20, 1861.

[35] *Chicago Weekly Democrat*, April 27, 1861.

[36] *Chicago Tribune*, May 30, 1861.

gomery Guards and Shields Guards, the Chicago Light Artillery, the United States Zouave Cadets, among others, made up the Sixtieth Regiment, State Militia. This regiment and that known as the Washington Independent Regiment presented a semblance of regular army organization at a time when trained forces were needed.[37] The politically-minded Wide Awakes, their object accomplished after the November election, turned their attention to military drill during the tense winter days in 1861.[38] The Chicago which heard the call to arms after the fall of Fort Sumter was not altogether unprepared.

With an ineffectual state militia Governor Yates was forced to requisition this ebullient enthusiasm.[39] So willingly was his call for six regiments met that Chicago could boast that the whole force could be obtained in that city alone, peopled by those anxious to make " short work " of " as desperate a band of traitors as ever infested the earth and conspired aganst republican institutions." [40] On the night of April 21, 595 men, the first to leave Chicago, boarded an Illinois Central train for Cairo. Among them were the Lincoln Rifles commanded by Captain Geza Mihalotzy, a company composed mainly of Hungarians, Bohemians, and men of Slavic blood, two companies of the Chicago Zouaves, the Turner Union Cadets made up of Germans, many of whom had seen service in the Revolution of 1848, the Chicago Light Artillery, and Captain Frederick Harding's company. Within two days after reaching Cairo the Chicago Artillery and Company B of the Chicago Zouaves saw service in capturing two steamers carrying munitions from St. Louis to the southern states.[41]

Others begged for the privilege to enlist but had to await the calls which came later. By May, Chicago proudly reported thirteen companies in actual service, with a reserve corps of twenty-five com-

---

[37] Several of the old military organizations existed only on paper in 1860, but the Chicago Light Artillery, a part of the Sixtieth Regiment, was ready for service in January, 1861. *Ibid.*, January 24, 1861.

[38] *Ibid.*, December 14, 1860, January 9, 1861.

[39] *Chicago Weekly Democrat*, January 12, 1861; *Chicago Weekly Tribune*, January 19, 1861; Illinois, *Report of the Adjutant General*, . . . *1861–66* (8 v. Springfield, 1886), I, 7.

[40] *Chicago Tribune*, April 17, 18, 1861.

[41] Two Chicago companies were accepted by April 19. *Ibid.*, February 6, April 17, 19, 1861; Illinois, *Report of the Adjutant General, 1861–66*, I, 7–9.

panies "ready to march at the tap of the drum." [42] And when men
of eighteen to forty-five years of age were assured by some employers
that salaries would go on while they were in the service of the government, those who might have hesitated because of family responsibilities rushed to the Chicago recruiting stations to sign up for
three months at $11 a month. [43]

The universality of the war spirit in Chicago was further shown
by the quick formation of a Home or Frontier Guard of men from
twenty-eight to forty-five and a company of those above forty-five,
groups from the University of Chicago, a Naval Brigade of the
fresh water sailors of Chicago, and a Company of Sappers and
Miners from the mechanics of the city. When Lincoln called for
three hundred thousand men in the summer of 1862, the answer was
almost as enthusiastic as it had been in the spring of 1861 when only
seventy-five thousand were asked for. Organized groups from the
Y.M.C.A. and the *Chicago Tribune,* and a Chicago Railway Battalion attested to the urge men had to rush to the colors. [44]

By June, 1861, citizens had raised over $36,466 to equip com-
panies and to aid soldiers' families. A War Finance Committee, organized April 18, collected money and paid for necessary supplies.
After August 10 the Union Defence Committee, a group of leading
citizens, absorbed the activities of the War Finance Committee. The
Mercantile Association, the Y.M.C.A., and others joined in the all-
absorbing enterprises of the hour — the sending of men to the front
and the care of soldiers' families left in Chicago. Regiments were
outfitted and sponsored by businessmen and other public-spirited
citizens. The Board of Trade, for example, gave its support and special blessing to the Seventy-second Illinois Regiment, mustered into
federal service in August, 1862. [45]

[42] *Chicago Tribune,* May 2, 1861. For tabular treatment of Chicago military participation see Appendix, pp. 504-5.

[43] *Chicago Tribune,* April 17, 18, 25, 1861; Fred Albert Shannon, *The Organization and
Administration of the Union Army, 1861-1865* (2 v. Cleveland, 1928), I, 29-31. By Act
of August 6, 1861, the pay of privates in the regular army and of volunteers was raised to
thirteen dollars a month. United States, *Statutes at Large,* XII, 326.

[44] *Chicago Tribune,* April 24-27, July 30, 1861, July 23, August 8, 1862; Cole, *The
Era of the Civil War,* p. 280.

[45] *Chicago Weekly Democrat,* June 1, 1861; *Chicago Tribune,* April 20, May 11, August
11, 1861, July 18, 23, 30, August 2, 24, 1862; Andreas, *History of Chicago,* II, 166, 227-28,
235; United States, "Government Contracts," *op. cit.,* II, li.

Foreign-born as well as native Americans were caught in the contagion of a great patriotic emotion, and ethnic barriers fell away in the common cause. During the winter of 1861, Hungarians, Bohemians, and numerous Slavs had organized a regular military company and had besought the governor of the state to call them into service at the first moment of danger to the Union. French-Canadians, Belgians, and Swiss were associated in the French Battalion. The Irish Brigade, in the Twenty-third Illinois under Col. James A. Mulligan, was accepted outside the regular quota and mustered into service on June 5, 1861. As early as January the Scots, through their military organization, the Highland Guards, had offered their services to the government. Chicago Scandinavians joined the Wisconsin Scandinavian Regiment as well as volunteering in Chicago. Germans, more strongly Republican than most other groups, responded valiantly. Indeed, so wholehearted was their support that the *Chicago Democrat* thanked God that Germans were in Chicago in the hour " of danger." [46]

For those who could not shoulder arms other ways of supporting the war were found. Shortly after Governor Yates's call for troops, women offered themselves as nurses. " A corps of Christian women " under the direction of Edmund B. Tuttle, city missionary of the Episcopal church, soon awaited a call to duty, but their offer was rejected by the state legislature.[47] The preparation of lint and bandages by those who must remain at home betokened an early consciousness of what war would bring. Sewing circles became at the same time fashionable and patriotic. A Ladies War Committee provided garments for which materials were furnished by the Board of Trade for the regiments of that organization, while women as

[46] *Chicago Tribune,* January 29, February 6, April 22, 23, May 28, 1861, August 13, 1862, August 24, 1863; Frederick F. Cook, *Bygone Days in Chicago* . . . (Chicago, 1910), pp. 10–13; MacMillan, " The Scots and Their Descendants in Illinois," *loc. cit.,* pp. 71–76; *Illinois Staats-Zeitung,* May 2, 7, June 21, December 2, 1861; Illinois, *Report of the Adjutant General, 1861–66,* I, 13, 214, II, 276; *The Irish Republic,* May 18, 1867.

[47] The first two women to volunteer as nurses were Jane A. Babcock and Mary E. M. Foster. (Andreas, *History of Chicago,* II, 314.) Among others who volunteered early were Mrs. D. M. Brundage, Miss J. S. Kellogg, Mrs. A. M. Beaubien, Mrs. E. B. Graves, Mrs. Mary Evens, Mrs. E. S. Johnson, and Miss Annette Sleightley. After Fort Donelson, the Sanitary Commission sent a group of volunteer nurses south. Mrs. Sarah Edwards Henshaw, *Our Branch and Its Tributaries* . . . (Chicago, 1868), pp. 52, 56; Mary A. Livermore, *My Story of the War* . . . (Hartford, 1892), chap. ii; *Chicago Tribune,* April 20, 23, 1861; Illinois, *House Journal, 1861,* p. 104.

an auxiliary of the Young Men's Christian Association attempted to care for needy families of men at the front. A similar purpose actuated the Ladies Relief Society for Soldiers Families, who carried on their work through visitors or supervisors and hired a manager for a weekly salary of seven dollars.[48] National brigades had their "Ladies' Associations" to collect money for special delicacies and necessities for the group to which they were attached, as well as to devise ways and means for the aid of widows and orphans.[49]

In nearly all these endeavors the church and secular bodies went hand in hand. Within a few months much of the relief, although co-operative in spirit and method, was carried on by the Chicago branch of the United States Sanitary Commission, created to promote the welfare of sick and wounded soldiers and their families. As the war progressed, camps were inspected to discover the needs of the soldiers, and agents were delegated to distribute donations.[50] To the Chicago branch or Northwestern Sanitary Commission, as it was later called, came supplies for distribution from the states of Illinois, Wisconsin, and Iowa whose generous support, in proportion to their means, gained for them an enviable record. A supply depot, set up on Wabash Avenue, received everything from bed sacking, sheets, and quilts to bandages and soap.[51]

---

[48] In April, 1861, James H. McVicker furnished a room which was fitted up with thirty sewing machines. L. Cornell and Company, W. C. Mason and Company, E. Richards and Company, and Cook, Stone and Company offered machines. The sales room of George R. Chittenden was used in 1862 by one group of women "in their busy labors at the Wheeler and Wilson Sewing Machines." The Ladies War Committee was organized in 1862. The Ladies Relief Society for Soldiers' Families was organized December 12, 1863. United States Sanitary Commission, *The Sanitary Commission of the United States Army . . .* (New York, 1864), p. 278; *Chicago Tribune,* April 22, 26, 27, 1861, April 21, 1862, September 11, December 14, 21, 27, 1863.

[49] For example, the Ladies' Association of the Irish Brigade collected $476.92 for a banner and devised plans for the care of orphans and widows. *Chicago Evening Journal,* April 26, 1861.

[50] The United States Sanitary Commission was set up in June, 1861. In September, 1861, Dr. Daniel Brainard, Isaac N. Arnold, and Col. John W. Foster were appointed a sub-committee for Chicago under the General Sanitary Committee of the United States. With representatives from other parts of the state the committee was to make up a state board. Since these men did not have time to devote to the undertaking, a number of Chicago citizens organized the Chicago Sanitary Commission October 17. Mark Skinner became its president. It was named by the United States Sanitary Commission as a branch for the Northwest. *Chicago Tribune,* September 19, October 18, November 5, 1861. See pp. 452-55.

[51] Charles J. Stillé, *History of the United States Sanitary Commission . . .* (Philadelphia, 1866), p. 184; *Chicago Tribune,* November 9, 1861.

With Illinois troops located chiefly in the Mississippi Valley, the battle of Fort Donelson, February 12–16, 1862, was the first which really tested the mettle of Chicago humanitarian and relief agencies, for hospitals at Paducah, Mound City, and Cairo were filled with the wounded. Sixteen physicians, fifty-two nurses, and a citizens' committee carrying $3,000 worth of supplies hurried to the scene of distress. A depot in the vicinity of Pittsburg Landing and one near the battleground at Shiloh furnished medicine and other necessities. Similar generosity and kindness were manifested in the weeks which followed. Bibles and religious tracts, as well as secular literature, became a part of the heavy shipments from Chicago to those at the front. Tons of foodstuffs and medicine were forwarded, and in 1863, when scurvy was reported as having attacked the army at Vicksburg, vegetables and dried or canned fruits in bountiful quantities were added to other supplies sent there and to the armies of Tennessee and the Cumberland.[52]

The spirit of humanitarianism was apparent on all sides. It was reflected in the gifts of workmen who shared a portion of their pay to help the families of those in service;[53] it was demonstrated in the benefactions of well-to-do businessmen who gave unsparingly not only of their wealth but of their time to carry on relief activities. The Chicago Medical Society offered free services to petitioning families of soldiers at the front, and fuel and other necessities were provided the needy.[54]

Despite military enthusiasm, frequent and unselfish displays of patriotism, and an outward appearance of agreement in the purposes of the war, it was rumored, as early as the summer of 1861, that "more secessionists" than such demonstrations would indicate were within the city's gates. Not all Southern sympathizers had followed the lead of Douglas, who, on the day that Sumter fell, announced that he no longer faced South. On May 1, visiting his home in Chicago, "the Little Giant" told his fellow citizens that there could be no neutrals in the war, "*only patriots,—or traitors.*" At least for

---

[52] *Ibid.*, February 19, 26, April 10, 12, May 23, 1862, January 5, 12, 1863; Henshaw, *op. cit.*, pp. 53, 116–38; Andreas, *History of Chicago*, II, 316–17; Stillé, *op. cit.*, pp. 323, 327, 338–39; United States Sanitary Commission, *op. cit.*, p. 278.

[53] *Ibid.*; *Chicago Tribune*, April 23, 1861, February 6, September 26, 1863. For the Northwestern Sanitary Fair and other relief activities see pp. 377–78, 452–55.

[54] *Chicago Tribune*, April 23, 1861, February 6, September 26, 1863.

the moment he was able to revive the flickering loyalties of some of his followers. But he had only a month to plead the cause of the Union. He died on June the third.[55]

The failure of the North at Bull Run on July 21 for a short time spurred to unified action, but by late August the *Tribune* warned its readers that a lodge of the Knights of the Golden Circle, formed in the spring, was secretly sowing seeds of discord, and that the New York *News*, "a violently treasonable sheet," had found five hundred or more readers a day in and near Chicago. So alarmed had the city fathers become by rumors of defection that the following oath, at the request of Mayor Rumsey, was prescribed for all citizens suspected of disloyalty:

> I, AB, do solemnly swear that I will support the Constitution of the United States; that I will true and faithful allegiance bear to the Government existing, and the laws enacted in pursuance thereof, and that I will not assist, aid or abet, by word or deed, any who are seeking to overthrow the Government, destroy the Constitution, or nullify the laws — so help me God.[56]

Dissatisfaction with the treatment given General Frémont found frequent expression as the hot summer months dragged on. German Republicans, in particular, were outraged by Lincoln's annulment of the General's emancipation proclamation in Missouri and announced that they would back Frémont and not Lincoln for President in 1864. When in November "the Pathfinder" was removed from command, Germandom offered mass protests, Caspar Butz apologized to his fellow nationals for his support of Lincoln in 1860, Hesing compared Frémont to the venerated Washington, and Hielscher declared that Nativism had been enthroned in the federal capital. These declarations tended to confirm the rumor that the war was being fought not to save the Union but to perpetuate the principles of abolitionism.

Alarmed by the growing dissatisfaction, the Union Defence Committee on August 24 sent out a call for a citizens' meeting to rally men of all creeds for the "defence and perpetuation of the Union

---

[55] *Ibid.*, May 2, August 28, 1861; *The Chicago Times*, June 12, 14, 15, 16, 18, 19, 1861.

[56] For a general discussion of the Knights of the Golden Circle see Mayo Fesler, "Secret Political Societies in the North during the Civil War," *Indiana Magazine of History*, XIV (September, 1918), 183–224; *Chicago Tribune*, August 28, 29, September 1, 1861.

and the constitution." The call set forth that no other than the Union party existed except "that of traitors and their abettors."[57] On October 8, the Republican and Democratic Central committees of Cook County, in an effort to stem the growing tide of opposition, issued jointly a call for a Union convention at Bryan Hall on the twenty-fourth to nominate men for county offices and as delegates to a state constitutional convention. The Union ticket, although it held the names of both Republicans and Democrats, met opposition, and on October 29 candidates were chosen on a "People's Union" ticket. On the thirty-first, another group put its ticket in the running. When the votes were counted after the election in November, it was found that the Union ticket, first in the field, was generally last in votes received. In spite of the victory of some Democratic aspirants, the *Times* felt that the Republicans had been undeservedly successful. These attempts for union in its opinion were unwise; straight tickets and distinct parties should be their unfailing practice.[58]

In the meantime preparations went forward for a forthcoming constitutional convention which met at Springfield, January 7, 1862, with Elliott Anthony, Melville W. Fuller, John H. Muhlke, and John Wentworth attending from Chicago. Organization of the convention was effected under the direction of southern Illinois Democrats representing the agricultural interests of the state. To them John Wentworth gave his support, deserting his erstwhile Republican fellows. The convention took the opportunity to castigate banks, corporations, and the judiciary, not to mention the Republicans' conduct of the war. On the question of banks and the currency as well as on corporations Wentworth's attitudes were as well known as they were detested by Republicans of the Joseph Medill brand. It was, therefore, expected that measures relating to these subjects would provoke vituperative assault. Into the discussions of the convention was injected a consideration of the conduct of the administrative officers of the state, tending to accentuate bitterness and partisanship in the deliberations. On January 13, Wentworth asked the

[57] *The Chicago Times,* August 13, 24, 30, September 9, 1861; *Illinois Staats-Zeitung,* September 16, 19, 25, October 1, November 11, 1861.

[58] *Chicago Tribune,* October 8, 30, 31, November 1, 12, 1861; *The Chicago Times,* October 25, 31, November 7, 1861; J. L. Scripps to George Schneider, November 27, 1861, George Schneider, *Papers* (Ms. Chicago Historical Society).

governor, among other things, for information concerning the indebtedness of the state, for the names of all contractors paid by the
state, for copies of contracts, and for statements as to whether the
general government had sent quartermasters to take charge of
the soldiers from Illinois.[59]

In an effort to free Chicago from state control, "Long John" on
March 18 introduced a measure providing that a special election
be held in April in Chicago that the people might decide whether
the city should select all of its own officers or whether some should
continue to be named by the governor or the General Assembly.
On March 24, the new constitution was adopted by the convention. Articles affecting banking, Congressional apportionment, and
the admission of Negroes to the state were to be submitted separately
to the vote of the people on June 17. Other provisions were to be
considered with the constitution itself.[60]

Adjournment was the signal for a concerted attack on the proposed constitution by those who saw in it a revival of the proslavery
party and the demise of Republicanism in Illinois. This "Egyptian
swindle" was the work of "Breckinridge secessionists," declared
the discontented, who beheld in the apportionment clause control
passing to southern Illinois, a section with interests less commercial
and industrial than those of the North. Certainly it did not fulfill
the objects for which the convention had been called, said Chicagoans of the Republican brand, for its primary purpose was to
draw up a document fitted to a population and livelihood which had
changed from the time of the old grant. In the midst of war, moreover, in the face of an increasing national taxation, it seemed to them
unwise to multiply state expenditure almost fourfold, as would be
the case if the provision increasing salaries and providing new
officers were allowed to pass. As for the mechanics' lien law, that
represented class legislation not afforded other laborers.[61]

[59] Illinois, *Journal of the Constitutional Convention of the State of Illinois, . . . 1862*
(Springfield, 1862), p. 59; for Governor Yates's answer, *ibid.*, pp. 132–34, 156–67, 198–206;
Oliver M. Dickerson, *The Illinois Constitutional Convention of 1862* (University of Illinois,
The University Studies, I, no. 9. Urbana, 1905), pp. 4, 12; *Chicago Evening Journal,* January
14, March 20, 1862; *Chicago Tribune,* January 7, 1862; Cole, *The Era of the Civil War,* pp.
267–68, 270.

[60] The election was to be held on the third Tuesday of April, 1862. The measure passed
on March 21. Dickerson, *op. cit.,* pp. 13, 15–18; *Chicago Evening Journal,* March 20, 1862;
Chicago Tribune, April 25, 1862.

[61] The apportionment adopted appeared a practical gerrymander. So much discussion

Among the provisions of the constitution to which great objection was raised was that relating to corporations. By this the state legislature had the power to modify and repeal charters issued after the constitution was adopted, whether for railroads or factories. This article was especially obnoxious to those seeking corporate grants. Furthermore, it specifically denied to succeeding legislatures release for the Illinois Central Railroad from its obligations to the state. The whole constitution was assailed as the nefarious design of politicians coveting profit and fat offices.[62]

To meet these charges, proponents of the proposed changes assembled in Metropolitan Hall and heard John Wentworth attack "stump-tail bankers" as "robbers" of the school fund, declare that some $112,000 of fees and perquisites had been received by certain judges and officeholders in the hall, and charge that officeholders and prominent men had entered into an alliance with the banks with the aim of defeating the constitution. In his efforts, Wentworth received the support of his erstwhile press competitor, the *Chicago Times*. In his arguments he was abetted by the presiding officer, Mayor Francis C. Sherman, who favored the new constitution because it contained a homestead exemption clause, because "females" were given the right to own property, and because it was against equality of Negroes. Besides these points, Sherman held that the new constitution would make the Illinois Central pay its debt for land grants.[63]

When the day of decision came, the *Tribune,* under a stirringly captioned editorial, "Down with the Secession Constitution," called upon Chicagoans to put an end to argument. Captain Schneider returned from his Danish consulship to swing the Germans into line against the constitution; Republican press and officials joined in what seemed to them a deadly struggle to preserve northern Republicanism and Unionism. Until the final votes came in, it appeared that not only Chicago but the state had endorsed the constitution.[64]

---

attended the consideration of this in the convention that it was decided to put it separately to popular vote. Dickerson, *op. cit.,* pp. 17–18; Van H. Higgins to E. B. Washburne, May 25, 1862, *Washburne Papers,* XXV; *Chicago Evening Journal,* March 22, April 2, 4, June 12, 16, 1862; Illinois, *Journal of the Constitutional Convention, 1862,* p. 1082.

[62] *Ibid.;* Dickerson, *op. cit.,* p. 21; *Chicago Evening Journal,* June 14, 16, 1862.

[63] *The Chicago Times,* June 15–17, 1862.

[64] *Chicago Tribune,* June 17, 20, 1862. See for opposing view, *The Chicago Times,* June 17, 1862; Andrew J. Townsend, *The Germans of Chicago* (unpublished Ph.D. Thesis,

To the *Tribune,* such a result meant that Wentworth would again be in political power, for it was alleged that " Old Liberty and Economy " had made " terms at Springfield with the Egyptian gang, and his price was the United States Senatorship." " For this," said the *Tribune,* " he was willing to sell out Northern Illinois, relying upon his old time tricks to deceive the people of this section of the State into voting for the swindle." The majority given in the state against the banking and currency provision was 3,801, while in Chicago it was 1,241 in favor — telling indication of diverging attitudes of the city and agricultural sections of the state; for the provision forbidding the immigration and settlement of Negroes and mulattoes in the state 100,590, in Chicago 1,604; in the state, 176,271 forbidding Negroes the suffrage, in Chicago 8,397; the state majority against Congressional apportionment was 7,230, that of Chicago, 152 in favor; whereas the state majority against the constitution was 16,051, that of Chicago was 995 in its favor.[65]

While the debate on the proposed constitution was at full heat, the spring municipal election had taken place. The Republicans "regretted" that Democratic politicians persisted in partisanship rather than patriotism and insisted on running candidates in order " to reclaim the city's government." They themselves were not in favor of "reviving party strife," they said, but in " self-defense " they found it necessary to nominate a ticket. On April 12, the convention met and named for mayor Charles N. Holden, who had been an alderman in 1855-56 and city treasurer in 1857, and a full slate of city officers. It adopted resolutions endorsing the President and his administration, pledged support to the prosecution of the war, opposed the proposed state constitution as a Democratic scheme in lower Illinois to gain control of the legislature and deprive northern Illinois of its influence, favored city economy and the right of a municipality to select its own officers, promised to use influence in Congress for a bill providing confiscation of all rebel property, and approved the work of Isaac N. Arnold of the Second District, in the House of Representatives. The Democrats retorted with similar

---

The University of Chicago, 1927), pp. 32, 218; Van H. Higgins to E. B. Washburne, May 25, 1862, Wm. H. Bradley to Washburne, June 13, 1862, J. R. Jones to Washburne, June 18, 1862, J. W. Sheahan to Washburne, June 19, 1862, *Washburne Papers,* XXV; Dickerson, *op. cit.,* pp. 23-24.

[65] *Chicago Tribune,* June 17, 23, 1862; Dickerson, *op. cit.,* p. 24.

charges against the Republicans, saying that the latter selected a man for the office of mayor who was an abolitionist tinged with Know-Nothingism and temperance. Their own candidate, Francis C. Sherman, on the other hand, represented all that the times needed, for he was a "Union man . . . whose principles of temperance and all other reforms" were not "of the Procrustean standard." The Democrats won in nearly all offices. This victory was explained by the Republicans as due in part to the fact that many of their voters absented themselves from the polls, and in part to the split between Wentworth and anti-Wentworth factions in the party, the former going so far as to support Sherman to prove that Wentworth only could carry the Republicans to victory. It was apparent that the old Democracy had reclaimed itself.[66]

New-found Democratic confidence marked the Congressional and state campaigns of the autumn of 1862. Democrats believed, not without reason, that Republican ranks were breaking. Arbitrary arrests, military failures, and economic uncertainties worked toward this disintegration. In September, Lincoln issued his preliminary proclamation of emancipation and the proclamation of the suspension of the writ of habeas corpus. Radical Chicago Republicans seized upon these pronouncements as an effective means of offsetting the irritation which had been mounting throughout the summer of 1862. Mass meetings heralded the President's announcement that on January 1 he would free all slaves in states in rebellion. "Let no one think to stay the glorious reformation," admonished the *Tribune*.[67]

To this the *Times* protested that there was no constitutional warrant for such a proclamation because, said the editor, "Military law does not destroy the fundamental civil law." And when Secretary Stanton ordered Brigadier-General J. M. Tuttle, commanding at Cairo, to colonize and find work for confiscated Negroes sent him by northern officers in the South, the Democrats felt they had ample proof that Illinois would be flooded by free and untrained Negroes. To few was this a welcome prospect. Only three months before, the people of Chicago had endorsed a constitutional provision to prevent Negro immigration.[68]

[66] *Chicago Evening Journal*, April 5, 11, 12, 14, 16, 1862; *The Chicago Times*, April 15, 1862; *Chicago Tribune*, April 14, 16, 1862.

[67] *Ibid.*, September 23, 1862.

[68] *Ibid.*, September 20, 1862; *The Chicago Times*, September 23, October 2, 6, 10, 1862.

Arbitrary arrests were also denounced by Democratic journals as un-American in principle and as an evidence of a growing despotism on the part of the Washington administration. Even Senator Trumbull questioned the power of the executive to suspend the writ of habeas corpus until such time as Congress should give its consent.[69] In general, the preliminary emancipation proclamation and the proclamation suspending the writ of habeas corpus gave strength to the Democrats. It was hoped, however, that a union of Republicans and war Democrats would stem the tide which seemed running toward an anti-administration victory.

On August 13, the Cook County Republican Convention renominated for Congress Isaac N. Arnold, called contemptuously by his opponents " the abolition candidate." The convention went on record in favor of the freeing of slaves in the District of Columbia, the confiscation of the property and emancipation of the slaves of " rebels and traitors " as a war measure. It warned against inflated paper currency and the lack of party unity. On October 14, the Democrats nominated Francis C. Sherman on a platform which opposed secession and deplored administrative inefficiency in the conduct of the war. They urged the enlargement of the Illinois and Michigan Canal by the government and censured Arnold, who had, in their opinion, neglected this measure so important to his city. They disapproved of Arnold's vote for a tax bill which they felt benefited New England and not the West. They demanded a change in the President's cabinet, and urged that the pay of soldiers be increased because of the depreciated currency. They condemned the " Africanization " of the state by federal military authorities, a condition which the *Times* declared was but " the policy of abolitionism to make all men free, and then to make all men equal, . . . to elevate negroes to the level of white men at the polls, and to degrade white men to the level of negroes in the workshops and fields of labor." [70]

The Republicans charged that their opponents reflected the views

---

The *Times* felt that Lincoln had fallen under the spell of abolitionists. *Ibid.,* September 23, 24, 26, 30, October 2, 1862.

[69] *Cong. Globe,* 37 Cong., 3 sess., pp. 31, 1090–92, 1185–87, 1205–8; White, *op. cit.,* p. 198.

[70] *Chicago Tribune,* August 14, 1862; *The Chicago Times,* June 15, August 14, October 6, 10, 15, 1862; *Chicago Evening Journal,* October 15, 1862.

of the Knights of the Golden Circle and of Vallandigham, and sought to prove that Arnold did not favor the influx of Negroes into the state and that his action regarding the Illinois and Michigan Canal was occasioned purely by a sense of Congressional deference. In view of the seriousness of the situation the *Tribune* urged that soldiers be allowed to vote, in the hope that it would strengthen the hands of the Republicans.[71]

Just before election day a feverish money market and the fear of a war with Europe unsettled business. This strengthened the appeal of the Republican-Union party that its candidates be supported so that unity in the prosecution of the war might not be jeopardized. Despite emotional and economic pressures, however, the legislature of the state went Democratic, and the Democrats were thus able to name a senator from their own ranks. Cook County remained in the Union fold, returning Arnold to Congress and voting for Ebon C. Ingersoll of Peoria, as representative at large.[72]

When the election was over, the Republicans consoled themselves with the usual regrets that not all voted who should have gone to the polls. But honest men knew that this was not the real cause for Democratic gains. Soon candor replaced subterfuge. Peace advocates openly characterized the war as " unwise, injurious, and unnecessary." Men counseled resistance to arbitrary arrests by the militia and urged repudiation of the Proclamation of Emancipation if it were put into effect January first. Even Medill experienced a sense of frustration because the proclamation was not extended to all slaves. And radicals, in general, trained their guns on programs initiated by Lincoln and his advisers, who included the much-disliked Stanton, " pro-slavery Blair and Bates and envious, ambitious Seward." [73]

Under this barrage, voters went to the polls in the spring mu-

---

[71] *Chicago Tribune*, October 17, 18, 1862; *Chicago Evening Journal*, October 15, 18, 1862. In 1865, the desired legislation granting votes to soldiers was enacted. Arnold's bill for the enlargement of the canal was postponed in order that an official government survey might be made.

[72] *Chicago* [Tri-Weekly] *Tribune*, November 7, 1862; *Chicago Evening Journal*, November 10, 1862; *Chicago Tribune*, November 10, 1862. For a discussion of disaffection during the Civil War in the Old Northwest, see Wood Gray, *The Peace Movement in the Old Northwest, 1860–1865* . . . (unpublished Ph.D. Thesis, The University of Chicago, 1933).

[73] *The Chicago Times*, November 10, December 11, 15, 1862; *Chicago Evening Journal*, November 10, 1862; Strevey, *op. cit.*, p. 144; I. Maple to Lyman Trumbull, December 28, 1862, *Trumbull Papers*, LII.

nicipal election on April 21, 1863, and again a Democrat, Francis C. Sherman, won the mayoralty race over Thomas B. Bryan, his Republican-Union opponent. With Sherman went all candidates of the Democratic party for city offices, in an election said by the *Tribune* to be fraudulent and dominated by Copperheads and the Irish. Thus Chicago, in the words of this newspaper, was now ranked as "among the disloyal cities," despite the work of the Young Men's Union Working Club, Union leagues, and other organized efforts.[74]

In the autumn, Union party success in Ohio, Pennsylvania, and Iowa was the signal for a hundred-gun salute by Captain James Smith's battery and the lighting of neighborhood bonfires, and a three-hour open meeting in the Union League rooms in Warner Hall voiced the satisfaction of those in attendance. Heartened also by Union successes on the field of battle Republicans urged a united front of all loyal to the North. In the county election of November this appeal bore the fruits of victory. The war party could now rest more comfortably after the tension and strain of peace movements both unofficial and official, which, in the legislature, had gone so far that Governor Yates had been impelled to prorogue that "Copperhead" body, which, the Governor held, had interfered with his prerogatives and had refused to make appropriations so that private capital had to finance the state. Among the leaders of opposition to Governor Yates was a Chicago member of the lower house, Melville W. Fuller, who had voted to condemn the suspension of the writ of habeas corpus and the Emancipation Proclamation and openly expressed his belief that the Constitution could not be maintained by the adoption of coercive powers by the government. After the Governor's prorogation, Fuller, on behalf of others of like mind, submitted a protest to what he termed a "monstrous and revolutionary usurpation of power." But one group of Chicago citizens applauded Yates's move as vigorously as Fuller raised objections.[75] Unanimity of thought in such days was impossible.

The Republican successes of November paved the way for the consideration of Lincoln's re-election. There was little agreement

[74] *The Chicago Times*, April 24, June 2, 1863; *Chicago Tribune*, March 5, 16, April 4, 22, 23, 24, 27, 1863.
[75] *Ibid.*, June 12, October 10, 15, November 9, 1863; *The Chicago Times*, November 4, 9, 1863; Illinois, *House Journal, 1865*, p. 27, *House Journal, 1863*, pp. 76, 372–75, 526–28. The legislature also approved a convention of all states at Louisville.

among the diverse elements of the party as to his fitness, and booms for Chase and Frémont threatened the very foundations of the party.[76] Even the editors of the *Chicago Tribune* were prepared to discard Lincoln if it seemed best, and even they objected to his lack of aggressiveness in dealing with the South. Others felt that they knew better than the President who should be named to military command. His cabinet choices still were a focus of criticism. The amnesty policy, proclaimed in December, 1863, was at first received by Chicagoans with considerable enthusiasm, but the *Tribune* was soon cautioning its readers that the proclamation should not be interpreted so broadly as to constitute an offer to release rebel prisoners should they take the oath. But some of the most critical realized that it would be unwise to abandon Lincoln in so grave a crisis.[77] The *Tribune* warned continuously that a departure from the policy prescribed by the radical Republicans meant defeat and declared that it was "a great historical fact that in revolutions the radical party always wins."[78]

As early as December, 1863, a Salmon P. Chase boom was on. In February, 1864, promoters of Lincoln's Secretary of the Treasury distributed "the Pomeroy Circular" which criticized the President's "manifest tendency toward compromises" and pointed to the fitness of Chase.[79] In late May, 1864, ultra-radicals, including a number of Illinois delegates led by Chicago Germans, met at Cleveland and nominated John C. Frémont and General John Cochrane. Their platform, which expressed views held by Caspar Butz and Ernest Pruessing, of Chicago, demanded the confiscation of rebel property for redistribution among the soldiers and insisted that reconstruction must be controlled by Congress.[80]

On June 7, the Republicans assembled at Baltimore, although this

[76] Arthur Charles Cole, "President Lincoln and the Illinois Radical Republicans," *The Mississippi Valley Historical Review*, IV (March, 1918), 430–32.

[77] I. N. Arnold to Abraham Lincoln, May 18, 1863, Lincoln to Arnold, May 26, 1863 (photostats. *Lincoln Collection*, Chicago Historical Society); J. Medill to E. B. Washburne, April 12 [1864], *Washburne Papers*, XLV; *Chicago Tribune*, December 11, 17, 1863; W. A. Baldwin to Lyman Trumbull, April 4, 1864, *Trumbull Papers*, LVII; Schurz, *op. cit.*, III, 98–101; Julian, *op. cit.*, p. 243.

[78] *Chicago Tribune*, November 3, 1863.

[79] *The Chicago Times*, February 26, 1864; J. W. Schuckers, *The Life and Public Services of Salmon Portland Chase* (New York, 1874), pp. 499–500; George Fort Milton, *The Age of Hate* (New York, 1930), pp. 27–28.

[80] *Deutsch-Amerikanische Monatshefte für Politik, Wissenschaft und Literatur*, I, 568–73, II, 74–86; *Illinois Staats-Zeitung*, January 14, February 5, 27, 1864. Butz was editor of

early convention date had been opposed by prominent members of the party. Patronage, the distribution of contracts, and a well-oiled machine brought about Lincoln's nomination. "Once more," declared the *Tribune,* "we triumphantly and hopefully unfurl to the breeze the standard of the Union with Abraham Lincoln of Illinois as the standard bearer."[81] On the ninth, loyal followers gathered in the Court House Square to ratify the nomination. The Dearborn Light Artillery fired a national salute, the Great Western Band performed, and those assembled listened to speeches by Wentworth, Hesing, and others as lighted rockets played across the sky and found reflection in the dark waters of the lake.[82]

But the breach between Lincoln and the radicals did not heal as the summer wore on. On July 2, those opposed to Lincoln's proclamation of pardon to Southerners sanctioned the Wade-Davis Bill. This opened still wider the already deep fissures in the ranks of Republicanism. Conferences seeking to bring about a cessation of hostilities served to confirm the skeptical. Horace Greeley's unsuccessful meeting with unofficial agents from the Confederacy at Niagara added tinder to the flames, fanned by cries for peace from the Democrats. The war must cease, declared these anti-administration forces. The Democrats, said the *Times,* must "remedy one by one the grievances inaugurated by the republican administration and against which the South is fighting. They would offer the South the Constitution, and with it the guarantee that for all time the rights of the States under that Constitution should be preserved inviolate. This would be a victory over the rebellion more potent than the taking of a dozen Richmonds or the slaughter of an hundred thousand rebels in arms."[83] Chicago was in a ferment, to which not only political animosities made their contribution but in which economic disturbances in the usual channels of trade played their part.[84]

---

the *Deutsch-Amerikanische Monatshefte.* He favored giving Negroes the lands of their former masters. Ernst Schmidt, Pruessing, and Butz signed a call for the Cleveland convention. Theodore Hielscher, "a German schoolmaster," was among the discordant. *Chicago Tribune,* May 26, 1864.

[81] J. Medill to E. B. Washburne, April 12 [1864], *Washburne Papers,* XLV; *Chicago Tribune,* June 9, 1864.

[82] *Ibid.,* June 10, 1864. A second meeting was held the following night.

[83] Koerner, *op. cit.,* II, 432; *The Chicago Times,* July 2, 25, August 3, 1864; Cole, *The Era of the Civil War,* pp. 319–22.

[84] E. B. McCagg to Charles Butler, January 20, 1863, Charles Butler, *Papers (Ms. Library of Congress).*

Not even the amazing prosperity which the war was bringing to Chicago served to deter critics of the Washington government. The whir of busy factory wheels, the bustle of the market place where exchanges had been quickened to an unprecedented degree, the tread of marching feet, and the noise of beating drums did not longer still the voices of the opposition. Objectors found little satisfaction in the fact that Chicago, in the first months of the war, had won fifteen of the thirty-six contracts for army supplies awarded at Springfield and had obtained large orders from Washington to furnish beef to the army.[85] They preferred that the merchants who were profiting abundantly get rich by other means than by orders from agencies like the County War Committee and the Union Defence Committee. There was, to these men who did not like the conduct of the war, little occasion for pride in the activities in their midst of the quartermaster's depot, set up by the federal government in 1861 to supply troops from Iowa, Wisconsin, Minnesota, and Illinois. Peace men preferred to send south other things than guns, bullets, and field ambulances, tents and uniforms, saddles and harnesses for horses, for which Chicago became one of the leading markets just as she did for oats, salt, pork, beef, bread, and lumber for the armies in the Department of the Cumberland.[86] There were those, too, who thought that they could find evidence that, although avowed war ideals were high, practices were sometimes corrupt; that efficiency and unselfishness did not characterize all business transactions; and that profiteering was making some men very wealthy; that bribes to army officers made it possible for some railroads to get the contracts for troop transport; and the prices paid by the government did not always mean that the product was good.[87]

But the critics of the war were by no means confined to those who from forum and press cried for peace. In 1862 and 1863 the call for troops had been answered. The draft had been avoided, but more and more, bounties and special offerings from the local govern-

---

[85] Shannon, op. cit., I, 53.

[86] In 1864, for instance, the quartermaster's department purchased $2,664,038.54 of supplies in Chicago in addition to $1,000,000 spent by other departments. Many mules as well as horses were sold. Colbert, op. cit., p. 96. See also pp. 90, 91, 101 ff.

[87] The Michigan Southern and Northern Indiana was charged with exerting influence of this kind. United States, "Government Contracts," op. cit., II, 55, 62–68, 118–19.

ments, from individuals, and from business and other groups were used to spur recruiting. As early as 1862 the County Board of Supervisors voted to levy a tax of $200,000 to be disbursed in bounties of $60 each to volunteering soldiers. The Board of Trade at the same time offered premiums amounting to $200,000, thereby drawing recruits from villages unable to meet the competition of Chicago, and thus saving the city from the ignominy of low enlistments. Other attempts of like kind continued. By 1863 the enlistment of Negro soldiers, with increased pay and with a bounty of $300, as in the case of white men, was agitated by those who would spare men of fair skin.[88] By the next year the situation was so disturbing that the county resorted to the sale of bonds, but response was lukewarm, and only ninety-four cents on the dollar were realized on a hoped-for $50,000. Reports that Chicago soldiers in the field were refusing to obey orders and had suffered arrest were added proof that many were becoming weary of the war.[89]

An increasing number of substitutes went to battle for those who could not or would not shoulder arms for the Northern cause. The Common Council joined with others in condoning the practice — in August, 1863, for instance, setting aside $120,000 to purchase substitutes for married men. As the war wore on prices for these substitutes followed the market, and brokers enjoyed prosperity. By summer, 1864, three-year men could demand from $550 to $650, and by spring of the next year $900 was sometimes asked. The " flesh brokers " of Chicago carried on a far-flung business, sending substitutes into communities where the cash return seemed greatest. In so doing, they reduced the number available for service in Chicago and Cook County.[90] Under the system it was charged that the police worked hand in hand with the brokers; criminals were reported to have gained their freedom, preferring the army to the jail; men of wealth and leaders in civic life and commercial enterprises were

---

[88] *Chicago Tribune,* May 10, July 10, 11, 23, 24, 25, 30, August 4, 7, 1862, October 6, 7, December 8, 11, 12, 23, 29, 1863, January 15, 16, March 3, 11, April 12, May 16, July 16, August 16, 1864; *Oquawka Spectator,* July 11, 1862; *The Workingman's Advocate,* September 17, 1864; *Official Records of the Rebellion,* ser. 3, III, 710.

[89] In 1864, for example, members of the Mercantile Battery were arrested for disobedience to orders. *Chicago Tribune,* May 23, 1864.

[90] *Ibid.,* August 6, 13, 1863, August 13, 17, 31, September 9, 17, 21, 1864, January 27, 30, 1865. The newspapers did not always use the word " substitute " in the military sense.

said to have become the beneficiaries of a practice held to be a concession to the well-to-do.[91]

The summer of 1864 brought fears of conscription. The *Tribune* joined long-time critics of the war in protesting the number set for the county in the call for troops in August. It seemed of no avail that the quota was reduced from 4,920 men to 1,816, that bounties were increased, and that attempts were made to stop recruiting in Chicago for other places. On September 26, a draft was imposed. In the First District of Illinois, in which Chicago lay, 1,770 names were drawn, of which 428 were held to service. With their cost ranging from $250 to $500, 322 persons including 88 from Chicago furnished substitutes. Most of these went in place of business and professional men and skilled workers, while unskilled laborers bought by far the smallest number.[92]

Once more in December, 1864, Chicago faced the draft when Lincoln again called for troops.[93] For the next few weeks defiance was the controlling emotion. Three years before Chicagoans had begged the privilege of going to war; now mass meetings protested what was considered an unfair assessment upon her man power. Mutual protective associations were organized to buy freedom for draftees; as many as three or four hundred men liable to conscription were reported as leaving daily for Canada or "for parts unknown"; aliens, particularly the Irish, eagerly sought papers which insured freedom from call; and bounty jumpers from other cities and states in increasing numbers passed through the city usually at the solicitation of Chicago brokers.[94]

[91] *The Chicago Times,* September 9, 1864, published lists of persons said to have bought exemptions, but government records do not substantiate the *Times's* statement. United States Provost Marshal General, *Final Report Made to the Secretary of War . . . March 17, 1863, to March 17, 1866* (Washington, 1866), part I, pp. 190, 196. See substitute certificate for George F. Rumsey, August 13, 1864 (*Ms.* Chicago Historical Society).

[92] *Ibid.; Chicago Tribune,* August 14, 24, 26, 27, 29, September 9, 11, 20, 21, 27, 1864; Colbert, *op. cit.,* pp. 96–97; United States Provost Marshal General, *Report, Illinois, First District,* LVII (*Ms.* War Department Archives, Washington). When, on October 22, conscription was ended, only fifty-nine drafted Chicagoans were reported held to service.

[93] Lincoln's call was on December 19, 1864, for three hundred thousand volunteers. He set February 15, 1865, as the day for imposing the draft, but complaints throughout the nation led the President to appoint a board to investigate quotas. Its findings were to be conclusive, and drafts were to be imposed as soon after February 15 as possible. Illinois, *Report of the Adjutant General, 1861–66,* I, 83–86, 92–93, 98–99.

[94] *Chicago Tribune,* January 2, 4, February 15, 24, March 15, 17, 1865. For similar incidents earlier see *ibid.,* July 2, 1863, September 4, 1864.

On February 7 a special meeting of the Board of Supervisors of Cook County decided to increase its bounty to $400, and the next day it became known that only 528 men had been obtained out of the 5,200 asked of the county.[95] Something had to be done. On the fifteenth a committee of prominent Chicagoans went to Springfield to protest the quota assignment, and two days later the announcement that prominent Chicagoans would carry their complaint to Washington gave heart to Chicago citizens.

Eagerly they awaited the appeal which Medill, S. S. Hayes, and R. M. Hough were to make to the federal authorities. Eagerly citizens of other towns also awaited the outcome, for they too had emissaries in Washington on similar errands. The Chicago delegation visited the provost marshal general and the secretary of war who denied their plea. Then they called upon Lincoln, the favorite son of Illinois, who listened to the arguments of Secretary Stanton and of General Fry as well as the statements of Medill and his colleagues. As they finished speaking he turned to those soliciting relief.

" Gentlemen," he said in a voice full of bitterness, " after Boston, Chicago has been the chief instrument in bringing this war on the country. The Northwest has opposed the South as New England has opposed the South. It is you who are largely responsible for making blood flow as it has. You called for war until we had it. You called for Emancipation, and I have given it to you. Whatever you have asked you have had. Now you come here begging to be let off from the call for men which I have made to carry out the war you have demanded. You ought to be ashamed of yourselves. I have a right to expect better things of you. Go home, and raise your 6,000 extra men. And you, Medill, you are acting like a coward. You and your ' Tribune' have had more influence than any paper in the Northwest in making this war. You can influence great masses, and yet you cry to be spared at a moment when your cause is suffering. Go home and send us those men." [96]

---

[95] Colbert, *op. cit.,* pp. 96–97.

[96] Illinois, *Report of the Adjutant General, 1861–66,* I, 91–93. " We all got up and went out, and when the door closed, one of my colleagues said: ' Well, gentlemen, the old man is right. We ought to be ashamed of ourselves. Let us never say anything about this, but go home and raise the men.' And we did — 6,000 men — making 28,000 in the war from a city of 156,000. But there might have been crape on every door almost in Chicago, for every family had lost a son or a husband. I lost two brothers. It was hard for the mothers." This

The order of the President was obeyed. Governor Oglesby proclaimed, on March 6, that Chicago's request had been refused and asked that the quota be filled without a draft. The battle of Five Forks on April 1 and the evacuation of Petersburg by the Confederate forces on the day following were the prelude of Appomattox on the ninth. Chicago was spared a second draft. On the twelfth the county abandoned further bounty payments, and the following day recruiting ceased.

In spite of discordant voices, Chicago and Cook County had given generously in defense of the Union. Along with the state they shared the tribute of the Maine legislature, which, after the battle of Fort Donelson, commended the valor of the soldiers of Illinois. In bounties the county had spent $2,571,172, and Chicago had paid out some $119,475 more, and 22,436 men from Cook County had shouldered arms.[97]

In these trying weeks in which Chicago was faced with the necessity of finding a way to recruit her war strength, the activities of the Democrats, especially those insisting on peace, gave added cause for anxiety. During the summer of 1864 they met in Chicago to nominate a president and vice-president. This meeting had been preceded by conferences of the war and the peace Democrats of the Northwest in Chicago in November and December, 1863. The latter met without the blessings of the *Times* and the *Post,* which at the moment, in the words of the *Times,* held that "true Democrats" must express to "the whole world . . . their earnest love for the Union cause, and their advocacy of a vigorous prosecution of the war."[98]

---

is reported as a conversation of Ida M. Tarbell with Medill in June, 1895. See Ida M. Tarbell, *The Life of Abraham Lincoln* (New York, 1909), II, 148–49.

[97] *Chicago Tribune,* April 8, 1862; *Chicago* [Tri-Weekly] *Tribune,* February 17, March 1, 8, 20, 1865; Colbert, *op. cit.,* pp. 96–97; Illinois, *Report of the Adjutant General, 1861–66,* I, 166–67, 199–200. For the battles in which Illinois and Chicago troops participated see Appendix, pp. 504–5. Cook County, constituting the First District of Illinois, paid a total internal revenue of about $46,703,000 from 1862–63 through 1870–71. Income taxes accounted for about 20 per cent, or $9,416,858; license fees, $2,281,189; sales taxes, $1,537,490; and taxes on amusements and communication, $3,383,548. Over $28,000,000 came from taxes on manufactures, spirits, and like products and were passed on to the consumers. United States Commissioner of Internal Revenue, *Report . . . on the Operations of the Internal Revenue System for the Year Ending June 30, 1863* (Washington, 1863), p. 179. See also reports for succeeding years through 1871.

[98] *The Chicago Times,* November 25, 26, December 12, 1863; *Chicago Morning Post,* November 8, December 15, 1863. The war Democrats met November 25, the peace Democrats on December 3.

The convention to nominate a man to serve as President in the troublous days to come, originally scheduled to assemble July 4, was postponed until August 29, because, said the *Tribune,* the Democrats dared not define their principles at that time and because the war faction feared what the peace group might do.[99]

Unable to find a hall to house their convention, Democratic promoters decided to erect a building on Park Row to accommodate fifteen thousand people and to cost $16,000. But these plans were blocked by an injunction obtained by Sanford B. Perry and other property owners on the ground that the proposed " wigwam " in the public park facing Michigan Avenue was against the rights of property owners and prohibited by the city charter.[100] But the Democrats were not deterred, and by August 20 most of the prominent figures of the national Democracy had found quarters in the hotels of the city. On the twenty-sixth Clement L. Vallandigham of Ohio spoke in the Court House Square. His charges against the Washington administration were answered by John Wentworth in what the *Tribune* was forced to describe as " a thorough Union speech." As the two men addressed the crowd of several thousand, cheers of approval mingled with " catcalls " and " howlings," the prelude of the convention's consideration of national candidates on the twenty-ninth.[101]

The war Democrats had already determined to recommend General George B. McClellan for the presidency, although his candidacy had been opposed by the promoters of Ulysses S. Grant, whose military record, if not his Democracy, offered an appeal similar to McClellan's. But Grant was not receptive — an attitude which greatly relieved the *Tribune* and others of like mind, who thought that he was needed in the military field and furthermore feared his vote-getting powers.[102]

99 *Chicago Tribune,* June 23, 1864.

100 *Ibid.,* May 29, 31, June 1, 23, August 20, 1864. For the charter provision by which the protestants prohibited the building of the " wigwam " see *Private Laws, 1863,* p. 96.

101 *Chicago Tribune,* May 31, August 20, 24, 27, 28, 1864. John M. Douglas of Chicago was a delegate-at-large to the convention, Melville W. Fuller and B. G. Caulfield were delegates from the first district, and Lambert Tree and John C. Garland were alternates. *Official Proceedings of the Democratic National Convention Held in 1864 at Chicago* (Chicago, 1864), p. 18.

102 A meeting of " Conservatives " had been held in Cincinnati on December 3 and 4, 1863, and agreed upon McClellan. *Chicago Evening Journal,* December 5, 1863; J. Medill to E. B. Washburne, May 30, 1864, *Washburne Papers,* XXXVIII.

On August 31, McClellan was nominated. For him, the candidate of the war Democrats, the "peace" faction drew up a platform which demanded the restoration of peace on the basis of "the federal union of all the states." The next day the delegates started their homeward trek. Their departure brought a sense of relief to those Chicagoans who had not enjoyed the presence of men whom an unfriendly press described as "smooth tongued Copperheads from the East," Missouri bushwhackers, and plug-uglies, who kept the city from the conduct of everyday business and disturbed the sleep of good Republicans by shouts of "Hurray for Little Mac," or "Bully for 'Ratio Seemore' [sic]."[103] The enthusiasm manifested at Chicago, thoughtful administration men feared, was prophetic of Democratic success in November. McClellan pleased his promoters by emphasizing his desire for the preservation of the Union rather than stressing the peace plank in the platform. For Chicago Republicans, days were indeed dark.

Nor did their gloom lift as they looked back upon the spring election for police commissioner and members of the council, for Republicans had hoped for success for all their candidates. But the electorate had been unmoved by charges that the Democratic administration had raised the tax total by at least 56 per cent, part of which had gone out of the school fund to support "the secesh Chicago *Times*" as the corporation newspaper. The Republicans had then called upon workingmen to maintain the dignity of labor and to remember that John F. Sendelbach, a German Catholic and Democratic candidate for police commissioner, had refused to pay the prices demanded by the Mason's Union, although they were "an advance of but twenty-five per cent." From excessive taxes and the unfair treatment of labor it was easy enough to speak of the high cost of living. This, too, was laid at the door of all Democrats to whom for political reasons was applied that most destructive term of hate, "Copperhead."[104]

But opponents countered with the declaration that the Republican party was accountable "for all the blood and treasure that had been poured out" in a war which was still unsuccessful, a war started in

---

[103] *The Chicago Times,* September 1, 1864; *Chicago Tribune,* August 30, 31, September 1, 1864.

[104] *Chicago Evening Journal,* April 14, 16, 18, 1864; *Chicago Tribune,* April 16, 19, 1864.

1861 to save the Union but now being waged to free the slaves. The national administration, particularly the cabinet and the President, was incompetent and corrupt, the Democrats insisted, and the state executive was both publicly and privately " defiant of the laws of the State and the rules of common decency." Municipal problems were thus engulfed in national issues, and the election became more than local in importance. The results reflected the general state of mind, for a Union man, Thomas B. Brown, became police commissioner, and the Common Council was evenly divided with Sherman, a war Democrat, the first two-year term mayor, holding the deciding vote.[105]

From local to national arenas flitted the fear of the passing of Republican control. Chicagoans of that credo watched apprehensively the results of a private call issued in late summer for a new national convention to be held in Cincinnati September 28, at which Lincoln would be replaced by a more popular candidate. But before that day came, military victory had turned the tide. On September 2, Atlanta fell into the hands of the North. The war was not a failure. Plans for the Cincinnati meeting were laid aside, and on September 22 Frémont withdrew his name from the presidential list. Immediately bets in Chicago of fifty to one on Lincoln's re-election repeated the optimism of 1860. The " Wide Awakes " took on life. Long lines of people, with " lanterns, transparencies, illuminations," and mottoes, marched to the stirring music of the Great Western Light Guard Band. Speeches by the great and well known again became the political tools of crusaders now united by a common enthusiasm.[106]

In spite of the cold rain which fell throughout the day, a large vote was cast. Unremitting electioneering brought Republicans hoped-for rewards. Chicago, in the words of a party protagonist, had given an emphatic and overwhelming verdict against " the disgraceful and traitorous platform that unpatriotic politicians concocted and adopted " in the Democratic convention held only a few weeks before in their city. Still, Lincoln's Chicago majority was less

---

[105] *The Chicago Times,* April 15–20, 1864; *Chicago Evening Journal,* April 20, 1864; *Chicago Tribune,* April 20, May 11, 1864. Mayors were chosen for two rather than the one-year term beginning in 1863.

[106] *Chicago Tribune,* September 4, 13, October 27, 28, November 4, 5, 1864; Randall, *op. cit.,* pp. 618–19, 621, 692. Mobile was taken August 5, 1864, by federal forces.

than two thousand out of the twenty-seven thousand votes cast. His re-election seemed to his Chicago foes a threat to " The Last Remnants of American Liberty," the establishment of a " perpetual dictator " in a government said to be free.[107]

The election scene had been clouded still more by the revelation of a plot to free Confederate prisoners at Camp Douglas, to plunder and burn Chicago, and to sever the Northwest from its national allegiance. The camp, occupying about sixty acres in the south section of the city, had been, since 1862, a year after its opening as a place to recruit and train Northern soldiers, a prison for captured Confederates. Between five and seven thousand had reached the camp after the Northern success at Fort Donelson, February 16, 1862.[108] The coming of these men, the representatives of a hated cause, created fear in the hearts of many and served to keep alive the animus so necessary to prosecute a war.[109]

In the spring of 1864, Confederate agents had gone to Canada to co-operate with the Sons of Liberty and others of like mind in their campaign for peace. In June, Jacob Thompson, a member of Buchanan's cabinet, and Clement L. Vallandigham, Grand Commander of the Sons of Liberty, were reported to have drawn up plans designed to detach the Northwest from the Union, to force the East to sue for peace, and eventually to provide for a close and permanent alliance of the Northwest with the South.

Difficulties beset these agitators. Several times they had hoped to carry through their schemes, but lack of preparation prevented. When the Democrats met in Chicago on August 29, hope was high that Vallandigham's peace platform might be accepted in the autumn election. Then, too, rumors of the attack on Camp Douglas had

[107] Koerner, op. cit., II, 435–36; Chicago Tribune, November 9, 1864; Chicago Evening Journal, November 9, 1864; The Chicago Times, November 28, 1864. Lincoln's vote was reported as 14,388 and McClellan's as 12,691.

[108] Camp Douglas lay on the west side of present-day Cottage Grove Avenue between Thirty-first and Thirty-third streets. (Chicago Tribune, September 30, 1861, February 21, 22, 1862; William Bross, " History of Camp Douglas," Mabel McIlvaine, ed., Reminiscences of Chicago during the Civil War [Chicago, 1914], pp. 165–68.) Estimates of the number of Confederate prisoners brought from Fort Donelson vary in different sources. The Official Records of the Rebellion put the number at five thousand, while the mayor of Chicago gave the number as seven thousand. William B. Hesseltine, Civil War Prisons . . . (Columbus, Ohio, 1930), pp. 41–42.

[109] Regret, however, was expressed about the high sick and death rate among the prisoners and the poor hospital accommodations. Official Records of the Rebellion, ser. 2, V, 587–89, VI, 4; Chicago Tribune, February 26, March 3, 1862, February 1, 1864.

resulted in redoubled vigilance over the prisoners. November the eighth seemed perhaps the best time to move.

Gradually the undertaking took form under the Confederate agent, Captain Thomas H. Hines, and his followers at Mattoon, Illinois. In Chicago, Charles Walsh, wealthy contractor and Brigadier General of the Chicago district of the Sons of Liberty, accumulated stores of munitions in his residence near the camp. As election day drew near, bands of armed men in "butternut" uniform were reported arriving in the city. Fears mounted hourly as the number of guards at Camp Douglas appeared insufficient to provide protection from prisoners ten times their number.

During the first week of November, Captain Hines and his followers entered Chicago. Colonel Benjamin J. Sweet, commanding at Camp Douglas, moved quickly. Early Monday, November 7, he sent three detachments through the city, who arrested the chief conspirators, including Judge Buckner S. Morris, Whig mayor in 1838; and at the home of Walsh they took the store of munitions. To protect Union commerce on the Great Lakes from rumored attacks by the Confederates, the steamer *Michigan* was sent to Canadian waters; and to help protect fellow citizens the Board of Trade of Chicago organized mounted and street patrols.[110]

It was in this tense atmosphere that the election had taken place. As men went to the polls, federal soldiers stood watch to preserve the peace. Along with Lincoln, Republican state and Congressional candidates rode to success. Radical labor, with others, had criticized the conduct of the administration and had demanded commitments particularly embarrassing to Republican candidates.[111] William Bross of the *Tribune* was opposed by labor as lieutenant governor of the state because of his anti-union attitude. Wentworth, con-

[110] John Wentworth was police commissioner at this time. Thomas H. Hines, "The North-Western Conspiracy," *The Southern Bivouac*, n.s. II (December, 1886–February, 1887), 442–44; Fesler, *loc. cit.*, pp. 244–45, 270–71; John B. Castleman, *Active Service* (Louisville, 1917), pp. 145, 157–59; Elbert J. Benton, "The Movement for Peace Without a Victory During the Civil War," The Western Reserve Historical Society, *Collections,* Publication no. 99 (Cleveland, 1918), pp. 55, 66; I. Winslow Ayer, *The Great North-Western Conspiracy in all its Startling Details* (Chicago, 1865), pp. 39–40; *Official Records of the Rebellion,* ser. 1, XLV, pt. I, 1082; *Chicago Tribune,* November 6, 7, 8, 11, 16, 18, 1864, February 10, 13, 15, April 24, 1865; *Chicago Evening Journal,* November 7, 8, 1864; John W. Headley, *Confederate Operations in Canada and New York* (New York, 1906), pp. 285–86, 299–300; Benn Pitman, ed., *The Trials for Treason at Indianapolis, Disclosing the Plans for Establishing a North-Western Confederacy* (Cincinnati, 1865), especially pp. 336–39.

[111] See pp. 169–70.

tending on the Republican ticket against Cyrus H. McCormick, the Democratic nominee, for the post of Congressman from the First District, was bitterly attacked by the labor press. "Will you vote for a man who, when mayor of this city, declared that fifty cents was a fair day's wages for a fair day's work?" asked the *Working-man's Advocate* in an effort to prove that Wentworth would grind under the heel of the well-to-do all who were "poor and unfortunate." [112] McCormick had squared himself with union labor at the outset of the campaign, because he had answered the *Advocate's* queries to candidates in the confident tone of a man who knew that "money and work were equally necessary to each other," addressing other men of like mind.[113]

The contest between Wentworth and McCormick was one of the high spots of the campaign. It deepened the lines between Republicans and Democrats and emphasized in colorful terms the platforms upon which they stood. The *Workingman's Advocate* hounded Wentworth with charges that unsavory combinations and money saved from "the sanitary fair and draft fund" were being used to win the *Journal* to his support. With Republicanism thus impaled, the *Tribune* came to his defense. It pointedly declared that $4,000 was the price the *Advocate* had asked for its support of the proposed candidacy of Charles Walker for Congress, but that this labor journal had eventually given its endorsement to the rich manufacturer, Cyrus McCormick. The inference was clear.

The *Times* added what it could to the *Advocate's* thrusts against the politically versatile Wentworth. He was accused of refusing poor relief when mayor during the panic of 1857; he was assailed as an enemy of the Germans of the city; his patriotism was chal-

---

[112] *The Chicago Times*, November 7, 1864; *Chicago Evening Journal*, September 7, 1864; *The Workingman's Advocate*, September 17, November 5, 1864. In an editorial on "The Town Bull," the *Advocate*, November 5, declared: "We have already suggested in a plain way to workingmen (what everybody who has watched Wentworth's administrations knew before) that John Wentworth ground to death, degradation and infamy every person who was unfortunate enough to break the laws and had not money enough to bribe his under-officers, or influence enough to help elect Wentworth to office. We have notified the people how he kept up a continued stench in the public nostrils by a system of 'pulling' small houses of low unfortunates and petty gaming houses of negroes, and others who had little money, and no votes or influence, while first class prostitutes and fancy gambling houses, where rich men reveled in vice, were protected, and allowed to flourish in the very heart of the city . . . with perfect impunity."

[113] *The Workingman's Advocate*, September 17, 1864.

lenged on the score that he had not contributed to the draft funds of the city. But McCormick's stand regarding an early peace, his alleged support of Breckinridge in 1860, and his financial assistance to the Democratic party militated against him with an electorate blinded by war's partisanship. In spite of radical labor's support, the reaper king lost. Voters rushed onto the Wentworth band wagon, and the Democrats could only console themselves in this defeat, as in the results of the election in general — that their mission was now to realize an early peace.[114]

The wish for peace was to be realized sooner than the Democracy had thought. Union military successes in the winter of 1865 forced the South to bow in despair before the conquerors from the North. On April 3, Richmond fell into the hands of Union forces, and Chicago spent the night in revelry and celebration. One short week later the news of Lee's surrender had been rung out by the Court House bell to a waiting city. Quickly the crowds gathered to read the " special sheet " distributed by the press; and cheers and shouts of joy, mingled with the strains of the Doxology, released the pent-up feelings of a war-tired people. At midnight the Dearborn Light Artillery boomed forth one hundred rounds, and by dawn the streets were filled with a jubilant populace. Merchants opened their places of business only to shut them; the courts adjourned early in the morning; banks and schools closed; and night forsook darkness and silence in fireworks, bonfires, booming cannon, and shouting parades.[115]

But these manifestations of joy soon turned to mourning. At four o'clock on the morning of April 15, Chicago heard that Abraham Lincoln had been assassinated. Flags, which a few days before had been unfurled from public buildings in ungoverned joy, soon rested at half mast; civilians cast aside the small flags, " stuck jauntily into their caps," for rosettes of white and black upon the breast and bands of crape upon the arm; the Board of Trade departed from their black-draped rooms; law courts adjourned; places of amusement and saloons did not open. Even the *Times* was mindful of

[114] *The Chicago Times,* November 7, 16, 1864; *Chicago Tribune,* September 18, 19, November 4, 1864; *Chicago Evening Journal,* November 11, 1864; *The Workingman's Advocate,* November 5, 1864; Hutchinson, *op. cit.,* II, 41, 42, 58–60.

[115] Chicago Tribune, *Annual Review, 1865,* pp. 14–15; *Chicago Tribune,* April 10, 11, 1865.

the loss sustained, for Lincoln's course in Southern restoration was already recognized to be conciliatory, whereas that of his successor was an uncertainty. On the nineteenth when funeral services were held in Washington, Chicago paused in her mad commercial race and devoted herself to church attendance and the passing of resolutions by assembled citizens. On May 2, the body of the dead President was escorted by at least forty thousand Chicagoans through muddy streets to the Court House, where a crowd estimated at one hundred twenty-five thousand saw his remains. In the minds of many, John Wilkes Booth was not solely to blame; to them it appeared that the South had unleashed the emotional forces which had laid Lincoln low. The years to come were to witness Chicago participating in a dreary and vindictive punishment of those held guilty of the "infernal rebellion." [116]

Four days after Lincoln's assassination, saddened Chicagoans went to the polls and cast their votes for city officers. The *Tribune* reminded them that choice lay between the enemies and the friends of "the martyred Abraham Lincoln," and that a vote against Republican candidates meant that Chicago would "cover herself with ignominy." The results of the election prevented that. Mayor John B. Rice, local theatrical manager, the recipient of a large majority, with twenty-four councilmen of the Union faith and eight Democrats, took charge of the government of the city.[117] A well-oiled machine in November also brought success in the county election, putting to rout the candidates of a soldiers' party, whose motto, "soldiers before politicians," if not the party itself, was destined to appear for many years at each succeeding election.[118]

Lincoln's death had raised to the presidency Andrew Johnson, his vice-president. An early pronouncement from the new chief executive that he would not pursue a policy which would prevent the punishment of the South brought him the praise of radical Republicans. "We ask not vengeance, but the justice which Abraham Lincoln's clemency would have withheld," said the *Tribune*. To this antagonist of the South, Illinois' election promised a reconstruction to its liking. "Johnson's little finger will prove thicker than

---

[116] *Ibid.*, April 16, 18, 19, 20, May 2, 3, 1865; *The Chicago Times*, April 17, 1865.

[117] *Chicago Tribune*, April 18, 19, 1865. Francis C. Sherman was the Democratic candidate for mayor to succeed himself.

[118] *Ibid.*, November 1, 6–8, 10, 11, 1865.

were Abraham Lincoln's loins," it significantly pointed out. "While he whipped them gently with cords, his successor will scourge them with a whip of scorpions. . . . There will be thorough work made of those who hatched and led the rebellion." [119]

But Johnson's proclamation on May 29 revealed his plan of restoration as essentially like Lincoln's. It roused disappointment and distrust. By July, disapproval had become clamorous. To men still laboring under a war psychosis it did not matter whether Southerners worked or died. Why should not these "traitors" either "dig or starve," for there were pick and shovel if hunger pricked. "Many a better woman" than Mrs. Jefferson Davis had worked for a living by taking in sewing. And why should the government furnish rations for General Lee, who had slain its citizens by the tens of thousands? Far better would it be for the country to cut him from the list of recipients or feed him in some penitentiary where his work in hammering stone would be some small compensation for the bread he ate. Perhaps, suggested the *Tribune,* he might prefer "to tote paper" in its press rooms, a job he might have if no Union soldier cared for it. Thus in Chicago, as in the North in general, an emotionally unbalanced victor thought of the restoration of the South in terms of revenge and fury. [120]

The openly expressed relief of the Democrats at the President's declarations soon convinced radicals that Johnson meant to abandon Republican support for Southern favor. Press and pulpit conspired to persuade Chicagoans that to Southerners should be meted out the punishment deserved by "fiends" and the followers of that "venomous creature," Jeff Davis. [121] If, for a moment, the flames of vengeance might have died down, satirical and unfriendly reports in the press or words spoken by men of the cloth served to rekindle them. In the winter of 1865–66, the *Tribune* sent its special correspondent, Sidney Andrews, through the Carolinas and Georgia. In the columns of the *Boston Advertiser* and his Chicago paper he ventilated his views on Southern life as he saw it — a life in which uncleanliness was general, where ignorance was the lot of both

[119] *Ibid.,* April 17, 18, 1865.

[120] *Ibid.,* May 31, June 30, July 10, 1865; F. A. Eastman to Lyman Trumbull, January 4, 1866, *Trumbull Papers,* LXII.

[121] *The Chicago Times,* February 20, 21, 23, 24, 1866; *Chicago Tribune,* April 17, May 15, 1865, February 6, 1866; *The Irish Republic,* May 11, 1867; *The Christian Times* [Baptist], April 13, 20, 27, 1865.

Negroes and white men, and where labor was disdained. When shortly afterwards Midwesterners read Andrews' book, *The South Since the War,* which reflected the same views as his newspaper articles, blood pressures rose to a dangerous high. His advocacy of a military control of the South met the approval of his readers, who with him desired that "justice be not overborne," and that reconstruction be pushed forward slowly.[122]

On January 5, 1866, Senator Trumbull, chairman of the Judiciary Committee, introduced a civil rights bill and a bill to continue and enlarge the powers of the Freedmen's Bureau. Designed to care for the civil and physical wants of the emancipated Negroes, these bills were generally endorsed by Republicans who also gave approval to Congressional reconstruction. When President Johnson's veto of the Freedmen's Bureau Bill became known in Chicago, Germans, who already had begun to doubt the wisdom of unswerving devotion to Republicanism, met in the German Workingmen's Hall in protest. Other irate and disappointed citizens assembled at the old Board of Trade Hall to voice their disapproval of Johnson's acts and to make declarations in favor of the Congressional plan of reconstruction. In April, the Civil Rights Bill was passed over a presidential veto. Heartened by this success another Freedmen's Bureau Bill was brought before Congress. It too was vetoed by Johnson, but both houses joined in overriding the President's objections.[123]

In both Senate and House, Chicago representatives had voted to override Johnson's veto of the Civil Rights Bill, thereby joining those opposed to the program of the President. Thus they bowed to the wish of radical Republicanism; thus they held that they had done their part in preventing the outcome of the war from being "blasted and nullified by the perverseness of the executive." Their reward came in the fall election. Throughout the summer and autumn canvass, the acts of Johnson were scrutinized by eyes inflamed by a persisting and infectious war hatred. Impeachment of the President was common talk.[124]

---

[122] Sidney Andrews, *The South Since the War* . . . (Boston, 1866), especially pp. 87, 111, 222–27, 390, 400.

[123] United States, *Senate Journal,* 39 Cong., 1 sess., p. 62; *Cong. Globe,* 39 Cong., 1 sess., pp. 421, 688, 936–43, 1679–81, 1809, 1861, 2743, 3850, 3842; *Chicago Tribune,* February 6, 24, 27, 1866.

[124] United States, *Senate Journal,* 39 Cong., 1 sess., p. 317; United States, *House Journal,*

Upon this antagonism to the chief executive, county, state, and Congressional officers rode into power, garnering, in several cases, two or three times the number of votes cast for the opposition. The Republicans had wooed the soldier vote by naming, among others, General John A. Logan as Congressman at large, Major A. F. Stevenson and General J. S. Reynolds as representatives in the state legislature, and General John L. Beveridge as sheriff. The Irish vote, on which the Republicans could seldom count, had been assiduously sought also. On August 15, the Fenian Brotherhood gathered at Haas's Park in what was described as the "Liberty Birthday of the Brotherhood." Beveridge presided, while Governor Richard Oglesby not only criticized President Johnson's reconstruction policy but belabored the British government both for its attitude toward Ireland and for its support of the Confederacy. The Fenians listened also to Schuyler Colfax, Speaker of the House of Representatives, who liked Johnson not a whit better than did Oglesby, and who with Oglesby played upon the Irish dislike of the President because of his attitude toward the invasion of Canada by the Fenians. But the Irish found the Democrats equally willing to join in their lamentations regarding their homeland.[125]

The Democrats sought support also from conservative Republicans who had not deserted Johnson. There were in Chicago men like Charles H. Ray, now retired from the *Tribune* staff, who could not uphold a policy of visiting upon the South a punishment born of vindictiveness. Political guillotines seemed to them the designs of a partisanship destined to postpone the swift conciliation they so much desired. Negro suffrage they regarded as "the final penal enactment for the punishment of the South," and they opposed those who advocated that the freedmen have all rights accorded others under the Constitution.[126]

But moderates in the Republican ranks and Democrats were met with the unflinching and determined opposition of radical Repub-

---

39 Cong., 1 sess., p. 528; *Chicago Tribune*, February 21, August 15, October 18, November 9, 1866.

125 C. M. Hawley to Lyman Trumbull, July 1, 1866, Norman Judd to Trumbull, July 11, 1866, *Trumbull Papers*, LXVII, LXVIII; *Chicago Tribune*, August 16, 30, October 20, November 9, 13, 1866; *The Irish Republic*, May 11, 1867. For important selections in the 1866 election see Appendix, p. 508.

126 C. H. Ray to J. R. Doolittle, May 24, 1866 (*Ms.* Chicago Historical Society); *Chicago Tribune*, January 4, 1866.

A HISTORY OF CHICAGO

licans. To men convinced that arming "white rebels" with the ballot and denying the same right to "loyal Negroes" were rank injustice, Johnson's policy of restoration seemed devoid of patriotism and party loyalty. By December, 1866, when Congress assembled, antagonism toward the President had reached such a pitch that some men would be satisfied with nothing short of his impeachment. Joining hands with Thaddeus Stevens, Wentworth cried out against a chief executive whom he described as a wolf who went upstream and stirred up the water so that it was unfit for the lamb [Congress] to drink.[127]

With a not unwarranted elation at the success of the November elections, the radicals set about to push through their program of national reconstruction. Trumbull, returned to the Senate, joined with those voting to override the President's veto of the Reconstruction Bill of February, 1867, and the supplementary legislation. Although he acquiesced at this moment in an acceptance of the Fourteenth Amendment, he was, undoubtedly, not as wholehearted in his support as were some of his Illinois colleagues.[128]

Animus toward the South rather than community concerns won the spring municipal contest for the Republicans. Mayor Rice, in spite of his opposition in 1866 to the demands of labor for an eight-hour day, was re-elected over Francis C. Sherman, war Democrat and mayor 1862–1865. A vote for Sherman, his opponents declared, would be a vote to obstruct reconstruction in the South "on the basis of equal suffrage and equal rights." Striking closer home, the Republicans played upon the threat of increased taxes in case of a Democratic victory. Reductions in city expenses would be achieved by Sherman, they asserted, only if the workers of the city were laid off by a suspension of labor on sewers, water and street improvements, and by a cut in the pay of policemen and firemen.[129] Gossips repeated the story circulated in 1863 that the North Chicago City Railway Company had offered Sherman $10,000 worth of stock as an advance reward for an ordinance permitting a connection with the Chicago City Railway on North and South Clark streets. The use

[127] Cong. Globe, 39 Cong., 2 sess., pp. 139–40, 320–21.
[128] White, op. cit., pp. 293–99; Chicago Tribune, January 13, 1867.
[129] Ibid., April 16, 17, 1867; The Chicago Times, April 15, 1867.

of the rumor as a political tool was not always countered by the statement that even the *Tribune,* organ of the opposition, had doubted its truth at the time of its inception.[130] The alleged use of money in the election by the North Chicago City Railway Company to prevent the re-election of Alderman Samuel Shackford of the Fifteenth Ward and company dictation of employee votes marked the day when public utilities and city politics had apparently established a mutually advantageous friendship.[131]

Good majorities for most Republican officials characterized the county election in November. Although local in nature, Republican forces declared the example of Chicago might have national influence, and they pointed to their demonstration of gratitude to the "boys in blue" from whom they had chosen nearly half their candidates.[132] It was, in their eyes, the sign of a patriot to vote for those who had fought in the war, and not to do so stamped one as disloyal.

But by spring, a fighting Democracy caused much worry in the ranks of Republicanism, although the Democrats elected only seven of the seventeen aldermen chosen in this election, and the council had a Republican majority.[133] The contest was focused on the issues of the war, now three years in the past. The success of the Democrats the Republicans laid in part to the widespread and frequently illegal naturalization of foreigners by a clerk of the Recorder's Court, which increased the number casting votes for "Copperheadism."[134] But the Democrats, in turn, declared their victory would have been greater had the Republicans not engaged in stuffing ballot boxes, made possible through boards of election judges of one party, contrary to custom. Although the office of alderman provided no salary, the race was keen. Charges of the outright purchase of votes by candidates themselves and by interested business organizations, including dealers in school textbooks, were heard on all sides. But in

---

[130] The purported contract between Sherman and the railway companies is printed in full in the *Chicago Tribune,* April 14, 1867. See also *ibid.,* December 7, 1863, July 15, 1864.

[131] *Ibid.,* April 18, 1867.

[132] *Ibid.,* November 3, 5, 6, 7, 1867.

[133] *Ibid.,* April 22, 1868; *The Chicago Times,* April 24, 1868.

[134] *Chicago Tribune,* April 19, 22, 23, 1868; *The Chicago Times,* April 23, 1868. Among the successful candidates were two Democrats, William McAllister as Judge of the Recorder's Court and Daniel O'Hara as clerk. O'Hara, who was charged prior to the election with issuing naturalization papers fraudulently, was to emerge in the 'seventies as one of the leading local Democratic politicians. *Chicago Tribune,* April 22, 1868.

a day when defalcations and malfeasance in office had become almost a habit, such reports fell on deaf ears.[135]

Similar conditions existed in the state legislature where "stealing" was reported a "fine art." Rings for plunder directed their attention, among other things, to the construction of a new state house, an industrial university, a bill incorporating the Casino Park Association in Chicago, the Illinois Southern Penitentiary, a new Chicago horse railroad, a Chicago Dock and Pier Company, and the exploitation of convict labor by lessors at the state prison at Joliet. In the case of the Chicago Dock and Pier Company alone, the *Tribune* believed that the city would be robbed of $20,000,000 worth of property by a bill giving land to that organization. It was equally exercised by a proposed bill to grant the Washington Street Horse Railway the right to use the tunnel under the river. The rejection of a bribe of $25,000 of stock in the Washington Street Horse Railway by a senator of the Chicago district brought special comment from the *Tribune* reporter at Springfield.[136]

All these legislative measures, "clustered together like a bunch of grapes," played upon jealousies between northern and southern Illinois and thus retarded a public opinion which might have prevented like schemes in the future. Northern interests were under fire because of their stake in a proposal to build a lock and dam on the Illinois River and to create a Board of Canal Commissioners empowered either to make plans to extend the Illinois and Michigan Canal to the Mississippi River or to plan river improvements between Chicago and La Salle; and the "Southern Penitentiary swindle" served as grist for the mill of northern critics. The construction of a new state house, whose architect was John C. Cochrane of Chicago, created the greatest scandal. Press and pulpit united in berating the frailty of man displayed in such scheming.[137]

[135] *The Chicago Times*, April 23, 1868. See also *ibid.*, March 24, 25, 27, April 1, 7, 14, 1868. See also pp. 297–99.

[136] *Chicago Tribune*, February 18, 19, March 6, 1867, August 26, 1868. Chicago and Cook County were represented in the state senate by Francis A. Eastman and Jasper D. Ward; in the house by Lester L. Bond, Joseph S. Reynolds, H. M. Singer, M. W. Leavitt, H. M. Shepard, A. F. Stevenson. Fremont O. Bennett, comp., *Politics and Politicians of Chicago* . . . (Chicago, 1886), p. 606.

[137] *Chicago Tribune*, March 6, 1867; Act of February 28, 1867, *Public Laws, 1867,* pp. 81–86; Cole, *The Era of the Civil War,* pp. 405–8. The act creating the Board of Canal Commissioners was made a dead letter by the refusal of the senate to confirm Governor Oglesby's appointments to the board. *Ibid.*, pp. 407–8; " Reports of a Special Committee ap-

The liquor traffic rendered rich rewards to officials who were willing to accept bribes from those wanting to evade the tax of $2.00 a gallon on whiskey. It was common knowledge that a "whiskey ring" operated with apparent immunity. By 1867, a great deal of whiskey was said to pass untaxed, and it was reported that "large quantities of alcohol" dispatched from New York and elsewhere and sold in Chicago privately at low rates were seized "almost daily." In Chicago and Peoria, too, whiskey made rich those who dealt in its manufacture and distribution. When a new law, passed in 1868, reduced the tax to fifty cents a gallon to be paid by distillers before the removal of their product, and provided for supervisors of internal revenue, the *Tribune* applauded.[138] That paper was likewise pleased with the levy made on tobacco and chronicled its belief that bribery would thereafter be more difficult and more expensive because of the greater number of officials required by the new law. But wholesale manufacturers and retailers of tobacco were not so enthusiastic and drafted resolutions protesting the placing of stamps on their stock at the time prescribed.[139]

A public mind diseased and distorted by looseness in public morals and by the practices of war thus could condone the partisan spirit which brought about the impeachment trial of President Johnson. By late February feeling in Chicago was running so high that the Common Council was emboldened to vote two to one for conviction;[140] and an impassioned assembly loudly applauded Charles V.

pointed to examine into the Management of the Illinois Agricultural College," Illinois, *Reports, 1869*, I, 523–28; "Report of the Committee of Investigation from House of Representatives, Illinois, to inquire into the affairs of the New State House," Illinois, *Reports, 1871*, I, 913–1113; "Report of the Joint Committee appointed to Investigate into the Discipline, Management, and Financial Condition of the Illinois State Penitentiary, at Joliet, January 24, 1872," *ibid.*, II, 645–711; "Report of the Committee on Printing, House of Representatives, February 27, 1869," Illinois, *Reports, 1869*, I, 31–32.

138 Government detectives were stationed in Chicago and received in addition to their pay one-half the fines they collected from parties convicted. *Chicago Tribune*, January 26, 1867, July 18, 1868; U. S. Vidocq [Franklin Eliot Felton], *The Secrets of Internal Revenue* (Philadelphia, 1870), pp. 54, 55, 197.

139 *Chicago Tribune*, July 18, November 18, 1868. The law required revenue stamps on tobacco products and announced that on January 1, 1869, all smoking and chewing tobacco, after April 1, 1869, all cigars, and after July 1, 1869, "all other manufactured tobacco" of every description would be considered as having been manufactured since July, 1868, and hence be subject to revenue tax. Tobacco dealers said the tobacco turnover was not that fast and that consequently much of their stock on which they had already paid the old tax would be subjected to a second tax.

140 The resolution was introduced by Arthur Dixon and was adopted February 24, 1868. *Ibid.*, February 25, 1868; Chicago, *Common Council Proceedings, 1867–68*, p. 370.

Dyer, Isaac N. Arnold, E. C. Larned, the Rev. R. M. Hatfield, and others who demanded that Johnson be made to pay for his opposition to Congressional reconstruction.[141]

The Illinois delegation, however, was not united in sentiment. In the House, Norman B. Judd from the First District, with other radicals including Congressman at large John A. Logan,[142] cried for impeachment. But Lyman Trumbull, joining six other Republicans in the Senate, refused to be carried away by mob psychology despite pressure from politicians, electorate, a partisan press, and even the church itself. But even when nerves were most tense the *Tribune,* to the surprise of some, protested against " any warfare by the party " on any senator constrained to vote in opposition to conviction. " To denounce such Senators as corrupt, to assail them with contumely and upbraid them with treachery for failing to understand the law in the same light as their assailants, would be unfortunate folly, to call it by the mildest term," declared the editor.[143]

That Johnson would not be convicted the *Tribune* had prophesied in early May. When the final vote was recorded, it joined moderates throughout the country and rationalized the acquittal for its radical readers by pointing out that Johnson's successor could have accomplished little in the few months he would have served and would only have been blamed for failure to accomplish more.[144]

The trial had taken place when presidential nominees for the election of 1868 were being considered. General Grant appeared to some Republicans the only person who could unravel the tangled threads of the vexing problems of the day. " Grant for President " clubs among native and foreign born organized sentiment for their candidate. They proved pillars of strength both before and after his nomination May 21 at Chicago. That the Republican party alone could perpetuate the liberties of the people and preserve the unity of America became again the text of Republican editorials and Republican campaign speeches.

[141] *Chicago Tribune,* February 26, 1868; see *The Chicago Times, passim,* particularly April 11, 1868, for opposing view.

[142] Logan moved to Chicago in 1871.

[143] *Cong. Globe,* 40 Cong., 2 sess., pp. 1351–53, 1396, supplement, pp. 417–20; White, *op. cit.,* pp. 317–19; *Chicago Tribune,* May 14, 15, 1868.

[144] *Ibid.,* May 2, 6, 11, 12, 13, 14, June 18, 1868.

Chicagoans liked the platform with its pledge to continue reconstruction and the Congressional guarantee of equal suffrage of " all loyal men at the south "; they rejoiced in the reiterated hostility to Johnson and in the commendation given the " thirty-five Senators " who pronounced him guilty. In the words of the *Tribune,* these articles of faith were " a living, moving, breathing platform," in spite of the omission of a plank on the tariff, about which Chicagoans of all political creeds were much concerned.[145]

During the war, Chicago Republicans had, in the name of patriotism, accepted high tariff rates. The bill in 1866, because it failed to reduce rates, revived in Chicago the attitude prevalent in the 'forties and 'fifties toward duties not solely for revenue as tending to favor the manufacturing classes of the East. Even the few Westerners not openly hostile to the principle of protection felt that a continuation of high tariff rates would create dissatisfaction among the masses, particularly laborers and farmers. To most Chicagoans, the bill of 1866 which again raised rates was designed as " a corrupt scheme of public plunder to put hundreds of millions into the pockets of those who have stocks of goods on hand." [146]

True to American custom and practice, these Midwestern antiprotectionists, therefore, formed an association to implement their conviction that " men should have the right to exercise their industry, to dispose of its fruits in any market " which to them seemed best, and " with the proceeds to buy whatever and wherever " they pleased. Under the name of the Free Trade League, this association opposed the demands of capitalists; it protested against the " paternal interference of Government with private pursuits "; and it took to its arms men of both parties whose economic aspirations for the moment outweighed political traditions of mutual distrust.[147]

[145] *Ibid.,* November 24, 1867, January 1, 20, March 10, May 20, 22, 26, August 1, 10, October 27, 1868.

[146] *Ibid.,* March 23, June 27, 1861, November 27, 1865, January 30, February 2, 9, 21, 1867; E. C. Larned to Lyman Trumbull, July 2, 1866, J. Medill to Trumbull, July 1, 1866, Horace White to Trumbull, July 5, 1866, *Trumbull Papers,* LXVII, LXVIII.

[147] *Chicago Tribune,* January 5, 17, 1866. The League had for its president Dr. Charles H. Ray, Republican; Thomas Hoyne, old-time Democrat and during the war a war Democrat as a vice-president; Andrew Carr Cameron, one-time member of the *Times* staff and later in charge of the *Workingman's Advocate,* the radical labor paper, was recording secretary; George W. Rust, of the *Times* and probably a Democrat, was corresponding secretary; Robert Clark, Republican, and James W. Sheahan, Douglas Democrat and in 1866 editor of the *Chicago Republican,* were members of the executive committee.

The League's activities were so vigorous that about five thousand businessmen of the city allied themselves against it and formed the Industrial Union to promote the theory of protection.[148] Had these Republican Midwesterners been consistent, they might well have openly endorsed the tariff plank in the Democratic platform of 1868, which declared for a tariff for revenue upon imports and such incidental protection to domestic manufactures as would, without impairing the revenue, impose the least burden upon and best encourage the great industrial interests of the country. But to have acknowledged kinship with the Democracy even on what was so vital an issue would have seemed to the radical Republicans little short of treason.

Other planks in the Democratic platform provoked bitter controversy in a partisan press. This was especially true of the stand taken on the payment of wartime bonds in greenbacks. The *Tribune* chose to interpret this proposal as "repudiation," a line of argument which the *Times* indignantly characterized as "a monstrous attempt to deceive and impose on the people," since, it asserted, the government had not agreed to pay the principal of the debt exclusively in gold. Instead of "gold for the bond-holder," advised the paper, let the cry be "God and Pendleton's plan for the people."[149] The Democratic nomination of Horatio Seymour of New York, representative of the sound-money theories of the East, for the presidency, comforted the Republican press in that it seemed to make clear the hopelessness of Pendletonism. But Seymour appealed to western sympathies by announcing his opposition to the contraction of the currency, and the Democratic press of Chicago gave enthusiastic support to both the platform and the candidates.[150]

The campaign was enlivened by Tanner Clubs patterned after the Wide Awakes of the early 'sixties. By September, enthusiastic young Republicans lighted the streets in their torchlight parades to demonstrate their will to put the "tanner" in the White House.

148 *Ibid.*, February 22, 1866. Among those connected with the organization were George Armour, of the Armour, Dole and Co., grain elevators; Roselle M. Hough, of R. M. and O. S. Hough and Co., pork and beef packers; Rollin Sherman, commission merchant; and Joseph Medill of the *Tribune*.

149 *Ibid.*, April 24, July 8, 10, August 19, 1868; *The Chicago Times*, July 5, 1868.

150 United States, *House Journal*, 39 Cong., 1 sess., p. 458; United States, *Senate Journal*, 39 Cong., 1 sess., p. 322; *Chicago Tribune*, April 17, September 4, 5, 8, 16, 19, 23, October 22, 28, 1868.

Uniformed in oilcloth cape and cap and tanner's apron, the Tanners at times suffered competition from the "White Boys in Blue," campaigning for Seymour and Blair. Faithful to the Democracy these too lighted the streets of Chicago with "transparencies," as they marched with banners announcing the canons of their political faith: "Let the Niggers Pay for their Own Soup," "No Nigger Voting," and "White Supremacy." Although the greater number of the "White Boys in Blue" was said by the *Tribune* to be Irish, the Republicans were not averse to receiving Irishmen into their own clubs. This was not always accomplished easily, for Democrats, said to be active in the Ku Klux Klan, did not hesitate to oppose, with physical force if need be, attempts to alienate those they held were of their blood and of their political faith.[151]

During the summer Chicagoans listened to Carl Schurz, Charles Ladd of Massachusetts, Lyman Trumbull, and General Grant, as well as state and local Republican celebrities. They heard also the counterblasts of the Democrats, as Senator James R. Doolittle of Wisconsin, Horatio Seymour, and his running mate, Francis P. Blair, Jr., joined in condemning Johnson's impeachment, Congressional reconstruction, and "black rule in the South."[152]

From May 28 to November 12, a campaign weekly published by the *Tribune* reported the principal happenings not only for residents of Chicago but for the whole Northwest. The same presses turned out campaign documents. Root and Cady, musical publishers, distributed a rallying song, "It is an Age of Progress," and H. M. Higgins in "a stirring" song and chorus, "We'll Win Every Time," recounted the "glorious deeds" of "the brave boys in blue."

Despite operations of a "blackleg ring" in Wall Street, alleged to have locked up $20,000,000 in currency to depress stocks and create a business crisis, the Republicans won in the state and nation. A partisan press in Chicago rejoiced that "the temporary disgrace" of the municipal election of the spring had been removed, and that the Democratic party and the Irish had ceased "to be one and the same thing in Chicago." So great was the Republican victory that the *Tribune* felt impelled to speak a word of caution as to the

151 *Ibid.*, August 28, 29, September 5, 29, October 3, 4, 11, 1868.
152 *Ibid.*, July 16, August 14, 30, September 20, 24, October 22, 24, 25, 26, 28, November 3, 1868.

dangers of a big and unwieldy majority in a government designed to be representative and democratic.[153]

About two months after the election, the state legislature assembled at Springfield bent on special legislation and shady activities similar to those of 1867. Ignoring the recommendations of Governor John M. Palmer, it jammed through another appropriation to the " penitentiary ring," an act for the transfer to the Illinois Central Railroad of " a portion of the submerged lands and lake park grounds lying on and adjacent to the shore of Lake Michigan, on the eastern frontage of the city of Chicago," and railroad legislation including rate regulation and the assignment of a portion of state taxes to provide for paying railroad debts of counties, townships, cities, and towns. It sought also to remedy defects in the 1867 act creating a Board of Canal Commissioners, and at the same time make the earlier law operative by an amendment more carefully limiting board authority and appropriating a maximum of $400,000 to build the lock and dam on the Illinois River and to dredge the mouth of the canal at La Salle.

In all of these bills, Chicagoans were deeply interested. They had objected to the system of leasing prison labor to private contractors and were glad to see the legislature of 1869 appropriate $300,000 for the penitentiary at Joliet. But in the act relating to the lake front lands, Chicago had an immediate concern, for it permitted the Illinois Central, the Chicago, Burlington and Quincy, and the Michigan Central railroads to pay only $800,000 for land valued at $2,600,000 or more. The governor's veto not only had stressed this important point for the citizens of Chicago but had expressed his objection to confirming " rights " to the Illinois Central without defining precisely what those rights were. He was of the opinion that the interest of Chicago in harbor development was not safeguarded in the bill because the railroad was not obligated to make improvements in the mile of lake bed which the act gave it.

The legislature's generosity in assigning a portion of state taxes for the payment of the debts incurred by governmental units hit Chicago especially hard, since the city had no railroad debt and was now forced to contribute, through the " tax-grab " law, to the payment of such obligations. Although rendered unconstitutional by

153 *Ibid.*, May 2, 20, 28, June 16, July 8, November 1, 4, 5, 1868.

the Constitutional Convention in 1870, the practice did not end until 1874 by virtue of a decision of the Illinois Supreme Court.[154]

As in the previous session, the people of the state welcomed the day of adjournment of a legislature the *Tribune* held "reckless beyond precedent," and one in which lobbying for special interests had run without restraint.[155]

This looseness of official morals was found also in city and county governments. Headed by Roswell B. Mason for mayor, a citizens' or "People's Ticket," to overthrow "the ring" and to restore Chicago to decent government, was swept into power in November, 1869, in the first autumn mayoralty contest. To Mason and his ticket radical labor gave valiant support. Endorsed by many of the best citizens and by practically the entire press, the People's ticket did not, however, permanently transform the political morals of the city.[156]

Charges of graft in the Common Council multiplied during the next few years. Excessive appropriations to extend the park system, made in committee of the whole, led the *Tribune* to characterize the majority "as dishonest and corrupt as any that has ever disgraced any municipal government." The newspaper urged Mayor Mason to exert his influence and power to put an end to such "ravages." That executive was, in the opinion of the *Tribune,* equal to the best the city had ever had. But the honest minority, which seemed barely able to exist in the company of the council ring called "McCauley's Nineteen," were unable to block bloated appropriation bills, and it was seldom that nominations made outside "the ring" got aldermanic confirmation.[157]

[154] *Ibid.,* March 5, 1869; Illinois, *Senate Journal, 1869,* II, 152, 735, 876, 922; Illinois, *House Journal, 1869,* III, 282–83, 638, 659; Illinois, *Reports, 1869,* II, 1053–67, 1069–75; Acts of February 25, March 10, 11, April 16, 1869, *Public Laws, 1869,* pp. 60, 309–12, 31, 245–48, 316–21. See pp. 75–76. For resolution on lake front question, see Pierce, *A History of Chicago,* III, in preparation.

[155] *Chicago Tribune,* March 2, April 17, 1869.

[156] *The Workingman's Advocate,* October 16, November 13, 1869; *Chicago Tribune,* September 25, October-November 3, 1869.

[157] On June 21, 1871, the council in a preliminary vote decided to buy from Sam Walker and others land which they wished to annex to Union Park from Warren to Madison. The sum of $100,000 was to be the first payment on an indefinite sum. (*Ibid.,* June 23, 24, 25, 27, 29, July 1, 24, 26, August 1, 4, 9, 16, 23, October 5, 1871.) "McCauley's Nineteen" in the council, 1870–71, was alleged to exact "ample pecuniary consideration" from applicants for any favor which the council might bestow. Several members were swept out of office in the 1871 election, but enough remained to organize a new ring of thirteen Republicans and eight Democrats. *The Chicago Times,* December 14, 1871.

Individually and collectively the Common Council laid themselves open to charges of accepting and even of soliciting bribes. The *Tribune* complained that Chicago suffered as did New York from Tammany, Tweed, and Sweeney. Among the charges leveled at the notorious " McCauley's Nineteen " was release from the contract of a foundryman for the consideration of $2,500.[158] Candidates for office paid tribute to attain their goals,[159] individuals and corporations dependent upon city legislation purchased privileges desired,[160] a newspaper could buy the corporation printing job,[161] and the taxpayers' money went into purchases made by the council at higher than the minimum bid.[162] Appointments connected with the police power of the city were disposed of with unconscionable callousness by " the ring," made up of thirteen Republicans and eight Democrats, who met in caucus.[163]

The Cook County Board of Supervisors also fell into evil ways.

[158] *Chicago Tribune*, December 14, 1871; *The Chicago Times*, December 14, 1871, January 1, 1872. The *Times* said that in voting for local improvements some aldermen received $250 to $4,000 for their votes. (*Ibid.*, January 1, 1872.) " Two citizens " informed the *Tribune* that " a direct and unequivocal demand was made upon them for money." *Chicago Tribune*, December 14, 1871.

[159] For example, Louis Amberg, reported the *Times*, was told by Alderman George Powell that " it would cost him something " to get the office of clerk of the West Side Police Court. Amberg, according to the *Times*, told the alderman that " he would not bleed worth a cent." William Baragwanath, leading candidate for boiler inspector, refused to pay $500 to Powell, and Fritz Metzke, the candidate of the *Staats-Zeitung*, was awarded the job. (*The Chicago Times*, December 14, 1871.) Metzke was a hat and cap maker. *Ibid.*, December 15, 1871.

[160] A bribe of $40,000 was said to have been paid the council by the Chicago Gas Light and Coke Company to prevent the creation of a rival gas company on the South Side. (*Ibid.*) Later when the grand jury investigated this allegation, the officials were suddenly called out of town. *Chicago Tribune*, January 15, 1872.

[161] *The Chicago Times*, December 14, 1871. In the case of the city printing the *Mail* and the *Republican* charged bribery when the work was awarded the *Evening Post*. The *Post* had not been a sponsor of the People's ticket of 1869. Joseph B. McCullagh of the *Republican* asserted that J. J. McGrath of the Fifteenth Ward and George Powell of the Ninth Ward wanted a bribe of $2,500 if the newspaper were to continue to do the corporation's business. McCullagh also declared that twenty-one aldermen signified that he could have their votes if he paid. The *Times* asserted that the editor of the *Post* offered a $3,000 bribe on the night of election. *Ibid.*, December 14, 1871.

[162] For instance, the question of a site for a proposed South Side pumping works was referred to a council committee of nine. C. C. P. Holden reported in favor of purchasing a lot on Loomis Street for about fifty-nine cents a square foot. John H. McAvoy and G. S. Whitaker favored the Hilliard Hopkinson lots recommended by the Board of Public Works at forty-six and one-half cents a square foot. J. J. McGrath, Alexander Bengley, George Powell, Edward Kehoe, and James McCauley favored the purchase of the O'Neill lot costing $1.06 per square foot. *Chicago Tribune*, November 1, 1870.

[163] *The Chicago Times*, December 14, 1871; *Chicago Tribune*, December 16, 1871.

This the *Tribune* attributed to the overwhelming Republican majority of November, 1868, which led officials to believe they had "a perpetual lease" on appointments. "Forthwith they entered upon a grand system of plunder and of personal aggrandisement," declared the editor. In spite of the reform election the next year, it was not a matter of surprise to the *Tribune* that the chairman had the temerity to vote for the location of a normal school in Englewood after receiving the gift of a lot.[164] What went on behind the scenes when these "brokers" met was, of course, sometimes a matter of conjecture. It seemed a grand era of acquisition. Citizens sometimes wondered why aldermen so frantically sought re-election to an office in which there was no salary.

Eventually the corruption became so flagrant that a grand jury was impaneled to investigate the bulging contents of strong boxes in John Buehler's bank. Incriminating evidence brought about the indictment of aldermen Busse, Glade, Bailey, Carney, Powell, Clarke, and McGrath, and ex-aldermen Whitaker, McCauley, Hildreth, Robinson, Montgomery, Walsh, and Sheil, of whom four, Busse, Glade, Montgomery, and Walsh, were convicted and sentenced to serve six months in the county jail and pay a fine of one hundred dollars. McCauley, Powell, and Busse on a second charge were acquitted by an instructed verdict, and charges against others of the "ring" were either dismissed or forgotten.[165]

The Congressional and state campaign of 1870 witnessed the anomaly of John Wentworth entering the arena, at the behest of the *Tribune,* to represent the First District in Congress as an independent Democrat. In the contest for nomination on the Republican ticket Joseph Medill had been worsted by Charles B. Farwell, a situation which brought upon the *Tribune* the charge of poor sportsmanship when it came out for "Long John," also supported by radical labor. Farwell, like the Republican candidates for the other Congressional, state, and county offices, won by a comfortable majority in the November election. This contest tended to outdistance in interest other political events of the year, although there had also been the judicial

164 *Ibid.,* March 10, 23, 1870.
165 *Ibid.,* December 17, 19, 30, 1871, January 20, 23, 27, February 1, 24, 25, March 3, 17, June 12, 1872; *The Chicago Times,* December 27, 30, 1871, January 6, 20, 23, 31, February 1, 2, 3, 10, 24, 29, 1872.

election in July. Of the three Circuit Court judges to be chosen the Republicans were successful in electing two. But a Democrat, Judge William McAllister, was named to the Illinois Supreme Court.

But the reform elements united the next year in selecting Medill to run as their representative for mayor on the " Fire Proof " ticket of 1871. No mayor had been faced with tasks of larger proportions, for in October of that year Chicago was leveled to the ground by the great fire. If Medill needed solace by service for the defeat in the Congressional nominating convention of 1870, he had it. His friends could console themselves also with the thought that their opponents and not they had sent a man to Washington to whom they ascribed a subserviency to " the ring." [166]

In the meantime, a constitutional convention met in December, 1869, to consider changes in the state document adopted in 1848. When discussions relating primarily to Chicago came up, representatives from the rural sections of Illinois engaged in forensics tinged with rancor. One of the chief concerns of the deliberators related to the suffrage for women and Negroes, as well as for incoming foreigners. The passage of the Fifteenth Amendment to the Federal Constitution served to solve difficulties relating to the Negro. Eventually, Illinois gave the franchise only to male citizens of the United States who were over twenty-one years of age and who had satisfied the residence requirements of one year in the state, ninety days in the county, and thirty days in the election district; to all electors of Illinois on April 1, 1848; and to foreigners who had " obtained a certificate of naturalization, before any court " in the state by January 1, 1870. The *Tribune* had early advocated the extension of suffrage to the Negro, and Joseph Medill, as a member of the convention, consistently stood by his earlier convictions. Other Republican leaders had been of like mind, and even some Chicago Democrats eventually came to accept and tolerate the idea. Temporarily, at least, the issue seemed closed. A proposal to submit to voters the question of woman suffrage was favorably considered in the convention but later abandoned, men being unable to bear the

---

[166] Bennett, *op. cit.,* pp. 135, 137; *The Workingman's Advocate,* October 29, 1870; *Chicago Tribune,* July 3, 10, October 30, 31, November 5, 7, 10, 1870. McAllister had run as an independent in the judicial election, but had been a life-long Democrat and was elected by Democratic votes. His election gave the Democrats a majority of four out of the seven seats in the court for the next nine years. *Ibid.,* June 29, July 3, 1870.

prospect of an old maid or widow tax collector or to picture women in the rôle of politician.[167]

Of far-reaching significance to Chicago were the regulations affecting the management of public warehouses and railroads and the constitutional provision which forbade the legislature to pass special legislation for cities. From the latter came the general incorporation law of 1872 and, in 1875, a new charter for Chicago. Assured by the *Tribune* that there was "more money to be saved and more rights protected by the adoption of the new Constitution" than would ever be at stake in a man's lifetime in Illinois, Chicagoans overwhelmingly approved the new document at the polls on July 2, 1870, by a vote of 19,575 to 216.[168]

The adoption of the constitution marked the belated recognition of problems which had been confronting the city for twenty years — years in which her citizens had turned their faces from the local scene to the great national struggle, in which local affairs of pressing importance had been subordinated to the issues of slavery, secession, and the preservation of the Union. Significant of the preoccupation with matters of national concern was the fact that although mayoralty elections during the early 'fifties had often been conducted without national party designations, after the agitation on the Kansas-Nebraska Act the contests were fought between national political parties, usually upon national rather than local issues. In the years 1861–70 the city wavered from her traditionally Democratic allegiance to elect three Republican mayors, two Democrats, and one belonging to the Citizens' party.[169]

As the decade of the 'seventies dawned, Chicago, like the rest of the North, although still waving the "bloody shirt" to maintain its hold on the electorate, heard occasionally a voice urging "a cessation of partisan turbulence." Some saw in the cultivation of happier relations with the defeated section a stimulus to business advance, and still others wished a restoration to a happy life of those who were also Americans.[170] There were those, too, who felt that, burdensome

[167] *Debates and Proceedings of the Constitutional Convention, 1869–1870,* II, 1286, 1290–94, 1309, 1725–26, 1873, 1878; *The Illustrated Chicago News,* May 29, 1868; *Chicago Tribune,* November 4, 1868, March 1, 1869, June 4, 1870. See pp. 66, 83–86, 185, 457.

[168] *Chicago Tribune,* June 26, July 4, 1870.

[169] See Appendix, pp. 506–7.

[170] *The Workingman's Advocate,* May 8, 1869; Document 645, 1868, *Common Council Documents.*

as were the problems of the reconstruction of the South, the re-establishment of honest and efficient local government in Chicago merited attention which had been diverted for too long a time. They raised the cry of political bossism as such local leaders as Anton C. Hesing and Daniel O'Hara emerged to dominate the German and Irish groups in political affairs. As they saw city aldermen "selected by ward bummers to represent ward bummers and their venal desires," critics ineffectually protested against such servants of the people's will and began to question the existence of popular government in this growing metropolis. So common was a betrayal of trust in these days of private and public profiteering and dishonesty, that one city collector's "spotless record" evoked astonished comment in the press as he passed on the duties of his office to his successor. Indeed, so saddened was the *Tribune* by the spectacles of human weakness in Chicago official life that it was impelled to remark:

> We have often wondered what posterity must think of the moral character of our age, in view of the practice now so rife of presenting men with costly gifts for simply doing the duties of their calling. By some it may be regarded as a proof of our generosity; but the cynical must consider it as a biting satire on the degeneracy of the times.[171]

[171] *The Chicago Times,* December 15, 1871; *Chicago Tribune,* May 21, 1862, February 16, 1868.

CHAPTER VIII

THE FORM AND FUNCTION
OF GOVERNMENT

THE INSTRUMENTS of government in Chicago, during the 'fifties and 'sixties, were, in many respects, like those of other cities, but their development was hastened to fit the changing and expanding needs of the rapidly growing community.[1] Like the legislatures of many other states the Illinois General Assembly continued to exercise control over city affairs. During these years governmental activities multiplied; a clearer differentiation between the functions of the executive and the legislative branches became apparent; the office of mayor tended gradually to take over executive powers formerly exercised by the Common Council; and administrative boards of a semi-independent character were set up, sometimes to supersede council committees. To these general characteristics Chicago gave its own particular color through the quickness with which changes occurred and through the personalities who appeared on the local political stage to direct the changes.

Chicago owed its basic governmental structure to a series of special laws passed by the state legislature, often at the behest of special interests in the city. In 1848 the framework of government rested upon the charter of 1837 and the general amendment of

[1] Limits of the city in 1848 were roughly Twenty-second Street on the south, Wood Street on the west, North Avenue on the north, and the lake on the east. By 1871 the city was bounded by Thirty-ninth Street on the south, by Fortieth Avenue and Western Avenue on the west, by North and Fullerton avenues on the north, and by the lake on the east. George H. Gaston, *The History and Government of Chicago* (Reprint, *The Educational Bi-Monthly*, June, 1914), pp. 9–10. See map, p. 307.

1847 together with a number of special local laws passed by the General Assembly.[2] By 1851 such confusion had resulted from this mass of legislation and so much more complex had urban problems become that the so-called charter of 1851 was enacted by the legislature.[3] This consolidating act represented, in a sense, a document of cumulative special legislation that had been required as the charter of 1837 gradually became outmoded. Another thorough revision to the charter was made in 1857 and marked the effective demarcation of administrative functions.[4] Again in 1863 a new charter was voted by the legislature, and this charter with its amendments remained the basis of local government until the city adopted the provisions of the general incorporation act of 1872.[5]

Fundamental in the governmental structure, of course, were the mayor and council. Under the 1837 charter the mayor was an elective official, but his executive powers were limited, and he was in many respects subordinate to the council. By the consolidating act of 1851, or under the preceding special laws which were combined in the 1851 law, his powers were increased. The responsibility for the enforcement of laws and ordinances, the obligation to give information and make recommendations to the council, the right to appoint the council committees, and perhaps most important of all the suspensive veto power made the mayor a figure of some importance in the municipal organization.[6] In 1857 the mayor's power was still further strengthened by the grant of the right to appoint, with the consent of the council, certain administrative officers, notably the comptroller, and by the provision that a two-thirds vote was necessary to override his veto.[7]

That the mayoralty in spite of its still limited authority was a position to which honor and influence were attached was evidenced by the type of men who sought the office. Lawyers, physicians, bankers, real estate promoters, grain and commission merchants, and

---

[2] For a detailed discussion of the charter of 1837 see Pierce, *A History of Chicago*, I, 322–27.

[3] Act of February 14, 1851, *Private Laws, 1851*, pp. 132 ff.

[4] Act of February 16, 1857, *Private Laws, 1857*, pp. 892 ff.

[5] Act of February 13, 1863, *Private Laws, 1863*, pp. 40 ff.

[6] Act of February 14, 1851, *Private Laws, 1851*, pp. 137–38. By the terms of the charter of 1851, if the mayor did not return a bill within three days it automatically became law. By this law also the mayor's veto could be overridden by a majority of the aldermen.

[7] Act of February 16, 1857, *Private Laws, 1857*, pp. 892–93.

other prominent leaders of the community coveted the prestige which would be gained. Such wealthy men as Cyrus McCormick, who had a taxable income in 1867 of $169,760, and Francis C. Sherman, whose taxable income in that year was $34,069, were not unwilling to be candidates for mayor. John Wentworth, after achieving prominence in the legislative halls at Washington, returned to direct the business of the city. Indeed, only two of the twenty-seven men running for the office between 1848 and 1869 — Isaac L. Milliken, a blacksmith, and Timothy Wait, a barkeeper — had not attained enviable standing in the business life of the city.[8]

The increasing importance of the mayor's office was temporarily slowed up by a law of 1869 which deprived the chief executive of his function of presiding over the council meetings.[9] But until then, as the powers of the mayor expanded, those of the Common Council came to be more and more of a purely legislative character. During this period two aldermen were elected by popular vote from each ward of the city. The number of these wards varied from time to time as the growth in population and the expansion of area made redistricting necessary. After 1847 there were nine wards, each represented by two aldermen; in 1857 the city was divided into ten wards; and in 1863 the city was made into sixteen wards, each of which elected two aldermen in alternate years for two-year terms. In 1869 the number of wards was increased to twenty.[10]

The council enjoyed the usual powers of a local legislative body. It was required to meet regularly, and attendance at its meetings could be made compulsory. Yet citizens complained that members frequently absented themselves, so that ordinances designed for the

8 Four of the candidates listed their primary occupation as commission merchant; three as lawyers; two as each of the following: flour miller, hotel proprietor, manufacturer, and physician; and one each as engineer, theater owner, newspaper owner, lumberman, real estate operator, contractor, wholesaler, engraver, blacksmith, barkeeper, banker, and insurance man. In addition many of these men also engaged in real estate speculation and had subsidiary business interests. Of the twenty-one living in 1867 fifteen reported taxable incomes ranging from $600 to $34,000, the average being $9,400. It is probable that others had substantial incomes from sources exempt from taxation under the federal income tax law. *Chicago Tribune*, May 2, 1867; *The Chicago Times*, May 2, 1867.

9 Act of March 10, 1869, *Private Laws, 1869*, I, 334. The so-called " Mayor's Bill " of March 9, 1872, restored to the mayor the powers of which he was deprived in 1869. *Public Laws, 1871*, pp. 218–20.

10 Act of February 14, 1851, *Private Laws, 1851*, pp. 134, 135; Act of February 16, 1857, *Private Laws, 1857*, pp. 892, 912; Act of February 13, 1863, *Private Laws, 1863*, pp. 41–42, 44; Act of March 10, 1869, *Private Laws, 1869*, I, 330–32.

municipal welfare were delayed and neglected.[11] The council also had authority to determine its own procedure and to pass judgment upon the qualification and election of its members. The mayor presided at the meetings, casting a deciding vote in case of tie until a law of 1869 temporarily withdrew these powers.[12] As early as 1850 city legislation had become so complex that fourteen committees were needed to supervise its several branches.[13] Gradually the influence of these committees grew to the point that their recommendation of a measure was tantamount to its acceptance and enactment into an ordinance. After 1857 the council, except by unanimous consent, could not act on matters of ordinances and petitions and communications to itself until a report had been made by the appropriate committee.[14] In addition to its legislative power the council exercised control over administrative matters by its share in the appointive power, by its power, subject to the control of the legislature, to define the functions of administrative officers, and, especially in the earlier years, by the direct supervision of administrative duties by council committees.

[11] *The Daily Democratic Press,* June 16, July 3, 18, August 31, 1855, July 17, 30, 1856. A majority of the aldermen constituted a quorum. Act of February 14, 1851, *Private Laws, 1851,* p. 141.

[12] *Ibid.,* pp. 138, 141, 142.

[13] These committees were concerned with finance, judiciary, claims, schools, police, harbors and bridges, fire and water, wharves and public grounds, printing, markets, wharfing privileges, and streets and alleys (in the last case one for each division of the city). *Chicago Daily Journal,* March 19, 1850.

[14] Act of February 16, 1857, *Private Laws, 1857,* p. 892.

Key to map showing additions to Chicago (on opposite page):

ANNEXATIONS	DATE	AREA (sq. mi.)
A Original town platted by Canal Commissioners	Aug. 4, 1830	.417
B Extension by trustees	Nov. 6, 1833	.458
C Extension of town limits when incorporated	Feb. 11, 1835	1.652
D Extension of city limits when incorporated	Mar. 4, 1837	7.659
D¹ Withdrawn in 1843; re-annexed	Feb. 14, 1851	.875
E Extension by legislature	Feb. 14, 1851	3.309
F Extension by legislature	Feb. 12, 1853	3.997
G Extension by legislature	Feb. 13, 1863	6.216
H Added to Lincoln Park by the legislature	Feb. 8, 1869	.082
I Extension by legislature	Feb. 27, 1869	11.362

From Grosser, *op. cit.,* pp. 9–10; Chicago, Department of Public Works, Bureau of Maps and Plats, *Map of Chicago Showing Growth of the City by Annexations and Accretions* ([Chicago], 1933).

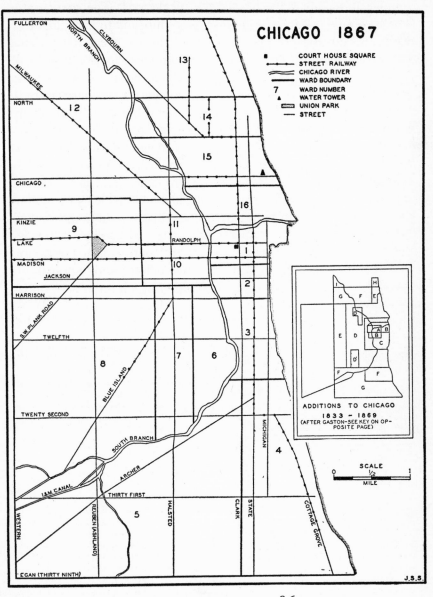

MAP OF CHICAGO, 1867

(From Rufus Blanchard, *Guide Map of Chicago, 1867.*)

Development in the judicial branch of government lagged behind that in the legislative and executive branches. In 1851, cases involving ordinances of the council were heard by two or more justices of the peace designated by the Common Council. The mayor was authorized to hold a police court.[15] Such a court had been established under Mayor Woodworth in 1849. It had, during the period from April 25, 1849, to February 11, 1850, heard 913 cases and assessed fines to the amount of $2,400. The mayor imposed small fines as a rule, because it was hard to collect large amounts. Those unable to pay had to be put in the county jail where the city paid for the prisoners' lodging and the jailer's fees.[16]

In 1857 the justices of the peace, designated by the council under the act of 1851, became the police court of the city, and provision was made for a police court clerk who was to be elected biennially by the people. The council was also permitted to appoint a prosecuting attorney for this court. In 1865 a police court was established for each of the three divisions of the city.[17]

In 1853 the legislature set up a " Recorder's Court of the city of Chicago," to consist of a judge and clerk elected by voters of the city for a term of five years. A system of grand and petit juries was also established and the jurisdiction of the court defined.[18] Shortly thereafter the legislature prescribed a police magistrates' court for each city of the state. Magistrates were popularly elected every four years, their number to be dependent on the population of the city. In Chicago, three were selected.[19]

[15] Act of February 14, 1851, *Private Laws, 1851*, pp. 168–69. The justices of the peace had power to fine or imprison, or both, in their discretion, where such discretion was vested in them by ordinance or regulation of the city, or by act of the state legislature.

[16] The mayor's court in the 1849–50 period collected only $1,658.24 out of which the marshal, constables, and witnesses were paid. Aside from the costs, judgments averaged $2.50. *Chicago Daily Journal*, March 7, 1850; *Daily Democrat*, April 26, 1849.

[17] Act of February 16, 1857, *Private Laws, 1857*, pp. 905–8; Act of February 16, 1865, *Private Laws, 1865*, I, 285. Appeals from the police court were taken to the Recorder's Court. An earlier ordinance of September 8, 1851, had made justices of the peace subject to call as a police court for cases arising under the ordinances. Chicago, *The Revised Charter and Ordinances of the City of Chicago* . . . (George Manierre, ed., Chicago, 1851), p. 184.

[18] In 1867, three official shorthand reporters were authorized by the legislature for the courts of Chicago and Cook County. (Act of March 6, 1867, *Public Laws, 1867*, pp. 146–48.) The Recorder's Court had concurrent jurisdiction with the Circuit Court within Chicago in all criminal cases except murder and treason and in civil cases where the amount did not exceed $100. Act of February 12, 1853, *General Laws, 1853*, pp. 147–50.

[19] Act of February 27, 1854, *Laws, 1854*, pp. 11–12. Two acts of 1855 provided for filling

The legal affairs of the city had been put in charge of a city attorney in 1837. In 1847 this office was made elective. By 1863 this single office was expanded into a department under the direction of the corporation counsel with the assistance of the city attorney. Members of this department were entrusted with the conduct of the corporation's law business, with the drafting of ordinances and other legal documents requested by the city, and with giving opinions on legal matters to officials.[20]

Perhaps the outstanding feature of the governmental development of these years was the multiplication of governmental functions. Activities which had been of private concern became matters of public interest and were controlled by governmental organizations either through the medium of the Common Council or, more and more as the years went on, through the activity of semi-independent boards.

In 1861 a board of three commissioners, one from each division of the city, was authorized to assume all police powers hitherto conferred on the mayor and council. The first board was appointed by the governor with the consent of the senate and had supervision over all members of the police force. The successors to the first commissioners were elected by those enjoying the franchise to serve six years. The council decided the size of the patrol and could increase the police force upon application of the police board.[21]

This change in the city constabulary had come about after other forms of law enforcement had been tried and after a period of agitation by citizens aroused by unchecked misdemeanors and crimes. Until the appointment of the police board by the authorities at Springfield, the mayor and council had supervised the police force. In 1855

---

vacancies and allowed the first election of such officers to take place in any year following 1854 if none had been elected. Acts of February 15, 1855, *Laws, 1855*, pp. 34, 44.

[20] Pierce, *A History of Chicago*, I, 329, 330; Act of February 14, 1851, *Private Laws, 1851*, pp. 138–39; Act of February 13, 1863, *Private Laws, 1863*, p. 50.

[21] Act of February 21, 1861, *Public Laws, 1861*, pp. 151–60. The police commissioners were required to have lived at least one year in the division they represented and five in the city. They must retire biennially. They could be removed by the judge of the Circuit Court of Cook County for misdemeanors, malfeasance, or delinquency in office upon charges preferred by the mayor. Annual salaries of police department members ranged from $1,500 for the general superintendent to $600 for patrolmen. No member of the force could receive other compensation without the unanimous consent of the police board. Any town within the county could call upon the police board to appoint men for duty in such jurisdiction and was required to bear the cost of such officers.

they had organized the police department into three districts and increased the number of policemen from forty-nine to eighty. The mayor was head of this force, and a city marshal was acting chief. At this time a separate night watch was abolished and day and night duty shared. This arrangement must have pleased those who, for some time, had felt that the night watch had not prevented robbery, incendiarism, and other disorders and crimes.[22]

The direct control of police appointments by mayor and council had, moreover, tied the police too closely to politics. A new city administration could dismiss the entire force, and "the guardians of the law" seemed mere flunkies of the political machine then in power. Election disorders ran their course and, at times, protection by the police was sadly lacking in the heat of political combat.[23] In March, 1861, when the new police board was appointed, Mayor Wentworth, unpopular with some of the Republican fraternity in spite of the fact that he was the mayor of that party, dismissed the police force in order, the *Tribune* said, to make the newly established police commissioners organize their department immediately. In this organization, the *Tribune* feared, the commissioners would disappoint nineteen out of every twenty applicants, leading the disappointed possibly to bolt the Republican party.[24]

As a result of Wentworth's action the newly appointed police commissioners hurriedly set to work.[25] Preference was given to applicants over five feet six inches in height, and by summer those chosen were garbed in new uniforms: blue frock coat with silver buttons embossed "Chicago Police," gray trousers with blue stripe down the

[22] In 1855, the force consisted of a captain, three or more lieutenants, three or more second lieutenants, three or more sergeants, police constables, and policemen. *The Daily Democratic Press,* August 7, 1854, May 1, 1855.

[23] In 1856, for example, Chicago was without police protection in April, while a new city administration was taking shape. The election had resulted in the choice of Thomas Dyer, Democrat, for mayor, who succeeded Levi D. Boone, the Know-Nothing candidate of 1855. *Ibid.,* March 5, April 18, 1856. See also *ibid.,* November 3, 5, 1856, March 3, 1858; *Chicago Daily Journal,* November 5, 1856, March 5, 1857.

[24] *Chicago Tribune,* March 27, 1861. Wentworth in his own defense ascribed his action to the tardiness of the police commissioners in the discharge of duty. This delay was unfortunate for both the city and the applicants for positions on the force. One of the commissioners, according to Wentworth, "contented himself with imbibing unbounded quantities of free liquor, bought for him by the men who were anxious to secure his favor." *Chicago Daily Democrat,* March 28, 1861.

[25] Governor Yates appointed Frederick Tuttle, William Wayman, and A. C. Coventry as commissioners. *Chicago Tribune,* February 25, 1861.

seam, and blue cloth cap " with a neat number." Even so distinctive a uniform, desired for some time in order " to distinguish a policeman from a drayman or a baggage wagon driver," must have been small comfort on the payless paydays, which occurred at not infrequent intervals. Some may have also found distasteful the regulations which made " moustaches " taboo and required that whiskers be " *a la militaire.*" [26]

By 1862, the force included a general superintendent, three captains, six sergeants, fifty-nine patrolmen, and one constable specially appointed, as well as extra squads detailed for special duty. In 1864, policemen employed by the city were given a bonus of $25 a month, effective from May of that year, and their pay was raised to the utmost limit allowed by the new charter when in February, 1865, salaries were increased to $800 a year. By 1869–70, the appropriation for the police department had mounted to $525,218, and expenditures for police protection had soared over 210 times within a twenty-year period. [27]

Despite the reassuring inscription " At danger's call we'll promptly fly, And bravely do or bravely die," on the policemen's flag carried in parades, citizens sometimes found it necessary to hire special guards to protect their business houses and private homes. Not always, it was charged, were the police " physically or morally brave." To them, one newspaper declared, a drunken man was " a glorious subject for club practice," a " nigger," unless " a brawny one," was worth no more than " an insult," and women were often treated as if they were " demons instead of human beings." Prisoners were sometimes clubbed into submission by plain-clothes men, and women of the street, unable to pay for immunity, received the cruelest kind of treatment. [28] So disruptive of confidence were charges of mis-

---

[26] *Ibid.*, March 28, May 9, July 6, November 2, 1861; *The Press and Tribune*, April 5, 1859; *The Chicago Times*, April 12, 1870; *Chicago Daily Democrat*, January 2, 1860.

[27] In 1849–50 Chicago paid $2,485.74 for police. In addition the marshal was paid $925.37. (*Chicago Daily Journal*, March 1, 1850.) In the year 1861–62 the city paid $43,700 for regular police services in addition to $499.34 for the special guard at Camp Douglas, $881 for elections, the state fair, and such occasions, and $1,463.88 for the mayor's special guard. From 1865 to 1868 the police department appropriation mounted from $169,117 to $390,738. *Chicago Tribune*, May 12, 1862, December 13, 22, 1864, March 1, 1865, April 16, August 13, 1866; *Hunt's Merchants' Magazine*, LVII (July, 1867), 33; Colbert, *Chicago*, pp. 92–93; *The Chicago Times*, April 30, 1870, April 29, 1871; Chicago, *Council Proceedings, 1868–69*, p. 469.

[28] *Chicago Tribune*, July 31, August 4, 1866, February 7, May 5, 1867.

conduct, inefficiency, bribery, and corruption that investigations were demanded in 1864 by the police themselves and again in 1868.

Nor was criticism confined to the patrolmen. The commissioners were under fire also. In 1864, the *Tribune* charged that the board had been driven by the "copperhead slave-driver" to oust the "branch of the city police force known as the ' detective corps,' " an important instrument in "municipal efficiency"; and four years later a "nearly unanimous vote" of the Common Council recommended that Mayor Rice appoint a committee of seven aldermen to investigate the police commissioners and officers of the police department, including the regular and detective forces. Despite legal tangles which prevented the council from compelling the presence of witnesses, the committee held sixteen meetings and collected testimony from eighty-nine persons including burglars, pickpockets, saloonkeepers, brothel keepers, and prostitutes. Some of the witnesses refused to testify, but others told of making gifts and of other forms of bribery to escape punishment for violation of the law. Still others testified that they had never given the police anything but that they had paid fines for their infringements of the law.[29] Upon the completion of testimony the committee recommended that charges be preferred against Captain Michael Hickey and Sergeant Adam Mergenthaler, but the whole investigation, in spite of the high hopes of promoters, ended " ingloriously for the prosecution," according to the *Tribune*.[30]

Until 1858 fire protection was in the hands of a volunteer force, whose membership was increased by those anxious to gain the social privileges of the fire companies and the exemption from jury service, from the militia except in war, and from payment of the road tax which this service offered. Added to the regular force were all citizens who, when needs were special, could be called upon to fight fires.

[29] *Ibid.*, February 13, April 30, 1864, January 1, 1868. For charges against the police see *The Chicago Times*, January 1, 6, 7, 12, 15, 30, February 1, 4, 8, 13, 1864; *Chicago Tribune*, January 1, 4, 10, 15, 17, 19, 27, February 3, 5, 10, 15, 17, 21, 25, March 2, 4, 1868.

[30] Because the committee did not have the power to compel testimony, it did not feel legally justified in preferring charges against any member of the board of police. In view of the seriousness of some of the testimony heard, however, the committee recommended that the council urge the police board officially to investigate the conduct of some of the members of the police force. A further recommendation suggested that the council make provision for prosecution and that the board place detectives in railroad stations to guard against confidence men. *Ibid.*, February 21, 1868. See p. 434.

By the terms of the consolidating act of 1851, as well as by earlier legislation, members of the council were fire wardens. The council was granted, in 1851, power to prescribe " fire limits " within which no wooden structures could be built and, in general, to take such measures as were necessary for fire prevention. The purchase of fire apparatus and the formulation of the fire wardens' duties were also a part of council procedure. The Chicago City Hydraulic Company was required in 1851 to place hydrants of sufficient size and capacity in localities where needed.[31]

In October, 1857, a great fire laid low a large part of Lake and South Water streets, causing the deaths of twenty-two people, some of whom were firemen, as well as an estimated $700,000 loss in property. The necessity of better fire equipment was realistically demonstrated. In February, 1858, the first steam engine to fight fire arrived in Chicago and was given the name of " Ye Great Skwirt 'Long John.' " Within a year of the 1857 fire, the city fathers ordered the formation of a paid fire department. The members of the new force were to receive regular wages and to become the beneficiaries of a municipal firemen's relief fund, derived from the tax on fire insurance premiums later turned over to the Firemen's Benevolent Association.[32]

Yet even with improved equipment and an organized force, many property owners provided themselves with hand equipment such as the Hydropult, advertised to throw water fifty feet. Indeed, the householder could also use the Hydropult to clean cisterns, water gardens, wash windows, and to give himself " a Spray Bath." In 1864, the municipal telegraphic fire alarm was installed. By a turn of the handle the alarm could be sent to the head office, whence a

[31] Chicago, Revised Charter and Ordinances, 1851, p. 111, Charter and Ordinances, 1856, p. 208; Act of February 14, 1851, General Laws, 1851, p. 92; Acts of February 14, 15, 1851, Private Laws, 1851, pp. 138, 161–63, 216; Act of February 28, 1854, Laws, 1854, p. 218; The Daily Democratic Press, January 2, 1854.

[32] Chicago Daily Journal, February 8, 11, 1858; Chicago Daily Democratic Press, October 20, 24, 1857; Chicago Daily Press and Tribune, February 21, August 9, 1858, January 21, 1860. See p. 445. The Citizen's Fire Brigade was formed in autumn, 1857, and in June, 1859, it became a part of the Chicago fire department. (Tanner, Halpin and Co., comp., D. B. Cooke & Co.'s Directory of Chicago for the Year 1858 [Chicago, 1858], p. 435 [hereafter cited as Tanner, Halpin and Co., D. B. Cooke & Co.'s Directory, 1858]; Andreas, History of Chicago, I, 227; Regular meeting of June 20, 1859, Chicago, Council Proceedings, 1858–61.) The firemen's relief fund received one-eighth of the fire insurance tax, amounting to $3,270 in 1867–68. Colbert, op. cit., pp. 92–93; Act of March 5, 1867, Private Laws, 1867, I, 148.

general signal was transmitted to the fire brigade stations of the city. At the sound of a bell designating the district where the fire had broken out, horses began " to tramp and snort," and within five minutes firemen and engines were on their way to the scene of conflagration.[33]

Still, losses by fire were considerable, in 1866 alone passing the two million dollar mark with slightly over two-thirds of that amount covered by insurance. Insurance rates advanced markedly under the sponsorship of the Chicago Board of Underwriters. In the winter of 1868, twenty-two firms were burned out in a fire " unparalleled, in the magnitude of its operations," at an estimated loss of $2,070,000, of which $1,486,000 was covered by insurance. In September, 1870, commercial life received another setback when fire destroyed buildings on Wabash between Madison and Washington valued at about $3,000,000, and several people were burned to death. A little more than a year later the holocaust now called the " Great Fire " laid Chicago in ashes.[34]

The cost of maintaining the fire department mounted yearly. For the fiscal year 1871–72 it had reached a budgetary estimate of $407,121. In 1865, the general supervision of the fire department was given to the Board of Police Commissioners which had to define and supervise the duties of members of the department. Two years later the board was empowered to arrange for the inspection of buildings, to impose building regulations, to prohibit manufactories creating fire hazards, to forbid or to regulate the sale or use of fireworks in the city, and to demolish any dangerous wall or building. At the same time came a reaffirmation of the council's power of regulation and prohibition of combustibles within the city and one mile beyond its limits and the right to forbid assemblages in any building not provided with safe egress.[35]

[33] Rev. Newman Hall, *From Liverpool to St. Louis* (London, 1870), pp. 152–53; *Chicago Tribune*, June 7, 1861, July 2, 1864.

[34] *Ibid.*, October 6, 1866, January 3, 1867, January 29, 1868, September 5, 1870. See pp. 477–78.

[35] *Chicago Tribune*, May 22, 1871; Act of February 16, 1865, *Private Laws, 1865*, I, 289, 291; Act of March 9, 1867, *Private Laws, 1867*, I, 766, 772; Act of February 14, 1851, *Private Laws, 1851*, p. 162. In 1867 the legislature permitted the city to pay as salaries $3,000 to the fire marshal; $1,800, $1,600, and $1,400 to the three assistants; $1,400 to engineers of fire engines; $1,200 to foremen of fire companies; $900 to fire policemen; and $720 to watchmen of engine houses.

From 1848 to 1871 several laws directed toward the control of election machinery passed the state legislature. The general law of 1851 guaranteed the right of the council to determine places of holding elections in each ward and forbade the arrest on civil process on election day of persons entitled to vote.[36] Two years later each ward became an election precinct with general regulations provided by the council.[37] By 1857 wards were divided into smaller election districts, and the council was empowered to name places for elections. In 1861, special elections, except those provided for in the charter, were abolished, and a legislative attempt was made to eliminate illegal voting.[38]

The Board of Registry created under a law of February 15, 1865, supervised election procedure. Fines and penalties for violations of election ordinances were provided for in the act which created the board. In 1869, the time of municipal elections was changed from spring to autumn; officers were to be elected on the first Tuesday after the first Monday in November and to take office on the first Monday in December after election. The names of all municipal officers were to be on the same ballot with state officials. All white males who were twenty-one years of age or older, and who had lived in Illinois at least a year and in Chicago for six months, and who had resided in the election precinct or ward at least thirty days directly preceding an election had the right to vote.[39] In 1861, bills provided punishment for those who voted or permitted others to vote without proper qualifications. The registry act of 1865 required all voters to register by the week preceding election. After 1869, the Board of Supervisors of Cook County chose this board of election inspectors, and the returns of elections, ballots, poll and registry lists or books

[36] *Ibid.*, pp. 134, 136, 137.

[37] Act of February 12, 1853, *General Laws, 1853*, p. 203. Under the power to regulate city elections granted by the charter of 1851, the Common Council passed an ordinance, July 8, 1851, naming the first Tuesday in March as the time when city officers were to be chosen. Places of election in each ward were to be designated by the council. The city clerk was to give six days' previous notice in written or printed form. The marshal was to post notices in three of the most public places in each ward. Special elections were to be held and conducted in the same manner as general elections. Chicago, *Revised Charter and Ordinances, 1851*, p. 96.

[38] Act of February 16, 1857, *Private Laws, 1857*, p. 892; Act of February 18, 1861, *Private Laws, 1861*, pp. 118, 144.

[39] Act of February 15, 1865, *Public Laws, 1865*, pp. 54-59; Act of March 10, 1869, *Private Laws, 1869*, I, 330. See also *Chicago Evening Journal*, April 18, 1864, for other voting requirements and qualifications.

were placed in the hands of the clerk of the County Court.[40] In spite of such regulations, charges of illegal voting were heard in nearly every election, and the efforts of parties in power to retain their grip ranged from the importing of illegal voters and the stuffing of the ballot box to suggested gerrymandering in apportionment acts considered by the state legislature.[41]

Expanding problems attendant upon a rapid urbanization led in 1861 to the creation of a semi-independent, elected Board of Public Works which assumed the functions earlier performed by the street commissioners and city superintendent. Made up of three members chosen to serve six-year terms in rotation, this board regulated the duties of subordinate officials and employees and tended to absorb certain powers formerly exercised by the council. The general amending act of 1863 placed the mayor on the board, while a law of 1867 provided for the appointment of the three board members by the mayor and council.[42]

The opening and care of thoroughfares were among the most pressing municipal problems facing Chicago. But so absorbed was the city in matters other than civic beautification that impassable and unclean streets seemed at times to claim little attention. Main avenues were the highway of wandering beasts as well as the thoroughfare of man. Under sagging wooden sidewalks lived " millions of rats " which at night regarded the streets as " their domain "; and " old boots, shoes, spoiled meat and fish, the garbage of the kitchens, dead dogs, cats and rats " befouled the places where man must walk. Even when attempts to clean the streets were made, the refuse was

---

[40] Acts of February 21, 22, 1861, *Public Laws, 1861,* pp. 267–69; Act of February 15, 1865, *Public Laws, 1865,* pp. 54–59; Act of March 10, 1869, *Private Laws, 1869,* I, 333–34; *Chicago Evening Journal,* March 15, 1865. Under the 1865 law the board of ninety-six inspectors, named by the council, was to make lists of qualified voters in election districts three weeks before election and to revise these lists one week prior to election.

[41] On January 21, 1865, a bill to redistrict the state for Congressional elections was introduced into the Illinois Senate and passed on February 9. The next day it was moved to reconsider the vote, and further consideration was postponed until July 4. Since there was no session on July 4, the bill was not considered. (Illinois, *Senate Journal, 1865,* pp. 232, 538, 546.) The *Chicago Times* of January 23, 1865, said the bill had been " manufactured by Joe Medill " in such a way that " abolition counties " would benefit, and Democratic strength would be minimized. See pp. 214, 263–65, 289.

[42] Act of February 18, 1861, *Private Laws, 1861,* pp. 118–19, 120; Act of February 13, 1863, *Private Laws, 1863,* pp. 44–45; Act of March 9, 1867, *Private Laws, 1867,* I, 760–61. Each of the three divisions of the city was to be represented on the board. The first commissioners were to retire at two-year intervals, their successors serving for six-year terms.

not always carried away but was simply pushed aside. And not always were sidewalks cleared, although from the 'thirties hindrances to a traveler's progress were forbidden. In the 'fifties enactments of a similar nature required owners or occupants of premises to keep sidewalks free from ice, snow, and dirt.[43]

Because ice and snow on the thoroughfares were frequently left for disposal to the offices of the sun, the city was made the defendant in occasional suits for negligence brought by those who suffered broken arms or legs. Nature's obstructions to free and safe movement seemed bad enough, but to encounter overenthusiastic merchants hawking their goods in the manner of " Chatham street " on some of the main avenues was more than some citizens could bear. And the wandering cow perpetuated a rural atmosphere strikingly incongruous amidst signs of urban sophistication. To wade ankle deep in mud and water so that he felt as if he were crossing " a Rubicon " was the lot of the pedestrian during wet weather in parts of the town where streets were unpaved. And where sidewalks were laid, teamsters frequently monopolized them to avoid " the sticky and Styx-like " roadways.[44]

To rescue Chicago from the mud which nearly engulfed pedestrians and vehicles alike, regrading was attempted. In 1849, a series of street grades was decided upon which, it was hoped, would effectually drain off surface waters. Damp and unhealthful streets, however, kept the problem of drainage constantly before the citizens, and in 1852 a Drainage Commission was incorporated by the legislature. Soon land which had been considered valueless was made available for gardens, and houses could be constructed with cellars which remained dry. New grades established by the council in 1855 and 1856 necessitated the lifting of buildings to new elevations above the low water level of the river as adopted by the canal trustees

[43] See Carl Schurz's amusing description of Chicago streets in 1854 in Schafer, *Intimate Letters of Carl Schurz, 1841–1869*, p. 128; *Chicago Tribune*, December 3, 1863, July 3, 4, 1865; *Oquawka Spectator*, April 25, 1856; *The Press and Tribune*, March 29, 1859; *The Daily Democratic Press*, February 25, 1854, April 16, 1855; *Chicago Daily Democrat*, April 7, 1860; Chicago, *Revised Charter and Ordinances, 1851*, p. 18, *Charter and Ordinances, 1856*, pp. 404–5.

[44] *Chicago Tribune*, March 8, April 1, June 13, 1861, May 20, 1862, July 25, 1866, January 30, 1867, April 1, 1868, November 13, 1870; *Chicago Daily Democrat*, March 11, 1857, March 26, 1860; *Chicago Evening Journal*, July 11, 1863; *The Press and Tribune*, September 26, 1859. The rumor that some dry goods merchants hired tobacco spitters to ruin women's dresses was circulated but denied. *Chicago Tribune*, July 25, 1866.

in 1847. In 1857 and 1868 the elevation was raised again. This jacking up of buildings made Chicago a city of "ups and downs" over whose grotesque and unattractive thoroughfares pedestrians passed with fear and danger.[45]

Irregularity and differences in street width complicated the situation still more. South of Twenty-second Street, especially, streets continued intermittently, some stopped, while others turned off abruptly. By 1869 the press was outspoken against the unplanned condition of the municipal thoroughfares. Citing the example of Baron Haussmann who had done much to rebuild Paris, the *Times* clamored for a long-time plan which would provide that "all streets, and public buildings and improvements should conform to the idea that Chicago is not only a great city now, but that it will become a vastly greater one." There was also complaint that in the South Division difficulties were increased during the winter season when the lamplighter found it impossible to get the gas street lamps lighted before darkness. Failure to number the houses and to post street names where they could be seen hampered the movement of persons unfamiliar with their surroundings even in the daytime.[46]

When grading the streets had failed to lift Chicago out of the mud, paving with planks was tried. In 1847, Lake Street between State and Dearborn was so planked, and the success of that effort led the city fathers to undertake similar paving on all the main thoroughfares. By 1851 almost ten miles had been planked. But this method of paving proved little better than ordinary gradings, for the planks rotted or became loose, sheltering pools of stagnant and filthy water. Cobblestones, the pine block or Nicholson paving, boulder stone, block limestone, and macadam were then tried as well as the more accessible cinders. In 1871, however, the city had nearly seven hundred miles of streets which could not be surface drained, a condi-

[45] *The Daily Democratic Press*, March 16, 1854; *Weekly Chicago Democrat*, October 12, 1850; *Chicago Tribune*, March 27, 1866, May 7, 1867, March 10, 1868, May 5, 1870; Bross, *History of Chicago*, p. 50; Chicago, *Charter and Ordinances, 1856*, pp. 230–47; Andreas, *History of Chicago*, I, 190; James Stirling, *Letters from the Slave States* (London, 1857), pp. 2–3; Rev. N. Hall, *op. cit.*, pp. 143–44; Lillian Foster, *Way-Side Glimpses, North and South* (New York, 1860), pp. 204–5. The elevations established in 1855 and 1856 were eight to fifteen and one-half feet above the low water level of the river in 1847.

[46] *Chicago Tribune*, October 8, 1866, February 28, 1868; *The Daily Democratic Press*, February 22, 23, 1855; *Chicago Daily Press and Tribune*, March 15, 1859; *The Chicago Times*, July 10, 1869.

tion due to indifference on the part of some citizens and opposition to increased taxation on the part of others.[47]

A tax of three days' labor each year from every male between the ages of twenty-one and sixty, or its equivalent in cash, provided in part for the care of the streets. Added to this was the yearly assessment not to exceed 3 per cent on the real estate of any natural division of the city which would be benefited by the proposed improvement. General upkeep, lighting, and sprinkling of thoroughfares were among the responsibilities of the Common Council until the establishment of the Board of Public Works in 1861.[48] During the fiscal year 1849–50, exclusive of ward expenses and commissioners' salaries, over $40,000 was spent on the thoroughfares, of which about $30,000 went for planking in the three divisions. By 1858 the government was dipping into the public funds for over $180,000 for special improvements of sidewalks, streets, and alleys and for the raising of the grade, and for eleven months in 1870–71, $357,202 went for street cleaning and repair and $400,476 for street intersections.[49] In September, 1867, for the first time contracts were let for sweeping and cleaning of the paved streets. Still, much complaint was directed toward the board because dirt remained upon the streets and sprinkling was left to owners of property. When nails in cleats on the sidewalks tore women's dresses, and when the sprinkling of crossings smeared and bedaubed foot gear and the "arrears of dry goods" belonging to "lady" pedestrians, the board was again blamed.[50]

The lighting of the streets appears to have become a matter of general municipal concern when gas was first used for illumination in street lamps in September, 1850. In spite of their extinguishment

47 *Chicago Daily Democrat*, August 27, 1849, January 4, 1851; William Ferguson, *America by River and Rail* . . . (London, 1856), p. 363, quoted also in Pierce, *As Others See Chicago*, p. 149; *The Daily Democratic Press*, July 11, September 26, 1855, February 15, July 30, November 28, 1856; *Chicago Daily Press and Tribune*, August 20, 1858; *Chicago Tribune*, February 5, 1861, July 31, November 1, 10, 1866, October 14, 1870, February 8, 1871; Hugo S. Grosser, *Chicago: A Review of Its Governmental History from 1837 to 1906* (Chicago, 1906), chap. ii, p. 7.

48 Act of February 14, 1851, *Private Laws, 1851*, pp. 145–46, 150, 155; Act of February 18, 1861, *Private Laws, 1861*, pp. 122–24.

49 *Chicago Tribune*, March 24, 1871; Chicago, *Council Proceedings, 1858–61*, pp. 71a, 75; *Chicago Daily Journal*, March 1, 1850.

50 *Chicago Tribune*, July 24, December 18, 1861, April 8, 1871; Chicago Board of Public Works, *Seventh Annual Report of the Board of Public Works to the Common Council, 1868* (Chicago, 1869), pp. 16–17 (hereafter cited as Board of Public Works, *Annual Report*).

by midnight, this service was preferable to the privately cared for posts with their sputtering oil lamps. By the close of the 'fifties the Common Council had provided for the lighting of the street lamps during all the night hours. The extension of municipal service after 1850 is graphically shown in the increase in the $2,160 initial valuation of lamp posts to $29,540.08 in 1859, and in the rise of the $502.95 cost of gas in the former year to the $22,817 in the latter. In 1869–70, over $245,900 was expended for the "lamp districts," and the tax imposed for such support had reached $404,488 in 1870–71.[51]

The city was first supplied with gas by the Chicago Gas Light and Coke Company, chartered by the state legislature in perpetuity on February 12, 1849, and headed by Hugh T. Dickey as president until 1873. Its charter gave the company the sole right to sell gas to the city and to Chicagoans for ten years, and the right to lay gas pipes and mains in the city streets provided no permanent damage was done. An initial capital stock of $300,000 was increased by $1,000,000 in 1855, and the company was empowered to issue bonds. High rates for service and charges of monopoly practices were among the causes which brought about the chartering of the People's Gas Light and Coke Company, also in perpetuity, in 1855 with the right to extend its pipes anywhere within the city. This charter forbade the People's Company from operating before February 12, 1859, unless the earlier company consented; it also introduced the principle of rate-setting by the legislature with stipulations that this company furnish gas to the city for no more than $2.00 a thousand cubic feet and to private consumers at no more than $2.50. The People's Company was slow in organizing, and it was not until 1862, a year after Albert M. Billings and Cornelius K. Garrison leased the concern for ninety-nine years, that it began to manufacture and sell gas. The threat of competition led the Chicago Company between 1862 and 1864 to come to an agreement with the People's Company by which the former supplied the South and North divisions and the latter furnished gas to the West Division.

[51] *Chicago Daily Democrat,* September 9, 1850; *The Daily Democratic Press,* July 1, 1854; *Chicago Daily Journal,* May 4, 28, August 26, September 5, 6, 18, October 3, 1850, January 28, February 27, 1851; Colbert, *op. cit.,* pp. 92–93; *The Chicago Times,* April 30, 1870, April 29, 1871; Chicago, *Charter and Ordinances, 1856,* pp. 431–32; Sparling, *op. cit.,* p. 53; Regular meeting of March 28, 1859, Chicago, *Council Proceedings, 1858–61,* pp. 93a–94; Annual Statements of the Finances of the City of Chicago for 1851, 1858, and 1859.

In 1865, the state legislature permitted an unlimited increase in the capital stock of the People's Company; the rate-setting features of the 1855 act were abolished; and the Common Council was empowered to regulate the price of gas after ten years, but the price was not to be set at less than $3.00 per thousand cubic feet. With the two companies in substantial agreement and with rate limitations temporarily removed, the monopoly was able to raise prices. Enraged at the situation, citizens met in mass meetings during the winter of 1866–67 and vainly protested. They petitioned the General Assembly, which held the key to relief, for enabling laws which would allow the city government either to buy the existing gas company properties or to build in competition with them. But even in 1870 Chicagoans were paying from $3.50 to $4.25 a thousand cubic feet for their gas, their hope unrealized for a municipally-owned plant which would furnish gas at the actual cost of production. They had entered upon the era of long-term franchises and concessions to those who were in control of the utilities.[52]

Because the city is situated on two sides of the Chicago River, the Common Council had to consider also the construction and repair of bridges. When the flood of March, 1849, destroyed the bridges, the city was forced to resort again to ferries, such as once had been a common means of transport across the river. During the following year ferries cost the city nearly $3,400.[53] Throughout the 'fifties and 'sixties agitation for bridges frequently became the theme of newspaper report and editorial as well as of the consideration of the council, and under this community pressure, city expenditures for bridges mounted from about $6,900 in 1849–50 to $142,267 in 1867–68.[54] But the late 'sixties found such accommodations sadly

---

[52] Act of February 12, 1849, *Private Laws, 1849*, p. 41; Acts of February 9, 12, 1855, *Private Laws, 1855*, pp. 642–43, 614–15; Act of February 7, 1865, *Private Laws, 1865*, I, 589–90; Wallace Rice, *75 Years of Gas Service in Chicago* . . . (Chicago, 1925), pp. 4–5, 6–7, 10, 18, 19, 21–22; *Chicago Daily Journal*, September 5, 6, 1850, January 28, 1851; *The Daily Democratic Press*, October 11, 1853; *Chicago Tribune*, May 9, 1862, December 15, 1866, January 8, 9, 1867, December 18, 1870. In various acts the state legislature gave the council rights to extend gas pipes to residences and to order the construction of street lamps. Act of February 14, 1851, *Private Laws, 1851*, p. 146; Acts of March 6, 9, 1867, *Private Laws, 1867*, I, 708, 761–62.

[53] *Chicago Daily Journal*, March 13, 1849, March 1, 1850; *Daily Democrat*, March 30, April 10, 1849.

[54] *Chicago Daily Journal*, March 1, 1850; Board of Public Works, *Seventh Annual Report, 1868*, pp. 123–27.

inadequate for the increasing trade of Chicago, and " mere apologies for bridges " vexed those wishing to cross the river. By 1866 the city had built twenty-two bridges, of which six were floats and the rest were pivots. Except for one of iron and another of iron and wood, these were all wooden structures which none too certainly bore the strain of traffic jams.[55] Extra policemen were needed to prevent disorder and accidents when bridges had to be cleared as tugs chugged noisily through the turbid waters of the river. By the dawn of the 'seventies, however, Chicago had twenty-seven truss bridges hinged on central piers.[56]

Tunnels under the river were discussed as early as 1853. The next year the Common Council gave attentive ear to a plan for such tunneling presented by the American Sub-Marine Tunnel Company of New York. Work was to be completed by May 1, 1855, at State, LaSalle, or Franklin Street as the council decided. As planned, the tunnel was to be privately operated, but the city was to have control of its opening, closing, lighting, cleaning, police regulations, and rates for passengers and vehicles, as well as the right to purchase the tunnel.[57]

In 1855 the Chicago Tunnel Company was incorporated, and the city was empowered to make a contract with it for the construction of tunnels under the river, for the use of which tolls could be exacted from the public.[58] But apparently no further action was taken for the next ten years. A tunnel under the river at Washington Street " to accommodate the great rush of travel and traffic " between the South and West divisions, for which bridges were not sufficient, was begun in 1866 and completed December 31, 1868, at a cost of $517,000. Its estimated cost was $200,000, a sum which boosters of Chicago were willing to pay for an undertaking described as " the first and only work of the kind in America and the second in the world." A tunnel

[55] *Chicago Tribune*, January 15, December 24, 31, 1866, July 20, 1867, February 13, 1870. There were also four railroad bridges and three slip bridges (over the Ogden and Brainard slips, and Scanlon Slough). There were twenty-nine bridges in all within the city.

[56] *The Daily Democratic Press*, April 26, 1854; Board of Public Works, *Tenth Annual Report, 1871*, pp. 48, 112.

[57] *The Daily Democratic Press*, February 15, July 23, 1853, June 28, 1854. Acts of February 14, 1851, and February 28, 1854, gave the council the right to authorize the building of tunnels and the charging of tolls for use. *Private Laws, 1851*, p. 155; *Laws, 1854*, p. 219.

[58] Act of February 15, 1855, *Private Laws, 1855*, pp. 571–76.

at LaSalle Street was begun in October, 1869, and completed July 1, 1871, at a cost of $566,276.48.[59]

As the city grew, the municipal government had not only to establish and maintain streets and bridges, it had to supervise and regulate in the public interest the various means of transportation developed by private business. In the 'fifties most Chicagoans, untroubled by long distances, walked to their destinations. Of course, the well-to-do had their carriages, and for those who wished to hire a means of transport there were the livery stables which advertised "carriages and horses at all hours." On Sundays, so popular a diversion was driving that it was almost impossible to meet the demand. A coach or carriage, drawn by two horses, might be had with driver for five dollars a day, and a cab with a single horse could be hired for three. By 1869 eight dollars were needed to go forth in style in a vehicle with a span of horses.[60]

Ordinances controlled fares charged for hacks or cabs. For one passenger going no more than a mile thirty cents was the fee in the early 'fifties, but by the end of the decade and throughout the 'sixties he had to pay fifty cents. Regardless of well-directed efforts at control by the government, extortion and other irregular practices sometimes led people, particularly after nightfall, to walk rather than trust themselves to avid and unscrupulous hackmen. A falling off in patronage eventually brought some reform and prompted the hackmen to organize for the purpose of regaining confidence.[61]

Following the example of older cities, transportation in Chicago was facilitated also by the omnibus, which was, in reality, an intracity stage. The first line, started in 1850, ran from the business center to what is now Lincoln Park. Soon others followed the spread of population or broke the way into sections of the city where real estate promoters had envisaged additions. By 1852 a traveler could

[59] *Chicago Tribune,* November 10, 1866, January 1, 1869; Andreas, *History of Chicago,* II, 64; Board of Public Works, *Ninth Annual Report, 1870,* pp. 19, 128; Grosser, *op. cit.,* chap. iii, p. 9.

[60] James W. Norris and L. S. Taylor, *Chicago Directory for 1848–1849* (Chicago, 1848), "Advertisers' Directory," p. 17 (hereafter cited as Norris and Taylor, *Directory, 1848–49*); *Weekly Chicago Democrat,* June 26, 1849; Edward H. Hall, comp., *The Chicago City Directory and Business Advertiser, 1855–56* (Chicago, 1855), p. 205 (hereafter cited as Hall, *Directory, 1855–56*); Edwards, *Directory, 1869–70,* p. 958.

[61] *Ibid.;* Tanner, Halpin and Co., *D. B. Cooke & Co.'s Directory, 1858,* p. 431; *Chicago Daily Democrat,* June 18, 1856; *Chicago Tribune,* March 20, 1867.

go by "bus" on Randolph Street from State to Bull's Head at the junction of the Southwestern Plank Road and West Madison, from the Lake Street bridge to State Street, thence to Twelfth Street. At first, service was hourly; then in some cases half-hour service was established. In 1852, J. Frink and Company operated hourly from the Lake House on the northeast corner of Rush and North Water streets to Clark Street and from there to the Michigan Southern Railway Station. By 1854, Parker and Company and Martin O. and Samuel B. Walker dominated the omnibus business. Over twenty-two miles of Chicago streets were then served by eighteen carriers on eight routes, making a total of 408 trips daily. Special buses at this time ran from the hotels to the railroad depots and similar places. Two buses were run each day to and from Holstein, Jefferson, and Niles.[62]

As early as 1854 suggestions were made that horse railroads be introduced by the simple expedient of placing omnibuses on tracks, although opposition quickly developed from those who mistrusted real estate promoters or who preferred that the peace of their neighborhoods be undisturbed. A proposal to construct a line to some point south of the city also received some support that year, but the Common Council apparently failed to act on the petition.[63] It was not until May 26, 1855, that an ordinance was passed. This required that the railroad company plank or otherwise improve the streets, that only animal power be used, and that the fare for a mile or less be five cents. For greater distances within the city limits a ten-cent fare was allowed. The franchise was granted for a period of twenty-five years with the privilege of renewal thereafter until the council elected to purchase the railways with their appurtenances.[64] Ap-

[62] See directories of the city for lines operating. *Oquawka Spectator*, May 24, 1854; *The Daily Democratic Press*, September 16, October 30, 1852, March 16, May 10, 1854; John A. Fairlie, "The Street Railway Question in Chicago," *The Quarterly Journal of Economics*, XXI (May, 1907), 372. For regulation by the Common Council see Chicago, *Charter and Ordinances, 1856*, pp. 435–45.

[63] *The Daily Democratic Press*, July 7, 11, August 1, 1854, May 7, 1855. A petition was filed on July 31 by C. B. Phillips praying the privilege to construct such a railroad. Stock was to be offered to Chicagoans first. What was not taken then was to be open to New York investors. Among other promoters of horse railroads were Stephen A. Douglas, Dr. William B. Egan, and Charles Cleaver. These men, who had real estate in the vicinity, wished to run a railroad from the Calumet River to Chicago, but the council did not grant permission for tracks to be laid in the city. Cleaver, *Early-Chicago Reminiscences*, p. 46; Gates, *The Illinois Central Railroad*, p. 108; *Chicago Tribune*, June 16, 1868.

[64] *The Daily Democratic Press*, May 28, 1855. The council could obtain the railways by

parently no railway took advantage of the new ordinance, and on February 7, 1856, it was repealed. On February 28, a substitute making a similar grant to the same petitioners passed the council.[65] It provided that the incorporators must obtain the assent of owners of land fronting the streets to be improved, until authorization of use came from the legislature.[66] Provision was made for purchase by the city after twenty-five years.[67] On March 4, the council passed an ordinance which gave to Roswell B. Mason and Charles B. Phillips, incorporators, the right to construct a horse railway. Some track was laid in the North Division, but the panic in 1857 curtailed activities. Mason sold out to Phillips. The road's further development was also blocked by the refusal of property owners along the line of the projected railway to give the necessary consent and by legislative indifference which Phillips charged was due to underhanded motives.[68]

On July 19, 1858, the council voted to give Henry Fuller, Franklin Parmelee, and Liberty Bigelow the right to construct and operate a horse railway in the South and West divisions for twenty-five years and after that until such time as the city might purchase the lines.[69] This ordinance was opposed by the press and by property owners because it failed to include requirements as to time of completion,

four annual payments, the amount to be determined by common agreement or by referees. The streets over which the proposed railroad was to go were State Street and Cottage Grove south from Water Street to the city limits; Washington Street, State to Market; Dearborn from Water Street north to North Avenue, west to Green Bay Road (North Clark Street), north to the city limits; north on Franklin from Water Street to Division, west to Clybourn, north on Clybourn and Racine to the city limits; on Sedgwick from Division to Green Bay Road. Document 497, 1855, *Common Council Documents.*

[65] Documents 1993, 2077, 1855, *ibid.; The Daily Democratic Press,* February 8, 29, 1856.

[66] Documents 2077, 2145, 1855, *Common Council Documents.* The prescriptions about fares, animal power, the paving of streets, and the streets to be improved were substantially the same as in the repealed grant. Archer Avenue from State to the city limits, however, was added, and construction was to start within six months and be completed within four years. If the routes were not finished within this time, the company had to release them.

[67] " The purchase price was to equal a sum of money, the interest on which at six per cent should equal the net earning of the railways for the year next preceding the date of purchase," according to Samuel Wilber Norton, *Chicago Traction* . . . (Chicago, 1907), pp. 16–17.

[68] Chicago, *Charter and Ordinances, 1856,* pp. 359–63; Andreas, *History of Chicago,* II, 119; *Chicago Daily Journal,* August 14, 1858. The charters of 1837 and 1851 did not grant the council rights to make such grants.

[69] At the same council meeting R. L. Fabian and W. S. Woodward petitioned that this same grant be made them. *Ibid.,* July 20, 1858; *Chicago Daily Press and Tribune,* July 21, 1858.

it did not stipulate definitely the price for which the city might eventually purchase it, and it made no restrictions as to the use of omnibuses.[70] The mayor vetoed this ordinance but approved the one replacing it, which attempted to meet the points of criticism. The first rail of the new road was laid with ceremony on December 2, 1858. But when the promoters of the project started work they were enjoined by the Circuit Court from laying any tracks.[71] Thus, with doubt as to the authority of the council to make such a grant, Fuller, Parmelee, Bigelow, and David A. Gage, like Mason and Phillips, sought a charter from the state legislature. This they were granted on February 14, 1859, for twenty-five years, and by late April four cars of the Chicago City Railway, laden with Chicagoans enthusiastic over the new method of transportation, made the initial trip from Lake to Twelfth Street.[72]

A complete system of lines, however, did not appear at once, nor did the omnibus discontinue its service. In some instances a close relationship existed between the horse railroad and the omnibus. Franklin Parmelee, one of the incorporators of the Chicago City Railway Company, was also the owner of an omnibus line which had operated on State Street. It was quite easy, therefore, to arrange that passengers be transferred to and from omnibuses at the end of the unfinished line on this street. But bitter rivalry between competing horse railways and omnibuses was the rule. Rate wars at times destroyed the fruits of profit. One such feud was that between Samuel B. Walker

[70] *Ibid.*, July 21, 23, August 2, 1858; *Chicago Daily Journal*, July 23, August 2, 1858.

[71] *Ibid.*, August 3, 1858; *Chicago Daily Democrat*, August 18, 1858; Chicago, *Municipal Code, 1881*, pp. 473–76; *Chicago Daily Press and Tribune*, August 20, 1858; Norton, *op. cit.*, p. 19. A number of property owners on State Street applied to Judge Manierre of the Cook County Circuit Court for an injunction to restrain the horse railway company from laying tracks and operating on State Street. The injunction was granted on the ground that the Common Council had no right to make such a grant without authority from the legislature. *Chicago Daily Press and Tribune*, January 4, 1859.

[72] Harry P. Weber, *An Outline History of Chicago Traction* (Chicago, 1936), p. 5; Ralph E. Heilman, " Chicago Traction. . . ," American Economic Association, *Publications*, ser. 3, IX (1908), 313; Act of February 14, 1859, *Private Laws, 1859*, p. 530. The company was authorized to construct and operate in the South and West divisions and was required to build and operate two railways in the city limits, within two years. Horse cars were provided for. The capital stock of the company was set at $100,000 but could be increased when the company desired. The Chicago City Railway served those who lived in the South and West divisions, but was permitted to extend its lines anywhere in Cook County. In the same act as that in which the Chicago City Railway received its grant from the legislature the North Chicago City Railway Company was granted similar rights in the North Division, also for twenty-five years, and on May 23, 1859, it was given a franchise by the city council. *Ibid.*, pp. 530–32; Chicago, *Municipal Code, 1881*, pp. 484–87, 502–4, 512–13.

and the Chicago City Railway, which ended when in 1860 Walker, owner of the bus line, withdrew his carriers from State and Randolph streets and left the horse cars in undisputed possession of these thoroughfares.[73] By 1864, both Walker and Parmelee had retired from the omnibus business, but others had taken their places.[74]

Street railway lines and services were extended as Chicago grew. The city fathers had early decided to give franchise rights to a few large companies rather than to many small ones. By 1863, the Chicago West Division Railway, incorporated in 1861, had purchased the rights and property of the Chicago City Railway Company in the West Division for $300,000, thereby consolidating holdings in that section.[75] In the summer of 1861 the North Chicago City Railway Company extended its track three quarters of a mile beyond the city limits to Wright's Grove, and later it built its line to Lake View. In 1867, the Chicago and Calumet Horse and Dummy Railroad Company was incorporated to give streetcar service to those living south of the city limits. The next year the Cook County Board of Supervisors, acting upon the recommendations of the trustees of the town of Hyde Park, granted this company the right to lay tracks in that neighborhood.[76]

Great excitement was aroused in 1863 when the state legislature passed a bill, sponsored by a downstate senator, that gave to a group of Chicago incorporators, using the misleading title "Wabash Railway Company," rights to construct and operate horse railways in Chicago without the consent of property owners or the Common Council. Unaware of the nature of the bill Chicago citizens had therefore offered little opposition to its passage. But when the purpose became known, the council, press, the existing railway companies, and citizens joined in a protest against such a secretive and highhanded measure, characterized by the *Tribune* as *"stolen* through the Senate and *bribed* through the House" to the tune of

---

[73] Gager, *Directory, 1857*, Appendix, pp. xxix; *The Chicago Times*, April 26, May 18, 1859; *Chicago Daily Democrat*, March 23, 1860; *The Press and Tribune*, May 19, 1859, January 14, 30, 1860; *Chicago Tribune*, January 22, March 14, June 7, 1861.

[74] Parmelee remained in the transfer business. Andreas, *History of Chicago*, II, 118, 119, III, 164.

[75] *The Chicago Times*, May 19, 24, 25, 1859; Act of February 21, 1861, *Private Laws, 1861*, pp. 340–42; *Chicago Tribune*, July 31, 1863.

[76] *Ibid.*, July 15, 1861; Weber, *op. cit.*, pp. 16–17; Act of March 5, 1867, *Private Laws, 1867*, II, 30–31.

an alleged $100,000 in stock.[77] The bill was vetoed by Governor Yates June 19, 1863, partly on the ground that it was an unwarranted intrusion in city affairs. Further action had been forestalled by the proroguing of the legislature by the governor on June 10. Aroused by the dangers lurking in possible future legislation of a similar character the city council in November, 1863, ordered that for twenty years no railway tracks could be constructed along Michigan, Wabash, and Third avenues, Lake Street east of Peck, Monroe, Washington, Adams, or West Jackson streets, although the General Assembly could override the city ordinance.[78]

Within two years street traction companies had fortified their existing grants under the protection of the legislature in a bill which extended their corporate lives and franchise rights to ninety-nine years and included other sweeping privileges.[79] The bill was strongly opposed in Chicago and was vetoed by Governor Oglesby. Board of Trade resolutions, protests of the Chicago Working Men's Society, and the objections of others, however, proved of no avail.[80] The legislature passed the measure over the governor's veto, to the dis-

---

[77] Special meeting, June 8, 1863, Chicago, *Council Proceedings, 1863;* Document 61, 1863, *Common Council Documents; Chicago* [Tri-Weekly] *Tribune,* June 8, 10, 12, 1863; Illinois, *Senate Journal, 1863,* pp. 130, 139. An additional clause at the end of the list of streets made it possible for construction to take place on almost any street in the adjacent towns of Cook County. A penalty of thirty to one hundred dollars or a maximum of a year's imprisonment was imposed for any obstacles placed in the way of construction or operation.

[78] *Ibid.,* pp. 381, 386–90; Chicago, *Municipal Code, 1881,* pp. 494–95; J. R. Jones to E. B. Washburne, December 13, 1863, *Washburne Papers,* XXXII; Willard E. Hotchkiss, "Chicago Traction: a Study in Political Evolution," *The Annals of the American Academy of Political and Social Science,* XXVIII (November, 1906), 386; *Chicago* [Tri-Weekly] *Tribune,* June 12, 1863. By the Constitution of 1848 the governor had the right to adjourn the General Assembly. (Verlie, *Illinois Constitutions,* p. 69.) Peck Street is today's Union Park Court. Third Avenue is Dearborn Street south of Jackson Boulevard.

[79] On January 4, 1865, Andrew H. Dolton, a member of the legislature from Cook County, introduced "An act concerning horse railways in the city of Chicago." (Illinois, *House Journal, 1865,* p. 103.) A clause which stated that contracts and franchises in existence between the city and the companies should be continued during "the life hereof" was included in the act. Companies involved were to run the railways by consent of or contract with the city government, and any contract providing for a fare of more than five cents could be modified by the council or by the legislature. Act of February 6, 1865, *Private Laws, 1865,* I, 597–98. For difficulties which arose under the ambiguous clause see Pierce, *A History of Chicago,* III, IV (in progress).

[80] Illinois, *Senate Journal, 1865,* pp. 243, 277–80; Illinois, *House Journal, 1865,* pp. 308–9; *Chicago Tribune,* January 23, 25, 27, 30, February 1, 1865; *The Chicago Times,* January 24, 30, February 4, 1865; *Chicago Evening Journal,* January 30, 1865; *Horse Railway Monopoly . . . Proceedings of Public Meeting of Citizens* (Chicago, 1865).

may of those who wanted to save the streets of Chicago for the public.[81] Other laws passed in 1867 and 1869 made provision for the regulation of street railway fares and for the introduction of steam or " dummy " engines by the traction companies.[82]

Although the state constitution of 1870 contained a provision that the General Assembly could not grant the right to construct and operate a street railroad in any city, town, or incorporated village without the consent of local authorities, and other acts offered some protection to municipalities, Chicago did not gain complete control of her traction concerns.[83] Meanwhile, horse railways gained great popularity. From 1860 through 1862 the number of passengers carried by the Chicago City Railway Company rose from 2,492,503 to 3,512,272, and the receipts mounted from $124,625 to $141,783. By 1863, the company was employing two hundred men, and the monthly pay roll was over $5,000.[84]

Municipal control of the Chicago River was dictated by the demands of commerce and of public health. The development and regulation of river and harbor were matters of prime importance to a community whose commercial leaders still looked to the lake and canal as outlets for local products. The late 'forties saw only a beginning of this development. The office of harbor master was created, and after 1851 the Circuit Court of Cook County was authorized to appoint three port wardens.[85]

Under the charter grants the council could lease wharfing privileges for no more than three years and could remove and try to prevent obstructions in the waterways, chiefly the much disliked sandbars made by spring freshets. The administration of funds and other matters relating to the harbor passed into the hands of the Board of Public Works after its creation. Under the board's direction harbor improvement costs advanced until, in 1871, $120,500 was spent for

[81] In the senate the veto was overridden 18 to 5; in the house, 55 to 22. Illinois, *Senate Journal, 1865*, pp. 415–16; Illinois, *House Journal, 1865*, pp. 596–97. For interpretation of the ninety-nine-year act see Blair *v.* City of Chicago, 201 U. S. 400 (1906).

[82] Act of March 9, 1867, *Private Laws, 1867*, I, 773; Act of March 10, 1869, *Private Laws, 1869*, I, 335.

[83] Verlie, *op. cit.*, p. 157.

[84] *Chicago Tribune*, January 11, March 3, 1863.

[85] Act of February 16, 1847, *Private Laws, 1846–47*, pp. 88–89; *Chicago Daily Journal*, March 1, 1849; *Daily Democrat*, May 29, 1849; Act of February 17, 1851, *General Laws, 1851*, pp. 156–59. In 1863 the duties of harbor master were redefined. Act of February 13, 1863, *Private Laws, 1863*, p. 51.

dredging the harbor, a telling contrast to $1,393 put out in 1849–50. Paralleling this advance in harbor improvement was the increase in amounts devoted by the city to river improvements in general, which jumped from $4,032 in 1850–51 to $1,337,000 in 1871.[86]

Even in the 'sixties, despite all the efforts which had been directed toward dredging and the aid received from the federal government, no solution for the frequent blocking of the channel had been found; and almost annual recommendations were still made to widen the river and straighten the entrance to the harbor for which, in the words of Henry Ward Beecher, nature had done little and the government less.[87]

Cleansing and draining the waters of the river, " a sluggish, slimy stream, too lazy to clean itself," were other problems for the city fathers.[88] In 1849, two plans for drainage were proposed by Mayor Woodworth. One was to build sewers on the river level in order to take advantage of what was thought to be a daily ebb and flow of the lake into the river, and the other was to build them level with the ground and connect them with the reservoirs of the water works to obtain an artificial flow of water. The early sewers followed the gravity plan, however, and a series of street grades was adopted which, it was hoped, would effectually drain off the surface waters. The first sewers were built of oak planks, but the later ones were made of brick and stone. A Board of Sewerage Commissioners was created in 1855 to supervise the sewerage system in the three " natural divisions " of the city and to plan for a co-ordinated system for the future. The following year this board sent Ellis S. Chesbrough, chief engineer, abroad to study systems used in larger European cities. In 1861, when the Board of Public Works was set up, the care of the sewerage

[86] Act of February 14, 1851, *Private Laws, 1851*, p. 142; *Chicago Tribune*, March 24, 1871; *Chicago Daily Journal*, July 3, 1849, March 1, 1850, February 27, 1851.

[87] *Weekly Chicago Democrat*, April 8, 1854; *Daily Democrat*, April 17, 1849; *Chicago Daily Journal*, March 17, October 18, 1849, March 9, 1852; *Chicago Daily Democratic Press*, August 21, 1857; *Chicago Tribune*, December 7, 1863; Henry Ward Beecher, *Eyes and Ears* (Boston, 1862), p. 99. In 1865, the Board of Public Works was permitted to make river and harbor improvements without employing contractors if three fourths of the aldermen consented. Soon thereafter the right to change the dock lines of the river and harbor was granted the council in the hope that navigation would thus be facilitated. Act of February 15, 1865, *Private Laws, 1865*, I, 274; Acts of March 6, 9, 1867, *Private Laws, 1867*, I, 708, 761, 774. See also pp. 68–69, 296.

[88] John Lewis Peyton, *Over the Alleghanies and Across the Prairies* (2d ed. London, 1870), p. 325.

system was placed among its duties. But the system of disposal remained defective; by 1866 only one eighth of the city was served by it, although expenditures for sewer construction had mounted from $3,700 in 1850–51 to $1,204,100 in 1869–70, and the 6 miles of sewers in 1854 had become 140 miles by 1871.[89]

The sewers were financed by special assessments and by bond issues, sometimes sold through New York brokers. Bond issues were more commonly used, but there was complaint that the annual interest was very high, amounting in 1870 to a sum sufficient to build ten miles of sewer. But despite the expense involved in the construction of sewers by the sale of bonds, the council in February, 1871, voted against special assessments for the purpose on the ground that it would be unjust taxation and inadequate to pay off the existing debt. In April, 1871, the legislature aided in settling the problem by passing a bill permitting cities to levy a general tax of one mill on the dollar on taxable real and personal property for constructing sewers.[90]

To remedy the unfortunate condition caused by the pollution of the river, diversion of the waters of the Calumet or Des Plaines into the Chicago River and pumping at Bridgeport to reverse the river's flow were tried. As early as 1860 a "Deep Cut Canal" was suggested as a permanent means by which to remove the disease-breeding filth of the river.[91] In 1865, legislative permission was given the Board of Public Works to lower the bed of the canal and to dredge the river and reverse its current in order to carry the city's sewage from the river to the Illinois and Michigan Canal and thence to the Illinois River and eventually to the Gulf of Mexico. At a cost of approximately $3,000,000, on July 18, 1871, the hand of man reversed

[89] *Chicago Daily Journal*, May 17, September 6, 1849, February 23, April 10, 1850, February 27, 1851; Andreas, *History of Chicago*, I, 190; William Bross, " What I Remember of Early Chicago," Mabel McIlvaine, ed., *Reminiscences of Chicago during the Forties and Fifties* (Chicago, 1913), p. 21; Acts of February 14, 1855, *Private Laws, 1855*, pp. 93–108; Act of February 18, 1861, *Private Laws, 1861*, pp. 132–34; Ellis S. Chesbrough, *Chicago Sewerage, Report of the Results of Examinations made in Relation to Sewerage in Several European Cities* . . . (Chicago, 1858), pp. 88–91, 94–95; *Weekly Chicago Democrat*, May 2, 1857; *The Daily Democratic Press*, March 16, 1854; *Chicago Tribune*, March 27, 1866, February 8, 1871; *Chicago Daily Democrat*, September 5, 1850; The Daily Democratic Press, *Fifth Annual Review, 1856*, p. 5; *The Chicago Times*, April 30, 1870.

[90] *Chicago Daily Journal*, August 21, 1849, February 23, 1850; *The Daily Democratic Press*, March 16, 1854; *Weekly Chicago Democrat*, May 2, 1857; *Chicago Tribune*, May 22, 1870, February 8, 27, March 1, 16, April 20, 1871; Act of April 22, 1871, *Laws, 1871*, p. 15.

[91] *Chicago Tribune*, May 30, 1862, January 16, 1863, January 6, 12, 1868, May 7, October 4, 1870; *Chicago Daily Democrat*, September 7, 8, 1860.

the sluggish movement of the Chicago River and forced the city's sewage downstream instead of into the green-blue waters of Lake Michigan from which the city obtained its water supply.[92]

At first, private companies chartered by the state supplied water to the residents of Chicago. But the service given by the Chicago Hydraulic Company was not always satisfactory. Frozen pipes in the winter and cisterns which did not always work in the summer meant hardship and bred discontent as well as bacteria. Moreover, the impurity of the water fed the ever-present fear of cholera.[93]

Under public pressure the city moved to take over the task of supplying water to its people. In 1851 the Chicago City Hydraulic Company, a municipal corporation, was incorporated by the legislature, but its efforts met the opposition of the Chicago Hydraulic Company on the ground of charter rights to a monopoly. This furnished ammunition for political battles. Injunctions requested by the company in 1853 were denied by the court, and in 1854 the city agreed to purchase the franchise of the Chicago Hydraulic Company for $15,000 due with interest on May 1, 1855. Apparently the transfer did not take place as soon as planned, for the following year the legislature extended the corporate powers of the company until such time as its affairs could be wound up satisfactorily. In 1857 the water commissioners were given additional borrowing power, assuring a bonded indebtedness of as much as $1,000,000 if necessary. It was not until 1861, however, that the Board of Public Works took over full responsibility for the city water supply, and the Chicago City Hydraulic Company ceased to exist.[94]

Increased demands by 1866 necessitated the purchase of an engine capable of pumping eighteen million gallons a day. This engine was to be used in connection with a tunnel to run out two miles under the

92 Act of February 15, 1865, *Private Laws, 1865*, pp. 277–80; [John Walter III], *First Impressions of America* (London, 1867), p. 93; *Chicago Tribune*, July 15, 18, 1871; Putnam, *The Illinois and Michigan Canal*, p. 143.

93 Pierce, *A History of Chicago*, I, 352–53; *Daily Democrat*, January 18, March 8, June 23, 1849.

94 Act of February 15, 1851, *Private Laws, 1851*, pp. 213–15; Act of February 14, 1855, *Private Laws, 1855*, p. 721; *The Daily Democratic Press*, January 12, April 2, 1853, January 27, 1854; Act of February 16, 1857, *Private Laws, 1857*, p. 1051; Act of February 18, 1861, *Private Laws, 1861*, pp. 132–34; Chicago Board of Water Commissioners, *Semi-Annual Report . . . to the Common Council of the City of Chicago, 1854* (Chicago, 1854), p. 12; *Chicago Daily Journal*, April 24, 1850. See p. 200.

bottom of the lake.[95] In spite of efforts directed toward improvement, especially before the completion of this tunnel in 1867 and the installation of good filters, Chicago housewives sometimes found it almost impossible to keep small fish from squirming out of the hydrant into their cooking receptacles, providing many a dish with an unwanted piscatorial flavor. Even the temperate threatened to cook food in lager beer or ale. "Dead fish, newts, and various specimens of watery animalculae known to the books," were said to make bathing a fisherman's pastime, while quenching one's thirst gave one a strangely ticklish sensation as "finny fellows" wriggled down the throat. When the wind blew from the west and southwest, moreover, "fetid accumulations from slaughter houses, tanneries, distilleries and glue factories" joined the minnows and gave Chicagoans "a brackish, fishy, glutinous, dirty, odoriferous fluid," which the editor of the *Tribune* felt was "fit only for the purposes of cleansing the dirtiest of Augaean stables." [96]

The average Chicagoan, however, had not even the questionable blessing of running lake water. He still used the pump in his back yard. Advice that frequent bathing and clean clothes served as a cholera preventive found him sometimes willing but helpless. Criticism of the "great unwashed" led the valiant editor of the *Tribune* to call attention to the fact that many lived in houses "entirely innocent of plumbers' work," and that there were many for whom "no plated faucets" suggested "'hot' and 'cold' at will." For the "many acres of epidermis" not housed in the mansions of the rich, the *Tribune* urged that public bathing houses on the beaches be established where "the Scriptural mandate of 'wash and be clean'" might be obeyed. Public bathing in the lake in the built-up section of the city met with opposition from the council and religious and other groups, but when an ordinance concerning bathing came before the city fathers in August of 1861 as the temperature hovered near one hundred degrees for six days, they capitulated and permitted seekers of cleanliness to avail themselves within prescribed hours and sections of the city of the cooling waters of the lake. But the late 'sixties still found citizens asking better public bathing facilities. A

[95] *Chicago Tribune,* September 11, 16, October 6, 1863, March 18, 1864, March 2, December 31, 1866, March 25, 26, 1867.
[96] Bross, *Reminiscences,* p. 18; *Chicago Tribune,* December 5, 1861, March 12, 1862.

stock company to open a public bathhouse for the poor was suggested in 1867, since the Board of Health had apparently not met the demands made upon it from the municipal coffers.[97]

By April, 1870, 239 miles of pipes carried to the citizenry of the city the water which they might use. For such improvements Chicagoans were grateful, giving thanks to Ellis S. Chesbrough, who, as city engineer, had not only tried to solve the problem of supplying good water but had developed plans for the sewerage and the drainage of the river. In 1861, meters for large consumers were installed for the first time. As early as 1850 pipes ran to all sections of the city although supplying none very adequately. By 1870 the servicing of the water debt was costing $200,000 a year, and operating expenses of the water department totaled $190,000, but the "revenue from water rents" of $477,000 left a surplus of $87,000 for the purchase and laying of new pipes. Early in 1869 the castellated Gothic water tower, from whose top the whole city was spread to view like "a distant smoking forest of pines," rose to symbolize what they hoped would be a new era in the history of a municipal water supply.[98]

Contaminated water and noxious odors kept before the public the problem of the preservation of health. Although the charter of 1837 had established a Board of Health, and although again in 1851 such a board was authorized and the council was again confirmed as regulator of all matters concerning the public health, neither served effectually. From 1857 to 1860, the Board of Health practically ceased to function, and in 1860 the council abolished it and transferred its duties to the police. The Board of Police Commissioners, established in 1861, continued jurisdiction over health matters until in 1866 a serious epidemic of cholera led to the creation of an independent Board of Health which was organized March, 1867.[99]

[97] Daily Democrat, May 7, 1849; Chicago Tribune, August 2, 13, 1861, June 24, 1867, July 12, 1868; Chicago, Charter and Ordinances, 1856, pp. 274, 296.

[98] Board of Public Works, First Annual Report, 1861–62, p. 19, Seventh Annual Report, 1868, p. 4; Testimonial concerning the Work of E. S. Chesbrough, City Engineer (Ms. Chicago Historical Society); Moses K. Armstrong, The Early Empire Builders of the Great West (St. Paul, 1901), pp. 184–85; Chicago Tribune, March 18, 1864, March 26, 1867, February 27, 1871; Chicago Daily Democrat, July 19, 1850.

[99] Chicago Board of Health, Reports of the Board of Health of the City of Chicago, 1867–69 (Chicago, 1870), pp. 49, 54–55, 61; Act of February 14, 1851, Private Laws, 1851, pp. 142–48, 163–65; Act of February 21, 1861, Public Laws, 1861, p. 152; Act of February 16, 1865, Private Laws, 1865, I, 591; Act of March 9, 1867, Private Laws, 1867, I, 768–70; Andreas, History of Chicago, II, 549; Pierce, A History of Chicago, I, 347–48.

In the 'fifties quarantine grounds had been blocked out near the city hospital. Later, detention at the quarantine station of immigrants or other persons affected with communicable diseases was prescribed. In the consolidating act of 1863 Chicago was again given a city physician, and in 1867 an ordinance made mandatory the vaccination for smallpox of all children in public or private schools.[100]

These were high points along the road to better health, a road beset by the dread scourge of cholera, sporadic outbreaks of erysipelas, and epidemics of smallpox, besides frequently reported " sore throats," " consumption and other forms of chronic pulmonary disease," typhoid, and diarrhoea. " Teething " and cholera infantum during the summer months exacted a heavy toll among infants, and whooping cough, measles, scarlet fever, and other so-called children's diseases claimed enough victims to create fear.[101] With city expenses to improve community health mounting from $2,132 in the fiscal year 1851–52 to $80,745 in 1868–69, the death rate of Chicago dropped from the high points reached during the cholera epidemics of 1849 and 1854, averaging in the 'fifties and 'sixties about the same as the death rate of Baltimore, somewhat more than that of Philadelphia, and less than that of New York.[102]

Food inspection began to assume an importance unknown in the first years of municipal life. In 1857, the legislature provided for a city fish inspector to determine and certify the weight, condition, and content of barrels of fish shipped. Other barreled foods such as meal, flour, salt, pork, and beef also were inspected under regulations of the council.[103] Bread, too, came within the list of foods regulated, an act of 1861 prescribing the weight and quality of loaves; in the 'sixties milk was examined; and in 1870 an ordinance required that skimmed milk be so labeled.[104]

---

[100] Board of Health, *Reports, 1867–69,* pp. 22, 29, 39, 143–47, 327; Chicago, *Charter and Ordinances, 1856,* pp. 268–73; Act of February 13, 1863, *Private Laws, 1863,* p. 53; *The Daily Democratic Press,* July 10, 1854, May 18, 1855.

[101] For statistics on diseases see Board of Health, *Reports, 1867–69,* pp. 27, *passim.*

[102] *Ibid.,* p. 271, *Reports, 1870–73,* p. 136; also health reports of Baltimore, Philadelphia, and New York.

[103] The fees for such examination constituted the income of the fish inspector, and the period of his appointment by the council was for two years. Act of February 18, 1857, *Private Laws, 1857,* pp. 1203–4; Act of February 13, 1863, *Private Laws, 1863,* pp. 46, 51–52, 60. See for earlier acts Pierce, *A History of Chicago,* I, 348, 351.

[104] Act of February 18, 1861, *Private Laws, 1861,* p. 148; Board of Health, *Reports, 1867–69,* pp. 219, 229, 256, 329. When the Board of Health attempted to limit to three the

After the organization of the Board of Health in 1867 sanitary inspectors for each district of the city were appointed to look into the quality of meats and other foods. In June of that year the inspectors were given a set of instructions on how to tell good from bad meat, probably because the sanitary committee of the Board of Health had just reported that of all meat sold in Chicago for local consumption 7 per cent was unfit for use and about 3 per cent was diseased. An outbreak of the dreaded " Texas cattle disease " in the stockyards the next year resulted in an order levying a fine not less than $5.00 or more than $500 for selling tainted meat. In 1868, too, the sanitary superintendent reported that meat and vegetable markets were frequently inspected, that cattle at the Union Stock Yard fell under his critical eye, and that the general sanitary condition was " better than ever known before " though " by no means what it should be." [105]

While many of these functions were those performed by growing cities everywhere, not all had within their jurisdictions a thriving business such as slaughtering and packing, which by its very nature necessitated regulation. A charter provision in 1851 empowered the council to control the location of these plants, and a city ordinance forbade them within the city limits without express permission. That year also a slaughterhouse inspector was appointed. But so important was the slaughterhouse in the commercial life of the city even in the 'fifties that Mayor Gurnee wishfully remarked that the adoption of " judicious measures " might prevent evils complained of without depriving the city of the benefits accruing from pay envelopes furnished by the industry under public attack.[106]

---

number of cows which could be kept on one lot, whereas the Common Council by ordinance had set the number at ten, the Supreme Court declared the board had no power to regulate in contravention of rules made by the council. Tugman *v.* City of Chicago, 78 Ill. 405 (1875); Board of Health, *Report, 1874–75,* pp. 92–93. See also p. 462.

[105] Board of Health, *Reports, 1867–69,* pp. 74 ff. Municipal markets from which the city got rent numbered three in 1849, all in the South Division. In 1851 a market was built on the North Side and in 1852 one on the West Side. To raise funds for the building of the markets in the North and West divisions, bonds were issued, and provision was made to supplement the income from the markets if it proved insufficient to pay the interest and principal on the bonds by an annual tax on the real estate and personal property of those divisions. Such a tax was levied on the three divisions of the city in 1855 and 1856. Act of February 14, 1851, *Private Laws, 1851,* p. 149; Chicago, *Revised Charter and Ordinances, 1851,* p. 153; *Chicago Daily Journal,* March 1, 1849, August 11, 1851, April 15, 1852; Chicago, *Charter and Ordinances, 1856,* pp. 432–34.

[106] Act of February 14, 1851, *Private Laws, 1851,* pp. 143–44; see also Act of February

CHICAGO IN 1858 AS VIEWED FROM THE COURT HOUSE.

PHOTOGRAPHS BY ALEXANDER HESLER

TOP. *Looking east and northeast toward Lake Michigan, showing center of business district. Among buildings are Second Presbyterian Church, Sherman House, Matteson House, and Tremont House.*

LEFT. *Looking southwest toward intersection of Washington and LaSalle. Area occupied chiefly by poorer residents.*

RIGHT. *Looking toward West Division; LaSalle Street in foreground; Metropolitan Hotel, right center.*

Dirty stables, pigsties, and ditches filled with animal refuse continued, however, to offend those concerned with city sanitation. The offal depot of Wahl Brothers and Lighthall, slaughterhouse owners, at Twenty-sixth Street and Stewart Avenue, provoked much complaint, for during the packing season in the late 'sixties twenty cars disposed of a daily average of 120 wagonloads of blood and offal. Ordinances which fixed penalties for allowing offal to run into the river and forbade the rendering of tainted matter in the city or within two miles of its limits were constantly disobeyed by these business enterprises. Distilleries sent their refuse riverward, and glue factories and hide and tallow works ignored commandments for cleanliness.[107]

Agitation for publicly supported scavengers led in 1849 to an ordinance calling for the appointment of one for each division of the city. Twice weekly from April 1 to November 1 garbage collectors assigned to hotels, taverns, eating places, and dwellings drove down the thoroughfares of Chicago. At the sound of their clanging bells tubs or buckets must be ready if the owner of the premises did not wish to be liable for a three dollar fine. But collecting refuse from one section often meant dumping it in another less thickly settled part of the city. By 1867 the citizens of Hyde Park, trespassed upon to the point of exasperation, protested against the use made of their section to deposit "every species of filthy and decaying matter, from loads of night soil to dead animals of all descriptions." Even in mid-'sixties private scavengers had to be called upon, for in 1865 there were only two municipally supported scavengers for the whole city.[108]

Burial of the dead likewise was a concern of the city government. In 1850, Chicago acquired a little over twelve acres for such a purpose to be added to the one hundred acres previously owned. Lots were sold, and the city was thus reimbursed for its initial expenditure, al-

---

16, 1865, *Private Laws, 1865,* I, 590; Chicago, *Revised Charter and Ordinances, 1851,* pp. 214, 216; Act of March 9, 1867, *Private Laws, 1867,* I, 774; *Chicago Daily Journal,* March 11, June 24, 1851.

107 *Chicago Tribune,* May 22, 1862, July 4, 8, August 10, 1864, February 9, April 22, 23, 1867, September 19, 1868; *The Daily Democratic Press,* December 14, 21, 1852; Board of Health, *Reports, 1867–69,* pp. 61 ff.

108 The council in 1849 was to furnish each scavenger with a harness and a tight wagon, but the scavenger provided his own horse. *Daily Democrat,* May 7, 9, 1849, January 20, 1860; *Chicago Tribune,* January 29, 1866, June 11, 1867.

though the cemeteries did not always pay for themselves.[109] In 1857, the city was empowered to buy tracts of land outside of the city limits for the establishment of cemeteries, which were to be tax exempt.[110] Cemeteries such as Graceland and Rosehill cared for the relatives and friends of those who did not want to use the one provided by the city, and paupers were given their last resting places in the cemetery at the Poor Farm. In late 1858, North Side residents begged the council to forbid further burial in the grounds provided by the city, at that time located at the southern end of what later became Lincoln Park. Although an arrangement was reached by the municipal government with Rosehill, interments continued in the old cemetery until 1865.[111]

Governmental activities dealing with the care of dependents on society expanded during the 'fifties and 'sixties, but they did not encompass the wide range of agencies which were known at a later day. Humanitarianism and theories of correction expressed themselves in city ordinances attempting to cope with problems demanding solution by the community. Within the two decades following 1850 private and public agencies went hand in hand, the council of the city shifting its burdens as much as possible to the shoulders of private benefactors and reformers.[112] Humanitarians seemed well aware of this and not always without resentment. Where the government did assume responsibility, conditions sometimes reflected an inability to control or an insensitiveness to understand. In particular the situation in the bridewell was held a matter of lamentation, but in 1871 a new jail, built at a cost of $343,968, relieved somewhat the congestion known until then.[113]

At the same time government control over public education expanded. The act of February 14, 1851, consolidated the provisions of previous acts and gave the city power over the school fund of town-

---

[109] *Chicago Daily Journal*, November 30, 1850, February 18, 1851.

[110] Act of February 16, 1857, *Private Laws, 1857*, p. 910; see also Act of February 13, 1863, *Private Laws, 1863*, p. 63. An act of March 9, 1867, stipulated that the council should have power to prevent interment within the limits of the city. *Private Laws, 1867*, I, 771.

[111] Rosehill was dedicated July 28, 1859. (*Chicago Press and Tribune*, July 28, 1859.) Graceland Cemetery received a charter in 1861. *Chicago Tribune*, February 26, 1861; Board of Health, *Reports, 1867–69*, pp. 95–96. See the legal compulsion for the city to move part of the cemetery in 1865, Conrad Schnell *et al. v.* The City of Chicago, 38 Ill. 383 (1865).

[112] For a detailed discussion of these activities see pp. 440–51.

[113] Grosser, *op. cit.*, chap. iii, pp. 9–10; *Chicago Tribune*, August 10, 1864, August 14, 1865, August 10, 1871.

ship 39, range 14, within which Chicago was situated. The council was the general manager of school affairs in Chicago and appointed school inspectors and trustees. A law of February 16, 1857, provided for the financial support of the schools by a city tax, levied annually on real and personal property. This tax could not exceed two mills on the dollar, a limit which was raised in the 'sixties. The administration of the school system was reorganized in 1857 under a Board of Education, composed of fifteen men chosen by the council, whose duties were prescribed by city ordinance. An act of 1861 forbade the members of the Board of Education to receive any compensation for their services as such.[114]

Besides confirming earlier legal provisions in regard to education, the consolidating act of 1863 contained a group of specific regulations for the conduct of the schools. At least one common school was provided in each district for the free instruction of all children over five years of age. And at a time when a war was being waged to free Negroes, one or more schools were required to care for colored children who were not to attend schools for white children after such schools were provided.[115] Not until 1872 were fundamental changes again made in the administration of the school system, although in 1865 an enactment was passed which declared that all children over six years should be given free instruction in the common schools of which there was to be at least one in each school district of the city. Children from adjoining towns of Cook County also could be admitted on conditions prescribed by the Board of Education.[116]

The late 'sixties saw the real beginning of the park system. In 1869 a park commission for each division of the city was set up. This had been foreshadowed as early as 1849 by a concern as to the abrasion of the "public ground" along the shores of the lake. During the 'fifties official and unofficial sanction to use the land between Michi-

114 These school lands were those reserved for public education in the government survey. *Private Laws, 1851*, pp. 165–67; *Private Laws, 1857*, pp. 909–10; Act of February 18, 1861, *Private Laws, 1861*, p. 146. See also pp. 392–93.

115 Act of February 13, 1863, *Private Laws, 1863*, p. 129.

116 Act of February 16, 1865, *Private Laws, 1865*, I, 285–86. The act of April 1, 1872, placed control of schools in the hands of a Board of Education in cities of over one hundred thousand. Even in levying taxes for educational support the board could direct in its function of budgetmaking and expenditures. The board could not, however, levy or collect taxes nor require the Common Council to collect a tax at its demand or under its direction. With the advice and consent of the council the board was named by the mayor. *Public Laws, 1871–72*, pp. 740–42. See pp. 390–94 for further discussion of the schools.

gan Avenue and the Illinois Central tracks had indicated a desire to provide a recreation place similar to the Battery of New York. Shade trees were planted in 1850 in the public square in block 39 of the original town plat, and citizens opposed the erection of public buildings on this open space which they called "the lungs" of the city. In 1851 an act of the legislature forbade the city authorities to sell block 39 of the original town, reserved it as a public square, and gave the council the power to grade and improve it.[117]

In February, 1854, a tract of less than twenty acres was purchased near Lake, Reuben, and Warren streets and christened "Union Park." Here, in fancy, graded land would be intersected by gravel walks dividing the park into thirteen beds "fringed with elm, maple, and other forest trees" and enclosed by a "highly ornamental" fence with "handsome gateways." But ten years passed, and the park was not so beautified.[118]

Jefferson Square and Dearborn and Lake parks had earlier received public funds for their improvement. Spots of shrubbery and grass amidst the scraggly and unkempt streets of Chicago, these tiny oases were protected by city ordinance from those who would use them for playing ball or cricket and even for resting on the grass. Soon they became little more than cow pastures overgrown with weeds, the receptacles of rubbish, and the abode of dead animals.[119]

In 1857, the legislature authorized the judge of the Cook County Court of Common Pleas to appoint three "discreet and disinterested freeholders" as commissioners to lay out a recreational park in the South Division. The plan was ambitiously pointed toward possibly

[117] Grosser, *op. cit.*, chap. iii, p. 10; *Chicago Daily Democrat*, August 9, 1849, September 3, 5, November 1, 1850, March 14, 1851; *Chicago Daily Journal*, March 17, 1849, April 10, 30, June 12, 1850, February 4, May 22, 1851; Act of February 4, 1851, *General Laws, 1851*, pp. 19–20; Act of February 14, 1851, *Private Laws, 1851*, pp. 147, 155; *The Daily Democratic Press*, August 19, 1853.

[118] *Ibid.*, February 8, 1854, May 5, 1855; *Chicago Tribune*, October 23, 1863.

[119] *Ibid.*, September 25, 1863. In 1857, however, $3,100 was spent for park improvement. (*Chicago Weekly Democrat*, February 6, 1858.) Jefferson Square, according to the ordinance of August 25, 1851, was "the block of ground known as block thirty-nine in the original town, upon which the court house is erected." The public land east of Michigan and south of Randolph and north of lot 8 in block 21 in section 15 was Lake Park. The public ground in Fort Dearborn Addition west of Michigan Avenue and between Randolph and Washington was Dearborn Park. The ordinance gave these parks their names. (Chicago, *Revised Charter and Ordinances, 1851*, p. 175.) In 1848, Jefferson Park, between Adams, Monroe, Throop, and Loomis streets, was bought from Jesse B. Thomas. Chamberlin, *Chicago and its Suburbs*, p. 340.

as many as three hundred acres. Similar grounds could be provided citizens of the North and West divisions, upon petition of all the aldermen of the division presented to the Court of Common Pleas. Within two years such plans were found premature and not desired by the people, and the act was repealed. But the Board of Public Works in 1861 was given the right to open or improve any park upon the approval of the council, and two years later similar powers were granted the Common Council. Railroad companies were prohibited in 1863 from encroaching on land or water west of a line four hundred feet east of Michigan Avenue.[120]

During 1861 a park of eighty acres in the North Division, embracing the northern section of the cemetery grounds, was laid out and improved by the landscape gardener, John C. Ure. The new park was called La Frambois Park in memory of an old Indian chieftain. One day it was to be a part of Lincoln Park. A sixty-acre tract north of the old cemetery along the lake shore was acquired in 1864 and was named Lake Park. Demands for its improvement echoed similar appeals of a few years before, when residents of the North Division asked that they be furnished more resorts than Washington Square, which had been donated to the city in 1842 by the original owners of Bushnell's Addition.[121]

But these advances in giving Chicago citizens recreational spaces seemed small indeed as they thought of parks provided in other cities, particularly Paris, London, and Boston. Public discontent was rewarded in 1867 when the legislature passed a bill for the establishment of a park in the "towns" of South Chicago, Hyde Park, and Lake. The act, however, was voted down by the electorate. Its supporters declared the election fraudulent and applied for a writ of mandamus to compel canvassers to count only votes from the precincts where a town election was held, but the writ was denied.[122]

Undismayed by reverses, promoters continued their propaganda.

120 Act of February 16, 1857, *Private Laws, 1857*, pp. 912–15; Act of February 19, 1859, *Private Laws, 1859*, p. 125; Act of February 28, 1861, *Private Laws, 1861*, p. 123; Act of February 13, 1863, *Private Laws, 1863*, p. 96. The council had as early as 1851 power to levy taxes when required for "the purchase of market grounds, public squares or parks, or any other permanent improvements." Act of February 14, 1851, *Private Laws, 1851*, p. 149.

121 *Chicago Tribune*, September 5, 8, 1861; *Chicago Evening Journal*, November 4, 1864; *The Daily Democratic Press*, April 12, 1855.

122 Act of February 27, 1867, *Private Laws, 1867*, II, 472–78. The vote by the Chicago voters was 3,049 to 2,750. *Chicago Tribune*, February 2, 23, April 24, 1867; People ex rel. Wallace *v.* Salomon, 46 Ill. 415 (1868).

Lincoln Park could serve Northsiders, they said, but it was too far from the West and South divisions of the city. That real estate could be procured reasonably because of a slow market in the winter months seemed an argument which might whip the opposition into line. In the latter part of 1868 an extensive plan for a South Side park system was drawn up, and in February, 1869, the legislature passed an act similar to the bill of two years before. On March 23, this was ratified by the people in spite of vigorous opposition from the residents of the North Side. At once a new South Park Commission began proceedings to obtain land for their park. The Circuit Court denied their application for the appointment of assessors to levy assessments on the property benefited by park improvement in order to get funds to buy the land. Later, however, the state Supreme Court ordered the lower court to make the appointment. Olmstead and Vaux, landscape experts of New York, were then employed to lay out the park.[123]

In 1869, the legislature also provided for the creation of a park fund to be distributed among the three divisions of the city on the basis of the assessed value of the taxable real estate in each. This fund was to be realized from the sale of the area four hundred feet wide, bounded by the west line of Michigan Avenue on the west, by the south line of Monroe Street on the north, and by Park Row on the south. The title of the Illinois Central Railroad to the water and lands lying immediately to the east of the strip of four hundred feet was confirmed, and the state transferred to that railroad the inalienable title to a certain section of submerged lands, extending eastward for one mile, which lay to the east of the Illinois Central tracks and breakwater. The title of the state to the land bounded by Randolph and Monroe streets, and between Michigan Avenue and the Illinois Central tracks, was transferred to the Illinois Central, Chicago, Burlington and Quincy, and the Michigan Central railroad companies for the erection of a passenger depot and other uses. In consideration of this grant the railroads were required to pay Chicago $800,000 for the park fund.[124]

---

[123] *Chicago Tribune,* December 4, 1868, March 18, 24, 1869; Act of February 24, 1869, *Private Laws, 1869,* I, 358–66; Andreas, *History of Chicago,* III, 167; People ex rel. Wilson *v.* Salomon, 51 Ill. 37 (1869). For pamphlet propaganda favoring the creation of a park system see [Anon.], *The Parks and Property Interests of the City of Chicago* (Chicago, 1869).

[124] Act of April 16, 1869, *Public Laws, 1869,* pp. 245–48. By this act the state of Illinois

Park boards were set up at the same session of the legislature for the West and North divisions of the city as well as for the South. Court decisions arising from disputes about their relationship to the Common Council eventually made these boards municipal corporations not subject to control by the council.

The Lincoln Park Board, composed as was the South Park Board of five commissioners appointed by the judge of the Cook County Circuit Court, was authorized February 8, 1869.[125] The board for the West Division was created on February 27 and was made up of seven commissioners appointed by the governor and empowered to obtain certain tracts of land for park purposes "by condemnation, contract, donation or otherwise," at a cost not to exceed $900,000. This amount was to be assessed on the property benefited.[126]

Charges of sectional favoritism and of unfair advantages reaped by holders of real estate, as well as allegations of dictatorial and needless powers granted the commissioners indicated that not all citizens rejoiced in the prospect of a planned system of parks.[127] Apparently because of dissension, modifications of the provisions of the law regarding park financing were almost immediately passed to equalize the amount of municipal funds expended.[128]

---

surrendered its title to the four-hundred-foot area stipulating that Michigan Avenue should be left ninety feet wide. See p. 296.

[125] See People ex rel. Miller v. Brislin, 80 Ill. 423 (1875); People ex rel. Bransom v. Walsh, 96 Ill. 232 (1880); Kedzie v. West Chicago Park Commissioners, 114 Ill. 280 (1885); West Chicago Park Commissioners v. McMullen, 134 Ill. 170 (1890); West Chicago Park Commissioners v. City of Chicago, 152 Ill. 392 (1894). The Lincoln Park Board could certify to the clerk of the court of Cook County the money necessary for the improvement and repair of the park so that he could apportion this amount on the taxable property of the towns of North Chicago and Lake View and compute it as a part of the taxes due and payable by the property owners of these towns. The board had the right to require the city to issue twenty-year, 7 per cent bonds for the purpose of paying for the land taken for the park and the property of the city, and the park lands acquired were pledged for the payment of the principal and interest of the bonds. Act of February 8, 1869, Private Laws, 1869, I, 372–74.

[126] Act of February 27, 1869, ibid., pp. 342–43, 374.

[127] South and West Chicago objected to paying taxes for Lincoln Park, for example. The increase in value of property near Lincoln Park, it was felt, should be reflected in assessments. The "automatic" character of the board was also assailed. Real estate speculators were said to be back of the South Side Park bill. (Chicago Tribune, February 7, 9, 10, 1869.) The Workingman's Advocate defended the bills to establish a park along the lake in the South Division on the site of the present-day Jackson Park. The Workingman's Advocate, March 27, 1869.

[128] The city could issue bonds bearing interest at a rate not to exceed 7 per cent for parks in the South and West divisions equal to the amount allowed for Lincoln Park. Subsequently it was provided that bonds of the city for financing Lincoln Park could not exceed $500,000. Finally, in 1871, provisions for the appropriation by city authorities of funds not

The expanding sphere of government during the years before the great fire of 1871 meant mounting costs as well as increased services to the citizens of this busy city. Complaints against these growing costs were frequent, and there were rumors that civil servants did not always discharge their duties with honesty. But little was done to reverse the trend of annual increases. In 1857 city finances were placed under the control of the treasury department, composed of a comptroller, treasurer, collectors and receivers of revenue whose offices were prescribed by state law, together with such clerks and assistants and an auditor, as the council might provide for. Subordinates in this department were nominated by officers of the treasury department to the council which authorized such appointments.[129] Appointments were, therefore, a joint responsibility of the council and treasury department, and the system probably tended to encourage the choice of qualified persons.

The increase of expenditures of the municipal government from approximately $45,000 in 1848-49 to over $6,000,000 in 1868 seemed as startling and unreal to the taxpayer of 1848 as did the multiplicity of demands for revenue. By 1870, the annual expenditures of the Board of Public Works alone had risen to $5,429,793, and in 1870-71 it cost almost as much to run the government of Chicago for a single day as it had cost for the entire fiscal year of 1847-48.[130]

Between 1848 and 1871 there were two distinct periods of rapid expansion in municipal expenditures. The first, beginning in 1848, lasted for ten years, when, apparently because of the derangement in property values during the panic, expenditures tended to level off for several years. The second, beginning in 1865, continued, with only a slight drop in 1870, until the great fire of October, 1871. In the ten years between 1848 and 1858, municipal governmental expenditures appreciated over twenty-eight times. The years 1858

---

to exceed $80,000 annually for park maintenance and improvement were made, the levy not to exceed three mills. Acts of March 10, 30, 1869, *Private Laws, 1869,* I, 368, 378; Act of June 16, 1871, *Public Laws, 1871,* pp. 593–94.

[129] Act of February 28, 1854, *Laws, 1854,* p. 218; Act of February 16, 1857, *Private Laws, 1857,* pp. 893–94, 900. The 1854 act provided that a city marshal "shall be elected," but merely says that the council "may whenever it shall deem it expedient so to do" elect a superintendent of special assessments. The marshal collected license fees and fines.

[130] *Chicago Daily Journal,* March 1, 1849; Chicago, *Council Proceedings, 1868–69,* pp. 469–70; *Chicago Tribune,* March 24, 1871. Municipal expenditures in 1847–48 were about $33,650. *Chicago Daily Journal,* March 3, 1848.

to 1865 had an approximate increase of only 121 per cent, but with the return of prosperity governmental costs went up 277 per cent from 1865 to 1870.[131]

Increases in the 'fifties were occasioned to a large extent by expenditures for planking and improving the city streets,[132] the discharge of municipal indebtedness, and the payment of interest on loans and outstanding obligations.[133] Expenditures rose above $1,000,-000 for the first time in 1858–59, the payment of city obligations and their servicing accounting for over one fifth of this total. No other single expense item approached so large a percentage. New municipal functions took their toll. For example, the sewerage commissioners drew on the treasury for over $60,000. Ten years earlier their services had not figured in municipal costs.[134]

The panic in 1857 left its mark on city finances, and so did the derangement of markets and fall in prices which attended the outbreak of the Civil War,[135] but returning prosperity, the war and postwar booms were accompanied by a rise in municipal expenditures. By 1865, they had increased over 109 per cent over those of 1862, and totaled $2,918,023. Of this sum, about $202,000 was spent on servicing and reducing the liabilities of the city; over $1,433,000 was used by the Board of Public Works. For the fire department, lighting the city, the police fund, the schools, and the special assessment projects the total amount appropriated was $936,941.[136] From

---

[131] The figures upon which these percentages are based represent the total annual expenditures of the city government, including operating expenses and the servicing of the municipal floating and bonded debt. In 1870, however, the expenditures of the park boards, as independent governmental agencies, were not included.

[132] See, for example, *ibid.*, March 1, 1849, March 1, 1850, February 27, 1851; Chicago, *Annual Financial Statement of the City of Chicago for the Municipal Year 1851* (Chicago, 1852), pp. 4–5.

[133] While the costs of paying interest and principal on the bonded debt amounted to but $3,080 in 1847–48, in 1850–51 the retirement of liabilities and payment of interest occasioned a total expense of $51,688. By 1853–54 these items cost $136,300. *Chicago Daily Journal,* March 3, 1848, February 27, 1851; *The Daily Democratic Press,* March 3, 1854.

[134] *Chicago Daily Journal,* March 1, 1849; " Annual Financial Statement, 1858," Chicago, *Council Proceedings, 1858–61,* pp. 71a, 72a. Expenditures for the year 1858–59 amounted to $1,318,435.

[135] In the fiscal year 1859–60, for example, expenditures totaled $1,320,500, or almost the same as during the preceding year. But in 1859–60, one third of the expenditure was to the payment of interest and principal on the debt of the city, as a result of which other municipal departments had to curtail costs drastically. " Annual Financial Statement, 1859," *ibid.*, pp. 167a–171.

[136] Chicago City Comptroller, *Annual Statement, 1862–63* (Chicago, 1863), p. 4; *Chicago Tribune,* April 16, 1866.

1865 until the fire of 1871, the cost of the city government continued its upward trend increasing over $4,000,000 between the fiscal years 1868–69 and 1869–70.[137] The reports for the year 1871–72 show the effect of the great fire, but even the estimates of expenditures as tabulated by the comptroller at the beginning of that year indicate that a substantial increase was expected.[138]

The salaries of city officers showed a frequently protested upturn. In the fiscal year ending February 26, 1848, the committee on finance of the Common Council reported that, exclusive of the police force and fire department, these salaries amounted to over $2,900.[139] In 1849–50, city officials were paid two and a half times that amount. Four years later, the annual financial report of the city indicated that salaries of the general officers of the city had reached $18,119 for the year.[140]

The practice of paying certain officers a percentage of moneys collected prevailed for a time. The city treasurer, city clerk, marshal, attorney, collector, street commissioners, and others were so compensated in part. The amount of these charges against the city purse attained considerable size as the years went by. Meanwhile, accusations of corruption directed against those officers whose income was based on the amount of money which they handled, focused the spotlight of public opinion upon their activities until the Illinois legislature in 1857 prohibited all officers paid a fixed salary by the city from receiving any income from fees.[141] With this act the prin-

---

[137] *Hunt's Merchants' Magazine*, LVII (July, 1867), 33; Colbert, *op. cit.*, pp. 92–93; Chicago, *Council Proceedings, 1868*, pp. 469–70; Chicago City Comptroller, *Annual Statement, 1869–70*, p. 6; *The Chicago Times*, April 30, 1870. The total expenses for 1868–69, $6,338,567; for 1869–70, $10,440,916; for 1870–71, $11,009,951. For further details see Appendix, p. 510.

[138] *Chicago Tribune*, May 22, 1871; *The Chicago Times*, April 29, 1871.

[139] *Chicago Daily Journal*, March 3, 1848. The offices specifically mentioned as included in this figure were the city clerk, attorney, marshal, treasurer, health officer, the three divisional assessors, street commissioners, and bell ringer. In the next year the amount was $5,882. The city collector, harbor master, and market clerk also received pay in 1848–49. *Ibid.*, March 1, 1849.

[140] *Ibid.*, March 1, 1850; *The Daily Democratic Press*, March 3, 1854.

[141] Act of February 16, 1857, *Private Laws, 1857*, p. 909. For example, in 1857 Mayor Wentworth charged street commissioners with negligence in collecting street taxes or crediting the city with their collections. The street commissioners in 1856–57 had a fixed salary of $600, relatively small as compared with some other salaries. Still, their positions were much in demand, because of the fees involved. *The Daily Democratic Press*, September 24, 1856; *Chicago Daily Democrat*, March 11, 1857. See also *Chicago Daily Journal*, March 17, 1849, for the inaugural speech of Mayor Woodworth in which he recommended paying officers a percentage of funds handled as an incentive to "faithful discharge of their duties."

ciple of payment of fixed salaries, specifically appropriated, was established for all the major city offices.

How to get funds to meet these expenses was ever present in the minds of the officials of the city. In 1848, the per capita tax levied on real and personal property amounted to $1.10, and the debt was $1.01 per capita. In 1870, with a population fifteen times as large, the total taxes levied amounted to $13.50 per capita or $1.50 per $100 of property value, and the bonded debt had increased to $36.01 per capita.[142]

To meet expenditures it seemed necessary to find fresh sources of revenue. This was attempted through increased assessments, new levies for the benefit of new services, loans, and the imposition of user charges for utilities of a public nature. The annual municipal receipts increased in the years 1848–71 from about $48,000 to more than $11,000,000.[143]

The regular annual city tax on personal and real property, exclusive of special assessments and loans, maintained a fairly constant relationship to the total revenue. In general, from 1848 to 1871, this tax produced between 30 and 40 per cent of the municipal receipts.[144] Chicagoans complaining of the municipal tax burden they bore could, however, derive some satisfaction from comparing their

[142] In 1848, taxes amounting to $22,051 were levied on its real and personal property assessed at $6,300,440, and total liabilities of the city amounted to $20,338. In 1870, the population of Chicago was 306,605, real and personal property was assessed at $275,986,550, taxes levied amounted to $4,139,798, and the bonded indebtedness to $11,041,000. (Chicago City Comptroller, *Annual Statement, 1893*, pp. 130–31.) The official assessed valuations of property on which taxes were based did not represent the full cash value of property until 1867. Before that year they were equivalent, roughly, to the credit value which was one third or one fourth of the cash value. Colbert, *op. cit.*, p. 23. See also Appendix, p. 510.

[143] *Chicago Daily Journal*, March 1, 1849; *The Chicago Times*, April 29, 1871. Special assessments, for permanent improvements, rose from $5,100 in 1848 to $2,836,800 in 1869. Hoyt, *op. cit.*, Appendix, p. 492.

[144] There were exceptions, as in 1864–65 when income from taxes amounted to some $974,700, or over 55 per cent of the total income of $1,757,300. The reported total for this year, however, did not include income from special assessments. (Chicago, *Council Proceedings, 1865–66*, p. 11.) In 1850–51, tax income totaled only about $19,500 or 13.7 per cent of the total income of $141,800. (*Chicago Daily Journal*, February 27, 1851.) Tax collections in Chicago, 1848–71, were seldom, if ever, lower than 80 per cent of the total taxes levied. Between 1849 and 1852 they averaged over 92 per cent, and from 1865 to 1871 over 86 per cent. *Ibid.*, March 1, 1849, March 1, 1850, February 27, 1851; Grosser, *op. cit.*, chap. i, p. 6, chap. ii, p. 7, chap. iii, p. 7; Chicago, *Annual Financial Report, 1851–52*, p. 3; Chicago, *Council Proceedings, 1865–66*, p. 11, *Council Proceedings, 1868*, p. 469; Hunt's *Merchants' Magazine*, LVII (July, 1867), 32–33; Colbert, *op. cit.*, p. 93; *The Chicago Times*, April 30, 1870, April 29, 1871.

taxes with those in other cities.[145] During the early 'fifties loans sometimes were greater in amount than the tax collections.

Other sources of revenue developed, such as the water fund which paid the cost of providing water to the city and its residents. In 1861, the legislature provided that the water fund be placed in the city treasury in a separate account and the Board of Public Works be responsible for its collection. In the fiscal year 1864-65 the water fund received over $430,000, including rates and $168,200 in proceeds from the sale of bonds, and in 1870-71, a total of over $2,000,000. Street planking and paving, grade raising, and similar improvements were paid for in the form of special assessments.[146]

License fees brought some income to the city. The power of the city to license and regulate extended to various enterprises. Its most important bearings were on the liquor business, in which attempts to control came through ordinances for Sunday closing and those demanding a license for the sale of liquor.[147] Owners of theaters, ferries, and vehicles, venders of such commodities as gunpowder, auctioneers, peddlers, and butchers, among others had to pay license fees to the city. During the fiscal year 1848-49 over $8,500 was paid into the city treasury for licenses, which represented almost 18 per cent of the total income of the city. By 1870-71 the percentage had fallen to less than 2 per cent, although income from licenses had increased to $190,366.[148] A tax of 2 per cent collected in Chicago on fire insurance premiums of companies not incorporated under the laws of Illinois provided some return, and interest and rents paid to the city by those using its property helped also to fill the municipal strongbox. In 1848-49, a little over 15 per cent of the total income came from these rentals, but by 1870-71 they produced less than .5 per cent of the total.[149]

---

[145] For figures on the taxes paid in New York see Edward Dana Durand, *The Finances of New York City* (New York, 1898), Appendix, pp. 372–73, 376.

[146] Act of February 18, 1861, *Private Laws, 1861*, p. 133; Chicago, *Council Proceedings, 1865–66*, p. 11; *The Chicago Times*, April 29, 1871.

[147] *Chicago Daily Journal*, July 20, 1849, June 29, 1850. See pp. 435, 436–38.

[148] Act of February 14, 1851, *Private Laws, 1851*, pp. 143–44; Act of February 13, 1863, *Private Laws, 1863*, pp. 57–58; Act of February 15, 1865, *Private Laws, 1865*, I, 284; *Chicago Daily Journal*, March 1, 1849, February 25, June 5, July 10, 1851; *The Chicago Times*, April 29, 1871. While billiard halls and bowling alleys were operated in violation of the law forbidding them, the fines levied on their proprietors were treated as license fees. See, for example, *Chicago Weekly Democrat*, February 6, 1858; *Chicago Tribune*, April 16, 1866.

[149] Act of February 18, 1861, *Private Laws, 1861*, pp. 146–47. The total of interest and

Income from all these sources, however, did not pay all of the expenses of the city. Short-term loans at high rates of interest had to be resorted to, and these were more often than not paid off by the flotation of long-term bonds. Mayor Woodworth, in 1848, urged such a bond issue to bolster up the depressed credit of the city.[150] The charter limitation which restricted the bond-issuing power of the city to $100,000 per annum, for the liquidation of the debts and permanent improvements, worked a hardship by the later 'fifties on those entrusted with expanding municipal functions.[151] But grants of power to incur new loans for the construction of schools, the bridewell, tunnels, streets, bridges, and similar public necessities allowed the issuance of bonds in addition to the annual $100,000 limit.[152] A large proportion of such debts was to be retired not by municipal taxes, but by other means such as the liquidation of the water debt by sums collected from consumers, and the assumption by the state of the river improvement debt.[153]

As early as 1854, the city began to feel the effect of the curb which the legislature had placed upon its borrowing power. The Common Council, during the 'fifties, increasingly used its power of bond issuance until by 1856 and 1857 city bond issues were up to the limit. This trend in municipal financing Wentworth declared had received sanction from those who looked upon the statutory grant of $100,000 annual bonding power as almost a mandate to borrow this amount.[154]

As a result, large floating debts, in the form of scrip, warrants, city orders, and other short-term loans, which bore interest at high rates, were incurred. When Wentworth took office as mayor in 1857 the floating debt of an unprecedented quarter of a million dollars became a source of embarrassment to the city. Both mayors Wentworth and Haines refused to replace the short-term debt with

---

rents of the city's property was $7,212 in 1848–49, and $31,622 in 1870–71. *Chicago Daily Journal,* March 1, 1849; *The Chicago Times,* April 29, 1871.

[150] *Chicago Daily Journal,* March 15, 1848; *Weekly Chicago Democrat,* March 21, 1848.

[151] Act of February 14, 1851, *Private Laws, 1851,* p. 147. This $100,000 limitation was also in the charter of 1837, and was reaffirmed in 1861. Edmund James, *The Charters of the City of Chicago* (Chicago, 1898), p. 67; Act of February 18, 1861, *Private Laws, 1861,* p. 137.

[152] See, for example, Act of February 28, 1854, *Laws, 1854,* p. 218; Acts of February 14, 15, 1855, *Private Laws, 1855,* pp. 94, 95, 566; Act of February 14, 1859, *Private Laws, 1859,* pp. 533–34.

[153] *Hunt's Merchants' Magazine,* LVII (July, 1867), 32; *Chicago Tribune,* May 7, 1867.

[154] *The Daily Democratic Press,* March 16, 1854; *Chicago Daily Democrat,* January 27, 1858. See Appendix, p. 510, for chart showing conditions of municipal finance.

long-term bonds, with the result that the floating debt still amounted to $230,000 in 1859. The city tried to fund this debt in long-term bonds in 1859 to effect savings on interest payments, but the Superior Court issued an injunction on the ground that such funding constituted an increase of the debt and hence was subject to the charter limitation.[155] The floating debt of the city, therefore, grew until by 1861 it stood at $500,110.[156] Then the legislature allowed the city to pay off the floating debt as it stood in April, 1861, by issuing twenty-year bonds at interest rates not to exceed 7 per cent.[157]

Objections to these rapid debt increases were not long in coming. Excessive taxes and increasing indebtedness were driving people from the city, declared the *Democrat* in 1852, as it urged the election of only those officials who would promise to contract no new debts and who would retire outstanding obligations. Improvements were sometimes delayed until their installation costs had been paid into the treasury by tax, special assessment, or subscription, so that the flotation of loans for their construction might be avoided. But the attitude toward the contracting of debts persisted that, cost what they might, public works should go on.[158]

As a result of the public demand for improvements, the indebtedness of the city soared from $20,338 in 1848 to $14,103,000 in 1871. Property valuation, tax levies, and total annual expenditures of the city during these years had by no means increased in the same proportion.[159] By 1871, the municipal funded debt, including school and school construction bonds, but excluding sewerage, water, and river improvement bonds, amounted to $3,707,000, or over 26 per cent of the entire long-term debt of the city of Chicago. The sewerage bonds outstanding at that time totaled $5,576,000, over 39 per cent of the total, while the water debt accounted for the remaining

---

[155] *Chicago Weekly Democrat,* July 9, 1859; " Annual Financial Statement, 1859," Chicago, *Council Proceedings, 1858–61,* pp. 167–69; *The Press and Tribune,* May 26, 1859.

[156] *Chicago Tribune,* May 7, 1861. This floating debt which was mostly in scrip bearing 10 per cent interest was larger than the city debt proper, for the latter amounted only to $484,000 at this time.

[157] Act of February 28, 1861, *Private Laws, 1861,* pp. 136–37.

[158] *The Press and Tribune,* April 11, 1859; *Weekly Chicago Democrat,* February 21, 1852; *Chicago Daily Journal,* September 18, 1850, April 22, 1852; *Chicago Daily Democrat,* October 16, 1851.

[159] *Weekly Chicago Democrat,* March 21, 1848; *The Chicago Times,* April 29, 1871. The " floating orders " in 1848 amounted to about $4,000; the floating liabilities in 1870–71 were $314,421. See chart showing tax, property value, and debt figures, Appendix, p. 510.

$4,820,000, or over 34 per cent.[160] The debt had been fairly evenly divided among these three items for the previous decade.[161]

A series of measures were tried to reduce the cost of servicing the debt. In 1851, when Mayor Gurnee was inaugurated, the part of the city debt maturing that year was bearing interest at the rate of 12 per cent per annum. Following a suggestion made in the previous administration, he undertook to refund the debt at much lower interest rates and made it a definite part of his policy to issue new bonds at a lower rate of interest and to refund at lower rates and for longer periods some 12 per cent bonds which matured.[162] Toward the end of Gurnee's administration, the interest rate on the city bonded debt averaged about 9.1 per cent.[163] By 1854 the cost of servicing averaged a little over 7 per cent on the total funded debt of $248,666.[164] By April, 1867, the average interest on the debt of $4,757,500 had decreased to about 6.67 per cent.[165] Equally important for the city were the fluctuations in the sale prices of municipal bond issues, reflecting the economic conditions of the time not only in Chicago but throughout the country.[166] The panic of 1857 sent city bonds far below par, but by 1862 a more favorable financial situation

[160] These computations are based on statements in the *Chicago Times*, April 29, 1871. The sewerage debt included the bond issues for river improvement, of which there were $2,896,000 outstanding. From the sources available, it is impossible to tell with certainty whether park bonds are included in the "municipal debt" for 1871 as given above.

[161] In April, 1866, for instance, out of a total bonded debt of $4,369,500, municipal bonds amounted to $1,383,500, water bonds to $1,657,000, and sewerage bonds to $1,012,500. (*Chicago Tribune*, April 16, 1866.) In 1861, the various items which made up the bonded debt were: the municipal debt proper, $484,000; sewerage debt, $885,000; and water debt, $1,105,000. *Ibid.*, May 7, 1861.

[162] In 1850 the issue of $80,000 in 7 per cent ten-year bonds was recommended to retire floating debts paying high interest and to erect certain needed public buildings. However, later in the same year, certain 10 per cent bonds held by George F. Lee were extended two years at the same interest rate. *Chicago Daily Journal*, June 13, September 18, 1850, March 11, 1851, March 9, 1852.

[163] Board of Water Commissioners, *Semi-annual Report, 1851*, p. 7.

[164] Computations cited here were based on itemized statement of the debt, appearing in *The Daily Democratic Press*, March 3, 1854.

[165] *Hunt's Merchants' Magazine*, LVII (July, 1867), 31–32.

[166] In 1851–52, the 7 per cent ten-year bonds sold for 90, and the 7 per cent fifteen-year bonds at 86.9, while it was only the 10 per cent two-year bonds which were quoted at par. (*Chicago Daily Journal*, March 9, 1852.) The city's 6 per cent twenty-year bonds reached a high quotation of 98 and a low of 85 in 1855. (*The Bankers' Magazine*, X [February, 1856], 606.) In 1857, municipal bonds began to suffer from the panic which began in that year. Six per cent twenty-year bonds sank from 83, offered in July, to 75 in October, while 7 per cent bonds of no redemption date were quoted at 99, asked, in July, and 97½ in October. (*Ibid.*, XII [July-October, 1857], 76, 156, 252, 332.) The 6 per cent bonds had recovered somewhat by the first half of 1859. *Ibid.*, XIII (February-May, 1859), 672, 831, 911.

and the fulfillment of contractual obligations by the city made possible the sale of $75,000 of 7 per cent bonds at 109. The payment by Chicago of the interest on its bonds in gold coin enhanced the credit of the city, and when, in 1870, 7 per cent bonds amounting to $2,800,000 were put on the market they were quoted at ninety-seven and one half with no commissions or deductions.[167]

Throughout the years 1848 to 1871 much of the governmental life of Chicago had been determined by the state legislature. Indeed it had seemed to Chicagoans at times that the legislature was acting as a superior municipal council, that Springfield was outlining the acts of the Chicago government. From representatives, frequently rural in point of view, had come direction. Even by 1870 Representative James McCoy of the Forty-eighth District reflected this growing hostility when he said: ". . . I believe it has become a nice question, whether the city of Chicago is in the State of Illinois, or the State of Illinois is in the city of Chicago. I believe that depends whether you live in Chicago or not." [168]

More hampering was the fact that as the legal calendar became overcrowded with special, local, and private bills, the lawmakers sometimes succumbed to the pleas of pressure groups to whose private interests those of the public were subordinated. To remove these evils, the state constitutional convention, assembled in December, 1869, entirely abolished the power of the legislature to enact special laws for cities. In 1872 the legislature passed a general municipal incorporation act, accepted by Chicago in 1875, which outlined charter provisions applicable to any city upon the consent of its voters.

[167] *Ibid.*, XVII (January, 1863), 567, XXV (August, 1870), 150; *Chicago Tribune*, July 7, 1870. Quotations on city scrip followed much the same course as did quotations on bonds, scrip selling at 10 per cent discount in April, 1849 (*Daily Democrat*, April 18, 1849), and rising to par when the sale of bonds gave the city funds with which to redeem the scrip. (*Ibid.*, June 9, 1849.) Issue of scrip fell off to some extent in the early 'fifties, none being issued unless funds for redemption were available. (*The Daily Democratic Press*, March 8, 1853.) During the panic years, the amount of scrip increased to about half a million dollars drawing interest at 10 per cent by 1861 (*Chicago Tribune*, May 7, 1861). The total of scrip and warrants was less than $300,000 by 1871. *The Chicago Times*, April 29, 1871.

[168] See, for example, *Debates and Proceedings of the Constitutional Convention, 1869–70*, I, 387, II, 1511; Verlie, *op. cit.*, p. 119; Samuel E. Sparling, *Municipal History and Present Organization of the City of Chicago* (University of Wisconsin, *Bulletin*, no. 23. Economics, Political Science, and History Series, II, no. 2. Madison, 1908), pp. 55–65. The government of Chicago under the operation of the Constitution of 1870 is more fully treated in Pierce, *A History of Chicago*, III (in preparation).

During the years from 1850 to 1870 adjustments had been made, in a sometimes haphazard fashion, to meet the changes resulting from the rapid growth of the city. Duties formerly performed by private enterprise were taken over by the municipal authorities. The power of the mayor was somewhat strengthened in an attempt to give a degree of unity to local policies. New boards, chosen in many different ways, were set up to direct increasingly complex administrative functions.

This adjustment of governmental structure to expanding needs, necessary though it was, was complicated by the dichotomy between opposing groups. Some feared a growth in the influence of the executive while others feared the indiscretions of the legislature of the city. Protests about governmental agencies and semi-independent executive boards created since 1850 arose from those who thought the day of responsible government was passing. But there were those who wished, for the sake of " unity, order, or economy," that consolidation might take place, and that more authority might be vested in the hands of the mayor. Conflicting pressures hindered the solutions of many problems in a day when purity in legislative bodies, national, state, and local, was sometimes sadly lacking. Nor did the electorate rise above their chosen representatives. If they had, their servants would have reflected the views of an aroused constituency.

CHAPTER IX

THE CHURCH AND THE CHANGING ORDER

THE CHURCHES, TOO, faced the problem of keeping pace not only with the physical expansion of the city, but also with the adjustment necessary to the unprecedented conditions created by an urban civilization and by a rapidly increasing wealth. The physical manifestations of church growth paralleled other aspects of development. From the South Side religious bodies spread into the North and West divisions as these sections were built up. Within sixteen years after Chicago was incorporated as a town, her citizens proudly acclaimed her "the city of churches," the place of a "congregation of spires."[1] But the twenty-five churches of 1848 seemed few indeed in comparison with the one hundred ninety churches, missions, and convents of 1870,[2] just as the homely frame buildings erected for a few thousand dollars stood in sharp contrast to the Gothic-styled structures which cost as much as $150,000.[3]

As urban sophistication developed, class and ethnic lines came to be more and more clear-cut. Well-to-do Protestants flocked in increas-

---

[1] *Daily Democrat,* May 4, 1849.

[2] *Weekly Chicago Democrat,* September 19, 1848. There were twelve convents included in the one hundred ninety churches in 1870. See Appendix, p. 511.

[3] For example, the First Baptist Church used in 1848 cost about $4,500. The edifice used by this congregation in 1870 had cost $150,000. (J. W. Norris, *A Business Advertiser and General Directory of the City of Chicago, for the Year 1845-6* [Chicago, 1845], pp. 4-7 [hereafter cited as Norris, *Directory, 1845-46*]; [Cyrus Bentley], *History of the First Baptist Church, Chicago* . . . [4th ed. Chicago, 1889], p. 39.) Some writers place the cost of this church at $175,000. Andreas, *History of Chicago,* II, 434.

ing numbers to the Episcopal, Congregational, New School and Old School Presbyterian churches, located on the fashionable avenues of the city. Of the twenty-nine churches listed for these denominations in 1865, twenty were in sections inhabited chiefly by middle-class and wealthy Chicagoans, while only two were in the parts where dwelt the poor and had memberships made up largely of immigrants.[4]

Foremost in numbers among the predominantly American Protestant groups stood the Methodists, and next came the Baptists. Although they too had houses of worship located along the fashionable streets of Wabash, Michigan, Indiana, and West Washington, both had good followings among Negroes, immigrants, and the poor.[5] The Methodists experienced a growth of 487 per cent in the two decades following 1850, and the Baptists had the still more flattering expansion of 681 per cent during the same period. While Chicago Methodists and Baptists in 1870 still outnumbered the Presbyterians and Congregationalists, the latter in the older cities of the East had maintained their lead.[6]

Regardless of the increases made by the predominantly American Protestant groups, their gains lagged proportionately behind population gains. But the Lutherans were at this time expanding from less than five hundred members in 1850 to over seventy-five hundred in 1870. Like the Roman Catholic, the Lutheran church drew to itself many of the new foreign dwellers in Chicago. In 1870, seventeen edifices reflected the expansion of the Lutheran membership over that of 1848 when three houses of worship could care for persons of that faith. During these same years the Roman Catholics had outgrown their four churches and were housed in twenty-five churches located in all three divisions of the city. Most of the Lutheran churches were in the North and West divisions where they could

[4] Episcopalians had an increase, 1850–70, of 631 per cent; Congregationalists increased 685 per cent, 1855–70.

[5] In 1865, the Methodist Episcopal organization had under its wing two Negro, four German and Scandinavian, and three or more churches located among " the poor." The total number of Methodist churches was sixteen. The Baptists had a total of eleven churches of which one was Negro, three were German and Scandinavian, and one (or possibly two) cared for the poor. See Appendix, p. 511.

[6] These five Protestant denominations accounted for about 7 per cent of the population in 1850, and 5 per cent in 1870. These figures must be considered as approximate because of the failure of denominations to keep exact membership rolls, and because of the difference in meaning of the term " membership." The population of Chicago grew from 29,963 in 1850 to 298,977 in 1870.

serve the workingmen and shopkeepers, who made up a good part of their membership.

In the South Division, at the fringe of the business district, were found the first three Jewish synagogues established in Chicago. These were attended chiefly by German Jews, living not among other Germans on the North Side, but having their homes in the South Division, west of State Street.[7]

Expansion in church memberships and in the numbers of church buildings had their counterpart in better salaries paid the ministers of the well-to-do congregations and in the large offerings and subscriptions made to wipe out debts for new buildings and upkeep. At the dedication of the Methodist Centenary Church in 1868, for example, subscriptions totaled $33,000 to cancel a debt of about $29,000; and at the dedication of Grace Methodist Episcopal Church pledges amounted to $38,130 on a debt of about $37,000.[8] Although there was not always generosity when demands were made, further evidence of greater prosperity was reflected in the salaries of $5,000 or more paid, in 1868, by such congregations as the First Presbyterian and Plymouth Congregational.[9] To the near-by country parson it must have seemed an unfair distribution of this world's goods when even congregations of small shopkeepers, clerks, and others of modest income, such as Leavitt Street Congregational Church or the Swedenborgian group, paid an annual salary of $2,000 or more in the postwar years.[10] A few churches even sought to care for the old age of

---

[7] Figures on Roman Catholic membership are not available. The Negro Methodist and Baptist churches were in the South Division west of State Street. Halpin, *Directory, 1865–66*, " City and County Record," pp. xxvii–xxxii; Reports of denominational bodies. See pp. 11 ff.; for more details, see Appendix, p. 511.

[8] *The Advance*, March 19, July 16, 1868. See also *Congregational Herald*, November 18, 1858.

[9] *The Advance*, July 9, August 27, December 3, 10, 1868. The First Presbyterian paid the Rev. Arthur Mitchell $6,000 in 1868, and, in the same year, Plymouth Congregational paid $7,000 to the Rev. William A. Bartlett to bring him from Brooklyn.

[10] *Ibid.*, February 25, 1869; [Rudolph Williams], *The New Church and Chicago, a History* (Chicago, 1906), pp. 69, 108, 138, 160. The salaries paid to ministers in the Rock River Conference of the Methodist Episcopal Church, which included Chicago and its hinterland, reveal the rural-urban contrast. In 1869, out of eleven Methodist churches listed in Chicago, two paid their clergymen, for salary and rent, $5,000 a year, another $3,300, another $3,000. The average of all eleven was about $2,300, and only one Chicago pastor of this denomination received less than $1,200. Of the 163 " charges " in the Rock River Conference, only seventeen outside of Chicago, churches in towns such as Freeport, Galena, Ottawa, and Aurora, paid salaries of $1,200 or more, and only one — the pastorate in Evanston — had a salary in excess of the average paid to Chicago pastors. Rock River Annual Conference of

their pastors. Wabash Avenue Baptist Church provided a $5,000 fund to the Rev. Robert Boyd when he retired, and the Methodists used some of the profits from their book concern as partial support for retired ministers and the widows and children of deceased clergymen.[11]

The renting of pews provided a source of income. Although this practice was considered by some as undemocratic in theory and application and therefore as conducive to class consciousness, others held that the system assured a means of promoting religious activities.[12] Gradually, congregations composed principally of the moderate-income group gave up this means of gaining revenue and proclaimed themselves " free " churches where support depended upon voluntary contributions. Even among the Episcopalians, who generally carried on pew-renting, a free church, the Church of the Holy Communion, was opened in 1859 with the blessing of the wealthy St. James's Church.[13] The invidiousness invariably felt by the poor man in the sale of seats, openly advertised by pulpit and press with prices for one pew sometimes more than his annual pay envelope, tended to keep the workingman from attending church services and led in some cases to the setting of one price for all pews and the provision for those who could not pay a full rental.[14] By the late 'sixties the implications of pew-renting had become so plain that insurgents were openly hoping that the day would speedily come when Christian worship and preaching should not be " sold out at so much a seat " but should be free to all, when rich and poor could meet on " a level before one God and Savior." [15]

the Methodist Episcopal Church, *Register of the Thirtieth Session, . . . 1869* (Chicago, 1869), pp. 50–55.

[11] *The Christian Times,* September 16, 1863; *Northwestern Christian Advocate,* January 5, 1853 (sometimes *North-Western Christian Advocate,* but cited in this book as *Northwestern Christian Advocate*); Rock River Annual Conference of the Methodist Episcopal Church, *Register of the Twenty-fourth Session, 1863,* p. 52.

[12] *Oquawka Spectator,* November 16, 1853; *Northwestern Christian Advocate,* October 26, November 30, 1853; *Congregational Herald,* May 5, 1854; *Chicago Tribune,* December 28, 1861; *The Advance,* March 31, June 23, 1870, January 26, 1871; *Weekly Chicago Democrat,* January 1, 1853; *Chicago Record,* I (October 1, 1857), 52.

[13] H. B. Whipple, *Sermon Preached at the Opening of the Free Church of the Holy Communion, Chicago, February 6, 1859* (Chicago, 1859), pp. 3–6; *Chicago Tribune,* March 30, 1861.

[14] *Chicago Daily Democrat,* December 27, 1850, January 2, March 13, 1860; *Weekly Chicago Democrat,* January 1, 1853; *Northwestern Christian Advocate,* October 26, November 30, 1853; *Chicago Tribune,* March 30, 1861; *The Advance,* October 24, 1867, June 23, 1870, January 26, 1871.   [15] *Ibid.,* March 31, 1870.

The income for religious instruction was, at times, further supplemented by the sale of church property, often openly encouraged by the governing boards. Church lands, like other realty holdings centrally located, appreciated greatly in value as these sites became desirable as business locations. For example, the First Baptist Church, which had been given its lot, 180 by 80 feet, at the corner of Washington and LaSalle, by the canal commissioners in the 'thirties, disposed of it to the Chamber of Commerce in 1864 for $65,000, sharing the proceeds with six other Baptist churches. In 1869 the First Congregational sold for $50,000 its house and lot at Washington and Green streets. Only sixteen years before the lot had been valued at $6,000.[16]

Serving as social functions as well as sources of revenue were the church fairs, dinners, oyster suppers in cold weather, and strawberry lunches in June, benefit performances by lecturers and by musicians such as Ole Bull, tableaux and amateur theatricals, although the last were condemned by the evangelical groups as stumbling blocks " over which sinners were eternally ruined." [17] Some few of the more liberal churches such as the Unitarians and Swedenborgians went even further and held " social " dances to care for depleted revenues.[18] Of all these, donation parties for ministers were perhaps the most popular, for they served as expressions of affection for a spiritual leader as well as providing for his support. Gifts ranging from money and watches to potatoes and shoes represented far more than their intrinsic worth. They were especially welcome to the minister's family when, as was occasionally the case, they proved to be the chief return the pastor received if he preached in a poor

[16] Bentley, *op. cit.*, pp. 14, 35–36; [First Congregational Church of Chicago], *The Quarter-Centennial of the First Congregational Church of Chicago, May 21st and 22d, 1876* (Chicago, 1876), pp. 14–15. The Methodists, who had also received their lot on the southeast corner of Clark and Washington from the canal trustees in the 'thirties have retained their control of it until the present day. Since the 'fifties it has been the site of a business block as well as of a church auditorium and has been for the Methodists a lucrative source of income. *Northwestern Christian Advocate*, January 27, 1858; Andreas, *History of Chicago*, I, 326. See also *The Advance*, April 15, 1869, July 28, 1870; *The Chicago Times*, January 31, 1855.

[17] *The Christian Times*, January 5, 1865. See also *ibid.*, March 7, 1855, December 23, 30, 1857, January 6, 1858, December 8, 22, 1864; *Chicago Daily Democrat*, November 8, 10, 17, 1849, May 18, October 10, 15, November 19, 20, December 4, 19, 23, 1850, June 23, 1851; *Northwestern Christian Advocate*, February 16, 23, April 27, May 4, 1853, July 19, 1854; *The Advance*, March 31, June 16, 1870; *Chicago Tribune*, January 7, 1857, May 23, 1861.

[18] *The Advance*, May 12, 1870; R. Williams, *op. cit.*, p. 135.

parish.[19] Once in a while, the churches benefited from the loyalty of members who, as merchants, contributed to church funds premiums from the sale of goods. Hulburd, Herrick and Company supported the Tabernacle Congregational Church's Mission School at Holstein through the sale of their " Sabbath School Boot Jack," and the Singer Sewing Machine Company offered the net profits of one hundred machines to the Wicker Park Congregational Church after a windstorm demolished its structure in 1870.[20]

Both native and foreign born came under the influence of the church, for church-going was indeed the outward sign of respectability. As the numbers of aliens grew, separate houses of worship arose to typify unity in religious practice. Some turned to Protestantism, joining with those of like belief, but others followed the lead of many immigrants before 1848 and found their religious haven within the Roman Catholic faith.

The first church of the Catholics had been built in 1833, and soon they had the largest number of communicants of any denomination in the city. Upon the death of Bishop Quarter in 1848, Bishop James Oliver Van de Velde succeeded to the diocese and carried on the work of expansion begun by his predecessor. Other men of vision and ability followed and strengthened this faith in the rapidly growing community. Their work was often sad and taxing, for cholera, smallpox, and consumption took a heavy toll among their parishioners, and poverty was the lot of many. Nor was a bountiful living theirs during these early years, for their congregations were made up chiefly of immigrants, farmers, mechanics, and poorly paid laborers who were able to aid but little in providing proper means for the celebration of the Mass and in furnishing comfortable residences for their priests. But vestments came in 1850 to the diocese from France, and financial aid came from Germany to St. Michael's when its funds ran especially low, and these gifts revived faltering spirits as well as failing finances. Fairs and the popular sociable lent their re-

[19] See, for example, *Northwestern Christian Advocate*, July 19, 1854, March 3, 1858; *The Christian Times*, February 9, 1865; *The Advance*, June 2, 1870; *The Interior*, September 28, 1871. On New Year's Day, 1868, Dwight L. Moody was presented with a house " furnished from top to bottom " and portraits of himself and Mrs. Moody painted by Healy and Antrobus. In 1860, the Rev. Zephaniah M. Humphrey of the First Presbyterian Church received an insurance policy worth $5,000. *The Advance*, January 9, 1868; *Chicago Daily Democrat*, January 5, 1860.

[20] *The Advance*, November 21, 1867, April 7, 1870.

turns, and profits realized in a speculation of lands supplemented other sources of revenue.[21]

Financial worries were enough, but there were, in addition, vexing administrative problems, particularly in the ministries of Bishop Van de Velde, Bishop O'Regan, and Bishop Duggan. The regimes of the last two priests suffered devastating attacks by Father Chiniquy, a French-Canadian priest, who sometimes preached at St. Louis Church in Chicago, and whose renunciation of his vows provided rich food for gossip.[22] Taking refuge in a law of 1845 investing in the Bishop of Chicago and his successors the power to control and convey all church property, Bishop Van de Velde objected to the holding of property for religious purposes by a group of nuns and in so doing aroused much opposition.[23] Disapproval of the Bishop by some of the faculty of the University of St. Mary further disturbed what should have been an atmosphere of religious harmony and eventually brought about Bishop Van de Velde's resignation. Such unhappy incidents assumed an undue importance in a setting of physical hardships and in a time when Roman Catholicism was feared by many Protestants as threatening the American principle of the separation of church and state.[24]

Despite such obstacles the Catholic faith steadily gained in membership. The most rapid expansion took place in the episcopate of Bishop Duggan from 1859 to 1870. New parishes sprang from older

[21] The bishops who followed Van de Velde were Bishop O'Regan, 1854; Bishop Duggan, 1859; Bishop Foley, 1870. Rev. James J. McGovern, " The Catholic Church in Chicago," *Souvenir of the Silver Jubilee in the Episcopacy of His Grace the Most Reverend Patrick Augustine Feehan, Archbishop of Chicago, November 1st, 1865–1890* (Chicago, 1891), pp. 95–97, 103, 169–70, 186–88, 196 ff.; Gilbert J. Garraghan, *The Catholic Church in Chicago, 1673–1871* . . . (Chicago, 1921), pp. 162–64; Sisters of Mercy, *Leaves from the Annals of the Sisters of Mercy* (3 v. New York, 1889), III, 246; George S. Phillips, *Chicago and her Churches* (Chicago, 1868), pp. 260 ff.; Francis J. Epstein, ed., " History in the Annals of the Leopoldine Association, Letters of the Bishop William Quarter, D.D.," *Illinois Catholic Historical Review,* I (July, 1918), 226–27.

[22] Charles P. T. Chiniquy, *Fifty Years in the Church of Rome* (3d ed. Montreal, 1886), chaps. xlviii-lxvi, *Forty Years in the Church of Christ* (Chicago, 1900), chaps. v, xvii. Chiniquy later joined the Presbyterian church.

[23] Act of February 24, 1845, *Laws, 1844–45,* pp. 321–22. For example, Father Walter Quarter had conveyed property to the Sisters of Mercy whose right to hold it was questioned by Bishop Van de Velde. Mother Agatha finally yielded. (A Sister of the Community, " The Sisters of Mercy," *Illinois Catholic Historical Review,* III [April, 1921], 350.) Another quarrel over deeds to a church lot induced the Bishop to have the church raised four feet off the ground to prevent attendance. Andreas, *History of Chicago,* I, 296–97.

[24] D. J. Riordan, " University of St. Mary of the Lake," *Illinois Catholic Historical Review,* II (October, 1919), 143–44.

ones; St. Jarlath's was an offshoot of St. Patrick's in 1869. Others like St. Columbkille's, at Grand and Paulina, grew out of a mission. St. Columbkille's, in turn, gave protection to another mission, the Church of the Annunciation, organized to care for the spiritual needs of an increasing number of immigrants in the rolling-mill district.[25] In 1868 this first Catholic church on the Northwest Side was strong enough to have its first resident priest. Into other industrial areas the Catholics pushed their ministrations. As early as 1855 they set up the Church of St. James near the American Car Works. In the stockyards district, Father Michael Lyons obtained a lot on Thirty-ninth Street between Halsted and Emerald Avenue, and upon this lot in 1868 he moved an old stable to serve temporarily as a house of worship. Christened the Church of the Holy Angels, it later became the Church of the Nativity.[26]

The Roman Catholics carried their faith also into sections beyond the boundaries of the city. In 1865, the Church of St. James established two missions, St. Thomas the Apostle at Fifty-fifth and Kimbark for families in Hyde Park and St. Anne's farther west on the South Side.[27] Separate parishes met the needs of ethnic groups whose mother tongues were not the same, and whose mastery of English was not great enough to permit religious instruction in that language. Services for Germans could be heard in four churches, and French-Canadians could attend the Church of St. Louis or, later, the Church of Notre Dame.[28]

[25] Garraghan, *Catholic Church in Chicago*, pp. 191–92, 199–201; *Minutes of St. Columb-kille's Church, December, 1858* (*Ms.* Chicago Historical Society); *Chicago Daily Democrat*, November 21, 1859; Rev. Thomas L. Hormer, *Fifty Years of Parish History, Church of the Annunciation, 1866–1916* (Chicago, 1916), p. 5.

[26] *Ibid.*, p. 5; Garraghan, *Catholic Church in Chicago*, pp. 190, 200.

[27] *Ibid.*, p. 199. St. Anne's was located at Fifty-fifth and Wentworth. Both missions became parishes in 1868.

[28] German Catholic churches included St. Joseph's, Cass and Chicago Avenue; St. Peter's, at first on Washington Street between Wells and Franklin and in 1853 at Clark and Polk; St. Michael's, North Avenue and Hudson; St. Francis of Assisi, Clinton and Mather streets. (McGovern, *loc. cit.*, pp. 78, 80; Garraghan, *Catholic Church in Chicago*, pp. 84, 146–47, 149–50, 198; J. C. Bürgler, *Geschichte der Kathol. [sic] Kirche Chicago's* . . . [Chicago, 1889], pp. 28, 29, 33.) The Church of St. Louis was located on Clark Street between Jackson and Adams. Before this church was built, temporary quarters had been at Clark and Quincy. A mission of St. Patrick's also served French-speaking Catholics. The Church of Notre Dame on the West Side, in reality a successor of the Church of St. Louis, also cared for these Catholics. Garraghan, *Catholic Church in Chicago*, pp. 149–50, 198; *Chicago Daily Democrat*, November 13, December 17, 1850; Halpin, *Directory, 1865–66*, " City and County Record," p. xxxiii; *Chicago Evening Journal*, February 26, 1863; *Chicago Tribune*, October 2, 1864.

Of all foreigners, the Irish were probably the most numerous and frequently the most prominent among the Catholics. They were the chief supporters of St. Patrick's, at Desplaines and Randolph, and its offshoots. They gave help after 1857 to the Church of the Holy Family, near Twelfth Street and Blue Island Avenue, under the direction of the Jesuit Father Arnold Damen. This church, although constructed at a time when money was hard to get, prospered throughout its history. It drew to its arms the workingmen who lived in the small wooden houses scattered over the windswept prairie near the railroad buildings and lumber yards. A college, parochial schools, and, in the 'seventies, a sodality building with halls for social gatherings and a reading room were physical evidences of the far-flung activities which Father Damen and other priests promoted for their followers.[29] In 1865, the Church of the Holy Family boasted that its newly dedicated altar surpassed in beauty and artistic finish anything of the kind in America, and that its many statues were " overhung by rich canopies resting on pillars of burnished gold." At Bridgeport, where many Irish lived, was St. Bridget's, recognized as a separate parish in 1854, but not provided with a dedicated building until 1857.[30]

Among other aliens who sought spiritual guidance from the Roman Catholic church were the Poles who, in 1866, founded the Society of St. Stanislaus and a year later petitioned Bishop Duggan for a church. The Bohemians, at first the charge of the Church of the Holy Family, later were received into the Church of St. Wenceslaus.[31]

Social, religious, and benevolent societies welded these foreigners into compact bodies devoted to common aims and bound by a common language. Festivals and celebration days cemented loyalty to church and a national identity, and lectures, periodicals, and other forms of sectarian education entrenched Catholicism in their hearts.

[29] Garraghan, Catholic Church in Chicago, pp. 119, 169–71, 204–5; McGovern, loc. cit., pp. 191–95; Thomas M. Mulkerins, Holy Family Parish . . . (Chicago, 1923), chap. xxiii; Gilbert J. Garraghan, " Beginnings of Holy Family Parish, Chicago, 1857–1871," Illinois Catholic Historical Review, I (April, 1919), 447.

[30] Garraghan, Catholic Church in Chicago, p. 189; The Chicago Times, November 28, 1857; The Monthly [Roman Catholic], II (1865), 474–75.

[31] [Joseph J. Thompson], The Archdiocese of Chicago: Antecedents and Developments (Des Plaines, Illinois, 1920), pp. 377 ff.; X. W. Krusska, History a Polska w Ameryce, I, 76; Garraghan, Catholic Church in Chicago, pp. 197, 200; Mulkerins, op. cit., p. 134. The petition of the Poles was granted, and a church was built at Noble and Bradley streets in the northwest part of the city.

Various orders of the priesthood and nuns instilled into trusting young minds the religion of their fathers and made loyalty to church man's first duty.[32] A separate cemetery with hallowed ground tended further to emphasize the oneness of those of the Catholic faith.[33] With few defections from the ranks of the faithful and an increasing immigration chiefly of Roman Catholics, the church expanded many times in the years after 1848, attaining a reported total membership of 108,500 persons by 1868, more than all the Protestant denominations claimed.[34]

Among the leading Protestant denominations were the Methodists, Baptists, and Presbyterians. As immigration of the Scandinavians and Germans increased, the Lutheran and Evangelical churches gained in importance. The Methodist church early asserted leadership because of its age and numbers. Its membership was made up chiefly of native Americans, but there were in the city by the late 'sixties four German Methodist congregations and two Scandinavian.[35] In the 'fifties there had been a Welsh Methodist group, but in the late 'sixties their acceptance of Calvinistic teachings attached them more to Presbyterianism than to Methodism.[36]

In 1853, twenty-five Scandinavian Methodists organized a church. Within a little over a decade their numbers increased to thirteen times the original membership. Germans were attracted into Methodism somewhat later, but by 1865 a considerable group worshipped as Methodists in addition to the members of the three German Evangelical *Gemeinschaften* which resembled Methodist churches in theology and mode of worship. Within the portals of the Methodist church, Negroes found their first religious haven in Chicago.

[32] See, for example, *The Monthly*, II (1865), 296. Some of the important orders and dates of arrivals are as follows: Religious of the Sacred Heart, 1858; Sisters of Charity of St. Vincent, 1858; Sisters of the Good Shepherd, 1859; Brothers of the Christian Schools, 1861; Alexian Brothers, 1866; Franciscan Sisters, 1867; the Poor Handmaids of Christ, 1868. Garraghan, *Catholic Church in Chicago*, pp. 202 ff.

[33] The largest Roman Catholic cemetery was Calvary, opened in November, 1859. No religious service other than Catholic could be held there, although non-Catholics were not denied burial. *Chicago Daily Democrat*, November 3, 30, 1859.

[34] Colbert, *Chicago*, p. 114.

[35] *Chicago Daily Democrat*, January 15, 1851; Edwards, *Merchants' Census Report, 1871*, p. 1242.

[36] As early as 1844 Welsh Methodist settlers met in private homes to hold services. In 1850 a room was rented at the corner of Randolph and Canal streets. *A Brief History of Hebron Presbyterian Church* (privately printed); Rev. Vyrnwy Morgan, *The Cambro-American Pulpit* (New York, 1898), p. 51; Gager, *Case & Co.'s Directory, 1857*, Appendix, p. xxxviii; Austin, *Bailey's Directory, 1867–68*, p. 1039; Edwards, *Directory, 1868*, p. 995.

At Quinn's Chapel in the late 'forties and early 'fifties " one of the best appearing and best conducted congregations in the city " met each Sunday under the guidance of a regular pastor. By 1854, efforts to provide a new church had succeeded, and at the time of the outbreak of the war the Bethel African Methodist Episcopal had been added.[37]

Although not so great in numbers as the Methodists, the Baptists were also a force in the early religious life of the city. Like the Methodists, they attracted Negroes into their fellowship, and as early as 1853 Zoar Baptist Church became the Negroes' special shrine. In 1862, Zoar and Zion, which had been organized in 1858, united to form Olivet, and within three years four hundred souls were listed among the faithful. German, Danish, and Swedish immigrants had their own Baptist churches in which to worship, edifices generally modest in appearance, as befitted the small numbers and slender purses of the congregations.[38]

The divisions which split the Presbyterians throughout the country at this time affected the Chicago churches of that denomination. The New School, liberal in attitude, was represented in the First Presbyterian Church started in 1833. Differences over the question of slavery led those not rabidly opposed to that institution to separate themselves from the First Church in 1842 and establish the Second Church. An exponent of the New School theology, this church by

---

[37] *Northwestern Christian Advocate,* January 12, 1853. The First German Methodist Church was organized in 1847; the Second or the Van Buren Street Church organized in 1852 (*ibid.,* February 16, 1853); the Third or Maxwell Street Church in 1854; and the fourth or Portland Avenue German Church was added in 1869. Andreas, *History of Chicago,* I, 332, II, 428; *Chicago Daily Democrat,* July 3, 1851; Halpin, *Directory, 1865–66,* " City and County Record," pp. xxix, xxxi.

[38] *Ibid.,* p. xxvii; Andreas, *History of Chicago,* I, 323–24. The First Baptist Church was organized in 1833. The Tabernacle, the pioneer church on the West Side, was organized because of disagreement regarding the slavery issue. It became the Second Baptist Church in 1864 when it joined others withdrawing from the First. (Halpin, *Directory, 1865–66,* " City and County Record," p. xxvi; Bentley, *op. cit.,* pp. 24–26, 36–37.) The First German Baptist Church was organized with fourteen members in 1851. (*Watchman of the Prairies,* July 22, 1851.) Others were established later. A Danish church appeared in mid-'sixties. (Halpin, *Directory, 1865–66,* " City and County Record," p. xxvii.) In 1853, the first Swedish church was founded and in 1855 was called the Scandinavian Baptist Church. In 1864 this church was disbanded and was followed two years later by what is generally known as the First Swedish Baptist Church. *The Christian Times,* November 22, 1854, June 20, 1855; Olson and others, eds., *History of the Swedes of Illinois,* I, 569–73; Edwards, *Merchants' Census Report, 1871,* p. 1241.

1851 found its tenets upheld in two other churches of the city.[39] Two Old School churches at the same time promoted their special doctrines. The year 1865 found Chicago with five Old School, eight New School, and two United Presbyterian churches.[40] Especially energetic in propagating its faith through colonization in the new parts of the city was the Second Presbyterian Church, which helped the First Presbyterian Church of Hyde Park, and the Olivet, Westminster, and Lake Forest churches. But the Presbyterians set up no establishments for Negroes, and few foreign groups other than the Scotch and Welsh were attracted by their denominational teachings.[41]

Out of the controversy over slavery, the Congregational church in Chicago was born. Its beginnings were in the Third Presbyterian Church which had many Congregationalists within its membership. This group in 1850 sent to the Christian Anti-Slavery Convention in Cincinnati a delegate with resolutions condemning the institution of slavery.[42] This action led to conflict within the Chicago church, and when several valiant but vain attempts to harmonize the discordant forces failed, the refractory antislavery element was cut off by the local presbytery. The ousted faction then organized the First Congregational Church in May, 1851. Those within the Presbyterian church who were opposed to slaveholding and who looked with favor on local autonomy in church government set up other

[39] By 1865, the membership of the First Presbyterian was nine hundred. (Philo A. Otis, *The First Presbyterian Church* . . . [2d ed. Chicago, 1913], pp. 34, 39–41; Halpin, *Directory, 1865–66*, " City and County Record," p. xxxii.) The Second Presbyterian was one of the wealthiest in the city. It directed its energies chiefly toward benevolent enterprises and home missions, in a ten-year period contributing $13,000 to the former. It claimed a membership of 285 in 1852 and 600 to 700 in 1865. *The Daily Democratic Press*, September 21, 1852; *Chicago Tribune*, June 26, 1892; Phillips, *op. cit.*, p. 194.

[40] The first of the Old School churches was the Reformed Presbyterian, organized in 1845, but without a building until 1850. By 1865, it had only three hundred members. (*Chicago Daily Democrat*, August 27, 1849, January 15, 1851; Halpin, *Directory, 1865–66*, " City and County Record," p. xxxiii.) The North Presbyterian was organized in 1848, the South Presbyterian in 1853, Edwards Church in 1861, and Fullerton Avenue Church in 1864. (*Ibid.*, pp. xxxii–xxxiii.) The Reunion Church in 1870 represented the reunion of the two schools. *The Advance*, July 7, 1870.

[41] *Chicago Tribune*, June 26, 1892; Andreas, *History of Chicago*, II, 417. There was a Scotch church from the 'sixties on. (Edwards, *Directory, 1870*, p. 932.) The Welsh church, originally called Calvin Methodist Church, affiliated with the New School Assembly in the 'sixties. Halpin, *Directory, 1865–66*, " City and County Record," p. xxxii.

[42] Andreas, *History of Chicago*, I, 307, 339; *Chicago Tribune*, January 31, 1862, June 26, 1892; *The Daily Democratic Press*, February 13, 1855.

units. By 1871 there were thirteen Congregational churches and two missions in the city.[43]

The Episcopalians, in spite of a flattering growth in membership, were less numerous than some of the other Protestant groups. In 1871 they could worship in fifteen churches, in which the average attendance was reckoned as 9,198, although the number of members was considerably less.[44] Four missions were organized, and St. Ansgarius, founded in the late 'forties, cared for Swedish communicants, the only foreign unit under Episcopalian authority.[45]

But growth did not always indicate harmonious expansion, for dissension over "high church" practices sometimes led to the organization of new congregations. This was the case when the Rev. C. E. Swope and some of his parishioners seceded in 1851 from Trinity Church and set up Grace Church where high church services were to be conducted.[46] In the late 'sixties, the refusal of the Rev. Charles E. Cheney of Christ Church to abide by the exact phraseology of the Book of Common Prayer brought to a head an issue which was tried in both church and secular courts. His open defiance came after protests had been made by a group of "Low Church" clergymen and laity against what they called "strong Romanizing tendencies," and the refusal by the General Convention of the Church, in 1869, of their petition to liberalize the use of the Prayer Book and to abandon phraseology held archaic. By the ecclesiastical court Cheney was found guilty of dropping a word in the church service and was sentenced to deposition from his ministry. But before sentence had been pronounced, Cheney and his attorney, Melville W. Fuller, had obtained an injunction from the Superior Court in

---

[43] John H. Hollister, "History of Plymouth Church," Papers (Ms. Chicago Historical Society), pp. 6–7; Chicago Daily Democrat, May 14, 1851; Chicago Tribune, January 31, 1862, June 26, 1892; Edwards, Merchants' Census Report, 1871, p. 1241; Watchman of the Prairies, April 15, May 13, 1851; Congregational Herald, April 21, 1854.

[44] Edwards, Merchants' Census Report, 1871, p. 1241. See Appendix p. 511.

[45] St. Ansgarius, which was the recipient of donations by Jenny Lind in 1850 and 1851, had the services of Gustaf Unonius, 1848–58. He was succeeded by the Rev. E. B. Tuttle, Episcopal city missionary, who advertised it as a "Free Church." Tuttle was succeeded in 1864 by the Rev. Jacob Bredberg. Eric Norelius, De svenska lutherska församlingarnas och Svenskarnas historia i Amerika (2 v. Rock Island, 1890), I, 367; Olson, op. cit., I, 413–17; Chicago Daily Democrat, April 26, December 7, 1850, July 2, September 1, November 10, 1860.

[46] Rev. Francis J. Hall, A History of the Diocese of Chicago . . . (Dixon, Illinois, n.d.), pp. 63–64; [Grace Church, Chicago], The Parish Year Book . . . (Chicago, 1896), pp. 9–13; Chicago Daily Democrat, May 21, 22, June 23, 1851.

Chicago restraining the church court from proceeding with the trial on the grounds that the profession of minister was property and, therefore, that Cheney was entitled to demand an examination of the dispute by the secular courts. The case was appealed to the Supreme Court of Illinois, and, in January, 1871, this court reversed the Superior Court decree and dissolved the injunction. Cheney's suspension from the church by the ecclesiastical court then followed.

The trial had repercussions in both secular and ecclesiastical ranks throughout the country. Ministers of the Protestant Episcopal church intent on " reform " joined laymen holding similar opinions in demanding that Cheney continue his rectorship, while members of other Protestant groups urged withdrawal from the Episcopal authority and alliance with the more evangelically-minded sects. The implications in an appeal from a church to a secular court on ecclesiastical matters led even those sympathetic with Cheney's stand to question the tie-up which might result between state and church. When Cheney eventually withdrew from the Protestant Episcopal church and became identified with the Reformed Episcopal, those disturbed by such intellectual controversies felt frankly relieved.[47]

Universalists, Unitarians, and Swedenborgians, as well as other Protestant groups, showed a satisfying although not spectacular growth as the years advanced.[48] Into the Lutheran church flocked German and Scandinavian immigrants. By 1849 there were three congregations of this denomination which received both spiritual and earthly guidance from the ministers to whom they entrusted themselves. The first German Lutheran church was established between 1843 and 1846, and the first Norwegian church in 1848. The first Swedish church was organized in 1853 by persons who had received ministrations before that time from Paul Andersen, the pastor of the Norwegian Lutheran congregation. By 1871 the city had seventeen Lutheran churches. About five of these were Scandinavian, and only one was English, a fact which indicated the increased number of

[47] *The Advance,* February 2, 16, March 2, April 6, May 25, June 15, 1871; Chase *et al. v.* Cheney, 58 Ill. 509–42 (1871); *The Nation,* XII (January 26, June 15, 29, 1871), 50, 409–10, 447–48; Andreas, *History of Chicago,* II, 413–15, III, 786–87. The word which Cheney wished to omit was " regenerate " as found in the baptismal service in the Prayer Book.

[48] See, for example, *The New Covenant,* November 22, 1862; *The Advance,* November 11, 1869; Edwards, *Merchants' Census Report, 1871,* p. 1242. The Swedenborgians added to their original group a German mission, organized as an independent congregation in 1864 as the First German New Church Society, and, by 1871, had two missions. R. Williams, *op. cit.,* pp. 128–29, 153.

Scandinavians and Germans who were finding homes within Chicago.[49]

By 1870 the Jews propagated the faith of their fathers in five congregations, having enrolled as members, according to reports, some two thirds of the Jews in Chicago. Their allegiance to religious belief and practice steadily resisted the efforts of would-be proselyters although the Presbyterians, especially, bravely and hopefully placed a missionary in the midst of these Jews, and the Western Hebrew Christian Brotherhood, an auxiliary of the Hebrew Christian Brotherhood of New York, sought uniformity in religious expression through the creed of Christianity.[50]

With vigor and earnestness missionaries as well as regular pastors battled to save unchristian souls for Protestantism. They labored tirelessly among the seamen who came into the port of Chicago, and who were thought to occupy " a position between the church and the heathen." The salvation of those at hand may have seemed motive enough, but there appeared even a greater incentive when it was remembered that these same subjects could be " light-bearers " to heathendom, and thus their conversion would result in an " economy of missionary effort." [51] In the Seamen's Bethel Church, erected in 1844, were heard the prayers of the righteous, and by 1851 the work of caring for the spiritual needs of sailors passed into the hands of the Seamen's Friend Society. From 1854 until 1871 the Rev. Joseph H. Leonard, a Methodist, so effectively whipped up emotions by his revivalistic methods that converts were many, and the public applauded his success by giving employment to "praying" sailors more frequently than to the unconverted.[52] Indeed, so well done were these missionary endeavors that in 1854 the mission was organized as a church, interdenominational in polity and independ-

49 See Pierce, *A History of Chicago*, I, 230–31, for years before 1848. Andreas, *History of Chicago*, I, 348–49; Norelius, *op. cit.*, I, 224; Stephenson, *Religious Aspects of Swedish Immigration*, pp. 172–73; Hatheway and Taylor, *Directory, 1849–50*, p. 12; Edwards, *Merchants' Census Report, 1871*, p. 1242.

50 Edwards, *Directory, 1870*, p. 931; *The Advance*, May 21, 1868, February 24, 1870. It was reported that six thousand of the nine thousand Jews in Chicago belonged to the Jewish churches.

51 *Northwestern Christian Advocate*, May 10, 1864. These were sailors on the Great Lakes! See also Rock River Annual Conference of the Methodist Episcopal Church, *Register of the Twenty-eighth Session, 1867*, p. 37.

52 Pierce, *A History of Chicago*, I, 246; Norris and Taylor, *Directory, 1848–49*, p. 8; *Watchman of the Prairies*, June 24, 1851; *Congregational Herald*, February 3, 1854; *The Christian Times*, February 14, 1855; *Northwestern Christian Advocate*, May 12, 1858.

ent of any ecclesiastical body. In 1869, a brick church was erected on Michigan Street near Market Street to provide a place for religious services, a reading room, and a library.[53]

Mission Sunday schools, like Sunday schools connected with well-established churches, sought to promulgate religious doctrines among those believed outside the fold. The Chicago City Missionary Society began in 1853 to care for the " destitute and ignorant " who, like the seamen, seemed in need of redemption. In 1854, the Rev. D. B. Nichols, a representative of the Massachusetts Sabbath School Society, came to Chicago as a missionary and as a promoter of Sabbath schools and education for the underprivileged. With the co-operation of the local Congregational churches and others Nichols organized a mission in connection with the Ragged School in the " Sands," which lay in the midst of shanties in the region near the lake north of the mouth of the river.[54]

Some missions flowered and passed away. Still others grew in strength and sometimes became small but independent churches which sent out missionaries in their turn as their financial resources permitted.[55] The same zeal which promoted the work among seamen and the poor extended also to the missions set up among Roman Catholics. Teachers and converts from the Shields Mission of the Baptists visited Catholic homes and labored earnestly to reclaim souls from the teachings of the Church of Rome.[56] Other Protestant denominations wholeheartedly joined in their efforts at con-

[53] *Congregational Herald*, April 21, 1854. The church was opened in 1869 as the Mariner's Church. (Andreas, *History of Chicago*, II, 445.) Mark Skinner became the president of the Chicago Seamen's Friend Society which was organized in 1867 to succeed the Seamen's Friend Society. *The Advance*, November 21, 1867.

[54] *Northwestern Christian Advocate*, January 5, 1853; *Congregational Herald*, February 17, 1854; Gager, *Directory, 1857*, Appendix, p. xl.

[55] For example, the Congregationalists established the Union Mission in 1854. By 1857 it had three hundred in its Sunday school. Union Park Church (Congregational), an outgrowth of a mission, undertook in 1868 the support of Bethany Chapel at Paulina and Second streets. (*The Advance*, June 18, 1868; Gager, *Directory, 1857*, Appendix, p. xxxvi.) The North Star Mission, organized by the Baptists in 1859 as the Bremer Avenue Sunday School, in 1860 moved to Division and Sedgwick streets, taking the name North Star Mission. It was reported to have a membership of one thousand in 1863. Supported by the First Baptist Church, in 1870 it became an independent congregation with land, parsonage, and missions valued at $30,000. *The Advance*, January 16, 1868; *The Christian Times*, October 7, 1863.

[56] The Shields Mission was first established in 1856 as the " New Street Mission Sabbath School." In seven years it had fifty teachers engaged in the instruction of five hundred pupils. In 1860, it took the name " Shields " in honor of a donor of several thousand dollars. The mission was moved to Twenty-fifth Street near Wentworth, in 1869, into a home costing

versions. The Presbyterians were especially active in attempts to redeem from "wickedness and unthrift" the Irish and Negroes who lived near the Michigan Southern Railroad. The mission known as the "Railroad Mission" was, at first, housed in a railway car on a siding, and here both whites and Negroes were taught in the same classes.[57] By 1871, city missions numbered thirty-three, and many more had attained the status of accredited churches. Five independent missions were also sustained by the united efforts of the Protestant denominations.[58] The Sabbath School Union and a Sabbath School Association reflected further an interdenominational unity of purpose to fix "during the first ten years" of life "the eternal destiny" of souls.[59]

The Illinois Street Mission was undoubtedly the leader among the independent Sunday school missions. Founded by Dwight L. Moody during the great revival of 1858 and three years later placed under the auspices of the Young Men's Christian Association, this mission sought to insure immunity from temptation in the "notorious Wells and North Clark street" neighborhood. By 1865 its average attendance of 750 children ranked it next to the Railroad Mission of the First Presbyterian Church. Under the impetus of the success of its Sunday school, the mission organized an independent church around its adult group and in 1864 built a "brick chapel of respectable dimensions." The simplicity of the church and its free seating arrangement appealed to its poor communicants and visitors. Under the peerless evangelism of Moody, this mission conducted a simple experiment in real Christian fellowship at its weekly Sunday evening teas. Within three years its chapel, built to seat twelve hundred, could not accommodate the many "helpless souls searching for Christ." Each evening its doors swung invitingly open, and during 1868 eight hundred meetings were held.[60]

Just as Moody sought in the Wells and Clark Street section to re-

---

$20,000 and able to accommodate twelve hundred children. *Ibid.*, September 30, 1863; Halpin, *Directory, 1865–66*, "City and County Record," p. xxxv; Bentley, *op. cit.*, pp. 27–28.

[57] This "Railroad Mission" by 1865 was housed in a brick chapel at Griswold Street near the Michigan Southern station. *The Advance*, December 12, 1867.

[58] Edwards, *Merchants' Census Report, 1871*, pp. 1241–42.

[59] *Watchman of the Prairies*, January 22, April 16, 1850, January 28, 1851, July 27, 1852; *Northwestern Christian Advocate*, August 23, 1854; *The Advance*, December 19, 1867. See also Pierce, *A History of Chicago*, I, 267.

[60] *The Advance*, November 7, 1867, March 19, April 23, 1868; Phillips, *op. cit.*, p. 560; Halpin, *Directory, 1865–66*, "City and County Record," p. xxxv.

NEWSBOYS' AND BOOTBLACKS' MISSION, 1868

(From *The Illustrated Chicago News*, June 6, 1868.)

claim those called depraved, so did Martin Van Arsdale, a student of theology acting under a commission from the Chicago Sunday School Union, endeavor to organize religious activities among newsboys, bootblacks, and sailors. But the sailors objected to being classed with minors, and the old Board of Trade Hall which housed the mission soon saw an assemblage of newsboys and bootblacks only, whose religious zeal was undoubtedly heightened by the Sunday noon lunch, the reward of a supper given for attendance at Sunday school three consecutive times, the entertainments by the magic lantern, and the showings of " relics and treasures " on weekday nights. Soon a home for those who were orphans gave forty boys sleeping accommodations in its two dormitories and provided " substantial and good " food in its dining room.[61]

Not content with the converts swept into the fold by intracity missions, Chicago missionaries directed their attention afield, going as far west as San Francisco and sometimes into the deep South. Northern Illinois and the neighboring states seemed, however, to provide a particularly fertile field for their work, which was carried on at times, as in the case of the Congregationalists, in co-operation with sectional or national organizations.[62] The world was larger than the United States, and therefore more favor attended foreign missions, for less than one fifteenth of the world's people were accounted " Christians," a term to these soldiers of the gospel synonymous with " Protestants." Nor did they fail to recognize that their mission into lands afar could, in addition to bringing those in darkness and error " to the spiritual body of Christ," lift the heathen to a new standard of living, change their economic pursuits, and open their doors to the commerce of the world.[63]

[61] The name " Newsboys' and Bootblacks' Mission " was adopted in March, 1867. (*The Advance*, February 6, 1868; *Chicago Tribune*, March 29, 1867.) The boys who lived in the home paid a nominal fee for the privilege, the deficit being made up by outside contributions. Of course many more than the forty who lived there attended the Sunday School of the Newsboys' and Bootblacks' Mission. Rules governed the activities of the inmates. For instance, a bath was part of the daily regimen. *The Advance*, February 6, 1868.

[62] The Congregationalists had a North Western Home Missionary Association organized in July, 1852. It became an auxiliary of the American Missionary Association. Episcopalians entered the home field somewhat later than other Protestant groups. *Watchman of the Prairies*, December 26, 1848; *Northwestern Christian Advocate*, September 28, October 12, 1853; *Congregational Herald*, February 17, 1854; *The Advance*, December 26, 1867; *Chicago Tribune*, September 16, 1863.

[63] *Watchman of the Prairies*, January 6, 1852; *Northwestern Christian Advocate*, April 27, 1853.

All major Protestant denominations in Chicago by the mid-'sixties supported foreign missions, although their work was sometimes hampered by insufficient funds. Aims were high and reached in fancy into the very center of " Popery," whither, it was urged, a missionary should be sent. Fires of enthusiasm were kept burning by lectures delivered by missionaries on vacation, inspiration to enroll in the movement came from the lips of eager preachers, and the energetic endeavors of the women's missionary societies served to loosen purse strings at the church suppers, fairs, and teas, while they liberated the promoters of these festivities from the drabness of household duties.[64]

As the movement grew, women's missionary societies from Congregational and Presbyterian churches attempted to co-ordinate their activities, holding a meeting in Chicago in October, 1868, to form the Woman's Board of Missions for the Interior.[65] When its first semiannual meeting was held at the Second Presbyterian Church on April 28, 1869, it was announced that contributions since December 1, 1868, had amounted to $1,944.56, and that the officers had assumed responsibility for the support of women missionaries in India, China, and Persia, as well as of " several native Bible-readers." Both income and activities of the board increased rapidly. Because of the divisions which had split the Presbyterians, the ladies of that denomination joined with their sisters in the Congregational church in this organization. When a rapprochement had been effected between the erstwhile warring divisions of their own church, however, the Presbyterian women and societies amicably separated from the Woman's Board of Missions to set up a similar organization of their own. At the meeting of the board which followed " the separation," allusion was made to the fact that women were really improving their status by their efforts on behalf of missions, and that by their example they were helping their sisters in the Orient who had traditionally been regarded and treated as chattels.[66]

[64] Ibid., June 29, 1853; The Advance, October 24, 1867, March 24, 1870. Lack of funds to support missionary enterprises is illustrated by the deficit of $26,000 faced by the Methodist Missionary Society in 1853. Northwestern Christian Advocate, February 9, 1853.

[65] The Advance, November 5, 1868. Like the missionary societies already organized in New York and Boston, the Woman's Board of Missions for the Interior was affiliated with the national Board of Foreign Missions. The board was to encourage the organization of local church societies.

[66] At the first semiannual meeting of the Woman's Board it was announced that the dues were $1.00 a year, or $25 for a life membership, and that to date twenty-six life mem-

The growing importance of Chicago as a center of missionary activity in the Middle West was reflected in the number and variety of its religious newspapers and publications, which wielded a considerable, if unmeasurable, influence. Newspapers and tracts, designed to convert readers to evangelical Christianity, were circulated among foreigners, inmates of prisons, drunkards, bawdy women and their guests, and, indeed, quite generally among those who were thought in need of salvation. All important denominations and even some of the smaller churches had their own journals which kept church members informed of religious activities and aided in the creation of public opinion.

Numerous Sunday school quarterlies, papers, and teachers' publications were also printed and widely circulated throughout the Northwest. It was with good reason that the *Advance* in 1867 called Chicago the "Religious Metropolis" of "newspapers and magazines" of the interior, for at that date almost twenty religious journals were printed regularly in the city,[67] and in 1871 as many as twenty-eight periodicals were being sent to readers outside the city. Between 1848 and 1871, over fifty had been published at one time or another; almost half of these had been weekly and a somewhat smaller percentage monthly. Denominational book depositories and bookstores further spread the points of view of the churches which maintained them.[68]

Besides these devices to consolidate their position, the churches continued the practice of sending out colporteurs, who distributed pamphlets and other publications about the streets, particularly in neighborhoods frequented by foreigners, the poor, and the underprivileged. Usually conference, synod, or district appointees, colporteurs at first did not restrict their services to Chicago, but as the city grew in the 'fifties and 'sixties some were commissioned to carry on work only there in order to supplement that of the city missionaries.[69]

---

bers and twenty-six affiliated or auxiliary societies had joined the board. Mrs. J. V. Farwell was selected to succeed Mrs. C. G. Hammond as treasurer of the board. The treasurer announced in July, 1870, that contributions from eight affiliated church societies during the preceding four months had amounted to $1,464.13. *Ibid.*, June 24, 1869 (Supplement), July 28, 1870, January 12, 1871.

[67] *Ibid.*, November 21, 1867; *Chicago Tribune,* June 29, 1861.

[68] For further discussion see pp. 408–12.

[69] *Northwestern Christian Advocate,* August 17, 1853.

The life of the colporteur was filled with a variety of tasks, for he had not only to sell books but also, upon occasion, to serve as evangelist, to help in the social meetings of churches, to visit desti-tute and "vicious" neighborhoods, "praying, exhorting, preach-ing" (if he were a preacher), as well as to collect all the funds he could. He urged children to attend Sunday school, and he preached against intemperance and other vices of the day.[70] For these varied duties, he was paid $150 a year in addition to traveling expenses, which, it was hoped, he could largely extract from "the brethren" among whom he sojourned.[71] But the conviction that this was the best way to spread religion appeared to be in itself sufficient com-pensation for some of these workers. By 1850, in the twelfth year of its existence, the Chicago Tract Society reported that almost three thousand families were visited monthly and given tracts and Bibles, and that volunteer distributors were aiding regular colporteurs in this work.[72]

The war stimulated to greater endeavors than before the distribu-tion of this type of literature. By 1871 the high regard in which tracts were held is in no way better told than in the expenditure of $52,274 by the Chicago Tract Society and in the receipt in Chicago of such pamphlets in consignments of tons.[73] A local Bible Society, affiliated with the American Bible Society, left copies of the Old and New Testaments in jails, hotels, ships, schools, and the homes of the destitute. As early as 1852 this organization reported that, through sale and gift, it had been responsible for placing 24,867 Bibles in the hands of those held especially in need of them. When Chicago

[70] *Ibid.*, August 10, 17, 1853; American Tract Society, *Twenty-Third Annual Report, 1848* (New York, 1848), p. 100, *Twenty-Seventh Annual Report, 1852,* p. 57, *Twenty-Eighth Annual Report, 1853,* pp. 64–65, *Thirty-Second Annual Report, 1857,* pp. 52–53, 60, *Thirty-Fifth Annual Report, 1860,* pp. 139–40.

[71] The American Tract Society and all the other societies used this method of payment, although the Methodist Tract Society had an alternative plan by which a colporteur was given all of the profit on his sales in lieu of salary and expense account. The advantage of the former and more widespread method was that it enabled a colporteur to feel " more at liberty to do the work of an evangelist, rather than that of the salesman." *Northwestern Christian Advocate,* August 17, 1853.

[72] *Watchman of the Prairies,* March 4, 1851; American Tract Society, *Twenty-Third Annual Report, 1848,* p. 142, *Twenty-Fourth Annual Report, 1849,* pp. 81–82. In 1854, the American Tract Society set up a depository in Chicago, later to be withdrawn, and after 1860 the literature of the group was distributed from the bookstore of William G. Holmes at 170 Clark Street. American Tract Society, *Thirty-Fifth Annual Report, 1860,* p. 139.

[73] American Tract Society, *Forty-Sixth Annual Report, 1871,* p. 77; *The Advance,* March 5, 1868.

volunteers prepared for war, the society armed each man with the " fortress " of a Bible.[74]

But the most effective means of saving souls was by the time-honored camp meeting and revival, where men were warned of the judgment to come and told of the " treasures of happiness or misery " laid up in " the future life." These " outpourings of the Holy Spirit " came with periodic regularity; revivals generally took place in the midwinter and camp meetings in the summer. In the heat of July and August, it was no great hardship for Chicago Methodists to seek the open tent in a wooded section sixteen and a half miles away at Des Plaines station where these meetings were often held. In the winter, the Baptists and Methodists in particular found recruits through a series of meetings; the years of 1850, 1852, 1855, and 1858 were high points in the decade before the Civil War. Counted a means of increasing " the spirituality of churches " and thereby insuring their prosperity, revivals were thought to be, in the words of the Baptist *Watchman of the Prairies,* " pillars of virtue and good order without which the structure of society would be dissolved." And when a winter passed in 1854 without a revival of stirring appeal, the *Northwestern Christian Advocate* regretfully noted that the " flame of revival " in " days of infidelity, luxury and wealth-worship " was hard to kindle in any city.[75]

But if the years of prosperity failed to create the need and interest which proponents of this form of conversion may have desired, those marked by the devastation wrought by cholera and by financial blight more than made up. With death at hand conversion was common, and nightly meetings resulted in growing membership rolls, particularly in 1850 and in 1852. In the latter year, the Rev. Jacob Knapp assisted in the First Baptist Church, and the Rev. Morgan Edwards each evening added his convincing admonitions to those of the regular minister of the Tabernacle Baptist so effectively that in a short time over 225 members were added to these two churches. At the same time, gratifying results came from similar

[74] American Bible Society, *Thirty-Second Annual Report, 1848,* p. 454, *Thirty-Third Annual Report, 1849,* p. 513; *Chicago Tribune,* April 22, 1861; *Watchman of the Prairies,* April 6, December 21, 1852.

[75] *The Interior,* March 17, 1870; *Chicago Tribune,* June 27, July 19, 1861, June 3, 1862, August 10, 1870, August 24, 1871; *Chicago Daily Democrat,* September 1, 1860; *The Advance,* August 18, 1870; *Watchman of the Prairies,* February 26, 1850, April 6, 1852; *Northwestern Christian Advocate,* March 8, 1854.

efforts in the Methodist, Congregational, and Presbyterian churches. Particularly moved at this time to renounce evil for good were the youth of the community, many of whom were counted among the faithful members of the Sunday schools.[76]

But if some of the meetings of the early 'fifties reaped rich rewards, particularly among the young, the revival which came with the financial wreckage of 1857 swept hundreds of men and women into salvation. During the pitiless winter of 1857–58, men of the cloth spoke in daily meetings and by mid-March, 1858, recorded over 250 conversions. Morning and noon prayer meetings brought about " very striking manifestations of the Spirit's power." Testimonials from gamblers, drunkards, and degenerates of all stripes added to the gatherings " something wholly new in the annals of Chicago." So great was the attendance at the noonday meetings of businessmen, as well as of women, " solemnly and seriously worshiping God," that fear crept into the hearts of the promoters lest it might become fashionable to attend and that the meetings might be resorted to as was the opera or places of amusement. Seamen's Bethel was the scene of similar fervor, and many mariners and landsmen were converted.[77] Cottage prayer meetings cared particularly for the women who could not go far from their own firesides at midday.[78] By May, conversions had broken all previous records; the Methodist churches and missions boasted 560 new members, several Congregational churches reported 143, and the First Baptist Church, 92 new communicants.[79]

It was in this atmosphere, in the midst of a city distraught by a nationwide economic disaster, that Dwight L. Moody began his revivalistic activities. In September, 1856, he had come from Boston, where his split infinitives and distressing solecisms had offended more than they did in the Chicago of that day. Puritan and abolitionist, he spent his leisure moments from work as salesman in a shoe

[76] *Watchman of the Prairies,* January 9, 1849, January 22, February 26, 1850, March 9, 23, April 6, 27, 1852; *Chicago Daily Democrat,* July 30, 1849, February 6, March 18, 1850, January 21, 24, April 28, 1852.

[77] *The Christian Times,* March 24, 31, 1858; *Northwestern Christian Advocate,* March 17, 31, May 12, 1858; *Chicago Daily Democrat,* April 6, 20, May 10, 1858.

[78] Rev. A. W. Williams, *Life and Work of Dwight L. Moody* . . . (Philadelphia, 1900), p. 101.

[79] *The Christian Times and Illinois Baptist,* May 19, 1858; *Northwestern Christian Advocate,* May 12, 1858; *Chicago Daily Democrat,* May 11, 1858.

store in distributing religious tracts. His arresting question, " Are you a Christian? " put without regard to sex, age, and color as he passed down the crowded streets of the city, gained for him an unparalleled reputation for ardor and devotion to the cause of religion.

Moody's energies soon found a further outlet in the Young Men's Christian Association, organized May 17, 1858, as one of the fruits of the revival, with Cyrus Bentley as its first president, and open to members of the evangelical churches only. In the association Moody could hope to "reclaim" young men, just as in the Illinois Street Mission Sunday School he was recruiting young boys.[80] Standing outside the entrance of the Methodist Church Block, which housed the association's headquarters after 1860, he industriously hailed passers-by and urged them to attend the noonday and other prayer meetings. Soon he and other association members undertook conversion by the time-honored method of street preaching and by visiting saloons, gambling dens, and other places of bad repute. During the war they carried on missionary endeavors among the soldiers of Camp Douglas.[81] Patriotism as well as religious zeal led in 1861 to the establishment of a recruiting station in Bryan Hall. Here the association raised five companies which united with those recruited by the Board of Trade. The association's activities also extended to Cairo and various battlefields, including Shiloh and Fort Donelson, where delegates served until regular army chaplains appeared.[82]

Into the hands of the association in 1861 also fell a relief organiza-

[80] A. W. Williams, *op. cit.*, p. 51; *The Advance*, November 21, 1867, March 19, 1868. Earlier in the 'fifties a Y. M. C. A. had been organized, composed principally of fathers looking after the young men who had no homes. ([Y. M. C. A.], *Monthly Bulletin*, XIX [May, 1892], 4.) Moody was at first connected with the Sunday School Mission work of the Plymouth Congregational Church, but he was soon inspired to start his own, for which he hired an empty tavern on the North Side. Dwight L. Moody, *Moody's Gospel and Sermons* . . . (New ed. 2 v. Chicago, 1889), I, 21. See p. 370.

[81] *The Advance*, September 12, 1867, March 19, 1868; Ferry, *Reminiscences of John V. Farwell*, II, 24; *Chicago Tribune*, December 20, 1861. Some 248,418 tracts, papers, and periodicals, and 3,500 hymn books were distributed by the association among the soldiers at Camp Douglas. Sometimes the attendance exceeded one thousand at the daily prayer meetings conducted by the association in its soldiers' chapel.

[82] Four of the companies raised by the association made up part of the Seventy-second Regiment of Illinois Volunteers. The other company became a part of the Eighty-eighth Regiment of Illinois Volunteers. The association appointed 219 delegates to the armies of the North. The delegates served 8,979 days. *The Advance*, March 19, 1868; *Chicago Tribune*, December 20, 1861.

tion which had been set up by Moody. In that winter alone 554 families received aid.[83] Then followed the establishment of the employment agency, which had been projected by the association from the start.[84] Library facilities added to the inducements of membership in the association, and after 1860 general growth attended the efforts of its promoters, lashed to enthusiastic endeavors by the ever-zealous Moody. Thus, by 1871, were brought into the communion of this non-sectarian fellowship 1,838 persons, inspired, in the words of their tireless and redoubtable evangelist, to " work in union with God's plan " to rid Chicago of her vices and her resorts of crime, which included by mid-'sixties a reported two thousand saloons and gambling houses which were dispensing, according to a horrified observer, the unbelievable total of twenty million gallons of liquor yearly to an estimated fifty thousand patrons.[85]

Lectures, denominational and interdenominational in spirit, added other avenues by which the gospel was introduced. " Justification by Faith Alone," the " Resurrection," and the " General Character of the Spiritual World and the Execution of the Last Judgment " might have been the titles of discourses delivered in any Protestant church. During Lent the Catholic churches, to which at times ad-

[83] The Advance, March 19, 1868. See also regarding such activities, 1861–62, Chicago Tribune, January 22, 1862. From 1865 to 1868, the association expended a yearly average of $25,000 for poor relief. (The Advance, March 19, 1868.) The distribution of relief by public charities was placed in the hands of the association during the war. The Christian Times, December 1, 1864.

[84] The employment agency was started informally in 1863 by J. M. Chapman and J. M. Cutler, two members of the association, who spent fifteen minutes daily taking names of those desiring help. During the first year positions for some five hundred persons were found. This success brought about an employment department which found jobs for 3,411 in 1867–68, for 5,081 in 1869–70, for 3,490 in 1870–71. The Advance, March 19, April 30, 1868, April 15, 1869, June 23, 1870, May 25, 1871.

[85] Ibid., September 17, 1867; Chicago Tribune, November 5, 1866. Memberships in the Y. M. C. A. totaled 229 in 1861, the large increases occurring during Moody's presidency in the late 'sixties. (Meetings of March 11, 1861, August 12, September 16, 1867, Young Men's Christian Association, Minutes of the Board of Managers June 21, 1858, to March 17, 1879 [Ms. Chicago Board of Managers of the Y. M. C. A.], pp. 65, 198, 202.) The Y. M. C. A. obtained most of its funds from membership dues, admission fees to literary and scientific lectures, and donations. Membership charges in the late 'sixties, for example, were $20 for a male life membership, $10 for female life membership, $5.00 a year for sustaining membership, and $2.00 a year for male and $1.00 for female associate memberships. (The Christian Times, October 21, 1869.) John V. Farwell donated the site of the Y. M. C. A. building on Madison between Clark and LaSalle streets (dedicated 1867 and destroyed by fire January, 1868). In January, 1869, a new Farwell Hall was dedicated. (The Advance, September 19, October 3, 1867, January 9, 16, March 19, 1868, January 28, 1869.) Farwell also donated $30,000 of stock in Farwell Hall to be used for a theological library open to all clergymen and young men preparing for the ministry in and around Chicago. Ibid., September 22, 1870.

mission was charged as a means of augmenting church revenues, were the rendezvous of interested auditors.[86]

Divided as at times they were over doctrinal manifestations, Protestant sects met on common ground in their opposition to "Romanism." Indeed, as they saw it, Protestantism stood apart from the practices and preachments of Catholicism as widely as "the difference between truth and error," almost as widely as "the difference between mythology of the heathen and the scriptures of the Old and New Testament." In theological diatribes directed against "Papists," Protestants disputed the Catholic assumptions as to the nature of the Church, the rule of faith and practice, the use of the Bible, the object of worship, the nature of sin, the agency by which the sinner was regenerated, salvation, the mediation of Christ with the Father, and the state into which souls went on departure from the body. Although Protestants were none too glad to welcome Catholics within their community, the "unfair treatment" at Rome of Americans, who were said to have been prevented by the Pope's police from conducting Protestant services, proved to the fearful that vigil must be kept to avert similar action in the United States.[87]

When Catholics attempted to divert public funds for parochial schools, Chicago Protestants were convinced that they constituted "a most troublesome, factious, and expensive religico-politico element." But this was not the sole cause of worry, for a request that Catholic priests be admitted to the public schools to instruct the children of Catholic parents in "their religious duties" provided Protestants with additional proof that these churchmen, who bent to their will the communicants of their churches in a solid Catholic vote, were antirepublican in political faith. To resist what Protestants characterized as "arrogant pretensions of the disciples of Rome" who insisted upon "Catholic Schools or no Schools," all non-Catholics were urged to act in unity to preserve America's much-vaunted religious freedom.[88]

When other arguments weakened, Protestants could, they said,

---

[86] McGovern, *loc. cit.,* pp. 117–18. In 1851, St. Louis Church charged admission of fifty cents to an English discourse "Evidence and Social Advantages of Christianity." *Chicago Daily Democrat,* May 3, 1851. For religious lectures see among others, *ibid.,* February 17, 1849, January 26, March 23, April 30, May 3, 1850. For discussion of religious seminaries see pp. 396–97.

[87] *Watchman of the Prairies,* December 11, 1849, March 12, 1850.

[88] *Northwestern Christian Advocate,* January 5, February 16, 1853; *The Press and Trib-*

prove that if school funds were allotted on the basis of the payment of taxes, the share of the Catholics would be insignificant. Nearly three fourths of the paupers at one time in the County Poor House under public care were Catholic, they declared, and the majority of these were Irish. " Superstition " as evinced in a worship of the saints and the veneration of relics, ceremony and form in church rituals, and the confessional were further signs of Catholic ignorance and depravity in the minds of the evangelical Christians of Chicago. Unless America were watchful, cried the Methodist journal, Catholics would foist upon all " ignorance, superstition and slavery." [89]

Lecturers lifting pleading voices over the threat of riots, tracts designed to expose allegedly nefarious undertakings of the Catholics, passages from the Bible selected to strengthen orthodox Protestantism or to aid in proselyting appealed to the bigoted ear and eye.[90] Books such as William Hogan's *Popery: as it was and as it is* had a reading public which thrived on sensationalism and unreality.[91] Aspiring office-seekers sometimes found it politically wise to be members of a Protestant church. The fact that Douglas's wife was a Catholic and that he was reported to have become one militated against him in his race for political preferment.[92]

All this agitation the Catholics regarded as the sign that Protestants feared their own " fast approaching dissolution," and that fanatics led the attack. Indeed, said the Catholic *Western Tablet*, words unmarked by " even the ordinary courtesies " characteristic of

une, April 19, 1859; *Watchman of the Prairies*, November 14, 1848; *The Irish Republic*, April 25, 1868; *The Interior*, March 24, 1870.

[89] *Northwestern Christian Advocate*, February 16, March 23, 1853. For example, a story for children entitled " The Holy Coat " ridiculed the veneration of relics. (*Watchman of the Prairies*, July 9, 1850.) One of the few pictorial cuts which appeared in the *Watchman of the Prairies* was of a sacred relic, the impression of the foot of the Virgin Mary preserved in Europe, on which were written words which, translated, indicated a three-hundred-year indulgence for all who kissed the footprint and repeated three " ave Marias." Such a ceremony the Protestants abhorred. *Ibid.*, August 13, 1850.

[90] *Ibid.*, April 22, 1851; *Northwestern Christian Advocate*, March 2, 1853.

[91] Hogan's book was published by S. Andrus & Son, Hartford, in 1859. See also *Northwestern Christian Advocate*, March 16, 1853, for an article recommending an anti-Catholic publication, John Thomas's *Popery as it was in the Middle Ages; and as it is in the Nineteenth Century*.

[92] George Fort Milton, after considerable research and correspondence with Father Gilbert J. Garraghan, is unable to conclude with assurance that Douglas had become a Catholic. Certain " inferential " evidence leads to that conclusion, however. Milton, *The Eve of Conflict*, pp. 568–69.

the speech of gentlemen seemed proof enough that Satan had taken "a vacation from his employments in the infernal world, and had established himself, for the time being, in the editorial sanctums of certain Presbyterian and Methodist prints."[93]

But Protestants did not always love one another. Lutheranism was attacked on the ground that it bore the earmarks of the "metaphysics and exegesis" of German universities; Methodist and Baptist quarreled about the merits of child baptism and of baptism by immersion; Universalism and Unitarianism were assailed for their "latitudinarian morality," although not quite so despised as Mormonism, which was said to live in "harmony with all the lusts of the natural heart"; Swedenborgianism was regarded as having a membership no more Christian than "the followers of Mahomet"; and the Disciples of Christ reaped a heavy harvest of criticism because of their attitude toward regeneration. Not content with this devastation of religious tenets, these same Protestant critics inveighed also against all apocalyptic cults which foretold the imminent end of the world. And when they thought of Spiritualism, their rebukes turned to scoffing, for "spirit-rappings" were to them a consummate piece of "irreverent jugglery."[94]

"Free-thinkers" received the heaviest condemnation of all. No greater reproach could be directed against a man than to call him infidel, agnostic, atheist. Into such unsavory company were cast all who admired the works of Thomas Paine and who indulged in celebrations of his birthday. Acknowledgment of disbelief in the immortality of the soul served to disqualify at least one Chicagoan's testimony in a court of law. Children were warned against the snares of unbelief by stories which depicted the sad and untimely end of any who indulged in "the pleasures of sin" condoned by those given to infidelity.[95] A literal interpretation of the Bible closed some

[93] Editorial entitled "Violence of the Sectarian Press," *Western Tablet*, November 27, 1852. See also "The Church and the War," *The Monthly*, II (July, 1865), 13–14.

[94] *Watchman of the Prairies*, July 30, December 10, 1850, November 4, 1851, November 30, December 14, 1852; *Northwestern Christian Advocate*, January 26, February 9, July 27, 1853, November 15, 1854; *The New Covenant*, February 5, 1859; *The Advance*, November 21, 1867. Inability of the Chicago clergy to co-operate at certain times was experienced by the Y. M. C. A. shortly after its creation. Y. M. C. A., *Minutes of the Board of Managers*, p. 17.

[95] *Watchman of the Prairies*, January 23, 1849, April 9, September 24, 1850; *Chicago Tribune*, November 20, 1868. The disqualification of testimony was in the case of David K. Orcutt *v.* Thomas A. Hill and Company.

minds also to pronouncements of Darwin and Huxley. Even in the late 'forties, David Hume was attacked as a promoter of " impiety," and the science of geology was classed by many with clairvoyance, mesmerism, psychology, and spiritualism.[96] But comfort was had in the thought that " God . . . allowed the geologists . . . to fall into such preposterous blunders that even the children of the next generation will make them their laughing sport." [97]

But the churches, perforce, considered more than purely doctrinal matters. Closely linked with theological problems were all those of the day which touched the life of man. The years before 1850 had seen the rise of antislavery societies in protest on moral grounds to labor in bondage. Frequent suggestions that slaveholders be excluded from the ministry and even from church membership seemed indeed the negation of pulpit disquisitions on brotherly love. The decade of the 'fifties beheld a striking correlation between Congressional debates and Sunday sermons, particularly in the evangelical groups.[98]

The Fugitive Slave Law was particularly distressing. A horrified religious press defined the contest as a battle between divine right and " injustice, inhumanity, and national disgrace." Even disunion was preferable to such obeisance to the friends of slavery.[99] And when the " colored citizens " of Chicago met at the African Methodist Church and characterized the law as another " glaring instance of northern subserviency to slaveholding dictation," they were but echoing the sentiments of their white brethren.[100] To a law requiring the return of fugitive slaves the Baptist *Watchman of the Prairies* boldly counseled disobedience. " No law can make it right to sin," said the editor, " and no Christian rightly understanding his duties

[96] *Watchman of the Prairies*, September 4, 1849; *The Advance*, June 24, July 8, 29, August 19, 1869. Edward Hitchcock's *Elementary Geology* (New York, 1840), a textbook, was attacked, and parents were reported as banning attendance at colleges which used it. *Northwestern Christian Advocate*, March 23, 1853.

[97] *The Interior*, March 24, 1870.

[98] See, for example, *Watchman of the Prairies*, January 22, 1850; *Northwestern Christian Advocate*, February 23, 1853; *The Christian Times*, August 26, 1857.

[99] *Watchman of the Prairies*, February 19, March 26, October 22, 1850.

[100] A preliminary meeting of Negroes was held on September 30. The resolution was passed October 2, 1850. (*Chicago Daily Journal*, October 3, 1850.) The African Methodist Church on October 7 organized a Liberty Association for " the general dissemination of the principles of Human Freedom." A vigilance committee was appointed to examine any attempts on the part of individuals to presume upon the liberties of their brethren in any way. *Weekly Chicago Democrat*, October 12, 1850.

can engage in it." [101] The Illinois Black Laws were also repudiated as "wicked and inhuman" by Protestants in general, who saw no justice or mercy for the Negro, nothing save chains and slavery. [102]

Perhaps, said these Negro sympathizers, colonization might solve perplexities, for even they held that the two races could "never live on terms of civil and social equality." Then, too, free Christian Negroes would be missionaries for the evangelization of the "Dark Continent." But Chicago Negroes organized and demonstrated their disapproval of any plans for emigration and colonization. This behavior seemed to the editor of the *Northwestern Christian Advocate* so "impolitic" and ungrateful that he, with a strikingly unchristian attitude toward those holding an opposing opinion, threatened to withdraw his support of the solicitation of funds for the struggling little African Methodist Church. [103]

The Kansas-Nebraska Act brought faltering opinions into line. Until its passage in 1854, editorial comment and pulpit declamation were not always united in a wholesale condemnation of the South and its institutions, nor did editors and preachers always appear consistent in their attacks. The dangers of unbridled denunciation, based upon confounding exceptions with general rules, were sometimes recognized and even prompted the spokesman of the unrestrained *Northwestern Christian Advocate* to advise in 1853 abandonment of "mere exaggeration." [104] Nor was his position unique, for in the membership of each church there were those at one time who considered abolitionism of the Garrisonian school quite as mischievous as slavery itself. [105] In 1854, however, issues to be fought out later on the field of battle were debated on Sunday not only in Methodist and Baptist pulpits but also in Congregational, Universalist, and Unitarian churches. Even in the conservative North Presby-

[101] *Watchman of the Prairies*, May 21, October 22, 1850. The First Presbyterian Church, although deprecating disobedience to law, resolved that laws might be so oppressive that citizens should not obey them. For the action of the antislavery Third Presbyterians in criticizing the stand of the General Assembly, see the *Western Citizen*, February 11, March 4, 1851. See pp. 195–99.

[102] *Watchman of the Prairies*, May 21, 1850, January 11, 1853; *Congregational Herald*, April 30, 1853; *The Christian Times*, August 31, 1853; *Northwestern Christian Advocate*, March 16, 1853.

[103] *Ibid.* See also *ibid.*, February 19, 1853; *The Christian Times and Illinois Baptist*, August 18, 1858.

[104] *Northwestern Christian Advocate*, February 23, 1853.

[105] *Ibid.* Officially, however, Congregationalists did not dissent from expressions opposed to slavery. David Christy, *Pulpit Politics* . . . (Cincinnati, 1862), p. 421.

terian Church, the Rev. Richard H. Richardson assailed the makers of a bill which would wipe out the Missouri Compromise line established in 1820.[106]

Late in March of that year, almost all the Protestant clergymen of Chicago met and drew up resolutions similar to those framed by their confreres of New England and New York. These sentiments, couched in biting and denunciatory language, they directed to the House of Representatives and the Senate at the national capital. They protested the repeal of the Missouri Compromise and the extension of slavery into Nebraska and Kansas as "a great moral wrong" and declared themselves divinely appointed to rebuke such wrongs. The petition was subsequently circulated in the Northwest and called forth from Douglas a vigorous attack on men of the cloth who participated in political discussions.[107] But these clerics were not deterred. Into Kansas they dispatched missionaries not only to gain converts to orthodox Christianity but also to carry the word of freedom. Suppliants for "free capital" as well as for "free men" petitioned for help through the columns of the religious press, which apparently saw no inconsistency in the church's officiating at the marriage of these two principles. Memories of Bunker Hill and Lexington, invoked to fight the ruffianism of the Kansas of 1855, called "Northern men of principle" to volunteer against "black King Slavery," as the fathers had shouldered "the musket against their ruddy King George."[108] The political vane of Kansas determined editorial lines of Baptist, Methodist, and Congregational organs, just as it came to be the theme of pastoral descant on these exciting Sundays.

The presidential campaign of 1856 in the same way was the vehicle

---

[106] *The Daily Democratic Press*, February 18, April 1, 1854. The North Presbyterian Church was affiliated with the Old School Assembly. Because of Richardson's growing anti-slavery attitude, some members of his church, including Cyrus H. McCormick, were led to consider the organization of a more orthodox Old School church. Hutchinson, *Cyrus Hall McCormick*, II, 8, 10.

[107] *The Daily Democratic Press*, March 29, April 13, 1854; *Northwestern Christian Advocate*, April 5, 19, 1854; *The Free West*, May 18, 1854. Church bells were tolled upon the receipt of news of the passage of the Kansas-Nebraska Act. *Northwestern Christian Advocate*, May 31, 1854.

[108] *Congregational Herald*, May 3, 24, 1855. Numerous reprints of letters and of resolutions of meetings in Kansas, summaries of Congressional activities relating to Kansas, and similar material appear in the columns of the religious press. See, for example, *The Christian Times*, October 31, December 19, 26, 1855, November 4, 1857; *Congregational Herald*, April 3, May 22, 1856; *Northwestern Christian Advocate*, May 23, August 1, 1855.

of diatribes fortified by texts from the Scriptures which sought to show that the election of Buchanan or Fillmore was the " deliberate sanction of the American people to the policy of terrorism and slavery," whereas a vote for Frémont was one for " justice, freedom and right — a vote for Kansas and a free territory, a rebuke to slavery, ruffianism." [109]

Still, hope burned that the day would come when slavery would be abolished without the dissolution of the Union. When men representing the views of Wendell Phillips and William Lloyd Garrison met in Cleveland on October 28, 1857, and recommended to slaves that they " rise in the spirit of Seventy-Six and achieve their freedom," the editor of the *Christian Times* looked with dismay upon what he considered the misguided zeal and unwisdom of such counsel. The religious conscience on the whole was not yet ready to go that far to enforce its principles as to the equality of labor. Pen and speech were the weapons they would then employ.[110] But the tension caused by tales of a " bloody Kansas " and an emotionalized discussion of the South and its institutions soon found an outlet in opposition to the Dred Scott Decision. Into the hands of slavery, to paraphrase the words of the watchful editor of the *Congregational Herald,* had now passed every equipment of law and power and usage. At the same time his fellow editors of the *Christian Times* solemnly chronicled the fall " one by one of the defenses of Freedom " which had culminated in the decision, and declared that its legal unsoundness must be obvious even to men untrained in the law.[111]

The raid at Harpers Ferry aroused much the same reaction in the religious as it did in the secular press. In their minds John Brown, as the leader of the movement, became at first a misguided monomaniac, although the country was admonished to take to heart the warning of the occasion. Brown's death, however, lifted him from the doubtful place to which he had been consigned and rendered him immortal; death bestowed the breath of a new life into

---

[109] *Congregational Herald*, September 4, 1856.

[110] *The Christian Times*, November 11, 1857. See also *ibid.*, February 4, 1857; *Chicago Tribune*, October 29, 1857. But when the executive committee of the American Tract Society announced its intention to discontinue a treatise on the subject of slavery offensive to the South, the Chicago Congregational Association and other antislavery groups in the city voiced both sorrow and alarm. *Chicago Daily Democratic Press*, October 15, 1857; *Congregational Herald*, September 24, October 1, 8, 15, 22, 29, 1857.

[111] *Ibid.*, March 26, 1857; *The Christian Times*, March 20, 1857.

his principles.[112] As time wore on clergymen more and more gave a helping hand to politicians as they prepared the way for coming events. These ministers of the gospel unashamedly laid claim to leadership in educating the " moral sentiment " so " manufactured to their hand." Nearly all, save the Roman Catholics, came to the support of the new Republican party and thus gave to it the strength of a great religious crusade. Even some Catholic priests as individuals came later to take a similar stand in what was commonly called " Freedom's battle." [113]

Yet some in the Protestant fold, despite the jibes of their fellows, did not as yet join the rapidly growing caravan. In the North Presbyterian Church, Dr. Nathan L. Rice undertook in January, 1860, to show that slavery was not necessarily sinful. At once the *Press and Tribune* called him the willing and obedient servant of the devil.[114] But secession accomplished the unity of opinion which had been lacking in all Presbyterian groups and in the Episcopal and Catholic churches. The Episcopalian *Chicago Record* heralded this change in an editorial, " The Church's Duty in Secession," which charged the politicians with duping " simple clergymen " by referring to the Episcopal church as the great tie between the sections. And when South Carolinian rectors refused to read prayers for the President, Chicago Episcopalians felt that the first act of secession had been committed.[115] Within the Presbyterian church, the act of secession wrought an equally great change. So complete was the reversal of its stand that the Chicago *Presbyterian Record* in January, 1861, cautioned the North against any compromise which might bring about an " *unrighteous* peace." Unified by the crisis, the Old and New School Presbyterians of Chicago for the first time since 1838 met at a season of fasting and prayer in early January, in compliance with

[112] *Ibid.,* November 2, 1859; *Congregational Herald,* December 29, 1859.

[113] *Ibid.,* June 7, 1860, March 14, 1861. Leaders in the Northwestern Christian Antislavery meeting in the First Congregational Church in autumn, 1859, urged continued activity. It was reported that about two hundred delegates from Iowa, Illinois, Indiana, Ohio, and Michigan attended. (*The Press and Tribune,* October 22, 1859.) By autumn, 1860, the editor of the *Democrat* declared that probably five-eighths of the members of the Congregational, Baptist, Methodist, and Universalist churches were Republicans. *Chicago Daily Democrat,* October 22, 1860; *The Monthly,* II (July, 1865), 11.

[114] *The Press and Tribune,* January 19, 1860. See, for example, attacks on Rice by the Rev. Samuel Wolcott of New England Congregational Church. *Ibid.,* February 24, 25, 1860.

[115] *Chicago Record,* December 15, 1860, March 15, 1861.

President Buchanan's request.[116] As the rallying cry called men to arms, the Catholics also fell into line.[117] The unity of Chicago men of the gospel was complete!

In the trying months of the winter and spring of 1861 sermons from Chicago pulpits intensified the animus which converted citizens to the belief that "the southern character" was essentially different from that of the North, where, it was said, a Puritan background had committed men to the principle of "human equality." It was, therefore, easy for "a Christian" to look upon "the troublous times" as "God's Providence bringing about great changes for good, and for the progress of humanity." Thus guided in his thoughts by the stirring eloquence of the Rev. William W. Patton of the First Congregational Church, the Chicagoan of that faith was willing to obey the command from his pastor's lips to "rise from his knees, and shoulder his rifle." [118] On the same day others listened with equal attentiveness and acquiescence. Lincoln's call for troops on April 15 stimulated further ministerial oratory, and in nearly all Protestant churches congregations were urged to illustrate to the world "the power of true religion to break every yoke." [119] Impressive farewells marked the enlistment and departure of men for the front, and so eloquent were the sermons preached that audiences, although moved to tears, were hardly able to restrain their enthusiasm as they heard compared the scenes at Lexington and Concord with those in Baltimore, April 19, 1861.[120]

As the years of the war wore wearily on, ministerial oratory kept

---

[116] *Chicago Tribune*, January 12, 15, 1861. This act of fellowship among the Presbyterians had its reward when the two groups reunited at the end of the 'sixties.

[117] *Ibid.*, August 27, 1861. Bishop Duggan during the unsettled days of January, 1861, directed the priests in his diocese to pray for the Union. (*Chicago Daily Journal*, January 7, 1861.) With the call for troops, flag-raisings at the Bishop's mansion and at St. Mary of the Lake were attended with patriotic fervor. *Chicago Evening Journal*, April 25, 26, 1861.

[118] *Chicago Tribune*, April 15, 1861; *Congregational Herald*, March 7, 1861. "The history of these colonies from the very first shows them [Southerners] to have been of a proud, overbearing, domineering spirit, turbulent and restless under the restraints of government, and by no means scrupulous as to the measures employed to reach a given end." *Ibid.*

[119] *Chicago Tribune*, April 15, 1861. The words quoted are those of the Rev. Dr. Robert W. Patterson of the Second Presbyterian Church. Special sermons were also delivered, among others, in the Baptist, West Side Universalist, First Methodist, and Third Presbyterian churches. *Ibid.*, April 22, 1861. See also *Chicago Record*, May 1, 1861.

[120] *Chicago Tribune*, April 22, 1861. See in particular the sermon of the Rev. William H. Ryder, Universalist.

alive the fires of hate, just as in the South the words of clergymen failed to sow the seeds of reconciliation. Arrows of vindictiveness which dealt death and destruction upon the foe met with applause as each in its turn indicated the negation of brotherly love.[121] The "clapping" of hands became the popular symbol of as complete agreement as had the deep-throated "amen" in the past.[122] And if for a moment leniency triumphed, listeners were recalled by stories of the barbarities of the Confederates upon wounded and dying Union soldiers, tales related particularly when Northern morale was weakened by Southern military victories. Accounts of the crushing of Northern skulls by the heel of enemy boots, the cutting off of ears as trophies to be carried into the "Land of Cotton," and the poisoning of food and drink given under the white flag of truce served as vehicles to arouse the fury so needed to carry on the war.[123] To a people in this mood, the fall of Richmond could mean nothing short of a moral victory, that "the Lord alone is 'the God of battles.'"[124] To them in victory charity was not the first emotion. Hand in hand with the politician went many ministers in plans of reconstruction.[125] They took their task seriously, for was not the North now commissioned to redeem a misguided Southern people from the devastation wrought by the hands of their own leaders?

The death of Lincoln gave strength and courage to those who would keep burning the fires of hate. "Perhaps," said the *Christian Times*, "it [the assassination of Lincoln] was needed that the rebel-

<hr/>

[121] Memorial sermons for the dead of Chicago's soldiers, such as that of the Rev. William W. Everts of the First Baptist Church in June, 1863, served to bring the "wicked rebellion . . . to the homes and hearts of . . . all." (*The Christian Times*, June 17, 1863.) The religious press was employed to this end, one paper declaring to healthy young men who were not serving their country: "YOU ARE UNFIT TO LIVE!" *Northwestern Christian Advocate*, August 13, 1862.

[122] Hutchinson, *op. cit.*, II, 33. Bishop Duggan of the Roman Catholic faith was strongly pro-Union. His support of the Irish Brigade was considerable. The Rev. Dr. John McMullen, president of St. Mary of the Lake, declared that were he not "a priest and a man of peace [he] would be down South . . . fighting under the Stars and Stripes for the preservation of the Union." (Garraghan, *Catholic Church in Chicago*, pp. 183–86.) Clergymen offered their services to the government as chaplains or in other capacities. See, for example, *The Christian Times and Illinois Baptist*, July 2, September 17, 1862.

[123] *Ibid.*, August 20, 27, 1862. See also *The Congregationalist* [Boston], July 11, 1862; *Northwestern Christian Advocate*, July 31, August 7, 1861, August 13, September 3, 10, 1862.

[124] *The Christian Times*, April 6, 1865.

[125] For official statements of the clerical attitude see Rock River Annual Conference of the Methodist Episcopal Church, *Register of the Twenty-eighth Session, 1867*, p. 33, *Register of the Twenty-ninth Session, 1868*, pp. 27–28. See also *Northwestern Christian Advocate*, February 28, 1866.

lion should consummate its crimes thus, in order that it might not escape a righteous retribution." Even the Catholics joined in a demand that Congressional plans of reconstruction replace those of leniency for the fallen foe.[126] So inflammatory were the words of some preachers during these trying years that a resolution to silence, by mayoral proclamation, a continuation of name-calling from the pulpit was presented to the city council by one would-be pacifier.[127]

But gradually the questions raised in peacetime turned men's thoughts into channels other than revenge. More and more it seemed the part of wisdom to restore the South economically and to re-establish trade relations. Problems of readjustment claimed attention. Waves of intemperance spread through the city and made the saloon the rendezvous of sinners and sometimes of those who delegated themselves the saviors, for into " dens of wickedness " went the faithful servants of the Gospel to kneel in prayer and supplication. Revivalism again had its day, and in 1868 the " boy preacher " Henry Morehouse of London came to Chicago and importuned his thousands of listeners to desist from evil-doing. But as the 'sixties grew old, appeals to hyper-emotionalism seemed to have less effect at least on the young than they had once had. This, thought the editor of the *Advance*, should not be too readily deplored for it was, in his mind, as it should be if one could " live intellectually and morally " in one's own generation. That his opinion was not commonly accepted by youth's elders need not be said, for then as always a return to old-fashioned religion seemed the only sure means of attaining "everlasting life." [128]

126 *The Christian Times*, April 20, 1865; *The Irish Republic*, May 11, 1867; " Catholics and the Missouri Constitution," *The Monthly*, II (October, 1865), 290–92.
127 Document 645, 1868, Chicago, *Common Council Documents*.
128 *The Advance*, February 20, March 19, 1868, January 12, 1871; Ferry, *op. cit.*, II, 24; *The Christian Times*, January 26, 1865.

CHAPTER X

THE QUEST FOR THE
REFINEMENTS OF LIFE

FROM THE WIDE ARRAY of forces which made Chicago the focus of the economic expansion of Middle America welled also its cultural life. Just as the 'fifties were marked by an accelerated commercial pace, so also was that decade distinguished by a significant educational advance. In 1854, John C. Dore left his home in Boston to become the first superintendent of schools in Chicago. In the next year a public high school was authorized; in autumn, 1856, it opened with an attendance of 169 boys and girls.[1]

The roots of elementary instruction, however, were deeply implanted by this time, for Chicago, since its incorporation as a town, had carried on the educational traditions of its early settlers. By ordinances passed in 1849 and 1851 all children five years and over were eligible to attend the schools, but in the former year only 1,794 children were enrolled. By 1871 education was provided for nearly 41,-000, an increase in school registration almost twice as great as the phenomenal increase of the total population within these years. This number represented a decreasing proportion of children of alien parentage in school, for, although in 1849 they had made up about

[1] An ordinance of the Common Council, November 28, 1853, created the office and defined the duties of superintendent of schools. Johnston, "Historical Sketches," *Twenty-Fifth Annual Report of the Board of Education*, pp. 32–33, 51; Chicago Superintendent of Schools, *Second Annual Report of the Superintendent of Public Schools of the City of Chicago, for 1855* (Chicago, 1856), pp. 6–7 (Reports of Superintendent and Board of Education hereafter cited as *Annual Report*).

39 per cent of public school enrollment, in 1870 they composed only about 16 per cent.

Despite this increase in the number enrolled, attendance was irregular, and many parents made no pretense of sending children to school at all. In 1856 alone, over four thousand children, or about one fourth of those between five and fifteen, were estimated as nonattendants, while many more went for less than a month. The situation in 1870–71 was also bad, for slightly over one half of those enrolled availed themselves of the opportunity.[2] Even so, Chicago was confronted with a lack of accommodations, for the number of buildings constructed failed to keep pace with the increasing school population. Sometimes so inadequate were facilities that children were forced to take turns sitting, and teachers were obliged to care for 120 pupils with equipment and space for half that number. In winter, conditions were particularly distressing for those children who attended school in ramshackle wooden structures built for other purposes, where ventilation came only through the chinks in the walls and warmth was furnished solely by a small stove. Despite legislative permission to the Common Council in 1865 to borrow $25,000 a year for four years for school property and the authorization in 1867 of a construction bond issue up to $500,000, the decade of the 'sixties closed with only 35 per cent of the school population accommodated in a fairly satisfactory way.[3]

Still, those buildings which were constructed, though generally made of wood, raised costs on permanent improvements in little more than five years from $8,820 (in 1861) to $135,354 (in 1867). Expenditures for other aspects of public education soared from a little under $5,000 in 1849 to more than $547,000 in 1871, and costs per pupil based on average daily enrollment mounted from $4.93 to $24.46 — an amount, however, below that of New York, Boston, and Cincinnati. At the same time the teacher in Chicago frequently had the sole instruction of more than one hundred pupils and even under the

[2] In 1865, the legislature permitted Chicago authorities to raise the age of entrance to six years. *Annual Report, 1864–65,* pp. 14–15; *Daily Democrat,* February 20, 1849; Johnston, *loc. cit.,* p. 47; *Annual Report, 1869–70,* pp. 172–73. See for conditions in 1856, *Annual Report, 1856,* pp. 5–6. See Appendix, p. 512.

[3] *Chicago Tribune,* February 19, 1866; Act of February 15, 1865, *Private Laws, 1865,* I, 283; Act of March 9, 1867, *Private Laws, 1867,* I, 778–79; *Annual Report, 1864–65,* pp. 6–7; *Annual Report, 1869–70,* p. 94. In 1869, the legislature authorized construction bonds totalling $700,000. Johnston, *loc. cit.,* pp. 39–40; *Private Laws, 1869,* I, 341.

best conditions carried a far heavier load than did teachers in the East.[4]

Part of these costs included salaries to teachers and other officials, which reached $444,634 in 1871, although the amount represented not so much higher salaries as pay to more teachers, whose number jumped from 19 in 1849 to 570 in 1871. As early as 1854 women exceeded men by nearly five to one, and by 1871 the proportion was sixteen to one. Although outnumbered, men could find consolation in the fact that they commanded the best positions and received as a rule at least twice as much salary as did their sisters.[5] In many cases, however, so poor was the quality of instruction said to be that it seemed as if the laborer were literally worthy of his slender hire, and a normal department was provided in 1856 in the hope of raising standards. Further efforts in this direction resulted in a model practice school under the direction of Ella Flagg in 1865–66, which, with the Teachers Institute started in 1850 and the publication of the *Chicago Teacher* in 1856, aimed at training better teachers. In spite of these efforts, however, by 1870 many elementary school teachers had only grammar school educations, and less than half the women teachers in all levels of instruction had graduated from high school or the normal.[6]

The cost of these educational endeavors was met in part by special taxes levied for the purpose, in part by the school fund income, and, especially after 1865, in part by the issue of bonds, primarily for the construction of buildings. The school fund, the most important source of revenue until the 'fifties, included rents from school lands and interest on money gained from the sale of other school lands, to which was added a state appropriation or dividend. The maximum amount of tax which might be levied for school purposes was regu-

---

[4] Figures for costs, pupil attendance, courses of study, and similar information have been found in the *Annual Reports*. For table summarizing some of the facts see Appendix, pp. 512–13.

[5] For example, in 1869–70, salaries were as follows: superintendent, $4,500; assistant to superintendent, $2,200; high school principal, $2,500; his male assistants, $2,200; female high school teachers, $1,000; male principals of district schools, $2,000 to $2,200; principals of primary schools and head assistants in district schools (mostly women), $1,000 to $1,200; women assistants in grammar and primary grades, beginning salary, $450; grammar teachers, a maximum of $800 after three years' service; primary teachers, a maximum of $700. *Annual Report, 1868–69*, pp. 114–15.

[6] *The Daily Democratic Press*, January 9, 1855; *Chicago Tribune*, August 25, 1868; *Chicago Daily Democrat*, December 31, 1850; *Annual Reports*.

lated by the state, being raised by law to two mills on the dollar in 1857 and to three mills in 1865, although the actual tax levied sometimes was less than the statutory limit. Failure to take advantage of the legal limit was probably occasioned by official fear of alienating popular support for the schools by raising the tax levy. Minor sources of income were the endowed funds left for specific objects, such as the purchase of textbooks for indigent children by educationally-minded citizens like Flavel Moseley and Jonathan Burr.[7]

In the elementary grades, instruction was offered in spelling, reading, grammar, penmanship, arithmetic, geography, and morals; singing and drawing received irregular attention until the 'sixties, when the work was systematized. In 1860–61, under the superintendency of William H. Wells, a graded course of ten years' instruction was adopted, and this became the pattern for similar efforts in the more remote sections of the state and of the Northwest. After the opening of the high school on October 8, 1856, those who desired more advanced instruction but who were unable to afford the tuition schools could get Latin and Greek, astronomy, physiology, natural philosophy, mathematics, English literature, and eventually the natural sciences. Only a small number, however, took the opportunity to go beyond the primary and grammar grades. In 1869–70, less than 1 per cent of the school population was enrolled in the high school.[8]

The 'sixties witnessed an expansion of the curriculum, particularly in the offerings designed to inculcate patriotism. Emphasis upon the lives of illustrious men, the singing of patriotic songs, and compulsory attention to the study of American history and government expressed the spirit of the day. Even so, efforts to introduce military drill into the schools met the disapproval of Superintendent Wells, although volunteer companies of high school boys armed with

[7] Act of February 16, 1857, *Private Laws, 1857*, p. 909; Act of February 15, 1865, *Private Laws, 1865*, I, 282–83; *Annual Reports*. For school finances, see Appendix, p. 513. The investment of the school fund was questioned in the late 'forties by Chicago citizens. (*Daily Democrat*, February 5, 28, 1849.) The state dividend was derived by Illinois from its share of the surplus revenue divided by the United States government in 1836, from the share given Illinois of the proceeds of public land sales within her boundaries, and, after 1855, from a state school tax.

[8] *Annual Reports* for 1856, 1859–60, 1860–61. The high school building was the boast of the city. It was made of Athens stone and was three stories high. (*The Daily Democratic Press*, August 20, 1855; Johnston, *loc. cit.*, p. 51.) In 1860, there were only ten public high schools in Illinois, 321 in the United States. Ellwood P. Cubberley, *The History of Education* (Boston, 1920), p. 701.

wooden wands marched up and down the school grounds after school hours. As always, the temper of the times reflected itself in special offerings introduced to meet popular demands. In 1865, at the behest of a group of patrons, German became a part of the curriculum. Courses in navigation, drafting, bookkeeping, and chemistry mirrored a desire to equip the great majority of pupils who did not go on to college.[9]

Indeed, so deeply embedded was the faith of man in the efficacy of education that the press successfully carried on an agitation for the establishment of evening schools for working children and adults in order to fit them for more complete living. In the mid-'fifties public school teachers volunteered to staff such a school held in a hall provided by the city, but such instruction did not go beyond the winter of 1856. In 1863, the Board of Education again inaugurated a plan to help " laboring youth." [10] Despite questions as to whether public funds could legally be used for this purpose, five evening schools opened in the various divisions of the city the next year, and by 1870 over thirty-eight hundred were reported enrolled.[11] In 1871, Superintendent Josiah L. Pickard urged the establishment of a trade school and part-time day schools for those employed part of the day, thereby voicing official agreement with the demands of the working classes for public technical schools.[12]

While trade schools were urged to equip better those who must en-

[9] *Chicago Tribune*, July 29, 1865; *Annual Reports* for 1861, 1863, 1865–66, 1867–68; *Illinois Staats-Zeitung*, July 30, October 31, 1861.

[10] *The Daily Democratic Press*, June 19, 1854; *The Free West*, June 29, July 6, 1854; *Weekly Chicago Democrat*, December 13, 1856; *Annual Report, 1856*, pp. 53–55. See plea from Sister M. Angela, St. Mary's University, to Stephen A. Douglas [March, 1858], for a donation for an industrial school, *Douglas Papers*. In 1856 three fourths of the 208 students were persons who worked as laborers and servants.

[11] *Chicago Tribune*, December 3, 1863; *Annual Reports* for 1863, 1864–65, 1869–70. An evening school was organized for Negroes to give them " the rudiments of a thorough English education." Rooms were provided by the pupils, who were at first " totally ignorant of the very meaning of letters." In the second season of the school the pupils were reported as reading fluently and writing " better than a great many of their white brethren." (*Chicago Tribune*, April 1, 1864.) As early as 1850, language instruction was offered in special schools. (*Chicago Daily Democrat*, July 13, 1849.) Other special schools included one for deaf mutes and several for physical training. *The Workingman's Advocate*, October 16, 1869; *Chicago Tribune*, April 1, 1864; *Annual Report, 1870–71*, pp. 130–32; Johnston, *loc. cit.*, p. 42.

[12] *The Workingman's Advocate*, August 21, 1869; *Annual Report, 1870–71*, pp. 130–32. The endorsement by workers of an industrial university extended from the 'fifties. *The Daily Democratic Press*, November 25, 27, 1852, January 23–26, 1854, January 15, 1855; *Chicago Tribune*, May 18, 25, 29, June 1, August 11, 1868; *Prairie Farmer*, n.s. XXI (May 30, 1868), 352.

gage in the grim realities of earning a living, instruction in the esoteric sphere of the arts was provided for those at the other end of the economic ladder who could afford to learn how to sing or to play some instrument. Many private teachers satisfied the desire, while the Chicago Conservatory of Music, established in 1867, and the Chicago Academy of Music, opened by Florenz Ziegfeld in 1870, trained musicians not only to give pleasure to themselves and others but also to supply the need for teachers when occasion demanded.[13] Teachers of painting and drawing furthered the aspirations of embryo artists, and the Academy of Design, chartered in 1865 to maintain an art gallery and a school of design, encouraged local talent to embark on a then uncertain financial sea.[14]

Until the 'fifties the education which the publicly supported schools provided was chiefly elementary in scope. When mid-century dawned, Chicago had more pupils in private than in public schools. By the late 'fifties the situation was reversed. In these private institutions, instruction often ranged from the elementary through the literary or college preparatory department and included music, painting, drawing, and foreign languages, particularly French. In 1848 eleven girls' schools, each with an attendance of from six to sixty-one, offered the daughters of the well-to-do the advantages of a " polite education." About the same time, boys could attend the Boys' Classical School and, shortly thereafter, A. J. Sawyer's High School for Boys. But the number of schools for girls exceeded that for their brothers, although shortly after 1850 coeducational private schools such as the Chicago Male and Female Institute, the English and Classical High School, the Franklin Institute, and the Garden City Institute appeared.[15]

In the score of years after 1850 about two hundred schools were opened, offering to their limited clientele the education denied those

---

[13] *Chicago Tribune,* April 18, May 26, 1867, August 20, 1870. Among the teachers at the Academy were Hans Balatka and William Groscurth, singing; Alfred H. Pease, S. N. Penfield, Louis Falk, Dudley Buck, and Florenz Ziegfeld, piano; Heman Allen and Ziegfeld, violin and viola. Instruction cost $15 for twenty lessons. *Ibid.,* September 2, 1870.

[14] *Private Laws, 1865,* II, 12–13. See advertisements and items regarding George Davis, H. D. Thielcke, and Miss B. I. Finlayson, among others. *Chicago Daily Democrat,* November 1, 1850; *The Daily Democratic Press,* October 25, 1854, February 23, 1856.

[15] *Annual Report, 1858–59,* p. 58. In 1848, Chicago had nineteen private schools and only three public. Norris and Taylor, *Directory, 1848–49,* pp. 11–12; *Daily Democrat,* May 24, 1849, April 27, October 5, 1852, February 27, 1860; *Chicago Tribune,* August 26, 29, September 1, 15, 1868; *The Daily Democratic Press,* September 18, October 11, 1852.

financially unable to attend. Of these, the Dearborn Seminary, organized in 1854 for girls, catered to a select patronage and lingered as a force of cultural uplift during a day when many other schools of similar intent lasted but a short time. In these privately promoted educational organizations, tuition rates were at times five or six dollars a course, with costs of instruction in piano and boarding and rooming accommodations additional.[16]

Besides these private institutions which usually took the place of the later-day high school, special Roman Catholic, Lutheran, and ethnic schools served a selected following. Under the guidance of Bishop Van de Velde, parochial Catholic schools increased to twelve by 1853, and in 1871 there were twenty-one parochial schools with an aggregate attendance of ten thousand. These offered chiefly elementary training, but the University of St. Mary of the Lake, opened in 1844, provided education above that level. In the 'sixties, law and divinity courses were offered by St. Mary's, and an affiliation with Rush Medical College was effected. Because of financial difficulties, St. Mary's closed its doors in 1866, but the cause of Catholic education was again served when the Jesuits opened St. Ignatius College in 1870. The various Lutheran groups, the German Methodists, and the Jews also had their special schools, generally directed toward elementary education, although by 1870 the Germans had established a high school of their own.[17]

The cause of Protestant higher education was served through the incorporation of Northwestern University at Evanston in 1851 under the aegis of the Methodist Episcopal Church;[18] through Augustana College, sponsored by the Lutherans in Chicago from 1860 to 1863;

16 Gager, *Directory, 1857,* Appendix, p. xxxii; *Chicago Daily Democrat,* April 1, 1850, February 27, 1860.

17 Garraghan, *Catholic Church in Chicago,* pp. 150–53, 202, 205–6, 213–16; *Chicago Tribune,* August 26, 1870; Edwards, *Directory, 1868–69,* pp. 999–1000. Taken together the Scandinavian and German schools had an enrollment in 1867–68 of 3,457. (*Annual Report, 1867–68,* p. 151; *Chicago Tribune,* January 18, May 7, 1870.) In 1871, there were eighteen of these special schools. In 1871 there were 12,275 pupils enrolled in church, private, and select schools. Edwards, *Merchants' Census Report, 1871,* p. 1241.

18 Act of January 28, 1851, *Private Laws, 1851,* p. 20; *Chicago Daily Democrat,* April 21, 1851. The University opened November 5, 1855, with literary, scientific, and eclectic courses. (*Weekly Chicago Democrat,* October 18, 1856.) In 1870, the Northwestern Female College, incorporated in 1857 as a private institution, became part of Northwestern University. Act of January 19, 1857, *Private Laws, 1857,* p. 6; Estelle F. Ward, *The Story of Northwestern University* (New York, 1924), p. 110; *The Daily Democratic Press,* August 9, 1855.

through Lind University, later called Lake Forest University; [19] and in 1857 through the University of Chicago under the direction of the Baptists.[20] In addition to the customary classical courses, the University of Chicago after 1859 was prepared to train in the law and to send men into a calling where fees ranged from ten to fifty dollars; and Chicago carried on agricultural education in its experimental farm.[21] Men were trained for the ministry at the Chicago Theological Seminary under Congregational auspices, at the Methodist Garrett Biblical Institute located on the Northwestern campus, at the Presbyterian Theological Seminary of the Northwest, and at the Baptist Union Theological Seminary affiliated with the University of Chicago.[22]

While these schools represented the enlarged educational structure of the 'fifties, medical training had received an early impetus in the establishment of Rush Medical College. In 1859, the Chicago Medical College was organized by resigning members of the Rush faculty, at first as a part of Lind University, but later affiliated with Northwestern University. Medical education of the homeopathic persuasion was carried on at Hahnemann Medical College; the Bennett College of

[19] Evangelical Lutheran Augustana Synod of North America, *After Seventy-five Years, 1860–1935; a Jubilee Publication, Seventy-fifth Anniversary of the Augustana Synod and Augustana College and Theological Seminary* (Rock Island, Illinois, 1935), pp. 28–32; T. M. Halpin and Co., *D. B. Cooke & Co.'s Chicago City Directory for the Year 1860–61*, p. 20 (hereafter cited as Halpin and Co., *D. B. Cooke & Co.'s Directory, 1860–61*); Act of February 13, 1857, *Private Laws, 1857*, p. 514; Act of February 16, 1865, *Private Laws, 1865*, I, 21, 53.

[20] The University of Chicago, *First Annual Catalogue of the University of Chicago, 1859–60* (Chicago, 1860), pp. 33–34; Act of January 30, 1857, *Private Laws, 1857*, p. 100; Thomas Wakefield Goodspeed, *A History of the University of Chicago* . . . (Chicago, 1916), p. 17. Stephen A. Douglas was its first president. In 1861 he was succeeded by William B. Ogden. (J. C. Burroughs to S. A. Douglas, June 24, 1856, *Douglas Papers.*) Douglas's critics declared his gift of land was to increase the value of his holdings and was not inspired by a love of education. Cole, *The Era of the Civil War*, p. 237; *Weekly Chicago Democrat*, October 18, 1856.

[21] Chicago opened a law department in 1859. In the same year Northwestern planned a department, but did not open it until 1873. *The Press and Tribune*, April 5, 1859, March 6, 1860; Goodspeed, *op. cit.*, p. 14; J. C. Burroughs to S. A. Douglas, March 30, 1859, *Douglas Papers;* Zebina Eastman, "Union College of Law," *Autograph Letter Book*, XL, 22 (*Ms.* Chicago Historical Society); *Prairie Farmer*, n.s. VIII (September 5, 1861), 136.

[22] The Chicago Theological Seminary was incorporated in 1855 and was opened in 1858. (Act of February 15, 1855, *Private Laws, 1855*, pp. 375–76.) Garrett was incorporated February 15, 1855. (*Ibid.*, pp. 511–13.) The Presbyterian Theological Seminary of the Northwest was incorporated February 16, 1857. (*Private Laws, 1857*, pp. 845–50.) The Baptists opened their school in 1867. The Baptist Theological Union was incorporated to establish a seminary February 16, 1865. *Private Laws, 1865*, I, 38–41; Goodspeed, *op. cit.*, p. 22.

Eclectic Medicine and Surgery and a school of pharmacy served others. The Woman's Hospital Medical College cared for the professionally unwelcome female, adding to a somewhat pretentious list of institutions in a city but a short time before an outpost of American civilization.[23]

Formal education was only a part of the vehicle of learning, for a variety of other means was at hand. The Chicago Lyceum and the Young Men's Association continued the laudable undertaking of adult education which they had begun in an earlier day. The latter institution, known after 1868 as the Chicago Library Association, served the city so well that its library, although not free, was considered virtually the public library of Chicago. Its limitations, however, by 1871 had convinced persons like Daniel L. Shorey that Chicago needed a tax-supported library.[24] The Mendelssohn Literary Association of the 'fifties was made up of young men interested in lecturing, debating, and composing, while the Zearing Literary Institute, organized in 1863, represented cultural aspirations of a similar kind.[25] A Western Association for the Promotion of Social Science, open to all interested in the problems of society, in 1868 directed attention particularly to such diverse subjects as prison reform, divorce, lodging houses and reformatories for women, the care of deaf-mutes, criminal abortion, and progressive taxation.[26]

[23] Pierce, A History of Chicago, I, 284; James Nevins Hyde, Early Medical Chicago . . . (Fergus Historical Series, no. 11. Chicago, 1879), p. 43. Hahnemann Medical College was incorporated by act of February 14, 1855. (Private Laws, 1855, pp. 530–33; Edwards, Directory, 1870, p. 938; Edwards, Directory, 1871, p. 48; Woman's Hospital Medical College, Annual Announcement of the Woman's Hospital Medical College of Chicago, Ill., 1870–71 [Chicago, 1870], pp. 5–6.) Mrs. Ada H. Kepley received an LL.B. at the University of Chicago in 1871. (The University of Chicago, Twelfth Annual Catalogue, 1870–71, p. 48.) Women were admitted as early as 1854 to the business colleges, of which Chicago had several. The Daily Democratic Press, February 28, 1854; The Press and Tribune, May 20, 1859.

[24] Pierce, A History of Chicago, I, 284–88; Watchman of the Prairies, December 17, 1850; Mary Onahan Gallery, Life of William J. Onahan . . . (Chicago, 1929), p. 6; Northwestern Christian Advocate, February 22, 1854; Gwladys Spencer, The Chicago Public Library: Origins and Backgrounds (unpublished Ph.D. Thesis, The University of Chicago, 1939), pp. 80, 89. There were several private libraries of size and value. That of Isaac N. Arnold had about eight thousand volumes. J. Y. Scammon had one of the world's outstanding Swedenborgian collections. Henry S. Monroe and Ezra B. McCagg had splendid libraries. These private collections were burned in the fire, 1871. Ibid., pp. 140–46.

[25] J. O. Heyworth, Diary and Notebook, 1856–57 (Ms. Chicago Historical Society); Chicago Tribune, November 11, 1863. See program and similar material dated May 11, 1858, in Douglas Papers.

[26] A. R. Brockway, Superintendent of House of Correction, Detroit, was the first president;

A decade earlier, the Chicago Academy of Natural Sciences had undertaken the promotion of its special interest. Delayed somewhat in its activities by the panic of 1857, it did not incorporate for two years, and then under the name Chicago Academy of Sciences. In 1862, Robert Kennicott, one of the most active of its promoters, returned from the Arctic after a three years' stay in search of specimens to use in the study of natural history. Although the collections he obtained went to the Smithsonian Institution, an understanding between its authorities and Kennicott gave Chicago a full set of specimens. In the winter of 1863–64 the purposes and plans of the academy were greatly strengthened and dignified by the presence of Louis Agassiz, whose lectures the following year gave to the cause of science a vitality much needed.[27] By 1871, a large collection of birds, insects, minerals, and marine shells was available for scientific study or for the enlightenment of the curious sight-seer.[28]

The presence in the city of men like Dr. Daniel Brainard of Rush Medical College, competent enough to take an active part in the French Academy of Sciences; the engineering feats of Newton Chapin and Daniel L. Wells, whose swing bridge became a model of instruction at the Royal Institute, Milan, Italy; and the advancement of astronomy through the Chicago Astronomical Society and the Dearborn Observatory at the University of Chicago seem proof enough that in some realms of knowledge Chicago was marching as though with seven league boots.[29] In 1856, the Chicago Historical

---

Sharon Tyndale, secretary; W. F. Coolbaugh, Chicago, treasurer; and the Rev. Fred H. Wines, Springfield, corresponding secretary. The new society was modeled after the British Social Science Association. It was hoped that the Western Association would do for that section what the American Association founded in Boston in 1865 was doing for the East. *The Chicago Times*, September 4, 1868; *Chicago Tribune*, September 4, November 7, 11, 1868; *The Workingman's Advocate*, May 21, 1870.

[27] The academy was placed on a solid financial foundation through the efforts of Eliphalet W. Blatchford, Ezra B. McCagg, George C. Walker, J. Young Scammon, and Daniel Thompson, among others. After Kennicott left for Alaska in 1865, he was succeeded as director and curator by Dr. William Stimpson, formerly in charge of the invertebrate department of the Smithsonian Institution. The Chicago Academy of Sciences was rechartered by act of February 16, 1865. *Private Laws, 1865*, II, 14; William K. Higley, *Historical Sketch of the Academy* (The Chicago Academy of Sciences, *Special Publication*, no. 1. Chicago, 1902), pp. 5–8; Colbert, *Chicago*, p. 108.

[28] By 1871, the collection included, among others, the Audubon Club Collection of Birds, Walsh Collection of Insects, Cooper Collection of Marine Shells, Hughes Collection of Minerals, Western Union Telegraph Collection from Alaska. Higley, *op. cit.*, pp. 7–8; Illinois, *Reports, 1867*, I, 453.

[29] *The Daily Democratic Press*, January 21, 1854; *Oquawka Spectator*, February 8, 1854;

Society was organized and in 1857 incorporated with the particular object " of providing at Chicago a Documentary Library of the most comprehensive character." By 1870, the library had grown to over fifteen thousand volumes and housed a large number of pamphlets and manuscripts.[30]

Adult education chiefly for mechanics was promoted by the Mechanics' Institute in a variety of ways, but particularly by its library and museum, by lectures and special fairs and exhibits. In 1855 its library was chosen by Congress as one of the three depositories for the scientific works of the Smithsonian Institution. By its fairs, beginning in 1847 and running for ten years, the prowess of Chicagoans in the manufacture of plows, cultivators, and other agricultural implements, in stoves and similar products was advertised. To these fairs came the folk of the countryside just as they came to Chicago for other exhibits in the fairs of the Chicago Horticultural Society, the Cook County Poultry Association, the Cook County Agricultural Society, and the Chicago Gardeners' Society.[31]

In March, 1858, the Chicago Academy of Medical Sciences was established to cultivate the science of medicine, to further the profession, and to advance the standards of public health. In 1868, Chicago was host to the American Association for the Advancement of Science in its first meeting west of Cleveland, a meeting which provoked

---

Pierce, *As Others See Chicago*, p. 122; The University of Chicago, *Seventh Annual Catalogue, 1865–66*, pp. 39–40; *Chicago Tribune*, January 24, August 1, 26, 1868. James Parton, when he visited Chicago after the mid-'sixties, remarked on the number of college men in the city, noting that " fifty graduates of Yale, all residents of the city, were gathered about one table." James Parton, " Chicago," *The Atlantic Monthly*, XIX (March, 1867), 344.

[30] William H. Brown was the first president of the Chicago Historical Society; William B. Ogden, vice-president; Dr. C. H. Ray, corresponding secretary; and S. D. Ward, treasurer. Gager, *Directory, 1857*, Appendix, p. xx; " Early Chicago," *Autograph Letter Book*, XVII, 19–20 (*Ms.* Chicago Historical Society); William Barry to Zebina Eastman, February 27, 1863, *ibid.*, XXXVII; William Barry to Stephen A. Douglas, January 19, February 19, 1858, *Douglas Papers;* Act of February 7, 1857, *Private Laws, 1857*, pp. 329–30.

[31] The Mechanics' Institute was incorporated in 1843. (Pierce, *A History of Chicago*, I, 288–89; Spencer, *op. cit.*, p. 117; Mechanics' Institute, *Awards and Address of N. S. Davis, 4th Fair, 1851* [*Ms.* McCormick Agricultural Library, Chicago]; *The Chicago Mechanics Institute* [Pamphlet, Chicago, 1913]; *Chicago Tribune*, March 27, 1861; *Weekly Chicago Democrat*, November 21, 1848, February 23, 1850; *The Daily Democratic Press*, October 9, 11, 16, 1852; *Oquawka Spectator*, December 21, 1853.) The following societies were active, particularly in the years noted: the Chicago Horticultural Society, 1847–50; the Mechanics' Institute, 1847–60; the Cook County Agricultural Society, 1858; the Chicago Gardeners' Society, 1859–60; National Agricultural Society, 1859; the Illinois State Agricultural Society, 1855, 1861, 1865, 1866; Cook County Poultry Association, 1868. See files of *Prairie Farmer* and press for years in which fairs were held.

enough interest to warrant several columns in the daily press during the sessions held.[32] This and other gatherings of men learned in science — along with frequent conventions of educators, musicians, and other professional workers — kept Chicago in touch with an advancing world. Each in its turn left the city enriched; each left it intellectually stirred and more receptive to the circulation of ideas.

But on the whole this was a rarefied atmosphere which most of the laity did not breathe. More popular were the lectures of the phrenologist, O. S. Fowler of New York, who for a sum could be prevailed upon to examine the heads of those who wished their characters "delineated." A Chicago Phrenological Society served those friendly to its " object." In the early 'fifties believers were attracted by a " mesmeric power " demonstrated by one Sharp, who was said to have convinced " the most incredulous of his power to control the actions " of those he brought " under the influence of his mysterious agency." " The science " named biology, an exponent declared before large audiences of Chicagoans, had no more connection with psychology or mesmerism than algebra had with common arithmetic. Indeed, in one demonstration, twenty-one of twenty-six persons who underwent experimentation were said to have been "biologically affected." But this was not a strange manifestation of the mind of a people in an age when the appearance of the planet Venus at midday meant to some " a dreadful portent of some impending evil," and when terror reigned in the hearts of others lest the end of the world was shortly to come because of a portended collision with some comet.[33]

Lectures on a myriad of topics, not only in English but in foreign tongue, were designed to enlighten and to entertain. In the 'fifties a plethora of political addresses dealt generally with aspects of the slavery question, just as in the 'sixties talks ventilated problems created by the war.[34] By temperance advocates and the exponents of women's

[32] The Press and Tribune, May 4, 1859; Chicago Tribune, August 1, 6, 13, 1868.

[33] Chicago Daily Democrat, February 1, 6, 21, 23, 25, March 4, 26, 28, 30, 1850, December 13, 18, 1855, August 27, 1860; Chicago Tribune, January 22, 1862, April 26, 1870; The Daily Democratic Press, January 9, 1855; Oquawka Spectator, June 12, 1857.

[34] Among others was Frederick Douglass in 1854 (The Free West, November 2, 1854; The Daily Democratic Press, February 13, 1856); Henry Ward Beecher in 1859 (The Press and Tribune, April 22, 1859); Edward Everett in 1862 (Chicago Tribune, May 12, 16, 1862); Orestes A. Brownson in 1863 (ibid., January 15, 1863); Wendell Phillips in 1867 (ibid., February 17, 22, 1867). The Germans in the Arbeiter-Verein, for example, listened to lec-

rights, by educators and dispensers of descriptive tales of lands far away, by technical experts expounding the mysteries of the spectrum or the pneumatic railways, ideas in Chicago were fertilized, and opinions were swayed.[35]

Much of the cultural uplift of the day, however, was gained from the printed page. Through the bookstores new books and periodical literature were available, a service of no mean significance at a time when no libraries in Chicago were free to all the public. Shops specializing in religious literature, or in foreign language publications, served a select clientele, while, all told, sixty-eight establishments represented the increased demand of the Chicago populace of 1871 over the sales of the six stores of 1849. Music publishers like Root and Cady distributed their own publications throughout the Middle West, and Lyon and Healy had begun a long-time service in the same field of culture.[36] Book and periodical publishers likewise distributed their productions and often combined their retail business with the sale of stationery and supplies. Among the prominent publishers in Chicago before 1871 were Robert Fergus, who put out historical materials; S. C. Griggs and Company, who were succeeded by Jansen, McClurg and Company; Rand, McNally and Company, early famed for their railroad and cartographic printing; and Church, Goodman and Donnelley, one of the largest book and periodical publishing houses in the West during the 'sixties and later known as the Lakeside Publishing and Printing Company.[37]

Fiction appealed to more readers than any other type of literature.

---

tures on historical and other subjects. (See, for example, *Illinois Staats-Zeitung*, September 6, October 8, 1861.) In addition there were, of course, the addresses of aspirants for political office.

[35] J. B. Gough, among others, lectured on temperance. Women's rights were discussed by Amelia Bloomer, Anna Dickinson, and Lucy Stone. Among speakers on education were Horace Mann, Jonathan B. Turner, advocate of agricultural and industrial education, Professor Goldwin Smith of Oxford University, and Catherine Beecher. Bayard Taylor, among other topics, discussed "Japan and the Japanese." (*Oquawka Spectator*, October 26, December 21, 1853, January 4, February 8, March 22, 1854, April 5, 1860, February 28, 1861; *Chicago Tribune*, September 18, 1864; *Daily Democrat*, May 7, 1849, September 24, 1850.) Professor W. C. Richards in 1871 spoke on "Light or the Spectrum Analysis" (*Chicago Tribune*, February 17, 1871); Dr. Cutcheon on "Anatomy and Hygiene" (*The Daily Democratic Press*, October 11, 1854); Dr. R. H. Gilbert on "Pneumatic Railways" (*The Workingman's Advocate*, March 12, 1870). Elihu Burrett, Theodore Parker, Horace Greeley, "Parson" Brownlow, and the Rev. W. H. Channing were popular lecturers.

[36] Edwards, *Merchants' Census Report, 1871*, p. 1239; Hatheway and Taylor, *Directory, 1849-50*, pp. 26-27; Andreas, *History of Chicago*, II, 593, III, 634. [37] *Ibid.*, II, 483-87.

Certainly this was true if advertisements in the press reflected popular desire. The sentimental novels of Mrs. Aline Grey, Mrs. E. D. E. N. Southworth, Mrs. Mary J. Holmes, Miss M. E. Braddon, and Mrs. Henry Wood, and the moralistic, poor-girl-to-rich-wife stories of Mrs. Madeline Leslie fitted the standards of the readers of the day. Adventure and mystery tales such as *Strange Stories of a Detective; or Curiosities of Crime,* " trap-door " and " wonderful accident " yarns, and novels by Oliver Optic found a reading public. The sectional conflict was intensified by the wide circulation given partisan discussions of slavery and politics. *Uncle Tom's Cabin,* advertised first in the *Chicago Democrat,* June 9, 1852, served as text for editorial comment and pulpit fulmination alike. To present a different picture from Mrs. Stowe's soul-stirring tale of Uncle Tom came W. L. G. Smith's *Life at the South, or " Uncle Tom's Cabin " As It Is,* and Mrs. Mary E. Eastman's *Aunt Phillis' Cabin.* During the war Henry Morford's *The Days of Shoddy* seemed a particularly timely theme, while books like Edward Everett Hale's *Man Without a Country* and J. T. Trowbridge's *Cudjo's Cave* served their purpose of propaganda.

Temperance advocates gained comfort in the lessons taught by T. S. Arthur's *Ten Nights in a Bar-Room,* and opponents of Roman Catholicism intensified the rancor they already felt by reading *Helen Mulgrave, or Jesuit Executorship, being Passages in the Life of a Seceder from Romanism; Carlington Castle; A Tale of the Jesuits;* and *Stanhope Burleigh: The Jesuits in Our Homes, a Novel.* In turn, the Catholics extolled the treatment given the controversial topics of Protestantism and Catholicism in Milner's *End of Controversy.*

Less ephemeral books also had their place in the reading of the time. The works of Alexander Dumas, Victor Hugo, Dickens, Thackeray, George Eliot, Sir Walter Scott, and Jane Austen were known by many, and contemporary American writers, including James Fenimore Cooper, Herman Melville, Nathaniel Hawthorne, and Oliver Wendell Holmes, were familiar to the more literate.

By the lover of history the works of Parkman, Motley, Hildreth, Prescott, and Bancroft could be had. Curiosity about aspects of local history was satisfied by Mrs. John H. Kinzie's *Wau-Bun,* Thomas Ford's *History of Illinois,* Bross's *History of Chicago,* and Fred Gerhard's *Illinois as It Is.* Devotees of biography could turn to Thomas Carlyle and Jared Sparks as of old, and some found pleasure in James

Parton's *Horace Greeley* and his *Life of Andrew Jackson.* Isaac N. Arnold's *History of A. Lincoln* and James W. Sheahan's *Life of Stephen A. Douglas,* besides chronicles of outstanding characters in national life such as William H. Seward, Sam Houston, and John Brown, were sold by subscription. When D. B. Cooke and Company advertised Barnum's autobiography in 1854, the claim of ninety-five thousand advance orders was used as an indication of the importance of this book. In 1868, *Biographical Sketches of the Leading Men of Chicago,* outlining the lives of prominent merchants, professional men, and politicians, indicated an interest in collective biographies of local personages.

Besides a wealth of fiction condemning or condoning the institution of slavery, the Civil War, politics, and current problems in general, the presses turned out an abundance of more serious treatises on these absorbing aspects of the 'fifties and 'sixties. Spooner's *Unconstitutionality of Slavery,* Gerrit Smith's *Constitutional Argument,* William Goodell's *Slavery and Anti-Slavery,* and Hinton R. Helper's *The Impending Crisis* are but a sampling of the books made available. The war quickened, as war always does, the production of volumes on military tactics, pocket guides for soldiers, personal reminiscences, and diaries. Political theory was expounded in William Whiting's pamphlet, *The War Powers of the President, and the Legislative Powers of Congress, in Relation to Rebellion, Treason and Slavery;* and in the Rev. Dr. Junkin's *Political Fallacies: An Examination of the False Assumptions, and Refutation of the Sophistical Reasonings which have brought this Civil War.*

As the center of an agricultural area, Chicago provided books such as Charles R. Baker's *Practical and Scientific Fruit Culture,* M. Quinby's *Mysteries of Bee-Keeping Explained,* and Edward Enfield's *Indian Corn: Its Value, Culture, and Uses.* In 1863, the editor of the *Evening Journal* significantly remarked that agricultural books continued to appear and to find a ready sale even in the midst of war.[38] This comment could have applied also to religious books. Sermons by Henry Ward Beecher and Matthew Hale Smith's *Mount Calvary, with Meditations in Sacred Places* pleased many readers, just as in the 'fifties did G. S. Weaver's *Ways of Life,* which showed "The Right Way and Wrong Way; The High and the Low Way; The True Way

[38] *Chicago Evening Journal,* June 6, 1863.

and the False Way; The Upward Way and the Downward Way; the Way of Honor and the Way of Dishonor." The Catholic laity at the same time were urged to absorb such manuals of devotional exercises as the *Christian's Guide to Heaven, or a Manual of Spiritual Exercises.*[39] Gifts of the Bible and prayer books, elaborately illustrated and well-bound volumes of *The Women of the Bible, Scenes in the Life of the Savior,* and Bunyan's *Pilgrim's Progress* were recommended especially at the Christmas season.

The publication of guidebooks and other writings on foreign countries, in a day when an increasing number of Chicagoans were finding it possible to cross the Atlantic, coincided with a greater interest in literature about America. Works on the various sciences including Sir Charles Lyell's *Geological Evidences of the Antiquity of Man,* which gave support to Charles Darwin's *Origin of Species,* were offered interested frequenters of the bookshops. At the same time, Louis Agassiz's *Introduction to the Study of Natural History* led a Chicago reviewer to remark that the " bare announcement " of the work would " lead thousands to embalm it in their private libraries," [40] a fate which probably befell many books of this type. The publication of a *History of Medical Education and Institutions in the United States, from the First Settlement of the British Colonies to the Year 1850,* by Dr. N. S. Davis of Chicago, justly aroused local pride, although it is likely that more households in the city possessed *The American Remedy and Toilet Receipt Book* which promised cures to those suffering with chronic diseases or aid to those who desired a beautiful complexion, a fine head of hair, a luxuriant beard or moustache. In the early 'fifties Mrs. E. Oakes Smith's *Woman and Her Needs* was highly advertised, and W. W. Evert's *Manhood — Its Duties and Responsibilities,* for one dollar, was reported to have found nearly four thousand inquisitive buyers in ten days. At the same time, books on etiquette, such as *The American Gentleman's Guide to Politeness and Fashion* by Henry Lunettes, prepared against possible pitfalls those hoping to play a part in polite society.[41]

[39] *Daily Democrat,* December 28, 1848. At the bookstore of Charles McDonnell the Catholics could find a good supply of Catholic literature. Hatheway and Taylor, *Directory, 1849–50,* p. 26.

[40] *Chicago Evening Journal,* September 26, 1863.

[41] *The Daily Democratic Press,* December 23, 1854; *Chicago Daily Democrat,* June 1, 1851, June 16, 1852, October 31, 1860; *Chicago Evening Journal,* August 15, October 17,

This increasing list of books represented a wide range of fancy, from the compulsory study of Goodrich's *History of the United States* to the unbidden delight of the essays of Ruskin, Emerson, and Lowell. Artemus Ward and Petroleum V. Nasby excited risibilities, while Longfellow, Whittier, and Thomas Bailey Aldrich joined with others of the day to please Chicagoans who liked poetry. Children's books passed from dinginess into a more attractive format than that of the 'thirties and 'forties and exemplified an improvement in bookmaking in all lines.[42]

A wide array of periodicals was also found, many of them published in Chicago and giving to the city a cultural leadership of great significance over the surrounding region. Those bearing the Chicago imprint were western in content and frequently in title. They breathed the air of the prairie, from the center of which they sprang: *The Prairie Leaf, Lady's Western Magazine, Western Garland, Youth's Western Banner, The Chicago Magazine: The West As It Is.* Their westernism, however, was that of the Northwest and just as partisan whether they were the so-called literary magazines, miscellanies, or vehicles of politics.

Most of these efforts were short-lived. Like the *Literary Budget,* the majority of these magazines strove to supply the channel by which there might be described the " undulating prairies, deep-wooded highlands, mighty rivers, and remnants of aboriginal races." This laudable enterprise was the undertaking of William W. Danenhower, the bookseller, as one means to advertise his books and periodicals. At first issued monthly, it became a weekly in January, 1854; it cultivated a high literary tone; and at one time it had a circulation of three thousand.[43] *Sloan's Garden City* also began as an advertising agent, this time for Sloan's patent medicines, although after a few issues that

---

1863. *A Physiological View of Marriage,* a volume of three hundred pages, was advertised for some time during 1863.

[42] *Chicago Jokes and Anecdotes* represents an effort to chronicle local humor. The Chicago newspapers and periodicals of the time contain much descriptive material relating to available reading in Chicago.

[43] *Literary Budget,* II (January 14, 1854), 12. Subscription price, $2.00 a year. Sometimes called the *Chicago Literary Budget.* Scott, *Newspapers and Periodicals of Illinois, 1814–1879,* p. 64, gives beginning date as January, 1852. A complete file is unavailable, but that at the Chicago Historical Society starts with number 7, volume I, December 1, 1853. This would lead to the assumption that the first issue was June, 1853. Probably it ran from June, 1853, to August 25, 1855. (Herbert E. Fleming, *Magazines of a Market-Metropolis* . . . [Chicago, 1906], pp. 384, 389.) As special features, the *Literary Budget* presented music, book reviews, a youth's department, a " scientific and artistic " column, a section of

purpose was abandoned. Costing $2.00 a year for weekly issues, the magazine specialized in the family story, patriotism, some music, short news items, and similar features. Its first issue appeared July 23, 1853, and it probably ceased publication in 1855.[44]

Not discouraged by the failure of other publishers in efforts to improve the literary taste of the West, the Chicago Mechanics' Institute enriched the community by its five issues of the *Chicago Magazine: The West As It Is,* under the editorship of Zebina Eastman. The panic of 1857 put an end to the undertaking, which had been so optimistically pointed toward history, biography, and a plenitude of illustrations.

The *Chicagoan,* the *Chicago Literary Messenger, Golden Hours,* and others suffered fates similar to that of the *Chicago Magazine.* In 1868, the *Illustrated Chicago News* offered its readers material designed to compete with *Frank Leslie's Illustrated Newspaper* and *Harper's Weekly,* while the *Lakeside Monthly,* succeeding the *Western Monthly* of 1869–71, started in 1871 as a magazine of biography and literature, shortly was transformed into a purely literary organ, and became the *Atlantic Monthly* of the Middle Region. In 1870 it had become a major enterprise of the Lakeside Publishing and Printing Company, a relationship similar to that of *Harper's Magazine* to Harper and Brothers, publishers. The war brought into being the *National Banner,* distinctly military and patriotic in viewpoint and published by Miss Delphine P. Baker.

Periodicals primarily for women or for family readers bloomed and withered. Such were the *Home Eclectic* and the *Lady's Western Magazine.* Under the sparkling editorship of Mrs. Martha L. Rayne, the *Chicago Magazine of Fashion, Music, and Home Reading* attained a circulation of about three thousand in the short period of its publication, 1870 to 1876. Its chief attraction lay in the fashion and household items, the former often lithographs in color, but sometimes there appeared discussions on such topics as to whether the recently married should " set up housekeeping " or " board out." [45] Art and

humor styled " Quirks and Quiblets," a column of proverbs called " The Reflector," and a column called " Facts and Fancies."

[44] *Sloan's Garden City* advertised Sloan's Family or Horse Ointment or Life Syrup. *Sloan's Garden City,* I (July 23, 1853), 5; Scott, *op. cit.,* p. 67; H. E. Fleming, *op. cit.,* pp. 390–404.

[45] *The Chicago Magazine of Fashion, Music, and Home Reading,* II (May, 1871), 63–64.

music periodicals such as the *Western Journal of Music* and the *Chicago Musical Review* lasted only one year, while scientific and legal magazines naturally found a relatively small clientele.[46] Of the last, the *Chicago Legal News,* founded in 1868 by Mrs. Myra Bradwell, had a far longer existence than was commonly accorded Chicago publications.[47]

In the realm of juvenile magazines Chicago early assumed a leadership through the publication of the *Little Corporal.* Its first number appeared in July, 1865, the offspring of the Northwestern Sanitary Fair when children were organized into the "American Eagle," with rank based on the number of pictures of the war eagle sold. Although the *Little Corporal* was avowedly nonreligious in purpose, a highly moralistic tone pervaded its pages, and readers were warned that if one wished to become a model Little Corporal, swearing, lying, tattling, chewing tobacco, intoxication, and disobedience to parents and teachers must be abjured. By 1869, a subscription list of eighty thousand spelled success for this magazine and served to stimulate other publishers to undertake similar ventures. Between 1865 and 1871, fifteen juvenile magazines were started; seven survived the fire of 1871.[48]

Despite the short life of many of these fresh western magazines, each attempt meant a cultural gain. Their failure to endure may be attributed to the instinct of subscribers to cling to the old. That meant the reading of *Harper's New Monthly Magazine, Putnam's Magazine,* the *Independent,* and others of eastern vintage.

Along with secular organs went the religious press. Before 1847,

---

[46] Of medical periodicals the *North-western Medical and Surgical Journal* had the longest life during the years treated in this volume. In 1844 it was the *Illinois Medical and Surgical Journal,* in 1846 the *Illinois and Indiana Medical and Surgical Journal,* in 1848 the *Northwestern Medical and Surgical Journal,* in 1858 the *Chicago Medical Journal,* in 1875 the *Chicago Medical Journal and Examiner.* The *People's Dental Journal* began in 1863 and discontinued publication probably in 1865.

[47] The first issue of the *Chicago Legal News* was October 3, 1868. Publication continued until July 16, 1925. Myra Bradwell was the wife of James B. Bradwell, judge of the Cook County Court, and was an ardent woman's rights advocate. In 1869, she passed the Illinois Bar examinations, but the state Supreme Court rejected her application to practice law on the ground that she was married. In a retrial, she was rejected on the ground of sex. In 1873, the United States Supreme Court upheld the decision. In 1885, Mrs. Bradwell got her license after the Illinois legislature passed an act guaranteeing the choice of profession to any person regardless of sex. *Dictionary of American Biography,* II, 581.

[48] *The Little Corporal,* [I] no. 1 (July, 1865), pp. 1–3; H. E. Fleming, *op. cit.,* pp. 406–7.

no periodicals or newspapers having denominational affiliations were published in Chicago, but in that year two were started. One of these was the *Herald of the Prairies,* " devoted to the promotion of practical religion, the maintenance of essential truth, and the advancement of the benevolent enterprises of the age." This organ of the New School Presbyterians and the Congregationalists became the *Prairie Herald* in 1849. The separation of the Congregationalists from the Presbyterian congregations led to the ascendency of the views of the former in the *Prairie Herald,* with the result that, in 1853, a group of Congregational clergymen took over the paper and issued it as the *Congregational Herald* until 1861. It was followed in 1867 by the *Advance,* one of the most ambitious religious papers published up to that time in Chicago. Eight pages of feature articles, editorials, and news items, besides sermons of such outstanding preachers as Henry Ward Beecher, attempted to capture the fancy not only of a local and denominational clientele but of readers in the states and territories, and in Canada.[49]

In 1847, also, a Baptist organ, the *Watchman of the Prairies,* was established, becoming by 1850 an implacable foe of slavery. Although it stopped abruptly with the issue of February 22, 1853, its policies continued under Baptist publications which succeeded it. The first of these was the *Christian Times,* which began with the issue of August 31, 1853, and changed its name to the *Christian Times and Witness* in 1865. In 1867 this paper became the *Standard.*[50]

Toward the end of 1852, the *Northwestern Christian Advocate* was established in Chicago by the General Conference of the Methodist Episcopal church. Among Protestant newspapers it became one of the most important published in Chicago, exerting an influence throughout the entire upper Mississippi Valley. It was the first of Chicago's religious papers to increase its size to eight pages, a change which took place with its issue of January 2, 1861.[51]

To set forth their views, the New School Presbyterians began the *Chicago Evangelist* in the same year in which the *Congregational Herald* was first issued. But the life of this paper was short, and in

---

[49] *Weekly Chicago Democrat,* February 12, 1853; *Congregational Herald,* April 7, 1853; *The Advance,* September 5, 12, 1867. The *Advance* was published until 1917, when it merged with the Boston *Congregationalist.* Scott, *op. cit.,* pp. 58, 60–61.

[50] The *Standard* was in existence until 1920.

[51] The *Northwestern Christian Advocate* was published in Chicago until 1930.

three years it was merged with the *New York Evangelist,* on whose staff was a resident Chicago editorial writer.[52] Presbyterian efforts to establish a periodical were attended by wavering success, and the *Presbyterian Expositor* and the *Christian Instructor and Western United Presbyterian,* among others, attested to an uncertainty not pleasing to their publishers. Not until 1870, after the reconciliation of different schools of thought within the denomination, was it possible to start a journal comparable to the *Advance* and the *Northwestern Christian Advocate.* Then the *Interior* made its weekly appearance among families of the Presbyterian credo.[53]

Episcopalians followed the lead of others, and in 1862 the *Chicago Record,* started in 1857 and sometimes called the *Church Record,* passed into the editorship of the Rev. Thomas Smith, who undertook a new journal, the *Northwestern Church.* In 1862, the *American Churchman* carried items of interest to those affiliated with the Episcopal persuasion, and by 1865 it was their leading Chicago journal.[54]

The *Western Tablet,* with the motto " where the spirit of the Lord is, there is liberty," each week during its brief life gave Catholic readers contact with their native Ireland, news of their adopted country and their new city, as well as discussions of religious topics. For a short time in mid-'sixties the *Monthly* was edited at the University of St. Mary of the Lake, followed in 1868 by the *Western Catholic,* which was available until 1905. The *Katholisches Wochenblatt* by 1859 furnished German Catholics, not always familiar with English, a means of religious sustenance.[55] The *New Covenant,* which appeared in 1848 as " A Family Paper: Devoted to Religion, Theoreti-

---

[52] Considerable rivalry between the Presbyterians and the Congregationalists attended the publication of their respective papers, the *Chicago Evangelist* and the *Congregational Herald.* (*Weekly Chicago Democrat,* April 2, 1853.) The Congregationalists brought their first issue from the press on April 7, one day before the Presbyterians dated their publication. *Northwestern Christian Advocate,* April 20, 1853; Scott, *op. cit.,* pp. 58, 66–67.

[53] The *Presbyterian Expositor* was an Old School Presbyterian publication, edited by the Rev. Dr. Nathan Rice and subsidized by Cyrus Hall McCormick. (Hutchinson, *Cyrus Hall McCormick,* II, 16; *Northwestern Christian Advocate,* June 12, 1861.) The *Northwestern Presbyterian* (1857–69) and the *Presbyterian Recorder* (1861–62) were the others. (Scott, *op. cit.,* pp. 71, 78; *The Advance,* January 20, March 24, 1870.) The *Interior* was in existence until 1910.

[54] The *Northwestern Church* ceased publication in 1865. The *American Churchman* started in 1862 and ceased publication in 1871.

[55] *The Western Tablet,* March 13, 1852; Scott, *op. cit.,* pp. 76, 83, 94. The *Katholisches Wochenblatt* was being published in 1939. The *Western Tablet* ceased publication in 1855.

cal and Practical: Social Reform Literature, and News," carried on as a fearless organ of the less orthodox group, the Universalists. Subject to countless attacks by the evangelical press, the *New Covenant* fought bravely on until the 'eighties.[56]

So popular was the religious periodical that even separate congregations such as the Salem Baptist Church undertook publication. The *Olive Branch of the West*, " full of moral and religious reading," initiated this type of venture in 1853. The Swedenborgians, probably at the instance of Jonathan Young Scammon, an important communicant, began their *New Church Independent and Monthly Review* in the same year. Although the first published organ of a small denomination in Chicago, this paper nevertheless carried on with greater success than some of those which represented larger and more prosperous groups. In 1864 the Second-Adventists started publication of their weekly, *Advent Christian Times,* and in the same year, the Mennonite monthly, *Herald of Truth,* also came from the press. The *Herald of Peace,* said to be the only Friends' paper in the West, first appeared as a semimonthly in 1867. The first Lutheran paper, the semimonthly *Lutherischer Kirchenfreund,* was the second religious German newspaper of Chicago, and the third among the foreign religious newspapers, although two others were organized in quick succession in 1870 — *Missionären,* the Swedish Lutheran monthly, and *Missionœren,* the Norwegian and Danish Methodist. The Swedish Methodists in 1864 moved their *Sändebudet* from Rockford to Chicago, where it came out under the auspices of the Methodist Book Concern.[57]

Journals for Spiritualist groups seemed appropriate enough in the age of Rochester spirit-rappings, and the weekly *Religio-Philosophical Journal* appeared in 1865 and cost " three Dollars per annum, invariably in advance." This paper was still in existence in 1895, outliving by many years the Spiritualist *News from the Spirit World* of 1868–70.[58]

---

[56] In 1881 the *New Covenant* was changed to the *Star and Covenant* through absorption of an older paper. In 1884 it became the *Universalist*. It soon ceased publication in Chicago and moved to Boston. In 1939 it was still published.

[57] The *Lutherischer Kirchenfreund* appeared in 1869 and continued publication until 1881. *Sändebudet* was being published in 1939. The Swedish *Missionären* ceased publication in 1873. The Norwegian and Danish Methodist organ continued after 1877 through 1939 under the name *Kristelige Talsmand*. Scott, *op. cit.,* pp. 93, 103.

[58] Halpin, *Directory, 1865–66,* p. 29; Scott, *op. cit.,* pp. 84, 92.

The popularity of these religious journals among the laity was almost as great as that of the secular press, whose aggregate daily circulation exceeded only slightly that of church publications.[59] In appearance and sometimes in editorial expression the secular and the religious were alike, but in the latter the opinion of lay writers acquired a sanctification and an authority not always accorded to the former.

Along with the publishing activities of churches sometimes went the establishment of book depositories, which indicated the strength of Chicago in the denominations which maintained them. When the General Conference of the Methodist Episcopal church resolved in 1852 to establish a depository in Chicago, it paid tribute to the city " as a great central point," a tribute justified within a year when sales of the new Methodist Book Concern exceeded $34,000.[60] Such success attracted the attention of the Baptists, who were equally anxious for more members, and the American Baptist Publication Society set up headquarters in the office of the *Chicago Times,* the first of its depositories west of Philadelphia. By the mid-'sixties the American Sunday School Union, the American Tract Society, the Chicago Bible Society, and a Swedish Lutheran Publication Society had official agents or depositories located in Chicago, while the bookstore of William Tomlinson served a similar purpose for the Presbyterian Publication Committee and two Episcopal publication societies.[61]

Of all secular publications, newspapers undoubtedly played the most effective rôle in crystallizing public opinion. The earliest news-

[59] The circulation of religious weeklies was probably greater during the ante-bellum period than was that of daily secular newspapers. The *Northwestern Christian Advocate,* with a circulation of 7,000 in 1854 and 13,000 in 1857, had risen to 21,000 in 1861 and 16,000 in 1870. The *Christian Times* rose from 4,000 in 1854 to 9,000 in 1864, and its successor, the *Standard,* printed 17,000 a week in 1870. Weekly circulations of secular papers, however, were larger than daily circulations. The *Democrat* had 5,000 in 1853, the *Tribune* 8,000 in 1857, and the *Times* 45,000 in 1870. *Northwestern Christian Advocate,* January 11, 1854, December 9, 1857; *The Christian Times,* August 30, 1854, August 11, 1864; *Chicago Tribune,* January 21, June 29, 1861, August 21, 1864, April 11, 1865; Hall and Smith, *Chicago City Directory for 1853–'54* (Chicago, 1853), pp. 248–49 (hereafter cited as Hall and Smith, *Directory, 1853–54*); Geo. P. Rowell & Co., *American Newspaper Directory, 1870* (New York, 1870), pp. 632–33.

[60] *Chicago Daily Democrat,* May 27, 1852; *Watchman of the Prairies,* November 2, 1852. The Methodist Book Concern controlled sales in Michigan, Illinois, Wisconsin, Iowa, and northern Indiana. *Northwestern Christian Advocate,* October 26, 1853.

[61] *The Christian Times,* April 18, 1855; Austin, *Bailey's Directory, 1867–68,* pp. xxxiv, xxxvi; *Chicago Tribune,* April 1, 1861.

paper of Chicago had appropriately borne the title *Democrat*. Not unfittingly did this title persist for the period of the editorship of John Wentworth, who assumed charge in November, 1836. By 1850, its four pages had carried news by telegraph for two years; it had tried political cartooning; and by crude illustrations it had offered its advertisers a graphic means of selling their goods. Shortly afterwards its circulation was said to be six hundred daily and thirty-five hundred weekly copies, for until 1861 a weekly as well as a daily paper appeared.

During much of its existence the *Democrat* benefited from its party views by being the official corporation journal, just as it profited from the editor's connection with corporations like the Illinois Central Railroad, for whose charter he had been an able lobbyist in the state legislature. Throughout, its editorial policy was stormy and effective; by the late 'fifties a libel suit and competition from the strongly Republican *Chicago Tribune* made it appear the better part of wisdom for Wentworth to retire from the field of newspaper ownership, and in 1861 John Wentworth's *Democrat* was merged with Joseph Medill's *Tribune*,[62] which, too, had its roots in the years before 1850. Established in 1847 as an offshoot of the literary paper, the *Gem of the Prairie,* to meet the demand for news alone, the *Tribune* passed through several changes in management and ownership in the 'fifties. In 1852, it absorbed the *Gem of the Prairie,* which was made the Sunday issue; in 1855, it took over the *Free West;* in 1858, it joined with the *Daily Democratic Press* and became known as the *Chicago Daily Press and Tribune*. On March 17, 1859, this title was shortened to the *Press and Tribune* and after October 24, 1860, the paper was called the *Chicago Daily Tribune*.

Under the guiding hand of John L. Scripps, who bought a one-third interest, a distinctive market review was inaugurated as early as 1848. After 1852 its strongly antislavery bias made the *Tribune* a leader in the movement for a new political party, a leadership in politics which it maintained consistently after the Republican party was founded. With the *Democratic Press* in the late 'fifties its cir-

[62] W. W. Danenhower, *Chicago City Directory, for 1851* (Chicago, 1851), p. 256; *Weekly Chicago Democrat*, May 13, 1854, July 27, 1861; *Chicago Daily Democrat*, June 25, 1850; *Chicago Tribune*, July 24, 1861; Gates, *The Illinois Central Railroad*, pp. 63, 173. Wentworth, in selling to the *Tribune*, was forced to agree to withdraw from the field of newspaper publishing until March, 1864. He did not again edit a paper. *Dictionary of American Biography*, XIX, 658.

culation was said to be the largest of any paper in the city, and by 1861, as news of the controversy over slavery stimulated interest, daily circulation was reported at 16,451 copies. War pushed circulation figures to unprecedented heights, reaching 53,000 with Lee's surrender, and this increase was accompanied by growth in size, improvement in format, and broadened influence. Circulation figures claimed by the *Chicago Tribune* kept pace with Greeley's *Tribune* of New York, although the weekly issue of the latter in 1861 circulated in Illinois approximately as widely as the daily *Tribune* of Chicago. In 1855, the Chicago paper began to use the Hoe one-cylinder steam press, and at the same time it became the first newspaper in Illinois to have copper-faced type. By 1864 the installation of an eight-cylinder press represented the expansion of its business.

Under the forceful direction of such men as Dr. Charles Ray, Joseph Medill, and Horace White, the *Chicago Tribune* was envisaged as an aggressive leader in the journalism of the Northwest. In the words of Medill, its journalism provoked readers to swear at the paper even while they swore by it. Especially in the late 'fifties did the *Press and Tribune* promote a political literacy; and during the war special *Tribune* correspondents with the army in the field and extensive telegraphic facilities kept anxious readers informed of the latest happenings.[63]

Of opposite political faith was the *Chicago Times*. In the summer of 1854 Douglas supporters started the publication of the *Chicago Daily Times,* with James W. Sheahan, later Douglas's biographer, as editor.[64] Although Sheahan's loyalty to Douglas was as unadulterated as later was Medill's advocacy of the candidacy of Lincoln,

---

[63] *Memorial of John L. Scripps* (Chicago, [1866]), p. 24. By 1862 Medill claimed a quarter million readers in the West. Certified circulation figures are not available. In 1865, the paper cost $12 a year by mail for the daily edition, $6.00 for the tri-weekly and $2.50 for the weekly. Dr. Charles H. Ray was editor of the *Tribune* from March 28, 1861, to November 20, 1863. Joseph Medill followed him to August 1, 1866, and Horace White served until October, 1874. Joseph Medill to Lyman Trumbull, July 4, 1862, *Trumbull Papers,* XLIX; Medill to E. B. Washburne, May 30, 1864, *Washburne Papers,* XXXVIII; *Chicago Daily Press and Tribune,* September 6, 1858, May 21, 1860; *Chicago Tribune,* January 21, 1861, April 8, 11, 25, 1865; Allan Nevins, *The Evening Post* (New York, 1922), p. 326; Rufus Blanchard, *Discovery and Conquest of the Northwest with the History of Chicago* (2 v. Chicago, 1898–1900), II, 231–33; Strevey, *Joseph Medill and the Chicago Tribune,* pp. 18–19; Scott, *op. cit.,* pp. lxxi–lxxii, 55–56, 59–60.

[64] Moses and Kirkland, *History of Chicago,* II, 16; Scott, *op. cit.,* p. 65; *Oquawka Spectator,* July 18, August 22, 1854. The *Times* was published by Isaac Cook, Daniel Cameron, and James W. Sheahan. When Douglas broke with Buchanan, Cook withdrew.

he failed to make the *Times* "a campaign paper," and thus provoked concern and dissatisfaction in Democratic ranks.[65] Financial troubles and political difficulties forced the owners to sell the paper in 1860 to Cyrus McCormick, who consolidated it with his *Herald* as the *Times and Herald,* later calling it the *Daily Chicago Times.* For a short time, McCormick seemed to steer a course none too close to the Douglas faction, raising a considerable apprehension in the hearts of the antiadministration Democracy. After the secession of South Carolina, although striving for peace, McCormick declared, just as Douglas had declared, his allegiance to the federal government, thereby creating the rumor that the extension of the patent on his reaper played a part in his declaration.[66]

On June 1, 1861, McCormick shifted the responsibilities attendant upon ownership of a newspaper in these trying days to Wilbur F. Storey, under whose colorful and energetic direction the *Times* became a provocative organ, critical and unafraid, which paid no man cowardly tribute. To Storey, emancipation of the slaves meant economic ruin to North and South, and his denunciation of the suspension of the writ of habeas corpus and of the arrest of Vallandigham shortly brought an order by Major General Burnside for the suppression of his so-called "Copperhead" sheet. In a sense, the order was but the official climax of open and hidden reproaches already leveled at the *Times*. Earlier, Governor Yates had written Secretary Stanton that there was an "urgent and almost unanimous demand" for its suppression; the Chicago Board of Trade had passed stinging resolutions against it and had excluded its reporters from their meetings; and the Galena and Chicago Union Railroad, mindful of the power of the press, had for a time forbidden its sale on their railway trains.[67]

[65] C. P. Button to S. A. Douglas, July 24, 1856, *Douglas Papers*. William Price bought Cameron's interest in 1858. The paper was not proving a profitable enterprise at that time. William Price to S. A. Douglas, May 10, 1858, *ibid.;* Helen E. Breckenridge, *The Chicago Times during the Civil War* (unpublished M.A. Thesis, The University of Chicago, 1931), p. 3.

[66] Hutchinson, *op. cit.,* II, 46–48; *Oquawka Spectator,* August 23, 1860; J. W. Sheahan to S. A. Douglas, December 17, 1860, P. A. Hoyne to Douglas, September 2, 1860, Charles H. Lanphier to Douglas, December 8, 1860, *Douglas Papers*. Lanphier attributed the "go-between course" of the *Times* to "McCormick's application for a renewal of his reaper patent," remarking: "Such renewal would amply pay him for fifty or seventy-five thousand sunk in a daily newspaper."

[67] Henry M. Hugunin, "The Late Wilbur Fisk Storey and his Chicago 'Times,'" *Auto-*

At four o'clock on the morning of June 3, 1863, soldiers from Camp Douglas marched into the office of the *Times*, although a temporary injunction had been issued by Judge Drummond at Storey's request. By noon, sane-minded citizens of both parties had petitioned President Lincoln to revoke the order. That night a reported twenty thousand men, including many "hard-fisted sons of toil," assembled to voice their conviction that in the correction of what was held one evil lay another still greater — the abrogation of the traditional rights of free speech and a free press. The following day Lincoln revoked the order of suppression, and on June 5 the *Times* resumed publication, with its editor more firmly convinced than ever that the war was being fought to overturn the Constitution and to destroy the rights of the American citizen.[68]

After the war, the *Times* enlarged its scope to include much more than it had before, maintaining its own cable service and a special correspondent in Europe. Articles on religion, literature, music, and amusements could be found by the reader who cared little for the sensational reports of corruption in the ranks of the opposing political party or for the bizarre and seamy side of life in general.[69]

As early as 1853 seven daily newspapers were reported published in Chicago. They were credited with having done much to make Chicago economically successful. Soon it could be said that nearly every week some new adventurer, ambitious to mold public opinion, tried his hand at the press, shortly to close his undertaking because of the persisting economic factors of supply and demand.[70] Some, besides the *Democrat*, the *Times*, and the *Tribune*, persisted long

graph Letter Book, LXVI, 181–84 (*Ms.* Chicago Historical Society); *Chicago Tribune*, June 3, 1861; Franc B. Wilkie, *Personal Reminiscences of Thirty-Five Years of Journalism* (Chicago, [1891]), p. 114; Scott, *op. cit.*, pp. 65, 66; *The Chicago Times*, January 31, February 2, March 6, 18, May 7, 22, 1863; *Official Records of the Rebellion*, ser. 1, XXIII, pt. 2, 381, ser. 3, II, 316; *Chicago Tribune*, January 3, 1863.

68 The petitioners included Judge Van H. Higgins, Lyman Trumbull, I. N. Arnold, Mayor Francis C. Sherman, W. B. Ogden, M. F. Tuley, S. S. Hayes, A. W. Arrington, Samuel W. Fuller, Wirt Dexter, and A. C. Coventry. *Ibid.*, June 5, 1863; *The Chicago Times*, June 5, 1863; *The Workingman's Advocate*, September 17, 1864; Cook, *Bygone Days in Chicago*, pp. 51–52.

69 Willis J. Abbot, "Chicago Newspapers and their Makers," *The Review of Reviews*, XI (June, 1895), 651.

70 Hall and Smith, *Directory, 1853–54*, pp. 248–49; John Reynolds, *Sketches of the Country on the Northern Route from Belleville, Illinois, to the City of New York, and Back by the Ohio Valley* (Belleville, 1854), p. 118; *Oquawka Spectator*, April 3, 1857. In 1871 the city directory reported ninety-one newspapers and publications in Chicago. Edwards, *Merchants' Census Report, 1871*, p. 1240.

enough to leave their mark. Among these were the *Chicago Daily Journal,* the *Daily Democratic Press,* and the *Gem of the Prairie,* which, describing itself as a family newspaper, combined the literary contributions with the news of the day.[71] The *Journal* was avowedly Whig and later Republican, and the *Press* was generally Democratic until driven by the Kansas-Nebraska question into the arms of the Republicans. In July, 1858, the *Democratic Press* joined forces with the *Tribune,* but the *Journal* carried on under its old name until 1929.[72]

In late 1860, the *Chicago Post* began its career under the general editorship of James W. Sheahan with the declaration of a devotion not to politics but to commercial, literary, and local happenings. Eagerness for war news forced retirement within five years, its plant being sold to the *Republican,* an organ of dissatisfied *Tribune* stockholders. In 1865, the name *Post* was taken by William Pigott for an evening newspaper, its editor being Dr. Charles Ray from 1867 until his death in 1870.[73]

In addition, a lusty foreign language press offered news to those who could not read English or preferred papers printed in the language of the homeland. The *Illinois Staats-Zeitung,* established in 1848 as a weekly, became a daily in 1851. In 1854 a Sunday edition, the *Chicago Sonntags-Zeitung,* was started. Republican in the 'fifties and on the whole favorable to Lincoln, this German paper opposed Andrew Johnson and Liberal Republicanism. Its opponent was the *National Demokrat,* a Douglas organ in 1855 and one of the more than thirty German periodicals published in Chicago from 1848 to 1871. In 1867 the Irish undertook the publication of the *Irish Re-*

---

[71] *Gem of the Prairie,* VI (March 2, 1850). The *Prairie Farmer* is similar and falls into the periodical-newspaper class.

[72] In 1851, the *Journal* reported a subscription list of 800 for its daily and 2,000 for its weekly issue. By 1867, its circulation was 7,000. (Scott, *op. cit.,* p. 57; Abbot, *loc. cit.,* p. 660; Danenhower, *Directory, 1851,* p. 256.) The *Journal* was owned and edited (at times jointly) by Richard and Charles Wilson. (Andreas, *History of Chicago,* II, 491; *Chicago Tribune,* August 21, 1864, March 5, 1867; *The Daily Democratic Press,* March 1, August 17, September 16, 21, 1854, April 12, 1855, June 11, 19, 20, 1856.) The *Daily Democratic Press* was established September 16, 1852, by John L. Scripps and William Bross. In 1854, the paper reported a circulation of 2,064 daily and 4,080 weekly. *Ibid.,* August 22, 1854; Winifred Gregory, ed., *American Newspapers, 1821–1936* (New York, 1937), p. 122; Scott, *op. cit.,* p. 63.

[73] Its subscription price was $7.50 a year. (*Chicago Evening Post,* December 18, 1865.) In August, 1878, the *Post* was merged with the *Chicago Daily News.* Scott, *op. cit.,* pp. 76–77, 84–85; "The Chicago Post" [December 17, 1860], *Douglas Papers.*

TABLE SHOWING THE AMOUNT OF ADVERTISING SPACE DEVOTED TO CERTAIN SELECTED ITEMS
IN CHICAGO NEWSPAPERS OF 1859 AND 1869

Chicago Tribune, 1859

	Jan. 31, 1859	Feb. 28, 1859	Mar. 31, 1859	Apr. 30, 1859	May 31, 1859	June 30, 1859	July 30, 1859	Aug. 31, 1859	Sept. 30, 1859	Oct. 31, 1859	Nov. 30, 1859	Dec. 31, 1859
Books.........	$13\frac{3}{4}''$ (7)	$8\frac{7}{8}''$ (5)	$6\frac{3}{8}''$ (5)	$33\frac{5}{8}''$ (11)	$14\frac{3}{8}''$ (8)	$15\frac{1}{4}''$ (6)	$17\frac{3}{4}''$ (6)	$19\frac{3}{8}''$ (7)	$19''$ (7)	$4''$ (3)	$22\frac{1}{8}''$ (8)	$20\frac{3}{8}''$ (7)
Drugs.........	$41\frac{1}{2}''$ (18)	$43\frac{1}{8}''$ (14)	$17\frac{5}{8}''$ (8)	$34\frac{1}{8}''$ (10)	$33\frac{1}{2}''$ (13)	$34\frac{3}{8}''$ (9)	$26\frac{5}{8}''$ (17)	$34\frac{1}{8}''$ (10)	$31\frac{3}{8}''$ (9)	$39\frac{3}{4}''$ (13)	$24\frac{1}{8}''$ (8)	$27\frac{1}{2}''$ (13)
Dry Goods....	$31''$ (17)	$31\frac{3}{4}''$ (17)	$88\frac{5}{8}''$ (30)	$100\frac{1}{8}''$ (35)	$87\frac{3}{8}''$ (35)	$47\frac{3}{4}''$ (21)	$41\frac{3}{4}''$ (21)	$44\frac{3}{4}''$ (20)	$81\frac{1}{2}''$ (35)	$72\frac{7}{8}''$ (30)	$63''$ (28)	$37\frac{3}{4}''$ (17)
Groceries.....	$17\frac{1}{8}''$ (15)	$22\frac{5}{8}''$ (28)	$36''$ (49)	$37\frac{5}{8}''$ (48)	$26\frac{7}{8}''$ (25)	$36\frac{1}{4}''$ (55)	$31\frac{3}{8}''$ (41)	$29\frac{5}{8}''$ (40)	$33\frac{1}{8}''$ (47)	$38\frac{1}{4}''$ (44)	$44''$ (45)	$57\frac{5}{8}''$ (45)
Musical Instruments......	$6\frac{3}{8}''$ (3)	$6\frac{1}{2}''$ (4)	$5\frac{1}{2}''$ (2)	$3\frac{7}{8}''$ (2)	$7\frac{1}{2}''$ (3)	$7\frac{7}{8}''$ (4)	$3\frac{1}{8}''$ (2)	$8\frac{3}{8}''$ (5)	$7\frac{3}{4}''$ (4)	$7''$ (4)	$3\frac{1}{2}''$ (3)	$8''$ (6)
Real Estate...	$14\frac{1}{4}''$ (16)	$15\frac{3}{4}''$ (22)	$43\frac{1}{8}''$ (58)	$46\frac{1}{2}''$ (61)	$36\frac{3}{8}''$ (41)	$25\frac{3}{4}''$ (28)	$20\frac{3}{8}''$ (20)	$11\frac{3}{4}''$ (18)	$19\frac{1}{8}''$ (22)	$14\frac{1}{4}''$ (18)	$9\frac{3}{8}''$ (14)	$10\frac{3}{8}''$ (14)
Transportation	$65\frac{5}{8}''$ (21)	$66\frac{5}{8}''$ (22)	$69''$ (24)	$74\frac{7}{8}''$ (25)	$19\frac{3}{4}''$ (6)	$8''$ (3)	$19\frac{7}{8}''$ (11)	$49\frac{7}{8}''$ (18)	$56\frac{1}{2}''$ (22)	$55\frac{3}{4}''$ (25)	$45\frac{3}{8}''$ (18)	$40\frac{1}{4}''$ (17)
Amusements..	$13\frac{5}{8}''$ (9)	$6\frac{1}{2}''$ (2)	$5''$ (3)	$11\frac{1}{4}''$ (5)	$4\frac{1}{4}''$ (2)	$4\frac{3}{4}''$ (3)	$8\frac{3}{4}''$ (4)	$15\frac{5}{8}''$ (4)	$8''$ (4)	$8\frac{1}{8}''$ (3)	$11\frac{1}{4}''$ (8)	$14\frac{7}{8}''$ (6)
Total Want Ads	$18\frac{1}{4}''$ (30)	$7\frac{5}{8}''$ (15)	$6''$ (13)	$4\frac{3}{4}''$ (10)	$2\frac{1}{4}''$ (4)	$6''$ (10)	$4''$ (8)	$4\frac{1}{2}''$ (8)	$4\frac{1}{2}''$ (9)	$5''$ (9)	$3\frac{1}{2}''$ (6)	$2\frac{7}{8}''$ (5)

	Chicago Tribune, 1869											
	Jan. 29, 1869	Feb. 27, 1869	Mar. 31, 1869	Apr. 30, 1869	May 31, 1869	June 30, 1869	July 31, 1869	Aug. 31, 1869	Sept. 30, 1869	Oct. 30, 1869	Nov. 30, 1869	Dec. 31, 1869
Books........	19¼″ (2)	9¾″ (2)	1¾″ (1)	9⅞″ (3)	10½″ (3)	5½″ (2)	0″ (0)	0″ (0)	6¼″ (2)	23⅛″ (5)	3¾″ (1)	4⅜″ (2)
Drugs........	59⅝″ (4)	60⅜″ (4)	4⅞″ (5)	37″ (7)	7⅛″ (4)	36″ (5)	32″ (6)	1¾″ (2)	⅝″ (1)	2¼″ (1)	2⅞″ (2)	1″ (1)
Dry Goods....	18½″ (4)	18¼″ (9)	40⅜″ (18)	13″ (9)	4¼″ (3)	14⅜″ (7)	25½″ (8)	26⅛″ (9)	12⅞″ (8)	30⅞″ (13)	13½″ (7)	5⅜″ (4)
Groceries.....	7″ (4)	11⅜″ (7)	7⅞″ (6)	6½″ (3)	3⅞″ (3)	14¾″ (6)	5⅜″ (3)	6⅜″ (3)	1⅛″ (1)	1¼″ (2)	6″ (4)	6″ (5)
Musical Instruments......	1¼″ (2)	1⅝″ (4)	1⅛″ (1)	3⅜″ (5)	1″ (3)	0″ (0)	1¾″ (4)	0″ (0)	⅜″ (1)	0″ (0)	14¾″ (4)	1¼″ (1)
Real Estate...	44⅜″ (87)	72¼″ (19)	84½″ (148)	101″ (197)	52½″ (70)	54⅛″ (95)	37¼″ (74)	34⅜″ (74)	57⅞″ (121)	43¾″ (94)	24⅜″ (58)	22⅛″ (50)
Transportation	13″ (11)	14⅛″ (11)	17″ (13)	9½″ (5)	21¾″ (16)	14⅞″ (14)	16⅝″ (16)	22″ (17)	14¾″ (14)	21¾″ (16)	14⅞″ (13)	9½″ (7)
Amusements..	19⅜″ (12)	17″ (12)	8¾″ (5)	16⅝″ (8)	14½″ (6)	15¾″ (6)	15⅞″ (8)	6¾″ (5)	7″ (5)	24½″ (13)	14¼″ (8)	18⅜″ (11)
Total Want Ads	113¾″ (350)	130½″ (265)	158″ (357)	168″ (413)	86″ (188)	124½″ (283)	100½″ (243)	110″ (267)	145″ (369)	116″ (277)	84″ (210)	69¼″ (195)

Figures not in parentheses indicate number of column inches of advertisements.
Figures in parentheses indicate number of advertisements.

public, especially intended to promulgate throughout the country the principle of Fenianism. In addition, however, some columns were devoted to political and other questions of the day, and poetry and fiction were included to please the less serious-minded. The Swedish *Hemlandet,* the Norwegian *Frihedsbanneret,* the Norwegian-Danish *Skandinaven,* besides papers published by the French, Italians, Dutch, and Bohemians, provided foreign residents of Chicago news of their native and adopted countries.[74] At the same time there appeared a host of special pleaders generally lasting only during a political campaign, as the *Rail Splitter* to support Lincoln, or during the height of emotional surges such as were found in the Know-Nothing movement or the temperance crusade.

Trade journals, like the *Commercial Advertiser,* under the editorship of Alfred Dutch, the *Chicago Commercial Index, Wells' Commercial Express,* and the *Western Produce Reporter* were but a few of the sheets designed to aid business. Particular trades, industries, and occupations had their organs, while the *Prairie Farmer* and the *Western Farmer* ranked high in popularity even among those not engaged in agriculture. The most important labor paper was the *Workingman's Advocate,* established in 1864 and having a circulation far beyond the confines of Chicago. As the exponent of radical labor it lashed into fury by its venomous attacks on capital all readers inclined to accept its interpretation of the relationship between employer and employee. By the late 'sixties even the outlying regions had their special chronicles, and the Sunday edition received a heartier welcome than it had a decade before.[75]

As Chicago read, so read most of the countryside. Into the hinter-

---

[74] Townsend, *The Germans of Chicago,* pp. 216–19; Emil Dietzsch, *Chicago's Deutsche Männer* . . . (Chicago, 1885), pp. 18–20, 28. The first editor of the *Illinois Staats-Zeitung* was Robert Hoeffgen. In 1851, George Schneider became editor. In 1862, Lorenz Brentano bought Schneider's interest. Anton C. Hesing became sole owner in 1867, with Hermann Raster as editor. The *Irish Republic* was published by the Republic News Company, incorporated February 21, 1867, with incorporators from various cities of the country. (*Private Laws, 1867,* II, 501; *The Irish Republic,* May 4, 1867.) Among foreign language newspapers was the semiweekly, *Le Journal de l'Illinois,* which was moved to Chicago from Kankakee, September, 1857, to serve the French. The weekly *L'Unione Italiano,* begun August 6, 1867, was succeeded November 21, 1868, by *Il Messaggiere Italiano dell' Ouest.* Two Bohemian weekly papers, *Narodní Noviny* and the *Nová Doba,* were begun in 1868.

[75] The *West Chicago Banner,* the *Union Stock Yards Daily Sun,* and the *Hyde Park Daily Sun* are typical of the papers of the outlying regions. The first exclusively Sunday paper was the *Sunday Vacuna,* which appeared in 1856. (Scott, *op. cit.,* p. 70.) The war broke down much of the opposition to a paper issued on the Sabbath.

land went small editions of Chicago papers parading under a caption chosen by the local prairie editor. The effect of this wide distribution of news was readily recognized by astute editors, who saw not only financial gain but the promotion of their articles of faith by this means, as well as by an increased subscription list of their own papers. Chicago journals and those in the outlying regions dependent upon Chicago benefited by the organization of the Western Associated Press in 1865, which effected co-operation among members in getting the latest dispatches. In 1861, John R. Walsh opened a news depot which became the seed of what was called after 1866 the Western News Company, a branch of the American News Company, New York, distributor of periodicals, books, and newspapers. Soon the business built up by Walsh was second only to that done by the New York office, and it had become a chief factor in " the commerce of literature," distributing, for example, much of the total issue of the *Tribune* and the *Times*.[76]

While the written page was fashioning the public mind and in turn reflecting it, the theater in a different way at times served the same ends. Although still frowned upon by most churches, it was becoming increasingly popular, attracting many of the best citizens despite its alleged alliance with Satan.[77] As urban development took place, the small, badly lighted, and simple structures of mid-century, where crude theatricals were seen, gradually gave way to almost palatial buildings. The season became almost a twelve-month period after the coming of the railroads, while the rise in the price of tickets served to emphasize the fact that production had become a profitable business.

Indeed, as in other lines of endeavor, it seemed a far cry from the days of the small theater under the direction of John B. Rice in the late 'forties and early 'fifties to McVicker's in 1857, Crosby's Opera House of the 'sixties, the Globe Theater of 1870, and Hooley's Opera

[76] See, for example, C. H. Ray to Lyman Trumbull, February 25, 1861, J. Medill to Trumbull, March 4, 1861, *Trumbull Papers*, XXXVI, XXXVII; *Chicago Tribune*, April 13, December 12, 14, 1866; Scott, *op. cit.*, pp. xc, xci; *Chicago Republican*, April 26, 1866; *Chicago Evening Journal*, April 21, 28, 1866.

[77] *Chicago Tribune*, November 23, 1868; James H. McVicker, *The Theatre: Its Early Days in Chicago*, pp. 64–69 (Ms. Chicago Historical Society). " Should a christian, a child of God, be seen standing to gaze at a puppet show, or mingle with the clamoring, shouting, swearing, drinking, crowd that frequent races, fairs, and other worldly amusements? If the amusement itself were not sinful, to associate with such men is to disgrace the sacred profession of religion." *Watchman of the Prairies*, September 9, 1851.

House in 1871. The brick theater which Rice had built in 1851 at a cost of $11,000 symbolized the development of play production of the day, just as the $85,000 structure known as McVicker's betokened the changes which had occurred within less than ten years under the effective leadership of Rice. In April, 1865, Crosby's Opera House opened its doors to an admiring throng that marveled at the wonders wrought by the expenditure of $600,000.[78]

Under the management of Rice and McVicker, Chicagoans saw Edwin Forrest, the three Booths, the veteran James E. Murdoch, James W. Wallack, Jr., besides English tragedians including Henry Loraine and Barry Sullivan, and the Irish actors, Mr. and Mrs. Charles Kean. Comedy was brought to Chicago by James H. Hackett, Joseph Jefferson, Edward A. Sothern, Mr. and Mrs. John Drew, and John Brougham, and the city enthusiastically welcomed Julia Dean, Charlotte Cushman, Eliza Logan, Laura Keene, Mrs. Scott Siddons, and Maggie Mitchell. In addition to Shakespearean productions including " Richard III," " Othello," " Hamlet," " Romeo and Juliet," Chicagoans were privileged to see " She Stoops to Conquer," " Rip Van Winkle," " The Lady of Lyons," and indeed most of the mid-century popular plays.

Histrionics of local appeal, including " The Chicago Fireman " and " 180 Monroe Street," pleased the fancies of those who preferred " home-talent." In 1859, " Speculation," written by a local member of the press, delighted audiences at McVicker's, describing, as it did, a lot in Mud Lake in whose sale Calderon Cornerlotte, a successful speculator, carried on business in the mode of the day. " Our Eastern Cousin in Chicago " proved equally popular in its representation of the eastern Jonathan Bosting and his scrapes while seeing the sights of Chicago.[79]

---

[78] McVicker, op. cit., pp. 62, 69–73; James Napier Wilt, The History of the Two Rice Theatres in Chicago from 1847 to 1857 (unpublished Ph.D. Thesis, The University of Chicago, 1923), p. 6; Andreas, History of Chicago, II, 601–12; Chicago Daily Democrat, November 6, 1857; Chicago Tribune, March 20, 1864, January 3, 1871; Lois Mildred Bergstrom, The History of McVicker's Theatre, 1857–1861 (unpublished M.A. Thesis, The University of Chicago, 1930), p. 16; Tanner, Halpin and Co., D. B. Cooke & Co.'s Directory, 1858, p. 496. The Globe, the only theater not destroyed by the fire in 1871, was built in 1870.

[79] Chicago Daily Democrat, December 4, 1852, September 3, 1858, September 1, 3, 23, 28, 1859. For " Our Eastern Cousin in Chicago," McVicker's scenic artist, John W. Whytal, painted a new scene of a well-known view in Chicago. Another success was " The Three Fast Men " which included local scenes from the " Illinois Central Depot, looking from the lake; Views of Wells and Madison streets, looking south [to] the Tam O'Shanter; . . . the

Besides enjoying local jibes, the theater-devotee found pleasure in plays heightening his animus to the South. These included " Uncle Tom's Cabin," which he saw first in 1852; " Bleeding Kansas Gaining Friends," and " The Octoroon," which, according to the *Democrat,* vividly illustrated " the iniquity of slavery." [80] Throughout the war, plays became the vehicle to get funds for charitable and patriotic enterprises, in accordance with the honored practice of benefit performances long known to the American of that day. The theater valiantly did its part to keep patriotic fervor at high pitch through plays like " The Southern Refugee or False and True," which depicted a rebel prison in which a prisoner's sleep was " troubled with rats and other small deer." The " Seven Sisters " had long runs, attracting no less a personage than Major General Logan, whose name in the play drew hearty applause from his patriotic admirers. Dancers, too, gained favor, and Julia Turnbull, Lola Montez, and Mlle. Augusta stood high in popular demand.[81]

Although an increasing number of stars visited the city, Chicago theaters operated to a considerable extent through stock companies in which ability for a skillful doubling of parts was an actor's chief asset. To the regular players, stars were added whenever possible. The *Democrat* proudly announced in 1856 that Rice had arranged to furnish sixteen stars in six months. By 1863, matinee performances claimed attendance from parents with young children and the everpresent countryfolk who were in town for only a few hours.[82]

That the theater was reaching its majority during these years was shown not only by the lengthening of the season and the appearance of more stars, but by the addition of special assistants to the manager, such as scene director, scenic artist, and orchestra leader, and by the introduction in 1857 of an amusement column in the press. In 1857, a Chicago Dramatic Club, formed to give amateur dramatic entertainment, ambitiously undertook Shakespeare's " Othello," and

Tremont House; view near 'Young America'" [Isaac Cook's saloon]. (*Ibid.,* November 29, 30, 1858.) There also appeared at the Variety Theatre " The Three Fast Women of Chicago." *Chicago Tribune,* November 7–9, 1866.

[80] *Chicago Daily Democrat,* December 13, 17, 18, 20, 25, 1852, March 10, 11, 1858, November 2, 1860.

[81] *Chicago Tribune,* July 27, August 12, 21, December 7, 9, 1863, August 1, 1864.

[82] *Chicago Daily Democrat,* March 29, 1856; McVicker, *op. cit.,* p. 70; *Chicago Tribune,* August 21, 1863, May 7, 1864; *Chicago* [Tri-Weekly] *Tribune,* September 9, 18, 1863, February 15, 1865. By 1865 matinee performances were given on Wednesday as well as Saturday.

made its first appearance at the German Theatre, for some time the amusement hall of German residents in Chicago. During the 'sixties Irish theatricals took place in Arlington Hall where the "Robber Chief of Galloway" and "The Irish Emigrant" were among the most popular amateur performances.[83]

Opera, too, had its devotees. Even among those who held plays the breeding place of sin there was usually an enthusiastic reception of this form of art. Educated for a decade or more by touring artists who sang excerpts from opera, Chicagoans by 1858–59 were ready for their first season, which began in September when English opera opened with a performance of "La Somnambula," featuring Rosalie Durand, Georgia Hodson, and Frederick Lyster. This brave start was followed that winter and the next summer by other companies, including Maurice Strakosch's Italian Company, the English Cooper's Opera Company, the Parodi Italian Opera Troupe, and the Lucy Escott English Opera Company.[84]

In the score of years which followed 1850, despite hardships attending community growth and the palsying effect of a war, this new city was privileged to hear 433 operatic presentations in thirty-six opera engagements or seasons, although "a season" was, on the average, little over two weeks in length. "Martha" was given twenty-eight times; "Il Trovatore," twenty-seven; "Faust," twenty-one; "The Bohemian Girl," nineteen; and "Norma," seventeen. In addition others, including "Don Giovanni" and "Lucia di Lammermoor," were heard by audiences said to be enthusiastic, even if the musical appreciation of the day, in the real sense, was not the highest. With prices ranging at least twice as high as for theatricals, the opera apparently was attended by those of considerable means. As time passed, opera-going became the thing to do, some of the best families regularly having boxes. By 1863, the *Tribune* proudly prophesied that interest in opera seemed so great that it was probable that Chicago would thereafter have a regular season each year.[85]

[83] *Chicago Tribune*, August 10, 1862, May 18, 1864; *Chicago Daily Democrat*, April 19, 1856, July 2, 4, 16, 1857. See for German dramatics and amusements Dietzsch, *op. cit.*, pp. 38–43; *Chicago Daily Democrat*, August 15, 1859; *Illinois Staats-Zeitung*, July 30, 1861. For Irish amateur performances see *The Irish Republic*, August 31, 1867.

[84] *Chicago Daily Press and Tribune*, September 25, 28, 1858, January 11, March 10, July 13, December 2, 1859.

[85] In 1859, for example, at the opera private boxes sold for ten dollars, at the theater for four or five dollars. The gallery seats at the opera cost about fifty cents and at the theater were

Amateur performances of the German masters by Germans resident in the city, who were members of the Germania Männerchor or the Concordia Männerchor, swelled the number of opportunities of those who wished to hear such music.[86] Indeed, by 1868 so conversant were Chicagoans said to have become with opera that the *Tribune* was impelled to remark that even New York was " slowly beginning to recognize that Chicago was ahead of that city in opera as in other respects." [87] At the same time, artists then renowned and others to become so at a later day enriched Chicago musical life by vocal concerts ranging from the ballad to the aria. Adelina Patti appeared in concert in 1853, Karl Formes in 1858, Carlotta Patti and Christina Nilsson in 1870.

To the oratorio and other forms of music, local groups and individuals made their contributions, sometimes co-operating with visiting artists as did the Chicago Oratorio Society in January, 1871, in presenting " The Messiah " and " The Creation." [88] With the coming of Hans Balatka in 1860 the musical life of Chicago took on new vigor. Under his tutelage the Chicago Musical Union and the Chicago Oratorio Society, in particular, offered alike to participants and listeners opportunities to know the best musical literature. So well organized had Chicago groups become by 1868 that the North American Sängerbund held a five-day Sängerfest in June with representatives from both Europe and America in attendance,[89] and in 1869 ninety-five members of the Mendelssohn Society, under the direction of J. A. Butterfield, journeyed to Boston to participate in the National Peace Jubilee. With this chorus went representatives of Chicago newspapers, who sent back to the city glowing accounts of the celebration of the coming of peace to North and South.[90]

---

generally fifteen, and dress circle and parquet seats at the former cost one dollar, at the latter twenty-five cents. *Chicago Daily Democrat,* February 27, September 1, 1859; *Chicago Tribune,* July 6, 1863, January 12, 30, 1870.

[86] *Ibid.,* February 7, 8, May 9, 1870. In 1870, the opera " Stradella " was presented by the Germania Männerchor with one hundred voices and a sixty-piece orchestra.

[87] *Ibid.,* May 13, 1868.

[88] Christina Nilsson and her troupe co-operated in this case. General admission to these performances at Farwell Hall was two dollars, reserved seats costing from three to four dollars. *Ibid.,* January 9, 1871.

[89] *Ibid.,* June 1, 17–23, 1868. A chorus of twelve hundred and a seventy-piece orchestra performed at the Sängerfest.

[90] There were 10,404 voices in the chorus. Representatives of the press of Chicago included A. S. Parsons, *Chicago Republican;* James B. Runnion, the *Chicago Times;* L. P,

Although the visits of famous instrumentalists were less frequent than those of vocal virtuosi, appearances by Ole Bull, Louis M. Gottschalk, and Carl Wolfsohn evoked the plaudits of the musically interested. Popular fancies were gratified by the Swiss Bell Ringers, by concerts given by drummer boys, and by the Druids or Ox Horn Players who produced upon seventy ox horns "the strangest, wild, but pleasing melody ever presented to the public." [91]

Added to these were the concerts presented by local artists and local orchestras. The first of the latter to attain any eminence was organized in 1850 by Julius Dyhrenfurth, who was followed as director by Carl Bergmann and William H. Currie.[92] Other orchestras succeeded one upon the other as adverse conditions wrote finis to different attempts at organization. In 1860, Hans Balatka became the director of a new Chicago Philharmonic Society, whose monthly concerts continued in spite of the Civil War, although lack of popular interest seems to have caused dissolution within a short time after. Then came the Orchestral Union, which under Balatka's leadership planned concerts devoted to the compositions of Mendelssohn, Beethoven, Haydn, and other masters.[93] During the 'sixties, also, Chicagoans were privileged to hear Theodore Thomas, although on the whole opportunities to attend orchestra concerts of the best classical works were infrequent.[94]

While the more pretentious type of music was offered to the fastidious and well-to-do, strolling street musicians and the hurdy-gurdy

---

Dodge, *Chicago Western Railway Gazette;* George P. Upton, *Chicago Tribune;* P. B. Randolph, *Chicago Religio-Philosophical Journal;* P. B. Morgan, *American Churchman.* P. S. Gilmore, *History of the National Peace Jubilee and Great Musical Festival . . .* (Boston, 1871), pp. 15, 156, 345–46, 668–74, 728; *Chicago Tribune,* June 16–22, 1869; *The Chicago Times,* June 16–18, 1869; *Chicago Republican,* June 16–20, 1869.

[91] *Chicago Daily Democrat,* September 4, 5, 1851.

[92] Dyhrenfurth's orchestra usually furnished accompaniments for the Chicago Philharmonic Society, organized as a choral society in 1853. *The Daily Democratic Press,* March 27, May 3, June 1, September 12, November 23, 1854, February 25, March 17, 1856; Act of February 11, 1853, *Private Laws, 1853,* p. 340.

[93] By its fourth season the Philharmonic boasted of forty pieces, five first violins, five second violins, three violas, three 'cellos, three double basses, two flutes, two clarinets, four oboes, four horns, two trumpets, trombone, tuba, and tympani. *Chicago Tribune,* November 14, 1863, November 2, 1866, November 20, 21, 1868, January 30, 1870; *Chicago Daily Democrat,* October 11, 25, 1860; Halpin, *Halpin & Bailey's Directory, 1862–63,* Appendix, p. xxvii.

[94] George Putnam Upton, *Theodore Thomas* (2 v. Chicago, 1905), I, 35–36. In November, 1869, and again in 1871 he gave a series of concerts. *Chicago Tribune,* November 25, 1869, March 9, April 23, 1871.

INTERIOR VIEW OF CROSBY'S OPERA HOUSE

during the lottery drawing, January 21, 1867. The large drum contained the numbered tickets; the smaller drum held names of the various prizes.

GREAT CHICAGO SKATING RINK

Northeast corner of Jackson and Wabash, 1866.

man in colorful array paraded the thoroughfares of the city. Free public concerts in Dearborn Park, Lincoln Park, or from the steps of the Court House were provided by the Great Western Band, at one time subsidized by the Common Council, while numerous bands dispensed a wide selection of offerings.[95]

Painting lagged considerably behind the advance made in music, for, in the words of an unhappy contemporary, art and mammon were incompatible.[96] There was, of course, some individual enjoyment. In the homes of the wealthy, fresco-painting adorned the ceilings of reception rooms, and upon the walls could be found paintings allegedly by Titian, Corbould, Kensett, and by less-known artists such as Fiske Reed and Charles King, who had studied under Benjamin West.[97] The art gallery opened in 1868 by U. H. Crosby contained works chiefly of American artists, although some European pieces could be found. But the gallery received too little support, as did other ill-starred ventures of Crosby, and was later leased by the Academy of Design. The plaintive comment of the *Tribune* as to the spirit generally prevalent seems justified in this as in other cases, for much of the infrequent interest manifested seemed a " pseudo-enthusiasm." [98]

Still, Chicago, like other cities, had its art unions, which distributed to subscribing members pictures and engravings, and held exhibitions of the works of American and local artists — works gathered at times from the homes and shops of the city for the pleasure and cultural uplift of the less well-to-do. Art patrons such as William B. Ogden, William Blair, Walter L. Newberry, J. Young Scammon, Joseph T. Ryerson, and Ezra B. McCagg placed their possessions before interested Chicagoans, also, at benefit fairs and similar public gatherings, adding to opportunities provided by organizations and enterprising

---

[95] *The Daily Democratic Press*, November 4, 1854, July 31, 1855, August 19, September 16, 1856; *Chicago Daily Democrat*, July 3, 1860; *Chicago Tribune*, October 24, 1868.

[96] *Ibid.*, April 29, 1867.

[97] The home of William Bross is described in Rev. N. Hall, *From Liverpool to St. Louis*, p. 150. See also *The Press and Tribune*, September 17, 1860. James Robb, president of the Chicago, Alton and St. Louis Railroad, owned Corbould's " Mary at the Feet of the Savior." He also owned a Rubens. (*Chicago Tribune*, January 9, 1861.) " The Martyrdom of St. Lawrence," reported to be an original Titian, was owned by Col. James D. Graham. (*The Press and Tribune*, May 16, 1859.) Kensett's " View on the Hudson " was owned by Isaac N. Arnold. *Chicago Tribune*, January 9, 1861, January 26, 1866.

[98] *Ibid.*, November 7, 1865, April 29, 1867; Andreas, *History of Chicago*, II, 558; Colbert, *op. cit.*, p. 111.

individuals who brought in from other cities the masterpieces of Titian, Raphael, Correggio, Guido, Da Vinci, Rembrandt, as well as copies of the works of French and other European artists of a later day, including Chailly, Vernet, Jostelle, Giraud, and Meadows.[99] Local artists sometimes exhibited the portraits they had made in oil, their colored crayon drawings, or their oil and water colors of the vast western plains or of the rugged hills and valleys of the East. But such exhibitions seemed to be chiefly for those of wealth, whose social position dictated attendance even if they did not view the pictures intelligently.[100] They, too, were the ones who gave commissions for portraits to struggling artists, sometimes paying several hundred dollars that they might see themselves always in grand attire rather than as often reflected in the French plate mirrors in gilt frames which hung on the walls of their parlors.[101]

Most Chicagoans were satisfied with lithographs, steel engravings, enlarged photographs, and daguerreotypes, India ink pictures, and photographs, plain or colored on porcelain, costing a small fraction of what the plutocracy of the town expended.[102] By the mid-'fifties the stereoscope, a "new attraction," amazed its users,[103] and by the

[99] Among the exhibitions were those of the Chicago Art Union, the Western Art Union, the Cosmopolitan Art Association in the 'fifties and the Academy of Design in the later 'sixties. *Chicago Daily Democrat*, November 16, December 14, 1850, February 10, 1851; *Chicago Tribune*, December 12, 1860, August 15, 16, October 6, 1866, March 7, 1868; *The Press and Tribune*, May 14, 1859; Colbert, *op. cit.*, pp. 110–11. See also Chicago Exhibition of the Fine Arts, *Catalogue of the First Exhibition of Statuary, Paintings, &c., Opened May 9th . . . 1859* (Chicago, 1859).

[100] Among the local artists was George P. A. Healy, portrait painter, who was commissioned by the government to paint the portraits of national celebrities including Harrison and Tyler. (*Chicago Tribune*, January 7, 1862.) Among other local artists were E. St. Alary, pastel painter (*The Daily Democratic Press*, October 4, 1855); V. R. Sloan, landscape painter (*Chicago Tribune*, December 4, 1864); and James Forbes, a native of Scotland, portrait painter (*The Press and Tribune*, October 3, 1859). Among Chicago women portrait painters was Mrs. S. H. St. John. *Chicago Tribune*, August 9, 1868, February 11, 1870.

[101] E. L. Jillett paid Healy $500 for a full-size painting of his wife and $150 for a bust portrait of himself. E. L. Jillett, Bill for Painting Picture, March, 1864 (*Ms.* Chicago Historical Society); *The Daily Democratic Press*, October 25, 1854.

[102] Prices are given, for example, in *Chicago Daily Democrat*, August 24, 1849, September 19, 1860; *The Daily Democratic Press*, February 12, 1855; *Chicago Tribune*, February 6, 26, 1863, January 26, 1866.

[103] *The Daily Democratic Press*, July 27, 1855. The stereoscope was first shown in Chicago at the " art gallery " of Alexander Hesler, who had introduced one at the Mechanics' Institute Fair in 1854. Robert Taft, *Photography and the American Scene* (New York, 1938), pp. 173–77.

early 'sixties the photographic album had so struck the popular fancy that without it one was a " nobody." [104]

That entertainment rather than a love of art for art's sake in general prompted whatever interest was manifested is nowhere better illustrated than by the exhibitions of the much-advertised panoramas. " Hutchin's Grand Classical Panorama of the Sea and Shores of the Mediterranean," pronounced by the press as " the most magnificent painting " ever brought to America, could be viewed for twenty-five cents, and J. Insco Williams's " Panorama of the Bible " and Charles McEvoy's " The Hibernicon " were others among the variety of canvases unrolled for the enjoyment of Chicagoans at nominal admission charges. [105]

Sculpture was as little appreciated as painting, for here, too, the Chicagoan openly confessed his preference for a corner lot when its price was about the same as that of " an art gem." [106] Despite his willingness to leave " the products of the pencil and the chisel for the gilded future," he felt pride in the achievements of the sculptor, Leonard W. Volk, who made Chicago his home after his studies in Italy were finished. Volk's busts of Douglas, Lincoln, and other great Americans, and his statue of " the Little Giant," made at the request of ex-Governor Matteson of Springfield, were especially admired and commended. Volk's popularity among his fellow citizens is shown by the action of the board of trustees of the Firemen's Benevolent Association in accepting his plan for a fireman's monument in 1863. [107] His handiwork and that of others which met with general favor had, of course, the external trappings of civil dress or military uniform and conformed to the standards prescribed for modesty in a day when " The Greek Slave " met the disfavor of many. Indeed, even much of the alabaster statuary which graced the ornamentally carved parlor tables in the better homes of Chicago was the design of some fountain,

---

[104] Chicago Tribune, December 22, 1861; J. R. Jones to E. B. Washburne, February 26, 1862, Washburne Papers, XXII. Tintypes became popular in the 'sixties.

[105] Chicago Daily Democrat, October 3, 1850; Chicago Tribune, December 5, 1861; The Workingman's Advocate, October 9, 1869.

[106] Chicago Daily Democratic Press, August 20, 1857.

[107] Ibid.; Chicago Daily Press and Tribune, July 2, 1858; Leonard W. Volk to S. H. Kerfoot, November 7, 1892 (Ms. Chicago Historical Society); Leonard W. Volk to S. A. Douglas, April 14, 1858, Douglas Papers; Colbert, op. cit., p. 111; Beveridge, Lincoln, IV, 253-54; Chicago Tribune, July 7, 1863.

vase, or bowl. " The Fairy's Whisper " by John Rogers, portraying a little child resting on a bank of flowers as a fairy whispered in her ear, could occasion no improper thoughts.[108] Its popularity was assured.

The quest for the good life was rewarded increasingly as peacetime activities supplanted the rigors and grimness of war, and as men were able to rid themselves of the growing pains of a new urban society. The achievements of Chicago in cultural uplift during these years had an enduring value. In a sense, they were the apprenticeship to a wider and better learning, to more sophistication, and to deeper appreciation of the arts and the sciences. This appreciation was developed not only by contacts with the best in literature and the arts imported from American and world centers, but by less pretentious attempts made by Chicago writers and artists. The advance of the common schools and the spread of adult educational agencies gave promise of a better-educated citizenry; and they offered an assurance of the eventual assimilation of the foreign born into the American social body. Literary journals and newspapers, though their lives were sometimes brief, also left their impress upon the culture of this crude and busy metropolis.

[108] *Chicago Daily Democrat,* November 20, 1850; *Chicago Tribune,* December 25, 1860, March 7, 1868.

CHAPTER XI

THE WAYS OF AN URBAN WORLD

As THE AGE of machinery unfolded material triumphs and the city became the agent of dissemination, living lost its simplicity. Like other American cities Chicago eagerly seized opportunities for physical expansion and heedlessly abandoned the ruralism of its earliest years. More and more it was to provide avenues for cultural advance; there were to be more leisure and greater comfort for those who need not toil endlessly to gain the necessities of life. And along with benefits, injuries and wrongs multiplied and mirrored the changing scene in which they were placed.

In no aspect of life was the transit reflected more distressingly or more realistically than in the increased numbers of those accused of wrongdoing. Charges of disorderly conduct and intemperance proved frequent reasons for incarceration in the watchhouse, while seemingly less heinous offenses, such as fast or reckless driving, driving at night without lights, and bathing publicly within the city limits, appeared with striking regularity in statements issued by the police. Thievery ranged from horse stealing and purloining hen roosts to robbery of the mails, the express, and the banks; pickpockets plied their trade with daring and success; counterfeiters deceived the unwary; and organized gangs created terror on all sides. Calls upon private agencies, particularly Pinkerton's, became more frequent, and the formation of secret citizen organizations to practice pistol shooting was openly carried on.[1] Barrel murders and other crimes of vio-

1 *Chicago Tribune*, January 27, 1870; Rowan, *The Pinkertons*. For an advertisement offering extensions of special police service see *Chicago Tribune*, May 5, 1867.

lence won for Chicago the unenviable reputation as ranking city in crime, where criminals received protection, where bondsmen readily furnished bail when needed, and where detection was made difficult by aid given by "mock auction" houses and "pink dealers." [2]

By 1849, according to the report of a Chicago newspaper, more gambling establishments were flourishing in Chicago than in Philadelphia and more in proportion to population than in New York. Faro banks, keno tables, billiard rooms and ball alleys, and poker and brag houses could be found by the interested, particularly on Wells, Randolph, and Lake streets, while on North and South Water streets were " groggeries and stews " where both sexes under the influence of liquor could play prick the loop, thimblerig, and wheel of fortune.[3] Private clubs under the descriptive names of "Cork Screw" and "Late and Early," where chips substituted for money in faro and keno, enticed "hundreds of fashionably attired young men," just as others lured the youth of the country, sailors, cattle drovers, grain speculators, and an annually increasing number passing through the city.[4]

By mid-'fifties, $30,000 a year was reported paid by Chicago patrons for the use of billiard and gaming tables alone.[5] In Mayor Wentworth's administrations attempts to break up the more notorious resorts which were giving Chicago an unsavory reputation met with partial success. But in 1858 the press warned that gambling was more prevalent than ever and had spread to hotels and eating-houses where rooms were changed frequently to avert suspicion. Raids upon private establishments sometimes revealed trap floors, secret passages,

[2] The newspapers are filled with items concerning crime. See, for example, Weekly Chicago Democrat, February 5, 1853, April 8, 1854, January 6, May 12, July 7, 1855, June 21, 1856, August 21, September 11, 1858; Daily Democrat, February 3, 1849; Chicago Daily Press and Tribune, December 20, 1858, January 12, March 17, 18, August 6, 7, 1859, April 26, May 23, 1860; Chicago Tribune, February 8, March 27, October 9, 1865, August 16, 1866, February 22, 1867, January 24, 25, 1870; Oquawka Spectator, October 30, 1853; The Bankers' Magazine, XIX (December, 1864), 494–95.

[3] About one hundred gambling establishments were said to be on North and South Water streets. (Gem of the Prairie, January 27, 1849.) Wells Street was reported to have many resorts of vice. (The Chicago Times, February 25, 1866.) The First Ward (which lay south of the Chicago River and north of Monroe Street), The Workingman's Advocate, February 19, 1870, describes as " the acknowledged rendez-vous of the garroters, thieves, sandbaggers, and vagabonds." See Junius Henri Browne, The Great Metropolis, A Mirror of New York (Hartford, 1869) for conditions in that city.

[4] Gem of the Prairie, February 17, 1849; Weekly Chicago Democrat, January 13, 1855; Chicago Daily Democrat, March 26, 1860.

[5] Weekly Chicago Democrat, January 13, 1855.

double doors, and rooms richly carpeted with fine rugs and hung with French mirrors, where white-coated bartenders dispensed wines, whiskey, and cigars throughout the night.[6]

Lotteries, in which tickets were sold for five or more dollars, offering such prizes as a fast-sailing schooner, a farm of two hundred acres, a piano, paintings, and sculpture, apparently evoked little condemnation as games of chance. Indeed, so enthralled with the lure of risk did Chicagoans become, particularly in the mid-'sixties, that the stakes offered by a North American Prize Concert, an International Musical and Gift Concert Association, and the Union National Gift Concert enticed many to purchase tickets for one dollar. Crosby's Opera House in 1867 was rescued from financial embarrassment through an Opera House Association which sold 210,000 lottery tickets not only to Chicagoans but to people throughout the country.[7]

Alongside gambling establishments flourished houses of prostitution, saloons, and dram shops. Sometimes they were one and the same. By 1856, 110 houses of "ill-fame" were said to employ one thousand women besides having connections with forty houses of assignation. So flagrant and open were violations of city ordinances, and so common was the report that justices and constables pocketed the fines taken from prostitutes and their keepers[8] that in April, 1857, Mayor Wentworth placated an aroused public opinion by invading with a posse of thirty policemen and a deputy sheriff the vice area known as the "Sands," located on the north side of the Chicago River upon land which had been in litigation in the courts.[9]

Armed with huge steel hooks and chains, officers of the law, with the sanction of William B. Ogden who had recently purchased the interest of one of the litigants in the suit over the land, ordered the removal of household effects and then proceeded to demolish the rows of wretched wooden shanties. What hooks and chains had not torn down, fire destroyed later in the day. Thus the "Sands," the

---

[6] *Chicago Weekly Democrat*, June 6, July 4, 1857, February 6, December 18, 1858; *Chicago Daily Press and Tribune*, August 3, 1858. For the unsavory reputation of Chicago see *Delphi* [Indiana] *Dollar Journal*, March 29, 1855; [Washington] *Daily National Republican*, March 6, 1865.

[7] *Chicago Daily Democrat*, September 15, 1849, February 25, December 27, 1850; *Chicago Tribune*, August 1, 10, 1866, January 22, 27, 1867.

[8] *The Daily Democratic Press*, September 29, 1856; *Chicago Weekly Democrat*, November 7, 1857. See also *Chicago Tribune*, November 14, 1866, in which it was charged that raids occurred only when the treasury was empty and police did not receive their pay promptly.

[9] *Ibid.*, April 21, 1857; *Chicago Weekly Democrat*, January 30, 1858.

"Five Points" of Chicago, disappeared, but neither were criminals deterred nor did gambling houses and brothels disappear. Instead, scattered throughout the city, the former inmates of the "Sands" brought into hitherto law-abiding sections the fear and terror which only lawless elements create. Property values tended to fall, perhaps causing the public conscience to cry out more loudly than heretofore. With no abatement of "the social evil," the police commissioner by 1864 formulated regulations that tacitly recognized prostitution as a legal trade.[10]

Tacit recognition, however, did not stem the rising tide of protest from reformers and general public. Charges that the police levied blackmail upon "houses of ill-repute" and upon their patrons, and that these guardians of the law were given to accepting bribes and gifts weakened the faith of most citizens in the actual enforcement of city ordinances.[11] Such laxity, the *Tribune* protested, led to the invasion of Chicago by the prostitutes of other places less lenient in attitude. Upon the heads of the city officials this newspaper placed the blame for blasting the morality of young men and boys and for seducing "innocent girls." New police raids, which seemed periodically well-timed, again failed to blot out the much discussed social evil.[12] In the hope of discovering a solution of this apparently insoluble problem the Common Council, on September 26, 1870, passed resolutions which looked to methods of control of what could not be "suppressed" but might be "regulated."[13]

Seldom were attempts made to discover why girls entered houses

[10] The regulations set up were: the complaints of two respectable householders were necessary before a raid was legal; as far as possible all descents must be made in the daytime; no person was to be arrested as an inmate who was a casual visitor. *Chicago Tribune*, January 28, 1864. See also *ibid.*, June 4, 1870; *Chicago Weekly Democrat*, November 7, 1857; John J. Flinn, *History of the Chicago Police* . . . (Chicago, 1887), pp. 83–84.

[11] *The Chicago Times*, January 6, 7, 12, February 8, 1864. For example, Molly Grant, alias Nelly Davis, keeper of a brothel, at the investigation conducted in 1868, testified to irregularities of the police. She declared that she offered something "extra" over the fines paid. (*Chicago Tribune*, February 3, 1868.) "Madame [Eleanor] Herrick" subscribed twenty-five dollars for a horse and buggy for one sergeant. *Ibid.*, January 19, 1868. See also *ibid.*, January 27, February 5, 10, 17, 1868. See also pp. 311–12.

[12] *Chicago Tribune*, February 5, August 6, 7, 1864, March 7, 1866.

[13] The resolution was introduced by Alderman J. A. Montgomery of the Third Ward and called for a special committee of three to consider the best mode of regulation, one object being to avoid "the cruel and unjust distinction against the weaker sex which has been manifested in our police jurisprudence in the past." (*Ibid.*, September 27, 1870.) Three were appointed to the committee on September 26, 1870. (Chicago, *Council Proceedings, 1869–70*, p. 521.) Nothing seems to have come of this resolution.

of prostitution. Such explanations as were made seemed to come chiefly from the submerged themselves, who attacked a society which paid girls starvation wages and which prohibited women from working for the living which was given men. A social system, becoming more and more inured to inequalities, raised few criticisms, although the plain-spoken Lyman E. DeWolf placed the blame squarely upon what he described as " gold gambling and stock jobbing," in which the family was no longer desired by employers as a basis of social organization except for the employing class.[14] And the *Tribune,* with a gesture of fairness, urged the removal of the popular disfavor toward work for women and the opening of more employments at suitable rewards.[15]

The dram shop and the saloon also thrived. Much of their trade was carried on illicitly, many retailers failing to pay license fees required by law. As early as 1854 a temperance advocate charged that of the six hundred places in Chicago where liquor was dispensed only 160 were licensed, and that the liquor traffic at that time commanded a capital of $1,000,000.[16] Shortly thereafter the editor of the *Democrat* regretfully remarked that for every church there were seventeen drinking houses, with fifteen thousand worshippers of Bacchus to ten thousand church attendants.[17] In 1859 the city treasury was fattened by $44,548 in license fees, and ten years later $110,136 was realized from the same source.[18] To the saloons and dram shops flocked young and old, particularly on Saturday nights, for Saturday was pay day and the end of a week's work. Then the streets were filled with milling crowds, saloons were lined with customers, and the haunts of vice were wide open, offering girls, music, liquor, and dancing.[19]

In such conditions the moralists and the churchmen beheld their failure to rout the forces of sin. Driving home the dictum that " no drunkard shall inherit the Kingdom of God," advocates of reform

14 DeWolf, *The Social Evil,* p. 7.

15 *Chicago Tribune,* January 9, 1866. " One woman in every thirty-seven of our entire population is an adulteress," said the *Tribune.*

16 *The Daily Democratic Press,* January 21, 1854.

17 *Weekly Chicago Democrat,* January 26, 1856. These saloons presented a striking contrast to the orderly beer parlors and concert saloons of North Side Germans.

18 Chicago City Comptroller, *Annual Statement, 1859,* p. 3; *Chicago Tribune,* April 19, 1869. See p. 348.

19 *Chicago Tribune,* August 6, 1866.

laid upon " drink " the blame for the unrest of the day.[20] The first
" social glass " was to be shunned, and the housewife was warned not
to use brandy in her mince pie unless willing to revive an appetite
" for the poison " in someone bravely struggling to rid himself of it.
Indeed, so strong was the Baptists' aversion to everything connected
with the purchase or sale of intoxicating spirits that they refused communion to anyone concerned with selling liquor.[21]

Churches and temperance organizations came to be one and the
same, the blessing of the former leading to meetings of the latter in
church edifices.[22] The Chicago Juvenile Temperance Society in the
'fifties and the Bands of Hope a little later attempted to start the
young right. The Washington Temperance Society, the Good Templars with both white and colored lodges, the Total Abstinence
Benevolent Association, an outgrowth of the work of Father Mathew,
who first visited Chicago in 1850, and the Scottish Temperance Society, among others of like purpose, fought licensing the sale of ardent
spirits and urged state prohibition or the making of the sale of liquor
a crime.[23]

Failing to effect widespread reform by moral suasion, temperance
leaders turned to legal restrictions. Under the pressure of public

[20] Approval of temperance forces was given the Lake Street House, City Hotel, and the
United States Hotel which advertised in the 'fifties as temperance houses where " men of
principle " could find " comforts and company of the right kind," and to druggists who advertised brandies and wines " expressly for medical purposes " or for communion services
only. *Watchman of the Prairies*, January 2, 1849, January 8, 1850, April 22,
August 26, 1851; *Northwestern Christian Advocate*, February 16, 1853.

[21] *Watchman of the Prairies*, January 8, 1850; *Northwestern Christian Advocate*, March
23, 1853; Herbert Wiltsee, " The Temperance Movement [in Chicago] 1848–1871," Illinois
State Historical Society, *Papers in Illinois History and Transactions for the Year 1937*, pp.
82–92.

[22] For example, the Marine Temperance Society to reclaim mariners held meetings in
Bethel Mission. (*Watchman of the Prairies*, January 4, 1848.) Alonzo Hyde, a reformed
inebriate of New York, addressed a meeting at the Canal Street Methodist Church. (*Ibid.,*
June 20, 1848.) A nondenominational convention of " the friends of a prohibitory liquor law
in the State of Illinois " was held at the Clark Street Methodist Church on December 7, 8,
1853. See also *The Daily Democratic Press*, May 4, 29, June 1, 1855; *The Christian Times and
Illinois Baptist*, May 12, 1858.

[23] Halpin, *Halpin & Bailey's Directory, 1863–64*, Appendix, p. xxxv; *Weekly Chicago
Democrat*, September 26, 1848, May 24, 1851; *Chicago Daily Democrat*, October 15, 1850,
February 11, 20, 24, April 15, 1851, March 2, 1852, April 23, 1860; *Chicago Tribune*, March
20, 1862, March 13, August 10, 1866. The Total Abstinence Benevolent Association was
chartered in 1867. (Illinois, *Senate Journal, 1867*, p. 235.) A Catholic Temperance and
Benevolent Society of the Church of the Holy Name was active in temperance reform in the
'fifties. Father Chiniquy was also a temperance apostle. *Chicago Daily Democrat*, March 18,
1850, June 2, 1851.

opinion in early 1851, the Illinois legislature passed a law approved by temperance forces, which forbade the sale of less than one quart of wine or liquor, prohibited the sale of any liquor for drinking on the premises, and allowed no sale to minors under eighteen years of age. The Maine enactment of June, 1851, which prohibited the sale of all liquor except for medicinal purposes met, however, with unalloyed enthusiasm, and agitation for such a statute in Illinois began at once.[24] In December, 1853, under the leadership of the Sons of Temperance, Chicago citizens became hosts to an interdenominational convention " of the friends of a prohibitory liquor law in the State of Illinois." [25] From twenty-four counties some 240 delegates, of whom over five-sixths were clergymen, attended, and before adjournment they organized the Illinois Maine Law Alliance, which bound its members never to vote for a candidate who was " not unequivocally pledged to the Maine Law." A month later the local Cook County Maine Law Alliance was formed. Putting into practice their desire to place men of their opinion in political power, they named for mayor Amos Gaylord Throop, who was defeated, according to a sympathetic Methodist paper, because of an alleged opposition of the Catholic priests, the rum-sellers, Irish whiskey-drinkers, and the German beer-drinkers. Realizing the importance of publicity in their campaign to vanquish the advocates of liquor, the state alliance then began the publication of a weekly newspaper, bearing as title the name of the society, but this ill-starred venture, after several changes of management, was given up for want of subscribers.[26]

The political activity of the alliance did not cease with the initial defeat, however, and, with the election of Levi D. Boone as mayor on the anti-foreign or " Know-Nothing " ticket in 1855, the city felt the effect of enforcement of liquor restrictions. The fee for licenses was raised to $300, an action of the council which led to a mass meet-

---

[24] *Ibid.*, February 14, 1851; *General Laws, 1851*, pp. 18–19; *Watchman of the Prairies*, February 18, 1851, February 10, March 16, 1852; Maine, *Acts and Resolves passed by the Thirty-first Legislature, 1851* (Augusta, 1851), pp. 210–18; *Western Citizen*, February 17, 1852; *Congregational Herald*, April 7, 1853.

[25] In June, 1853, the national division of the Sons of Temperance representing more than three hundred thousand members in the United States and Canada met in Chicago and heard among others Neal Dow, author of the Maine Law. *Northwestern Christian Advocate*, June 15, December 14, 1853; also *Congregational Herald*, June 18, 1853; *Weekly Chicago Democrat*, June 18, 1853.

[26] *Northwestern Christian Advocate*, February 15, March 15, June 7, 1854.

ing by the sellers of liquor and others, who denounced the new requirement as the most tyrannical measure since the Stamp Act.[27] This licensing ordinance now caused open disobedience. When an attempt was made to bring to trial those who had broken the law, one hundred men, mostly Germans, marched on Saturday, April 21, to the courthouse. Soon Irishmen joined the others assembled to rescue those held malefactors in the eyes of the law but believed by their comrades more sinned against than sinning. As the crowd swelled and cried its defiance, officers tried to clear the corridors of the courthouse. Shots were fired, the police lost control of the mob, one man was killed, and several were wounded.

In late afternoon the National Guard, the Light Guard, Swift's Artillery, and a detail of special police were called out. By evening the city became fairly quiet, and by the next morning, fifty-six rioters had been arrested. Church bells signaled the hour of religious services to a city partly under martial law. In spite of the presence of the militia, a large number of armed Germans gathered that day at Washington Square. The Montgomery Guards had, by late afternoon, been added to other guardians of the law, and a second proclamation of the mayor begged citizens to remain at home to avoid danger. In this tense atmosphere the court decided the cases against the defendants. By mid-May fines imposed upon them fattened the city treasury by $420. But it had cost the city $4,223 to suppress the Lager Beer riots, and the strain upon the reservoir of goodwill was not measurable.[28]

The alliance at that time was appealing to the people on a referendum for a state statute similar to the Maine Law, the voting to take place on June 4. Clergymen, laymen, and politicians seemed a triumvirate not only worthy but certain of success. But Chicago by a wide margin defeated the forces of prohibition.[29] With this defeat, the

---

[27] *The Daily Democratic Press,* March 23, 1853. J. A. Huck, a brewer, was chosen president of the meetings. An association was formed to protect members prosecuted for violation of the law. The initiation fee was five dollars. (*Ibid.,* March 28, 1855; Ernest Hurst Cherrington, ed., *Standard Encyclopedia of the Alcohol Problem* [6 v. Westerville, Ohio, 1924–30], II, 570. See p. 211.) In 1867, the German Association protested aganist Sunday closing laws. *Chicago Tribune,* August 13, 1867.

[28] *The Daily Democratic Press,* April 23, 24, May 17, June 12, 1855; *Weekly Chicago Democrat,* April 28, 1855.

[29] *The Daily Democratic Press,* April 27–June 8, 1855, *passim.* The vote of June 4 follows: Chicago for prohibition law, 2,785; against, 3,964; Cook County for the law, 3,807; against, 5,182. *Ibid.,* June 8, 27, 28, July 3, 1855.

Maine Law Alliance as a political force seems to have disappeared, except for a union temperance movement which it sponsored at the time of the great revival of 1858, when practically every religious interest flourished.

Although the Civil War diverted the attention of the entire country from customary concerns, the cause of prohibition was not altogether deserted. Regular meetings of the Chicago Temperance Legion continued; new societies were set up, one of them at Bridgeport, the home of the Irish; a number of Chicago churches co-operated with others in the state to hire the services of a famous lecturer and physiologist for temperance education; and when the minister of the Clark Street Methodist Episcopal Church got drunk while serving on Governor Yates's Sanitary Commission delegation after the battle of Pittsburg Landing, the outcry which went up from the state and local secular press, to say nothing of the religious journals, bespoke an aggrieved public opinion still highly sensitive.[30] Compared to the high pitch reached before 1860, however, interest in temperance waned after that year, and did not regain its old strength for several years following the close of the war. By 1866 the press noted the growing consumption of beer rather than hard liquors, and pointed out that during 1865 alone nearly seven million gallons of the former were manufactured in the city, or thirty-nine gallons for each man, woman, and child.[31]

In 1867, at a temperance mass meeting held in Farwell Hall, the Rev. Dr. R. M. Hatfield counselled re-entry into politics on a national scale. Revivalistic methods quickened interest, and preachers boldly invaded saloons and prayed and preached for the besotted patrons. In 1870, the perennial non-enforcement of ordinances restricting hours and the Sunday opening of saloons offered temporary ballast to the wavering temperance lines. When the mayor refused to close the saloons in accordance with the laws and in spite of the petitions with twenty-two thousand names, which the temperance groups submitted, the salutary opposition had appeared which gave renewed vigor to the movement. Total abstinence pledges which obliged the signers to " touch not, taste not, handle not," were circu-

---

[30] *The Christian Times and Illinois Baptist*, May 12, 1858; *Chicago Tribune*, June 29, September 24, December 22, 1861, March 13, April 11, 30, May 17, 22, 1862.
[31] The exact amount was 6,924,168 gallons. *Ibid.*, February 1, 1866.

lated in ever increasing numbers. Programs of child education in the Sunday schools were undertaken, and temperance tract distribution went forward with a new impetus. Public meetings such as those held each week in Farwell Hall became the order of the day, and temperance " bars " where coffee and soup were available came into existence. The Washingtonian Home, founded in 1863, expanded its work of curing drunkards of their taste for liquor, the income from the sale of liquor licenses guaranteeing its existence.[32]

The fire of 1871 did not put a stop to this activity, for the " Fire-Proof " ticket on which Joseph Medill was candidate for the mayoralty was pledged to enforce the laws restricting the sale of liquor. The election of this ticket was the last important political success of the temperance forces in the line of municipal regulation of the traffic in spirits, however, for the victory of the foreign groups and particularly the Germans in 1873 put an end to any effective enforcement of the restrictive ordinances.[33]

Tobacco users, as well as those addicted to the consumption of liquor, also came under the ban of the more conservative members of society, to whom it appeared that " tobacco boys " made " tobacco men," who would " spit tobacco along their way through life to the annoyance of their neighbors and the displeasure of their wives and families." [34]

As crime statistics mounted in spite of church-going and other salutary influences, aroused citizens brought pressure to bear upon the Common Council to do something about the growing number of juvenile offenders. Obedient to the public will, the city fathers transmitted, in 1855, to the state legislature a memorial asking for the establishment of a reform school near Chicago.[35] The charter of 1851 had authorized the council to provide for " the safe keeping and education " of children " destitute of proper parental care, wandering about the streets, committing mischief and growing up in

[32] The Advance, November 28, 1867, March 19, 1868, January 6, 1870; Chicago Tribune, April 10, November 22, 1867, January 14, 1868, March 30, 1870, July 17, 1871; The Interior, March 17, 31, 1870.

[33] Cherrington, op. cit., II, 570, 572. See also Pierce, A History of Chicago, III (in progress).

[34] The New Covenant, May 3, 1862. See also Northwestern Christian Advocate, May 11, June 12, 1853, August 18, 1870; Watchman of the Prairies, January 18, 1848, September 11, 1849.

[35] The Daily Democratic Press, January 16, 1855.

mendicancy, ignorance, idleness, and vice." This grant was strengthened by legislative enactment in 1857 and by subsequent statutes.[36] In 1854, the legislature, however, had given to the council the right to purchase grounds and erect buildings.[37] In spite of these provisions the council was slow to act, and the numbers of offenders increased. When, in 1855, the state failed to accede to the request of the city fathers, the Chicago Asylum and Reform School was established to care for miscreants under sixteen years of age who were without proper parental care or who had been convicted before a Chicago justice of the peace or police magistrate and had not paid the prescribed fine.[38]

Commitment to the reformatory could be made by all courts having criminal jurisdiction in Cook County and by police magistrates. Because not all Illinois counties and cities had such facilities, provision was made by the consent of the Chicago council for the school to receive offenders from any locality which would bear expenses. In this capacity the Chicago Asylum and Reform School served the state until 1872, after which the courts of Chicago could sentence juvenile offenders to Pontiac.[39]

From the establishment of the school in 1855, moral instruction was provided the inmates, and some regular employment was taught. Boys, up to the age of twenty-one, were bound out for a term of

[36] Act of February 14, 1851, *Private Laws, 1851*, p. 148; Act of February 14, 1857, *Private Laws, 1857*, pp. 651–55; Act of February 22, 1861, *Private Laws, 1861*, p. 149; Act of February 13, 1863, *Private Laws, 1863*, p. 133; Act of March 5, 1867, *Private Laws, 1867*, III, 31.

[37] Act of February 28, 1854, *Laws, 1854*, p. 219; Chicago Reform School, *First Annual Report of the Superintendent of the Chicago Reform School, to the Board of Guardians, 1855–56* (Chicago, 1856), p. 7.

[38] Chicago, *Charter and Ordinances, 1856*, p. 339. Children so committed were to remain in the school until " discharged in due course of law," and if incorrigible they could be transferred to the bridewell to serve out the sentence. In 1857 those over twenty-one had to be discharged and sentenced by the court or magistrate who had originally committed them to the school. The Common Council had the right to levy a tax not exceeding two mills on the dollar on the real estate of Chicago for the support of the school. Act of February 14, 1857, *Private Laws, 1857*, p. 651.

[39] Act of March 15, 1872, *Public Laws, 1871–72*, pp. 663–64. In 1861, a commissioner appointed by the mayor upon request of the board of guardians passed on all commitments. The board of guardians was chosen by the council. (Act of February 22, 1861, *Private Laws, 1861*, p. 149; Act of February 13, 1863, *Private Laws, 1863*, p. 133.) The cost of upkeep was assessed upon such parents or guardians. (Act of March 5, 1867, *Private Laws, 1867*, III, 31.) Children so placed were subject to the same rules as those committed by the courts. In 1867 the facilities of the school were opened to parents or guardians who wished children between six and sixteen to be placed under such a regimen.

years as apprentices or servants in order to learn a trade. Girl offenders had no separate school until 1866, being placed in the same institution with boys. In 1861 a separate institution was provided by law, but it was not opened until spring, 1866.[40]

A growing public conscience regarding the prevalence of prostitution led in 1853 to the organization of the Chicago Female Guardian Association "to reclaim abandoned females, to afford aid and protection to those exposed to temptation, and by all justifiable means to promote the cause of moral purity."[41] In November, 1855, Mayor Boone appointed a committee "to obtain information respecting institutions for the reformation of unfortunate females," and in January those interested again assembled and resolved that an institution looking toward the reformation of "guilty females" should be established. A study of similar institutions in other cities convinced the committee that such an establishment in Chicago would prove "one of the greatest blessings to persons fallen from virtue and lost to moral and religious society." The committee also recommended that a Strangers' Retreat should be provided for "the virtuous," where they could get room and board at a low rate until employment was found. At the same time one public-spirited citizen offered the site for an asylum for "fallen women," and another pledged $5,000 toward the building and furnishings, provided $20,000 were raised from other sources. The venture so optimistically and humanely proposed, however, failed to materialize at this time.[42]

In 1858, the Magdalen Asylum, or House of the Good Shepherd, was established through the efforts of Father John McMullen of the Church of the Holy Name and through aid given him by three Sisters of the Good Shepherd of St. Louis. Easily approached by those for whom it was intended, the home soon assumed an enviable importance among reformatories and charitable institutions. From 1858

[40] Chicago, *Charter and Ordinances, 1856,* pp. 339–40; *The Daily Democratic Press,* September 20, 1855; Act of February 14, 1857, *Private Laws, 1857,* pp. 652–53; Act of February 22, 1861, *Private Laws, 1861,* pp. 151–52; Chicago Reform School, *Sixth Annual Report, 1860–62,* pp. vi-vii, *Seventh Annual Report, 1862–63,* p. vii, *Eighth Annual Report, 1863–64,* p. vi, *Ninth Annual Report, 1864–65,* p. vi, *Eleventh Annual Report, 1866–67,* p. 38. Eight girls were committed during the first year. Their average age was thirteen years. During the year 1855–56 one girl had been in the school.

[41] *Northwestern Christian Advocate,* September 14, 1853.

[42] *The Daily Democratic Press,* November 14, 1855, February 4, 1856.

to 1866 its average yearly number of inmates was seventy-three, and in these years 264 women were discharged as reformed.[43] A new building, four stories high and made of pressed brick, was dedicated in 1869. It symbolized the expanding activities of the asylum, which, in the words of a contemporary, had given shelter to " the weeping Magdalene whom the world had flattered for an hour only to despise for a lifetime." [44]

The House of the Good Shepherd shared with the Erring Woman's Refuge for Reform the care of female lawbreakers. The latter home had been established in 1863 by a group of socially minded women bent on reclaiming their "erring sisters." [45] To these homes the city government contributed equally from the fines collected from keepers, inmates, and visitors of houses of prostitution. To the city council annual accounts were rendered by the homes to which officials could commit malefactors.[46] Despite the stigma which inevitably was attached to anyone who emerged, admission was, by 1867, refused to applicants, and, in 1870, ninety were reported as inmates.[47]

As the number of women engaged in earning their own livelihoods increased, public-minded citizens turned their attention to the establishment of homes for working girls where board and room could be obtained at reasonable rates. In August, 1866, one was started on West Madison Street under the auspices of the Ladies Boarding House Association. Ten sleeping apartments and a dining hall for a small weekly charge offered pleasant surroundings.[48] Soon another house under the sponsorship of Seth Paine and other interested citizens was opened on West Jackson near Halsted Street at a cost of

---

[43] Garraghan, *Catholic Church in Chicago*, pp. 206–7; *Chicago Daily Journal*, June 28, August 15, 1859, May 28, 1860; *A Strangers' and Tourists' Guide to Chicago*, pp. 100–1; *The Chicago Times*, July 8, 1866.

[44] *Chicago Tribune*, August 9, 1869.

[45] Tuthill King gave $10,000 to the Erring Woman's Refuge for Reform. *The Chicago Times*, February 20, 1863; *Chicago Tribune*, February 19, 1863.

[46] Act of March 31, 1869, *Private Laws, 1869*, I, 254–55; Helen D. Haseltine, *A History of the Chicago Home for Girls Founded in 1863 as the Chicago Erring Woman's Refuge for Reform* (unpublished M.A. Thesis, The University of Chicago, 1934); *Chicago Tribune*, February 19, March 14, 15, 1863; *The Chicago Times*, February 20, 1863.

[47] Haseltine, *op. cit.*, p. 44; *Chicago Tribune*, February 3, 1871. See petition of property owners to the Common Council praying for the withdrawal of city financial support, since nearness to the home depreciated the value of their holdings. *Ibid.*, September 8, 1871; Chicago, *Council Proceedings, 1870–71*, pp. 287, 294–95.

[48] *Chicago Tribune*, August 7, 1866.

$15,000. Bakers and grocers provided supplies at cost for the inmates, whose weekly board bill was three and a half dollars. So successful was the home that it was soon enlarged to furnish a reading room, library, lecture room, and dormitory accommodations for three hundred women. By 1870, an industrial department gave opportunities to 125 residents to engage in a profit-sharing enterprise.[49] Working mothers were provided a place to leave children during their hours of employment outside their homes in the Chicago Nursery and Half-Orphan Asylum, founded in 1859,[50] and after 1861 homeless women over sixty were cared for in the Home for Aged and Indigent Females, later called the Old Ladies' Home of Chicago.[51]

Orphans, too, shared in public benefactions, and asylums for their care appeared early. Besides individuals seeking homes for children alone in the world, the church and press were actively interested. A Protestant organization, the Orphan Benevolent Association, started partly to care for children orphaned in the cholera epidemic in 1849, sponsored the Chicago Orphan Asylum, supported by membership dues, fairs, excursions, teas, benefit concerts, and public subscription. In 1869, the Uhlich Evangelical Lutheran Orphan Asylum was incorporated to serve homeless children of that special sect, and orphaned Catholics were cared for by the Sisters of Mercy in a home financed by the same measures as those which brought in funds for the Protestant homes. German Catholic orphans received attention in a separate institution in order that they might not be "alienated from their German kin and their German nationality."[52] The Chi-

[49] *Ibid.*, May 17, August 19, 1868, July 8, 1869, May 20, 1870.

[50] The Chicago Nursery and Half-Orphan Asylum was first located on Illinois Street near State. In 1860, it was moved to 151 North Market and organized permanently. In the period of the Civil War, the asylum had increased usefulness. By 1867 more ample quarters were found at Franklin and Wisconsin streets. As in the case of other houses caring for dependents on society, neighbors complained of the effect on the neighborhood. *Ibid.*, October 24, 1861, January 16, 1867; *The Press and Tribune*, July 28, 1860; Andreas, *History of Chicago*, II, 672.

[51] *Ibid.*, pp. 671–72; *Chicago Tribune*, November 16, 1861, January 25, 1862, February 6, 1863; Act of February 14, 1865, *Private Laws, 1865*, I, 76–79. The Old Ladies' Home was supported by contributions of philanthropic citizens. Voting members paid five dollars. Miss Caroline Smith, a liberal donor, served as the first matron. Tanner, Halpin and Co., *D. B. Cooke & Co.'s Directory, 1858*, p. 486.

[52] *Chicago Daily Democrat*, August 4, 9, 11, September 15, 1849, August 14, October 29, 1850, February 15, April 9, May 7, December 12, 1851, May 1, 1855; *The Daily Democratic Press*, November 27, 1852; *Weekly Chicago Democrat*, November 26, 1853; *Chicago Tribune*, November 17, 1860, November 20, 22, 1861, March 19, 26, 1866, January 7, 1867, July 13, 1871; *Chicago Evening Journal*, January 16, 1864; Mrs. Charles Gilbert Wheeler, *Annals*

cago Ministry-at-Large, another agency, incorporated by the Unitarian Church in 1863 to give relief, culture, education, and guardianship to destitute and neglected children, provided them not only suitable homes but employment.[53]

Benevolences were a part of the activities of various national groups and vocational associations. Among the latter were the Firemen's Benevolent Association, policemen in their protective association, the Bricklayers' and Masons' Benevolent Association, the Draymen's Benevolent Association, a Seamen's Mutual Benevolent Society, and the Laborers' Benevolent Association. Bakers and railroad employees furnished protection to themselves and their families from the adversities of the day,[54] and like organizations based on national affiliations afforded also a means for social contacts and community pleasures.[55] In addition to these societies, both men and women laborers received benefits from membership in the Chicago Sick Relief Association, which supplied through insurance weekly sick relief or accident compensation and, in the case of death, the sum of $100 toward funeral expenses.[56]

Care of the poor, undertaken at an early time, continued to be a public responsibility. The modern social worker and governmental aid had not yet assumed the direction of measures of alleviation. What was done was often a combination of public and private charity, although the city and county at an early day offered some help

---

of the Chicago Orphan Asylum from 1849 to 1892 (Chicago, 1892); Garraghan, Catholic Church in Chicago, pp. 154, 157, 208–9; Bürgler, Geschichte der Kathol. Kirche Chicagos, p. 97; Private Laws, 1869, I, 251.

[53] Chicago Daily Press and Tribune, October 20, 1858; Act of June 13, 1863, Private Laws, 1863, pp. 34–37. See pp. 159–60. Any person could become an annual member by paying five dollars. Life membership was fifty dollars or more.

[54] The Firemen's Benevolent Association was incorporated February 12, 1849. (Private Laws, 1849, p. 43. For the policemen's association see Chicago Tribune, February 7, 1868, January 23, 1871.) The Bricklayers' and Masons' Benevolent Association was incorporated February 16, 1865. (Private Laws, 1865, I, 65. For the Draymen's Benevolent Association see The Daily Democratic Press, May 2, 1855.) The Seamen's Benevolent Society was organized in September, 1860, and incorporated February 22, 1861. (Private Laws, 1861, p. 46. For the Laborers' Benevolent Association see Act of February 13, 1865, Private Laws, 1865, I, 82.) The Chicago Bakers' Relief Society was incorporated March 26, 1869. (Private Laws, 1869, I, 229.) The Illinois Central [Railroad] Relief Club was organized in 1862. (Chicago Tribune, March 10, 1863.) The Chicago Arbeiter-Verein, incorporated in 1865, cared for German laborers. Act of February 16, 1865, Private Laws, 1865, I, 63.

[55] See pp. 17–24, 160–73.

[56] Chicago Tribune, September 5, 1868. In a short time after its beginning the Chicago Sick Relief Association had $25,000 capital stock and a membership of 250. It was incorporated March 15, 1869. Private Laws, 1869, I, 237.

to the poverty stricken. By 1853 the Cook County Poor House was unable to satisfy the demands made upon it.[57] Private agencies, generally held the proper source of such relief, steadily and increasingly bore the burden. The Ladies' Benevolent Association, which had been in existence since 1843, raised money for the poor by benefit lectures, concerts, fairs, and parties.[58] In 1865, the Ladies' Relief Association organized for purposes similar to those of the Ladies' Benevolent Association and distributed the cast-off clothing of the well-to-do.[59] Soup kitchens, to which generous housewives and merchants contributed, supplemented the work of other charitable agencies and helped, particularly in moments of special stress, to fend off starvation.[60]

The Chicago Relief Society, organized in 1850, was, in a sense, the first really systematic attempt to face in modern manner the problem of caring for the destitute. The society divided the city into districts and employed visitors to distribute supplies to applicants in the hope of curbing unwise giving and curtailing the growing menace of begging.[61]

In 1857, when want attacked workers hitherto able to care for themselves, the Chicago Relief and Aid Society took up the work of alleviating suffering not only by contributions of fuel and other necessities, but by procuring employment for those out of work. The legislature, granting incorporation in 1857 to this organization, charged it with the duty of administering in an orderly fashion the private charity in Chicago, and empowered it to accept appropriations from the city council. Its activities were carried on by a general superintendent, a visitor, a messenger, and a caretaker for its woodyard and lodginghouse. Aid from the city reflected the mood of the council, but the society was given the right to occupy land belonging to the city rent free for the purpose of storing supplies. Private contributions were its chief means of support, and its annual canvass was

[57] *Weekly Chicago Democrat*, February 19, 1853; *The Chicago Times*, January 19, 1853; *Oquawka Spectator*, August 26, 1858.

[58] Pierce, *A History of Chicago*, I, 265; *Daily Democrat*, February 1, March 1, 1849.

[59] *Chicago Tribune*, March 7, 1866.

[60] *Chicago Daily Democratic Press*, November 4, 1857; *Chicago Daily Press and Tribune*, December 18, 1858, January 5, 1859; *Chicago Tribune*, January 9, 1864.

[61] *Chicago Daily Democrat*, December 27, 31, 1850, December 11, 1852; *The Daily Democratic Press*, December 29, 1854; Chicago Relief and Aid Society, *The Thirty-fourth Annual Report of the Chicago Relief and Aid Society to the Common Council of the City of Chicago, 1891* (Chicago, 1891), p. 6.

generally directed toward meeting needs intensified by cold weather.[62]

By 1867, the lack of co-ordination in charitable enterprises as carried on by numerous welfare groups led to a meeting which resulted in placing in the hands of the Chicago Relief and Aid Society more responsibility for poor relief. A plan of granting supplies in return for labor gave in 1868–69 twenty-five hundred days of work to the unemployed and disbursed the sum of $27,222 to the needy. But preference on the part of workers for the city over the country, where work seemed at times more plentiful, proved a source of discouragement and an obstacle to the highest fulfillment of hopes.[63]

Forsaken and homeless women and children were cared for by the Chicago Home for the Friendless, organized March 18, 1858, to find employment for the women and homes in the country for the children. Nineteen women, representing Protestant denominations in the city, made up the governing board of this home and sought financial aid for their undertaking by personal gifts and the usual forms of benefits. Within a year, the home was already overcrowded as were most places of refuge in the late 'fifties. Aided by a lot donated by Jonathan Burr and through their own tireless efforts, promoters soon raised $10,000 for a new structure more nearly fitted to the needs of the organization. Here, in the year 1860 alone, 243 destitute widows with children, children for whom parents made no provision, and other homeless persons found food and shelter. Occasionally children were sent to the home by the police court, but more often the destitute were rescued from the streets or some place of misery through the efforts of the vigilant humanitarian sponsors of the organization.[64]

---

[62] *Ibid.*, pp. 7–8; Chicago Relief and Aid Society, *Forty-third Annual Report, 1900*, p. 5; Act of February 16, 1857, *Private Laws, 1857*, p. 1123; Andreas, *History of Chicago*, II, 670; Marjorie Helen Coonley, *Private Relief Societies in Chicago, 1871–1910* (unpublished M.A. Thesis, The University of Chicago, 1921), p. 4; *Chicago Tribune*, November 23, 1870.

[63] Wirt Dexter, a prominent Chicago lawyer, was influential in establishing a common plan of action for charitable organizations. He continued his activity in this connection until his death in 1890. Chicago Relief and Aid Society, *Thirty-third Annual Report, 1890*, p. 3, *Fourteenth Annual Report, 1871*, p. 4, *Forty-third Annual Report, 1900*, p. 5; *Chicago Tribune*, December 1, 1867, February 8, 1868, November 8, 1869, March 27, 1870; Coonley, *op. cit.*, p. 12.

[64] Mrs. Lyman Baird, *History of the Chicago Home for the Friendless, 1859–1909* (Chicago, 1909), p. 2; Smith & DuMoulin, *Directory, 1859–60*, Appendix, p. 12; *Chicago Daily Press and Tribune*, July 17, 1858. Subscription papers were circulated for funds ranging from one to one hundred dollars. Among its first promoters were Mrs. Abraham H. Hoge,

At a time when the mentally sick were regarded in less compassionate light than today, the work of Dr. Edward Mead, pioneer neuropsychiatrist of Illinois, was conspicuous. His "Chicago Retreat," started in 1847, was the only hospital for the insane within several hundred miles of Chicago, and its record of cures stamped it as unique in a day of generally unscientific treatment. In 1852, the retreat was destroyed by fire, and over half a century passed before a private institution of like purpose was established in Chicago.[65] In the meantime, the county poorhouse was used. Here no special pathological treatment was provided, for human sympathy then included only food, clothing, and shelter for those so afflicted. Although there was some agitation for better care of the insane paupers of the community, it was not until 1870 that a brick building large enough to house two hundred patients was constructed.[66]

The physically sick received kindlier and more enlightened attention. Those who were able to purchase the services of qualified physicians were especially fortunate, but a number of free clinics took care of the poor. The Illinois Charitable Eye and Ear Infirmary, established in 1858, was one of these, and it received contributions of furniture, money, and other necessities from the churches. During the war this infirmary had the aid of the United States Sanitary Com-

---

Mrs. Daniel P. Livermore, Mrs. Norman B. Judd, and Mrs. Andrew F. Brown. The first home was on the corner of West Randolph and Peoria streets. (*Ibid.*, August 26, 1858.) The lot given by Burr was on Wabash Avenue, south of Twelfth Street, and given under the condition that $10,000 be raised for the home. (*Ibid.*, March 24, April 16, 1859.) By 1870, the home was at Wabash Avenue and Twentieth Street. The Irish predominated among inmates, having over twice as many entrants as those listed as American and about six times as many as German. In 1870 the total receiving aid was 1,603. *Chicago Tribune*, January 23, 1861, January 7, 1862, January 10, 1871; Baird, *op. cit.*, pp. 2–3, 7–8.

[65] Peter Bassoe, "A Sketch of the Development of Psychiatry and Neurology in Chicago," *Proceedings of the Institute of Medicine in Chicago* [Reprint], II, no. 9 (December 15, 1936), 1–2; George H. Weaver, "Edward Mead, M.D., the Pioneer Neuropsychiatrist of Illinois," The Society of Medical History of Chicago, *Bulletin*, III (December, 1924), 281–85.

[66] In 1853, press comments directed attention to the need of a county insane asylum on the ground that the "State Lunatic Asylum" provided each county with care for two persons only, regardless of the population or needs of the county. (*Weekly Chicago Democrat*, February 12, 1853.) The county poorhouse, erected late in 1854, gave over a special wing to the insane. Apertures for passing food through brick walls into cells about seven by eight feet were tell-tale signs of the use made of this part of the building. Vermin were plentiful, so it was said, and the only heat was from a stove in the near-by corridor. Weston A. Goodspeed and Daniel D. Healy, eds., *History of Cook County, Illinois* (2 v. Chicago, 1909), I, 541; Andreas, *History of Cook County*, pp. 484–85; Henry M. Hurd and others, *The Institutional Care of the Insane in the United States and Canada* (4 v. Baltimore, 1916–17), II, 280, 282–83.

mission and the Northwestern Sanitary and Christian Commission. From 1867 to 1871 the General Assembly of Illinois appropriated for its support $5,000 a year, and in 1871 it became a full-fledged state institution.[67]

Gratuitous treatment for the sick poor was furnished also by Rush Medical College, the Chicago City Dispensary of the Chicago Medical College, the Hahnemann Medical College, the Brainard Free Dispensary, and various physicians who volunteered to treat without charge those unable to pay for medical services.[68] Calamities such as the cholera epidemic led to the establishment of temporary hospitals for " indigent persons," and sick immigrants, in the early 'fifties particularly, were cared for by the city.[69]

But even so, these facilities were not sufficient to provide for those afflicted, and the city physician was importuned by the Board of Health as early as 1854 to give an opinion as " to the establishment of a hospital commensurate with the actual wants and population of the city." [70] It was three years before such a hospital with its two medical boards, one allopathic and one homeopathic, was completed. But disagreement prevailed between these two schools of medical practice, and the " city hospital " did not open. In 1859 the building was leased for five years to a group of allopathic physicians, who were placed under contract to receive and care for city patients

[67] " Several wealthy and charitable citizens of Chicago " were sponsors. (*Ibid.*, p. 535.) The first dispensary was in a small wooden building at 60 North Clark Street. In 1861, it was moved to Ewing's Block, 28 North Clark Street. In 1864, the infirmary was given the use of a lot for ten years by Walter L. Newberry. A wooden building cost $2,000. Hyde, *Early Medical Chicago*, pp. 50–51; Act of March 6, 1867, *Public Laws, 1867*, p. 37; Act of March 25, 1869, *Public Laws, 1869*, p. 43; Act of April 17, 1871, *Public Laws, 1871–72*, p. 137.

[68] When patients were unable to go to the dispensary, located at Dearborn and Indiana streets, they were visited at their homes. (Bailey, *Directory, 1864–65*, Appendix, p. xxii.) Within a year after the establishment of the Brainard Free Dispensary in 1867 it had treated 656 poor persons and vaccinated 163 children at a cost of $250. It was located at 79 West Madison Street, where patients on three days a week could have the attention of a physician who spoke German. In December, 1868, the dispensary was moved to Rice and Jackson's Building, northwest corner of Jefferson and Randolph streets. The women of St. Paul's Universalist Church opened a free dispensary in 1871. *Chicago Tribune*, October 13, 14, 1863, January 19, 1866, September 16, December 6, 1868, January 16, 1870.

[69] Board of Health, *Reports, 1867–69*, p. 28; *Daily Democrat*, May 17, 1849, July 15, 1852; Andreas, *History of Chicago*, I, 595–97.

[70] In 1853 the mayor was requested by the council to buy a lot. The following year a prize of $100 for the best plan for a permanent city hospital was offered. It was awarded in 1855 to Carter and Bauer, whose estimate for construction was $50,000. Board of Health, *Reports, 1867–69*, pp. 32, 35, 43; *The Daily Democratic Press*, May 4, 1853.

at a uniform rate of $3.00 a week. Here in this Chicago City Hospital could be found private wards, a much-needed change from the one-room establishments so general, and a special ward for diseased and lying-in women. Charity patients could receive treatment if recommended by city or county agents or " some responsible party." [71] In 1863, the hospital passed into the hands of the United States military authorities, and from July, 1864, to November, 1865, the government used the hospital exclusively for the treatment of the diseases of eye and ear under the name of Des Marres Eye and Ear Hospital. In November, 1865, after considerable public agitation about the lack of a city hospital, it was turned over to Cook County as a general hospital for the poor, and in January, 1866, it was opened to receive patients. Before this, the poor sick of the county had been sent to Mercy Hospital, the Poor House, and the Pest House, which was said to be " not fit for a dog." [72] The city, however, had maintained a pest house, or smallpox hospital, during these years. Since the county hospital would not accept persons afflicted with infectious diseases, the smallpox hospital received them. Called the Lake Hospital, it served the citizens of Chicago until destroyed by the fire in 1871. [73]

A United States Marine Hospital under government auspices, on the site of the barracks of old Fort Dearborn, the Illinois General Hospital of the Lake, and a hospital of the Sisters of Mercy, called Mercy Hospital, cared for the sick also.[74] Other Roman Catholic hospitals were opened as the years advanced, St. Mary's, under the

[71] Board of Health, Reports, 1867–69, p. 46. Daniel Brainard, George Schloetzer, and George K. Amerman were the surgeons and DeLaskie Miller, Joseph P. Ross, and Samuel C. Blake the physicians. Andreas, History of Chicago, II, 536; Halpin, Halpin & Bailey's Directory, 1862–63, Appendix, p. xxxv; The Press and Tribune, August 15, 1859; Chicago Daily Democrat, September 6, 1860; Chicago Tribune, May 8, 1862; Hyde, op. cit., p. 53.

[72] Chicago Tribune, June 9, November 13, 1865, January 8, 15, 1866.

[73] Board of Health, Reports, 1867–69, pp. 67, 69, 72, 73, 83. The city operated a cholera hospital at times. Chicago Tribune, January 1, 1868. See also Board of Health, Reports, 1867–69, pp. 39–40.

[74] In 1852 the Marine Hospital was granted $32,000 by the government. Grants had been made in 1848 and 1849. (Daily Democrat, January 16, February 6, June 16, 29, 1849, April 1, 1852.) The Illinois General Hospital of the Lake was incorporated October 29, 1849. (Laws, 1849, pp. 40–41.) Its income was from voluntary donations. It, however, received public charges " at the lowest possible expense consistent with care " given. (Chicago Daily Democrat, September 28, October 22, 1850, March 15, 1851.) The Sisters of Mercy opened their hospital in 1853. Garraghan, Catholic Church in Chicago, pp. 158–60; A Sister of the Community, " The Sisters of Mercy," loc. cit., p. 352.

auspices of the Alexian Brothers, and St. Joseph's, under the Sisters of Charity of St. Vincent de Paul, appearing in the 'sixties.[75]

Members of the Episcopal church were responsible for the first hospital of a Protestant denomination in Chicago. This was St. James's Hospital, opened in 1854, and designed primarily as a charity hospital. Supported partly by the collections taken at services the first Sunday of the month, the hospital in its first year cared for sixty-nine patients. In 1864, St. Luke's Hospital was established by Episcopalians as a charity or free hospital for the needy. After 1865 the Lutherans maintained the Protestant Deaconesses' Hospital, and the Jews had a hospital after 1868. One for women and children was founded through the efforts of Dr. Mary H. Thompson by an association of women and opened to patients May 8, 1865. A free dispensary furnished treatment without regard to race and color and was in part kept up by church organizations.[76]

Although Chicago made rapid strides in the construction of facilities for the care of the sick, and an increasing number of qualified physicians were available for treatment, many Chicagoans preferred to take matters into their own hands. Health cures which would purify the blood found ready purchasers among those receptive to high-pressure advertising and salesmanship. Supplementing the common spring purgative of molasses and sulphur, Old Sachem Bitters and Wigwam Tonic were reminiscent of a well-grounded faith in the effectiveness of Indian cures. One bottle of such a remedy as Kennedy's Medical Discovery was reported to be in very truth an absolute restorative for those afflicted with sixteen different ailments ranging from scrofula to dropsy. Hostetter's Celebrated Stomach Bitters, one of the many remedies classified as the " Female's Friend " promised to infuse " new vitality into the frame " and be

[75] St. Mary's was opened in 1866 and St. Joseph's in 1868. Garraghan, *Catholic Church in Chicago,* p. 208.

[76] St. James's Hospital provided apartments for young men who had in the city no relatives " to watch a sick bed." By paying " a moderate sum per week," they could obtain " that care and attention they will so much need, and will be so little likely to find in crowded hotels, or in their lonely sleeping rooms." (*The Daily Democratic Press,* March 10, 1854, May 1, 1855.) The group which organized St. Luke's was at first called the Camp Douglas Hospital Aid Society. The average cost per patient in 1869 in the Jewish hospital was sixty-three cents a day. Henry Greenebaum was an important promoter. *Chicago Tribune,* June 20, 1864, August 9, 1868, January 16, 18, 1870; Independent Order B'nai B'rith, *Annals of Ramah Lodge, No. 33* . . . ([Chicago], 1929), p. 13.

the savior from an untimely grave of women not strong enough " to undergo the trials of maternity." Advertisements as to contraceptive devices pointed to the day of smaller families.[77] Alleged remedies for venereal diseases, infirmaries devoted to their cure, and doctors who promised full restoration to health were advertised in the press.[78]

During the war reform movements which had been pointed toward the care of dependents and delinquents were temporarily halted, and energies were concentrated on relief for victims of the struggle. Within the city help for needy soldiers' families was the concern of many civic and church organizations as well as of the government. In addition to aid given soldiers on the field of battle, homes in Louisville, Cairo, and Chicago provided temporary headquarters for men in transit. In Chicago, the Sanitary Commission and the Y.M.C.A. worked in close co-operation. They were supported in their efforts by a board of directors made up of women representatives from the churches in the city. Soon this board of directors was expanded to include women from Wisconsin and Michigan. By September, 1863, wounded and paroled soldiers joined recruits at the Soldiers' Home. So successful was the institution that a plan for a permanent establishment for the disabled was launched in November, 1863. Meanwhile a " Soldiers' Rest " looked after soldiers or regiments passing through the city. During 1864, over sixty thousand men were cared for, and over one hundred sixty-seven thousand meals were prepared by Chicago housewives for this refuge alone.[79]

But just as in peacetime, the most successful way of getting money for relief was by the then-honored and popular fair, ice cream and strawberry festival, benefit musical, dinner, donation party, and " sociable." Of these the most profitable during the period of hostilities was the Northwestern Sanitary Fair of October and November, 1863.

[77] See, for example, Chicago Tribune, December 12, 1860, February 24, 1865; The Chicago Times, April 2, 1864. See also Chicago Daily Democrat, February 22, 1850, for advertisement of " The Original Philotoken or Female's Friend," for relief of diseases attendant on pregnancy.

[78] See, for example, The Chicago Times, September 16, 1863, April 20, May 3, July 12, 1864, May 1, 1865, December 27, 1867; Chicago Tribune, July 15, August 10, October 4, 1864, October 1, 1865, December 13, 1867.

[79] Organization, Constitution and By-Laws of the Soldiers' Home in the City of Chicago (Chicago, 1863); Chicago Tribune, June 15, December 5, 1863, January 19, 1864; Henshaw, Our Branch and its Tributaries, pp. 141, 279; Andreas, History of Chicago, II, 311–13; Stillé, History of the United States Sanitary Commission, p. 142. See pp. 258–60.

Heavy casualties in the summer had left the treasury of the Sanitary Commission depleted, and a continuing list of wounded, particularly in Tennessee, focused attention on the necessity of replenishing revenues. The idea of a soldiers' fair for the benefit of the Sanitary Commission was promoted by Mrs. Abraham H. Hoge and Mrs. Daniel P. Livermore in the hope of realizing $25,000. When the final receipts were in, the sum of $85,000 lay in the commission's coffers, earned through the combined efforts of " men, women and children, corporations and business firms, religious societies, and political organizations," and the schools of an enthusiastic Northwest.[80]

Into Chicago during the last week of October and the first week of November poured thousands of citizens from near-by villages and states. To some it was the first visit to the mushroom city of the Middle Valley. And was it not worth the journey by horse and wagon over the dusty, rough, and unpaved highways, or, if possible, by the slightly faster means of steam travel, when one could see the Emancipation Proclamation fresh from the pen of the President, who had sent it as his contribution to aid in the relief or comfort of soldiers? [81]

Free dinners furnished by the women of the city, to which " country friends " donated poultry, eggs, vegetables, fruit, cream, butter, and cheese, tempted the palate of at least the " 1,000 or 1,500 gentlemen " who " ordinarily " dined down town " at restaurants or eating-houses." In Bryan Hall was the " bazaar," and at its rear was a temporarily constructed Manufacturers' Hall for the display and sale of heavy manufactures. An art department, housed in rooms at McVicker's Theatre, enticed the lover of " remarkable landscapes, . . . superior historical pieces, fine specimens of portrait painting, . . . still life, and . . . *genre* pictures." Relics and trophies lured others,

---

[80] By autumn, 1863, the Sanitary Commission had sent to battlefields and hospitals " nearly 30,000 boxes of sanitary stores, worth in the aggregate almost a million and a half dollars." ([Anon.], *History of the North-Western Soldiers' Fair* . . . [Chicago, 1864], pp. 3, 4, 7–8.) An executive committee appointed at a meeting in Bryan Hall decided to hold a convention of delegates from Aid Societies, Union Leagues, and Good Templars in Illinois, Michigan, Wisconsin, Iowa, and Minnesota on September 1, 1863. Each society was asked to send at least one woman delegate to the convention. About 150 delegates attended the convention. Eliphalet W. Blatchford was treasurer of the fair, and Mrs. Daniel P. Livermore and Mrs. Abraham H. Hoge were the managers. *Chicago Tribune,* July 29, 1863.

[81] *Ibid.,* October 30, 1863; Mrs. D. P. Livermore to Abraham Lincoln, October 11, 1863, I. N. Arnold to Lincoln, October 13, 1863, Lincoln to the " Ladies having in Charge the North Western Fair. . . ," October 26, 1863 (*Mss.* Chicago Historical Society).

and in the evenings, "the talent and ingenuity of the Northwest" in "entertainments of the most brilliant character," from pantomime and tableaux to concerts and lectures, teased any lingering dollars from their hiding places.[82] The merriment of a fortnight gave way to a sense of the grim reality of war on the last day of the fair, for the maimed in battle and those recovering from wounds from Confederate bullets came as guests. To them Anna Dickinson spoke, extolling the glory of their sacrifices and offering to them the obeisance of a grateful nation.

The co-operation of the whole Northwest seemed to have marked the passage of events during the fair. The glamour of success helped also to eradicate, or at least lessen, charges infrequent, but nevertheless present, that agents of the commission sometimes took supplies intended for the wounded, and that the management was inefficient.[83]

To supplement the activities of the Sanitary Commission the United States Christian Commission was organized in November, 1861, by the Young Men's Christian Association, and soon thereafter the Northwestern Branch was established in Chicago. Besides visiting camps, maintaining diet kitchens, providing temporary lodging and employment bureaus, distributing tracts, Bibles, and secular reading material, the commission built a chapel at Camp Douglas for federal soldiers and prisoners. In all these activities John V. Farwell, who was a member of the United States Christian Commission, was a moving spirit, just as he had been in activities of the Y.M.C.A. His able and tireless confederates, including Dwight L. Moody, Benjamin F. Jacobs, and Tuthill King, were instrumental in extending the usefulness of the commission and in aiding in the disbursement of over $100,000 for the comfort of soldiers.[84]

[82] The receipts from the various entertainments at the fair were: Admission to Bryan Hall, Manufacturers' Hall, and Supervisors' Room, $41,423; to German Department in Bryan Hall, $3,799; sale of the *Volunteer* (Fair newspaper), $377; art gallery, $3,726; dining hall, $6,409; Metropolitan Hall entertainments, $4,419; Ellsworth Zouave Drill, $141; Emancipation Proclamation sale, $3,000. Total, $63,294. An additional $22,084 was received in cash donations. *History of the North-Western Soldiers' Fair,* pp. 6, 9, 13, 29, 35, 183. For the program of the fair see *Chicago Tribune,* October 23, 28, 29, November 2, 1863.

[83] Miss Dickinson concluded her salute to the war-torn veterans with this promise: "You shall have immortal crownings, and the world shall honor your graves!" *History of the North-Western Soldiers' Fair,* p. 43; Andreas, *History of Chicago,* II, 317–18, 321; *Chicago Tribune,* December 27, 1861; Henshaw, *op. cit.,* pp. 224, 228.

[84] The Northwestern Branch was established in Chicago November 16, 1861. It was said to be second only to New York in services rendered in the field by its army committee,

As the war drew to a close, scanty funds for charitable purposes signified the inevitable cooling of enthusiasm. A drive for money was imperative. Under the guiding hands of Mrs. Hoge and Mrs. Livermore, the Northwestern Sanitary Commission joined forces with the board of the Soldiers' Home in putting on another fair. On May 30, with Major General Joseph Hooker as honorary president, a fair of national and international proportions opened with Dearborn Park as its central site. Enthusiasm, particularly throughout the Northwest, had been roused to white heat by unprecedented advertising in which the *Voice of the Fair,* edited by Andrew Shuman of the *Chicago Evening Journal,* played a stellar rôle. Season tickets for five dollars, snapped up " like pancakes," betokened a widespread interest in seeing Lincoln's log cabin now become a shrine; there were contributions from China, Japan, Germany, Russia, England, Italy, Denmark, and Switzerland, not to mention John Brown's ox yoke and a plantation bell from the old home of the despised president of the Confederacy. Colorful figures, such as General Sherman and General Grant, elicited hysterical and worshipful enthusiasm which, in turn, served to provide the needed funds. As the last week of June approached, the fair came to a climactic end with an auction of all remaining goods, which swelled receipts to $358,070.[85]

The participation of women in war activities had taken them from duties restricted to the home and had contributed to the growing emancipation of the sex. No longer were these women satisfied to have no part in the great task of government; no longer did they wish to be kept from the challenging experience of earning a living; no longer did they like being denied the pleasures of educational advance. The sphere of " laying the foundation of society " and of " humanizing the world " solely through an influence on husband and children seemed less alluring than it had even little more than a decade before when the shelter of home life prohibited any direct

---

of which Farwell was chairman. Lemuel Moss, *Annals of the United States Christian Commission* (Philadelphia, 1868), pp. 309–11, 737; Phillips, *Chicago and Her Churches,* pp. 138–42; Andreas, *History of Chicago,* II, 323–24.

[85] When all accounts were settled, the Sanitary Commission had $84,364, the rest of the net proceeds going to the Soldiers' Home and the Christian Committee after expenses of $117,257 were paid. Henshaw, *op. cit.,* pp. 295, 296, 299, 315; *Chicago Tribune,* February 20, March 15, May 29, June 2–13, 1865; *Voice of the Fair,* April 27, May 18, 30, 31, June 15, 1865; *Chicago Tribune, Annual Review, 1865,* p. 15; W. T. Sherman, *Personal Memoirs of General W. T. Sherman* (3d ed. 2 v. New York, 1890), II, 41.

contact with the "sordid" life outside.[86] With increased wealth in the community there came also a greater amount of leisure time, which after the war gave opportunity for a consideration of the restraints to which women were subjected. The way had been prepared by lectures, books, and forum discussions in the 'fifties, but it was not until the war was over that the feminist revolt took place in Chicago.[87]

In June, 1868, a woman's association was organized " to increase the social relations of woman and mankind, and to advocate anything that will, in any way, tend to promote the welfare of both sexes — the female sex especially." Called the " Sorosis," after its New York predecessor, the new society dedicated itself to the belief that "woman should uphold herself; not cast the first stone; and should not be afraid of Mrs. Grundy."[88] A weekly paper, the *Sorosis,* and a weekly meeting were intended to carry forward the program so altruistically framed. The suffrage question soon became the absorbing theme of the Chicago organization at a time when it was assuming importance in other parts of the United States.

By late 1868 Mrs. Cynthia H. V. N. Leonard and Mrs. Mary L. Walker, prominent in the club's activities, found agreement on organization matters no longer possible and led their followers into two new organizations. Each issued its journal and prepared to sponsor a statewide suffrage convention February 11 and 12, 1869, at a time when a new state constitution was being considered. " Sorosis No. 1," with Mary A. Livermore, Myra Bradwell, and some leading men of the community at the helm, " ran off with the show " and obtained as speakers Elizabeth Cady Stanton, Anna Dickinson, and Edward Beecher, not to mention outstanding local exponents.[89] Efforts to reconcile the discordant elements in order to advance the principles of equal suffrage failed to materialize in the joint meet-

[86] *Watchman of the Prairies,* January 4, May 9, 1848, September 11, 1849, September 17, 1850; *The Advance,* May 5, 1870, January 12, 1871.

[87] For example, in 1854 Lucy Stone spoke on "The Social and Legal Disabilities of Women." (*The Daily Democratic Press,* January 2, 1854.) The admission price was twenty-five cents.

[88] *Chicago Tribune,* June 19, 1868. Mrs. J. W. Loomis presided.

[89] The Leonard faction, called by the press " Sorosis No. 2," named its journal the *Chicago Sorosis.* See *Chicago Tribune,* January 10, 14, 21, 28, 31, 1869, for the story of the differences in the two groups.

ing proposed, and the Illinois Woman Suffrage Association, under the blessings of the Livermore-Walker group, and a rival organization, the Universal Suffrage Association, emerged.[90] Soon the latter gave way to its stronger and more influential sister, whose official organ was realistically named the *Agitator*.[91]

While the question of suffrage was being considered at the meetings of Sorosis, a convention of the Western Female Suffrage Association, made up of women of the midwest states, was held in Chicago on September 9 and 10, 1869. Under the chairmanship of Mary A. Livermore, the convention proposed a sixteenth amendment to the Constitution. Those in attendance heard Lucy Stone, ever popular with the suffragists, and appointed Dr. Mary Safford and Mrs. Kate N. Doggett as delegates to the Women's Industrial Congress in Berlin.[92] A few months later the Illinois Suffrage Association under the chairmanship of Judge James B. Bradwell of Chicago held its first annual meeting at Springfield, where the state constitutional convention was in session. Neither eloquence nor unembellished arguments served to bring the lawmakers into line.[93] And when, in 1871, the Illinois Woman Suffrage Association met in Chicago it courageously began another campaign to insure equal rights in Illinois through the action of the next legislature.[94]

In the meantime, a struggle to amend the statute which allowed a husband to commit his wife to an insane asylum merely with the consent of the superintendent of the institution had resulted in a change in the law. This had come about following much public discussion of the case of Mrs. Elizabeth P. W. Packard of Manteno, Illinois, who, because of religious differences with her husband, a clergyman, had been incarcerated by his order from June, 1860, until June, 1863, in the state asylum. Prominent Chicago citizens, including Mayor Francis C. Sherman, Isaac N. Arnold, and J. Young Scammon, took an active part in urging repeal of the law, and their efforts

[90] *Ibid.*, January 21, 31, February 12, 13, 1869; *The Chicago Times*, February 13, 1869.

[91] The paper was edited by Mary Livermore, her husband, D. P. Livermore, and Mrs. Mary L. Walker. The *Agitator* was soon merged with the Boston publication, *Woman's Journal*, of which Mrs. Livermore became editor-in-chief. Livermore, *The Story of My Life*, p. 482.

[92] *Chicago Tribune*, September 10, 12, 1869; Elizabeth Cady Stanton, Susan B. Anthony, Matilda Gage, *The History of Woman Suffrage* (6 v. New York, 1881–[1922]), III, 570.

[93] *Debates and Proceedings of the Constitutional Convention, 1869–70*, I, 451, 479, 487, 510, II, 1077, 1277, 1392, 1528, 1551; Stanton, Anthony, Gage, *op. cit.*, III, 570.

[94] *Chicago Tribune*, January 24, 1871.

were furthered by an excited religious and secular press.[95] Other advances in legal equality, though slight, reflected the indomitable spirit of pioneers such as Myra Bradwell and her husband. Their endeavors were partly rewarded in 1869 when the state legislature gave to women the right to control their own earnings.[96]

In the laws governing divorce, modifications during these years further heartened those engaged in the crusade for equality. Although no change was made in the legal grounds for divorce, the Illinois law of 1859 permitted women to take their maiden names afterwards, and that of 1869 gave them the right to sue for divorce and receive alimony in cases where the marriage, through no fault of theirs, was bigamous.[97] Under these statutes, which were comparatively liberal for the day, an increasing number of divorces was granted. By the late 'sixties Chicago became a haven for those desiring expeditious separation, applicants coming from the Far West and cities of the East.[98] The year 1865 seems to have marked the peak of divorces granted, the number being equal to 9 per cent of the marriages performed that year. Indeed, so numerous were the applications for separation that the *Tribune* was impelled to deplore the " system of social education " of the day which trained so poorly that "incompatibility of temper" was an important reason for engaging in divorce proceedings.[99]

But ridicule, opposition, and closed minds proved for a time an invincible trinity against lifting limitations imposed on women.

[95] Act of February 15, 1851, *Laws, 1851,* p. 98; Act of February 16, 1865, *Public Laws, 1865,* pp. 85–86; Act of March 5, 1867, *Public Laws, 1867,* pp. 139–40; Mrs. E. P. W. Packard, *Marital Power Exemplified in Mrs. Packard's Trial, and Self-Defence from the Charge of Insanity* (Chicago, 1869), pp. 1–12, 50–51, 116, Appendix, pp. 1–6, 17–20. Mrs. Packard gained nationwide attention through the version of her experience in this book. She was said to have been instrumental in obtaining modification of the Massachusetts law similar to the Illinois statute. Act of May 16, 1865, Massachusetts, *Acts and Resolves . . . 1865,* p. 644. See also *Chicago Tribune,* February 21, March 12, 1864.

[96] Stanton, Anthony, Gage, *op. cit.,* III, 570; *Laws, 1869,* p. 255.

[97] The grounds for divorce included impotence, bigamy, adultery, desertion or habitual drunkenness for two years, extreme cruelty, and conviction for felony or other infamous crime. Act of March 3, 1845, *Revised Statutes, 1845,* p. 196; Act of February 18, 1859, *Laws, 1859,* p. 128; Act of April 5, 1869, *Laws, 1869,* p. 164.

[98] *Chicago Republican,* November 12, 1870; Colbert and Chamberlin, *Chicago and the Great Conflagration,* p. 180.

[99] *Chicago Tribune,* December 4, 1865; Colbert, *op. cit.,* pp. 17, 87. The divorce records of Cook County before 1872 were destroyed by the fire of 1871. However, those for 1872–76 indicated desertion as the cause in the greatest number of applications, followed by adultery, then cruelty. United States, *Marriage and Divorce, 1867–1906* (2 v. Washington, 1908–10), pt. II, p. 753.

Still, some of the restrictions, in spite of opposition, gradually gave way under continued assault, in which men joined their wives and sisters. More and more women entered industry and the professions. But the invasion of women into men's activities was not one to cause alarm. Even some of those men who confessed the prevalent treatment "wrong" still subscribed to the epigram:

> All honor to woman, the sweetheart, the wife,
> The delight of the fireside, by night and by day,
> Who never does anything wrong in her life,
> Except when permitted to have her own way.[100]

Most women, however, accepted and many defended the lot which had befallen them. Over them "Dame Fashion" gained increasing power as the rigors and privations of frontier life receded. Luxury and extravagance rather than necessity could dictate choice more often than in the days which had passed. Laces, silks, and embroideries in a variety of qualities were a token of more comfortable living; and calico and gingham symbolized the circumstances of the common folk.[101] For all, hoop skirts or crinoline were the vogue, a style which finally led inconvenienced males to petition boardinghouse keepers to provide separate tables for ladies and to agitate for wider doorways in buildings to be constructed. By the mid-'sixties, a "Duplex Elliptic or double spring skirt," which permitted the wearer to occupy less space if in a crowded place, was a boon to a woman's companion. A feminine revolt from the dictates of fashion appeared indeed remote. Even the most daring who, in 1851, had adopted the bloomer costume found insults and ridicule more than they could bear. By the end of the 'sixties fashion decreed that skirts have fewer steels and smaller hoops, but ruffles and puffs and bustles did not aid greatly in reducing milady's figure. By 1860, mantles, burnooses with round and square hoods, and ruched, tight sleeves were considered "distingué," and silk hair nets with bangles of gold or silver braid were "all the rage."[102]

---

[100] The Illustrated Chicago News, May 29, 1868.

[101] Silks cost about a dollar a yard, and calico and gingham ranged from six to twelve and a half cents in 1849. See, for example, Daily Democrat, January 1, 16, May 11, 23, 1849.

[102] See in particular The Chicago Magazine of Fashion, Music, and Home Reading, I (April, 1870), 20–22; Oquawka Spectator, April 16, September 19, 1856; Pierce, As Others See Chicago, p. 144; The Press and Tribune, June 10, 1859; Chicago Tribune, June 11, 1862, January 13, 1866; Chicago Daily Democrat, June 19, 25, 28, July 3, 15, November 24, 1851,

While women were generally forced to make their own clothes or to employ a seamstress, they could keep up-to-date through fashion periodicals such as *Godey's Lady's Book,* the *Report of Fashions,* the *Chicago Magazine of Fashion, Music, and Home Reading,* and the *Dressmakers' and Milliners' Guide.*[103] Lectures on the latest modes could sometimes be heard, and fashion notes and advertisements in the local newspapers educated in the latest styles from Paris. More than their sisters, men could find ready-to-wear clothing probably chiefly produced by local tailors. Fashion shows by the late 'sixties gave the dandy a chance to inspect what was the latest in daytime or evening wear.[104]

For both men and women many beauty aids were advertised. Laird's Bloom of Youth or Liquid Pearl; Hagan's Magnolia Balm to remove tan, freckles, sallowness, ring marks, and moth patches as well as to rid one of a " red, rustic face "; and Ween-Fun, or Chinese Skin Powder promised the bloom of youth to women. Concoctions such as " Depuys — New Perfume — Kiss-Me-Quick," distilled from fragrant tulips, seemed a sure sale, and hair dyes and pomades could be had by both sexes. At the better barber shops genuine bay rum and private combs, shaving cups, and brushes were advertised, where a shave or hair cut cost only ten to fifteen cents.[105]

A variety of foods was available, even more than the pleasing variety which earliest Chicago had boasted. These included fresh fruits

---

April 7, October 25, 1860. By 1868, heavy rolls or coils of braided hair replaced the " waterfalls " previously worn, but in either case a woman's head was by no means small, particularly if she donned her " Pyramid " or " Alpine " hat. Then, as at a later day, fads changed in shoes, especially for those who could afford evening slippers.

[103] The *Report of Fashions* was sold by Field and Benedict in 1852. (*Ibid.,* April 27, 1852.) The *Chicago Magazine of Fashion, Music, and Home Reading* carried full descriptions of the latest styles, most of which were furnished by Field, Leiter and Company. The *Dressmakers' and Milliners' Guide* provided pattern and chart service for three dollars a year. (*The Daily Democratic Press,* May 4, 1855.) In the 'sixties James McCall's *Royal Chart, A System of Cutting Ladies' and Children's Dresses by Measure* served a similar purpose for five dollars. *Chicago Tribune,* January 19, 1868.

[104] In 1871, there were listed 129 clothiers and 244 tailors. The latter number probably included seamstresses and seventeen clothing manufacturers. (Edwards, *Merchants' Census Report, 1871,* pp. 1239, 1240.) Hamlin and Company, Field, Palmer and Leiter, and Ross and Gossage held spring fashion shows. *Chicago Tribune,* April 9, 1868. For a description of correct dress for men see *The Chicago Magazine of Fashion, Music, and Home Reading,* I (April, 1870), 22.

[105] See, for example, *Daily Democrat,* January 4, 6, December 6, 1849, December 4, 1850; *The Daily Democratic Press,* April 19, June 27, 1856; *Chicago Daily Press and Tribune,* July 10, 1858; *Chicago Tribune,* January 9, 1862, October 3, November 24, 1863.

and vegetables in season. Although urban development had not robbed all Chicagoans of their own gardens, many products were imported, especially early season supplies which came from warmer climates. John Wandall's Great Western Fruit Depot, one of the first to engage in the distribution of such imports, was supplanted in the 'sixties by large scale operators including Washington Porter, who in 1869 brought the first whole carload of bananas to Chicago from Panama.[106] During the cold months dried fruits and vegetables and preserved fruits added variety to the usual diet.[107]

Beef, pork, mutton, and game meats such as venison, buffalo, prairie chicken, grouse, and quail graced the menus of hotels and homes, while the use of tripe, because it was inexpensive, increased. Sea foods were common, Chicago epicures by the early 'fifties " luxuriating " in fresh fish three days from the sea,[108] and white fish and trout could be had from the Upper Lakes.

Most of the perishable foods were retailed in the city markets. In 1849 there were three, at each of which butchers had their stalls. As the city grew, independent meat shops multiplied, 170 supplying the populace in 1871.[109] Trade in fish also kept the stallholders busy. At the same time the fruit and vegetable business shifted from the markets to outside dealers.

Milk in the early days had arrived principally on the hoof, the cows being driven morning and evening to the homes of owners by a member of the family or by a boy on horseback hired for twenty-five cents a week. Then the railroad began to destroy ruralism, and, if they wished, dwellers of the city as early as 1853 could buy milk shipped in by the Galena Railroad, soon to be called "the Milky Way."[110] In June, 1868, it was reported that Chicago consumed 38,400 quarts of milk daily. City dairies furnished about a thousand

---

[106] Pierce, A History of Chicago, I, 200–1; Inter Ocean, A History of Chicago, pp. 460–61. See pp. 48, 111. Wandall's name was sometimes given as Wandell.

[107] Daily Democrat, January 6, March 15, 1849, February 16, April 27, 1852, January 5, 1860.

[108] Illinois State Register, November 20, 1851.

[109] The establishment of meat shops at places outside the city markets was permitted by law in 1851. The butchers were required to take out licenses. Chicago, Revised Charter and Ordinances, 1851, p. 153; Edwards, Merchants' Census Report, 1871, p. 1240.

[110] Chicago Daily Democrat, June 26, 1850; The Daily Democratic Press, September 25, 1852, February 26, 1853; Chicago Daily Press and Tribune, July 28, 1858. The last seven months of 1854, 27,338 gallons of milk were brought to Chicago by the Galena. It retailed at six cents a quart. Weekly Chicago Democrat, January 20, 1855.

gallons; the rest was shipped in from countryside dairies.[111] But as the number of owners of cows decreased, drawbacks to the handy door to door service became more obvious, for the milk was often reported sour or watered,[112] and its purity was questioned when slops from such places as distilleries provided the food for the cows.[113]

Although many foods common at a later day were still classed as luxuries, ice cream, punch, nuts, and candies were among the delicacies available. Chewing gum had already made its appearance, a popular brand being the spruce gum manufactured by Curtis and Perkins of Bangor, Maine, advertised to clean and preserve the teeth and impart " a delicious fragrance " to the breath. Its use was unsuccessfully recommended in the place of " the filthy weed " for those who must chew, but an increasing number of tobacconists indicated that entreaties of such nature did not affect the growing number of purchasers of cigars, tobacco, and snuff. It may be, however, that these appeals to supplant tobacco by other products and the prevailing opposition of many to its use kindled the ingenuity of producers to bring out cigars advertised to put to rout such dread diseases as cholera.[114]

In a climate where the thermometer could for days hover around a hundred degrees, the preservation of foods was a problem of considerable magnitude. At an early day iceboxes were used by those who could afford to purchase ice, in the winter taken from the Calumet River and Calumet Lake and occasionally from lakes and bays of Wisconsin, from Mackinaw, and other northerly points. Ice from the contaminated water within the basin of the Illinois Central breakwater and the Chicago River was at times sold to disgusted consumers.[115]

111 *Chicago Tribune,* June 6, 1868.

112 *Prairie Farmer,* XIII (August, 1853), 317.

113 *Weekly Chicago Democrat,* April 30, 1853. In 1858, J. H. Wanzer advertised the purity of his product. *Chicago Daily Press and Tribune,* July 28, 1858. See pp. 335–36 for attempts of the city government to regulate practices.

114 In addition to the Chicago newspapers, 1848–71, for preceding sections see " Chicago in 1856," *Putnam's Monthly Magazine,* VII (June, 1856), 606–13; *Chicago Daily Democrat,* December 19, 1850; Annual Statements and Reports of the Board of Trade. By 1871, there were 290 cigar manufacturers and dealers, 16 wholesalers and retailers of cigars, and 26 tobacco manufacturers and wholesalers. (Edwards, *Merchants' Census Report, 1871,* pp. 1239, 1240.) " Anti-cholera camphorated cigars " appeared in 1849. *Chicago Daily Democrat,* July 10, 1849.

115 *Chicago Tribune,* February 10, 1863, July 18, 1868; *Chicago Daily Democrat,* January 10, May 19, 1851, January 21, 1852; Andreas, *History of Chicago,* III, 337–38.

The variety of foods which Chicagoans of the 'fifties and 'sixties might have did not guarantee, however, freshness, good quality, and careful cooking. Visitors to the city complained that the fish of the Upper Lakes was coarse and that meats were either almost raw or swimming in grease; and Chicagoans themselves held that much of the cooking done in the city was "only a few degrees removed from the savages" that had been driven "off the soil."[116] Even lectures and cooking schools to promote the education of cooks did not effect desired improvements, for attendance, on the whole, seemed to be from "the first families" where meals were less subject to criticism.[117] Lack of moderation in eating and ignorance as to the proper balance of foods and as to food combinations demanded a toll in digestive upsets, for which, however, there were advertised innumerable cures.[118]

Frequently, costs determined the selection of foods and made for an endless monotony in the average family's meals, most of which were prepared by an already heavily burdened mother. From 1860 to 1864, for example, some cuts of beef and ham had jumped 100 per cent in price, forcing the poor man's family to stick to mutton.[119] Consumers of butter suffered even greater levies on their purses, paying twelve cents a pound in the winter of 1853 but as much as forty-five cents in July, 1864, the latter approximating the cost in New York at the same time.[120] Eggs in the winter of 1864 cost fifty cents a dozen because farmers could not reach market, and the staple, potatoes, reached a dollar a bushel under the influence of wartime inflation.[121] Similar fluctuations, of course, attended prices of other necessities, just as in the case of imported fruits and luxury foods

[116] *Chicago Tribune,* July 26, 1865; Pierce, *As Others See Chicago,* pp. 144, 162.

[117] *Chicago Tribune,* October 16, 1866.

[118] Such were Kennedy's Medical Discovery (*ibid.,* November 13, 1860), or Sands' Sarsaparilla. *Daily Democrat,* January 4, 1849.

[119] In 1853, the best cuts of beef were ten cents a pound, and in 1861 the price was about the same. By 1864, beef steaks ranged from fifteen to twenty-two cents. Hams from 1860 to 1864 left the ten- or twelve-cent class and reached as much as twenty-five cents, while mutton cost thirteen and twenty cents. *Weekly Chicago Democrat,* February 12, May 7, 1853; *Chicago Tribune,* January 26, June 29, August 17, 1861, July 20, 1864.

[120] Quoted as part of family weekly budgets in Commons, *A Documentary History of American Industrial Society,* IX, 67, 69. See also Colby, *Our Family,* p. 191.

[121] *Chicago Tribune,* February 5, 8, 1864. In 1853, eggs reached a high of fifteen cents. (*Weekly Chicago Democrat,* February 12, 1853.) In 1860, eggs were quoted at ten cents. (*Chicago Daily Democrat,* November 1, 1860.) In the winter of 1853, potatoes ranged from sixty-two and one-half to seventy-five cents a bushel. *Chicago Weekly Democrat,* November 1, 1860; *Chicago Tribune,* January 26, 1861.

in general. By 1864 oranges had reached $1.25 a dozen, a price which completely excluded them as a part of the poor man's diet. Sugar increases reflected also the effects of wartime influences, a condition which seemed plausible enough. But Chicagoans found it hard to understand why vegetables and fruits were sometimes more expensive than in eastern cities. Realists were forced, in accounting for these price increases, to acknowledge the effect of speculation as well as that of poor roads and similar factors.[122]

For those who must live in one of the many boardinghouses which could be found along the tree-lined streets of Chicago, the same determinants for food prices, to which rental expense was sometimes added, entered into consideration. In 1853, board and lodging could be had for $2.25 to $3.00 weekly for a single workingman according to accommodations and distance from the central part of the city, but by mid-'sixties the cost hovered about $5.00 a week.[123]

For transients, coffee houses, restaurants, and hotels furnished accommodations ranging from the more elaborate and well-managed service of the Tremont and Sherman to that of those patronized chiefly by immigrants.[124] By 1858, Horace Greeley pleased Chicagoans, ever on the alert to hear praises of their city, when he declared that there were at least half a dozen hotels better than New York could boast of prior to the opening of the Astor.[125]

Even with increasing numbers, boardinghouses and hotels often could not care for the crowds of visitors to the city, some of whom had to take refuge in private homes or be satisfied with hotels where dormitory arrangements for sleeping prevailed. Here the lack of privacy may have seemed hard enough to bear, but having to sleep beneath a buffalo robe swarming with " living creatures " was often the crowning indignity of all. Greasy and badly cooked foods served

---

[122] In 1861, oranges could be bought for twenty-five to forty cents a dozen. *Ibid.*, January 26, June 29, 1861, July 20, 1864.

[123] See, for example, not only the Chicago newspapers but *Oquawka Spectator*, especially issues of November 9, 1853, December 4, 1857; also *Weekly Chicago Democrat*, February 19, 1853; *Chicago Tribune*, March 8, 1866.

[124] The better restaurants or " eating saloons " generally served on marble-topped tables and had a varied menu which included imported wines. The quick lunch appeared in the 'fifties. By 1871, there were 112 restaurants and 80 hotels listed. *Daily Democrat*, January 1, 16, June 23, 1849, September 3, 1852; *The Daily Democratic Press*, November 20, 1854, July 7, September 27, October 30, 1855; Edwards, *Merchants' Census Report, 1871*, pp. 1239–40.

[125] *Chicago Daily Press and Tribune*, December 28, 1858.

on dishes rinsed in long leaden sinks and wiped with soiled linen, the parlor, where the ubiquitous spittoon was not always used as it should have been, and where black beetles, ants, and other animals passed their lives undisturbed, gave to these dollar-a-day hotels a reputation none too enviable. Here, particularly in the 'fifties, could frequently be found Irish and Scotch immigrants. French traders and Mexicans mingled with adventurers from the far-away sections of the United States as they paused momentarily in this crossroads of east to west travel.[126]

This picture of accommodations for the stranger within Chicago's gates appeared the more drab in contrast to that of the Tremont with its five stories, in 1850 the highest brick building in the city, so high indeed that it seemed " to scrape acquaintance with the clouds." Furnishings alleged to have cost $30,000, mantles of Egyptian marble, stucco " elegantly done " by Chicago artists, transoms over the doors to improve ventilation, and both lower and upper sashes of the windows " hung on pullies " to be opened or closed at will seemed the quintessence of comfort and elegance. Damask curtains lined with silk, rosewood and mahogany chairs in the parlors, drinking fountains in the halls, steam counters in the kitchen, bedrooms so well furnished that a bachelor would " never miss the comforts of home," not to mention a Jackson Annunciator and speaking tube in each room, commended the Tremont to the well-to-do. By 1855, steam heat was introduced, which made possible the opening of parlors in winter which hitherto had been closed at that season, and the next year a bulletin board in the lobby made available up-to-date telegraphic dispatches on important events.[127]

Throughout the 'fifties the Sherman House offered similar comforts. In 1860, a new building of six stories took the crown from the Tremont, being eighty-four feet high. The Palmer House, opened

---

[126] *Chicago Daily Democrat*, June 28, 1849, May 24, 1852; *Weekly Chicago Democrat*, May 28, 1853; *The Press and Tribune*, April 6, 1860; *Chicago Tribune*, December 4, 1865; [Isabella Lucy (Bird) Bishop], *The Englishwoman in America* (London, 1856), quoted in Pierce, *As Others See Chicago*, pp. 142–45. As in the 'thirties and 'forties trains or boats were met by runners and wagons. (Villard, *Memoirs, 1835–1900*, I, 24.) This was particularly true of hotels for immigrants. Among hotels for such patrons was a French hotel, opened in 1851 on State Street. (*Chicago Daily Democrat*, June 19, 1851.) An immigrant hotel was conducted in 1856 by Henry C. Meyer at what was later Haymarket Square. Mrs. Bertha M. Severin, *Autobiography* (*Ms.* Chicago Historical Society).

[127] *Chicago Daily Democrat*, November 15, 17, 1849, July 18, 19, September 30, 1850; *The Daily Democratic Press*, November 6, 1855, March 20, 1856.

in September, 1870, acclaimed the most elegant up to that time in Chicago although not the largest, boasted a telegraphic fire alarm in each room and a fire hose on each floor, as well as huge tanks of water on the roof always ready to fight fire. Small wonder was it that these accommodations could command $4.50 a day by the mid-'sixties, a price which averaged from one to two dollars higher than charges in the smaller hotels of the city.[128]

Those living at home, to whom economic well-being had come, also had more physical comforts than in the past. Though most houses were warmed by stoves and open fireplaces, central steam and hot-air heating could be found. By 1854, Walworth and Company of Boston had established a branch office in Chicago to pipe through buildings the " exhausted steam " from steam engines for pumping and other purposes, and by the 'sixties hot-air furnaces and other devices for central heating were advertised as considerably improved over similar appliances of the 'fifties.[129]

Wood brought by boats from the Lower Lakes or from the interior by wagon and eventually by rail provided fuel to most Chicagoans, although coal could be procured from southern Illinois at first by way of the Illinois and Michigan Canal and also during the period of navigation by boat from Cleveland and Erie. The coming of the railroad aided in keeping a supply sufficient to care for needs, a condition unknown in an earlier day. To some extent this improved carriage led to a greater use of coal rather than wood for heating purposes.[130]

To the earlier use of cod, lard, sperm, and other oils which furnished fuel to light the dwellings of the day, kerosene was added.[131]

---

[128] Among other hotels were the Baltic House, Lake House, United States Hotel, Foster House, Briggs House, Metropolitan Hotel, and the Michigan Avenue Hotel built in 1870 by the Inter-Oceanic Hotel Company. *Daily Democrat,* May 19, June 15, 1849, August 27, 1860; *The Daily Democratic Press,* May 20, 1854, February 24, October 10, 1855, June 25, 1856; *Chicago Tribune,* December 4, 1865, August 4, September 8, 27, 1870.

[129] *The Daily Democratic Press,* May 11, August 24, December 12, 1854; *Chicago Tribune,* August 27, 1864, July 26, 1865; " Warming and Ventilating Houses," *Chicago Magazine,* I (June, 1857), 355-58. The first building in Chicago said to have been heated by steam was the Lake View House.

[130] *Chicago Daily Democrat,* July 30, 1849, September 19, November 1, 1860; *Oquawka Spectator,* January 4, 1854; *Chicago Daily Democratic Press,* August 27, 1857; *Chicago Tribune,* July 15, 1861; Chicago Daily Democratic Press, *Sixth Annual Review, 1857,* p. 21. See pp. 115-16, 181-82.

[131] Rosin oil was much discussed in 1855, and a company was formed to promote its use in lighting. (*Oquawka Spectator,* April 3, 1855.) In 1861, cod, sperm, and lard retailed at

Business houses, public buildings, and some of the main thoroughfares, not to mention the homes of the wealthy, as early as 1850 were
illumined sometimes by gas, made at first from the coal of the La Salle
mines. By mid-'fifties gas was proposed as a substitute for wood and
coal for culinary purposes, although its actual use was postponed for
about thirty years.[132]

These physical comforts represented what an advancing urbanization was bringing no more clearly than did the facilities for recreation. Survivals of the preceding generation still carried their portion
of pleasure, but they were more and more giving way to commercial-
ized forms of amusement. An increasing number of sedentary occupations led to the promotion of gymnasium associations to which
men in the early 'fifties and some women in the late 'sixties willingly subscribed.[133] Although dancing and theater-going were still
frowned upon by some, they proved alluring divertissements to
others.[134]

Games and other pastimes sometimes met similar disapproval, although not condemned as harshly as the " vices." Bowling, billiards,
rifle contests, and match games, if operated in connection with a
liquor saloon, as was often the case, were looked upon by moralists
as a waste of time and eventually leading down the dark path of
sin. Horse racing, in spite of the opposition, had many devotees,
and the courses at Garden City and Brighton were well patronized
by the mid-'fifties. Purses from $100 to $1,125 were offered for the
winner of a mile heat, the general run. " Racing matinees " became
popular. In 1871 the Dexter Park Driving Association leased the
park of that name for ten years and distributed in premium money
over $23,000 at its first meet.[135]

---

approximately $1.00 a gallon, kerosene and whale oil at $1.25 a gallon, and olive oil at $2.00
a gallon. *Chicago Tribune,* January 26, 1861.

[132] Rice, *75 Years of Gas Service in Chicago,* pp. 4, 9, 31–32; *Oquawka Spectator,* January 4, 1856.

[133] *Chicago Daily Democrat,* August 26, 1852, June 1, 1860; *The Daily Democratic
Press,* April 5, 1854; *Chicago Tribune,* January 7, 1861, October 8, 19, December 20, 1866,
January 28, 1868, December 4, 1870.

[134] *Watchman of the Prairies,* February 29, 1848, February 26, March 5, 1850; *The Interior,* September 21, 1871; *Northwestern Christian Advocate,* January 12, February 9, 1853;
The Advance, November 19, 1868, May 12, 26, 1870.

[135] *Chicago Daily Press and Tribune,* July 7, 1858; *The Daily Democratic Press,* June 6,
1855; *Chicago Daily Democrat,* October 20, 1860; *Chicago Tribune,* August 5, 26, 1863, June
27, September 14, 1864, April 27, July 26, 28, 1865, August 6, 18, 1866, August 22, 1867,
March 25, October 4, 1868.

Prize fighting, despite an unsavory reputation and the open disapproval of press and pulpit, proved an occasional attraction. " Prize fights between men are beastly exhibitions," declared the *Tribune,* "but there is an unutterable loathsomeness in the worse brutality of abandoned, wretched women beating each other almost to nudity, for the amusement of a group of blackguards, even lower in the scale of humanity than the women themselves." The rowdiness which accompanied these meets led to frequent raids by the police, whose activities eventually drove the sport across the state line to Indiana, to which special trains carried spectators.[136]

Even cruder and more brutal than the prize fighting of the day were the cock fights and the championship contests between dogs which were patronized by underworld characters. Gamblers wagered dollars by the thousands as several hundred of " the flash gentry " raucously cheered battling cocks or canines, as the case might be.[137] In 1868, an exhibition buffalo hunt was staged at the Chicago Equestrian Academy by a traveling show, whose buffalo had lost the use of its forelegs but nevertheless was tormented by two half-breed Spanish Californians with a blanket and a piece of rope.[138] Just as repellent as these evidences of coarseness and emotional depravity was the revelry of the onlookers at exhibitions of rat killing, which took place in pits especially designed for terriers to blot out life in these intrusive rodents which plagued householder, merchant, and pedestrian alike.[139]

Among the most popular diversions were the circuses and animal shows, which as early as 1836 had come to Chicago to dispense enjoyment. Among the sights which entranced Chicagoans were

[136] In 1860, a match between the world's heavyweight champion, John C. Heenan, and a sparring partner, Aaron Jones, took place in Bryan Hall. (*Ibid.,* November 27, 1860, July 2, 16, December 31, 1861, February 16, March 31, 1866, November 20, 1867.) In 1870, to get around a state law a fight between John Keenan and Jem Mace, two well-known pugilists, was promoted at Turner Hall, Clark Street, as a " Grant Musical Festival." The fight was March 18, 1870. (*Ibid.,* May 19, 1870.) The state law passed in 1869 was designed to prevent prize fighting and sparring or boxing exhibitions. Act of March 31, 1869, *Public Laws, 1869,* p. 307.

[137] In a fight in February, 1866, between a Chicago-owned dog and one from Boston, the original stakes were $500 plus gate money, but side bets swelled the amount until about $30,000 were reported to have changed hands. *Chicago Tribune,* February 15, 16, 1866.

[138] *Ibid.,* September 17, 18, 20, 1868. The attendance was said to have been small, only a few Wells Street " roughs " being amused. The proprietors of the Equestrian Academy were so disgusted that they cancelled the lease of the promoters for the last two nights.

[139] *Ibid.,* July 3, 1865, tells of the rats which that year seemed especially numerous under sidewalks, in walls of dwellings and stores — indeed, everywhere.

elephants drawing "the great car of Juggernaut," mechanical curiosities like "the great steam dispenser of discordant music," the calliope, a self-propelled carriage prophesied "to supersede the use of horses," not to mention Tom Thumb, "Mr. Nellis, the man without arms," who loaded and fired pistols with his toes, shot bow and arrow, and played an accordion. In 1853, P. T. Barnum's "Grand Colossal Museum and Menagerie" gave three performances daily, charging thirty cents to adults and fifteen cents to children. Other well-known circuses came also. Mabie's Grand Olympic Arena and United States Circus, the Great Western Railroad Circus, Tyler's Indian Exhibition, John Robinson's Great Circus, and G. F. Bailey and Company's Quadruple Combination Circus and Menagerie were among those which proved particularly enjoyable. Exhibitions, mechanical panoramas or dioramas of such spectacles as the "conflagration" of Moscow, or "a perfect moving and lifelike representation of every incident" of the funeral of Napoleon, contributed to what was considered proper enjoyment.[140]

Tableaux, pantomimes, pageants, ballets, and acrobatic feats afforded pleasure to the same "fashionable circles" that supported the legitimate drama and the opera. Others were entertained by numerous magicians, who declared themselves able to controvert "the laws and regulations of Nature,"[141] or by minstrels who delineated "Negro character," at whose performances one sometimes could enjoy a drink from a bar near by for five cents or a pony of brandy for ten cents.[142]

[140] The calliope, invented in 1855, came to Chicago in 1857. (*Chicago Daily Democrat*, May 12, 1857.) The self-propelled carriage, called the "Family Steam Carriage," was brought in 1864 by Spaulding and Rogers. It was propelled by a steam motor. (*Chicago Tribune*, October 7, 1864.) The newspapers are filled with items about amusements.

[141] Among the many entertainers and magicians were Signor Blitz with a flock of trained canaries (*Chicago Daily Democrat*, May 20, 24, 1850; *Chicago Tribune*, March 17, 1866, June 16, 1871); Monsieur Adrien (*Chicago Daily Democrat*, June 6, 12, 1850); the "Fakir of Siva," who engaged in spirit rappings (*ibid.*, April 28, 1852); Professor Barton, "the Great Magician, East Indian and Chinese Juggler" (*The Daily Democratic Press*, September 18, 1855); Madame Bosco, "The Original World-Renowned and only Magicienne" (*The Press and Tribune*, July 8, 1859); Robert Heller, the "renowned Illusionist, Master of the Occult Science, Interpreter of Ancient Necromancy, Inventor of Modern Miracles and Originator of the Wonderful and Mysterious Science of SECOND SIGHT" (*Chicago Tribune*, January 6, 1862); Hermann "with his feats of modern magic" (*ibid.*, January 20, 1870); Martin, the "wizard and Ventriloquist." *Ibid.*, March 24, 1871.

[142] The Christy Minstrels visited Chicago in 1855. (*The Daily Democratic Press*, October 1, 1855; *The Press and Tribune*, March 29, 30, 31, April 1, 2, 4, 1859; *Chicago Daily Democrat*, August 15, 1859, March 23, 1860.) This troupe belonged to George Christy and had no connection with E. P. Christy, the original founder of Christy's Minstrels, who re-

Baseball rivaled racing in the popular fancy. By 1860, there were four teams in the city, and by 1866 there were eight times that number, a brief ten years from the day when the first, or Union Base Ball Club, came into being. After the mid-'sixties contests took place with teams in the East and so stimulated interest that in 1870 the Chicago White Stockings were organized " not only to beat anything in the West " but to " indicate Chicago's importance as the first city on the continent, by bidding defiance to any and all clubs in America." [143]

In 1865 the Northwestern Baseball Association was established. A movement for uniform rules and better organization among the clubs within the city had been started in the summer of 1858.[144] By 1872 salaries for players on the Chicago professional team ranged from $2,500 down to $1,500,[145] and represented then, as at a later day, the growing commercialization of the sport although amateurs got their measure of fun in playing. Intercollegiate contests were held between the universities of Chicago and Northwestern and in 1870, a tournament to determine the championship among local amateurs drew as enthusiastic applause as did the professional games. Cricket and quoits, just as in earlier days, afforded pleasure to spectators and

---

tired in 1854. After George Christy's death, the company was taken over by R. M. Hooley, S. C. Campbell, and G. W. Griffin and the name changed to Hooley and Campbell's Minstrels.

[143] In 1860, the baseball teams were called the Atlantic, Columbia, Excelsior, and Olympic. (Smith & DuMoulin, *Directory, 1859–60,* Appendix, p. 8; *Chicago Tribune,* December 10, 1866.) The Columbia Club was organized in the spring of 1859. (*The Press and Tribune,* May 21, 1859; *The Daily Democratic Press,* August 12, 1856; *Chicago Tribune,* November 7, 1868.) Many games were played for the city championship or with teams in places near, but in 1868 the Excelsiors had played teams in Detroit, Cleveland, and Cincinnati. The White Stocking uniform was a white flannel shirt with a contrasting blue " C " on the pocket, bright blue flannel pants, white stockings and shoes. In their first year they visited St. Louis, New Orleans, and Memphis, among other places. They were defeated by the Mutual at New York the next year but beat the Athletics at Philadelphia. At the end of this season Chicago occupied third place. In 1871 they were also at Baltimore. (*Ibid.,* September 27, 1868, April 30, May 7, 14, June 17, 1870, June 6, 10, 13, July 15, 1871; George Wright, *Record of the Boston Base Ball Club* [Boston, 1874], pp. 18, 22.) After 1868 the Brooklyn Atlantics, the Philadelphia Athletics, the Buckeyes, and the Red Stockings from Cincinnati played in Chicago. *Chicago Tribune,* March 20, June 18, 19, 20, 21, July 22, 23, August 12, 1868, July 31, 1869.

[144] *Ibid.,* December 20, 1866; *Chicago Daily Press and Tribune,* July 9, 1858. The regulations which had been adopted by the New York teams and considered in Chicago required the ball to be ten inches in circumference and weigh six ounces. It had to be pitched and not thrown. The bat was to be round and not over two and a half inches in diameter. The bases were to be placed at each corner of a square, each side of which measured thirty yards. The pitcher was to stand fifteen yards from the home base.

[145] Calvin G. Stambaugh to George M. Moulton, October 8, 1871 (*Ms.* Chicago Historical Society).

amateur participants. All these games suffered condemnation if bet-
ting were indulged in, although the mantle of respectability fell upon
amusements in connection with fairs, benefit performances, and the
ever-popular summer-time picnic.[146]

The celebration of national holidays offered another outlet for exu-
berant spirits. On July Fourth Chicagoans attentively listened to oratory which was pointed to an American solidarity of thought and
punctuated by displays of fireworks. Men, women, and children forgot trouble in dances, excursions and picnics, baseball games, horse
racing, and balloon ascensions, the salvos of booming cannon and
the ringing of church bells; military drills and reviews mirrored the
American fondness of parade and offered to strangers, country cous-
ins, and curiosity-seekers, who mingled with Chicagoans, the thrill-
ing spectacle of uniformed men tramping rhythmically down the
streets.[147] In 1868, May 30 became " All-Heroes Day " by mandate
of John A. Logan, commander-in-chief of the Grand Army of the
Republic. But no holiday, besides the Fourth, seems to have had the
support accorded Washington's birthday, when processions, balls,
and banquets gave Americans and aliens alike an opportunity to pay
homage to " the Father of Our Country." [148] In addition to such patriotic celebrations were, of course, the festivities of Christmas, the calls
of New Year's, and the peculiarly American Thanksgiving. Gradually the banks, the post office, customhouse, and public offices closed
their doors to business on these days, and even some storekeepers restrained temporarily their consuming desire for profits.[149]

Such varied offerings left people free to choose the way in which
they might spend their hours of leisure. Besides other forms of re-

[146] *Chicago Tribune,* December 11, 1860, February 21, 1861, January 18, 1867, August 5,
1868, September 26, 1869, February 10, September 7, 9, 29, 1870; *The Daily Democratic
Press,* January 6, 1857; *The Workingman's Advocate,* June 25, 1870; Pierce, *A History of
Chicago,* I, 207–8.

[147] *Chicago Daily Democrat,* June 29, July 6, 1849, June 26, 1850, June 29, July 7, 1852,
July 2, 3, 1860; *The Daily Democratic Press,* July 6, 1855; *Chicago Tribune,* July 4, 1861,
July 2, 4, 1862, July 6, 1863, July 2, 3, 4, 6, 1864, July 4, 1865, July 5, 1868, July 4, 1871.

[148] *Ibid.,* June 2, 1868, May 29, 30, 31, 1869; *Daily Democrat,* February 23, 1849, February 22, 23, 1850, February 20, 1852; *The Daily Democratic Press,* February 23, 1855.

[149] *Chicago Daily Democrat,* December 24, 1849, December 24, 30, 31, 1850, November
25, 1852; *Chicago Tribune,* November 29, 1860, November 30, 1861, December 28, 1864,
December 25, 1866, January 1, 1870; *The Daily Democratic Press,* November 30, 1854, November 29, December 24, 1855, January 3, 1856; *Weekly Chicago Democrat,* November 5,
1853. The *Tribune* editor estimated that $340,000 had been expended for Christmas gifts
in 1863. *Chicago Tribune,* January 5, 1864.

laxation there were many clubs and societies. While many of these organizations were designed to give release from the daily round of business, there were others primarily focused upon the perpetuation of special points of view. It was, as de Tocqueville observed of Americans in the 'thirties, a time of associations of a thousand kinds other than the purely political. Indeed, in Chicago, as elsewhere, point was given to the comments of this keen observer of the American scene as one saw societies constantly springing up to promote joint action. Some were ephemeral, but others like the Ancient and Honorable Fraternity of Free and Accepted Masons and the Independent Order of Odd Fellows had their roots firmly embedded by mid-century, expanding appreciably their membership rolls during the next twenty years.[150] The Independent Order of the Sons of Malta, the United Ancient Order of Druids, the Independent Order of Chaldeans, and the Independent Order of the Sons of Herman claimed the allegiance of a smaller number than did the Masons and Odd Fellows, and at least the first had passed from the list of active secret fraternities after a few years.[151] College societies and social clubs, such as the Chicago Club for men, sometimes played an important part in the lives of members, and an Old Settlers Society in the 'fifties, followed by the Old Settlers Society of 1871, appeared an anomaly in a city less than forty years old.[152]

But the deeper values of leisure were not realized by the generation

[150] Halpin, *Directory, 1865–66*, " City and County Record," pp. xli-xliii; Edwards, *Directory, 1870*, " City and County Record," pp. 938–41.

[151] Tanner, Halpin and Co., *D. B. Cooke & Co.'s Directory, 1858*, p. 485; Halpin, *Directory, 1863–64*, " City and County Register," p. xxxiv. The Sons of Malta died during the period of the Civil War. (Arthur Preuss, comp., *A Dictionary of Secret and Other Societies* [St. Louis, 1924], p. 442.) The first " grove " of the Order of Druids, an importation from England, was organized in Chicago in November, 1860, with twenty-six members. By late 1864 there were over eight hundred members. (*The Chicago Times*, November 22, 1864.) Myron Lodge No. 1 of the Old Free Order of Chaldea was incorporated in 1851, and the Sons of Herman in 1863. From the names of the incorporators, it may be inferred that both were chiefly German organizations. (Act of February 17, 1851, *Private Laws, 1851*, p. 298; *Private Laws, 1863*, pp. 33–34; Halpin, *Directory, 1863–64*, " City and County Register," p. xxxiv.) Another German fraternity was the German order of Harugari, two Chicago lodges of 1863 having grown to nine in 1871 with a grand lodge and a special lodge for members of highest rank. *Ibid.;* Edwards, *Directory, 1871*, p. 51.

[152] *Chicago Tribune*, January 12, 1866, January 25, February 10, 1871; *The Christian Times*, November 7, 1855; Edward T. Blair, *A History of the Chicago Club* (Chicago, 1898), pp. 13–20; Act of March 25, 1869, *Private Laws, 1869*, II, 677. Among other social clubs in the earlier 'seventies was that called " The Grasshoppers " devoted primarily to dancing. Among its members were the socially prominent Honorés, Badgers, Wallers, Rogers, Krieghs, and Hayes. Carter H. Harrison to N. Thomasson, January 7, 1923, *Terrace Row Papers*.

of Chicagoans who during the 'fifties and 'sixties had, on the whole, more opportunities for enjoyment than had men in the 'thirties and 'forties. And there were many whose labors were so taxing and whose work hours were so long that little inclination for play was left in their tired bodies. The lights and shadows which were reflected during the 'fifties and 'sixties deepened as time went on and the urban body grew strong and matured. The score of years which followed mid-century brought with them many of the amenities of life, and in spite of contradictions civilization moved forward.

CHAPTER XII

THE PASSING OF OLD CHICAGO

As THE shrill-voiced whistle of the " Pioneer " sounded the departure of the first steam railway locomotive from Chicago, it heralded the end of land isolation and signalized Chicago's metamorphosis from town to city. The twenty or more years which followed that momentous event were crowded. In them Chicago became the leading entrepôt of the Middle Valley and a distributor of news information and other agencies of enlightenment. Great lines of rail stretched to market and reached into the outlying region to garner foods for hungry urban dwellers.

Toil was the price paid to accomplish these ends — toil sometimes so skillfully directed that vast fortunes became the order of the day in spite of a panic in 1857 and a depression after the Civil War. Speculation in lands rendered rich returns to the many who dared gamble on the future. Business was prosecuted without cessation, and in general society seemed immersed in secularism. Critics of the existing system complained that the sympathy of the old and the respect of the young were given the successful man of business, and that religion and the other refinements of life received but scanty homage. From bootblack to hack driver, one writer caustically declared, Chicagoans put on " real-estate airs, and a general talent for blowing " was " the highest Chicago merit." [1]

But America possessed no more interesting city than Chicago. Down its streets passed the recently arrived immigrant, pack on back,

[1] " Chicago," *Frank Leslie's Illustrated Newspaper*, II (July 12, 1856), 71.

CHICAGO FIRE OF OCTOBER, 1871

This view is from the West Division showing the fire on the South Side. In
the foreground is Randolph Street bridge over which crowds were fleeing
westward. The Lake Street bridge is at left center.

hands clutching household utensils and other possessions. Behind him trudged his children, each with his load, followed by the mother, often with a child in her arms. Occasionally they passed through this crossroads of the nation to points beyond; frequently they stayed in Chicago with their fellow aliens, who made up about one half of the population of the city from 1850 to 1870. Those who remained and took up the task of earning a living gradually adopted the ways of Americans. They often provided the man power necessary to the growing city, and sometimes they attained wealth and leadership, particularly in politics.

But political and economic dominance, on the whole, was in the hands of the native stock, scarcely any of whom had been born in Chicago. New captains of industry and business, such as Potter Palmer, Marshall Field, Cyrus H. McCormick, and Benjamin P. Hutchinson, had come upon the stage. They were, in a very real sense, the beneficiaries of the versatile Ogden, the bold and venturesome Hubbard, and the enterprising Newberry, soon to depart from active participation in the building of a metropolitan empire.

The inhabitants of this feverishly-moving Chicago, although not altogether inured to urban ways of life, had at hand many of the refinements and pleasures which the city of the day afforded. As early as the 'fifties the wealthy scattered during the summer for points of recreation or for their summer homes in the East, and travel abroad dignified still further the few who were seeking the culture of Europe.

But Chicago was not a beautiful city. There could be few fine buildings, wide promenades, and well-laid streets while Chicagoans were so hurried. The city had sprung up in less than a generation, and city beautification takes longer than that. To be sure, some attention had been paid these matters, and where improvements had been made gratification and pride followed. When plate glass windows were put in store fronts in the early 'fifties, the press remarked on the significance of the change and in doing so noted not only the commercial value of better displays but the improved appearance of the buildings. In the 'sixties marble fronts, mansard roofs, and some external decoration were the boast of the owners of a few business houses, and more than one or two stories as early as the 'fifties were heralded as the arrival of urban maturity. But even in the district which had the spectacular new Palmer House and Grand Pacific Hotel, there remained, in 1871, a substantial proportion of wooden buildings; and of the stone and brick structures in Chicago most had wood interiors.[2]

Along Michigan and Wabash avenues wealthy Chicagoans in the 'fifties were building new and expensive residences, and others were moving further into the South Division, while the homes of the well-to-do could also be found in the northern part of the city. But incongruities existed. Alongside the sections where the dwellings of the rich rose in impressive orderliness were workmen's cottages, uninteresting in design and uniform in appearance, with vegetable gardens and barns close at hand.

Adjacent were the insanitary, ramshackle houses of the poor, the abode of those on the lowest rung of the ladder of economic success. As early as the mid-'fifties cabins in the West Division, some only ten by sixteen feet, were shelters of families with five or more children, whose hospitality was often extended to at least one dog and a cat, to pigs, chickens, and a cow. By 1865 there were many more like this, lying near each other in the areas known as " Kilgubbin," " Kansas," " Healy Slough," and " Conley's Patch." [3]

Some recognized the hazards in a town made of pine, a city of boards and shingles. Not only had there been criticism of such fire traps, but there had been recommendations that buildings unsafe for human habitation be torn down and that no more poor houses be put up.[4] But Chicagoans paid little heed to forecasts and admonitions even in a summer such as that of 1871, when heat and drought had left the ground parched, an invitation to the holocaust soon to come.

On Saturday night, October 7, about ten o'clock, fire broke out in the West Division between Canal and Clinton streets and north of Van Buren. From wooden shacks to lumber yards, planing mills, and paper-box factory, the flames spread with deadly precision, mowing down property worth $1,000,000. It was many hours before bat-

[2] *The Daily Democratic Press*, October 5, 1852; Pierce, *As Others See Chicago*, p. 183; Mabel McIlvaine, ed., *Reminiscences of Chicago during the Great Fire* (Chicago, 1915), p. xxi; James W. Sheahan and George P. Upton, *The Great Conflagration* (Chicago, 1871), p. 51.

[3] *Chicago Tribune*, March 15, 1861, August 7, 1865, August 22, 1866; Board of Health, *Reports, 1867–69*, p. 171. See pp. 139–41, 145.

[4] *Chicago Tribune*, March 19, 1866, September 10, 1871; *The Chicago Times*, May 8, 1869.

tling firemen brought the conflagration under control; and along the docks lining the river, the coal which smouldered throughout Sunday was indisputable proof of the obstinacy of this enemy of man.

Scarcely had citizens recovered from the fear of the fire of the seventh, when about nine-thirty on the evening of the eighth a new fire broke out in the O'Leary barn on De Koven Street on the West Side, from which it rapidly spread. Legend has held Mrs. O'Leary's cow responsible for kicking over the lamp which ignited straw in the barn. But Mrs. O'Leary later denied the charge. Some laid the blame upon a group of Irish holding high festival in the neighborhood, who wished milk for punch and, while visiting Mrs. O'Leary's cow, upset the lamp which they had carried to give light in their quest for refreshment. Some saw in the disaster the plot of the lawless who wished to loot and rob the helpless. Others held the Communists responsible, while still others looked upon the disaster as the judgment of an angry God upon a wicked city, a modern Sodom and Gomorrah. But proof in no case was established, and the origin of the fire of October 8 is still unknown.

Whatever the cause, fire soon swept toward the river through the narrow streets and alleys of the West Division unchecked by the firemen, tired from their taxing labors of the day before and unable to fight effectively because of damaged equipment. To the northeast shot the flames, offering the vain hope that when they reached the area burned the day before they might be stayed. About midnight they leaped the river at Adams Street and laid in ruins the poverty-stricken, crime-filled "Conley's Patch"; a gas explosion plunged the South Division into darkness; and the flames raced onward to the south until checked by the use of gunpowder under the direction of General Phil Sheridan.

As the billows of fire were rolling over the South Division, the Oriental Flouring Mills on the West Side used their steam force pump to throw a constant stream of water on the building and in so doing saved the entire district. But in other parts of the city the steady onset " seemed to melt like lead " the buildings before it.[5] At about half past two Monday morning the Court House was reached; soon tongues of flame ate their way across the stationary bridge at

[5] Gilbert Merrill to Mosher, October 27, 1871, George Howland to S. H. Peabody, October 14, 1871, Hon. Thomas Hoyne, *Narrative of the Great Fire of Chicago,* p. 4 (*Mss.* Chicago Historical Society).

State Street to find new fuel in the North Western Railroad yards, the McCormick Reaper Works, the grain elevators, lumberyards, and the residences beyond. Then the castellated waterworks, the last defense against ravage, was gutted, and the North Division, with the exception of the palatial home of Mahlon D. Ogden, later the site of Newberry Library, was reduced to ashes.

Chicago was now literally a city of the earth. Even the block pavements had turned to charcoal. The material loss was estimated at about $196,000,000; at least three hundred persons are thought to have perished; and irreplaceable records and priceless possessions had disappeared. The symbols of the aspirations and the achievements of an industrious citizenry were now gone.

APPENDIX

PLACE OF BIRTH OF NATIVE-BORN CHICAGOANS BY SECTION, 1850–1870 [1]

	Old Northwest			Middle Atlantic			New England			South and Border States [a]		
	1850	1860	1870	1850	1860	1870	1850	1860	1870	1850	1860	1870
Number..................	6,635	31,462	101,284	4,683	13,906	30,410	1,861	6,574	13,752	495	1,939	7,303
Per Cent of Total Population......	22.14	28.79	33.88	15.63	12.73	10.17	6.21	6.02	4.60	1.65	1.77	2.44
Per Cent of Native-born Population	48.12	57.58	65.59	33.96	25.45	19.69	13.50	12.03	8.91	3.61	3.55	4.73

	States West of Mississippi River			Miscellaneous			Totals		
	1850	1860	1870	1850	1860	1870	1850 [b]	1860	1870
Number..................	19	138	1,589		617	82	13,693	54,636	154,420
Per Cent of Total Population......	.06	.13	.53		.565	.03	45.70	50.005	51.65
Per Cent of Native-born Population	.14	.25	1.03		1.13	.05			

[1] Based on figures in United States, *Statistical View . . . Being a Compendium of the Seventh Census* (J. D. B. DeBow, comp. Washington, 1854), p. 399, *Eighth Census, 1860,* "Population," p. 613, *Ninth Census, 1870,* I, "Population," 380–85.

[a] Includes Maryland, Texas, Arkansas, and Missouri.

[b] An additional 588 persons, or 1.96 per cent of the total population, were of unknown nativity.

PLACE OF BIRTH. FOREIGN-BORN CHICAGOANS, 1850–1870 [1]

	Germany [a]			Ireland			England			Wales		Scotland		
	1850	1860	1870	1850	1860	1870	1850	1860	1870	1860	1870	1850	1860	1870
Number	5,094	22,230	59,299	6,096	19,889	39,988	1,883 [b]	4,354	10,027	222	565	610	1,641	4,197
Per Cent of Total Population	17.00	20.35	19.83	20.35	18.20	13.37	6.28	3.98	3.35	.20	.19	2.04	1.50	1.40
Per Cent of Foreign-born Population	32.48	40.70	41.02	38.87	36.41	27.66	12.01	7.97	6.94	.41	.39	3.89	3.00	2.90

	Norway		Sweden		Denmark		Holland		France			Italy			Belgium	
	1860	1870	1860	1870	1860	1870	1860	1870	1850	1860	1870	1850	1860	1870	1860	1870
Number	1,313	6,374	816	6,154	150	1,243	305	1,640	234	883	1,418	4	104	552	152	392
Per Cent of Total Population	1.20	2.13	.75	2.06	.14	.42	.28	.55	.78	.81	.47	.01 +	.09	.18	.14	.13
Per Cent of Foreign-born Population	2.40	4.41	1.49	4.26	.27	.86	.56	1.13	1.71	1.62	.98	.03	.18	.38	.28	.27

	Switzerland		Poland		Russia		British America		Miscellaneous			Totals		
	1860	1870	1860	1870	1860	1870	1860	1870	1850	1860	1870	1850	1860	1870
Number	503	1,226	109	1,205	37	118	1,867	9,648	1,761	49	511	15,682	54,624	144,557
Per Cent of Total Population	.46	.41	.10	.40	.03	.04	1.71	3.23	5.91	.04	.17	52.34	49.995	48.35
Per Cent of Foreign-born Population	.92	.85	.20	.83	.07	.08	3.42	6.67	11.23	.09	.35			

[1] Based on figures in United States, *Statistical View . . . Being a Compendium of the Seventh Census*, p. 399, *Eighth Census, 1860*, "Population," p. 613, *Ninth Census, 1870*, I, "Population," 386–91. The census for 1870 distinguishes also 6,277 Bohemians, a figure included here.

[a] These figures include Austrians.
[b] This figure includes the Welsh.

RAILROAD DIRECTORS IN SELECTED YEARS SHOWING CHICAGOANS AND IMPORTANT FIGURES

(Names in italics indicate participation in two or more of these roads)

1854[1]

Road	Chicago	New York City and State (New York City, unless otherwise noted)	New England (Boston, unless otherwise noted)	Others
Galena and Chicago Union John B. Turner (Chicago) — Pres. Wm. M. Larrabee (Chicago) — Secy. Wm. H. Brown (Chicago) — Treas.	John B. Turner Walter L. Newberry Charles Walker Samuel Howe *Elisha S. Wadsworth* Thomas Dyer Benjamin W. Raymond George Smith Hugh T. Dickey			Thomas D. Robertson (Rockford, Ill.) Dexter A. Knowlton (Freeport, Ill.) Charles S. Hempstead (Galena, Ill.)
Chicago and Aurora J. F. Joy (Detroit) — Pres. I. H. Burch (Chicago) — Treas.	Mark Skinner I. H. Burch C. G. Hammond	A. H. Robbins G. C. Davisson (Albany)		J. F. Joy Henry Ledyard J. W. Brooks (all of Detroit) J. Van Nortwick (Batavia, Ill.)
Chicago and Milwaukee (under construction) *Walter S. Gurnee* (Chicago) — Pres. *A. S. Downs* (Chicago) — Secy.-Treas.	*W. S. Gurnee* *N. B. Judd* *E. S. Wadsworth* E. K. Rogers H. G. Loomis H. A. Tucker		E. G. Howe (Hartford, Conn.)	D. O. Dickenson (Waukegan, Ill.)

[1] Based on Hall & Co., *Directory, 1854-55*, Appendix, pp. 16-18; *Report of the Directors to the Stockholders of the Illinois Central Railroad Company, March 15, 1854* (New York, 1854), p. 2; *Annual Report of the President and Directors to the Stockholders of the Chicago and Rock Island Railroad Co. . . . Dec. 18, 1854* (New York, 1855), p. 2.

RAILROAD DIRECTORS IN SELECTED YEARS SHOWING CHICAGOANS AND IMPORTANT FIGURES (*continued*)

(Names in italics indicate participation in two or more of these roads)

1854[1]

Road	Chicago	New York City and State (New York City, unless otherwise noted)	New England (Boston, unless otherwise noted)	Others
Illinois and Wisconsin Wm. B. Ogden (Chicago) — Pres. Henry Smith (Chicago) — Vice Pres. *A. S. Downs* (Chicago) — Secy.-Treas.	Wm. B. Ogden *W. S. Gurnee* M. D. Ogden G. W. Snow J. C. Walter Geo. Steel J. P. Chapin C. V. Dyer Henry Smith	J. J. Phelps C. Butler	H. Hotchkiss (New Haven) Alfred Smith (Hartford)	
Illinois Central Wm. P. Burrall (New York) — Pres. David A. Neal (Boston) — Vice Pres. John F. Bunce (New York) — Secy. Matthias B. Edgar (New York) — Treas.		Joseph W. Alsop Jonathan Sturges Thos. W. Ludlow Geo. Griswold John F. A. Sanford Leroy M. Wiley Franklin Haven Robert Schuyler Morris Ketchum Wm. P. Burrall Gouverneur Morris (Morrisiana)	David A. Neal	Joel A. Matteson [Gov.] (Springfield, Ill.) *ex officio*
Chicago and Rock Island Henry Farnam (Chicago) — Pres. Nelson D. Elwood (Joliet, Ill.) — Secy. Azariah C. Flagg (New York) — Treas.	Henry Farnam Isaac Cook *Norman B. Judd*	Thomas C. Durant Azariah C. Flagg William Walcott (Utica) Clark Durant (Albany) John Stryker (Rome)	Joseph E. Sheffield (New Haven)	Nelson D. Elwood (Joliet, Ill.) Theron D. Brewster (Peru, Ill.) Lemuel Andrews (Rock Island) Ebenezer Cook (Davenport, Ia.)

1862[1]

Road	Chicago	New York City and State (New York City, unless otherwise noted)	New England (Boston, unless otherwise noted)	Others
Illinois Central W. H. Osborn (New York) — Pres. N. P. Banks (Chicago) — Resident Director W. M. Phillips (New York) — Secy. A. E. Burnside (New York) — Treas.	N. P. Banks	Thomas E. Walker J. N. Perkins G. W. Smith J. Sturges J. W. Alsop F. C. Gebhard A. S. Hewitt W. H. Osborn L. M. Wiley William Tracy	F. Haven	Richard Yates [Gov.] (Springfield, Ill.) *ex officio*
Chicago, Burlington and Quincy John Van Nortwick (Chicago and Batavia, Ill.) — Pres. Edward L. Baker (Boston) — Chairman of the Board Amos T. Hall (Chicago) — Secy.-Treas.		*Erastus Corning* (Albany)	*John M. Forbes* *John W. Brooks* Henry P. Kidder Sidney Bartlett Robt. S. Watson William Booth Edward L. Baker (New Bedford, Mass.)	John Van Nortwick (Chicago and Batavia, Ill.) C. S. Colton (Galesburg, Ill.) James F. Joy (Detroit)
Michigan Central *John W. Brooks* (Boston) — Pres. H. H. Hunnewell (Boston) — Vice Pres. Wm. B. Fowle, Jr. (Boston) — Secy. Isaac Livermore (Boston) — Treas.		D. D. Williamson Geo. F. Talman *Erastus Corning* (Albany)	*John W. Brooks* Nathaniel Thayer *John M. Forbes* R. B. Forbes H. H. Hunnewell	Elon Farnsworth (Detroit)

[1] See footnote on page 488.

RAILROAD DIRECTORS IN SELECTED YEARS SHOWING CHICAGOANS AND IMPORTANT FIGURES (continued)

(Names in italics indicate participation in two or more of these roads)

1862 [1]

Road	Chicago	New York City and State (New York City, unless otherwise noted)	New England (Boston, unless otherwise noted)	Others
Chicago and Rock Island Henry Farnam (Chicago) — Pres. Francis H. Tows (New York) — Secy. E. W. Dunham (New York) — Treas.	Henry Farnam *Norman B. Judd* John F. Tracy	Thomas C. Durant Francis H. Tows *David Dows* E. W. Dunham Wm. H. Macy James N. Cobb Charles W. Durant John B. Jervis (Rome)		Ebenezer Cook (Davenport, Ia.) [one vacancy]
Michigan Southern and Northern Indiana (Later, Lake Shore and Michigan Southern) *E. M. Gilbert* (Utica) — Pres. *M. L. Sykes, Jr.* (Chicago) — Vice Pres. D. P. Barhydt (New York) — Secy. Henry Keep (New York) — Treas.	*M. L. Sykes, Jr.*	*E. M. Gilbert* (Utica) Henry Keep Allan Campbell Albert Havemeyer Milton Courtright Hamilton White (Syracuse) Nelson Beardsley (Auburn) Wm. Williams (Buffalo)		*Stillman Witt* (Cleveland) John S. Barry (Constantine, Mich.) Philo Morehouse (Elkhart, Ind.) [one vacancy]
St. Louis, Alton and Chicago (In process of reorganization. No directors listed in 1862) James Robb (Chicago) — Receiver Joseph Price (Chicago) — Treas.				

1 See footnote on page 488.

Road	Chicago	New York City and State (New York City, unless otherwise noted)	New England (Boston, unless otherwise noted)	Others
Pittsburgh, Ft. Wayne and Chicago *Wm. B. Ogden* (Chicago) — Receiver Geo. W. Cass (Pittsburgh) — Pres. Samuel Hanna (Fort Wayne) — Vice Pres. Augustus Bradley (Pittsburgh) — Secy. John P. Henderson (Pittsburgh) — Treas.	John Evans *William B. Ogden*			Thomas A. Scott (Philadelphia) Geo. W. Cass Wm. Robinson, Jr. G. A. Smith Springer Harbaugh (all of Pittsburgh) Samuel Hanna Jesse L. Williams Pliny Hoagland (all of Fort Wayne) John Larwill (Wooster, Ohio) R. McKelley (Sandusky) A. L. Wheeler (Plymouth, Ind.) W. Merriman (Bucyrus, Ohio) Kent Jarvis (Massillon, Ohio)
Galena and Chicago Union Walter L. Newberry (Chicago) — Pres. Wm. H. Brown (Chicago) — Vice Pres. Wm. M. Larrabee (Chicago) — Secy. Wm. Larned (Chicago) — Treas.	Jason McCord Wm. Larned W. L. Newberry Jonathan Burr *Edw. K. Rogers* Wm. H. Brown Charles S. Hempstead Orrington Lunt John Wentworth Flavel Moseley	W. H. Ferry (Utica) D. A. Knowlton (Westfield)		T. D. Robertson (Rockford, Ill.)

[1] See footnote on page 488.

RAILROAD DIRECTORS IN SELECTED YEARS SHOWING CHICAGOANS AND IMPORTANT FIGURES (*continued*)

(Names in italics indicate participation in two or more of these roads)

1862 [1]

Road	Chicago	New York City and State (New York City, unless otherwise noted)	New England (Boston, unless otherwise noted)	Others
Chicago and North Western (Later combined with Galena) *Wm. B. Ogden* (Chicago) — Pres. P. H. Smith (Chicago) — Vice Pres. James R. Young (Chicago) — Secy. Geo. P. Lee (Chicago) — Treas.	*Wm. B. Ogden* George Smith P. H. Smith	Wm. A. Booth Lowell Holbrook *David Dows* C. S. Seyton H. H. Boody Austin Baldwin	G. M. Bartholomew (Hartford)	M. C. Darling (Fond du Lac, Wis.) A. L. Pritchard (Watertown, Wis.) J. J. R. Pease (Janesville, Wis.)
Chicago and Milwaukee Mahlon D. Ogden (Chicago) — Pres. *M. L. Sykes, Jr.* (Chicago) — Vice Pres. A. S. Downs (Chicago) — Secy. H. A. Tucker (Chicago) — Treas.	M. D. Ogden *N. B. Judd* E. K. Rogers H. A. Tucker *M. L. Sykes, Jr.*	J. Wadsworth *E. M. Gilbert* (Utica)		A. Stone, Jr. *S. Witt* (both of Cleveland)

[1] Based on John Ashcroft, comp., *Ashcroft's Railway Directory for 1862* . . . (New York, 1862).

1871[1]

Road	Chicago	New York City and State (New York City, unless otherwise noted)	New England (Boston, unless otherwise noted)	Others
Illinois Central John Newell (Chicago) — Pres. L. A. Catlin (New York) — Secy. Wm. K. Ackerman (Chicago) — Treas.	John M. Douglas	Abram S. Hewitt William Tracy W. H. Osborn Thomas E. Walker Jonathan Sturges	H. H. Hunnewell	John M. Palmer [Gov.] (Springfield, Ill.) *ex officio* Wilson G. Hunt R. Daniel Walterbeck Cunningham Borthwick Henry Chauncey George Bliss (Addresses not given)
Chicago, Burlington and Quincy *James F. Joy* (Detroit) — Pres. John N. Denison (Boston) — Chairman of Board Amos T. Hall (Chicago) — Secy.-Treas.		*Erastus Corning* (Albany) John C. Green	*Nathaniel Thayer* John M. Forbes *Sidney Bartlett* *John W. Brooks* Robt. S. Watson William Boott John N. Denison	*James F. Joy* (Detroit) Chauncey S. Colton (Galesburg, Ill.)
Michigan Central *James F. Joy* (Detroit) — Pres. *Nathaniel Thayer* (Boston) — Vice Pres. Isaac Livermore (Boston) — Treas.		*Erastus Corning* (Albany) Geo. F. Talman Moses Taylor John Jacob Astor	*John W. Brooks* *Nathaniel Thayer* *H. H. Hunnewell* *Sidney Bartlett*	*James F. Joy* (Detroit)

[1] See footnote on page 491.

RAILROAD DIRECTORS IN SELECTED YEARS SHOWING CHICAGOANS AND IMPORTANT FIGURES (continued)

(Names in italics indicate participation in two or more of these roads)

1871[1]

Road	Chicago	New York City and State (New York City, unless otherwise noted)	New England (Boston, unless otherwise noted)	Others
Chicago, Rock Island and Pacific (Formerly Chicago and Rock Island) *John F. Tracy* (Chicago) — Pres. Ebenezer Cook (Davenport, Ia.) — Vice Pres. Francis H. Tows (New York) — Secy.-Treas.	*John F. Tracy* *Henry H. Porter*	David Dows Francis H. Tows *A. G. Dulman* *Charles R. Marvin* Robt. A. Forsyth (Newburgh, N.Y.)		*Milton Courtright* *William L. Scott* John Hearn (all of Erie, Pa.) Ebenezer Cook Geo. L. Davenport (both of Davenport, Ia.) B. F. Allen (Des Moines)
Lake Shore and Michigan Southern (Formerly Michigan Southern and Northern Indiana) Horace F. Clark (New York) — Pres. Augustus Schell (New York) — Vice Pres. Geo. B. Ely (Cleveland) — Secy. James H. Banker (New York) — Treas.	Albert Keep	Horace F. Clark James H. Banker Augustus Schell Azariah Boody William Williams (Buffalo)	William D. Bishop (Bridgeport, Conn.)	*William L. Scott* *Milton Courtright* John A. Tracy (all of Erie, Pa.) H. B. Payne Amasa Stone, Jr. Stillman Witt (all of Cleveland)
Pittsburgh, Fort Wayne and Chicago Geo. W. Cass (Pittsburgh) — Pres. F.M.Hutchinson (Pittsburgh) — Secy.-Treas.	William B. Ogden	J. F. D. Lanier S. J. Tilden Louis H. Meyer		Geo. W. Cass Springer Harbaugh (both of Pittsburgh) J. Edgar Thomson Thomas A. Scott (both of Philadelphia) Jesse L. Williams

1871[1]

Road	Chicago	New York City and State (New York City, unless otherwise noted)	New England (Boston, unless otherwise noted)	Others
Pittsburgh, Fort Wayne and Chicago (*continued*)				Pliny Hoagland (both of Fort Wayne) R. R. Springer (Cincinnati) Kent Jarvis (Massillon, Ohio) John H. Sherman (Mansfield, Ohio)
Chicago and Alton T. B. Blackstone (Chicago) — Pres. Wm. M. Larrabee (Chicago) — Secy.-Treas.	T. B. Blackstone John B. Drake Peyton R. Chandler John Crerar	D. Willis James John A. Stewart	Wm. F. Weld Lorenzo Blackstone (Norwich, Conn.)	John J. Mitchell (Alton, Ill.)
Chicago and North Western *John F. Tracy* (Chicago) — Pres. M. L. Sykes, Jr. (New York) — Vice Pres. Albert L. Pritchard (New York) — Secy.-Treas.	Henry R. Pierson John B. Turner *Henry H. Porter* *John F. Tracy* George L. Dunlap	John M. Burke H. Henry Baxter George S. Scott *Anthony G. Dulman* M. L. Sykes, Jr. *Charles R. Marvin* Harvey Kennedy A. B. Baylis		J. L. Ten Have Frzn (Amsterdam, Holland) *William L. Scott* *Milton Courtright* (both of Erie, Pa.) R. P. Fowler (Watertown, Wis.)

[1] Based on Henry V. Poor, *Manual of the Railroads of the United States, for 1871–72* . . . (New York, 1871).

RECEIPTS AND SHIPMENTS OF SELECTED ITEMS IN CHICAGO'S COMMERCE, 1852[1]

Receipts

Commodity	Unit	Lake	Canal	Galena R.R.
Barley	bu.	1,687	8,785	90,248
Corn [a]	bu.		1,810,830	671,961
Oats	bu.		833,703	674,941
Wheat	bu.	129,251	108,597	504,996
Flour	bbl.	2,857	1,846	44,316
Wool	lbs.		525,632	244,662
Hides	lbs.	11,000	887,318	396,312
Hogs, Live	no.	280		
Hogs, Dressed	lbs.		86,800	10,881,510
Beef	bbl.	11	1,178	
Pork	bbl.	960	2,310	
Cured Meats	lbs.	3,300	303,576	1,836,084
Lard	lbs.		67,793	
Butter	pkgs.	866	2,818	9,587
Salt	bbl.	91,674		
Salt	tons	185		
Sugar	tons		1,604	
Molasses	lbs.		746,564	
Whiskey	bbl.	1,783		
Lumber	feet	149,419,482	163,548	5,658
Merchandise and Sundries	lbs.	8,892,000[d]	408,000	759,894
Agricultural Implements	tons		72	1,962,000
Iron	bdls. & bars	122,555	5,100	
Iron	lbs.	32,336,000[e]		
Coal	tons	42,933	3,310	
Lead	lbs.	5,147 kgs.[g]	642,027	715,300

Shipments

Commodity	Unit	Lake	Canal	Galena R.R.
Barley	bu.	70,818	508	
Corn	bu.	2,737,011		
Oats	bu.	2,930,317		
Wheat	bu.	635,196	807	
Flour	bbl.	61,196	2,901	
Wool	lbs.	920,113		
Hides	no.	47,875	40	
Cattle	no.	77		
Hogs, Live	no.	4,508		
Beef	bbl.	49,856[b]	175	
Pork	bbl.	9,938[c]	38	
Lard	bbl. & kgs.			22,248
Butter	pkgs.	4,638	90	
Salt	bbl.	9,062	27,457	
Salt	sacks	4,259	402,746	
Sugar	lbs.		768,871	
Molasses	lbs.		254,000	
High Wines and Whiskey	bbl.	14,021	2,868	
Lumber	feet		49,095,181	21,645,090
Merchandise and Sundries	lbs.	6,528 pkgs.	14,477,564	34,061,600
Agricultural Implements	tons		274	
Iron	lbs.	138,000	20,146,000[f]	3,936,000
Coal	tons		196	
Lead	lbs.	2,036,000	2,000	1,245

[1] Statistics from The Daily Democratic Press, Annual Review, 1852, pp. 10-11.

[a] In the original, these entries are erroneously listed for the lake and canal.

[b] Does not include 1,546 tierces. [c] Does not include 640 tierces.

[d] Does not include...

[e] Includes 22,454,000 pounds of railroad iron and 6,990,000 pounds of pig iron.

[f] Includes 19,294,000 pounds of railroad iron.

RECEIPTS OF SELECTED ITEMS IN CHICAGO'S COMMERCE IN 1864-65[1]

1865 Receipts	Chicago & North Western Railroad	Illinois Central Railroad	Chicago & Rock Island Railroad	Chicago, Burlington & Quincy Railroad	Chicago & Alton Railroad	Chicago & Milwaukee Railroad	Michigan Central Railroad	Michigan Southern Railroad	Pittsburgh, Ft. Wayne & Chicago Railroad	Chicago & Great Eastern Railroad	Lake	Illinois and Michigan Canal
Barley, bu.	301,300	111,920	226,286	133,130	17,170	6,252	467	188	190			26,741
Corn, bu.	2,141,291	1,665,120	2,032,485	2,461,070	535,772	35,198	528	731	12,281			4,310,864
Oats, bu.	6,571,412	1,247,199	1,983,484	3,016,257	657,894	266,360	450	1,278	5,627	355		2,015,125
Wheat, bu.	4,980,396	1,625,219	1,381,311	1,584,460	463,685	50,255	23,137	7,634	64,689	280,150	22,861	404,639
Flour, bbl.	477,719	212,066	140,356	133,142	57,754	12,916	17,484	5,611	4,093	11,974	12,414	84,715
Cotton, lbs.					815,280							
Wool, lbs.	1,861,296	2,227	564,640	1,507,536	959,038	259,948		7,400	28,401	235,704	49,000	23,940
Hides, lbs.	6,592,688	2,467,956	2,904,520	4,775,016	1,968,526	605,003		148,400	222,417	18	113,625	23,820
Cattle, no.	125,690	30,122	35,448	98,397	38,655	12,812	822	730	929		103	
Live hogs, no.	322,101	146,470	146,895	494,434	131,213	2,425	3,240	19,290	4,256		13	13
Dressed hogs, no.	34,413	11,032	45,603	31,297	4,434	2,806		137,110	2,591			
Cured meats, lbs.	2,251,265		1,039,105	10,335,658	8,200	2,283,025		5,700				1,097,924
Pork, bbl.	5,432	1,379	12,929	5,426	1,657	4,611			24			9,756
Beef, bbl.	3,837	1,299	1,226	195	71	2,020				45		521
Lard, lbs.	1,760,408	4,670	1,614,542	8,127,189	345,002	418,882		1,700				987,835
Butter, lbs.	6,187,119	81,432	779,775	761,973	66,920	922,798	597,033	50,800	95,705	10,655		17,825
Salt, bags		95				2,108					30,404[a]	54
Salt, bbl.		38						2,491		60	675,649	300 lbs.
Sugar, hhds.											7,131	
Sugar, bbl.											51,517	
Molasses and syrup, casks.											14,950	900 lbs.
Liquors and high-wines, bbl.	14,227	15,795	24,220	43,828	4,613	4,702		601	250	4,100	9,085 casks	9,696
Lumber, feet.	3,243,000	210,050		29,400	363,489		4,937,391	2,423,000	8,826,000	700,000	480,165,000	695,076
Merchandise and sundries, lbs.	52,012,920				10,727,706		100,645,557		80,576,828			42,516
Iron, bdls.											18,341	
R.R. iron, bars.											97,132	
Iron, lbs.									70,243,932		42,478,000	3,044,832
Lead, lbs.	7,237,624	3,198,560			256,234	3,060		2,700				
Coal, tons.	19	6,213	21,507	3,346	7,396	10		46	5,445		251,038	28,244

[1] Chicago Board of Trade, *Seventh Annual Statement, 1864-65*, pp. 26, 48, 50, 55, 57, 65, 74-104.

[a] This does not include 782 tons.

SHIPMENTS OF SELECTED ITEMS IN CHICAGO'S COMMERCE IN 1864-65 [1]

1865 Shipments	Chicago & North Western Railroad	Illinois Central Railroad	Chicago & Rock Island Railroad	Chicago, Burlington & Quincy Railroad	Chicago & Alton Railroad	Chicago & Milwaukee Railroad	Michigan Central Railroad	Michigan Southern Railroad	Pittsburgh, Ft. Wayne & Chicago Railroad	Chicago & Great Eastern Railroad	Lake	Illinois and Michigan Canal
Barley, bu.	2,935	12,834	18,200	12,271	25,469	45,317	6,381	13,278	14,700	....	173,425	2,588
Corn, bu.	28,198	14,981	....	320	....	38,732	247,296	320,988	42,943	4,350	11,993,475	48,760
Oats, bu.	963	698,537	510	260	1,970	372	815,211	668,166	992,847	546,568	12,098,000	647,525
Wheat, bu.	17,129	4,936	3,740	253	1,697	28,864	60,986	42,644	11,445	1,000	9,983,567	93,067
Flour, bbl.	5,206	8,874	11,812	1,225	11,023	3,562	36,110	71,750	100,887	1,170	1,034,793	1,133
Cotton, lbs.	....	....	....	....	....	....	....	....	....	....	13 bales	....
Wool, lbs.	1,500	....	13,540	....	....	....	508,444	2,901,047	1,777,847	....	1,786,500	....
Hides, lbs.	87,530	....	1,390	2,010	10,686	296,991	1,766,960	1,252,000	1,968,802	426,900	10,205,700	200
Cattle, no.	2,623	25,218	417	350	....	293	3,860,365	3,392,000	9,383,715	13,200	397	....
Live hogs, no.	300	2,930	5,730	1,108	....	3	63,071	39,081	107,110	180	690	200
Dressed hogs, no.	....	....	....	....	....	786	66,144	180,974	322,501	....	....	....
Cured meats, lbs.	71,500	....	....	1,750	....	4,500	38,006	137	17,858	....	3,651,500	62,910
Pork, bbl.	2,914	14,302	2,925	....	12,199	33	5,789,457	14,879,455	25,594,220	625[a]	106,835	65
Beef, bbl.	75	5,340	1,519	....	511	8	33,637	81,660	55,244	2,322	91,131	2,015
Lard, lbs.	21,830	51,300	37,450	....	120,301	137,055	3,431	27,356	6,919	....	10,183,500	....
Butter, lbs.	600	....	900	16,225	437,004	3,650	3,943,129	15,071,874	12,776,531	164,900	1,869,000	3,479
Salt, sacks.	....	13,908	6,516	209	100	154	597,033	398,389	2,435,889	....	....	10,080
Salt, bbl.	12,074	112,569	62,986	164,615	83,170	3,169	....	4,712	3,567	690	690	32,500
Sugar, lbs.	....	....	....	....	....	....	3,391	....	....	....	....	24,937
Sugar, bbl.	....	....	....	....	4,721	....	565,203	....	....	....	....	....
Molasses and sugar, lbs.	....	....	....	....	....	....	....	....	....	....	800	....
Liquors and high-wines, bbl.	3,322	2,557	2,851	4,569	743	1,907	....	11,443	59,713	4,555	43,990	69
Lumber, feet.	4,638,443	75,334,470	29,559,570	62,229,106	37,281,011	629,358	2,780,376	305,200	2,509,000	3,019,000	599,000,000	53,612,045
Merchandise and sundries, lbs.	....	....	....	....	33,063,664	....	42,191,132	....	27,387,822	....	....	469,783
Iron, bdls.	....	....	....	....	....	....	....	....	....	....	....	....
R.R. iron, bars.	....	....	....	....	....	....	....	....	....	....	680	....
Iron, lbs.	37,460	48,510	....	....	6,263,376	....	2,425,752	324,765	6,942,925	182,000	1,017	407,990
Lead, lbs.	7,813	2,052	....	....	900	33,570	847	851	2,922,203	....	306,000	....
Coal, tons.	....	....	2,136	2,445	....	453	....	....	60	50	3,205,125	1,488

[1] Chicago Board of Trade, *Seventh Annual Statement, 1864-65*, pp. 26, 38, 46, 48, 50, 55, 57, 61, 64, 65, 74-104.

[a] This includes beef and pork.

1871 Receipts	Chicago & North Western Railroad	Illinois Central Railroad	Chicago, Rock Island & Pacific Railroad	Chicago, Burlington & Quincy Railroad	Chicago & Alton Railroad	Michigan Central Railroad	Lake Shore & Michigan Southern Railroad	Pittsburgh, Ft. Wayne & Chicago Railroad	Pittsburgh, Cincinnati & St. Louis Railroad	Lake	Illinois and Michigan Canal
Barley, bu.	2,147,564	703,800	552,428	469,498	97,310	450	970	350	1,310	......	160
Corn, bu.	2,797,538	10,475,680	4,950,437	10,076,463	7,105,000	6,350	11,051	14,229	122,118	......	5,521,143
Oats, bu.	3,351,594	3,141,250	1,915,051	3,546,185	1,299,000	7,087	46,311	17,889	70,851	1,750	1,128,086
Wheat, bu.	7,049,883	4,051,780	1,638,313	1,347,385	116,500	10,502	24,851	12,690	51,173	77,540	11,289
Flour, bbl.	675,473	139,355	232,823	204,545	65,100	20,535	9,636	1,921	1,530	47,673	13,586
Cotton, lbs.	......	2,399,000	......	......	......	......	......	......	......	......	......
Wool, lbs.	7,159,480	629,500	6,711,270	12,020,906	270,800	......	3,515	8,141	23,248	194,100	5,661
Hides, lbs.	4,623,695	5,710,100	3,048,780	7,952,591	1,726,000	318,380	590,280	234,878	613,268	203,680	4,382
Cattle, no.	78,697	79,438	72,406	188,682	105,311	1,535	3,989	486	2,415	......	......
Hogs, live, no.	532,242	440,548	384,562	678,501	260,058	18,377	28,876	7,220	10,835	......	......
Dressed hogs, no.	109,607	84,035	28,857	35,942	4,486	2,910	370	2,224	4,035	......	......
Fresh and cured meats, lbs.	16,987,051	......	3,925,980	8,129,565	1,026,000	......	52,719	......	82,303	127	......
Pork, bbl.	46,159	2,126	4,522	15,488	......	......	7	520	......	50	......
Beef, bbl.	......	......	......	53,239	......	......	13	......	......	......	......
Lard, lbs.	1,795,787	1,898,700	3,271,550	8,154,212	1,415,000	......	102,326	20,442	4,781	......	......
Butter, lbs.	4,903,027	......	1,804,278	2,274,391	145,000	15,260	103,777	96,040	310,629	1,993,795	515
Salt, bbl.	......	1,025	......	......	......	......	......	4,094	15,128	668,410	......
Salt, sacks.	......	11,666 B. & Hg.	......	......	......	......	......	......	B. & P.	......	......
Sugar, hhds.	......	......	......	......	......	......	......	......	......	......	......
Sugar, bbl.	......	5,137 bbl.	......	......	......	......	......	......	......	......	......
Molasses and sugar, pkgs.	......	......	......	......	......	......	139,883	46,106	......	......	......
Liquors and high-wines, bbl.	21,948	11,466	35,078	10,961	4,300	6,813	7,349	1,509	21,545	......	......
Lumber, feet.	4,371,270	1,567,000	1,177,000	4,280,300	......	12,102,000	8,937,000	15,336,000	6,737,200	984,758,000	62,605
Merchandise and sundries, lbs.	162,455,900	96,714,700	41,465,680	41,390,743	26,840,000	251,615,940	210,762,769	272,173,046	113,210,533	......	762,592[a]
Iron & nails, lbs.	......	......	......	5,047,674	......	......	60,441,808	199,771,541	21,235,090	......	......
Pig & R.R. iron, tons	6,139	......	2,129	......	......	......	......	......	14,291	......	......
Iron, lbs.	424,416	10,291,000	2,195,170	......	......	......	430,674	......	934,515	......	932,273[b]
Lead, lbs.	46,348	47,140	8,762	4,395	267,300	......	2,518	76,186	107,652	515,253	4,176
Coal and coke, tons	......	......	......	......	......	......	......	......	......	......	......
Agricultural implements, lbs.	......	......	2,828,680	1,813,801	......	......	13,144,238	......	1,633,397	......	2,400

[1] Chicago Board of Trade, *Fourteenth Annual Report, 1871*, pp. 86-109. [b] Including 903,716 pounds of pig and scrap, 28,557 pounds of wrought and cast iron.
[a] This does not include 22 bbl.

SHIPMENTS OF SELECTED ITEMS IN CHICAGO'S COMMERCE IN 1871[1]

1871 Shipments	Chicago & North Western Railroad	Illinois Central Railroad	Chicago, Rock Island & Pacific Railroad	Chicago, Burlington & Quincy Railroad	Chicago & Alton Railroad	Michigan Central Railroad	Lake Shore & Michigan Southern Railroad	Pittsburgh, Ft. Wayne & Chicago Railroad	Pittsburgh, Cincinnati & St. Louis Railroad	Lake	Illinois and Michigan Canal
Barley, bu.	44,522	15,200	41,244	5,006	109,800	222,006	174,856	505,410	393,021	1,307,048	......
Corn, bu.	77,834	......	2,100	......	......	1,054,347	1,015,428	275,172	90,278	34,200,876	......
Oats, bu.	37,423	1,860	1,151	93	700	1,346,977	865,596	779,150	320,608	8,797,599	......
Wheat, bu.	29,839	13,950	21,483	19,836	25,000	368,090	87,752	64,450	56,176	12,110,923	97,950
Flour, bbl.	23,324	37,432	19,293	4,862	17,900	230,990	150,967	217,648	95,569	488,705	1,784
Cotton, lbs.	......	......	......	......	......	2,267,300	......	......	......	......	......
Wool, lbs.	77,090	83,300	33,090	32,430	41,000	8,646,270	5,887,520	8,963,460	412,660	174,700	......
Hides, lbs.	904,860	3,500	1,550	......	......	8,863,460	7,692,787	2,652,500	560,997	1,783,240	......
Cattle, no.	3,863	8,226	7,496	3,488	8,428	116,684	124,699	124,599	4,444	......	......
Live hogs, no.	1,544	461	135	276	792	377,671	484,251	290,062	7,094	......	......
Dressed hogs, no.	226	......	......	......	832	92,173	35,848	36,837	2,826	......	......
Fresh and cured meats, lbs.	20,000	6,345	1,413,150	2,227,236	8,100,000	18,243,470	47,076,113	63,529,400	26,910,091	155,600	......
Pork, bbl.	490	164	1,911	......	15,900	27,106	27,070	33,933	2,762	34,207	......
Beef, bbl.	......	......	......	......	450	5,650	18,488 tc. & bbl.	58,962 tc. & bbl.	135	5,603	......
Lard, lbs.	107,200	658,800	206,120	406,971	330,000	5,919,670	22,236,937	26,275,950	4,503,565	384,550	......
Butter, lbs.	121,133	......	518,680	71,161	......	3,297,186	1,543,517	4,801,635	147,732	528,330	......
Salt, bbl.	62,059	77,149	100,539	134,236	53,200	500	2,755	420	2,966 bgs. & bbl.	4,778	11,536
Sugar, pkgs.	......	45,034	......	......	......	......	......	......	......	......	9,990 lbs.
Molasses, bbl.	......	3,483	......	......	......	......	......	......	......	......	......
Liquors and high-wines, bbl.	10,700	2,981	18,676	5,268	6,800	18,511	23,800	81,026	3,269	......	......
Lumber, feet.	41,694,621	89,275,000	41,909,800	123,550,134	142,600,000	9,149,200	7,507,000	3,679,000	32,105,266	5,993,000	37,421,522
Merchandise and sundries, lbs.	308,104,438	239,484,500	117,635,630	210,936,048	210,640,000	87,738,240	64,264,609	87,026,100	54,964,620	......	......
Iron & nails, lbs.	576,830	......	......	105,846,139	86,750,000	......	3,477,307	6,968,600	5,804,736	......	201,791[a]
Pig & R.R. iron, tons.	17,254	22,406	......	......	......	......	2,739	......	......	......	17,950
Iron, lbs.	......	......	......	......	......	......	......	......	......	......	1,122,825[b]
Lead, lbs.	......	165,100	......	......	25,000	......	161,278	2,302,281	3,340,992	......	......
Coal, tons.	43,968	11,130	12,756	19,791	3,215	760	1,510	371	442	......	2,890
Agricultural implements & wagons, lbs.	11,731,424	......	14,056,080	13,879,235	......	......	715,055	......	1,526,760	......	443,555

[1] Chicago Board of Trade, *Fourteenth Annual Report*, 1871, pp. 87-109.
[a] This does not include 49 bbl.
[b] Includes 104,050 pounds of pig and scrap, 927,875 pounds of wrought and cast iron.

CHICAGO LABOR: OCCUPATIONS AND PLACE OF BIRTH OF LABORERS, 1870[1]

Classifications	Total	Place of Birth of Employed Persons											
		United States	Germany	British Isles			Scandinavia	British America	Other South Europe	France	Other North Europe	Italy	Others
				Ireland	England and Wales	Scotland							
Manufacturing and Mechanical Industries	51,114	12,519	14,251	11,445	2,814	1,138	3,811	2,130	2,075	366	232	81	252
Trade	21,931	11,684	4,271	2,401	1,004	305	462	610	508	151	368	137	30
Transportation	9,160	3,083	1,532	2,640	501	189	668	322	124	53	29	5	14
Domestic and Personal Service	14,168	4,409	2,452	3,991	394	140	1,611	452	515	94	65	24	21
Professional Services	2,665	1,905	279	117	108	30	54	84	49	18	7	3	11
Public Service	1,416	736	222	266	56	24	49	30	20	9	3	0	1
Agriculture and Mining	544	172	183	80	41	15	24	9	16	2	1	0	1
Clerical Service	154	105	16	10	11	2	1	6	0	1	0	0	2
Itemized Totals	101,152	34,613	23,206	20,950	4,929	1,843	6,680	3,643	3,307	694	705	250	332
Miscellaneous	11,808	5,142	2,572	1,387	759	223	533	422	387	53	57	48	225
Totals	112,960	39,755	25,778	22,337	5,688	2,066	7,213	4,065	3,694	747	762	298	557

[1] Based on itemized figures in United States, *Ninth Census, 1870,* I, "Population," 782.

PER CENT OF EMPLOYED BY NATIONALITY IN 1870[1]

Nationality	Number Employed As Reported	Per Cent of Total Employed Inhabitants	Per Cent of Nationality Employed
American..............	39,755	35.19	25.74
Irish...................	22,337	19.77	55.86
English and Welsh.......	5,688	5.04	53.70
Scotch.................	2,066	1.83	49.23
German................	25,778	22.82	49.27
Scandinavian...........	7,213	6.39	52.38
British American........	4,065	3.60	42.13
French.................	747	.66	52.68
Italian.................	298	.26	53.99
North European (unspecified)..........	762	.67	
South European (unspecified)..........	3,694	3.27	
Other foreign and unknown	557	.49	
Total..........	112,960	99.99	

Based on figures in United States, *Ninth Census, 1870*, I, "Population," 782.

WAGES OF SELECTED WORKERS[1]

(Per day except where indicated)

	1852	1853–54	1860	1863	1865–66
Blacksmiths and Ironworkers	$1.25	$1.25–2.00	$1.25–1.75	$2.25	$2.75–3.00
House Painters....	1.50	1.25–1.75	1.25–1.50	2.00	2.50–2.75
Masons and Plasterers.........	1.50	1.50–2.00	1.50–1.75	2.50–3.00	3.00–3.50
Machinists.......	1.50	1.25–2.00	1.75–3.00	2.35	2.50–4.00
Carpenters.......	....	1.50–2.00	1.25–2.00	2.00–2.25	3.00–4.00
Ship Carpenters...	2.00	1.50–2.25	2.50	....	4.00
Printers..........	8.00 (week)	1.67	1.67	2.33	....
Shoemakers......	....	6–12 (week)	7–8 (week)	....	14–15 (week)
Day Laborers.....	.87½	1.00–1.50	.75–1.00	1.75–2.00	1.50

[1] Taken from figures in *Chicago Daily Democrat*, July 10, 1852; *The Daily Democratic Press*, March 16, 1854; *Chicago Tribune*, October 8, 1863, January 14, 1864, January 1, 1867; *The Chicago Times*, November 25, 1865; Chicago Tribune, *Annual Review, 1865*, pp. 10–11; *Hunt's Merchants' Magazine*, XXXII (June, 1855), 692–93.

RESOLUTIONS PRESENTED BY THE CHICAGO TYPOGRAPHICAL UNION AND UNANIMOUSLY ADOPTED AT THE MASS MEETING OF THE GENERAL TRADES ASSEMBLY, SEPTEMBER 10, 1864.[1]

Whereas, The proprietors of the *Times,* in their recent action in discharging the men in their employ, have avowed their purpose to be to break up our labor organizations, and thus to place the laboring men in such a position that they will be completely at the mercy of their employers; and

Whereas, The *Chicago Times* is supported by the Democratic party in this State and county, therefore

Resolved, That we call upon the leaders of the Democratic party in this State and county, and the State and County Democratic Central Committee, to repudiate the *Chicago Times* as the organ of the party, and establish a new Democratic organ in this city, that will reflect the sentiments of the Democratic voters of the State and county, and of the whole Northwest.

Resolved, That to such an organ we will give our hearty and earnest support; and

Resolved, That unless such a course is adopted, the Democratic party stands in danger of losing both prestige and support with the masses of laboring men.

Resolved, That the National Democratic Executive Committee be requested to remove Wilbur F. Storey from such a committee, as being totally unworthy to represent the Democratic party in such an important position.

Whereas, the proprietors of the *Chicago Times* newspaper establishment have, in an underhanded, secret and discreditable manner, sought to injure the labor organization in this city known as the " Chicago Typograph-

[1] *The Workingman's Advocate,* September 17, 1864.

ical Union," by discharging from their employ, without a moment's warning, all the compositors engaged in that establishment (some thirty to forty in number), except those who would so far forget their manliness and their obligations to their fellow-craftsmen, and forfeit their honor, self-respect and independence, as to disown their allegiance to said organization and aid in its overthrow; and

Whereas, we believe the attempt on the part of said employers to use female labor upon their newspaper to be only a temporary expedient, until by further importation and employment of disreputable printers, who, either because of their incompetence or unworthiness, can obtain employment only in offices where they are allowed to work for less than the regular established and fair remuneration; the object of said employers being solely and only to thus get control of their employees to such an extent as eventually to dictate to them the price of their labor, with a view of reducing it to the lowest possible standard; and

Whereas, we believe that female labor is not available, to any great extent, upon daily newspapers, but that the labor and habits of life incident to a newspaper compositor are entirely unsuited to the delicate organizations and constitutions of females, and that the thousands of dollars expended by newspaper proprietors to partly educate girls to set type have been appropriated and used with no wish, design or expectation on the part of said proprietors to confer benefit upon such females, but only that the latter might become instruments in the hands of their employers to aid in breaking up the powerful and well-organized Typographical Union throughout the country, particularly in the Northwest; and

Whereas, we do not believe the compensation demanded and received by the Union printers of Chicago at all exorbitant, being below the standard in New York, St. Louis and other cities, and hardly sufficient to enable men with families to support to maintain themselves, by close application to their labor, and to provide aught for the future; and

Whereas, We believe there is a mutual interest existing among all classes of labor in the maintenance and support of labor organizations as against the machinations and encroaching selfishness of capitalists; therefore

Resolved, That we regard the recent action of the *Times'* proprietors as a direct blow aimed at the interest of labor in this city, and in behalf of the grinding capitalists, and that we hereby publicly denounce said proprietors as the enemies of the laboring man.

Resolved, That common decency would seem to demand that all newspaper publishers and politicians asking the laboring masses for their votes, either for their friends or themselves, should prove themselves, by their actions, openly the friends of labor, and that it is a direct insult to the intelligence of the people — " the bone and sinew of the land," as they sometimes term us — to ask us to give our suffrages and support to any publisher or candidate, either directly or indirectly, who is not in practice a friend of labor.

Resolved, That we do not regard the Printers' Union as at war against the true interest of female labor, but only as opposed to females being made the instruments of a base plot and conspiracy to overthrow and crush out the manly independence and dignity of labor, that capital may profit thereby; and that the very parties seeking to employ such female labor will only use it when contributing to their selfish ends, and when no longer available to them as a means of power, will cast it aside with no regard to the welfare or interest of their deluded victims, whatever fair promises and professions these proprietors may now make.

Resolved, That we hereby pledge our honor as intelligent and thinking men, that we will withhold all patronage and support from the *Times* establishment, from this time forth, so long as it remains in its present hostile attitude toward the Printers' Union; and that hereafter, at local, city and county elections, we will support for office, with our votes and influence, under any circumstances only such men as are unequivocably pledged to vote no public patronage or support to any newspaper, manufacturing or contracting interest which does not comply with the terms and pay the prices demanded by the labor unions.

Resolved, That, as laboring men, having a common interest in the elevation and promotion to office in our city and county such men only as will use all honorable means at their command in behalf of the interests of labor, to protect it from the grinding despotism of capital, we hereby mutually pledge ourselves to lay aside our party ties and predilections, in our municipal and county elections, and vote only for the known friends of the laboring man; and if deemed advisable that we will nominate and elect to office men from our own ranks in whom we have confidence; and

Whereas, The *Chicago Tribune* has been at all times the prompt and ready enemy of both the labor organizations and their friends, and a leader of even the *Times* in such opposition, so much so that it even refused to advertise for the Typographical Union for pay, in which they were in direct conflict with the more generous course of the *Journal;* therefore,

Resolved, That we include the *Tribune* in our denunciations against the enemies of Labor.

Resolved, That the morning, evening, and weekly English and German newspapers be requested to publish the resolutions in full.

CHICAGO TROOPS IN THE CIVIL WAR [1]

Western Campaigns	1861	1862	1863	1864	1865
Infantry: 12(1861-65); 19(1861-64); 23(1861-62);24(1861-64); 37(1861-66);42(1861-66); 51(1861-65);57(1861-65); 58(1862-66);65(1863-65); 72(1862-65);82(1863-65); 88(1862-65);89(1862-65); 90(1862-65);113(1862-65); 127(1862-65) *Cavalry:* 9(1861-65); 12(1864-66); 13(1861-65);16(1863-65); 17(1864-65); Hoffman Dragoons and Thielemann's Cavalry (1861-62, became 16th Cavalry in 1863) *Artillery:* Old Batteries "A" & "B" 1861-64, consolidated as Battery "A," 1864-65); Co. I (1862-65) of 1st Ill. Light Artillery; Co. M (1863-65) and Co. M (1863-64) of 2d Ill. Light Artillery; Bridges' Indep. Battery, 1863-64, Co. B of 1st Ill. Light Artillery, 1864-65); Colvin's Battery (1862-65); Chicago Board of Trade Battery (1862-65); Chicago Merc. Battery (1862-65)	*Sept. 13-20* — siege and surrender of Lexington (Mo.). *Inf.:* 23 (captured). *Nov. 7* — engagement at Belmont (Mo.). *Art.:* Old Battery "B"	*Feb. 6* — capture of Fort Henry. *Inf.:* 12; *Art.:* Old Battery "B" *Feb. 14-16* — capture of Ft. Donelson. *Inf.:* 12, 57, 58; *Art.:* Old Batteries "A" and "B" *Mar. 6-8* — battle of Pea Ridge (Ark.). *Inf.:* 37 *Mar. 15-Apr. 8* — siege of Island No. Ten. *Inf.:* 42, 51 *Apr. 6-7* — battle of Shiloh. *Inf.:* 12, 57, 58; *Cav.:* Thielemann's Cavalry Co.; *Art.:* Old Batteries "A" and "B" *Apr. 29-May 30* — siege of Corinth. *Inf.:* 12, 42, 51, 57, 58; *Art.:* Old Batteries "A" and "B", Co. I, Co. L *Oct. 3-4* — battle of Corinth. *Inf.:* 12, 57 *Dec. 7* — battle of Prairie Grove (Ark.). *Inf.:* 37	*May 18-July 4* — siege of Vicksburg. *Inf.:* 37 (from Je. 11), 72, 90 (from Je. 12), 113, 127; *Cav.:* Thielemann's Cav. Co.; *Art.:* Old Batteries "A" & "B," Co. I, Co. L, Chi. Merc. Battery *Aug. 16-Oct. 19* — Burnside's campaign in eastern Tenn. *Inf.:* 65 *Sept. 10* — engagement at Bayou Fourche and capture of Little Rock (Ark.). *Cav.:* 13 *Sept. 19-20* — battle of Chickamauga. *Inf.:* 19, 24, 42, 51, 88, 89; *Art.:* Chi. Bd. of Trade Battery, Bridges' Indep. Battery *Nov. 4-Dec. 23* — Knoxville campaign. *Inf.:* 65; *Art.:* Colvin's Battery, Co. M *Nov. 24-25* — assault and capture of Lookout Mt. and	*Apr. 8* — battle of Sabine Cross Roads (La.). *Art.:* Chi. Merc. Battery *Apr. 9* — engagement of Pleasant Hill (La.). *Inf.:* 58 *May 1-Sept. 8* — Atlanta campaign. *Inf.:* 12, 19 (to Je. 9), 24 (to Je. 28), 42, 51, 57, 65 (from Je. 4), 82, 88, 89, 90, 127; *Cav.:* 16 (from Je. 28); *Art.:* Old Batteries "A" & "B" (consolidated with Battery A on Jy. 12), Bridges' Indep. Battery, Chi. Bd. of Trade Battery *Nov. 15-Dec. 21* — march to the sea and siege of Savannah. *Inf.:* 12, 57, 82, 90, 127 *Nov. 30* — battle of Franklin (Tenn.). *Inf.:* 42, 51, 65, 72, 88, 89; *Cav.:* 9, 16; *Art.:* Bridges' Indep. Bat. *Dec. 15-16* — battle	*Jan.-Apr.* — campaign of the Carolinas. *Inf.:* 12, 57, 82, 90, 127 *Feb. 22* — occupation of Wilmington (N.C.). *Inf.:* 65 *Mar. 17-Apr. 12* — siege and capture of Mobile and defenses. *Inf.:* 37, 58, 72 *Mar. 19-21* — battle of Bentonville (N.C.). *Inf.:* 12, 57, 82, 90, 127 *Mar. 21* — occupation of Goldsborough (N.C.). *Inf.:* 65 *Apr. 12* — occupation of Montgomery (Ala.). *Art.:* Chicago Board of Trade Battery

Eastern Campaigns	1861	1862	1863	1864	1865
		Dec. 27-28 — attack on Chickasaw Bayou (Miss.). *Inf.*: 113, 127; *Cav.*: Thielemann's Cavalry Co.; *Art.*: Old Batteries "A" and "B," Chi. Merc. Battery Dec. 30-Jan. 3, 1863 — battle of Stone River (Murfreesborough). *Inf.*: 19, 24, 42, 51, 88, 89; *Art.*: Chi. Bd. of Trade Battery	Missionary Ridge. *Inf.*: 19, 24, 42, 51, 82, 88, 89, 90, 127; *Art.*: Old Batteries "A" and "B," Co. I	of Nashville. *Inf.*: 42, 51, 58, 65, 72, 88, 89; *Cav.*: 9, 16; *Art.*: Co. I, Bridges' Indep. Bat., Chicago Board of Trade Battery	
Infantry: 23(1862-65); 39(1861-65); 65(1862); 82(1862-63) *Cavalry:* 8(1861-65); 12(1862-63); Barker's Chicago Dragoons (joined 12th Cav. in 1862); Sturges' Rifles (1861-62) *Artillery:* Co. M, 2d Ill. Light Artillery (1862)	July 6-17 — campaign in W. Va. *Cav.*: Barker's Chicago Dragoons, Sturges' Rifles	May 31-June 1 — battle of Seven Pines. *Cav.*: 8 June 25-July 1 — battle of Seven Days' Retreat. *Inf.*: 39; *Cav.*: 8, Sturges' Rifles Sept. 15 — capture of Harpers Ferry. *Inf.*: 65 (captured); *Art.*: Co. M (captured) Sept. 17 — battle of Antietam. *Cav.*: 8	May 1-5 — battle of Chancellorsville. *Inf.*: 82 June 9 — engagement at Beverly Fort (Va.). *Cav.*: 8, 12 July 1-3 — battle of Gettysburg. *Inf.*: 82; *Cav.*: 8, 12 July 14 — engagement at Falling Waters (Md.). *Cav.*: 8, 12	May 12-16 — battle of Drewry's Bluff (Va.). *Inf.*: 39 July 24 — engagement of Kernstown. *Inf.*: 23 Sept. 22 — battle of Fisher's Hill (Va.). *Inf.*: 23 June 16, 1864-Apr. 2, 1865 — siege operations against Petersburg and Richmond. *Inf.*: 39	Mar. 28-Apr. 9 — campaign of Appomattox. *Inf.*: 23, 39 Apr. 2 — assault on Petersburg. *Inf.*: 39 Apr. 9 — engagement at Clover Hill and surrender of Lee. *Inf.*: 39

1 Showing chief engagements in which regiments containing an appreciable number of Chicagoans participated.

Information is taken from:

Report of the Adjutant General of the State of Illinois (8 v. Springfield, 1886);
Frederick H. Dyer, comp., A Compendium of the War of the Rebellion (Des Moines, 1908);
Andreas, History of Chicago, II.

CHICAGO VOTE FOR MAYOR [1]

Year	Candidates	Vote
1848	James H. Woodworth (Ind. Dem.) James Curtiss (Dem.)	1,971 1,361
1849	James H. Woodworth Timothy Wait L. C. Kercheval Samuel D. Childs	2,668 399 245 22
1850	James Curtiss Levi D. Boone L. C. Kercheval	1,697 1,227 805
1851	Walter S. Gurnee Eli B. Williams James Curtiss Edward K. Rogers	2,032 1,092 1,001 226
1852	Walter S. Gurnee James Curtiss Amos G. Throop (Temp.) Peter Page	1,749 1,294 1,142 269
1853	Charles M. Gray Josiah L. James	3,270 971
1854	Isaac L. Milliken (Dem.) Amos G. Throop (Temp.)	3,800 2,556
1855	Levi D. Boone (Know-Nothing) Isaac L. Milliken (Dem.)	3,186 2,841
1856	Thomas Dyer (Pro-Nebr. Dem.) Francis C. Sherman (Anti-Nebr. Dem.)	4,712 4,123
1857	John Wentworth (Rep.) Benjamin F. Carver (Dem.)	5,933 4,842
1858	John C. Haines (Rep.) Daniel Brainard (Dem.)	8,642 7,481
1859	John C. Haines (Rep.) Marcus D. Gilman (Dem.)	8,587 7,728
1860	John Wentworth (Rep.) Walter S. Gurnee (Dem.)	9,998 8,739
1861	Julian S. Rumsey (Rep.) Thomas B. Bryan (Union)	8,274 6,601
1862	Francis C. Sherman (Dem.) C. N. Holden (Rep.)	7,437 6,254

[1] Where party is not indicated, candidates are Democrats running without formal party nominations.

CHICAGO VOTE FOR MAYOR (*continued*)

Year	Candidates	Vote
1863	Francis C. Sherman (Dem.) Thomas B. Bryan (Union)	10,252 10,095
1865	John B. Rice (Rep.) Francis C. Sherman (Dem.)	11,078 5,600
1867	John B. Rice (Rep.) Francis C. Sherman (Dem.)	11,904 7,971
1869	Roswell B. Mason (Citizens') George W. Gage (Rep.)	19,826 11,410

CHICAGO VOTE FOR GOVERNOR

Year	Candidates	Vote
1848	Augustus C. French (Dem.)* Charles V. Dyer (Liberty)	2,098 462
1852	Joel A. Matteson (Dem.)* Edwin B. Webb (Whig) Lincoln B. Knowlton (Abol.)	2,704 1,506 481
1856	William H. Bissell (Rep.)* William A. Richardson (Dem.) Buckner S. Morris (Know-Nothing)	6,431 4,936 294
1860	Richard Yates (Rep.)* James C. Allen (Dem.)	10,815 8,023
1864	Richard Oglesby (Rep.)* James C. Robinson (Dem.)	14,397 12,690
1868	John M. Palmer (Rep.)* John R. Eden (Dem.)	22,265 17,064

* Won in state.

CHICAGO VOTE FOR CONGRESSIONAL REPRESENTATIVES

Date	Nominees	Vote
1848	John Wentworth (Dem.)* Owen Lovejoy (Abol.) J. Y. Scammon (Whig)	1,337 347 1,546
1850	Richard Moloney (Dem.)* Churchill Coffing (Whig) James H. Collins (Abol.)	1,938 1,464 60
1852	John Wentworth (Dem.)* Cyrus Aldrich (Whig) James H. Collins (Abol.)	2,216 1,929 410
1854	James H. Woodworth (Rep.)* John B. Turner (Nebr. Dem.) Robert S. Blackwell (Whig) Edward L. Mayo (Dem.)	2,813 991 357 75
1856	John F. Farnsworth (Rep.)* Wm. W. Van Nortwick (Dem.) Benjamin F. James (Know-Nothing)	6,382 4,947 258
1858	John F. Farnsworth (Rep.)* Thomas Dyer (Douglas Dem.) Breckenridge F. Blackburn (Admin. Dem.)	8,004 8,071 223
1860	Isaac N. Arnold (Rep.)* Augustus M. Herrington (Dem.)	10,763 8,047
1862	Isaac N. Arnold (Rep.)* Francis C. Sherman (Dem.)	6,649 6,799
1864	John Wentworth (Rep.)* Cyrus H. McCormick (Dem.)	13,501 12,446
1866	Norman B. Judd (Rep.)* Martin R. M. Wallace (Dem.)	11,378 4,560
1868	Norman B. Judd (Rep.)* Martin R. M. Wallace (Dem.)	19,232 17,143
1870	Charles B. Farwell (Rep.)* John Wentworth (Ind.)	16,533 13,087

* Won in the district.

CHICAGO PRESIDENTIAL VOTE

Date	Nominees	Vote
1848	Martin Van Buren (Free Soil) Zachary Taylor (Whig) Lewis Cass (Dem.)* Gerrit Smith (National Reform) †	1,543 1,283 1,016 ...
1852	Franklin Pierce (Dem.)* Winfield Scott (Whig) John P. Hale (Free Soil)	2,692 1,575 426
1856	John C. Frémont (Rep.) James Buchanan (Dem.)* Millard Fillmore (Know-Nothing)	6,397 4,946 332
1860	Abraham Lincoln (Rep.)* Stephen A. Douglas (Dem.) John Bell (Constitutional Union) John C. Breckinridge (So. Dem.)	10,697 8,094 107 87
1864	Abraham Lincoln (Union)* George B. McClellan (Dem.)	14,388 12,691
1868	Ulysses S. Grant (Rep.)* Horatio Seymour (Dem.)	22,300 17,029

* Won in state.
† No records available as to Smith's vote in Chicago.

MUNICIPAL FINANCE STATISTICS, 1848–71 [1]

Year	Real and Personal Property Valuation	Annual Per Cent Increase in Property Valuations	Yearly Taxes Levied	Annual Per Cent Tax Increase	Tax Rate on Dollar (in mills)	Debt[a]
1848	$ 6,300,440	7.72	$ 22,051.54	......	3.5	$ 20,338.38
1849	6,676,684	5.97	30,045.09	36.25	4.5	36,333.20
1850	7,220,249	8.14	25,270.87	15.89°	3.5	42,195.00
1851	8,562,717	18.59	63,385.87	150.83	7.4 −	93,395.00
1852	10,463,414	22.20	76,948.96	21.24	7.4 −	126,035.00
1853	16,841,831	60.96	135,662.68	76.30	8.1 +	189,670.00
1854	24,392,239	44.83	199,081.64[b]	46.74	8.1 +	248,666.00
1855	26,992,893	10.66	206,209.03	3.58	7.6 +	328,000.00
1856	31,736,084	17.57	396,652.39	92.35	12.5 −	435,000.00
1857	36,335,281	14.49	572,046.00	44.22	15.7 +	535,000.00
1858	35,991,732	1.22°	430,190.00	24.80°	11.9 +	1,601,000.00
1859	36,553,380	1.56	543,614.00	26.37	14.8 +	1,855,000.00
1860	37,053,512	1.37	573,315.29	5.46	15.4 +	2,336,000.00
1861	36,352,380	1.89°	550,968.00	3.90°	15.1 +	2,474,000.00
1862	37,139,845	2.17	564,038.06	2.37	15.1 +	3,028,000.00
1863	42,667,324	14.88	853,346.00	51.29	20.0 −	3,422,500.00
1864	48,732,782	14.22	974,665.64	14.21	20.0	3,544,500.00
1865	64,704,177	32.77	1,294,183.50	32.78	20.0	3,757,500.00
1866	85,953,250	32.84	1,719,064.05	32.83	20.0 −	4,369,500.00
1867	195,026,844	126.89	2,518,472.00	46.50	12.9 +	4,757,500.00
1868	230,247,000	18.06	3,223,457.80	27.99	14.0 −	6,484,500.00
1869	266,024,880	15.54	3,990,373.20	23.79	15.0	7,882,500.00
1870	275,986,550	3.74	4,139,798.60	3.74	15.0 −	11,041,000.00
1871	289,746,470	4.99	2,897,564.70	30.01°	10.0	14,103,000.00

[1] Figures and computations, in general, based on tables in Hugo S. Grosser, *Chicago: A Review of its Governmental History from 1837 to 1906* (Chicago, 1906), chaps. i, ii, and iii; Chicago, Department of Finance, *Thirty-Seventh Annual Statement of the City of Chicago from January 1, 1893, to December 31, 1893* (Chicago, 1894), pp. 130–31. For the basis of property valuation, see p. 347. Real and personal property valuations have been combined. During the years shown on this table, personal property averaged 20.43 per cent of the total property valuation. By individual years, personal property ranged from 15 to 25 per cent of the total except in 1861 and 1862 when it was slightly below 15 per cent and in 1865 and 1867 when it was above 25 per cent.

[a] Debt statistics have been taken from the above sources and from *Weekly Chicago Democrat*, March 21, 1848; *Chicago Daily Democrat*, March 1, 1852, January 27, 1858; *Chicago Daily Journal*, March 1, 1849, March 1, 1850, February 27, 1851, February 28, 1852; *The Daily Democratic Press*, March 3, 1854; *Chicago Tribune*, May 7, 1861, January 2, 1865, April 16, 1866, May 2, 1869, May 1, 1871; *The Chicago Times*, April 29, 1871; *The Bankers' Magazine*, IX (August, 1854), 131, X (February, 1856), 605; *Hunt's Merchants' Magazine*, LVII (July, 1867), 31–32; Colbert, *Chicago*, p. 93. Floating debt is included only in figures for 1848 and 1849. Sewerage, water, and river improvement debt is included in 1858 and after.

[b] Gager, *Directory, 1857*, Appendix, p. vi. Grosser gives this figure as $499,081.64, probably an error in printing.

[c] Decrease.

NUMBERS AND MEMBERSHIPS OF LEADING CHICAGO CHURCHES,
1850–1870 [1]

		1850	1855	1860	1865	1870
Methodist Episcopal[a]...	Members	688	873	1,410	2,045	4,036
	Churches	4	10	14	16	21
	Missions				5	
Baptist..............	Members	452	731	1,105[b]	1,881	3,528
	Churches	2	4	7	11	20
	Missions				5	8
New School Presbyterian	Members	597		1,147[b]	1,585	3,237[d]
	Churches	3	4	6	8	18[d]
	Missions				7	8[d]
Old School Presbyterian	Members	45	104	491	290[c]	
	Churches	1	2	2	5	
Congregational.........	Members		223	808	1,068	1,750
	Churches		5	6	6	13
	Missions		1		3	2
Protestant Episcopal....	Members	380	563	1,043	1,293	2,776
	Churches	4	6	9	11	15
	Missions				1	2
Lutheran (all branches)........	Members	480				7,567
	Churches	3	5	7	11	17
	Missions				1	1
Evangelical (all branches)........	Churches	1	2	2	3	6
Roman Catholic........	Churches	4	7	12	16	25
	Convents				10	12
Swedenborgian.........	Members	38	56	127		
	Churches	1	1	2	2	2
	Missions		1			2
Unitarian.............	Churches	1	1	2	2	4
Universalist...........	Churches	1	2	2	2	4
Jewish...............	Synagogues	1	2	2	4	5
Dutch Reformed.......	Churches	1	2	2	2	3
United Presbyterian....	Churches		1	1	2	2

[1] The sources are city directories, newspapers, reports of denominations. Information is not available for all churches. The table includes all large denominations and some with small memberships.

[a] One of these churches in 1855 and 1860 was African Methodist Episcopal; two in 1865 and 1870 were African Methodist Episcopal.

[b] Membership figure is for 1861.

[c] Membership figure is for 1866.

[d] Figures are of 1871 for the reunited old and new schools.

SCHOOL POPULATION [1]

Year Ending	Number in City under 21 Years of Age	Total Enrollment	Average Daily Enrollment	Number of Schools	Number of Teachers and Principals
1849		1,794		4	19
1850		1,919	1,224	4	21
1851	12,021	2,287	1,409	4	25
1852		2,404	1,521	6	29
1853	17,404	3,086	1,795	6	34
1854		3,500	1,629	7	35
1855	31,235	6,826	2,154	9	42
1856		8,542	3,688	11	61
February 1, 1858		10,786	4,318	11	81
February 1, 1859		12,873	5,516	13	105
February 1, 1860	52,861	14,199	6,649	14	125
February 1, 1861		16,547	7,582	14	138
December 31, 1861		16,441	8,217	14	160
December 31, 1862	58,955	17,521	8,962	15	190
December 31, 1863		21,188	10,820	19	212
August 31, 1865	82,996	29,080	13,507	18	240
August 31, 1866	89,150	25,241	14,609	18	265
August 31, 1867		27,260	16,393	22	316
July 3, 1868		29,954	19,261	25	401
July 3, 1869	109,583	34,740	22,838	31	479
July 1, 1870	136,333	38,939	25,258	36	535
July 1, 1871		40,832	28,174	39	570

[1] Figures for the column on "Number in the City under 21 Years of Age" and for the years 1849 to 1855 are taken from Johnston, *loc. cit.*, p. 47. Figures for 1856 to 1871 are from the Annual Reports of the Chicago Board of Education. City directories have been used for the number of public schools from 1849 through 1853.

SCHOOL FINANCES [1]

Year Ending	Amount of School Fund[a]	Tax Receipts	Total Receipts	Current Expenditures[b]	Expenditures plus 6%[c]	Cost per Pupil based on Daily Enrollment[d]
1849	$ 168,940	$ 6,677	$ 12,877	$ 4,896	$	$
1850	181,720	7,220	13,991	6,038		4.93
1851	205,188	12,844	21,294	7,399		5.25
1852	215,636	10,462	19,784	10,704		7.04
1853	230,636	25,663	36,711	12,130		6.76
1854	356,411	36,588	48,456	14,255		8.75
1855	406,374			16,546		7.68
1856	1,112,000			29,720	40,920	11.10
Feb. 1, 1858	977,000	68,000[e]	104,000	45,701	62,701	14.52
Feb. 1, 1859	977,000	71,000[e]	108,500	55,424	70,341	12.75
Feb. 1, 1860	977,000	56,500[e]	90,000	64,216	83,834	12.61
Feb. 1, 1861	977,000	48,000[e]	90,000	76,152	96,100	12.67
Dec. 31, 1861	1,006,180			86,260	106,487	12.96
Dec. 31, 1862	1,006,927	80,000[e]	118,000	91,544	112,110	12.51
Dec. 31, 1863	1,028,440	85,335	126,928	112,710	146,655	13.55
Aug. 31, 1865	1,038,170	97,466	146,013	176,004	209,688	15.53
Aug. 31, 1866	807,751	180,000[f]	269,637[g]	219,199	261,951	17.93
Aug. 31, 1867	807,751	234,446	388,266	296,673	346,732	21.15
July 3, 1868	807,751	371,275	717,600	352,002	421,074	22.98
July 3, 1869	808,761	551,372	813,344	446,787	556,551	24.49
July 1, 1870	2,774,675	365,841	628,487	527,742	652,980	25.35
July 1, 1871	2,774,675	370,443	1,019,569	547,462	689,185	24.46

[1] All figures are given to the nearest dollar. They are taken from Johnston, *loc. cit.*, p. 47; Gager, *Directory, 1857*, Appendix, p. vi; Annual Reports of the Chicago Board of Education.

[a] Consists chiefly of appraised value of real estate belonging to the School Fund. Income from this fund was to be used only for salaries.

[b] Includes money spent for salaries, supplies, clerical help, janitor service, fuel, etc.

[c] Beginning in 1856, 10 per cent of the valuation of city-owned school buildings and furniture was added to the figure for current expenditures in order to allow for rental costs. This estimated rental charge was reduced to 6 per cent in 1858–59 to conform with the basis used in other cities.

[d] Cost per pupil before 1856 is obtained by dividing the figure for current expenditures by the average daily enrollment. Beginning in 1856 the figures for expenditures plus 6 per cent are used.

[e] Figures for the school tax receipts are not available for 1855–63. These figures have been computed from total city tax receipts in the annual reports of the City Comptroller. They have been given to the nearest $500. This has necessitated the use of round numbers in the column of Total Receipts for corresponding years.

[f] School tax rate raised from two mills to three.

[g] This and succeeding figures in this column include proceeds from bond sales.

SELECTIVE BIBLIOGRAPHY

The following list does not include all sources used in the preparation of *A History of Chicago*, II. Instead, lists of selected and representative types of materials appear. Sources infrequently used and not primarily related to Chicago history have been omitted. Some of these are cited in the footnotes.

In the case of city directories, reports and publications of private and public institutions and organizations, a statement of the years surveyed and similar pertinent data are included in the bibliographical description.

PRIMARY

I. UNPUBLISHED

Ackerman, William K. *Collection, 1839–83. Mss.* Chicago Historical Society.

Atkinson, Charles H. *Diaries, 1867–73. Mss.* Chicago Historical Society.

Autograph Letter Books. Mss. Chicago Historical Society.

Brayman, Mason. *Mason Brayman Papers. Mss.* Chicago Historical Society.

Caton, John D. *John D. Caton Papers.* From December 16, 1840, to May 4, 1881. *Mss.* Library of Congress.

Chicago and North Western Railway Company. *Record " 2 " C. & N. W. Ry. Co., June 4, 1863, to Dec. 19, 1867; Record " 3 " C. & N. W. Ry. Co., Jan. 2, 1868, to June 2, 1881. Mss.* Chicago and North Western Railway Company.

Chicago City National Bank. *Record Book of Directors and Stockholders Meetings, 1865–87.* Ms. Chicago Historical Society.

Chicago, St. Paul and Fond du Lac Railroad. *Records " A " and " B."* Mss. Chicago and North Western Railway Company.

Christian, William H. *W. H. Christian Papers, 1853–1911.* Mss. Chicago Historical Society.

Colby, Francelia. *Our Family* [*Reminiscences of Chicago from 1854*]. Typescript. Chicago Historical Society.

Douglas, Stephen A. *Papers of Stephen A. Douglas, 1845–1861.* Mss. The University of Chicago Library.

Drummond, Thomas. *Letters.* Mss. Chicago Historical Society.

Ellsworth, Col. Elmer E. *Papers.* Mss. Chicago Historical Society.

Evangelical Lutheran Synod of Northern Illinois. *Minutes of the First Annual Convention, 1851.* Ms. Chicago Lutheran Theological Seminary.

Flaven, Lizzie. *Papers, 1865–68.* Mss. Chicago Historical Society.

Fricke, Gustav A. *Autobiographical Sketch.* Ms. Chicago Historical Society.

Galena and Chicago Union Railroad Company. *Record B.* Ms. Chicago and North Western Railway Company.

Gillett and King Lumber Company. *Gillett Papers, 1858–76.* Mss. Chicago Historical Society.

Greenebaum, Henry E. *Henry E. Greenebaum Papers.* Mss. Chicago Historical Society.

Hempstead, Charles S. *Hempstead Papers.* Mss. Chicago Historical Society.

Heyworth, J. O. *Diary and Notebook, 1856–57.* Ms. Chicago Historical Society.

Hollister, John H. *Papers.* Mss. Chicago Historical Society.

Hubbard, Gurdon S. *Gurdon S. Hubbard Papers.* Mss. Chicago Historical Society.

Illinois and Wisconsin Railroad Company. *Records.* Mss. Chicago and North Western Railway Company.

Illinois Central Railroad. *Memorandum of an Understanding Relative to Proposed Relations Between the Illinois Central Railroad and the Galena and Chicago Union Railroad, March 6, 1855.* Ms. Illinois Central Railroad Company.

Johnson, B. F. *Johnson Papers.* Mss. Illinois Central Railroad Company.

Jones, Fernando. *Papers.* Mss. Chicago Historical Society.

Kimberly, Edmund Stoughton. *Papers, 1811–63.* Mss. Chicago Historical Society.

Lamb, Chas. A. *Report of Sanitary Fair, Oct.–Nov. 1863*. *Ms*. Chicago Historical Society.

Lincoln, Abraham. *Lincoln Collection*. *Mss*. and photostats. Chicago Historical Society.

McVicker, James H. *The Theatre: Its Early Days in Chicago*. *Ms*. Chicago Historical Society.

Madison and Beloit Railroad Company. *Records, " A."* *Mss*. Chicago and North Western Railway Company.

Mason, Roswell B. *Correspondence*. *Mss*. Illinois Central Railroad Company.

Mead, A. B. *Diary, 1869*. *Ms*. Chicago Historical Society.

Mechanics' Institute. *Awards and Address of N. S. Davis, 4th Fair, 1851*. *Mss*. McCormick Agricultural Library, Chicago.

Michigan Central Railroad. *Opening of Road to New Buffalo* [March 1, 1849]. Bulletin in Chicago Historical Society.

Miscellaneous Manuscripts. Chicago Historical Society.

Ogden, William B. *Report of W. B. Ogden, President of the Galena and Chicago Union Rail Road Company, read before Stockholders at Annual Meeting, April 5, 1848*. *Ms*. Chicago Historical Society.

Osborn, W. H. *Manuscript Collection, 1854–1856*. Illinois Central Railroad Company.

Raymond, B. W. *Account and Letter Books, 1844–1876*. 15 v. *Mss*. Chicago Historical Society.

Real Estate. *City Clerk's Assessment Roll of North Division of Original Town; Plats and Data showing Owners of Property in Central Section with Dates Sold, down to 1882; Sale of Canal Lands, 1835–55*. *Mss*. Chicago Historical Society.

Rice's Theatre. *Account Book; Day Book, 1858–72*. *Mss*. Chicago Historical Society.

Rock River Valley Union Railroad Company. *Record Books, " A " and " B."* *Mss*. Chicago and North Western Railway Company.

Rumsey, George F. *Papers, 1862–70*. *Mss*. Chicago Historical Society.

St. Columbkille's Parish. *Minutes, . . . December 1858*. *Ms*. Chicago Historical Society.

Scharf, Albert F. *Memorandum regarding Camp Douglas Conspiracy, November 9, 1864*. *Ms*. Chicago Historical Society.

Schneider, George. *Papers*. *Mss*. Chicago Historical Society.

Severin, Mrs. Bertha M. *Autobiography*. *Ms*. Chicago Historical Society.

Starkweather, C. Robert. *Collection*. *Mss*. Chicago Historical Society.

Stuart, William. *Letters*. *Mss*. Chicago Historical Society.

Swift, William H. *William H. Swift Papers, 1843–1865. Mss.* Chicago Historical Society.

Terrace Row Papers. Mss. Chicago Historical Society.

Trumbull, Lyman. *The Papers of Lyman Trumbull, 1855–1877.* 77 v. *Mss.* Library of Congress, 1918.

United States Provost Marshal General. *Report, Illinois, First District.* LVII. *Ms.* War Department Archives, Washington.

Ward, Samuel Dexter. *Personal Reminiscences of Half a Century Ago.* Typescript. Chicago Historical Society.

Washburne, Elihu B. *The Papers of Elihu B. Washburne, 1829–1882.* 102 v. *Mss.* Library of Congress, 1935.

Withrow, Thomas F. *History of the Chicago, Rock Island and Pacific Railway Company, from its Inception February 27, 1847, to date.* Copied by B. Sienauk, 1894. *Ms.* John Crerar Library.

Young Men's Christian Association. *Minutes of the Board of Managers June 21, 1858, to March 17, 1879. Mss.* Chicago Board of Managers of the Y. M. C. A.

II. BOOKS AND PAMPHLETS

[Anon.] *History of the North-Western Soldiers' Fair, held in Chicago . . . 1863, including a List of Donations and Names of Donors, Treasurer's Report, &c., &c.* Chicago: Dunlop, Sewell & Spalding, 1864.

——. *Horse Railway Monopoly. Report of Committee, with Accompanying Documents. Proceedings of Public Meeting of Citizens.* Chicago: Tribune Book and Job Office, 1865.

——. *Memorial of John L. Scripps.* Chicago: Republican Job Printing Co., [1866].

——. *Memorial to the Government of the United States from the Citizens of Chicago, Illinois, Setting Forth the Advantages of that City as a Site for a National Armory and Foundry.* Chicago: n.p., 1861.

——. *Memorial to the President and Congress of the United States by the National Canal Convention, Assembled at Chicago, June 2, 1863.* Chicago: Tribune Company, 1863.

——. *The Parks and Property Interests of the City of Chicago.* Chicago: Western News Company, 1869.

——. *Statistical and Historical Review of Chicago, Rise and Value of Real Estate, Parks, Tunnels, Buildings, etc. . . . .* Chicago: City Directory Publishing House, 1869.

Arnold, Isaac N. *William B. Ogden; and Early Days in Chicago . . .*

(Fergus Historical Series, no. 17). Chicago: Fergus Printing Company, 1882.

Ayer, I. Winslow. *The Great North-Western Conspiracy in all its Startling Details*. Chicago: Rounds and James, 1865.

Chicago Exhibition of the Fine Arts. *Catalogue of the First Exhibition of Statuary, Paintings, &c., Opened May 9th . . . 1859*. Chicago: Press and Tribune, 1859.

Chicago Reform School. *Rules and Regulations of the Chicago Reform School*. Chicago: Guilbert and Clissold, 1870.

Chicago Tribune Campaign Documents. *Spirit of the Chicago Convention, 1864;* Issues of the Campaign, 1864. (Bound in *Pamphlets on Lincoln and the Civil War*, I, in Lincoln Collection, The University of Chicago Library.)

Cleaver, Charles. *Early-Chicago Reminiscences* (Fergus Historical Series, no. 19). Chicago: Fergus Printing Co., 1882.

Colbert, E[lias], and Chamberlin, Everett. *Chicago and the Great Conflagration*. Cincinnati: C. F. Vent, 1871.

Cook, Frederick Francis. *Bygone Days in Chicago; Recollections of the "Garden City" of the Sixties*. Chicago: A. C. McClurg and Co., 1910.

DeBow, J. D. B. *The Industrial Resources, etc., of the Southern and Western States: Commerce, Agriculture, Manufactures, Internal Improvements, Slave and Free Labor, Slavery Institutions, Products, etc., of the South, etc.* 3 v. New Orleans: DeBow's Review, 1852.

DeWolf, Lyman E. *The Social Evil. Whither Are We Drifting*. Chicago: privately printed, 1870.

[Ferry, Abby Farwell]. *Reminiscences of John V. Farwell by his Elder Daughter*. 2 v. Chicago: Ralph Fletcher Seymour, 1928.

Gilmore, P. S. *History of the National Peace Jubilee and Great Musical Festival, Held in the City of Boston, June, 1869, to Commemorate the Restoration of Peace Throughout the Land*. Boston: Lee and Shepard, 1871.

Guyer, I[saac] D. *History of Chicago; Its Commercial and Manufacturing Interests and Industries. . . .* Chicago: Church, Goodman & Cushing, 1862.

Henshaw, Mrs. Sarah Edwards. *Our Branch and its Tributaries; Being a History of the Work of the North-western Sanitary Commission and its Auxiliaries during the War of the Rebellion. . . .* Chicago: Alfred L. Sewell, 1868.

Joint Committee of the Board of Trade and Mercantile Association. *Produce and Transportation, The Railway and Warehouse Monopolies. Report. . . . A Review of the Warehouse and Grain Inspec-*

tion Trouble. Chicago: Evening Journal Job Printing House, 1866.

Kedzie, Rev. A. S. *Chicago Theological Seminary.* Chicago: n.p., [1860].

Kirkland, Caroline [ed.]. *Chicago Yesterdays; a Sheaf of Reminiscences.* Chicago: Daughaday and Company, 1919.

Koerner, Gustave. *Memoirs of Gustave Koerner, 1809–1896* . . . (Thomas J. McCormack, ed.). 2 v. Cedar Rapids, Iowa: The Torch Press, 1909.

Larned, E. C. *The New Fugitive Slave Law: Speech of Edwin C. Larned, Esq. at the City Hall in the City of Chicago, on the Evening of Oct. 25th, 1850, in Reply to Hon. S. A. Douglas.* Chicago: Office of the Democrat, 1850.

Livermore, Mary A. *My Story of the War.* . . . Hartford, Conn.: A. D. Worthington and Company, 1892.

——. *The Story of My Life.* Hartford: A. D. Worthington and Company, 1898.

McIlvaine, Mabel, ed. *Reminiscences of Chicago during the Civil War.* Chicago: R. R. Donnelley and Sons Company, 1914.

——. *Reminiscences of Chicago during the Forties and Fifties.* Chicago: R. R. Donnelley and Sons Company, 1913.

——. *Reminiscences of Chicago during the Great Fire.* Chicago: R. R. Donnelley and Sons Company, 1915.

[MacLeish, Andrew]. *The Life of Andrew MacLeish, 1838–1928.* Chicago: privately printed, 1929.

[May, Samuel]. *The Fugitive Slave Law and its Victims* (Anti-slavery Tracts, n.s. no. 15). Rev. ed. New York: American Anti-Slavery Society, 1861.

Merchants, Farmers and Mechanics Savings Bank. *The Labor Question . . . Labor, Trades Unions, Co-operative Societies, and Model Houses and Cottages.* . . . Chicago: Merchants, Farmers and Mechanics Savings Bank, 1867.

Moody, Dwight L. *Moody's Gospel and Sermons, Delivered in Europe and America.* New ed. 2 v. Chicago: Rhodes and McClure Publishing Co., 1889.

North-Western Sanitary Fair. *Circular Collection, 1865.* Chicago: n.p., 1865.

Packard, Mrs. E. P. W. *Marital Power Exemplified in Mrs. Packard's Trial, and Self-Defence from the Charge of Insanity.* . . . Rev. ed. Chicago: Clark and Company, 1869.

Pierce, Bessie Louise, ed. *As Others See Chicago.* Chicago: The University of Chicago Press, 1933.

Schnyder, A. *Ein Brief über Taubstummen-Erziehung an eine Mutter, deren Tochter eine Schülerin der Ersten Deutsch-Englischen Taub-stummen-Schule von Chicago ist, und Erster Jahresbericht über die Erste Deutsch-Englische Taubstummen-Schule.* Chicago: privately published, 1881.

Smith, A. Hyatt. *Letter . . . as to the Bonds of the Rock River Valley Union Railroad Company . . .* reprinted as an appendix to [Anon.] *Letter to the Hon. John Letcher of the House of Representatives, in Relation to the Rock River Valley Union R. R. Co., and its Application for a Grant of the Public Lands.* Milwaukee: n.p. [1854].

[Soldiers' Home, Chicago]. *Organization, Constitution and By-Laws of the Soldiers' Home in the City of Chicago.* Chicago: S. P. Rounds, 1863.

Thorn, W., & Co. *Chicago in 1860; a Glance at its Business Houses.* Chicago: Thompson and Day, 1860.

Trade and Labor Assembly of Chicago. *Constitution, By-Laws and Rules of Order . . . adopted May, 1880.* Chicago: n.p., 1886.

Unonius, Gustaf. *Minnen från en sjuttonårig vistelse i nordvestra Amerika.* 2 v. Upsala: W. Schultz, 1862.

Wentworth, John. *Congressional Reminiscences . . .* (Fergus Historical Series, no. 24). Chicago: Fergus Printing Co., 1882.

Whipple, H. B. *Sermon Preached at the Opening of the Free Church of the Holy Communion, Chicago, February 6, 1859.* Chicago: Scott and Co., 1859.

Wilkie, Franc B. *Personal Reminiscences of Thirty-Five Years of Journalism.* Chicago: F. J. Schulte and Co., [1891].

Wright, John S. *Chicago: Past, Present, Future.* Chicago: Horton and Leonard, 1868.

——. *Investments in Chicago.* Chicago: n.p., 1858.

III. ARTICLES

[Anon.] "Chicago," *Frank Leslie's Illustrated Newspaper*, II (July 12, 1856), 71.

——. "The Chicago Conspiracy," *The Atlantic Monthly*, XVI (July, 1865), 108–20.

——. "Chicago in 1856," *Putnam's Monthly Magazine*, VII (June, 1856), 606–13.

Epstein, Francis J., ed. "History in the Annals of the Leopoldine Association, Letters of the Bishop William Quarter, D.D.," *Illinois Catholic Historical Review*, I (July, 1918), 226–27.

Gallery, Mary Onahan, ed. " The Diaries of William J. Onahan," *Mid-America*, XIV, n.s. III (October, 1931), 152–77.

Hines, Thomas H. " The Northwestern Conspiracy," *The Southern Bivouac: A Monthly Literary and Historical Magazine*, n.s. II (December, 1886–February, 1887), 437–45, 500–10, 567–74.

Jevne, Christian H. " An Immigrant in Chicago, 1864," Norwegian-American Historical Association, *Studies and Records*, III (1928), 67–72.

Logan, Mrs. John A. " Recollections of a Soldier's Wife," *Cosmopolitan Magazine*, LIV–LV (December, 1912–September, 1913).

Onahan, William. " A Civil War Diary," *Mid-America*, n.s. III (July, 1931), 64–72.

Parton, James. " Chicago," *The Atlantic Monthly*, XIX (March, 1867), 325–45.

IV. NEWSPAPERS AND PERIODICALS

The Advance. I–IV, 1867–71. [Weekly. Congregational.]

The Bankers' Magazine [Baltimore]. IV–XXV, 1849–71. [Title varies.]

Chicago Bank Note List. 1853–64. [Semimonthly.]

Chicago Daily Journal. 1848–61. [Republican. Title varies: *Daily Chicago Journal*, January 26, 1853–February 9, 1855; *Chicago Daily Journal*, 1848–January 25, 1853, February 10, 1855–April 21, 1861. In 1861 becomes *Chicago Evening Journal.*]

Chicago Daily Press and Tribune. 1858–60. [Republican. Becomes *The Press and Tribune*, March 17, 1859.]

Chicago Evening Journal. 1861–71. [Daily. Republican.]

Chicago Evening Post. 1865–71. [Daily. Known as *Daily Chicago Post*, 1865–66.]

The Chicago Magazine of Fashion, Music, and Home Reading. 1870–71. [Monthly.]

Chicago Magazine: The West as It Is. I, March–August, 1857. [Monthly.]

Chicago Morning Post. 1860–65. [Daily. Becomes *Chicago Post*, 1863–65. Merged with *Chicago Republican.*]

Chicago Record: a Journal, Devoted to the Church, to Literature, and to the Arts. I–V, 1857–62. [Monthly. 1858–60, *The Church Record;* became *The Northwestern Church* in 1862. Protestant Episcopal.]

Chicago Republican. 1865–71. [Daily.]

The Chicago Times. 1854–71. [Daily. Democratic, Independent. Title varies: *Chicago Daily Times*, August 30, 1854–July 30, 1860; *The*

Times and Herald, July 31–November 26, 1860; *Daily Chicago Times,* November 27, 1860–June 20, 1861 (scattered issues).]

Chicago Tribune. 1847–71. [Daily. Republican. Title varies: *Chicago Daily Tribune,* June 10, 1847–June 30, 1858; *Chicago Daily Press and Tribune,* July 1, 1858–March 16, 1859; *The Press and Tribune,* March 17, 1859–October 24, 1860; *Chicago Daily Tribune,* October 25, 1860–August 21, 1864; *Chicago Tribune,* August 22, 1864–September 14, 1867; *The Chicago Tribune,* September 15, 1867–71.]

The Christian Times. I–XIII, 1853–65. [Baptist. Continues *Watchman of the Prairies;* 1858–62, *The Christian Times and Illinois Baptist;* 1862–65, *The Christian Times;* 1865–67, *Christian Times and Witness.* Merged into *Standard.*]

Commercial Advertiser. 1847–53. [Weekly to 1849, then daily. 1847–51 as *Chicago Commercial Advertiser.*]

Congregational Herald. I–IX, 1853–61.

Daily Democrat. 1845–61. [Known as *Chicago Daily Democrat,* June 7, 1849. Absorbed by *Chicago Tribune,* 1861.]

The Daily Democratic Press. 1852–58. [Non-partisan, Republican. Known as *Chicago Daily Democratic Press,* May 8, 1857. United with *Chicago Daily Tribune,* July 1, 1858, to become *Chicago Daily Press and Tribune.*]

DeBow, James D. B. *DeBow's Review. Agricultural, Commercial, Industrial Progress and Resources.* New Orleans. I–XXXIV, 1846–64; (ser. 2) I–VIII, 1866–71. [Suspended September 1864–December 1865. Title varies.]

Deutsch-Amerikanische Geschichtsblätter. I–XI, 1901–11.

Deutsch-Amerikanische Monatshefte für Politik, Wissenschaft und Literatur. I–IV, 1864–67.

L'Écho des deux mondes; journal littéraire et artistique, dévoué aux intérêts de la langue française en Amérique. I–X, 1904–13.

Die Fackel. Literaturblatt zur Förderung geistiger Freiheit. I–XVII, 1843–65.

The Free West. 1853–55. [Weekly. Organ of Freedom Party of Illinois. Merged with *Chicago Tribune.*]

Gem of the Prairie. 1848–52. [Weekly. Literary. Became Sunday edition of *Chicago Tribune.*]

Hunt, Freeman, ed. *The Merchants' Magazine and Commercial Review.* New York. XX–LXIII, 1849–70. [Merged into *Commercial and Financial Chronicle.*]

Illinois Staats-Zeitung. 1848–71. [Both weekly and daily editions after 1851.]

Illinois State Register. Springfield. January 7, 1848–December 28, 1854, January 1–December 31, 1857. [Library of Congress.]

The Interior. I–II, 1870–71. [Weekly. Presbyterian.]

The Irish Republic. May 4, 1867–April 25, 1868.

The Monthly. II. [Roman Catholic magazine edited at the University of St. Mary of the Lake. Chicago: James P. Byrne, 1865.]

The New Covenant. 1848–60. [Weekly. Universalist.]

New York Times. 1851–71. [Daily. 1851–57 as *New York Daily Times*.]

Northwestern Christian Advocate. I–XX, 1852–71. [Weekly. Methodist Episcopal.]

Oquawka [Illinois] *Spectator*. 1853–64. [Weekly. Non-partisan, Democratic.]

Prairie Farmer. 1849–71. [Monthly, 1849–57; weekly, 1857–71.]

The Rail Splitter. June 23–October 27, 1860. [Weekly. Republican campaign paper.]

Railroad Gazette: a Journal of Transportation, Engineering and Railroad News. I, 1870–71. [Weekly. Continues *Western Railroad Gazette*.]

Railroad Record, or Journal of Commerce, Banking, Manufactures and Statistics. I, 1853–54.

United States Economist and Dry Goods Reporter. n.s. I–V, 1852–56. [Library of Congress.]

Voice of the Fair. I, April 27–June 21, 1865.

Watchman of the Prairies. I–VI, 1847–53. [Weekly. Baptist. Continued as *Christian Times*.]

Weekly Chicago Democrat. 1846–61. [1857–61 as *Chicago Weekly Democrat*.]

Wells' Commercial Express and Western Produce Reporter. 1857–71. [Weekly, then weekly and monthly. Daily, 1861 on, called *Chicago Commercial Express* . . .]

Western Citizen. I–XI, 1842–53. [Temperance and antislavery paper; organ of Liberty Party.]

Western Tablet. I–II, 1852–53. [Roman Catholic.]

The Workingman's Advocate [Chicago]. I–XII, 1864–71.

V. DOCUMENTS AND REPORTS

A. *Official*

Chesbrough, Ellis S. *Chicago Sewerage, Report of the Results of Examinations made in Relation to Sewerage in Several European Cities in the Winter of 1856–57*. . . . Chicago: The Board of Sewerage Commissioners, 1858.

Chicago, City of. *Annual Financial Statement of the City of Chicago for the Municipal Year 1851*. Chicago: The Democrat Office, 1852.

——. *The Charter and Ordinances of the City of Chicago (to Sept. 15, 1856, inclusive,)* . . . (George W. and John A. Thompson, comps.). Chicago: D. B. Cooke and Co., 1856.

——. *Common Council Documents, 1848–71*. Not printed, Chicago City Hall.

——. *Council Proceedings, 1858–70*. [1858–65 *Proceedings* found in privately bound copy at the Chicago Historical Society.]

——. *Index to Council Documents*. I–III, 1837–70. Not printed, City Clerk's Office, Chicago City Hall.

——. *Laws and Ordinances Governing the City of Chicago* . . . (Murray F. Tuley, comp.). Chicago: Bulletin Printing Company, 1873.

——. *Laws and Ordinances Governing the City of Chicago, Jan. 1, 1866* . . . (Jos. E. Gary, comp.). Chicago: E. B. Myers and Chandler, 1866.

——. *The Municipal Code of Chicago: Comprising the Laws of Illinois Relating to the City of Chicago, and the Ordinances of the City Council* . . . (Egbert Jamieson and Francis Adams, eds.). Chicago: Beach, Barnard and Co., 1881.

——. *Ordinances of the City of Chicago; passed since the Publication of the Revised Ordinance of 1851, and now in Force* (Arno Voss, comp.). Chicago: Daily Democrat, 1853.

——. *Police Ordinance and Rules and Regulations for the Government of the Police Department and Instructions as to the Powers and Duties of Police Officers of the City of Chicago*. Chicago: Daily Democrat Printing Office, 1855.

——. *The Revised Charter and Ordinances of the City of Chicago* . . . (George Manierre, ed.). Chicago: Daily Democrat, 1851.

Chicago Board of Education. . . . *Annual Report*, 1858/59–1878/79. Chicago: printer varies, 1859–80. [Continues Chicago Superintendent of Schools, *Annual Report*.]

Chicago Board of Health. *Reports* . . . , 1862–75. Chicago: printer varies, 1863–76.

Chicago Board of Public Works. . . . *Annual Report* . . . *to the Common Council*, 1862–71. Chicago: printer varies, 1862–72.

Chicago Board of Water Commissioners. . . . *Semi-Annual Report* . . . *to the Common Council of the City of Chicago*, 1854–61. Chicago: 1854–62.

Chicago Bureau of Engineering. *A Century of Progress in Water Works, Chicago, 1833–1933*. Chicago: Bureau of Engineering, 1933.

Chicago City Comptroller. *Annual Statements,* 1858–71. Chicago: 1859–72.

Chicago Department of Public Works. *First Annual Report . . . Fiscal Year ending December 31, 1876.* Chicago: Clark and Edwards, 1877.

Chicago Reform School. . . . *Annual Reports,* 1855/56–64/65, 1866–67, 1868–69. Chicago: printer varies, 1856–69.

Chicago Superintendent of Schools. . . . *Annual Reports,* 1854–57. Chicago: printer varies, 1855–58. [Continued by Chicago Board of Education, *Annual Report.*]

Cook County Board of Supervisors. *Reports,* 1866–71. n.p., n.d. [Privately bound volume at Municipal Reference Library with binder's title: *Proceedings of the Board of Commissioners of Cook County, 1866–71.*]

Cook County Department of Public Charities. *Annual Report of the Superintendent and Medical Director of Public Charities, to the Board of County Commissioners of Cook County, 1872.* Chicago: n.p., 1872.

Illinois. *Biennial Report of the Auditor of Public Accounts, 1853,* bound with *General Laws of the State of Illinois. Passed by the Eighteenth General Assembly Convened January 3, 1853.* Springfield: Lanphier and Walker, 1853.

——. *A Compilation of the Statutes of the State of Illinois of a General Nature in Force January 1, 1857* (N. H. Purple, comp.). 2 v. 2d ed. Chicago: Keen and Lee, 1857.

——. *Debates and Proceedings of the Constitutional Convention of the State of Illinois, convened at the City of Springfield, Tuesday, December 13, 1869.* . . . 2 v. Springfield: E. L. Merritt and Brother, 1870.

——. *General Laws of the State of Illinois, passed by the . . . General Assembly,* 1851, 1853, 1859. Springfield: 1851–59.

——. *The General Statutes of Illinois . . . 1818 to 1869* (Eugene L. Gross, ed.). 3d ed. Springfield: E. L. and W. L. Gross, 1872.

——. *Journal of the Constitutional Convention of the State of Illinois, convened at Springfield, January 7, 1862.* Springfield: Charles H. Lanphier, 1862.

——. *Journal of the House of Representatives of the . . . General Assembly of the State of Illinois,* 1849–71. Springfield: printer varies, 1849–71.

——. *Journal of the Senate of the . . . General Assembly of the State of Illinois,* 1849–71. Springfield: printer varies, 1849–71.

——. *Laws of the State of Illinois, Passed by the . . . General Assembly,* 1849, 1852–59, 1871. Springfield: 1849–71.

——. *Private Laws of the State of Illinois Passed by the . . . General Assembly,* 1849–69. Springfield: printer varies, 1849–69.

——. *Public Laws of the State of Illinois, Passed by the . . . General Assembly,* 1849–72. Springfield: printer varies, 1849–72.

——. *Report of the Adjutant General of the State of Illinois, 1861–66.* . . . 8 v. Springfield: H. W. Rokker, 1886.

——. *Reports Made to the General Assembly of Illinois . . . ,* 1849–71. Springfield: printer varies, 1849–71.

——. *The Revised Statutes of the State of Illinois, A. D. 1874* (Harvey B. Hurd, comp.). Springfield: Illinois Journal Company, 1874.

——. *The Statutes of Illinois: an Analytical Digest of all the General Laws of the State in Force at the Present Time, 1818 to 1869* (Eugene L. Gross, ed.). 3d ed. Springfield: E. L. and W. L. Gross, 1872.

Illinois Department of Agriculture. *Transactions,* o.s. IX–XXII, n.s. I–XIV, 1871–84; State Printer, 1872–85.

Illinois Railroad and Warehouse Commission. *Second Annual Report . . . for Year ending Nov. 30, 1872.* Springfield: State Journal, 1873.

Illinois State Agricultural Society. *Transactions.* I–VIII, 1853–70. [Continued as Illinois Department of Agriculture, *Transactions.*]

Legislative Reference Bureau, comp. *Constitutional Conventions in Illinois.* 2d ed. Springfield: Schnepp and Barnes, 1919.

McAlpine, Wm. J. *Report to the Water Commissioners of the City of Chicago, Sept. 26, 1851, on Supplying the City with Water.* Chicago: Seaton and Peck, 1851.

New York [State]. *Proceedings of the Special Committee on Railroads, . . . to Investigate Alleged Abuses in the Management of Railroads chartered by the State of New York.* 5 v. Albany: Evening Post Steam Press, 1879–[1880].

Robinson, Chalfant. *History of the Reciprocity Treaty of 1854 with Canada.* United States, 62 Cong., 1 sess., S. Doc. XXVII, no. 17. Washington: Government Printing Office, 1911.

United States. *A Compendium of the Ninth Census (June 1, 1870)* . . . (Francis A. Walker, comp.). Washington: Government Printing Office, 1872.

——. *Congressional Globe.* 1849–71.

——. *Eighth Census, 1860.* 4 v. Washington: Government Printing Office, 1864–65.

——. " Government Contracts," *Reports of Committees of the House of Representatives, 1861–62.* 37 Cong., 2 sess., H. Rept. no. 2. Washington: Government Printing Office, 1862.

——. *Marriage and Divorce, 1867–1906.* 2 v. Washington: Government Printing Office, 1908–10.

United States. *Ninth Census, 1870.* 3 v. Washington: Government Printing Office, 1872.

——. *Official Army Register of the Volunteer Force of United States Army, 1861, 62, 63, 64, 65.* Washington: Government Printing Office, 1865.

——. *Preliminary Report on the Eighth Census, 1860* (Joseph C. G. Kennedy, comp.). Washington: Government Printing Office, 1862.

——. " Report of the Postmaster General," *Message of the President of the United States and Accompanying Documents to the two Houses of Congress.* 38 Cong., 2 sess., H. Ex. Doc. 1. 6 v. Washington: Government Printing Office, 1864.

——. " Report of the Postmaster General," *Message of the President of the United States and Accompanying Documents to the two Houses of Congress.* 40 Cong., 3 sess., H. Ex. Doc. 1. 4 v. Washington: Government Printing Office, 1868.

——. *Seventh Census, 1850.* Washington: Robert Armstrong, 1853.

——. *Statistical View of the United States . . . being a Compendium of the Seventh Census* (J. D. B. DeBow, comp.). Washington: Beverly Tucker, 1854.

United States Bureau of Statistics. *First Annual Report of the Internal Commerce of the United States,* by Joseph Nimmo, Jr., being Part Second of the *Annual Report of the Chief of the Bureau of Statistics on the Commerce and Navigation of the United States, for the Year Ending June 30, 1876.* Washington: Government Printing Office, 1877.

United States Census Office. *Report on the Agencies of Transportation in the United States, including the Statistics of Railroads, Steam Navigation, Canals, Telegraphs, and Telephones . . .* Washington: Government Printing Office, 1883.

United States Commissioner of Internal Revenue. *Report . . . on the Operations of the Internal Revenue System, 1863–71.* Washington: Government Printing Office, 1864–71.

United States Comptroller of the Currency. *Report . . . to the Second Session of the Forty-Second Congress of the United States, December 4, 1871.* Washington: Government Printing Office, 1871.

United States Federal Trade Commission. *Report of the Federal Trade Commission on the Grain Trade.* 5 v. Washington: Government Printing Office, 1920.

——. *Report of the Federal Trade Commission on the Meat Packing Industry.* 6 v. Washington: Government Printing Office, 1920.

United States General Land Office. *Report of the Commissioner of the*

General Land Office [1867, 1868]. Washington: Government Printing Office, 1867–68.

United States House of Representatives. *Report of the Industrial Commission on Agriculture and Taxation in Various States.* 57 Cong., 1 sess., H. Doc. 180. Washington: Government Printing Office, 1901.

——. *Extracts from Congressional Debates on the Reciprocity Treaty of 1854 with Canada.* 61 Cong., 3 sess., H. Doc. CXXIV, no. 1350. Washington: Government Printing Office, 1911.

United States Provost Marshal General. *Final Report Made to the Secretary of War . . . March 17, 1863, to March 17, 1866.* Washington: Government Printing Office, 1866.

United States Sanitary Commission. *The Sanitary Commission of the United States Army; a succinct Narrative of its Works and Purposes.* New York: published for the benefit of the United States Sanitary Commission, 1864.

——. *The United States Sanitary Commission.* Boston: Crosby and Nichols, 1864.

United States Senate. *Report of the Senate Select Committee on Interstate Commerce.* 49 Cong., 1 sess., S. Rept. 46. 2 v. Washington: Government Printing Office, 1886.

——. *Report of the Select Committee on Transportation-Routes to the Seaboard.* . . . 43 Cong., 1 sess., S. Rept. 307, pt. 2. 2 v. Washington: Government Printing Office, 1874.

United States Treasury Department. *Commerce and Navigation, Report of the Secretary of the Treasury,* 1847–72. Washington: Government Printing Office, 1848–73. [Title varies.]

United States War Department. *The War of the Rebellion: A Compilation of the Official Records of the Union and Confederate Armies.* 70 v. in 128. Washington: Government Printing Office, 1880–1901.

Verlie, Emil Joseph, ed. *Illinois Constitutions* (Illinois State Historical Library, *Collections,* XIII. Constitutional Series, I). Springfield: Illinois State Historical Library, 1919.

Wisconsin Railroad Commissioners. *First Annual Report.* Madison: Atwood and Culver, 1874.

B. *Private*

American Bible Society. *Annual Reports,* 1847/48–1871/72.

American Congregational Union. *Year Book for the Year 1855.* New York: American Congregational Union, 1855.

American Tract Society. *Annual Reports,* 1848–71. New York: The Society, 1848–71.

Annual Conference of the Methodist Episcopal Church. *Minutes for the year 1850.* New York: G. Love and L. Scott, 1850.

Chicago and North Western Railway Company. *Documents Relating to the Formation of the Chicago and North Western Railway Company.* New York: John W. Amerman, 1860.

——. *Annual Reports,* 1860–71.

Chicago and Rock Island Company. *Annual Report of the President and Directors to the Stockholders of the Chicago and Rock Island Railroad Company,* 1850/51–1865/66. New York: 1852–66. [Title varies.]

Chicago Baptist Association. *Minutes of the Fourteenth Anniversary . . . 1850.* Elgin: Western Christian Print, 1850.

——. *Proceedings of the Thirty-Fifth Anniversary . . . 1870.* Elgin: Watchman Print, 1870.

Chicago Board of Trade. . . . *Annual Report of the Trade and Commerce of Chicago, for the Year ending December 31 . . . Compiled for the Board of Trade, by Charles Randolph, Secretary.* 12th–15th, 1869–72. Chicago: printer varies, 1870–73. [Continues the Chicago Board of Trade, *Annual Statement.* 2d–11th, 1859–1868/69.]

[Chicago Daily Press and Tribune.] . . . *Annual Review of the Trade and Commerce and of the Public and Private Improvements of the City of Chicago . . .* 7th–8th, 1858–59. Chicago: Press and Tribune, 1859–60.

[Chicago Daily Tribune.] *Annual Review of the Trade and Commerce of the City of Chicago,* 1860, 1863–65, 1869–70. Chicago: Tribune Company's print, 1861–71. [Title varies.]

Chicago Home for the Friendless. *Annual Reports,* 1864–71. Chicago: printer varies, 1865–72.

Chicago Relief and Aid Society. *Annual Report, 1871.* Chicago: 1871.

Chicago, Rock Island and Pacific Railroad Company. *Annual Report of the President and Directors to the Stockholders of the Chicago, Rock Island and Pacific Railroad Company,* 1867–72. New York: L. H. Biglow and Co., 1867–72.

[The Daily Democratic Press, and others.] *Annual Review of the Commerce, Manufactures, and the Public and Private Improvements of Chicago,* 1852–57. Chicago: Democratic Press, 1853–58.

[Episcopal] Diocese of Illinois. *Journal of the Thirteenth Annual Convention . . . 1850.* Aurora: Jubilee Press, 1850.

——. *Journal of the Thirty-Third Annual Convention . . . 1870.* Chicago: Rounds and Kane, 1870.

Fox River Baptist Association. *Minutes of the Thirty-Fifth Anniversary . . . 1870.* Chicago: North-Western Printing House, 1870.

——. *Proceedings of the Fifteenth Annual Meeting . . . 1850.* Chicago: Jas. J. Langdon, 1850.

——. *The Thirtieth Anniversary . . . held in the Meeting House of the Somonauk Baptist Church, Ill., July 6th, 7th and 8th, 1865.* Chicago: Church, Goodman and Donnelley, 1865.

Galena and Chicago Union Railroad Company. *Annual Reports,* 1849–61.

General Assembly of the [New School] Presbyterian Church in the United States of America. *Minutes, 1850.* New York: Presbyterian Publication Committee, 1850.

General Assembly of the [Old School] Presbyterian Church in the United States of America. *Minutes, 1850.* Philadelphia: Presbyterian Board of Publication, 1850.

General Assembly of the Presbyterian Church in the United States of America. *Minutes . . . 1871.* New York: Presbyterian Board of Publication, 1871.

Illinois Central Railroad Company. *Reports and Accounts,* 1854, 1856–71.

Lake Shore and Michigan Southern Railway Company. *Eighth Annual Report of the President and Directors . . . to the Stockholders, for the Fiscal Year Ending December 31, 1877.* Cleveland: Fairbanks, Briggs and Co., 1878.

Michigan Central Railroad Company. *Annual Reports,* 1847–71. Boston and Detroit: printer varies, 1847–71.

Michigan Southern and Northern Indiana Railroad Company. *Annual Reports,* 1852–53, 1857–58, 1861–62.

Pittsburgh and Fort Wayne Railway Company. *Seventh Annual Report of the Board of Directors of the Pittsburgh, Fort Wayne and Chicago Railway Company to the Stock and Bondholders for the Year 1868.*

Poor, Henry V. *Manual of the Railroads of the United States . . . , 1868/ 69–1872/73.* New York: H. V. and H. W. Poor, 1868–72.

Rock River Annual Conference of the Methodist Episcopal Church. *Minutes of the Twenty-Third Session . . .* Chicago: Dunlop, Sewell and Spalding, 1862.

——. *Register of the Session. . . .* Chicago: Methodist Book Depository, 1863–70.

Scandinavian Evangelical Lutheran Augustana Synod. *Protokoll . . . tionde årsmöte . . . 1869.* Rock Island: Augustana Book Concern, 1917.

——. *Protokoll . . . elfte årsmöte . . . 1870.* Rock Island: Augustana Book Concern, 1917.

The University of Chicago. . . . *Annual Catalogue of the University of Chicago. Officers and Students for the Academic Year,* 1859/60–1870/71. Chicago: printer varies, 1860–71.

Wisconsin Railroad Commissioners. *Annual Report.* Madison: 1874.

Woman's Hospital Medical College. *Annual Announcement of the Woman's Hospital Medical College of Chicago, Ill., 1870–71.* Chicago: Robert Fergus' Sons, 1870.

Woolen Manufacturers' Association of the Northwest. *First Annual Report.* . . . Chicago: Printers' Co-operative Association, 1868.

VI. DIRECTORIES, GUIDE BOOKS, AND MAPS

[Anon.] *Chicago, A Strangers' and Tourists' Guide to the City of Chicago.* Chicago: Relig. Philo. Pub. Association, 1866.

Austin, Ed. S., comp. *John C. W. Bailey's Chicago City Directory for 1867–68.* Chicago: John C. W. Bailey, 1867.

Bailey, John C. W. *Chicago City Directory,* [1864–65, 1866–67]. John C. W. Bailey, 1864, 1866.

Bailey and Edwards. *Chicago Directory, 1868.* See Edwards, Richard . . . *Annual Directory.*

Blanchard, Rufus. *Citizen's Guide for the City of Chicago. Companion to Blanchard's Map of Chicago.* Chicago: Rufus Blanchard, 1866.

——. *Guide Map of Chicago, 1867.* Chicago: Rufus Blanchard, 1867.

——. *Map of Chicago, 1857.* Chicago: Rufus Blanchard, 1857.

Chicago Department of Public Works, Bureau of Maps and Plats. *Map of Chicago Showing Growth of the City by Annexations and Accretions.* [Chicago]: n.p., 1933.

Danenhower, W. W. *Chicago City Directory, for 1851.* . . . Chicago: W. W. Danenhower, 1851.

Edwards, Richard. . . . *Annual Directory of the Inhabitants, Institutions, Manufacturing Establishments and Incorporated Companies of the City of Chicago* . . . (9th)–15th, (1866)–1872. Chicago: Richard Edwards, 1866–72.

Edwards, Richard, comp. *Chicago (Merchants') Census Report; and Statistical Review, embracing a Complete Directory of the City.* . . . Chicago: Richard Edwards, 1871.

Gager, John, comp. *Case & Co.'s Chicago City Directory for the Year Ending June First, 1857.* . . . Chicago: John Gager and Co., [1856].

——. *Gager's Chicago City Directory for the Year Ending June 1st, 1857.* . . . Chicago: John Gager and Co., 1856.

Hair, James T., comp. *J. C. W. Bailey & Co.'s Chicago City Directory for the Year 1865-6.* Chicago: John C. W. Bailey, 1865.

Hall, Edward Hepple, comp. *The Chicago Almanac and Advertiser, for the Year 1855.* . . . Chicago: Chicago Printing Company, 1855.

——. *The Chicago City Directory and Business Advertiser, 1855-56.* Chicago: Robert Fergus, 1855.

Hall and Smith. *Chicago City Directory, for 1853-'54.* Chicago: Robert Fergus, 1853.

Hall, [Edward H.] & Co. *Chicago City Directory and Business Advertiser, for 1854-55.* . . . Chicago: R. Fergus, 1854.

Halpin, T. M., comp. *Halpin & Bailey's Chicago City Directory, 1861/62-1863/64.* Chicago: Halpin and Bailey, 1861-63.

——. *Halpin's . . . Annual Edition Chicago City Directory,* [7th-8th], 1864/65-1865/66. Chicago: T. M. Halpin, 1864-65.

Halpin, T. M., and Co., comp. *D. B. Cooke & Co.'s Chicago City Directory, for the Year 1860-61.* Chicago: D. B. Cooke and Co., 1860.

Hatheway, O. P., and Taylor, J. H. *Chicago City Directory and Annual Advertiser, for 1849-50.* . . . Chicago: Jas. J. Langdon, 1849.

Kennedy, R. V., and Co., comp. *D. B. Cooke & Co.'s City Directory for the Year 1859-60.* . . . Chicago: D. B. Cooke and Co., 1859.

Norris, James W., and Taylor, L. S. *Chicago Directory for 1848-1849.* Chicago: Norris and Taylor, 1848.

Smith & DuMoulin. *Chicago City Directory, for the Year Ending May 1, 1860.* Chicago: Smith and DuMoulin, 1859.

Tanner, Halpin and Co., comp. *D. B. Cooke & Co.'s Directory of Chicago for the Year 1858.* Chicago: D. B. Cooke and Co., 1858.

Udall and Hopkins. *Chicago City Directory, for 1852 & '53.* Chicago: Udall and Hopkins, 1852.

SECONDARY

I. UNPUBLISHED WORKS

[Anon.] *History of Crane Company.* Typescript. Crane Company [Chicago].

Atwood, Jane Kellog. *Development of the Commerce of the Great Lakes.* M.S. Thesis, The University of Chicago, 1915.

Bergstrom, Lois Mildred. *The History of McVicker's Theatre, 1857-1861.* M.A. Thesis, The University of Chicago, 1930.

Brown, James, IV. *The History of Public Assistance in Chicago, 1833–93.* Ph.D. Thesis, The University of Chicago, 1939.

Breckenridge, Helen Elizabeth. *The Chicago Times during the Civil War.* M.A. Thesis, The University of Chicago, 1931.

Coonley, Marjorie Helen. *Private Relief Societies in Chicago, 1871–1910.* M.A. Thesis, The University of Chicago, 1921.

Corliss, C. J. *Seventy-Two Years on Lake Front.* Outline *Ms.* Illinois Central Railroad Company.

Dailey, Don Marcus. *The Development of Banking in Chicago before 1890.* Ph.D. Thesis, Northwestern University, 1934.

Ellis, Lewis E. *A History of the Chicago Delegation in Congress, 1843–1925.* Ph.D. Thesis, The University of Chicago, 1925.

Espenshade, Esther Elizabeth. *The Economic Development and History of Chicago, 1860–65.* M.A. Thesis, The University of Chicago, 1931.

Field, Marshall. *Papers.* Typescript. Marshall Field and Company.

Fishback, Mason McCloud. *Illinois Legislation on Slavery and Free Negroes, 1818–1865.* M.A. Thesis, University of Illinois, 1901.

Goodwin, G. B. *The Street Railway Systems of Chicago, Their History and Present Condition.* Evanston, *Ms.* Dicke Collection, 1898.

Gray, Wood. *The Peace Movement in the Old Northwest, 1860–1865; a Study in Defeatism.* Ph.D. Thesis, The University of Chicago, 1933.

Halsey, Elizabeth. *The Development of Public Recreation in Chicago.* Ph.D. Thesis, University of Michigan, 1939.

Haseltine, Helen D. *A History of the Chicago Home for Girls Founded in 1863 as the Chicago Erring Woman's Refuge for Reform.* M.A. Thesis, The University of Chicago, 1934.

Johnson, Earl S. *The Natural History of the Central Business District of Chicago.* In progress, Ph.D. Thesis, The University of Chicago, 1939.

Kiler, Aureka Belle. *A History of the Free Soil Movement in Illinois; Together with a Review of the Kindred Anti-Slavery Movements Culminating in the Formation of the Republican Party.* M.A. Thesis, University of Illinois, 1896.

Mason, Mame Charlotte. *The Policy of the Segregation of the Negro in the Public Schools of Ohio, Indiana, and Illinois.* M.A. Thesis, The University of Chicago, 1917.

Merrifield, Charles Warren. *The Chicago Conspiracy: A Study of the Insurrectionary Phase of the Civil War Peace Movement in the Old Northwest.* M.A. Thesis, The University of Chicago, 1935.

Murphy, Mary Elizabeth. *Cultural Interests Indicated by Lectures before the Chicago Lyceum, 1837–1871.* M.A. Thesis, The University of Chicago, 1929.

Newton, Fred Earle. *Railway Legislation in Illinois from 1828 to 1870.* M.A. Thesis, University of Illinois, 1901.

Palmer, Vivien Marie. *The Primary Settlement as a Unit of Urban Growth and Organization.* Ph.D. Thesis, The University of Chicago, 1932.

Severson, Harry L. *History of Investment Banking in Chicago.* In progress, Ph.D. Thesis, The University of Chicago, 1939.

Smith, Marion Barnett. *History of the Chicago Home for the Friendless.* M.A. Thesis, The University of Chicago, 1930.

Spencer, Gwladys. *The Chicago Public Library: Origins and Backgrounds.* Ph.D. Thesis, The University of Chicago, 1939.

Strevey, Tracy Elmer. *Joseph Medill and the Chicago Tribune during the Civil War Period.* Ph.D. Thesis, The University of Chicago, 1930.

Thomas, Rollin George. *The Development of State Banks in Chicago.* Ph.D. Thesis, The University of Chicago, 1930.

Townsend, Andrew Jacke. *The Germans of Chicago.* Ph.D. Thesis, The University of Chicago, 1927.

Wilt, Napier. *The History of the Chicago Theater.* In progress, Chicago, 1939.

——. *The History of the Two Rice Theatres in Chicago from 1847 to 1857.* Ph.D. Thesis, The University of Chicago, 1923.

II. BOOKS AND PAMPHLETS

Ackerman, William K. *Early Illinois Railroads, a Paper Read before the Chicago Historical Society, Tuesday evening, February 20, 1883.* . . . Chicago: Fergus Printing Company, 1884.

——. *Historical Sketch of the Illinois-Central Railroad, together with a Brief Biographical Record of its Incorporators and some of its Early Officers.* Chicago: Fergus Printing Company, 1890.

Ahern, M. L. *The Political History of Chicago, 1837–1887.* Chicago: P. Donohue and Henneberry, 1886.

Ander, Oscar Fritiof. *T. N. Hasselquist: The Career and Influence of a Swedish-American Clergyman, Journalist and Educator* (Dr. Ira Oliver Nothstein, ed., *Augustana Library Publications,* no. 14). Rock Island: The Augustana Library Publications, 1931.

Andreas, A. T. *History of Chicago from the Earliest Period to the Present Time.* 3 v. Chicago: A. T. Andreas, 1884–86.

——. *History of Cook County, Illinois. From the Earliest Period to the Present Time.* . . . Chicago: A. T. Andreas, 1884.

[Anon.] *Biographical Sketches of the Leading Men of Chicago, Written by the Best Talent of the Northwest.* Chicago: Wilson and St. Clair, 1868.

——. *The Chicago, Rock Island and Pacific Railway System and Representative Employees.* Chicago: Biographical Publishing Company, 1900.

——. *Chicago und sein Deutschthum.* Cleveland: American Biographical Publishing Co., 1901–2.

——. *The First National Bank of Chicago, Charter Number Eight: A Brief History of its Progress.* . . . Chicago: privately printed, 1913.

——. *Industrial Chicago.* . . . 6 v. Chicago: The Goodspeed Publishing Company, 1891–96.

Baird, Mrs. Lyman. *History of the Chicago Home for the Friendless, 1859–1909.* Chicago: n.p., 1909.

Barrows, Harlan H. *Geography of the Middle Illinois Valley* (Illinois State Geological Survey, *Bulletin,* no. 15). Urbana: University of Illinois Press, 1910.

Beckner, Earl R. *A History of Labor Legislation in Illinois.* Chicago: The University of Chicago Press, 1929.

Bennett, Fremont O., comp. *Politics and Politicians of Chicago, Cook County, and Illinois.* Chicago: The Blakely Printing Company, 1886.

[Bentley, Cyrus.] *History of the First Baptist Church, Chicago, with the Articles of Faith and Covenant, and a Catalogue of its Members, December, 1889.* 4th ed. Chicago: R. R. Donnelley and Sons, 1889.

Bisbee, Lewis H., and Simonds, John C. *The Board of Trade and the Produce Exchange, Their History, Methods, and Law.* Chicago: Callaghan and Co., 1884.

Blair, Edward T. *A History of the Chicago Club.* Chicago: R. R. Donnelley and Sons Company, 1898.

Blanchard, Rufus. *Discovery and Conquest of the Northwest with the History of Chicago.* 2 v. R. Blanchard and Co., 1898–1900.

Bosse, Georg von. *Das deutsche Element in den Vereinigten Staaten unter besonderer Berücksichtigung seines politischen, ethischen, sozialen und erzieherischen Einflusses.* Stuttgart: Chr. Belsersche Verlagsbuchhandlung, 1908.

Boyle, James E. *Chicago Wheat Prices for Eighty-One Years, Daily, Monthly and Yearly Fluctuations and their Causes.* n.p., 1922.

Bregstone, Philip P. *Chicago and Its Jews; a Cultural History.* [Chicago]: privately published, 1933.

Bross, William. *History of Chicago. Historical and Commercial Statistics*

. . . *What I Remember of Early Chicago.* . . . Chicago: Jansen, Mc-Clurg and Co., 1876.

Brownson, Howard Gray. *The History of the Illinois Central Railroad to 1870* (University of Illinois, *Studies in the Social Sciences,* IV, nos. 3 and 4). Urbana: University of Illinois, 1915.

Bürgler, J. C. *Geschichte der Kathol. Kirche Chicagos. Mit besonderer Berücksichtigung des Katholischen Deutschthums.* Chicago: der office des Weltbürgers, 1889.

Chamberlin, Everett. *Chicago and Its Suburbs.* Chicago: T. A. Hungerford and Co., 1873.

[Chicago Academy of Sciences.] *Historical Sketch of the Chicago Academy of Sciences with the Act of Incorporation, Constitution, By-Laws, and Lists of Officers and Members, 1877.* Chicago: Jameson and Morse, 1877.

[Chicago and North Western Railway Company.] *Yesterday and Today; a History of the Chicago and North Western Railway System.* 3d ed. rev. Chicago: Winship Co., 1910.

[Chicago Medical Society.] *History of Medicine and Surgery and Physicians and Surgeons of Chicago.* Chicago: Biographical Publishing Co., 1922.

The Chicago Tribune. *The W. G. N.,* . . . . Chicago: The Chicago Tribune, 1922.

Clark, Hannah B. *The Public Schools of Chicago: A Sociological Study.* Chicago: The University of Chicago Press, 1897.

Clark, Thomas D. *A Pioneer Southern Railroad from New Orleans to Cairo.* Chapel Hill: University of North Carolina Press, 1936.

Clemen, Rudolf Alexander. *The American Livestock and Meat Industry.* New York: The Ronald Press Company, 1923.

Colbert, E[lias]. *Chicago: Historical and Statistical Sketch of the Garden City.* . . . Chicago: P. T. Sherlock, 1868.

Cole, Arthur Charles. *The Era of the Civil War, 1848–1870* (Clarence W. Alvord, ed., *The Centennial History of Illinois,* III). Springfield: Illinois Centennial Commission, 1919.

Currey, Josiah Seymour. *Chicago: Its History and Its Builders, a Century of Marvelous Growth.* 5 v. Chicago: The S. J. Clarke Publishing Company, 1912.

——. *Manufacturing and Wholesale Industries of Chicago.* 3 v. Chicago: Thomas B. Poole Company, 1918.

Dickerson, Oliver Morton. *The Illinois Constitutional Convention of 1862* (University of Illinois, *The University Studies,* I, no. 9). Urbana: University of Illinois Press, 1905.

Dietzsch, Emil. *Chicago's Deutsche Männer. Erinnerungs-Blätter an Chicago's Fünfzigjähriges Jubliäum.* . . . Chicago: Max Stern and Co., 1885.

——. *Geschichte der Deutsch-Amerikaner von Chicago (von der Gründung der Stadt an bis auf die neueste Zeit).* Chicago: M. Stern and Co., 1881.

Dowrie, George William. *The Development of Banking in Illinois, 1817–1863* (University of Illinois, *Studies in the Social Sciences,* II, no. 4). Urbana: University of Illinois Press, 1913.

Emery, Henry Crosby. *Speculation on the Stock and Produce Exchanges of the United States* (Columbia University, *Studies in History, Economics and Public Law,* VII, no. 2). New York: Columbia University Press, 1896.

Evangelical Lutheran Augustana Synod of North America. *After Seventy-five Years, 1860–1935; a Jubilee Publication; Seventy-fifth Anniversary of the Augustana Synod and Augustana College and Theological Seminary.* Rock Island, Illinois: Augustana Book Concern, 1935.

Felsenthal, Bernhard. *The Beginnings of the Chicago Sinai Congregation, A Contribution to the Inner History of American Judaism.* Chicago: S. Ettlinger Printing Co., 1898.

Felsenthal, B., and Eliassof, Herman. *History of Kehillath Anshe Maarabh [sic] (Congregation of the Men of the West), Issued under the Auspices of the Congregation on the Occasion of its Semi-Centennial Celebration, November 4, 1897.* Chicago: n.p., 1897.

Fergus, Robert. *Biographical Sketch of John Dean Caton, Ex-Chief-Justice of Illinois* (Fergus Historical Series, no. 21). Chicago: Fergus Printing Company, 1882.

[First Congregational Church of Chicago.] *The Quarter-Centennial of the First Congregational Church of Chicago, May 21st and 22d, 1876.* Chicago: Culver, Page, Hoyne and Co., 1876.

Fleming, Herbert E. *Magazines of a Market-Metropolis: Being a History of the Literary Periodicals and Literary Interests of Chicago* . . . (A reprint of papers entitled " The Literary Interests of Chicago," *American Journal of Sociology,* XI–XII). Chicago: The University of Chicago Press, 1906.

Fleming, Isaac A. *The Chicago Stock Exchange; an Historical Sketch with Biographies of its Leading Members.* Chicago: n.p., 1894.

Flinn, John Joseph. *History of the Chicago Police from the Settlement of the Community to the Present Time.* . . . Chicago: Police Book Fund, 1887.

Flint, Henry M. *The Railroads of the United States; their History and Statistics*. Philadelphia: John E. Potter and Company, 1868.

[Flint, Henry Martyn.] By a Member of the Western Bar. *Life of Stephen A. Douglas, United States Senator from Illinois with His most Important Speeches and Reports*. New York: Derby and Jackson, 1860.

Fuller, S. S., and others, comps. *Riverside, Then & Now, a History of Riverside, Illinois*. Riverside: The Riverside News, 1936.

Gallery, Mary Onahan. *Life of William J. Onahan; Stories of Men Who Made Chicago*. [Chicago]: Loyola University Press, 1929.

Garraghan, Gilbert J., S.J. *The Catholic Church in Chicago, 1673–1871; an Historical Sketch*. Chicago: Loyola University Press, 1921.

Gaston, George H. *The History and Government of Chicago*. Reprints from *The Educational Bi-Monthly*, February, 1914–February, 1916.

Gates, Paul Wallace. *The Illinois Central Railroad and Its Colonization Work* (*Harvard Economic Studies*, XLII). Cambridge: Harvard University Press, 1934.

Goldstein, Benjamin F. *Marketing: A Farmer's Problem*. New York: The Macmillan Company, 1928.

Goodsell, J. H., and C. M. *The Chicago Fire and the Fire Insurance Companies*. Chicago: publishers of the *Spectator*, 1871.

Goodspeed, Thomas Wakefield. *A History of the University of Chicago, founded by John D. Rockefeller; the first Quarter-Century*. Chicago: The University of Chicago Press, 1916.

Goodspeed, Weston A., and Healy, Daniel D., eds. *History of Cook County, Illinois*. 2 v. Chicago: Goodspeed Historical Association, 1909.

Gordon, Joseph Hinckley. *Illinois Railway Legislation and Commission Control Since 1870* (University of Illinois, *The University Studies*, I, no. 6). Urbana: University of Illinois Press, 1904.

[Grace Church, Chicago.] *The Parish Year Book of Grace Church Chicago, July 1896*. Chicago: Rogers and Smith Co., 1896.

Grant, John C., ed. *The Second Presbyterian Church of Chicago, 1842–1892*. Chicago: Knight, Leonard and Co., 1892.

Grosser, Hugo S. *Chicago: A Review of Its Governmental History from 1837 to 1906*. [Chicago: n.p., 1906.]

Hall, Rev. Francis J., D.D. *A History of the Diocese of Chicago, Including a History of the Undivided Diocese of Illinois from its Organization in A. D. 1835*. Dixon, Illinois: DeWitt C. Owen, n.d.

Harper, William Hudson, and Ravell, Charles H. *Fifty Years of Banking in Chicago, 1857–1907*. [Chicago]: The Merchants' Loan and Trust Company [1907].

Harris, N. Dwight. *The History of Negro Servitude in Illinois*. Chicago: A. C. McClurg and Co., 1904.

Haynie, J. Henry. *The Nineteenth Illinois. A Memoir of a Regiment of Volunteer Infantry Famous in the Civil War*. . . . Chicago: M. A. Donohue and Co., 1912.

[Hebron Presbyterian Church.] *A Brief History of Hebron Presbyterian Church*. Privately printed, n.d.

Higley, William Kerr. *Historical Sketch of the Academy* (The Chicago Academy of Sciences, *Special Publication*, no. 2). Chicago: Stromberg, Allen and Co., 1902.

Hormer, Rev. Thomas L. *Fifty Years of Parish History, Church of the Annunciation, 1866–1916*. Chicago: n.p., 1916.

Hoyt, Homer. *One Hundred Years of Land Values in Chicago*. Chicago: private edition, 1933.

Huston, Francis Murray. *Financing an Empire; History of Banking in Illinois*. 4 v. Chicago: The S. J. Clarke Publishing Co., 1926.

Hutchinson, William T. *Cyrus Hall McCormick*. 2 v. New York: D. Appleton-Century Company, 1930–35.

Hyde, James Nevins. *Early Medical Chicago: An Historical Sketch of the First Practitioners of Medicine, with the Present Faculties, and Graduates Since their Organization, of the Medical Colleges of Chicago* (Fergus Historical Series, no. 11). Chicago: Fergus Printing Co., 1879.

Independent Order of B'nai B'rith. *Annals of Ramah Lodge, No. 33: Independent Order of B'nai B'rith*. [Chicago]: n.p., 1929.

[Inter Ocean.] *A History of the City of Chicago, its Men and Institutions*. . . . Chicago: The Inter Ocean, 1900.

International Typographical Union. *Official Souvenir of the International Typographical Union, Forty-First Session at Chicago, June 12–17, 1893*. Chicago: Press of Henry O. Shepard Co., n.d.

James, F. Cyril. *The Growth of Chicago Banks*. 2 v. New York: Harper and Brothers, 1938.

Johnson, Eric, and Peterson, C. F. *Svenskarne i Illinois*. Chicago: W. Williamson, 1880.

Kelly, Fred C. *Seventy-Five Years of Hibbard Hardware; the Story of Hibbard, Spencer, Bartlett & Co.* Chicago: Hibbard, Spencer, Bartlett and Co., 1930.

Kirkland, Joseph. *Story of Chicago*. Chicago: Dibble Publishing Co., 1892.

Kohlmeier, A. L. *The Old Northwest as the Keystone of the Arch of American Federal Union.* Bloomington, Indiana: The Principia Press, 1938.

Lee, Judson Fiske. *Transportation as a Factor in the Development of Northern Illinois Previous to 1860* (Reprint of Illinois State Historical Society, *Journal,* X [April, 1917], 17–85). Chicago: n.p., 1917.

Leech, Harper, and Carroll, John Charles. *Armour and His Times.* New York: D. Appleton-Century Company, 1938.

Lewis, Lloyd, and Smith, Henry Justin. *Chicago: The History of its Reputation.* New York: Harcourt, Brace and Co., 1929.

Lueders, August. *Sechzig Jahre in Chicago.* Chicago: n.p., 1929.

McManis, John T. *Ella Flagg Young and a Half-Century of the Chicago Public Schools.* Chicago: A. C. McClurg and Co., 1916.

Mann, Charles W. *The Chicago Common Council and the Fugitive Slave Law of 1850* (An Address read before the Chicago Historical Society at a Special Meeting Held January 29, 1903). Chicago: Chicago Historical Society, n.d.

Milton, George Fort. *The Eve of Conflict; Stephen A. Douglas and the Needless War.* Boston: Houghton Mifflin Co., 1934.

Montgomery, Royal E. *Industrial Relations in the Chicago Building Trades.* Chicago: The University of Chicago Press, 1927.

Morgan, Vyrnwy. *The Cambro-American Pulpit.* New York: Funk and Wagnalls Co., 1898.

Morris, Henry C. *The History of the First National Bank of Chicago.* . . . Chicago: R. R. Donnelley and Sons Company, 1902.

Moses, John, and Kirkland, Joseph. *History of Chicago, Illinois.* 2 v. Chicago: Munsell and Co., 1895.

Moses, John. *Illinois, Historical and Statistical.* . . . 2 v. 2d ed. rev. Chicago: Fergus Printing Co., 1895.

Mulkerins, Thomas M., S.J. *Holy Family Parish Chicago, Priests and People.* Chicago: Universal Press, 1923.

Norelius, Eric. *De svenska lutherska församlingarnas och Svenkarnas historia i Amerika.* 2 v. Rock Island: Augustana Book Concern, 1890–1906.

Norton, Samuel Wilber. *Chicago Traction, a History Legislative and Political.* Chicago: n.p., 1907.

Olson, Ernst W., and others, eds. *History of the Swedes of Illinois.* 2 v. Chicago: Engberg-Holmberg Publishing Co., 1908.

Otis, Philo Adams. *The First Presbyterian Church, 1833–1913. A History of the Oldest Organization in Chicago with Biographical Sketches of the Ministers and Extracts from the Choir Records.* 2d ed. Chicago: Fleming H. Revell Co., 1913.

Paine, A. E. *The Granger Movement in Illinois* (University of Illinois, *Studies,* I, no. 8). Urbana: University of Illinois Press, 1904.

Phillips, George S. *Chicago and her Churches.* Chicago: E. B. Myers and Chandler, 1868.

Pooley, William Vipond. *The Settlement of Illinois from 1830 to 1850* (University of Wisconsin, History Series, I, no. 4). Madison: The University, 1908.

Putnam, James William. *The Illinois and Michigan Canal. A Study in Economic History* (Chicago Historical Society, *Collection,* X). Chicago: The University of Chicago Press, 1918.

Quaife, Milo M. *Chicago's Highways Old and New: from Indian Trail to Motor Road.* Chicago: D. F. Keller and Company, 1923.

Rice, Wallace. *75 Years of Gas Service in Chicago. . . .* Chicago: The Peoples Gas Light and Coke Company, 1925.

——. *The Chicago Stock Exchange, A History.* Chicago: The Chicago Stock Exchange, 1928.

Riley, Elmer A. *The Development of Chicago and Vicinity as a Manufacturing Center Prior to 1880.* Chicago: McElroy Publishing Co., 1911.

Rowan, Richard Wilmer. *The Pinkertons, a Detective Dynasty.* Boston: Little, Brown and Co., 1931.

Schlüter, Hermann. *Die Anfänge der deutschen Arbeiterbewegung in Amerika.* Stuttgart: J. H. M. Dietz, 1907.

Schotter, H. W. *The Growth and Development of the Pennsylvania Railroad Company; A Review of the Charter and Annual Reports of the Pennsylvania Railroad Company, 1846 to 1926, inclusive.* Philadelphia: Press of Allen, Lane and Scott, 1927.

Scroggs, William O. *A Century of Banking Progress.* Garden City, New York: Doubleday, Page and Company, 1924.

Sheahan, James W. *The Life of Stephen A. Douglas.* New York: Harper and Brothers, 1860.

Sisters of Mercy. *Leaves from the Annals of the Sisters of Mercy.* 3 v. New York: Burns and Oates, 1889.

Sparling, Samuel Edwin. *Municipal History and Present Organization of the City of Chicago* (University of Wisconsin, *Bulletin,* no. 23. Economics, Political Science, and History Series, II, no. 2). Madison: The University, 1908.

Stidger, Felix G. *Treason History of the Order of Sons of Liberty, Formerly Circle of Honor, Succeeded by Knights of the Golden Circle,*

Afterward Order of American Knights. Chicago: Published by Author, 1903.

Stockton, Frank T. *The International Molders Union of North America* (Johns Hopkins University, *Studies in Historical and Political Science,* XXXIX, no. 3). Baltimore: Johns Hopkins Press, 1921.

[Tabernacle Independent Church, Chicago.] *Directory . . . Containing a List of the Membership . . . 1878–79.* Chicago: The Church, [1879].

Taylor, Charles H., ed. *History of the Board of Trade of the City of Chicago.* 3 v. Chicago: Robert O. Law Company, 1917.

[Thompson, Joseph J.] *The Archdiocese of Chicago: Antecedents and Development.* Des Plaines, Ill.: St. Mary's Training School Press, 1920.

Tracy, George A. *History of the Typographical Union; its Beginnings, Progress and Development. . . .* Indianapolis: International Typographical Union, 1913.

Union Pacific Railway (Eastern Division). *Action of the Board of Trade of Chicago, and Extracts from leading Journals of Illinois, showing the Necessity and Advantages of its Immediate Construction to the Pacific.* Chicago: Rounds and James, 1868.

[Unity Church.] *. . . Chicago Year Book, 1885.* Chicago: Fergus Printing Company, 1885.

Upton, George Putnam. *Theodore Thomas.* Chicago: A. C. McClurg and Company, 1905.

Vandenbosch, Amry. *The Dutch Communities of Chicago.* Chicago: printed by Carlstrand-Rook Co., for the Knickerbocker Society of Chicago, 1927.

Visher, John W. *Handbook of Charities of Chicago.* 3d ed. Chicago: Charles H. Kerr and Company, 1897.

Ward, Estelle Frances. *The Story of Northwestern University.* New York: Dodd, Mead and Co., 1924.

Warren, George P. *Prices of Farm Products in the United States* (United States, Department of Agriculture, *Bulletin,* no. 999). Washington: Government Printing Office, 1921.

Weber, Harry P. *An Outline History of Chicago Traction.* [Chicago: n.p., 1936.]

Wheeler, Mrs. Charles Gilbert. *Annals of the Chicago Orphan Asylum from 1849 to 1892.* Chicago: published by the Board, 1892.

White, Horace. *The Life of Lyman Trumbull.* Boston: Houghton Mifflin Co., 1913.

Williams, Rev. A. W. *Life and Work of Dwight L. Moody, the Great*

Evangelist of the XIX Century. . . . Philadelphia: P. W. Ziegler and Co., 1900.

[Williams, Rudolph.] *The New Church and Chicago, a History.* [Chicago]: W. B. Conkey Co., 1906.

Wing, Jack. *The Great Union Stock Yards of Chicago.* Chicago: Religio-Philosophical Publishing Association, 1865.

Wood, David Ward, ed. *Chicago and its Distinguished Citizens, or the Progress of Forty Years.* . . . Chicago: Milton George and Company, 1881.

III. ARTICLES

Abbot, Willis J. "Chicago Newspapers and their Makers," *The Review of Reviews,* XI (June, 1895), 646–65.

Althaus, Friederick. "Beiträge zur Geschichte der Deutschen Kolonie in England," *Unsere Zeit,* n.s. IX, pts. 1 and 2 (1873).

[Anon.] "The French Colony in Chicago," *L'Écho des Deux Mondes,* VII (1909), 13–19.

——. "Review of the Chicago Live Stock Trade, during the Year 1868," *Griffith's Live Stock Reporter,* quoted in Illinois State Agricultural Society, *Transactions,* VII (1867–68), 402–80.

——. "Story of the Rock Island's Seventieth Anniversary Celebration, October 10, 1922," *Rock Island Magazine,* XVII (November, 1922).

——. "The Union Stock Yards of Chicago," Illinois State Agricultural Society, *Transactions,* VI (1865–66), 314–24.

Ander, Fritiof. "Some Factors in the Americanization of the Swedish Immigrant, 1850–1890," Illinois State Historical Society, *Journal,* XXVI (April–July, 1933), 136–50.

Babcock, Kendric C. "The Expansion of Higher Education in Illinois from 1865 to 1925," Illinois State Historical Society, *Transactions, 1925,* pp. 41–53.

Bassoe, Peter. "The Early History of Neurology and Psychiatry in the Middle West," The Society of Medical History of Chicago, *Bulletin,* III (October, 1923), 175–90.

——. "A Sketch of the Development of Psychiatry and Neurology in Chicago," reprint from *Proceedings of the Institute of Medicine of Chicago,* II, no. 9 (December 15, 1936).

Brooks, D. C. "Chicago and Its Railways," *Lakeside Monthly,* VIII (October, 1872), 264–80.

Brune, Adolf. "Einfluss deutscher Musiker auf die Entwicklung deutscher Musik in Chicago," *Jahrbuch der Deutschamerikaner für das Jahr 1918* (1917), pp. 131–43.

Cleveland, H. I. "Booming the First Republican President, a Talk with Abraham Lincoln's Friend, the Late Joseph Medill," *Saturday Evening Post,* CLXXII (August 5, 1899), 85–86.

Cole, Arthur Charles. "Illinois Women of the Middle Period," Illinois State Historical Society, *Transactions, 1920,* pp. 84–92.

——. "President Lincoln and the Illinois Radical Republicans," *The Mississippi Valley Historical Review,* IV (March, 1918), 417–36.

Cooley, Verna. "Illinois and the Underground Railroad to Canada," Illinois State Historical Society, *Transactions, 1917,* pp. 76–98.

Coulter, E. Merton. "Effects of Secession upon the Commerce of the Mississippi Valley," *The Mississippi Valley Historical Review,* III (December, 1916), 275–300.

Eliassof, Herman. "The Jews of Chicago," American Jewish Historical Society, *Publications,* XI (1903), 117–30.

Fairlie, John A. "The Street Railway Question in Chicago," *The Quarterly Journal of Economics,* XXI (May, 1907), 371–404.

Fesler, Mayo. "Secret Political Societies in the North during the Civil War," *Indiana Magazine of History,* XIV (September, 1918), 183–286.

Gallery, John Ireland. "The Chicago Catholic Institute and Chicago Lyceum," *Illinois Catholic Historical Review,* II (January, 1920), 303–22.

Garraghan, Gilbert J., S. J. "Beginnings of Holy Family Parish, Chicago, 1857–1871," *Illinois Catholic Historical Review,* I (April, 1919), 436–58.

Gates, Paul Wallace. "The Disposal of the Public Domain in Illinois, 1848–1856," *Journal of Economic and Business History,* III (1930–31), 216–40.

——. "The Promotion of Agriculture by the Illinois Central Railroad, 1855–1870," *Agricultural History,* V (April, 1931), 57–76.

——. "The Struggle for the Charter of the Illinois Central Railroad," Illinois State Historical Society, *Transactions, 1933,* pp. 55–66.

Goodspeed, Edgar J. "The Old University of Chicago, in 1867," Illinois State Historical Society, *Journal,* III (July, 1910), 52–57.

Heilman, Ralph E. "Chicago Traction, a Study of the Efforts of the Public to Secure Good Service," American Economic Association, *Publications,* ser. 3, IX (1908), 313–443.

Herriott, F. I. "The Germans of Chicago and Stephen A. Douglas in 1854," *Deutsch-Amerikanische Geschichtsblätter,* XII (1912), 381–404.

Hotchkiss, Willard E. "Chicago Traction: a Study in Political Evolution,"

The Annals of the American Academy of Political and Social Science, XXVIII (November, 1906), 385–404.

Huch, C. F. "Revolutionsvereine und Anleihen," *Mitteilungen des deutschen Pionier-Vereins von Philadelphia,* no. 18 (1910).

Jones, Alexander J. "The Chicago Drainage Canal and Its Forebear, the Illinois and Michigan Canal," Illinois State Historical Society, *Transactions, 1906,* pp. 153–61.

Knapp, Joseph G. "A Review of Chicago Stock Yards History," *The University Journal of Business,* II (June, 1924), 331–46.

Korey, Harold. "The Story of Jewish Education in Chicago Prior to 1923," *Jewish Education,* VI (January–March, 1934), 37–47.

Lee, Guy A. "The Historical Significance of the Chicago Grain Elevator System," *Agricultural History,* XI (January, 1937), 16–32.

McGoorty, John P. "The Early Irish of Illinois," Illinois State Historical Society, *Transactions, 1927,* pp. 54–64.

McGovern, Rev. James J., D.D. "The Catholic Church in Chicago," *Souvenir of the Silver Jubilee in the Episcopacy of His Grace the Most Reverend Patrick Augustine Feehan, Archbishop of Chicago, November 1st, 1865–1890,* pp. 1–261. Chicago: n.p., 1891.

MacMillan, Thomas C. "The Scots and Their Descendants in Illinois," Illinois State Historical Society, *Transactions, 1919,* pp. 31–85.

Miller, Rev. Samuel. "Historical Review of the Church (Old School Branch)," *Presbyterian Reunion. A Memorial Volume, 1837–1871.* New York: D. C. Lent and Company, 1870.

Nevins, Frank J. "Seventy Years of Service from Grant to Gorman," *Rock Island Magazine,* XVII (October, 1922), 5–43.

Norris, Joe L. "The Land Reform Movement [in Chicago]," Illinois State Historical Society, *Papers in Illinois History and Transactions for the Year 1937,* pp. 73–82.

Payne, Will. "The Chicago Board of Trade," *The Century Illustrated Monthly Magazine,* LXV, n.s. XLIII (March, 1903), 745–54.

Riordan, D. J. "University of St. Mary of the Lake," *Illinois Catholic Historical Review,* II (October, 1919), 135–60.

Schneider, Otto C. "Abraham Lincoln und das Deutschthum," *Deutsch-Amerikanische Geschichtsblätter,* VII (1907), 65–75.

Selby, Paul. "The Editorial Convention of 1856," Illinois State Historical Society, *Journal,* V (October, 1912), 343–49.

———. "Lincoln and German Patriotism," *Deutsch-Amerikanische Geschichtsblätter,* XII (1912), 510–35.

Senning, John P. "The Know-Nothing Movement in Illinois, 1854–1856," Illinois State Historical Society, *Journal,* VII (April, 1913), 7–33.

Sharp, Katharine L. " Chicago Libraries " (" Illinois Libraries," pt. IV), University of Illinois, *Studies*, II, no. 7 (1908).

A Sister of the Community. " The Sisters of Mercy," *Illinois Catholic Historical Review*, III (April, 1921), 339–70.

Stephenson, George M. " Nativism in the Forties and Fifties, with Special Reference to the Mississippi Valley," *The Mississippi Valley Historical Review*, IX, 185–202.

——. " The Stormy Years of the Swedish Colony in Chicago before the Great Fire," Illinois State Historical Society, *Transactions, 1929*, pp. 166–84.

Stevens, Frank E. " Stephen A. Douglas, The Expansionist," Illinois State Historical Society, *Transactions, 1913*, pp. 87–90.

——. " The Irish in Chicago," *Illinois Catholic Historical Review*, II–III (April, October, 1920), 458–73, 146–69.

——. " The Irish in Early Illinois," *Illinois Catholic Historical Review*, II (October, 1919–January, 1920), 223–28, 286–302.

Thompson, Taylor. " The Northwestern Confederacy," *Confederate Veteran*, XXIV (February, 1916), 87–88.

Tunell, George G. " The Diversion of the Flour and Grain Traffic from the Great Lakes to the Railroads," *The Journal of Political Economy*, V (June, 1897), 340–75.

Weaver, George H. " Beginnings of Medical Education in and near Chicago," The Society of Medical History of Chicago, *Bulletin*, III (September, 1925), 339–470.

——. " The Chicago Medical Relief Committee," The Society of Medical History of Chicago, *Bulletin*, II (March, 1922), 334–38.

——. " Edward Mead, M.D., the Pioneer Neuropsychiatrist of Illinois," The Society of Medical History of Chicago, *Bulletin*, III (December, 1924), 279–92.

Williams, John F. " The Work of the Physicians during the Chicago Fire," The Society of Medical History of Chicago, *Bulletin*, II (March, 1922), 339–42.

Wiltsee, Herbert. " The Temperance Movement [in Chicago] 1848–1871," Illinois State Historical Society, *Papers in Illinois History and Transactions for the Year 1937*, pp. 82–92.

INDEX

A NOTE ON THE TYPE
IN WHICH THIS BOOK IS SET

DEVICE OF
ROBERT GRANJON

This book is set in Granjon, a type named in compliment to ROBERT GRANJON, *but neither a copy of a classic face nor an entirely original creation. George W. Jones drew the basic design for this type from classic sources, but deviated from his model to profit by the intervening centuries of experience and progress. This type is based primarily upon the type used by Claude Garamond (1510–61) in his beautiful French books, and more closely resembles Garamond's own than do any of the various modern types that bear his name.*

Of Robert Granjon nothing is known before 1545, except that he had begun his career as type-cutter in 1523. The boldest and most original designer of his time, he was one of the first to practise the trade of type-founder apart from that of printer. Between 1549 and 1551 he printed a number of books in Paris, also continuing as type-cutter. By 1557 he was settled in Lyons and had married Antoinette Salamon, whose father, Bernard, was an artist associated with Jean de Tournes. Between 1557 and 1562 Granjon printed about twenty books in types designed by himself, following, after the fashion of the day, the cursive handwriting of the time. These types, usually known as " caractères de civilité," he himself called " lettres françaises," as especially appropriate to his own country. He was granted a monopoly of these types for ten years, but they were soon copied. Granjon appears to have lived in Antwerp for a time, but was at Lyons in 1575 and 1577, and for the next decade at Rome, working for the Vatican and Medici presses, his work consisting largely in cutting exotic types. Towards the end of his life he may have returned to live in Paris, where he died in 1590.

This book was composed, printed, and bound by The Plimpton Press, Norwood, Mass. The paper was manufactured by S. D. Warren Co., Boston. Designed by S. R. Jacobs. Binding adapted from designs by W. A. Dwiggins.